EIGHTH EDITION

THE
BUSINESS WRITER'S
HANDBOOK

Gerald J. Alred
University of Wisconsin–Milwaukee

Charles T. Brusaw
Consultant

Walter E. Oliu
Consultant

ST. MARTIN'S PRESS   New York

FOR BEDFORD/ST. MARTIN'S

Developmental Editor: Caroline Thompson
Editorial Assistant: Kaitlin Hannon
Senior Production Supervisor: Nancy J. Myers
Project Management: Books By Design, Inc.
Cover Design: Donna L. Dennison, Kim Cevoli
Cover Art: *Office Interior with Desk, Computer, and Telephone.* © Beth Galton,
   Workbook.com.
Composition: Pine Tree Composition, Inc.
Printing and Binding: R. R. Donnelley & Sons Company

President: Joan E. Feinberg
Editorial Director: Denise B. Wydra
Editor in Chief: Karen S. Henry
Director of Marketing: Karen Melton Soeltz
Director of Editing, Design, and Production: Marcia Cohen
Manager, Publishing Services: Emily Berleth

Library of Congress Control Number: 2005921354

Manufactured in the United States of America.

1   0   9   8   7   6

f   e   d   c   b   a

For information, write

St. Martin's Press
175 Fifth Avenue
New York, NY 10010

ISBN: 0-312-43612-2 (paperback)
          0-312-35268-9 (hardcover)
EAN: 978-0-312-43612-4

ACKNOWLEDGMENTS

Figure D–2: Source: Federal Emergency Management Agency.
Figure D–3: Entry for "regard" from *The American Heritage Dictionary of the English
   Language*, Third Edition. Copyright © 2000 by Houghton Mifflin Company.
   Reprinted with the permission of the publisher. All rights reserved.
Figure D–11: Reprinted with the permission of the De Santis Collection.

*Acknowledgments and copyrights are continued at the back of the book on page 583, which
constitutes an extension of the copyright page.*

Contents

Preface iv

Five Steps to Successful Writing ix

Checklist of the
Writing Process xvii

Contents by Topic xix

Model Documents
and Figures by Topic xxii

The Business Writer's Handbook:
Alphabetical Entries 1–582

Index 585

Commonly Misused
Words and Phrases 630

Preface

The eighth edition of *The Business Writer's Handbook*, like previous editions, is a comprehensive resource for both academic and professional audiences. The *Handbook*'s nearly 400 entries cover effective print, oral, and online communication in the workplace, offering advice for writing and designing many different types of professional documents in addition to thorough explanations of grammar, style, and usage. This edition includes many new sample documents and visuals, as well as expanded advice for integrating visuals, making appropriate rhetorical choices, and considering ethics in business writing.

How to Use This Book

The Business Writer's Handbook is made up of alphabetically organized entries with color tabs. Within each entry, underlined cross-references such as "proposals" link readers to related entries that contain further information. Many entries present advice and guidelines in the form of convenient Writer's Checklists.

The *Handbook*'s alphabetical organization enables readers to find specific topics quickly and easily; however, readers with general questions will discover several alternate ways to find information in the book.

- **Contents by Topic.** The complete Contents by Topic on pages xix–xxi groups the alphabetical entries into topic categories. This topical key can help a writer focusing on a specific task or problem browse all related entries; it is also useful for instructors who want to correlate the *Handbook* with standard textbooks or their own course materials.

- **Commonly Misused Words and Phrases.** The list of Commonly Misused Words and Phrases on pages 630–31 extends the Contents by Topic by listing all of the usage entries, which appear in italics throughout the book.

- **Model Documents and Figures by Topic.** The topically organized list of model documents and figures on pages xxii–xxiv makes it easier to browse the book's abundant sample documents and visuals to find specific examples of business writing genres.

- **Checklist of the Writing Process.** The checklist on pages xvii–xviii helps readers to reference key entries in a sequence useful for planning and carrying out a writing project.
- **Comprehensive Index.** The index lists all the topics covered in the book, including those topics that are not main entries in the alphabetical arrangement.

Helpful Features

ESL Tips boxes throughout the book offer special advice for writers of English as a second language. In addition, the Contents by Topic on the inside back cover includes a list of entries — ESL Trouble Spots — that may be of particular interest to ESL writers.

Digital Tips and Web Link boxes throughout the book direct readers to specific related resources on the companion Web site at *<bedfordstmartins.com/alredbus>*. Digital Tips in the book suggest ways to use workplace technology and word-processing software to simplify complex writing tasks such as designing a document or creating an index. Expanded Digital Tips on the Web site offer step-by-step instructions for completing each task. Web Links in the book point students to related resources on the companion site such as model documents, tutorials, and links to hundreds of useful related Web sites.

New to This Edition

Our focus in revising the *Handbook* for this edition has been to give greater attention to the rhetorical and ethical choices writers face — both in writing and in designing professional documents. In response to suggestions from many instructors and workplace professionals who use the *Handbook*, we have replaced, revised, and redesigned many sample documents — in fact, this edition contains more new and updated examples than any previous edition. In addition to thoroughly updated coverage of grammar, usage, and style, readers will find the following improvements.

- **New and redesigned sample documents and visuals.** New sample documents reflect the prominence of e-mail in the workplace. Abundant illustrations — many of them new — include charts, graphs, drawings, tables, internationally recognized symbols, illustrated descriptions and instructions, brochure and newsletter pages, presentation slides, and more.

- **A new entry on the context of the writing situation** discusses questions writers must ask to understand and respond effectively to different writing situations. This entry also shows writers how to convey enough background information to help their readers understand the value and purpose of a document. To complement this discussion, most examples and model documents throughout the book are now introduced with a description of the rhetorical situation that prompted them.

- **Ethics Notes** throughout the book describe ethical issues in business writing and help writers understand and address them.

- **Expanded treatment of visual communication.** A new chart in the entry <u>visuals</u> compares the functions of various types of graphics and can help writers make the best choices for their audience, purpose, and context. This entry also offers expanded advice for effectively integrating, labeling, and crediting visuals, and cautions readers about using misleading visuals.

- **Updated coverage of résumé writing.** Job seekers will find new advice for using résumé summary statements, combining chronological and functional formats, and sending résumés as e-mail attachments. New sample résumés designed by Kim Isaacs, the Résumé Expert at Monster.com, and new sample application letters provide up-to-date models.

- **Expanded discussions of copyright and plagiarism.** Revised and expanded entries explain when and how to seek permission to use copyrighted material, how to properly acknowledge sources, and how to distinguish common knowledge from sources that must be cited.

- **Streamlined coverage of research.** We have combined and revised the previous edition's separate entries on library and Internet research in one research entry with an expanded *Writer's Checklist: Evaluating Print and Online Sources.*

- **Updated coverage of documenting sources** provides current APA (American Psychological Association), *CMS* (*Chicago Manual of Style*), and MLA (Modern Language Association) documentation models.

- **An updated companion Web site at <*bedfordstmartins.com/ alredbus*>.** The Web site helps instructors take advantage of the *Handbook*'s potential as a classroom text by offering lesson plans, handouts, teaching tips, and assignment ideas. For students, the Web site includes additional sample documents, useful tutorials, expanded Digital Tips, and links to hundreds of useful Web sites keyed to the *Handbook*'s main entries.

Acknowledgments

For their invaluable comments and suggestions for this edition of *The Business Writer's Handbook*, we thank the following reviewers who responded to our questionnaire: William Allegrezza, Indiana University Northwest; Stuart Brown, New Mexico State University; Amy Dayton, University of Arizona; Anne Greenhalgh, University of Pennsylvania; Lou Ann Karabel, Indiana University Northwest; Charlene Keeler, California State University–Fullerton; Sonia Khatchadourian, University of Wisconsin–Milwaukee; Margaret Loring, New Mexico State University; Ron McNeel, New Mexico State University; David Rota, University of Missouri–St. Louis; Linda Van Buskirk, Cornell University; Dona Vasa, University of Nebraska–Lincoln; Julie Vedder, West Virginia University; and Terry Zambon, University of Colorado.

For their helpful reviews of the companion Web site, we thank Anne Bliss, University of Colorado–Boulder; Lesley Baker, Tulane University; Mary Connerty, Pennsylvania State University–Erie; Annette Gooch, Santa Rosa Junior College; Christina Grignon, University of Wisconsin–Milwaukee; Nancy Hightower, University of Denver; Matthias Jonas, Niceware International, LLC; Elizabeth Robinson, Texas A&M University; Charlotte Rosen, Cornell University; and Philip Tietjen, Virginia Tech University.

For their detailed reviews of the model documents, we thank Paul Frommer, University of Southern California; Joseph E. Gawel, University of Maryland; Charlene Keeler, California State University–Fullerton; Jeff Smith, University of Southern California; and James Stull. We thank Julie Dyke Ford, New Mexico Institute of Mining and Technology, and Rochelle Rodrigo, Mesa Community College, for reviewing the new entry on context. We gratefully acknowledge Eva Brumberger of Virginia Tech University for her thorough review of the visuals coverage, and Kim Isaacs of Advanced Career Systems, Inc., for her review of the résumés entry and her work on new sample résumés.

For this edition, we owe special thanks to Richard C. Hay, University of Wisconsin–Milwaukee, for revising the entry on documenting sources and for reviewing new entries; Randy Thompson, Computer Graphics Design, for developing new visuals; and Renee Tegge, whose keen eye, impressive knowledge of grammar, and insightful suggestions improved many entries. In addition, we are very much indebted to the many reviewers and contributors not named here who helped us shape the first seven editions.

We wish to thank Bedford/St. Martin's for supporting this book, especially Joan Feinberg, President, and Karen Henry, Editor in Chief. We are grateful to Emily Berleth, Manager of Publishing Services at Bedford/St. Martin's, and Herb Nolan of Books By Design for their patience and expert guidance. We are pleased to acknowledge the enthusiastic assistance of Kaitlin Hannon, Editorial Assistant. Finally, we wish to thank Caroline Thompson, our developmental editor at Bedford/ St. Martin's, whose editing, professionalism, and collegiality helped produce an outstanding edition.

We offer heartfelt thanks to Barbara Brusaw for her patience and time spent preparing the manuscript for the first five editions. We also gratefully acknowledge the ongoing contributions of many students and instructors at the University of Wisconsin–Milwaukee. Finally, special thanks go to Janice Alred for her many hours of substantive assistance and for continuing to hold everything together.

G. J. A.
C. T. B.
W. E. O.

Five Steps to Successful Writing

Successful writing on the job is not the product of inspiration, nor is it merely the spoken word converted to print; it is the result of knowing how to structure information using both text and design to achieve an intended purpose for a clearly defined audience. The best way to ensure that your writing will succeed—whether it is in the form of a memo, a résumé, a proposal, or a Web page—is to approach writing using the following steps:

1. Preparation
2. Research
3. Organization
4. Writing
5. Revision

You will very likely need to follow those steps consciously—even self-consciously—at first. The same is true the first time you use new software, interview a candidate for a job, or chair a committee meeting. With practice, the steps become nearly automatic. That is not to suggest that writing becomes easy. It does not. However, the easiest and most efficient way to write effectively is to do it systematically.

As you master the five steps, keep in mind that they are interrelated and often overlap. For example, your readers' needs and your purpose, which you determine in step 1, will affect decisions you make in subsequent steps. You may also need to retrace steps. When you conduct research, for example, you may realize that you need to revise your initial impression of the document's purpose and audience. Similarly, when you begin to organize, you may discover the need to return to the research step to gather more information.

The time required for each step varies with different writing tasks. When writing an informal memo, for example, you might follow the first three steps (preparation, research, and organization) by simply listing the points in the order you want to cover them. In such situations, you gather and organize information mentally as you consider your purpose and audience. For a formal report, the first three steps require well-organized research, careful note-taking, and detailed outlining. For a routine e-mail message to a coworker, the first four steps merge as you type the information on the screen. In short, the five steps expand, contract, and at times must be repeated to fit the complexity or context of the writing task.

Dividing the writing process into steps is especially useful for collaborative writing, in which you typically divide work among team members, keep track of a project, and save time by not duplicating effort. When you collaborate, you can use e-mail to share text and other files, suggest improvements to each other's work, and generally keep everyone informed of your progress as you follow the steps in the writing process.

Preparation

Writing, like most professional tasks, requires solid <u>preparation</u>.* In fact, adequate preparation is as important as writing a draft. In preparation for writing, your goal is to accomplish the following four major tasks:

- Establish your primary purpose.
- Assess your audience (or readers) and the context.
- Determine the scope of your coverage.
- Select the appropriate medium.

Establishing Your Purpose.   To establish your primary <u>purpose</u> simply ask yourself what you want your readers to know, to believe, or to be able to do after they have finished reading what you have written. Be precise. Often a writer states a purpose so broadly that it is almost useless. A purpose such as "to report on possible locations for a new research facility" is too general. However, "to compare the relative advantages of Paris, Singapore, and San Francisco as possible locations for a new research facility so top management can choose the best location" is a purpose statement that can guide you throughout the writing process. In addition to your primary purpose, consider possible secondary purposes for your document. For example, a secondary purpose of the research-facilities report might be to make corporate executive readers aware of the staffing needs of the new facility so that they can ensure its smooth operation in whatever location is selected.

Assessing Your Audience and Context.   The next task is to assess your <u>audience</u>. Again, be precise and ask key questions. Who exactly is your reader? Do you have multiple readers? Who needs to see or to use

*In this discussion, as elsewhere throughout this book, words and phrases shown as links—underlined and set in an alternate typeface—refer to specific alphabetical entries.

the document? What are your readers' needs in relation to your subject? What are their attitudes about the subject? (Skeptical? Supportive? Anxious? Bored?) What do your readers already know about the subject? Should you define basic terminology, or will such definitions merely bore, or even impede, your readers? Are you communicating with international readers and therefore dealing with issues inherent in global communication?

For the research-facilities report, the readers are described as "top management." Who is included in that category? Will one of the people evaluating the report be the Human Resources Manager? If so, that person likely would be interested in the availability of qualified professionals as well as in the presence of training, housing, and perhaps even recreational facilities available to potential employees in each city. The Purchasing Manager would be concerned about available sources for materials needed by the facility. The Marketing Manager would give priority to the facility's proximity to the primary markets for its products and services and the transportation options that are available. The Chief Financial Officer would want to know about land and building costs and about each country's tax structure. The Chief Executive Officer would be interested in all this information and perhaps more. As with this example, many workplace documents have audiences composed of multiple readers. You can accommodate their needs through one of a number of approaches described in the entry readers.

In addition to knowing the needs and interests of your readers, learn as much as you can about the context. Simply put, context is the environment or circumstances in which writers produce documents and within which readers interpret their meanings. Everything is written

---

ESL ESL TIPS FOR CONSIDERING AUDIENCES

In the United States, conciseness, coherence, and clarity characterize good writing. Make sure readers can follow your writing, and say only what is necessary to communicate your message. Of course, no writing style is inherently better than another, but to be a successful writer in any language, you must understand the cultural values that underlie the language in which you are writing. See also awkwardness, copyright, global communication, plagiarism, and English as a second language.

Throughout this book we have included ESL Tips boxes like this one with information that may be particularly helpful to nonnative speakers of English. See the Contents by Topic on the inside back cover for listings of ESL Tips and ESL Trouble Spots, entries that may be of particular help to ESL writers.

in a context, as illustrated in many entries and examples throughout this book. To determine the effect of context on the research-facilities report you might ask both specific and general questions about the situation and about your readers' backgrounds: Is this the company's first new facility, or has the company chosen locations for new facilities before? Have the readers visited all three cities? Have they already seen other reports on the three cities? What is the corporate culture in which your readers work, and what are its key values? What specific factors, such as competition, finance, and regulation, are recognized as important within the organization?

Determining the Scope.   Determining your purpose and assessing your readers and context will help you decide what to include and what not to include in your writing. Those decisions establish the <u>scope</u> of your writing project. If you do not clearly define the scope, you will spend needless hours on research because you will not be sure what kind of information you need or even how much. Given the purpose and audience established for the report on facility locations, the scope would include such information as land and building costs, available labor force, cultural issues, transportation options, and proximity to suppliers. However, it probably would not include the early history of the cities being considered or their climate and geological features, unless those aspects were directly related to your particular business.

Selecting the Medium.   Finally, you need to determine the most appropriate medium for communicating your message. Professionals on the job face a wide array of options—from e-mail, fax, voice mail, videoconferencing, and Web sites to more traditional means like letters, memos, reports, telephone calls, and face-to-face meetings.

The most important considerations in selecting the appropriate medium are the audience and the purpose of the communication. For example, if you need to collaborate with someone to solve a problem or if you need to establish rapport with someone, written exchanges could be far less efficient than a phone call or a face-to-face meeting. However, if you need precise wording or you need to provide a record of a complex message, communicate in writing. If you need to make information that is frequently revised accessible to employees at a large company, the best choice might be to place the information on the company's intranet site. If reviewers need to make handwritten comments on a proposal, you may need to provide paper copies that can be faxed or use word-processing software to insert comments electronically. The comparative advantages and primary characteristics of the most typical means of communication are discussed in <u>selecting the medium</u>.

Research

The only way to be sure that you can write about a complex subject is to thoroughly understand it. To do that, you must conduct adequate <u>research</u>, whether that means conducting an extensive investigation for a major proposal—through interviewing, library and Internet research, careful <u>note-taking</u>, and <u>documenting sources</u>—or simply checking a company Web site and jotting down points before you send an e-mail to a colleague.

Methods of Research. Researchers frequently distinguish between primary and secondary research, depending on the types of sources consulted and the method of gathering information. *Primary research* refers to the gathering of raw data compiled from interviews, direct observation, surveys, experiments, <u>questionnaires</u>, and audio and video recordings, for example. In fact, direct observation and hands-on experience are the only ways to obtain certain kinds of information, such as the behavior of people and animals, certain natural phenomena, mechanical processes, and the operation of systems and equipment. *Secondary research* refers to gathering information that has been analyzed, assessed, evaluated, compiled, or otherwise organized into accessible form. Such forms or sources include books, articles, reports, Web documents, e-mail discussions, business letters, minutes of meetings, and brochures. Use the methods most appropriate to your needs, recognizing that some projects will require several types of research and that collaborative projects may require those research tasks to be distributed among team members.

Sources of Information. As you conduct research, numerous sources of information are available to you.

- Your own knowledge and that of your colleagues
- The knowledge of people outside your workplace, gathered through <u>interviewing for information</u>
- Internet sources, including Web sites, directories, archives, and discussion groups
- Library resources, including databases and indexes of articles as well as books and reference works
- Printed and electronic sources in the workplace, such as brochures, memos, e-mail, and Web documents

Consider all sources of information when you begin your research and use those that are appropriate and useful. The amount of research you will need to do depends on the scope of your project.

Organization

Without <u>organization</u>, the material gathered during your research will be incoherent to your readers. To organize information effectively, you need to determine the best way to structure your ideas; that is, you must choose a primary <u>method of development</u>.

Methods of Development. An appropriate method of development is the writer's tool for keeping information under control and the readers' means of following the writer's presentation. As you analyze the information you have gathered, choose the method that best suits your subject, your readers' needs, and your purpose. For example, if you were writing instructions for assembling office equipment, you would naturally present the steps of the process in the order readers should perform them: the sequential method of development. If you were writing about the history of an organization, your account would most naturally go from the beginning to the present: the chronological method of development. If your subject naturally lends itself to a certain method of development, use it — do not attempt to impose another method on it.

Often you will need to combine methods of development. For example, a persuasive brochure for a charitable organization might combine a specific-to-general method of development with a cause-and-effect method of development. That is, you could begin with persuasive case histories of individual people in need and then move to general information about the positive effects of donations on recipients.

Outlining. Once you have chosen a method of development, you are ready to prepare an outline. <u>Outlining</u> breaks large or complex subjects into manageable parts. It also enables you to emphasize key points by placing them in the positions of greatest importance. By structuring your thinking at an early stage, a well-developed outline ensures that your document will be complete and logically organized, allowing you to focus exclusively on writing when you begin the rough draft. An outline can be especially helpful for maintaining a collaborative-writing team's focus throughout a large project. However, even a short letter or memo needs the logic and structure that an outline provides, whether the outline exists in your mind or on-screen or on paper.

At this point, you must begin to consider <u>layout and design</u> elements that will be helpful to your readers and appropriate to your subject and purpose. For example, if <u>visuals</u> such as photographs or tables will be useful, this is a good time to think about where they may be deployed and what kinds of visual elements will be effective, especially if they need to be prepared by someone else while you are writing and revising the draft. The outline can also suggest where headings, lists, and other special design features may be useful.

Writing

When you have established your purpose, your readers' needs, and your scope and have completed your research and your outline, you will be well prepared to write a first draft. Expand your outline into **paragraphs**, without worrying about grammar, refinements of language usage, or punctuation. Writing and revising are different activities; refinements come with revision.

Write the rough draft, concentrating entirely on converting your outline into sentences and paragraphs. You might try writing as though you were explaining your subject to a reader sitting across from you. Do not worry about a good opening. Just start. Do not be concerned in the rough draft about exact word choice unless it comes quickly and easily—concentrate instead on ideas.

Even with good preparation, writing the draft remains a chore for many writers. The most effective way to get started and keep going is to use your outline as a map for your first draft. Do not wait for inspiration—you need to treat writing a draft as you would any on-the-job task. The entry **writing a draft** describes tactics used by experienced writers—discover which ones are best suited to you and your task.

Consider writing an **introduction** last because then you will know more precisely what is in the body of the draft. Your opening should announce the subject and give readers essential background information, such as the document's primary purpose. For longer documents, an introduction should serve as a frame into which readers can fit the detailed information that follows.

Finally, you will need to write a **conclusion** that ties the main ideas together and emphatically makes a final significant point. The final point may be to recommend a course of action, make a prediction or a judgment, or merely summarize your main points—the way you conclude depends on the purpose of your writing and your readers' needs.

Revision

The clearer a finished piece of writing seems to the reader, the more effort the writer has likely put into its **revision**. If you have followed the steps of the writing process to this point, you will have a rough draft that needs to be revised. Revising, however, requires a different frame of mind than does writing the draft. During revision, be eager to find and correct faults and be honest. Be hard on yourself for the benefit of your readers. Read and evaluate the draft as if you were a reader seeing it for the first time.

Check your draft for accuracy, completeness, and effectiveness in achieving your purpose and meeting your readers' needs and expectations. Trim extraneous information: Your writing should give readers exactly what they need, but it should not burden them with unnecessary information or sidetrack them into loosely related subjects.

Do not try to revise for everything at once. Read your rough draft several times, each time looking for and correcting a different set of problems or errors. Concentrate first on larger issues, such as <u>unity</u> and <u>coherence</u>; save mechanical corrections, like <u>spelling</u> and <u>punctuation</u>, for later <u>proofreading</u>. See also <u>ethics in writing</u>.

Finally, for important documents, consider having others review your writing and make suggestions for improvement. For collaborative writing, of course, team members must review each other's work on segments of the document as well as the final master draft. Use the Checklist of the Writing Process on pages xvii–xviii to guide you not only as you revise but also throughout the writing process.

Checklist of the Writing Process

This checklist arranges key entries of *The Business Writer's Handbook* according to the sequence presented in Five Steps to Successful Writing, which begins on page ix. This checklist is useful both for following the steps and for diagnosing writing problems.

PREPARATION 394

- [x] Establish your **purpose** 441
- [x] Identify your **audience** or **readers** 50, 455
- [x] Consider the **context** 111
- [x] Determine your **scope** of coverage 503
- [x] **Select the medium** 504

RESEARCH 463

- [x] **Brainstorm** to determine what you already know 57
- [x] Conduct **research** 463
- [x] Take notes (**note-taking**) 350
- [x] **Interview for information** 284
- [x] Create and use **questionnaires** 444
- [x] Avoid **plagiarism** 386
- [x] **Document sources** 148

ORGANIZATION 364

- [x] Choose the best **methods of development** 331
- [x] **Outline** your notes and ideas 364
- [x] Develop and integrate **visuals** 558
- [x] Consider **layout and design** 305

WRITING A DRAFT 000

- [x] Select an appropriate **point of view** 387
- [x] Adopt an appropriate **style** and **tone** 523, 540
- [x] Use effective **sentence construction** 508
- [x] Construct effective **paragraphs** 369
- [x] Use **quotations** and **paraphrasing** 452, 374
- [x] Write an **introduction** 290

☑ Write a **conclusion** 107

☑ Choose a **title** 537

REVISION   495

☑ Check for **unity** and **coherence** 547, 82

  conciseness 104

  pace 369

  transition 541

☑ Check for **sentence variety** 515

  emphasis 184

  parallel structure 373

  subordination 526

☑ Check for **clarity** 78

  ambiguity 34

  awkwardness 51

  logic errors 315

  positive writing 391

  voice 562

☑ Check for **ethics in writing** 192

  biased language 53

  copyright 113

  plagiarism 386

☑ Check for appropriate **word choice** 575

  abstract/concrete words 6

  affectation and **jargon** 23, 298

  clichés 81

  connotation/denotation 110

  defining terms 134

☑ Eliminate problems with **grammar** 252

  agreement 26

  case 72

  modifiers 337

  pronoun reference 412

  sentence faults 512

☑ Review mechanics and **punctuation** 440

  abbreviations 2

  capitalization 69

  contractions 113

  dates 133

  italics 294

  numbers 355

  proofreading 418

  spelling 523

CONTENTS BY TOPIC

Use this list as a quick reference for finding entries by topic. To search this book in more detail, use the index. For a list of figures and model documents, see pages xxii–xxiv.

BUSINESS WRITING DOCUMENTS AND ELEMENTS

Business Plans   62
Description   139
Forms Design   234
Indexing   268
Instructions   274
Job Descriptions   298
Mission Statements   334
Policies and Procedures   389
Process Explanation   407
Promotional Writing   412
   Brochures   58
   Newsletter Articles   344
   Newsletters   346
   Press Releases   405
   Sales Letters   500
Proposals   420
Questionnaires   444
Report Components
   Abstracts   7
   Appendixes   42
   Conclusions   107
   Executive Summaries   195
   Glossaries   250
   Introductions   290
   Tables of Contents   529
   Titles   537
Reports   462
   Annual Reports   36
   Feasibility Reports   200
   Formal Reports   211
   Investigative Reports   294
   Progress and Activity Reports   408
   Trip Reports   543
   Trouble Reports   544
Writing for the Web   577

CORRESPONDENCE

Acknowledgment Letters   11
Adjustment Letters   17
Collection Letters   85
Complaint Letters   101
Correspondence   114
Cover Letters   127
E-mail   179
Form Letters   209
Inquiries and Responses   270
International Correspondence   279
Memos   326
Reference Letters   457

Refusal Letters   457
Sales Letters   500

JOB SEARCH AND APPLICATION

Acceptance / Refusal Letters   9
Application Letters   42
Interviewing for a Job   286
Job Search   300
Resignation Letters   474
Résumés   478
Salary Negotiations   498

DESIGN AND VISUALS

Layout and Design   305
   Forms Design   234
   Headers and Footers   260
   Headings   261
   Lists   314
Visuals   558
   Drawings   172
   Flowcharts   206
   Global Graphics   248
   Graphs   253
   Maps   319
   Organizational Charts   364
   Photographs   382
   Tables   529
Web Design   566

PRESENTATIONS AND MEETINGS

Listening   312
Meetings   321
Minutes of Meetings   332
Presentations   396

RESEARCH AND DOCUMENTATION

Bibliographies   55
Copyright   113
Documenting Sources   148
Interviewing for Information   284
Note-Taking   350
Paraphrasing   374
Plagiarism   386
Questionnaires   444

Quotations 452
Research 463

ORGANIZATION, WRITING, AND REVISION

Collaborative Writing 82
Description 139
Ethics in Writing 192
Exposition 199
Global Communication 246
Logic Errors 315
Methods of Development 331
　Cause and Effect 76
　Chronological 78
　Comparison 98
　Definition 136
　Division and Classification 145
　General and Specific 244
　Order of Importance 361
　Sequential 517
　Spatial 521
Narration 342
Organization 364
Outlining 364
Persuasion 380
Preparation 394
　Audience 50
　Brainstorming 57
　Context 111
　Purpose 441
　Readers 455
　Scope 503
　Selecting the Medium 504
Proofreading 418
Revision 495
Writing a Draft 576

DIGITAL TIPS

Creating an Index 269
Creating an Outline 367
Creating Styles and Templates 216
Incorporating Tracked Changes 496
Laying Out a Page (See Web Link:
　Designing Documents, 311)
Leaving an Away-from-Desk
　Message 183
Preparing an ASCII Résumé 494
Proofreading for Format
　Consistency 419
Reviewing Collaborative
　Documents 84
Sending an E-mail Attachment 181
Testing Your Web Site 571
Using PDF Files 580

ESL TROUBLE SPOTS

Adjectives 13
Agreement 26
Articles 47

Biased Language 53
Clauses 80
Comma Splice 90
Commas 91
Double Negatives 171
English as a Second Language 186
Gender 243
Idioms 266
Mood 339
Nouns 352
Number (Grammar) 354
Numbers 355
Periods 377
Phrases 383
Plagiarism 386
Point of View 387
Possessive Case 392
Prepositions 395
Pronouns 413
Quotation Marks 450
Run-on Sentences 497
Sentence Construction 508
Sentence Fragments 514
Spelling 523
Style 523
Syntax 528
Tense 532
Transition 541
Verbals 549
Verbs 552
Voice 562

ESL TIPS

Assigning Gender 243
Avoiding Shifts in Voice, Mood,
　or Tense 554
Choosing Voice 565
Determining Mood 340
Punctuating Numbers 358
Stating an Opinion 389
Understanding the Requirements
　of a Sentence 512
Understanding the Subject
　of a Sentence 509
Using Adjectives 16
Using Articles 45
Using Possessive Pronouns 415
Using the Progressive Form 535

STYLE AND LANGUAGE

Style 523
　Affectation 23
　Allusions 33
　Ambiguity 34
　Awkwardness 51
　Biased Language 53
　Business Writing Style 67
　Clarity 78
　Clichés 81
　Comparison 98
　Conciseness 104

Contractions 113
Defining Terms 134
Direct Address 144
Double Negatives 171
Emphasis 184
English, Varieties of 190
Euphemisms 194
Expletives 198
Figures of Speech 204
Gobbledygook 251
Idioms 266
Intensifiers 277
Jargon 298
Nominalizations 349
Pace 369
Parallel Structure 373
Point of View 387
Positive Writing 391
Repetition 461
Rhetorical Questions 496
Sentence Variety 515
Subordination 526
Telegraphic Style 531
Tone 540
"You" Viewpoint 581
Word Choice 575
Abstract / Concrete Words 6
Antonyms 41
Buzzwords 68
Connotation / Denotation 110
Dictionaries 141
Foreign Words in English 208
Functional Shift 240
Malapropisms 319
Synonyms 528
Thesaurus 537
Vague Words 549

USAGE

See pages 631–32.

SENTENCES AND
PARAGRAPHS

Sentence Construction 508
Appositives 46
Clauses 80
Complements 103
Expletives 198
Modifiers 337
Objects 359
Phrases 383
Restrictive and Nonrestrictive
Elements 476
Syntax 528
Sentence Faults 512
Comma Splice 90
Dangling Modifiers 131
Garbled Sentences 242
Mixed Constructions 337
Run-on Sentences 497
Sentence Fragments 514

Paragraphs 369
Coherence 82
Transition 541
Unity 547

PARTS OF SPEECH
AND GRAMMAR

Grammar 252
Agreement 26
Case 72
English as a Second Language 186
Gender 243
Mood 339
Number 354
Person 379
Possessive Case 392
Pronoun Reference 412
Tense 532
Voice 562
Parts of Speech 376
Adjectives 13
Adverbs 21
Articles 47
Conjunctions 109
Functional Shift 240
Interjections 278
Nouns 352
Prefixes 394
Prepositions 395
Pronouns 413
Suffixes 527
Verbals 549
Verbs 552

PUNCTUATION AND
MECHANICS

Mechanics
Abbreviations 2
Acronyms and Initialisms 12
Ampersands 35
Capitalization 69
Compound Words 104
Contractions 113
Dates 133
Italics 294
Numbers 355
Proofreaders' Marks 417
Spelling 523
Punctuation 440
Apostrophes 41
Brackets 56
Colons 89
Commas 91
Dashes 132
Ellipses 178
Exclamation Marks 195
Hyphens 263
Parentheses 375
Periods 377
Question Marks 443
Quotation Marks 450
Semicolons 506
Slashes 520

MODEL DOCUMENTS AND FIGURES BY TOPIC

Use the following list as a quick reference for finding samples of business writing and visuals by topic. See also the complete Contents by Topic on pages xix–xxi. For additional model documents and resources, see the companion Web site at <bedfordstmartins.com/alredbus>.

BUSINESS WRITING DOCUMENTS AND ELEMENTS

A–2   Informative Abstract 8

B–2   Brochure 59

C–18   Long Cover Letter (for a Report) 129

D–1   Simple Description 139

D–2   Illustrated Description 140

E–2   Executive Summary 196

F–1   Feasibility Report 202

F–6   Formal Report 217

F–7   Form (for Staff Reappointment) 235

F–8   Form (for a Medical Claim) 236

I–1   Index Entry 268

I–5   Illustrated Instructions 276

I–9   Investigative Report 295

M–6   Mission Statement 335

N–2   Newsletter Article 345

N–3   Company Newsletter (Front Page) 347

P–5   Press Release 406

P–6   Process Explanation 408

P–7   Progress Report 409

P–8   Activity Report 411

P–10   Formal Internal Proposal 425

P–11   Sales Proposal 429

Q–1   Questionnaire 445

T–3   Trip Report 544

T–4   Trouble Report 545

CORRESPONDENCE

A–5   Acknowledgment Letter (Sent as E-mail) 12

A–6   Adjustment Letter (When Company Is at Fault) 18

A–7   Partial Adjustment Letter (Accompanying a Product) 20

C–3   First-Stage Collection Letter 86

C–4   Second-Stage Collection Letter 87

C–5   Third-Stage Collection Letter 88

C–9   Complaint Letter 102

C–11   A Poor Bad-News Message 118

C–12   A Courteous Bad-News Message 120

C–13   A Good-News Message 121

C–14   Full-Block-Style Letter 123

C–15   Modified-Block-Style Letter 124

C–16   Headers for the Second Page of a Letter 126

C–17   Brief Cover Letter (Sent as E-mail) 128

C–18   Long Cover Letter (for a Report) 129

E–1   E-mail Signature Block 183

I–2   Inquiry 271

I–3   Response to an Inquiry (Indicating That It Has Been Forwarded) 272

I–4   Response to an Inquiry 273

I–6   Inappropriate International Correspondence (Marked for Revision) 280

I–7   Appropriate International Correspondence 281

M–4   Typical Memo Format 330

P–1   Persuasive Memo 381

R–1   Reference Letter 458

R–2   Refusal Letter (Sent as E-mail) 460

S–1   Sales Letter 501

JOB SEARCH AND APPLICATION

A–3   Acceptance Letter
      (Sent as E-mail) 10

A–4   Refusal Letter
      (Sent as E-mail) 11

A–10 Application Letter Sent as E-mail
      (College Student Applying for an
      Internship) 43

A–11 Application Letter (Recent College
      Graduate Applying for a Job) 44

A–12 Application Letter (Applicant with
      Years of Experience) 45

I–8   Follow-up Correspondence 289

J–1   Job Description 299

R–1   Reference Letter 458

R–7   Resignation Letter (to Accept
      a Better Position) 476

R–8   Resignation Memo (Under
      Negative Conditions) 477

R–9   Student Résumé (for an Entry-
      Level Position) 480

R–10 Résumé (Highlighting Professional
      Credentials) 481

R–11 Student Résumé (for a Graphic
      Design Job) 482

R–12 Résumé (Applicant with
      Management Experience) 483

R–13 Advanced Résumé (Showing
      Promotion Within a Single
      Company) 484

R–14 Advanced Résumé (Combining
      Functional and Chronological
      Elements) 485

R–15 Electronic Résumé (in ASCII
      Format) 487

DESIGN AND VISUALS

C–8   Comparison Using a Table 100

D–11 Conventional Line Drawings 173

D–12 Exploded-View Drawing 174

D–13 Cutaway Drawing 175

D–14 Clip-Art Images 175

F–2   Flowchart Using Labeled
      Blocks 206

F–3   Flowchart Using Pictorial
      Symbols 207

F–4   Common ISO Flowchart
      Symbols 207

G–3   Graphic for a U.S. Audience 248

G–4   Graphic for a Global
      Audience 249

G–5   ISO Symbols 249

G–6   Double-Line Graph 254

G–7   Distorted and Distortion-Free
      Expressions of Data 254

G–8   Bar Graph 255

G–9   Bar (Column) Graph 256

G–10 Pie Graph 257

G–11 Picture Graph 257

H–1   Header and Footer 261

H–2   Headings Used
      in a Document 262

I–5   Illustrated Instructions 276

L–3   Sample Page Illustrating Layout
      and Design Choices 309

L–4   Bulleted List 315

M–1   Map 320

N–3   Company Newsletter
      (Front Page) 347

O–3   Organizational Chart 365

P–2   Photo 382

P–4   Slides for a Brief Presentation 401

T–1   Elements of a Table 530

T–2   Informal Table 531

V–2   Chart for Choosing Appropriate
      Visuals 559

W–1   Site Map 568

PRESENTATIONS AND MEETINGS

M–2   Meeting Agenda 323

M–3   E-mail to Accompany
      an Agenda 324

M–5   Minutes of a Meeting 333

P–4   Slides for a Brief Presentation 401

RESEARCH AND DOCUMENTATION

D–5   APA Sample Page 155

D–6   APA Sample List
      of References 156

(continued)

D-7   *CMS* Sample Page
(with Footnotes) 162

D-8   *CMS* Sample Bibliography 163

D-9   MLA Sample Page 168

D-10 MLA Sample List
of Works Cited 169

Q-1   Questionnaire 445

Q-2   Long Quotation (MLA Style) 454

ORGANIZATION, WRITING,
AND REVISION

B-1   Cluster Map from a Brainstorming
Session 58

C-2   Chronological Method
of Development 79

C-6   Whole-by-Whole Method
of Comparison 99

C-7   Part-by-Part Method
of Comparison 100

C-8   Comparison Using a Table 100

C-10 Conclusion 108

D-1   Simple Description 139

D-2   Illustrated Description 140

D-4   Classification 147

G-1   General-to-Specific Method
of Development 244

G-2   Specific-to-General Method
of Development 245

N-1   Narration 343

O-1   Decreasing Order-of-Importance
Method of Development 362

O-2   Increasing Order-of-Importance
Method of Development 363

P-1   Persuasive Memo 381

P-9   Proofreaders' Marks 418

S-2   Sequential Method
of Development 518

S-3   Spatial Method
of Development 522

W-1   Site Map 568

GRAMMAR, STYLE,
AND LANGUAGE

A-1   Abstract-to-Concrete Words 7

A-8   Affected Writing 24

A-9   Affected Writing Revised
for Clarity 25

C-1   Pronoun Case Chart 73

V-1   Verb-Conjugation Chart 555

a / an

A and *an* are indefinite <u>articles</u> because the <u>noun</u> designated by the article is not a specific person, place, or thing but is one of a group.

- The insurance agent sold *a* policy.
  [not a specific policy but an unnamed policy]

Use *a* before words or abbreviations beginning with a consonant or consonant sound, including *y* or *w*.

- The office manager felt that it was *a* difficult situation.
- It was *a* historic event for the company.
- We were awarded *a* DOD contract.
- The year's activities are summarized in *a* one-page report.
  [*One* begins with the consonant sound "wuh."]

Use *an* before words or abbreviations beginning with a vowel or a consonant with a vowel sound.

- He seems *an* unlikely candidate for the job.
- He bought *an* SLR digital camera.
  [*SLR* begins with a vowel sound "es."]
- The applicant arrived *an* hour early.
  [*Hour* begins with a silent *h*.]

Do not use unnecessary indefinite articles in a sentence.

- I will meet you in *a* half *an* hour.
  [Choose one article and eliminate the other.]

See also <u>adjectives</u>.

a lot

A lot is often incorrectly written as one word (*alot*). The phrase *a lot* is informal and normally should not be used in business writing. Use *many* or *numerous* for estimates or give a specific number or amount.

- The staff raised ~~a lot of~~ *many* objections to the policy.

abbreviations

DIRECTORY
Using Abbreviations   2
Writer's Checklist: Using Abbreviations   3
Forming Abbreviations   3
   Names of Organizations   3
   Measurements   4
   Personal Names and Titles   4
   Common Scholarly Abbreviations   5

Abbreviations are shortened versions of words or combinations of the first letters of words (Corp./Corporation, URL/Uniform Resource Locator). Abbreviations, if used appropriately, can be convenient for both the reader and the writer. Like symbols, they can be important space savers in business writing.

Abbreviations that are formed by combining the initial letter of each word in a multiword term are called *initialisms*. Initialisms are pronounced as separate letters (SEC/Securities and Exchange Commission). Abbreviations that combine the first letter or letters of several words — and can be pronounced — are called *acronyms*. Acronyms are always written without periods (PIN/personal identification number, laser/light amplification by stimulated emission of radiation).

Using Abbreviations

The most important consideration in the use of abbreviations is whether they will be understood by your **readers**. Even the same abbreviation, for example, can have two different meanings (NEA stands for both the National Education Association and the National Endowment for the Arts). In business, industry, and government, specialists and people working together on particular projects often use abbreviations. Like **jargon**, shortened forms will be easily understood within a group of specialists; outside of the group, however, they might be incomprehensible. In fact, abbreviations can be easily overused, either as an **affectation** or in a misguided attempt to make writing concise, especially in **e-mail**. Remember that memos, e-mail, or reports addressed to specific people may be read by other people—you must consider those secondary readers as well. A good rule to follow: when in doubt, spell it out.

Writer's Checklist: Using Abbreviations

☑ Except for commonly used abbreviations (U.S., a.m.), spell out a term to be abbreviated the first time it is used, followed by the abbreviation in parentheses. Thereafter, the abbreviation may be used alone.

☑ In long documents, repeat the full term in parentheses after the abbreviation at regular intervals to remind readers of the abbreviation's meaning, as in "Remember to submit the CAR (Capital Appropriations Request) by. . . ."

☑ Do not add an additional period at the end of a sentence that ends with an abbreviation.

   ● The official name of the company is DataBase, Inc.

☑ For abbreviations specific to your profession or discipline, use a style guide recommended by your professional organization or company. (A list of style guides appears at the end of **documenting sources**.)

☑ Write acronyms in capital letters without periods. The only exceptions are acronyms that have become accepted as common nouns, which are written in lowercase letters, such as *scuba* (*s*elf-*c*ontained *u*nderwater *b*reathing *a*pparatus).

☑ Generally, use periods for lowercase initialisms (a.k.a., e.d.p., p.m.) but not for uppercase ones (GDP, IRA, UFO). Exceptions include geographic names (U.S., U.K., E.U.) and formal expressions of academic degrees (B.A., M.B.A., Ph.D.).

☑ Form the plural of an acronym or initialism by adding a lowercase *s*. Do not use an **apostrophe** (CARs, DVDs).

☑ Do not follow an abbreviation with a word that repeats the final term in the abbreviation (ATM location *not* ATM machine location).

☑ Do not make up your own abbreviations; they will confuse readers.

Forming Abbreviations

Names of Organizations.   A company may include in its name a term such as *Brothers, Incorporated, Corporation,* or *Company.* If the term is abbreviated in the official company name that appears on letterhead stationery or on its Web site, use the abbreviated form: *Bros., Inc., Corp.,* or *Co.* If the term is not abbreviated in the official name, spell it out in writing, except with addresses, footnotes, <u>bibliographies</u>, and <u>lists</u> where abbreviations may be used. Likewise, use an ampersand (&) only if it appears in the official company name. For names of divisions within organizations, terms such as *Department* and *Division* should be abbreviated only when space is limited (*Dept.* and *Div.*).

Measurements.   Except for abbreviations that may be confused with words (*in.* for *inch* and *gal.* for *gallon*), abbreviations of measurement do not require periods (*yd* for *yard* and *qt* for *quart*). Abbreviations of units of measure are identical in the singular and plural: 1 *cm* and 15 *cm* (*not* 15 *cms*). Some abbreviations can be used in combination with other symbols (*°F* for *degrees Fahrenheit* and *ft²* for *square feet*).

The following list includes abbreviations for the basic units of the International System of Units (SI), the metric system. This system not only is standard in science but also is used in international commerce and trade.

MEASUREMENT	UNIT	ABBREVIATION
length	meter	m
mass	kilogram	kg
time	second	s
electric current	ampere	A
thermodynamic temperature	kelvin	K
amount of substance	mole	mol
luminous intensity	candela	cd

For additional definitions and background, see the National Institute of Standards and Technology Web site at <http://physics.nist.gov/cuu/Units/units.html>. For information on abbreviating dates and time, see <u>numbers</u>.

Personal Names and Titles.   Personal names generally should not be abbreviated: Thomas (*not* Thos.) and William (*not* Wm.). An academic, civil, religious, or military title should be spelled out and in lowercase when it does not precede a name. (The *captain* wanted to check the orders.) When they precede names, some titles are customarily abbreviated (Dr. Smith, Mr. Mills, Ms. Katz). See also <u>Ms./Miss/Mrs.</u>

An abbreviation of a title may follow the name; however, be certain that it does not duplicate a title before the name (Angeline Martinez, Ph.D. *or* Dr. Angeline Martinez). When addressing <u>correspondence</u> and including names in other documents, you normally should spell out titles (The Honorable Mary J. Holt; Professor Charles Matlin). Traditionally, periods are used with academic degrees, although they are sometimes omitted (M.A./MA, M.B.A./MBA, Ph.D./PhD).

Common Scholarly Abbreviations.   The following is a partial list of abbreviations commonly used in reference books and for **documenting sources** in research papers and reports. Other than in formal scholarly work, generally avoid such abbreviations.

anon.	anonymous
bibliog.	bibliography, bibliographer, bibliographic
ca., c.	*circa*, "about" (used with approximate dates: ca. 1756)
cf.	*confer*, "compare"
chap.	chapter
diss.	dissertation
ed., eds.	edited by, editor(s), edition(s)
e.g.	*exempli gratia*, "for example" (see **e.g./i.e.**)
esp.	especially
et al.	*et alii*, "and others"
etc.	*et cetera*, "and so forth" (see **etc.**)
ff.	and the following page(s) or line(s)
GPO	Government Printing Office, Washington, D.C.
i.e.	*id est*, "that is" (see **e.g./i.e.**)
l., ll.	line, lines
ms, mss	manuscript, manuscripts
n., nn.	note, notes (used immediately after page number: 56n., 56n.3, 56nn.3–5)
N.B., n.b.	*nota bene*, "take notice, mark well"
n.d.	no date (of publication)
n.p.	no place (of publication); no publisher; no page
p., pp.	page, pages
proc.	proceedings
pseud.	pseudonym
pub.	published by, publisher, publication
rev.	revised by, revised, revision; review, reviewed by (Spell out "review" where "rev." might be ambiguous.)
rpt.	reprinted by, reprint
sec., secs.	section, sections
sic	so, thus; inserted in **brackets** ([*sic*]) after a misspelled or wrongly used word in quotations
supp., suppl.	supplement
trans.	translated by, translator, translation
UP	University Press (used in MLA style, as in Oxford UP)
viz.	*videlicet*, "namely"
vol., vols.	volume, volumes
vs., v.	*versus*, "against" (*v.* preferred in titles of legal cases)

WEB LINK USING ABBREVIATIONS

For links to Web sites specifying standard abbreviations and acronyms, including U.S. Postal Service abbreviations, see *<bedfordstmartins.com/ alredbus>* and select *Links for Handbook Entries.*

---

above

Avoid using *above* to refer to a preceding passage or <u>visual</u> because its reference is often vague. The same is true of *aforesaid, aforementioned, the former,* and *the latter.* To refer to something previously mentioned, repeat the <u>noun</u> or <u>pronoun</u>, or construct your <u>paragraph</u> so that your reference is obvious.

- Please fill out and submit ~~the above~~ *your travel voucher* by March 1.

Using such references can also be an <u>affectation</u>. See also <u>former/latter</u>.

absolute words *(see* **adjectives***)*

absolutely

Absolutely means "definitely," "entirely," "completely," or "unquestionably." Avoid it as a redundant <u>intensifier</u> to mean "very" or "much."

- We are ~~absolutely~~ sure we can meet the deadline.

abstract / concrete words

Abstract words refer to general ideas, qualities, conditions, acts, or relationships — intangible things that cannot be detected by the five senses (sight, hearing, touch, taste, and smell), such as *learning, leadership,* and *technology. Concrete* words identify things that can be perceived by the five senses, such as *diploma, manager,* and *keyboard.*

  Abstract words must frequently be further defined or described.

- The marketing team needs freedom *to survey customers*.

Abstract words are best used with concrete words to help make intangible concepts specific and vivid.

- *Transportation* [abstract] was limited to *buses* [concrete] and *commuter trains* [concrete].

Just how concrete a particular context might require you to be is shown in Figure A–1, which goes from the most abstract, on the left, to the most concrete, on the right. The example in Figure A–1 represents seven levels of abstraction; the appropriate level depends on your <u>purpose</u> in writing and on the <u>context</u> in which you are using the word. See also <u>word choice</u>.

FIGURE A–1. Abstract-to-Concrete Words

abstracts

An abstract summarizes and highlights the major points of a <u>formal report</u>, trade journal article, dissertation, or other work. Its primary purpose is to enable readers to decide whether to read the work in full. For a discussion of how summaries differ from abstracts, see <u>executive summaries</u>.

Although abstracts, typically 200 to 250 words long, are published with the longer works they condense, they can also be published separately in periodical indexes and by abstracting services (see <u>research</u>). For this reason, an abstract must be readable apart from the original document.

Depending on the kind of information they contain, abstracts are often classified as descriptive or informative. A *descriptive abstract* summarizes the <u>purpose</u>, <u>scope</u>, and methods used to arrive at the reported findings. It is a slightly expanded table of contents in sentence and paragraph form. A descriptive abstract need not be longer than several sentences. An *informative abstract* is an expanded version of the descriptive abstract. In addition to information about the purpose, scope, and research methods used, the informative abstract summarizes the results, <u>conclusions</u>, and any recommendations. The informative abstract retains the <u>tone</u> and essential scope of the report, omitting its details. The first two paragraphs of the abstract shown in Figure A–2 alone would be descriptive; with the addition of the paragraphs that detail the findings and conclusions of the report, the abstract becomes informative.

The type of abstract you should write depends on your <u>readers</u> and the organization or publication for which you are writing. Infor-

---

ABSTRACT

Purpose

This report investigates the long-term effects of long-distance running on the bones, joints, and general health of runners aged 50 to 72. The Sports Medicine Institute of Columbia Hospital sponsored this investigation, first to decide whether to add a geriatric unit to the Institute, and second to determine whether physicians should recommend long-distance running for their older patients.

Methods and scope

The investigation is based on recent studies conducted at Stanford University and the University of Florida. The Stanford study tested and compared male and female long-distance runners aged 50 to 72 with a control group of runners and nonrunners. The groups were matched by sex, race, education, and occupation. The Florida study used only male runners who had run at least 20 miles a week for five years and compared them with a group of runners and nonrunners. Both studies based findings on medical histories and on physical and X-ray examinations.

Descriptive section

Findings

Both studies conclude that long-distance running is not associated with increased degenerative joint disease. Control groups were more prone to spur formation, sclerosis, and joint-space narrowing and showed more joint degeneration than runners. Female long-distance runners exhibited somewhat more sclerosis in knee joints and the lumbar spine area than matched control subjects. Both studies support the role of exercise in retarding bone loss with aging. The investigation concludes that the health risk factors are fewer for long-distance runners than for those less active aged 50 to 72.

Conclusions

Recommendations

The investigation recommends that the Sports Medicine Institute of Columbia Hospital consider the development of a geriatric unit a priority and that it inform physicians that an exercise program that includes long-distance running can be beneficial to their aging patients' health.

iii

FIGURE A–2. Informative Abstract (from a Report)

mative abstracts work best for wide audiences that need to know conclusions and recommendations; descriptive abstracts work best for compilations, such as proceedings and progress reports, that do not contain conclusions or recommendations.

Writing Style

Write the abstract *after* finishing the report or document. Otherwise, the abstract may not accurately reflect the longer work. Begin with a topic sentence that announces the subject and scope of your report or document. Then, using the major and minor headings of your outline or **table of contents** to distinguish primary ideas from secondary ones, decide what material is relevant to your abstract. (See **outlining**.) Write with **clarity** and **conciseness**, eliminating unnecessary words and ideas. Do not, however, become so terse that you omit articles (*a, an, the*) and important transitional words and phrases (*however, therefore, but, in summary*). Write complete sentences, but avoid stringing together a group of short sentences end to end; instead, combine ideas by using **subordination** and **parallel structure**. Spell out all but the most common **abbreviations**. Typically, in a formal report, an abstract follows the title page and is numbered page iii.

accept / except

Accept is a **verb** meaning "consent to," "agree to take," or "admit willingly." (I *accept* the responsibility.) *Except* is normally used as a preposition meaning "other than" or "excluding." (We agreed on everything *except* the schedule.)

acceptance / refusal letters (for employment)

When you decide to accept a job offer, you can notify your new employer by telephone or in a meeting—but to make your decision official, you need to send an acceptance in writing to your new employer. See also **correspondence** and **e-mail**.

Figure A–3 shows an example of an acceptance letter written by a college student. Of course, the details you include in your own letter will vary depending on your previous conversations with your new employer. Note that in the first paragraph of Figure A–3, the student identifies the job he is accepting and the salary he has been offered—doing so can

From: Chad Johnston <chjohnston@hotmail.com>
To: Helen Castro <castro@cdc.com>
Sent: Monday, April 17, 2006 8:39 AM
Subject: Acceptance of Account Representative Position

Dear Ms. Castro:

I am pleased to accept your offer of $28,500 per year as an account representative at your Corporate Education Center.

After graduation, I plan to leave Boston on Tuesday, June 6. I should be able to find suitable living accommodations within a few days and be ready to report for work on the following Monday, June 12. Please let me know if this date is satisfactory to you.

I look forward to working with your sales and customer service staff at CDC.

Sincerely,

Chad Johnston

FIGURE A–3. Acceptance Letter (Sent as E-mail)

avoid any misunderstandings about the job or the salary. In the second paragraph, the student details his plans for moving and reporting for work. Even if the student discussed these arrangements during earlier conversations, he needs to confirm them, officially, in this letter. The student then concludes with a brief but enthusiastic statement that he looks forward to working for the new employer.

When you decide to reject a job offer, send a job-refusal letter to make that decision official, even if you have already notified the employer during a meeting or on the phone. Writing a letter is a gesture that the employer will appreciate. Be especially tactful and courteous — the employer you are refusing has spent time and effort interviewing you and may have counted on your accepting the job. Remember, you may apply for another job at that company in the future. In Figure A–4, an example of a job-refusal letter, the applicant mentions something positive about her contact with the employer and refers to the specific job

From: Emily Brazy <ebrazy@yahoo.com>
To: Roger Vallone <vallone@cdc.com>
Sent: Friday, January 27, 2006 3:47 PM
Subject: Account Representative Position

Dear Mr. Vallone:

I enjoyed talking with you about your opening for an account representative, and I was gratified to receive your offer.

After giving the offer serious thought, however, I have decided to accept a position with an advertising agency. I feel that the job I have chosen is better suited to my skills and long-term goals.

I appreciate your consideration and the time you spent with me. I wish you the best of luck in filling the position.

Sincerely,

Emily Brazy

FIGURE A–4. Refusal Letter (Sent as E-mail)

offered. She indicates her serious consideration of the offer, provides a logical reason for the refusal, and concludes on a pleasant note. For further strategy on handling refusals and negative messages generally, see **refusal letters**.

acknowledgment letters

One way to build goodwill with colleagues and clients is to send an acknowledgment letter, letting them know that something they sent arrived and expressing thanks. It is usually a short, polite note. If you have established a working relationship with someone, an e-mail message is appropriate. (See **correspondence**.) The example shown in Figure A–5 is typical and could be sent as a letter or an e-mail.

A

```
From:      Wilbur Kohn <kohn@kohns.com>
To:        Marsha Stein <stein39@macrofoods.com>
Sent:      Friday, February 24, 2006 5:52 PM
Subject:   Checkout Lane Reporting System
```

Dear Ms. Stein:

I received your comprehensive report today. When I finish studying it in detail, I'll send you our cost estimate for the installation of the Checkout Lane Reporting System.

Thank you for preparing such a thorough analysis.

Regards,

Wilbur Kohn

FIGURE A–5. Acknowledgment Letter (Sent as E-mail)

acronyms and initialisms

Acronyms are formed by combining the first letter or letters of several words; they are pronounced as words and written without periods (FEMA/*F*ederal *E*mergency *M*anagement *A*gency). Initialisms are formed by combining the initial letter of each word in a multiword term; they are pronounced as separate letters (ABC/*A*ssociation for *B*usiness *C*ommunication). See **abbreviations** for the use of acronyms and initialisms.

active voice (*see* voice)

ad hoc

Ad hoc is Latin for "for this" or "for this particular occasion." An ad hoc committee is one set up to consider a particular issue, as opposed to a permanent committee. The term has been fully assimilated into English and thus does not have to be italicized. See also **affectation** and **foreign words in English**.

adapt / adept / adopt

Adapt is a verb meaning "adjust to a new situation." *Adept* is an adjective meaning "highly skilled." *Adopt* is a verb meaning "take or use as one's own."

- The company will *adopt* a policy of finding executives who are *adept* managers and who can *adapt* to new situations.

adjectives

DIRECTORY
Limiting Adjectives   13
Comparison of Adjectives   15
Placement of Adjectives   15
Use of Adjectives   17

An adjective is any word that modifies a **noun** or **pronoun**. *Descriptive adjectives* identify a quality of a noun or pronoun. *Limiting adjectives* impose boundaries on the noun or pronoun.

- *hot* surface [descriptive]
- *three* phone lines [limiting]

Limiting Adjectives

Limiting adjectives include these categories:

- Articles (*a, an, the*)
- Demonstrative adjectives (*this, that, these, those*)
- Possessive adjectives (*my, your, his, her, its, our, their*)
- Numeral adjectives (*two, first*)
- Indefinite adjectives (*all, none, some, any*)

Articles.   Articles (*a, an, the*) are traditionally classified as adjectives because they modify nouns by either limiting them or making them more specific. See also <u>a/an</u>, <u>articles</u>, and <u>English as a second language</u>.

Demonstrative Adjectives.   A demonstrative adjective points to the thing it modifies, specifying the object's position in space or time. *This* and *these* specify a closer position; *that* and *those* specify a more remote position.

- *This* report is more current than *that* report, which Human Resources distributed last month.

- *These* sales figures are more recent than *those* reported last week.

Demonstrative adjectives often cause problems when they modify the nouns *kind*, *type*, and *sort*. Demonstrative adjectives used with those nouns should agree with them in number.

- *this* kind, *these* kinds; *that* type, *those* types

Confusion often develops when the preposition *of* is added (*this kind of*, *these kinds of*) and the object of the preposition does not conform in number to the demonstrative adjective and its noun. See also <u>agreement</u> and <u>prepositions</u>.

- *This kind of* human resources ~~policies are~~ *policy is* standard.

- *These kinds of* human resources ~~policy is~~ *policies are* standard.

Avoid using demonstrative adjectives with words like *kind*, *type*, and *sort* because doing so can easily lead to vagueness. Instead, be more specific. See also <u>kind of/sort of</u>.

Possessive Adjectives.   Because possessive adjectives (*my, your, his, her, its, our, their*) directly modify nouns, they function as adjectives, even though they are pronoun forms (*my* idea, *her* plans, *their* projects). See also <u>functional shift</u>.

Numeral Adjectives.   Numeral adjectives identify quantity, degree, or place in a sequence. They always modify count nouns. Numeral adjectives are divided into two subclasses: cardinal and ordinal. A *cardinal adjective* expresses an exact quantity (*one* pencil, *two* computers); an *ordinal adjective* expresses degree or sequence (*first* quarter, *second* edition).

   In most writing, an ordinal adjective should be spelled out if it is a single word (*tenth*) and written in figures if it is more than one word (*312th*). Ordinal numbers can also function as adverbs. (John arrived *first*.) See also <u>first/firstly</u> and <u>numbers</u>.

Indefinite Adjectives.   Indefinite adjectives do not designate any-thing specific about the nouns they modify (*some* CD-ROMs, *all* designers). The articles *a* and *an* are included among the indefinite ad-jectives (*a* chair, *an* application).

Comparison of Adjectives

Most adjectives in the positive form show the comparative form with the suffix *-er* for two items and the superlative form with the suffix *-est* for three or more items.

- The first report is *long*. [positive form]
- The second report is *longer*. [comparative form]
- The third report is *longest*. [superlative form]

Many two-syllable adjectives and most three-syllable adjectives are preceded by the word *more* or *most* to form the comparative or the super-lative.

- The new media center is *more* impressive than the old one. It is the *most* impressive in the county.

A few adjectives have irregular forms of comparison (*much, more, most; little, less, least*).

Some adjectives (*round, unique, exact, accurate*), often called *ab-solute words*, are not logically subject to comparison.

- We modified our design to follow more ~~exactly~~ closely the recommended changes.

- We modified our design to follow ~~more~~ exactly the recommended changes.

Placement of Adjectives

When limiting and descriptive adjectives appear together, the limiting adjectives precede the descriptive adjectives, with the articles usually in the first position.

- *The ten red* cars were parked in a row.
  [article (*The*), limiting adjective (*ten*), descriptive adjective (*red*)]

Within a sentence, adjectives may appear before the nouns they modify (the attributive position) or after the nouns they modify (the predica-tive position).

ⓔˢˡ   TIPS FOR USING ADJECTIVES

Do not add *-s* or *-es* to an adjective to make it plural.

* the *long* trip

* the *long* trips

Capitalize adjectives of origin (city, state, nation, continent).

* the *Venetian* canals

* the *Texas* hat

* the *French* government

* the *African* deserts

In English, verbs of feeling (for example, *bore, interest, surprise*) have two adjectival forms: the present participle (*-ing*) and the past participle (*-ed*). Use the present participle to describe what causes the feeling. Use the past participle to describe the person who experiences the feeling.

* We heard the *surprising* election results.
  [The *election results* cause the feeling.]

* Only the losing candidate was *surprised* by the election results.
  [The *candidate* experienced the feeling of surprise.]

Adjectives follow nouns in English in only two cases: when the adjective functions as a subjective complement

* That project is not *finished.*

and when an adjective phrase or clause modifies the noun.

* The project *that was suspended temporarily* . . .

In all other cases, adjectives are placed before the noun.

When there are multiple adjectives, it is often difficult to know the right order. The guidelines illustrated in the following example would apply in most circumstances, but there are exceptions. (Normally do not use a phrase with so many stacked <u>modifiers</u>.) See also <u>articles</u>.

The six extra-large rectangular brown cardboard take-out containers

number	*size*		*color*		*qualifier*	
determiner	*comment*	*shape*		*material*		*noun*

- *The small* jobs are given priority. [attributive position]
- The exposure is *brief*. [predicative position]

Use of Adjectives

Nouns often function as adjectives to make other nouns more precise.

- The *accident* report prompted a *product* redesign.

When adjectives modifying the same noun can be reversed and still make sense or when they can be separated by *and* or *or*, they should be separated by commas.

- The company seeks a *bright, energetic, creative* management team.

Notice that there is no comma after *creative*. Never use a comma between a final adjective and the noun it modifies. When an adjective modifies a phrase, no comma is required.

- We need an *updated Web page design.*
  [*Updated* modifies the phrase *Web page design.*]

Writers sometimes string together a series of nouns used as adjectives to form a unit modifier, thereby creating stacked (jammed) <u>modifiers,</u> which can confuse readers. See also <u>word choice.</u>

adjustment letters

An adjustment letter is written in response to a <u>complaint letter</u> and tells the customer what your company intends to do about the complaint. Although sent in response to a problem, an adjustment letter actually provides an excellent opportunity to build goodwill for your company. An effective adjustment letter, such as those shown in Figures A–6 and A–7, can both repair any damage done and restore the customer's confidence in your company.

No matter how unreasonable the complaint, your response and tone should be positive and respectful. Avoid emphasizing the problem, but do take responsibility for it. Focus on what you are doing to correct the problem. You should settle such matters quickly and courteously, and always try to satisfy the customer at a reasonable cost to your company. See also <u>refusal letters.</u>

INTERNET SERVICES CORPORATION
10876 Crispen Way
Chicago, Illinois 60601

May 10, 2006

Mr. Jason Brandon
4319 Anglewood Street
Tacoma, WA 98402

Dear Mr. Brandon:

We are sorry that your experience with our customer support help line did not go smoothly. We are eager to restore your confidence in our ability to provide dependable, high-quality service. Your next three months of Internet access will be complimentary as our sincere apology for your unpleasant experience.

Providing dependable service is what is expected of us, and when our staff doesn't provide quality service, it is easy to understand our customers' disappointment. I truly wish we had performed better in our guidance for setup and log-on procedures and that your experience had been a positive one. To prevent similar problems in the future, we plan to use your letter in training sessions with customer support personnel.

We appreciate your taking the time to write us. It helps to receive comments such as yours, and we conscientiously follow through to be sure that proper procedures are being met.

Yours truly,

Inez Carlson

Inez Carlson, Vice President
Customer Support Services

www.isc.com

FIGURE A–6. Adjustment Letter (When Company Is at Fault)

Full Adjustments

Before granting an adjustment to a claim for which your company is at fault, first determine what happened and what you can do to satisfy the customer. Be certain that you are familiar with your company's adjustment policy. In addition, be careful about your wording; for example, "We have just received your letter of May 7 about our *defective product*" could be ruled in a court of law as an admission that the product is in fact defective. Treat every claim individually, and lean toward giving the customer the benefit of the doubt.

Grant adjustments graciously; a settlement made grudgingly will do more harm than good. Not only must you be gracious, but you must also acknowledge the error in such a way that the customer will not lose confidence in your company. (See also <u>tone</u> and <u>correspondence</u>.) Emphasize early what the reader will consider good news.

- Yes, you were incorrectly billed for the delivery.

- Please accept our apologies for the error in your account.

- Enclosed is a replacement for the damaged part.

If an explanation will help restore your reader's confidence, explain what caused the problem. You might point out any steps you may be taking to prevent a recurrence of the problem. Explain that customer feedback helps your firm keep the quality of its product or service high. Close pleasantly, looking forward, not back. Avoid recalling the problem in your closing (Again, we apologize . . .).

The adjustment letter in Figure A–6, for example, begins by accepting responsibility and offers an apology for the customer's inconvenience (note the use of the pronouns *we* and *our*). The second paragraph expresses a desire to restore goodwill and describes specifically how the writer intends to make the adjustment. The third paragraph expresses appreciation to the customer for calling attention to the problem and assures him that his complaint has been taken seriously.

Partial Adjustments

You may sometimes need to grant a partial adjustment—even if a claim is not really justified—to regain the lost goodwill of a customer or client. If, for example, a customer incorrectly uses a product or service, you may need to help the reader better understand the correct use of that product or service. In such a circumstance, remember that your customer or client believes that his or her claim is justified. Therefore, you should give the explanation before granting the claim—otherwise, your reader may never get to the explanation. If your explanation establishes customer responsibility, do so tactfully. Figure A–7 is an example of a partial adjustment letter.

ADDISON COMPUTERS
6409 East Seventh Street
Hartford, Connecticut 06156

September 21, 2006

Mr. Carlos Sanchez
570 Masterfield Avenue
Baton Rouge, LA 70805

Dear Mr. Sanchez:

Enclosed is your Addison Laptop Computer, which you shipped to
us on August 29.

Our technical staff reports that the laptop was damaged by exposure
to high levels of humidity. You stated in your letter that you often
use your laptop on a covered patio. Doing so in a high-humidity environment, as is typical in Louisiana, can result in damage to the
internal circuitry of your computer—as described on page 32 of
your Addison Owner's Manual.

We have replaced the damaged circuitry and thoroughly tested your
laptop. To ensure that a repetition of your recent experience does not
occur, we recommend you avoid leaving your laptop exposed to high
humidity for extended periods.

If you should find that the problem recurs, please call me at
800-555-0990. I will be glad to work with you to find a solution.

Sincerely,

Stephen Winton

Stephen Winton
Customer Service Representative

www.addison.com

FIGURE A–7. Partial Adjustment Letter (Accompanying a Product)

adverbs

DIRECTORY
Types of Adverbs   21
Comparison of Adverbs   22
Placement of Adverbs   22

An adverb modifies the action or condition expressed by a <u>verb</u>.

- The wrecking ball hit the side of the building *hard.*
  [The adverb tells *how* the wrecking ball hit the building.]

An adverb also can modify an <u>adjective</u>, another adverb, or a <u>clause</u>.

- The brochure design used *remarkably* bright colors.
  [*Remarkably* modifies the adjective *bright.*]
- The redesigned brake pad lasted *much* longer.
  [*Much* modifies the adverb *longer.*]
- *Surprisingly,* the engine failed.
  [*Surprisingly* modifies the clause *the engine failed.*]

Types of Adverbs

A simple adverb can answer one of the following questions:

Where? (adverb of place)

- Move the display *forward* slightly.

When? or *How often?* (adverb of time)

- Replace the thermostat *immediately.*
- I worked overtime *twice* this week.

How? (adverb of manner)

- Add the solvent *cautiously.*

How much? (adverb of degree)

- The *nearly* completed report was deleted from his disk.

An interrogative adverb can ask a question (*Where? When? Why? How?*):

- *How* many hours did you work last week?
- *Why* was the disk reformatted?

A conjunctive adverb can modify the clause that it introduces as well as join two independent clauses with a <u>semicolon</u>. The most common conjunctive adverbs are *however, nevertheless, moreover, therefore, further, then, consequently, besides, accordingly, also,* and *thus.*

- *Therefore,* I should finish the project by the deadline.
- I rarely work on weekends; *however,* this weekend will be an exception.

In the second example, note that a semicolon precedes and a <u>comma</u> follows *however.* The conjunctive adverb (*however*) introduces the independent clause (*this weekend will be an exception*) and indicates its relationship to the preceding independent clause (*I rarely work on weekends*). See also <u>transition</u>.

Comparison of Adverbs

Most one-syllable adverbs show comparison with the suffixes *-er* and *-est.*

- This copier is *fast.* [positive form]
- This copier is *faster* than the old one. [comparative form]
- This copier is the *fastest* of the three tested. [superlative form]

Most adverbs with two or more syllables end in *-ly,* and most adverbs ending in *-ly* are compared by inserting the comparative *more* or *less* or the superlative *most* or *least* in front of them.

- She moved *more quickly* than any other company's sales representative.
- *Most surprisingly,* the engine failed during the final test phase.

A few irregular adverbs require a change in form to indicate comparison (*well, better, best; badly, worse, worst; far, farther, farthest*).

- The training program functions *well.*
- Our training program functions *better* than most others in the industry.
- Many consider our training program the *best* in the industry.

Placement of Adverbs

An adverb usually should be placed in front of the verb it modifies.

- The pilot *methodically* performed the preflight check.

An adverb may, however, follow the verb (or the verb and its object) that it modifies.

- The system failed *unexpectedly*.
- They replaced the hard drive *quickly*.

An adverb may be placed between a helping verb and a main verb.

- In this temperature range, the pressure will *quickly* drop.

Adverbs such as *only*, *nearly*, *almost*, *just*, and *hardly* should be placed immediately before the words they limit. See also <u>only</u> and <u>modifiers</u>.

affect / effect

Affect is a <u>verb</u> that means "influence."

- The new management could *affect* the company's stock value.

Effect can function as a <u>noun</u> that means "result."

- The change in management had a positive *effect*.

Effect can also function as a verb that means "bring about" or "cause." However, avoid using *effect* as a verb. A less formal word, such as *make* or *produce*, is usually preferable.

- The new manager will ~~effect~~ *make* several changes to improve morale.

affectation

Affectation is the use of language that is more formal, technical, or showy than necessary to communicate information to the reader. Affectation is a widespread writing problem in the workplace because many people feel that affectation lends a degree of authority to their writing. In fact, affectation can alienate customers, clients, and colleagues.

Affected writing forces readers to work harder to understand the writer's meaning. It typically contains abstract, highly technical, or foreign words and is often liberally sprinkled with trendy <u>buzzwords</u>.

⚡ ETHICS NOTE <u>Jargon</u> and <u>euphemisms</u> can become affectation, especially if their purpose is to hide relevant facts or give a false impression of competence. See <u>ethics in writing</u>. ✦

Writers are easily lured into affectation through the use of long variants—words created by adding prefixes and suffixes to simpler words (*orientate* for *orient*; *utilization* for *use*). Unnecessarily formal words (such as *penultimate* for *next to last*), created words using *-ese* (such as *managementese*), and outdated words (such as *aforesaid*) can produce affectation. (See also **above**.) Elegant variation—attempting to avoid repeating a word within a paragraph by substituting a pretentious synonym—is also a form of affectation.

- The use of robotics in the assembly process has increased
  , and it
  production. ~~Robotic utilization~~ has cut costs.
  ∧

Another type of affectation is **gobbledygook**, which is wordy, roundabout writing with many legal- and scientific-sounding terms (such as *herewith* and *quantum*).

Figure A–8 shows the original maintenance regulations for merchants with retail stores located on a military base. The revision of those regulations, which eliminates various forms of affectation, is much clearer (See Figure A–9).

In addition to performing interior housekeeping services, the concessionaire shall perform custodial maintenance on the exterior of the facility and grounds. Where a concessionaire shares a facility with one or more other concessionaires, exterior custodial maintenance responsibilities will be assigned by Post Exchange management on a fair and equitable basis. In those instances where the concessionaire's activity is located in a Post Exchange complex wherein predominant tenancy is by Post Exchange–operated activities, then Post Exchange management shall be responsible for exterior custodial maintenance except for those described in 1, 2, 3, and 4 below. The necessary equipment and labor to perform exterior custodial maintenance, when such a responsibility has been assigned to the concessionaire, shall be furnished by the concessionaire. Exterior custodial maintenance shall include the following tasks:

1. Clean entrance door and exterior of storefront windows daily.
2. Sweep and clean the entrance and customer walks daily.
3. Empty and clean waste and manage recyclable material disposal daily.
4. Check exterior lighting and report failures to the contracting officer's representative daily.

FIGURE A–8. Affected Writing

The merchant will, with his or her own equipment, perform the following duties daily:

1. Maintain a clean and neat appearance inside the store.
2. Clean the entrance door and the outsides of the store windows.
3. Sweep the entrance and the sidewalk.
4. Empty and clean wastebaskets and dispose of recyclable materials.
5. Check the exterior lighting and report failures to the representative of the contracting officer.

The merchant will also maintain the grounds surrounding the store, as specified in the merchant's contract. Where two or more merchants share the same building, Post Exchange management will assign responsibility for the grounds. Where the merchant's store is in a building that is occupied predominantly by Post Exchange operations, Post Exchange management will be responsible for the grounds.

FIGURE A–9. Affected Writing Revised for Clarity

Understanding the possible reasons for affectation is the first step toward avoiding it. The following are some causes of affectation.

- *Impression.* Some writers use pretentious language in an attempt to impress the reader with fancy words instead of evidence and logic.

- *Insecurity.* Writers who are insecure about their facts, conclusions, or arguments may try to hide behind a smoke screen of pretentious words.

- *Imitation.* Perhaps unconsciously, some writers imitate poor writing they see around them.

- *Intimidation.* A few writers, consciously or unconsciously, try to intimidate or overwhelm their readers with words, often to protect themselves from criticism.

- *Initiation.* Writers who are new to a field often feel that one way to prove their professional expertise is to use as much technical terminology and jargon as possible.

- *Imprecision.* Writers who are having trouble being precise sometimes find that an easy solution is to use a vague, trendy, or pretentious word.

See also clichés, conciseness, and nominalizations.

affinity

Affinity refers to the attraction of two persons or things to each other.

- The *affinity* between the company and its investors can be explained by the company's profit margins.

Affinity should not be used to mean "ability" or "aptitude."

- She has an ~~affinity~~ *aptitude* for marketing.

agreement

DIRECTORY
Subject-Verb Agreement   27
Compound Subjects   29
Pronoun-Antecedent Agreement   29

Grammatical agreement is the correspondence in form between different elements of a sentence to indicate <u>number</u>, <u>person</u>, <u>gender</u>, and <u>case</u>.
A subject and its <u>verb</u> must agree in number.

- The *design is* acceptable.
  [The singular subject, *design*, requires the singular verb, *is*.]
- The new *products are* going into production soon.
  [The plural subject, *products*, requires the plural verb, *are*.]

A subject and its verb must agree in person.

- *I am* the designer.
  [The first-person singular subject, *I*, requires the first-person singular verb, *am*.]
- *They are* the designers.
  [The third-person plural subject, *they*, requires the third-person plural verb, *are*.]

A <u>pronoun</u> and its antecedent must agree in person, number, gender, and case.

- The *employees* report that *they* are more efficient in the new facility.
  [The third-person plural subject, *employees*, requires the third-person plural pronoun, *they*.]

- *Kaye McGuire* will meet with the staff on Friday, when *she* will assign duties.
  [The third-person singular subject, *Kaye McGuire*, requires *she*, the third-person feminine pronoun, in the subjective case.]

See also **sentence construction**.

Subject-Verb Agreement

Subject-verb agreement is not affected by intervening **phrases** and **clauses**.

- *One* in twenty hard drives we receive from our suppliers *is* faulty.
  [The verb, *is*, must agree in number with the subject, *one*, not *hard drives* or *suppliers*.]

The same is true when **nouns** fall between a subject and its verb.

- Only *one* of the emergency lights *was* functioning.
  [The subject of the verb is *one*, not *lights*.]
- *Each* of the managers *supervises* a very large region.
  [The subject of the verb is *each*, not *managers*.]

Note that *one* and *each* are normally singular.

Indefinite pronouns such as *some*, *none*, *all*, *more*, and *most* may be singular or plural, depending on whether they are used with a mass noun (*Most* of the oil *has* been used) or with a count noun (*Most* of the drivers *know* why they are here). Mass nouns are singular, and count nouns are plural. Other words, such as *type*, *part*, *series*, and *portion*, take singular verbs even when they precede a phrase containing a plural noun.

- A *series* of meetings *was* held about the best way to market the new product.
- A large *portion* of most annual reports *is* devoted to promoting the corporate image.

Modifying phrases can obscure a simple subject.

- The *advice* of two engineers, one lawyer, and three executives *was* obtained prior to making a commitment.
  [The subject of the verb *was* is *advice*.]

Inverted word order can cause problems with agreement.

- From this work *have come* several important *improvements*.
  [The subject of the verb is *improvements*, not *work*.]

The number of a subjective __complement__ does not affect the number of the verb — the verb must always agree with the subject.

- The *topic* of his report *is* employee benefits.
  [The subject of the sentence is *topic*, not *benefits*.]

A subject that expresses measurement, weight, mass, or total often takes a singular verb even when the subject word is plural in form. Such subjects are treated as a unit.

- *Four weeks is* the normal duration of the training program.

A verb following the relative pronoun *who* or *that* agrees in number with the noun to which the pronoun refers (its antecedent).

- This is one of those management *problems* that *require* careful analysis.
  [*That* refers to *problems*.]
- She is one of those *employees* who *are* rarely absent.
  [*Who* refers to *employees*.]

The word *number* sometimes causes confusion. When used to mean a specific number, it is singular.

- *The number* of committee members *was* six.

When used to mean an approximate number, it is plural.

- *A number* of people *were* waiting for the announcement.

Relative pronouns (*who, which, that*) may take either singular or plural verbs, depending on whether the antecedent is singular or plural. See also __who/whom__.

- He is a bookkeeper *who takes* work home at night.
- He is one of those bookkeepers *who take* work home at night.

Some abstract nouns are singular in meaning but plural in form: *mathematics, news, physics,* and *economics*.

- *News* of the merger *is* on page 4 of the *Chronicle*.

Some words, such as the plural *jeans* and *scissors*, cause special problems.

- The *scissors were* ordered last week.
  [The subject is the plural *scissors*.]
- *A pair* of scissors *is* on order.
  [The subject is the singular *pair*.]

A book with a plural title requires a singular verb.

- *Basic Medical Laboratory Techniques* is an essential resource.

A collective noun (*committee, faculty, class, jury*) used as a subject takes a singular verb when the group is thought of as a unit and a plural verb when the individuals in the group are thought of separately.

- The *committee is* unanimous in its decision.
- The *committee are* returning to their offices.

A clearer way to emphasize the individuals would be to use a phrase.

- The *committee members are* returning to their offices.

Compound Subjects

A compound subject is composed of two or more elements joined by a **conjunction** such as *and, or, nor, either . . . or,* or *neither . . . nor.* Usually, when the elements are connected by *and,* the subject is plural and requires a plural verb.

- *Accounting and chemistry are* both prerequisites for this position.

One exception occurs when the elements connected by *and* form a unit or refer to the same thing. In that case, the subject is regarded as singular and takes a singular verb.

- *Bacon and eggs is* a high-cholesterol meal.
- Our greatest *challenge and business opportunity is* the Internet.

A compound subject with a singular element and a plural element joined by *or* or *nor* requires that the verb agree with the closer element.

- Neither the director nor the *project assistants were* there.
- Neither the project assistants nor the *director was* there.

If *each* or *every* modifies the elements of a compound subject, use the singular verb.

- *Each* manager and supervisor *has* a production goal to meet.
- *Every* manager and supervisor *has* a production goal to meet.

Pronoun-Antecedent Agreement

Every pronoun must have an antecedent—a noun to which it refers. See also **pronoun reference**.

- When *employees* are hired, *they* must review the policy manual.
  [The pronoun *they* refers to the antecedent *employees*.]

Gender.   A pronoun must agree in gender with its antecedent.

- *Mr. Swivet* in the accounting department acknowledges *his* share of
  the responsibility for the misunderstanding, just as *Ms. Barkley* in
  the research division must acknowledge *hers*.

Traditionally, a masculine, singular pronoun was used to agree with
such indefinite antecedents as *anyone* and *person*.

- *Each* may stay or go as *he* chooses.

Because such usage ignores or excludes women, use alternatives when
they are available. One solution is to use the plural. Another is to use
both feminine and masculine pronouns, although that combination is
clumsy when used too often.

- *All employees*   *their*   *cards*
  ~~Every employee~~ must sign ~~his~~ time ~~card~~.
  ^   ^   ^

- *or her*
  Every employee must sign his time card.
                           ^

Do not attempt to avoid expressing gender by resorting to a plural pronoun when the antecedent is singular. You may be able to avoid the
pronoun entirely.

- *a*
  Every employee must sign ~~their~~ time card.
                           ^

Avoid gender-related stereotypes in general references, as in "the
nurse . . . *she*" or "the doctor . . . *he*." What if the nurse is male or the
doctor female? See also <u>biased language</u>.

Number.   A pronoun must agree with its antecedent in number.
Many problems of agreement are caused by expressions that are not
clear in number.

- Although the typical engine runs well in moderate temperatures,
  it   *stalls*
  ~~they~~ often ~~stall~~ in extreme cold.
  ^   ^

Use singular pronouns with the antecedents *everybody* and *everyone* unless to do so would be illogical because the meaning is obviously plural.
See also <u>everybody/everyone</u>.

- *Everyone* pulled *his or her* share of the load.

- *Everyone* thought my plan should be revised, and I really couldn't blame *them*.

Collective nouns may use a singular or plural pronoun, depending on the meaning.

- The *committee* arrived at the recommended solutions only after *it* had deliberated for days.
  [*committee* thought of as collective]

- The *committee* quit for the day and went to *their* respective homes.
  [*committee* thought of as plural]

Demonstrative <u>adjectives</u> sometimes cause problems with agreement of number. *This* and *that* are used with singular nouns, and *these* and *those* are used with plural nouns. Demonstrative adjectives often cause problems when they modify the nouns *kind*, *type*, and *sort*. When used with those nouns, demonstrative adjectives should agree with them in number.

- *this* kind, *these* kinds; *that* type, *those* types

Confusion often develops when the <u>preposition</u> of is added (*this kind of*, *these kinds of*) and the object of the preposition does not conform in number to the demonstrative adjective and its noun.

- This kind of retirement ~~plans are~~ best.
  plan is

Avoid that error by remembering to make the demonstrative adjective, the noun, and the object of the preposition — all three — agree in number. The agreement makes the sentence not only correct but also more precise. Keep in mind that using demonstrative adjectives with words like *kind*, *type*, and *sort* can easily lead to vagueness. See <u>kind of/sort of</u>.

Compound Antecedents.   A compound antecedent joined by *or* or *nor* is singular if both elements are singular and plural if both elements are plural.

- Neither the *engineer* nor the *technician* could do *his* job until *he* understood the new concept.

- Neither the *executives* nor the *directors* were pleased at the performance of *their* company.

When one of the antecedents connected by *or* or *nor* is singular and the other plural, the pronoun agrees with the closer antecedent.

- Either the *computer* or the *printers* should have *their* serial numbers registered.
- Either the *printers* or the *computer* should have *its* serial number registered.

A compound antecedent with its elements joined by *and* requires a plural pronoun.

- *Seon Ju and Juanita* took *their* layout drawings with them.

If both elements refer to the same person, however, use the singular pronoun.

- The noted *economist and author* departed from *her* prepared speech.

all ready / already

All ready is a two-word phrase meaning "completely prepared." *Already* is an **adverb** that means "before this time" or "previously." (They were *all ready* to cancel the order; fortunately, we had *already* corrected the shipments.)

all right

All right means "all correct." (The answers were *all right*). In formal writing, it should not be used to mean "good" or "acceptable." It is always written as two words, with no hyphen; *alright* is nonstandard.

all together / altogether

All together means "all acting together" or "all in one place." (The new employees were *all together* at the orientation.) *Altogether* means "entirely" or "completely." (The trip was *altogether* unnecessary.)

allude / elude / refer

Allude means to make an indirect reference to something. (The report simply *alluded* to the problem, rather than stating it explicitly.) *Elude* means to escape notice or detection. (The discrepancy in the account *eluded* the auditor.) *Refer* is used to indicate a direct reference to some-thing. (She *referred* to the merger during her presentation.)

allusion / illusion

An *allusion* is an indirect reference to something not specifically men-tioned. (The report made an *allusion* to metal fatigue in the support structures.) An *illusion* is a mistaken perception or a false image. (The manager is under the *illusion* that the reorganization will cost very little.)

allusions

An allusion is an indirect reference to something from past or current events, literature, or other familiar sources. The use of allusion pro-motes economical writing because it is a shorthand way of referring to a body of material in a few words or of helping to explain a new and unfamiliar process in terms of one that is familiar. In the following ex-ample, the writer sums up a description with an allusion to a well-known story. The allusion, with its implicit reference to "right standing up to might," concisely emphasizes the writer's point.

- As it currently exists, the review process involves the consumer's attorney sitting alone, usually without adequate technical assis-tance, faced by two or three government attorneys, two or three attorneys from CompuSystems, and large teams of experts who support the government and the corporation. The entire proceed-ing is reminiscent of David versus Goliath.

Be sure, of course, that your reader is familiar with the material to which you allude. Allusions should be used with restraint, especially in **international correspondence**. If overdone, allusions can lead to **affec-tation** or can be viewed merely as **clichés**. See also **business writing style**.

almost / most

Do not use *most* as a colloquial substitute for *almost* in your writing.

- New shipments arrive ~~most~~ *almost* every day.

also

Also is an **adverb** that means "additionally." (Two 5,000-gallon tanks are on-site, and several 2,500-gallon tanks are *also* available.) *Also* should not be used as a connective in the sense of "and."

- He brought the reports, the letters, ~~also~~ ^and^ the section supervisor's recommendations.

Avoid opening sentences with *also*. It is a weak transitional word that suggests an afterthought rather than planned writing.

- ~~Also,~~ ^*In addition*^ he brought statistical data to support his proposal.

- ~~Also,~~ ^*He also*^ he brought statistical data to support his proposal.

ambiguity

A word or passage is ambiguous when it can be interpreted in two or more ways, yet provides the reader with no certain basis for choosing among the alternatives.

- Language is more valuable to a writer than a computer.
  [Does that mean a writer is more in need of language than a computer is? Or does it mean that language is more valuable to a writer than a computer is?]

Ambiguity can take many forms, as in ambiguous **pronoun reference**.

AMBIGUOUS	Inadequate quality-control procedures have resulted in more equipment failures. This is our most serious problem at present. [Does *this* refer to *inadequate quality-control procedures* or to *equipment failures*?]
SPECIFIC	Inadequate quality-control procedures have resulted in more equipment failures. *These failures* are our most serious problem at present.
SPECIFIC	Inadequate quality-control procedures have resulted in more equipment failures. *Quality control* is our most serious problem at present.

Incomplete **comparison** and missing or misplaced **modifiers** (including **dangling modifiers**) cause ambiguity.

- Ms. Lee values rigid quality-control standards more than Mr.
  Rosenblum. [Complete the comparison.]
  does

- He lists his hobby as cooking. He is especially fond of cocker
  spaniels. [Add the missing modifier.]
  also

The placement of some modifiers enables them to be interpreted in either of two ways.

- She volunteered *immediately* to deliver the toxic substance.

By moving the word *immediately*, the meaning can be clarified.

- She *immediately* volunteered to deliver the toxic substance.

- She volunteered to deliver *immediately* the toxic substance.

Imprecise <u>word choice</u> (including faulty <u>idioms</u>) can cause ambiguity.

- The general manager has denied reports that the plant's recent
  fuel-allocation cut will be ~~restored~~. [inappropriate word choice]
  rescinded

Various forms of <u>awkwardness</u> also can cause ambiguity.

amount / number

Amount is used with things that are thought of in bulk and that cannot be counted (mass <u>nouns</u>), as in "the *amount* of electricity." *Number* is used with things that can be counted as individual items (count nouns), as in "the *number* of employees."

ampersands

The ampersand (&) is a symbol sometimes used to represent the word *and*, especially in the names of organizations (Kirkwell & Associates). When you are writing the name of an organization in sentences, addresses, or references, spell out the word *and* unless the ampersand appears in the organization's official name on its letterhead stationery or Web site.

analogies (*see* figures of speech)

and / or

And/or means that either both circumstances are possible or only one of two circumstances is possible. This term is awkward and confusing because it makes the reader stop to puzzle over your distinction.

AWKWARD   Use A *and/or* B.

IMPROVED   Use A or B or both.

annual reports

The corporate annual report is, in effect, a state-of-the-company message, which publicly traded companies are legally required to publish annually but private companies are not. Written primarily for stockholders, the report also addresses such readers as bankers, the financial press, labor unions, employees, and local political officials. An annual report usually covers the high points of the previous year's operations and finances and forecasts the coming year's operations. It may also explain the company's current direction and highlight its strengths. If weaknesses have developed or failures have occurred, the annual report may analyze them and explain the efforts being made to overcome them.

Your company's annual report could be the most important writing you will ever be asked to do. Study your company's annual reports of the past several years for content, style, and format. Within reason, try to emulate past reports. Then review the writing process outlined in the "Checklist of the Writing Process" and use all the steps listed there. Finally, collaborate closely with your company's (or outside contractor's) graphics, print-production, and Web staffs. Meet with them regularly throughout the information-gathering and writing stages to discuss design, to learn their file-format requirements, to schedule photographs, and to schedule milestones for producing the print and Web versions of the report. See also business plans, collaborative writing, mission statements, and writing for the Web.

Structure and Parts

Some annual reports are lavishly produced publications that paint the company and its operations in glowing terms; others are spartan financial summaries that merely meet the legal requirements for annual financial reporting. Most are a combination of both. Annual reports vary greatly in organization, but they typically include five major sections:

- Financial highlights
- A statement to the stockholders or a letter from the president
- A narrative section on the company's operations
- A financial statement
- A listing of the company's board of directors and officers

Financial Highlights.   The financial highlights section is a brief review of the company's sales and earnings that usually precedes the statement to the stockholders, sometimes even appearing on the inside of the front cover. The most read part of the annual report, this section often compares sales and earnings for three years and typically includes the percentage of change from year to year.

Statement to Stockholders.   This section is a direct statement to stockholders from the company's president or the chair of the board of directors. The statement (sometimes in the form of a letter) is second in readership only to the financial highlights. It sets the stage for the rest of the report. This section should not repeat the financial facts already cited in the financial highlights; instead, it should interpret the entire year's performance, touch on plans and future directions, and give the company's explanations for any failures.

The statement to stockholders may be an in-depth review of the company's operations during the past year or a brief summary of the entire report. A brief summary of the annual report is sometimes followed by an article in question-and-answer format in which the president of the company reviews the past year's operations.

Narrative Section.   This section of the annual report is normally used to present company operations and new products or developments in a positive light. Select the topics for this section carefully, making certain they are timely and meaningful and that they contribute to the primary objective of the annual report. Topics for this section might include the following:

- Major profit factors in the last year's performance
- Current market performance of existing products or services
- Prospects for increasing stock dividends
- Significant new products or services
- Productivity and profits
- The company's performance compared with that of its competition
- Outlook for next year (for the company as a whole or by divisions)
- Major acquisitions and restructuring

- Significant organizational changes
- Research and development
- Global operations and economic climate (when appropriate)
- Service and support operations
- Social responsibilities (such as environmental responsibility and community service)

Financial Statement.   At the minimum, most financial statements include the following:

- A company balance sheet
- A statement of income
- Changes in financial position
- An independent auditor's statement
- Footnotes, as necessary

Most annual reports also include a fairly comprehensive comparison of financial results of the past three years. Footnotes in the financial section should be written in simple, direct language rather than in accounting terms. The auditor's statement should be limited to no more than one-third of a page.

The financial statement should be uncluttered and inviting. Although it may appear at the beginning, the middle, or the end of the report, it most often appears at the end. It is frequently prepared as a separate booklet, printed on colored paper, and bound into the report.

Board of Directors and Company Officers.   The final part of the annual report lists the company's board of directors and their corporate affiliations. Many annual reports also include a photograph of each director, as well as a listing of the company's officers by name and title (sometimes with photographs). The officers generally include the chair of the board of directors, the president, vice presidents, secretary, treasurer, and legal counsel. To avoid hard feelings about some being shown in photographs and others not, establish a logical cutoff point. For example, if there are too many officers to include photographs of them all, show only the executive committee. Do not, however, underestimate the importance of photographs, for they lend a human touch to what is essentially a financial report.

Preparing the Report

If you prepare an annual report, first interview the president of the company or the chair of the board of directors to determine the general direction the report is to take. Next, interview vice presidents or division heads to learn the highlights of each division's operations. Determine from them the proper emphasis to place on their divisions' performances (but stay within the general direction established by the president or chair). See <u>interviewing for information</u>.

The primary focus of the report often depends on which audience is primary: shareholders, bankers, business and financial analysts, the financial press, employees, labor unions, or the local communities in which your company operates. You cannot satisfy all those groups, so establish priorities among them.

Compose a list of primary topics and allot space as necessary to each division or subsidiary in order to make a number of decisions:

- Whether to show sales and earnings as a company total only or by division as well
- The contents of charts and graphs
- Whether to include photographs of the executives of branches, divisions, and subsidiaries
- How lavish or spartan the report should be in appearance and cost

Tone is critical in writing and designing an annual report. Avoid any <u>biased language</u>, <u>clichés</u>, and unnecessary technical terms. Use simple sentences, short <u>paragraphs</u>, and a straightforward and informal style. Companies are as different as people: some are well established and conservative, while others are aggressive start-ups. The annual report should convey the image your company has established or wants to establish.

Design and Visuals. Typography, graphics, and design communicate a message about a company as strongly as words do. Be sure to select visual elements that enhance your company's image and accurately reflect your industry. See <u>layout and design</u> and <u>visuals</u>. A classic, formal page layout with traditional typography suggests a conservative company, while bold graphics, a dynamic design, and nontraditional typography suggest a more cutting-edge company.

Most readers merely scan an annual report, but they do pause to look at photographs and <u>visuals</u> and read the captions. Therefore, use photographs and visuals liberally, although purposefully, in the narrative section to enhance the company's image, and complement the photographs and visuals with informative and well-written captions. Choose only those photographs and illustrations that will make the maximum contribution to the report's theme. Both photographs and their captions are critical in enlivening your annual report and putting a human face on your company. Colorful and well-shot photographs that show action or people enjoying themselves attract favorable interest.

Charts and **graphs** enable readers to grasp numerical material quickly and easily, provided those visuals are not so complex that they defeat the purpose. Some companies deploy graphs throughout the annual report at strategic locations near the financial highlights, in the statement to stockholders, and throughout the narrative section. Others group them in the financial statement. Subjects that most easily lend themselves to graphs and charts, usually shown in a three-year comparison arrangement, are the following:

- Assets
- Capital expenditures
- Dividends
- Earnings (by product groups or divisions)
- Industry growth
- Inventories
- Liabilities
- Net worth
- Price trends
- Reserves
- Sales (by product groups or divisions)
- Source and disposition of funds (taxes, wages, working capital)

The following information is normally printed on the inside front and back covers of the annual report:

- Notice of the annual meeting
- Corporate address
- Names of transfer agents, registrar, and stock exchange

Some annual reports use the inside front cover solely for the announcement of the annual meeting.

Writer's Checklist: Annual Reports

☑ Review past annual reports for their content, style, and format.

☑ Interview senior company officials to learn which issues they wish to highlight.

☑ Allocate topics and space to reach your company's target audiences.

☑ Adopt a writing style and layout and design consistent with your company's image.

☑ Collaborate with graphics specialists to ensure that photographs, charts, and graphs highlight images and information effectively for target outside audiences.

☑ Work closely with the graphics, print-production, and Web staffs to ensure that the report is professionally designed and produced.

antonyms

An antonym is a word with a meaning opposite that of another word (*good/bad, wet/dry, fresh/stale*). Many pairs of words that look as if they are antonyms, such as *limit/delimit*, are not. When in doubt, consult a thesaurus or dictionary. See also <u>synonyms</u>.

apostrophes

An apostrophe (') is used to show possession or to indicate the omission of letters. Sometimes it can be used to avoid confusion for certain plurals of words, letters, and <u>abbreviations</u>.

Showing Possession

An apostrophe is used with an *s* to form the possessive case of some nouns (the *report's* title). For further advice on using apostrophes to show possession, see <u>possessive case</u>.

Indicating Omission

An apostrophe is used to mark the omission of letters or <u>numbers</u> in a <u>contraction</u> or a date (*can't, I'm, I'll;* the class of *'06*).

Forming Plurals

An apostrophe can be used in forming the plurals of letters, words, or lowercase abbreviations if confusion might result from using *s* alone.

- The search program does not find *a*'s and *i*'s.
- Do not replace all *of which*'s in the document.
- *I*'s need to be distinguished from the number 1.
- Check for any c.o.d.'s.

Generally, however, add only *s* in roman type when referring to words as words or capital letters.

- Five *and*s appear in the first sentence.
  [The word itself is in <u>italics</u>.]
- The applicants received *A*s and *B*s in their courses.

Do not use an apostrophe for plurals of abbreviations with all capital letters (DVDs) or a final capital letter (ten Ph.D.s) or for plurals of numbers (7s, the late 1990s).

appendixes

An appendix, located at the end of a __formal report__, __proposal__, or other major document, supplements or clarifies the information in the body of the document. Appendixes (or *appendices*) can provide information that is too detailed or lengthy for the primary audience of the document. For example, an appendix could contain material of interest to secondary __readers__, such as __maps__, statistical analysis, or __résumés__ of key personnel involved in a proposed project.

A document may have more than one appendix, with each providing only one type of information. When the document contains more than one appendix, arrange them in the order they are mentioned in the text. Begin each appendix on a new page, and identify each with a letter, starting with the letter *A* (Appendix A: Sample Questionnaire). If you have only one appendix, title it simply "Appendix." List the titles and beginning page numbers of the appendixes in the __table of contents__.

application letters

When applying for a job, you usually need to submit both an application letter (also referred to as a *cover letter*) and a __résumé__. Employers may ask you to submit them by standard mail, fax, or __e-mail__. See also __job search__.

The application letter is essentially a __sales letter__ in which you market your skills, abilities, and knowledge. Therefore, your application letter must be persuasive. The successful application letter accomplishes four tasks: (1) it catches the reader's attention favorably by describing how your skills will contribute to the organization, (2) it explains which particular job interests you and why, (3) it convinces the reader that you are qualified for the job by drawing your reader's attention to particular elements in your résumé, and (4) it requests an interview. See also __correspondence__, __interviewing for a job__, __persuasion__, and __salary negotiations__.

The sample application letters shown in Figures A–10 through A–12 follow the application-letter structure described in this entry. Each sample's __emphasis__, __tone__, and __style__ are tailored to fit the applicant's experience and the particular audience.

From: Marsha S. Parker <msparker@ubi.edu>
To: Patrice C. Crandal <pcrandal@abels.com>
Sent: Monday, February 28, 2006 10:47 AM
Subject: Application for Summer Internship

Attachment: 📄 Parker_Resume.doc

Dear Ms. Crandal:

I have learned from your Web site that you are hiring under-graduates for summer internships. This internship is appealing because I have discovered through personal research that Abel's buyer training program is one of the most effective in the industry.

The professional and analytical qualities that my attached résumé describes match the job description on your Web site. My experience with the Alumni Relations Program and the University Center Committee have enhanced my communication and persuasive abilities as well as my understanding of compromise and negotiation. For example, in the alumni program, I persuaded both uninvolved and active alumni to become more engaged with the direction of the university. On the University Center Committee, I balanced the students' demands with the financial and structural constraints of the administration. With these skills, I can ably assist the members of your department with their summer projects and success-fully juggle multiple responsibilities.

I would appreciate the opportunity to meet with you to discuss your summer internship further. If you have questions or would like to speak with me, please contact me at (412) 863-2289 any weekday after 3 p.m., or you can e-mail me at <msparker@ubi.edu>. Thank you for your consideration.

Sincerely,

Marsha S. Parker

FIGURE A–10. Application Letter Sent as E-mail (College Student Applying for an Internship)

449 Samson Street, Apt. 19
Providence, RI 02906
September 19, 2006

Alice Tobowski
Employee Relations Department
Advertising Media, Inc.
1007 Market Street
Providence, RI 02912

Dear Ms. Tobowski:

I recently learned from Jodi Hammel, a graphic designer at Advertising Media, that you are recruiting outstanding advertising assistants. Your position interests me greatly not only because your firm is number one in the region but also because I am impressed with Advertising Media's Employee Development Program.

Ms. Tobowski, I am aware that hundreds of applicants are applying for this position, but I have a combination of qualities probably few can match. As noted in my enclosed résumé, I not only possess multilingual skills (Spanish, French, and English) but also hold a degree in advertising.

Through several internships in advertising companies, I have developed outstanding verbal and written communication skills as well as an ability to work well with colleagues. Most recently, I developed a successful advertising campaign for Quilted Bear in Providence, which resulted in a 25 percent increase in customer inquiries from the French Canadian and South American markets.

Could we schedule a meeting at your convenience to discuss this career opportunity further? Feel free to call me any weekday morning at 401-578-1241 or e-mail me at <singh@pcexec.com> if you have questions or need further information. Thank you for your consideration.

Sincerely,

Sarah Singh

Sarah Singh

Enclosure: Résumé

FIGURE A–11. Application Letter (Recent College Graduate Applying for a Job)

522 Beethoven Drive
Roanoke, VA 24017
November 15, 2006

Ms. Cecilia Smathers
Vice President, Dealer Sales
Hamilton Office Machines, Inc.
6194 Main Street
Hampton, VA 23661

Dear Ms. Smathers:

During the recent NOMAD convention in Washington, one of your sales representatives, Karen Jarrett, informed me of a possible opening for a district manager in your Dealer Sales Division. My extensive background in the office systems industry makes me an ideal candidate for the position.

I was with Technology, Inc., Dealer Division from its formation in 1992 until TI's merger and reorganization last year. During that period, I was involved in all areas of dealer sales both within Technology, Inc., and through personal contact with a number of independent dealers. From 1998 to 2004 I served as Dealer Sales Manager and Special Representative. As described in the enclosed résumé, I was the national winner of TI's "Outstanding Customer Service Award" for 1999, 2002, and 2003. I have strong contacts with key buyers at all the major firms in our industry.

I would be happy to discuss my qualifications in an interview at your convenience. Please telephone me at (804) 449-6743 or e-mail me at <gm302.476@sys.com>.

Sincerely,

Gregory Mindukakis

Gregory Mindukakis

Enclosure: Résumé

FIGURE A–12. Application Letter (Applicant with Years of Experience)

Opening

In the opening paragraph, provide <u>context</u> and show your enthusiasm. Indicate how you heard about the position and name the specific job title or area. If you have been referred to a company by an employee, a career counselor, a professor, or someone else, be sure to say so. ("I recently learned from Jodi Hammel, a graphic designer at Advertising Media, that you are recruiting outstanding advertising assistants.") Explain why you are interested in the job and demonstrate your initiative as well as knowledge of the organization by relating your interest to some facet of the organization. ("Your position interests me greatly not only because your firm is number one in the region but also because I am impressed with Advertising Media's Employee Development Program.")

Body

In the middle paragraphs, show through examples that you are qualified for the job. Limit each of these <u>paragraphs</u> to just one basic point that is clearly stated in the topic sentence. For example, your second paragraph might focus on work experience and your third paragraph on educational achievements. Do not just *tell* readers that you are qualified—*show* them by including examples and details. Come across as proud of your achievements and refer to your enclosed résumé, but do not simply summarize your résumé. Indicate how you with your talents can make valuable contributions to their company. ("I was the national winner of TI's 'Outstanding Customer Service Award' for 1999, 2002, and 2003. I have strong contacts with key buyers at all the major firms in our industry.")

Closing

In the final paragraph, request an interview. Let the reader know how to reach you by including your phone number or e-mail address. End with a statement of goodwill, even if only a "thank you."

Proofread your letter *carefully*. Research indicates that if employers notice even one spelling, grammatical, or mechanical error, they often eliminate candidates from consideration immediately. Such errors will give employers the impression that you lack writing skills or that you are careless in the way you present yourself professionally. See also <u>proofreading</u>.

---

appositives

An appositive is a <u>noun</u> or noun <u>phrase</u> that follows and amplifies another noun or noun phrase. It has the same grammatical function as the noun it complements.

- George Thomas, *the noted economist,* summarized the president's speech in a confidential memo.

- The noted economist *George Thomas* summarized the president's speech in a confidential memo.

For detailed information on the use of <u>commas</u> with appositives, see <u>restrictive and nonrestrictive elements</u>.

If you are in doubt about the <u>case</u> of an appositive, check it by substituting the appositive for the noun it modifies.

- My boss gave the two of us, Jim and I, *me* the day off.

  [You would not say, "My boss gave *I* the day off."]

articles

Articles (*a, an, the*) function as <u>adjectives</u> because they modify the items they designate by either limiting them or making them more specific. The two kinds of articles are indefinite and definite.

The indefinite articles, *a* and *an*, denote an unspecified item.

- *A* package was delivered yesterday.
  [This is not a specific package but an unspecified package.]

The choice between *a* and *an* depends on the sound rather than on the letter following the article, as described in the entry <u>a/an</u>.

The definite article, *the*, denotes a particular item.

- *The* package was delivered yesterday.
  [This is not just any package but one specific package.]

Do not omit all articles from your writing. Including articles costs nothing; eliminating them makes reading more difficult. (See also <u>telegraphic style</u>.) However, do not overdo it. An article can be superfluous.

- I'll meet you in *a* half *an* hour.
  [Choose one article and eliminate the other.]

Do not capitalize articles in titles except when they are the first word (*The Economist* reviewed *Winning the Talent Wars*). See also <u>capitalization</u> and <u>English as a second language</u>.

ESL TIPS FOR USING ARTICLES

Whether to use a definite or an indefinite article is determined by what you can safely assume about your audience's knowledge. In each of these sentences, you can safely assume that the reader can clearly identify the noun. Therefore, use a definite article.

- *The* sun rises in the east.
  [The Earth has only one *sun*.]

- Did you know that yesterday was *the* coldest day of the year so far?
  [The modified noun refers to *yesterday*.]

- *The* man who left his briefcase in the conference room was in a hurry.
  [The relative phrase *who left his briefcase in the conference room* restricts and, therefore, identifies the meaning of *man*.]

In the following sentence, however, you cannot assume that the reader can clearly identify the noun.

- *A* package is on the way.
  [It is impossible to identify specifically what package is meant.]

A more important question for some nonnative speakers of English is when *not* to use articles. These generalizations will help. Do not use articles with the following:

Singular proper nouns

- Utah, Main Street, Harvard University, Mount Hood

Plural nonspecific countable nouns (when making generalizations)

- Helicopters are the new choice of transportation for the rich and famous.

Singular uncountable nouns

- She loves chocolate.

Plural countable nouns used as complements

- Those women are physicians.

See also <u>English as a second language</u>.

---

as / because / since

As, *because*, and *since* are commonly used to mean "because." To express cause, *because* is the strongest and most specific connective; *because* is unequivocal in stating a causal relationship. (*Because* she did not have an MBA, she was not offered the job.)

Since is a weak substitute for *because* as a connective to express cause. However, *since* is an appropriate connective when the emphasis is on circumstance, condition, or time rather than on cause and effect. (*Since* it went public, the company has earned a profit every year.)

As is the least definite connective to indicate cause; its use for that purpose is best avoided. (See also <u>subordination</u>.) The word *as* can also contribute to <u>awkwardness</u> by appearing too many times in a sentence.

- ~~As we~~ realized ~~as soon as~~ we began the project, the problem needed a solution.

  We ... *the moment* ... *that*

Avoid colloquial, nonstandard, or wordy phrases sometimes used instead of *as*, *because*, or *since*. See also <u>affectation</u>, <u>as such</u>, and <u>due to/because of</u>.

PHRASE	REPLACE WITH
being as, being that	because, since
inasmuch as	because
insofar as	since
on account of	because
on the grounds of/that	because
due to the fact that	because

as much as / more than

The phrases *as much as* and *more than* are sometimes incorrectly combined, especially when intervening phrases delay the completion of the phrase.

- The auditors had as much~~, if not more,~~ influence in planning the program ~~than~~ the accountants.

  as ... *, if not more* ... *as*

as such

The phrase *as such* is seldom useful and should be omitted.

- Style sheets~~, as such,~~ are useful in designing Web pages.

as well as

Do not use *as well as* with *both*. The two expressions have similar meanings; use one or the other and adjust the <u>verb</u> as needed.

- Both General Motors ~~as well~~ *and* as Ford ~~is~~ *are* marketing hybrid vehicles.
- ~~Both~~ General Motors as well as Ford is marketing hybrid vehicles.

audience

Although the word *audience* can have a slightly different meaning for a writer than for a speaker, it is crucial to both. The writer and the speaker must know as much as possible about the people they are trying to reach with their message—**readers** or listeners—regardless of its method of delivery. For meeting the needs of some particular audiences, see **global communication**, **international correspondence**, and **presentations**.

augment / supplement

Augment means to increase or magnify in size, degree, or effect. (Many employees *augment* their incomes by freelancing.) *Supplement* means to add something to make up for a deficiency. (He will *supplement* his diet with vitamins.)

average / median / mean

The *average* (or arithmetic *mean*) is determined by adding two or more quantities and dividing the sum by the number of items totaled. For example, if one report is 10 pages, another is 30 pages, and a third is 20 pages, their *average* length is 20 pages. It is incorrect to say that "each report averages 20 pages" because each report is a specific length.

- ~~Each report averages~~ *The three reports average* 20 pages.

The *median* is the middle number in a sequence of numbers. For example, the *median* of the series 1, 3, 4, 7, 8 is 4.

awhile / a while

The **adverb** *awhile* means "for a short time." The **preposition** *for* should not precede *awhile* because *for* is inherent in the meaning of *awhile*. The two-word noun **phrase** *a while* means "a period of time."

- Wait ~~for~~ awhile before sending the e-mail.

- Wait for ~~awhile~~ before sending the e-mail.
  a while

awkwardness

Any writing that strikes the <u>readers</u> as awkward—that is, as forced or unnatural—impedes the readers' understanding. The following check-list and the entries indicated will help you smooth out most awkward passages.

Writer's Checklist: Eliminating Awkwardness

☑ Strive for <u>clarity</u> and <u>coherence</u> during <u>revision</u>.

☑ Check for <u>organization</u> to ensure your writing develops logically.

☑ Keep <u>sentence construction</u> as direct and simple as possible.

☑ Use <u>subordination</u> appropriately and avoid needless <u>repetition</u>.

☑ Correct any <u>logic errors</u> within your sentences.

☑ Revise for <u>conciseness</u> and avoid <u>expletives</u> where possible.

☑ Use the active <u>voice</u> unless you have a justifiable reason to use the passive voice.

☑ Eliminate jammed or misplaced <u>modifiers</u> and, for particularly awkward constructions, apply the tactics in <u>garbled sentences</u>.

B

bad / badly

Bad is the <u>adjective</u> form that follows such linking <u>verbs</u> as *feel* and *look*. (We don't want to look *bad* at the meeting.) *Badly* is an <u>adverb</u>. (Our stock performed *badly* last year.) To say "I feel *badly*" would mean, literally, that your sense of touch is impaired. See also <u>good/well</u>.

balance / remainder

One meaning of *balance* is "a state of equilibrium"; another meaning is "the amount of money in a bank account after deposits and withdrawals have been credited and debited." *Remainder*, in all applications, means "what is left over."

be sure to

The <u>phrase</u> *be sure and* is colloquial and unidiomatic when used for *be sure to*. See also <u>idioms</u>.

- When you sign the contract, be sure ~~and~~ to keep a copy.

beside / besides

Besides, meaning "in addition to" or "other than," should be carefully distinguished from *beside*, meaning "next to" or "apart from." (*Besides* two of us from Marketing, three people from Production stood *beside* the president during the ceremony.)

B

between / among

Between is normally used to relate two items or persons. (Preferred stock offers a middle ground *between* bonds and common stock.) *Among* is used to relate more than two. (The subcontracting was distributed *among* three firms.)

between you and me

The expression *between you and I* is incorrect. Because the <u>pronouns</u> are <u>objects</u> of the <u>preposition</u> *between*, the objective form of the personal pronoun (*me*) must be used. See also <u>case</u>.

- Between you and ~~I~~, Joan should be promoted.

me

bi- / semi-

When used with periods of time, *bi-* means "two" or "every two," as in *bimonthly*, which means "once in two months." When used with periods of time, *semi-* means "half of" or "occurring twice within a period of time." *Semimonthly* means "twice a month." Both *bi-* and *semi-* normally are joined with the following element without a space or hyphen.

biannual / biennial

In conventional usage, *biannual* means "twice during the year," and *biennial* means "every other year." See also <u>bi-/semi-</u>.

biased language

Biased language refers to words and expressions that offend because they make inappropriate assumptions or stereotypes about gender, ethnicity, physical or mental disability, age, or sexual orientation.

⬆ ETHICS NOTE The easiest way to avoid bias is simply not to mention differences among people unless the differences are relevant to the discussion. Keep current with accepted usage and, if you are unsure of

B

the appropriateness of an expression or the tone of a passage, have several colleagues review the material and give you their assessments. ✦

Sexist Language

Sexist language can be an outgrowth of sexism, the arbitrary stereotyping of men and women—it can breed and reinforce inequality. To avoid sexism in your writing, treat men and women equally, and do not make assumptions about traditional or occupational roles. Accordingly, use nonsexist occupational descriptions in your writing.

INSTEAD OF	CONSIDER
chairman, chairwoman	chair, chairperson
foreman	supervisor, manager
man-hours	staff hours, worker hours
policeman, policewoman	police officer
salesman, saleswoman	salesperson

Use parallel terms to describe men and women.

INSTEAD OF	USE
man and wife	husband and wife
Ms. Jones and Bernard Weiss	Ms. Jones and Mr. Weiss; Mary Jones and Bernard Weiss
ladies and men	ladies and gentlemen; women and men

Sexism can creep into your writing by the unthinking use of male or female pronouns where a reference could apply equally to a man or a woman. One way to avoid such usage is to rewrite the sentence in the plural.

- *All employees* ~~Every employee~~ will have *their managers* ~~his manager~~ sign *their travel vouchers.* ~~his travel voucher.~~

Other possible solutions are to use *his or her* instead of *his* alone or to omit the pronoun completely if it is not essential to the meaning of the sentence. See also **pronoun reference**.

- Everyone must submit *an* ~~his~~ expense report by Monday.

He or she can become monotonous when used repeatedly, and a pronoun cannot always be omitted without changing the meaning of a sentence. Another solution is to omit troublesome pronouns by using the imperative **mood** whenever possible.

- *Submit all*
  Everyone must submit his or her expense *reports*
  report by Monday.

Other Types of Biased Language

Identifying people by racial, ethnic, or religious categories is simply not relevant in most workplace writing. Telling readers that an accountant is Native American or an attorney is Jewish almost never conveys useful information. Linking a profession or characteristic to race or ethnicity reinforces stereotypes, implying that it is rare or expected for a person of a particular background to have achieved a certain position.

Consider how you refer to people with disabilities. If you refer to "a disabled employee," you imply that the part (*disabled*) is as significant as the whole (*employee*). Use "an employee with a disability" instead. Similarly, the preferred usage is "a person who uses a wheelchair" rather than "a wheelchair-bound person," an expression that inappropriately equates the wheelchair with the person. Likewise, references to a person's age can also be inappropriate, as in expressions like "middle-aged manager" or "young Web designer."

In most workplace writing, such issues are simply not relevant. Of course, in some contexts, race, ethnicity, religion, disability, or age should be identified. For example, if you are writing an Equal Employment Opportunity Commission report about your firm's hiring practices, the racial composition of the workforce is relevant. In such cases, you need to present the issues in ways that respect and do not demean the individuals or groups to which you refer. See also **ethics in writing**.

bibliographies

A bibliography is an alphabetical list of books, articles, Web sources, and other works that have been consulted in preparing a document or that are useful for reference purposes. In a **formal report** or other document, a bibliography can provide a convenient alphabetical listing of sources in a standardized form for readers interested in getting further information on the topic or in assessing the scope of the research.

While a list of references, footnotes/endnotes, and a works-cited list refer to works actually cited in the text, a bibliography includes works consulted for general background information. For information on using various citation styles, see **documenting sources**.

Entries in a bibliography are listed alphabetically by the author's last name. If an author is unknown, the entry is alphabetized by the first word in the title (other than *A*, *An*, or *The*). Entries also can be arranged by subject and then ordered alphabetically within those categories.

An annotated bibliography includes complete bibliographic information about a work (author, title, publisher, and publication date) followed by a brief description or evaluation of what the work contains. The following is an annotation of a book on style and format:

> Sabin, William A. 2005. *The Gregg Reference Manual: A Manual of Style, Grammar, Usage, and Formatting.* 10th ed. New York: McGraw Hill/Irwin. 688 pp.
>
> The author states that the tenth edition of this standard office guide "is intended for anyone who writes, edits, or prepares material for distribution or publication" (p. viii). The book begins with a section titled "How to Look Things Up," which includes a reference to an online index at <www.gregg.com>. The book is then divided into three parts. Part 1: "Grammar, Usage, and Style" contains 11 sections on topics such as punctuation, abbreviations, spelling, and usage. Part 2: "Techniques and Formats" contains seven sections on such topics as proofreading, correspondence (letters, memos, and e-mail), and other elements of manuscript preparation. Part 3: "References" includes four appendixes: several essays on style, rules for alphabetic filing, a glossary of grammatical terms, and an alphabetical list offering appropriate pronunciation for words used in business, legal, and professional contexts.

both . . . and

Statements using the *both . . . and* construction should always be balanced grammatically and logically. See also **parallel structure**.

- For success in management, you must be able *both* to develop
  to master
  writing skills *and* mastering presentation skills.

brackets

The primary use of brackets ([ ]) is to enclose a word or words inserted by the writer or editor into a quotation.

- The text stated, "Hypertext systems can be categorized as either modest [not modifiable] or robust [modifiable]."

Brackets are used to set off a parenthetical item within parentheses.

- We should be sure to give Emanuel Foose (and his brother Emilio [1812–1882]) credit for his role in founding the institute.

Brackets are also used to insert the Latin word *sic*, which is a scholarly abbreviation that indicates a writer has quoted material exactly as it appears in the original, even though it contains a misspelled or wrongly used word. See also quotations.

- Dr. Smith wrote that "the earth does not revolve around the son [*sic*] at a constant rate."

brainstorming

Brainstorming, a form of free association used to generate ideas, can be done individually or in groups. Brainstorming can stimulate creative thinking about a topic and reveal fresh perspectives and new connections. When preparing to write, jot down as many random ideas as you can think of about the topic. When a group brainstorms, a designated person writes down the words or phrases as the other group members suggest them. Do not stop to analyze ideas or hold back looking for only the "best" ideas; just write down everything that comes to mind. After compiling a list of initial ideas, ask *what, when, who, where, how,* and *why* for each idea, then list additional details that those questions bring to mind. When you run out of ideas, analyze each one you recorded, discarding those that are redundant. Then group the items in the most logical order, based on the purpose of the document and the needs of the readers; that will result in a tentative outline of the document. Although the outline will be sketchy and incomplete, it will show where further brainstorming or research is needed and provide a framework for any new details that additional research yields.

Many writers find a technique called *clustering* (also called *mind mapping*), as shown in Figure B–1, helpful in recording and organizing ideas created during a brainstorming session. To cluster, begin with a blank sheet of paper or a flip chart. Think of a keyword or key phrase that best characterizes your topic and put it in a circle at the center of the paper. Figure B–1 shows brainstorming about the best way to communicate with customers, so that topic could be "Customer communication." Then, think of subtopics most closely related to the main topic. In Figure B–1, the main topic ("Customer communication") might lead to such subtopics as "Advertising," "Internet," "Direct mail," and "Conferences and trade shows." Draw circles or boxes around the subtopics, connecting each to the center circle, like adding spokes to a wheel hub. Repeat the exercise for each subtopic. Each subtopic should stimulate additional subtopics, which you add in circles connected to the parent subtopic, as you did with the main topic at the center of the page. In Figure B–1, for example, one subtopic is "Internet," which could stimulate additional subtopics like "E-mail" and "Web page."

B

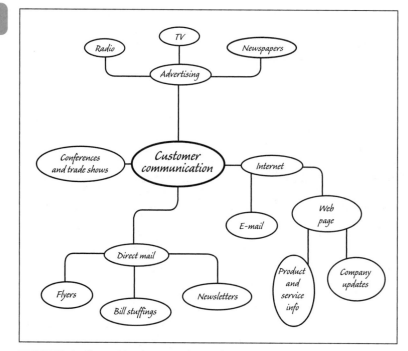

FIGURE B–1. Cluster Map from a Brainstorming Session

Continue the process until you exhaust all possible ideas. The resulting "map" will show clusters of terms grouped around the central concept.

brochures

Brochures are printed publications that promote the products and services offered by a business or that promote the image of a business or an organization by providing information important to a target audience. The goal of a brochure is to inform or to persuade or both. See also <u>clarity</u>, <u>persuasion</u>, and <u>promotional writing</u>.

Types of Brochures

The two major types of brochures are sales brochures and informational brochures. *Sales brochures* are created specifically to sell a company's products and services. For example, a brochure for a cell phone company might describe the various phones and calling plans available;

B

a brochure for a consulting company would detail its seminars or specific services. *Informational brochures* are created to inform and educate the reader as well as to promote goodwill and raise the profile of an organization. For example, a health-food company might create an informational brochure that shows the reader how to clean fruits and vegetables before they are eaten and offers healthful recipes; a psychiatric center might create a brochure describing how to recognize depression in teenagers.

Designing the Brochure

Before you begin to write, determine the specific **purpose** of the brochure—to provide information about a service? to sell a product? You must also identify your target audience—general reader? expert? potential or existing client? Understanding your purpose, audience, and **context** is essential to creating content and design that will be both rhetorically appropriate and persuasive to your target audience. Once you make these decisions, gather samples of brochures for similar products or services to stimulate your thinking.

Cover Panel. The main goal of the cover panel of a sales or promotional brochure is to gain the audience's attention. The cover panel should clearly identify the organization or product being promoted as well as provide a carefully selected visual image or headline geared toward the interest of the audience. Accompany the image with a minimal amount of text—for example, a statement about the company's mission and success or a brief promotional quotation from a satisfied customer. Figure B-2 shows a brochure produced by the National Cancer Institute,

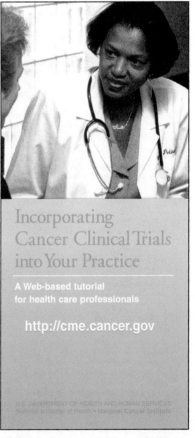

Incorporating
Cancer Clinical Trials
into Your Practice

A Web-based tutorial
for health care professionals

http://cme.cancer.gov

U.S. DEPARTMENT OF HEALTH AND HUMAN SERVICES
National Institutes of Health • National Cancer Institute

FIGURE B-2. Brochure (Cover Panel)

B

which hopes to attract health-care professionals to a course on conduct-ing clinical trials in their practices. The cover photo features a health-care professional wearing a stethoscope and apparently counseling a patient.

First Inside Panel.   The first inside panel of a brochure should again identify the company and attract the reader with headlines and brief, readable content, such as that used in advertising. The first inside panel of the National Cancer Institute brochure uses boldface <u>headings</u> to highlight brief descriptions of the course and those participants who may benefit.

Subsequent Panels.   Subsequent panels should describe the prod-uct or service with your readers' needs in mind, clearly stating the ben-

What is "Incorporating Cancer Clinical Trials Into Your Practice?"

It's a free Web-based tutorial for health care professionals that emphasizes the importance of participating in cancer clinical trials, either through patient referral or becoming a clinical trials investigator.

The course begins with a brief overview of cancer clinical trials and explains ways one can become involved in clinical trials. It continues with practical information and guidance for professionals interested in referring patients to, or conducting, clinical trials.

Participants will hear from experienced clinicians about some of the issues they have faced and how these issues were addressed.

Who should take this course?

The course is designed for health care professionals who are new to the clinical trials process, including oncologists, family physicians, internists, nurses, and other clinical staff. Specifically, it is for those clinicians that are referring patients to cancer clinical trials for the first time, and clinical research staff who are new to conducting clinical trials in their practices.

What are the course objectives?

At the end of the course, participants should be able to:

• Describe the role of clinical research in advancing cancer care

• Explain how clinical trials are conducted

• Describe the sponsorship of clinical trials

• Demonstrate how to locate clinical trials

• Understand how clinical trial sites are set up, staffed, and funded

• Make successful patient referrals to clinical trials

• Know how a physician may become a cancer clinical trials investigator

• Understand regulatory, record keeping, and reporting requirements in conducting clinical trials

• Identify key issues in communication among the patient, referring clinician, and clinical trials investigator

To register for this course, go to **http://cme.cancer.gov**, where you will be given further instructions.

Participants may receive continuing medical education (CME) credits or contact hours for course completion.

FIGURE B–2. Brochure (*continued*) (Inside Panels)

B

efits and solutions to problems that your product or service offers. Include relevant and accurate supporting facts and <u>visuals</u>. You might further establish credibility with a company history, a product history, and a list of current clients or testimonials. Use subheadings and bulleted lists to break up the text and make the brochure easy to read. In the final panel, be clear about the action you want the reader to take, such as calling to order the product or visiting a Web site for more information. In Figure B–2, the second inside panel describes the course objectives and tells readers how to register.

Layout-and-Design Features. As you plan the design for a brochure, create a rough planning sketch. To find the best way to present your content, experiment with margins, spacing, and the arrangement and amount of text on each panel (you may want to make changes to content or length based on concerns of layout). Allow adequate white space for readability. Experiment with various fonts and formatting. Consider, for example, enlarging the first letter of the first word in a paragraph, but do not overdo the use of unusual fonts or alternative styles (such as running type vertically). Choose a style that unifies your brochure, and use it consistently throughout. Be judicious about color choices. For some brochures, black and white, which is cheaper, is more effective; in other circumstances (such as brochures for travel) color, although more expensive, is a must. Depending on your budget and the scale of your project, consider using a professional printer. See also <u>layout and design</u>.

Writer's Checklist: Creating Sales or Informational Brochures

☑ Collect other brochures to stimulate your thinking as you consider the goals and content for your brochure and each panel.

☑ Create a rough sketch that maps out the content of each panel to help you select <u>visuals</u>, color schemes, and the number of panels.

☑ Experiment with margins, spacing, and the arrangement and amount of text on each panel; make appropriate changes to content or length and allow adequate white space for readability.

☑ Experiment with fonts and formatting, such as enlarging the first letter of the first word in a paragraph, but do not overuse unusual fonts or alternative styles, such as running type vertically.

☑ Consider color choices: black and white, which is cheaper, can be effective; in some circumstances color, although more expensive, is a must.

☑ Evaluate the impact of the design with your content. Does the design complement the content and make the brochure more persuasive? Have you adequately considered the needs of your readers? When your brochure is distributed, will it fulfill its purposes?

B

☑   Depending on your budget and the scale of your project, consider using a professional printer.

🌀 WEB LINK   **SAMPLE BROCHURES**

For links to Web sites with sample brochures, see *<bedfordstmartins.com/ alredbus>* and select *Links for Handbook Entries*.

---

business plans

A business plan is a **proposal** that allows potential supporters to evaluate ideas for a new business venture. Business plans usually describe the framework of a business venture, from marketing to financial applications. They often are written primarily for bankers and other outside funders or consultants, but they also are written for internal audiences consisting mostly of upper management. Usually **readers** are targeted to provide funding, resources, cooperation, or, in the context of a large corporation, permission and financial support to run a division in a certain way. Because business plans typically are internal, they are often kept confidential, unlike **annual reports**.

Purposes and Audience

A business plan can fulfill a single **purpose** or several purposes. Some of the most common purposes are the following:

- *To persuade potential investors or lenders to finance a business venture.* A comprehensive business plan allows investors to review objectively the company's assumptions, facts, and future outlook.

- *To allow reviewers (usually upper management) within a company to assess the profitability and goals of a new, internal business venture.* These readers typically want to evaluate economic forecasts and determine future profitability of the new venture and perhaps to provide creative direction.

- *To provide employees with guidance and direction.* A business plan can help employees formulate a corporate philosophy and develop strategies for pursuing and realizing new business ideas. In addition to providing financial information to outside readers, business plans can provide readers inside the company with guidance, motivation, and a spirit of company unity.

- *To convince customers and suppliers that a company's business ventures are stable with a promising future.* The business plan can help build a pool of loyal customers. In particular, potential customers for a large contract will want to see a company's business plan for reassurance that the company can deliver what it promises.

- *To create strategic alliances with other businesses.* A business partner in a joint venture, depending on the <u>context</u>, may need reassurance that the company is financially solid for a secure future.

Before you write a business plan, you must identify and analyze your audience. The purposes of a business plan can differ dramatically, depending on which audience you are trying to convince. If you are addressing a banker, the central purpose of the business plan is to obtain funding for the new venture; to accomplish that, you need to demonstrate credibility by documenting a solid history of financial success. If you are addressing upper management, the central purpose is to demonstrate how the venture is likely to add value to the company.

When you are writing a business plan, find out which issues are of most interest to your audience and respond directly to those issues. If you are writing a plan for multiple audiences with diverse interests and needs, be comprehensive in addressing all interests and needs in your plan.

Format, Length, and Sections

Because the audiences and purposes of business plans vary, their lengths and designs vary as well. Business plans can be as brief as one page, but typically they run between four and ten pages. Whether they are short or long depends on the audience, the purpose, and the nature and complexity of the proposed business ideas. For a business plan to be fully persuasive, tailor it to the business's specific audience and situation. (See also **persuasion**.) Design each plan differently and avoid copying the features of another company's plan.

The contents and sections will vary from one company to the next, but many plans (like **formal reports**) include a title page, a **table of contents**, and an **executive summary**. (See also **formal reports**.) Most plans cover the following topic areas in subsequent sections:

- Company description and strategy
- Market analysis and strategy
- Marketing plan
- Financial analysis
- Supporting documents

B   Company Description and Strategy

The first section of a business plan typically describes the following:

- The business and the company's functions, products, and services
- The overall strategy or philosophical orientation in the form of a vision and mission statement
- Goals and milestones
- The management team and key members likely to be involved in the business venture

Business Description.   A business plan should begin with a concise but complete description of the type of organization, its products, and its services, as well as a brief mention of the company's place in the market.

- Identify the company's legal name and status.
- Explain exactly what the company does.
- Define the percentage and growth opportunity of each product or service and describe the customer base.
- Describe current products or services and what makes them unique and competitive.
- Mention products and services in development.

You can use this section to indicate the company's business location, rent or mortgage expenses, and maintenance and insurance costs; to discuss whether the current location offers a competitive advantage; and to mention supplies and suppliers, current and projected machinery, equipment, and facilities to indicate anticipated expenses.

Vision and Mission Statements.   Vision and **mission statements** can be one and the same; however, they usually are written separately and serve different purposes. They may vary in length from one-sentence statements to multiple pages that begin with the mission statement, which outlines why the business exists, followed by the vision statement, which broadly discusses the future direction of the company.

Goals and Milestones.   State short-term as well as long-range goals with a timetable showing when the company expects to achieve specific milestones. Be realistic, especially when defining and setting short-term goals. Identify in specific, measurable terms what the company can reasonably achieve within a specified time frame.

Management and Key Team Members.   Identify all members of management. Describe their strengths, including any experiences or skills that particularly contribute to the business or to a particular venture. Also describe company procedures that demonstrate how the business is run, such as cash-flow analysis, regular meetings, and yearly reviews.

Identify those who will work closely with management, such as accountants, lawyers, insurance agents, and partners. Briefly describe their backgrounds and qualifications. If you are proposing that new positions be added to the company, mention that in the plan and describe basic elements of a human resources policy such as working hours, wages, vacation time, and sick leave. You can include <u>résumés</u> of candidates for the new positions in <u>appendixes,</u> along with other supporting documents.

Market Analysis and Strategy

Perhaps most important, the business plan needs to define and analyze the market and the competitive climate in which the writer proposes to launch the business venture. Once a solid understanding of the market is demonstrated, describe the new venture or the new product or service and propose your strategy for launching the new venture and managing it over time to contribute to overall profits.

This section of the business plan also needs to identify and analyze the major competitors and to examine how the company will address the competition to ensure that its products and services will make a strong entry into the marketplace. See also <u>research</u>.

Marketing Plan

Provide a specific plan for advertising and promoting products or services. Indicate the specific actions—in the form of specific projects and actions—the company will take to achieve its sales and promotional objectives. This section often is written by a marketing director, who includes discussions of promotional strategies and costs in different market channels as well as sales projections for each market segment. See also <u>collaborative writing</u>.

Financial Analysis

In one or more subsections, present the company's financial plan and financial statements, especially if the business plan's purpose is to obtain venture capital. Provide historical information about financial status as well as projections about the company's financial growth. Identify both strengths and weaknesses, including new opportunities for growth, areas where the company can control costs, and ways of restructuring to make the company more efficient. Predict problems and describe the company's strategy to prevent or minimize their effects. These sections often benefit from strategically placed <u>graphs</u> and <u>tables</u>.

B

Provide complete and detailed financial statements (perhaps in an appendix). Bankers and other investors typically want to see a balance sheet, profit-and-loss statements, a three-year cash-flow projection, and source and use-of-funds statements. Until the business venture is up and running, the company might be able to provide only projections of profit-and-loss statements or balance sheets. Also describe the company's liability and property insurance. Make estimates of calculations conservative by using slightly low or low-end sales and margin figures and by slightly overstating expected costs.

Supporting Documents

In appendixes, provide **résumés** of key members of management and any other supporting information that demonstrates the company's potential and management's credibility. Other documents might include positive reviews of a new product, service, or venture, or positive articles about the company from industry or the popular press. Finally, you could provide copies of contracts with impressive clients (with the clients' permission) or information that would demonstrate relationships between the company and such clients.

Writer's Checklist: Preparing Business Plans

☑ Identify and analyze the audience for your business plan and tailor your writing accordingly.

☑ Determine your purpose, such as convincing potential investors to finance a business venture or allowing upper management to assess the profitability and goals of a new business venture.

☑ Ensure that the business plan contains the following sections:
  • Company description and strategy
  • Market analysis and strategy
  • Marketing plan
  • Financial analysis
  • Supporting documents

☑ Update and revise the plan regularly. If the plan is not working, carefully review each section and reconsider your presentation.

WEB LINK   SAMPLE BUSINESS PLANS

Business Resource Software, Inc., and Palo Alto Software, Inc., makers of business software, offer numerous sample business plans online. See *<bedfordstmartins.com/alredbus>* and select *Links for Handbook Entries*.

business writing style   **B**

Business writing has evolved from a very formal and elaborate style to one that is more personal and direct. Yet, even though business writing style is less formal today, it must adhere to the conventions of standard English with the use of conventional <u>spelling</u> and standard grammatical forms. See also <u>English, varieties of</u> and <u>style</u>.

Business writing legitimately varies from the conversational style you might use in a note sent by <u>e-mail</u> to the formal, legalistic style found in contracts. In most e-mail messages, letters, and <u>memos</u>, a style between those two extremes generally is appropriate. Writing that is too formal can alienate <u>readers</u>, and an overly obvious attempt to be casual and informal may strike the reader as insincere or unprofessional. See also <u>correspondence</u>.

● Dear Jane,/

Your proposal arrived today, and it looks good.
~~Just got your proposal. It's awesome!~~

The use of personal <u>pronouns</u> is important in letters and memos. In fact, one way you can make your business writing persuasive is through the use of the <u>"you" viewpoint</u>, which often, but not always, uses the pronoun *you* to place the readers' interest foremost.

⚡ ETHICS NOTE Be careful when you use the pronoun *we* in a business letter that is written on company stationery because it commits your company to what you have written. In general, when a statement is your opinion, use *I*; when it is company policy, use *we*. Do not refer to yourself in the third person by using *one* or *the writer*. It is perfectly natural and appropriate to refer to yourself as *I* and to the reader as *you*. In a <u>report</u>, however, you may be writing to more than one reader and may not necessarily want to refer to collective readers as *you*. See also <u>ethics in writing</u>, <u>persuasion</u>, and <u>point of view</u>. ✦

The best writers strive to write in a style that is so clear that their message cannot be misunderstood. In fact, you cannot be persuasive without being clear. One way to achieve <u>clarity</u>, especially during <u>revision</u>, is to eliminate overuse of the passive <u>voice</u>, which plagues most poor business writing. Although the passive voice is sometimes necessary, often it not only makes your writing dull but also is ambiguous, uninformative, or overly impersonal.

You can also achieve clarity with <u>conciseness</u>. Proceed cautiously here, however, because business writing should not be an endless series of short, choppy sentences. (See also <u>sentence variety</u> and <u>telegraphic style</u>.) Don't be so concise that you become blunt or deliver too little information to be helpful to the readers. Appropriate and effective

B

<u>word choice</u> is also essential to clarity. Finally, you can achieve clarity through the wise use of <u>punctuation</u>. A misplaced <u>comma</u> or other punctuation mark can cause misunderstanding and confusion. See also "Five Steps to Successful Writing."

buzzwords

Buzzwords are words or phrases that suddenly become popular and, because of an intense period of overuse, lose their freshness and preciseness. They may become popular through their association with technology, popular culture, or even sports. We include them in our vocabulary because they *seem* to give force and vitality to our language. Actually, buzzwords sound pretentious in business writing. See also <u>word choice</u>.

interface [as a verb]	deliverables	dialogue [as a verb]
impact [as a verb]	24/7	bleeding edge
skill sets	dot-com	cash cow

Obviously, some buzzwords are appropriate in the right context.

- We must establish an *interface* between the computer and the satellite hardware.
  [*Interface* is appropriately used as a <u>noun</u>.]

When writers needlessly shift the normal function of a word, they often create a buzzword that is imprecise.

- We must ~~interface~~ *cooperate* with the Human Resources Department.

  [*Interface* is inappropriately used as a verb; *cooperate* is more precise.]

⚙ WEB LINK **BUZZWORDS**

Former newspaper editor John Walston offers BuzzWhack, a lighthearted site dedicated to the meaningful use of buzzwords. See *<bedfordstmartins.com/alredbus>* and select *Links for Handbook Entries*.

C

can / may

In writing, *can* refers to capability (I *can* have the project finished today). *May* refers to possibility (I *may* be in Boston on Monday) or permission (*May* I leave early?).

cannot

Cannot is one word.

- We can not meet the deadline specified in the contract.
  cannot

capital / capitol

Capital refers either to financial assets or to the city that hosts the government of a state or a nation. *Capitol* refers to the building in which a state or the national legislature meets. *Capitol* is often written with a small *c* when it refers to a state building, but it is always capitalized when it refers to the home of the U.S. Congress in Washington, D.C.

capitalization

DIRECTORY

Proper Nouns   70
Common Nouns   70
First Words   70
Specific Groups   70
Specific Places   71
Specific Institutions, Events,
   Concepts   71

Titles of Works   71
Professional and Personal Titles   71
Abbreviations   72
Letters   72
Miscellaneous Capitalizations   72

C

The use of capital, or uppercase, letters is determined by custom. Capital letters are used to call attention to certain words, such as proper <u>nouns</u> and the first word of a sentence. Use them carefully, especially when they affect a word's meaning (march/March, china/China, turkey/Turkey) and because a spell checker would fail to identify an error.

Proper Nouns

Proper nouns name specific persons, places, things, concepts, or qualities and are capitalized (Business Writing 205, Microsoft, Pat Wilde, Peru).

Common Nouns

Common nouns name general classes or categories of people, places, things, concepts, or qualities rather than specific ones and are not capitalized (business writing class, company, person, country).

First Words

The first letter of the first word in a sentence is always capitalized. (Of the plans submitted, ours is best.) The first word after a <u>colon</u> is capitalized when the colon introduces two or more complete sentences or if the colon precedes a statement requiring special emphasis.

- The meeting will address only one issue: What is the firm's role in environmental protection?

If a subordinate element follows the colon or if the thought is closely related, use a lowercase letter following the colon.

- We kept working for one reason: the approaching deadline.

The first word of a complete sentence in **quotation marks** is capitalized.

- Peter Drucker said, "The most important thing in communication is to hear what isn't being said."

The first word in the salutation (Dear Mr. Smith:) and complimentary close (Sincerely yours,) is capitalized. See also <u>correspondence</u> and <u>e-mail</u>.

Specific Groups

Capitalize the names of ethnic groups, religions, and nationalities (Native American, Christianity, Mongolian). Do not capitalize the names of social and economic groups (middle class, working class, unemployed).

Specific Places

Capitalize the names of all political divisions (Ward Six, Chicago, Cook County, Illinois). Capitalize the names of geographical divisions (Europe, Asia, North America, the Middle East). Do not capitalize geographic features unless they are part of a proper name.

- The mountains in some areas, such as the *Great Smoky Mountains,* make television transmission difficult.

The words *north, south, east,* and *west* are capitalized when they refer to sections of the country. They are not capitalized when they refer to directions.

- I may travel *north* when I relocate, but my family will remain in the *South.*

Specific Institutions, Events, Concepts

Capitalize the names of institutions, organizations, and associations (U.S. Department of Health and Human Services). An organization usually capitalizes the names of its internal divisions and departments (Aeronautics Division, Human Resources Department). Types of organizations are not capitalized unless they are part of an official name (a business communication association; Association for Business Communication). Capitalize historical events (the Great Depression of the 1930s). Capitalize words that designate holidays, specific periods of time, months, or days of the week (Labor Day, the Renaissance, January, Monday). Do not capitalize seasons of the year (spring, autumn, winter, summer).

Titles of Works

Capitalize the initial letters of the first and last words of the title of a book, an article, a play, or a film, as well as all major words in the title. Do not capitalize articles (*a, an, the*), coordinating **conjunctions** (*and, but*), or **prepositions** unless they begin or end the title (*The Lives of a Cell*). Capitalize prepositions within **titles** when they contain more than four letters (*Between, Within, Until, After*), unless you are following a style that recommends otherwise. The same rules apply to the subject line of an **e-mail** or a **memo**.

Professional and Personal Titles

Titles preceding proper names are capitalized (Ms. Berger, Senator Lieberman). Appositives following proper names normally are not capitalized (Joseph Lieberman, *senator* from Connecticut). However, the

C

word *President* is capitalized when it refers to the chief executive of a national government.

Job titles used with personal names are capitalized (Ho-shik Kim, *Division Manager*). Job titles used without personal names are not capitalized.

- The *division manager* will meet us tomorrow.

Use capital letters to designate family relationships only when they occur before a name (my uncle; Uncle Fred).

Abbreviations

Capitalize <u>abbreviations</u> if the words they stand for would be capitalized, such as M.B.A. (Master of Business Administration).

Letters

Capitalize letters that serve as names or indicate shapes (vitamin B, T-square, U-turn, I-beam).

Miscellaneous Capitalizations

The first word of a complete sentence enclosed in <u>dashes</u>, <u>brackets</u>, or <u>parentheses</u> is not capitalized when it appears as part of another sentence.

- We must make an extra effort in safety this year (accidents last year were up 10 percent).

Certain units, such as parts and chapters of books and rooms in buildings, when specifically identified by number, are capitalized (Chapter 5, Ch. 5; Room 72, Rm. 72). Minor divisions within such units are not capitalized unless they begin a sentence (page 11, verse 14, seat 12).

---

case

DIRECTORY

Subjective Case   73
Objective Case   74
Possessive Case   75

Appositives   75
Determining the Case of Pronouns   75

Grammatical case indicates the functional relationship of a <u>noun</u> or a <u>pronoun</u> to the other words in a sentence. Nouns change form only in the possessive case; pronouns may show change for the subjective, the objective, or the possessive case.

The case of a noun or pronoun is always determined by its function in a phrase, clause, or sentence. If it is the subject of a phrase, clause, or sentence, it is in the subjective case; if it is an <u>object</u> in a phrase, clause, or sentence, it is in the objective case; if it reflects possession or ownership and modifies a noun, it is in the possessive case. Figure C–1 is a table of pronouns in the subjective, objective, and possessive cases.

SINGULAR	SUBJECTIVE	OBJECTIVE	POSSESSIVE
First person	I	me	my, mine
Second person	you	you	your, yours
Third person	he, she, it	him, her, it	his, her, hers, its
PLURAL	SUBJECTIVE	OBJECTIVE	POSSESSIVE
First person	we	us	our, ours
Second person	you	you	your, yours
Third person	they	them	their, theirs

FIGURE C–1. Pronoun Case Chart

The subjective case can indicate the person or thing acting (*He* sued the vendor), the person or thing acted upon (*He* was sued by the vendor), or the topic of description (*He* is the vendor). The objective case can indicate the thing acted on (The vendor sued *him*) or the person or thing acting but in the objective position (The vendor was sued by *him*). (See also <u>voice</u>.) The possessive case indicates the person or thing owning or possessing something (It was *his* company). See also <u>modifiers</u>.

Subjective Case

A pronoun is in the subjective case (also called the *nominative case*) when it represents the person or thing acting or is the receiver of the action but in the subject position.

- *I* wrote a proposal.

- *I* was praised for my proposal writing.

A linking <u>verb</u> links a pronoun to its antecedent to show that they identify the same thing. Because they represent the same thing, the pronoun is in the subjective case even when it follows the verb, which makes it a subjective complement.

- *He* is the head of the Quality Control Group. [subject]
- The head of the Quality Control Group is *he*.
  [subjective complement]

The subjective case is used after the words *than* and *as* because of the understood (although unstated) portion of the clauses in which those words appear.

- George is as good a designer as *I* [am].
- Our subsidiary can do the job better than *we* [can].

Objective Case

A pronoun is in the objective case (also called the *accusative case*) when it indicates the person or thing receiving the action expressed by a verb in the active voice.

- They informed *me* by letter that they had received my résumé.

Pronouns that follow action verbs (which excludes all forms of the verb *be*) must be in the objective case. Do not be confused by an additional name.

- The company promoted *me* in July.
- The company promoted John and *me* in July.

A pronoun is in the objective case when it is the object of a gerund or a **preposition** or the subject of an infinitive.

- Between *you* and *me*, his facts are questionable.
  [objects of a preposition]
- Many of *us* attended the conference. [object of a preposition]
- Training *him* was the best thing I could have done.
  [object of a gerund]
- We asked *them* to return the deposit. [subject of an infinitive]

English does not differentiate between direct objects and indirect objects; both require the objective form of the pronoun. See also **complements**.

- The interviewer seemed to like *me*. [direct object]
- They wrote *me* a letter. [indirect object]

Possessive Case

A noun or pronoun is in the possessive case when it represents a person, place, or thing that possesses something. To make a singular noun possessive, add *'s* (the *manufacturer's* robotic inventory system). With plural nouns that end in *s*, show the possessive by placing an apostrophe after the *s* that forms the plural (a *managers'* meeting). For other guidelines, see **possessive case**.

Appositives

An **appositive** is a noun or noun phrase that follows and amplifies another noun or noun phrase. Because it has the same grammatical function as the noun it complements, an appositive should be in the same case as the noun with which it is in apposition.

- Two auditors, Jim Knight and *I*, were asked to review the books. [subjective case]

- The group leader selected two members to represent the department—Mohan Pathak and *me*. [objective case]

Determining the Case of Pronouns

One test to determine the proper case of a pronoun is to try it with some transitive verb such as *resembled* or *hit*. If the pronoun would logically precede the verb, use the subjective case; if it would logically follow the verb, use the objective case.

- *She* [*He, They*] resembled her father. [subjective case]

- Angela resembled *him* [*her, them*]. [objective case]

In the following example, try omitting the noun to determine the case of the pronoun.

SENTENCE	(*We/Us*) pilots fly our own airplanes.
INCORRECT	*Us* fly our own airplanes. [This incorrect usage is obviously wrong.]
CORRECT	*We* fly our own airplanes. [This correct usage sounds right.]

To determine the case of a pronoun that follows *as* or *than*, mentally add the words that are omitted but understood.

- The other sales representative is not paid as well as *she* [is paid]. [You would not write, "*Her* is paid."]

- His partner was better informed than *he* [was informed].
  [You would not write, "*Him* was informed."]

C

If pronouns in compound constructions cause problems, try using them singly to determine the proper case.

> **SENTENCE**   (*We/Us*) and the Johnsons are going to the Grand Canyon.
>
> **CORRECT**   *We* are going to the Grand Canyon. [You would not write, "*Us* are going to the Grand Canyon."]

For advice on when to use *who* and *whom*, see who/whom.

cause-and-effect method of development

The cause-and-effect method of development is a common strategy to explain why something happened or why you think something will happen. The goal of the cause-and-effect method of development is to make as plausible as possible the relationship between a situation and either its cause or its effect. The conclusions you draw about the relationships should be based on evidence you have gathered. Like all methods, this one is often used in combination with others. If you were examining a problem with multiple causes, for example, you might combine cause-and-effect with order-of-importance as you examine each cause and its effect.

Evaluating Evidence

Because not all evidence will be of equal value, keep the following guidelines in mind as you gather evidence:

- *Your facts and arguments should be relevant to your topic.* Be careful not to draw a conclusion that your evidence does not lead to or support. You may have researched some statistics, for example, showing that an increasing number of Americans are licensed to fly small airplanes. You cannot use that information as evidence for a decrease in new car sales in the United States—the evidence does not lead to that conclusion.

- *Your evidence should be adequate.* Incomplete evidence can lead to false conclusions.

  - Driver training classes do not help prevent auto accidents. Two people I know who completed driver training classes were involved in accidents.

A thorough investigation of the usefulness of driver training classes in keeping down the accident rate would require more than one or two examples. It would require a systematic comparison of the driving records for a representative sample of drivers who had completed driver training and those who had not.

- *Your evidence should be representative.* If you conduct a survey to obtain your evidence, do not solicit responses only from individuals or groups whose views are identical to yours; be sure you obtain a representative sampling.

- *Your evidence should also be demonstrable.* Two events that occur close to each other in time or place may or may not be causally related. For example, that new traffic signs were placed at an intersection and the next day an accident occurred does not necessarily prove that the signs caused the accident. You must demonstrate the relationship with pertinent facts and arguments. See also **logic errors**.

Linking Causes to Effects

To show a true relationship between a cause and an effect, you must demonstrate that the existence of the one *requires* the existence of the other. It is often difficult to establish beyond any doubt that one event was the cause of another event. More often, a result will have more than one cause. As you research a subject, your task is to determine which cause or causes are most plausible.

When several probable causes are equally valid, report your findings accordingly, as in the following excerpt from an article on the use of an energy-saving device called a furnace-vent damper. The damper is a metal plate that fits inside the flue or vent pipe of a natural-gas or fuel-oil furnace. When the furnace is on, the damper opens to allow gases to escape up the flue. When the furnace shuts off, the damper closes, thus preventing warm air from escaping up the flue stack. The dampers are potentially dangerous, however. If a damper fails to open at the proper time, poisonous furnace gases could back up into the house and asphyxiate the occupants. Tests run on several dampers showed a number of probable causes for their malfunctioning.

- One damper was sold without proper installation instructions, and another was wired incorrectly. Two of the units had slow-opening dampers (15 seconds) that prevented the [furnace] burner from firing. And one damper jammed when exposed to a simulated fuel temperature of more than 700 degrees.

—Don DeBat, "Save Energy but Save Your Life, Too," *Family Safety*

The investigator located more than one cause of damper malfunctions and reported on them. Without such a thorough account, recommendations to prevent malfunctions would be based on incomplete evidence.

center on

Use the phrase *center on* in writing, not *center around*. (Our discussions should *center on* hiring practices.) Often the idea intended by *center on* is better expressed by other words.

- The hearings on computer security ~~centered on~~ *dealt with* access codes.

chronological method of development

The chronological **method of development** arranges the events under discussion in sequential order, emphasizing time as it begins with the first event and continues chronologically to the last. **Trip reports**, **instructions**, work schedules, some **minutes of meetings**, and certain **trouble reports** are among the types of writing in which information is organized chronologically. Chronological order is typically used in **narration**.

In the memo shown in Figure C–2, a retail store manager describes the steps taken over a one-year period to reduce shoplifting at his store. After providing important background information, the writer presents the steps taken in chronological order.

cite / sight / site

Cite means "acknowledge" or "quote an authority." (The speaker *cited* several famous economists.) *Sight* is the ability to see. (He feared that he might lose his *sight*.) *Site* is a plot of land (a construction *site*) or the place where something is located (a Web *site*).

clarity

Clarity is essential to effective communication with your **readers**. You cannot achieve your **purpose** or a goal like **persuasion** without clarity. Many factors contribute to clarity, just as many other elements can defeat it.

The Rack

Interoffice Memorandum

To: Joanna Sanchez, Vice President for Marketing
From: Larry Brown, Manager, Downtown Branch   *LB*
Date: September 18, 2006
Subject: Reducing Shoplifting at the Downtown Store

Over the past year, my staff and I have taken a number of measures to try to reduce the amount of shoplifting in the downtown store. As you know, we have spent much time, effort, and money on the problem, which we hope will be alleviated during the Christmas shopping season. Let me recap the specific steps we have taken.

Task Force
We formed a task force of salespeople, buyers, managers, and executive staff to recommend ways of curtailing shoplifting and methods of implementing our recommendations. We met four times during January and twice in March to reach our final recommendations.

Mark IV Surveillance System
In April, we installed a Mark IV System, which uses closed-circuit TV cameras at each exit. The cameras, which are linked with our security office, are capable of taping signals from all exits simultaneously. The task force felt the Mark IV System might be useful in detecting a pattern of specific individuals entering and leaving the store. This system, which became operational on April 20, has been very helpful in reducing the number of thefts.

Employee Training
During May and June, we held employee workshops on detecting shoplifters. Security, Inc., a consulting firm, led the workshops and provided not only lectures and tips on spotting shoplifters but also demonstrations of common techniques shoplifters use to divert store personnel. All those who attended thought the workshops were quite helpful.

Other Steps Taken
Because the task force determined that certain items were particularly vulnerable to shoplifters, we decided in July to restructure some of the display areas. Our purpose was to make those areas less isolated from the view of clerks and other store personnel. The remodeling, most of which was relatively minor, was completed over the summer months.

For the fall and holiday sales, we have hired extra uniformed security guards. The guards from Security, Inc. should be able to deter first-time shoplifters, although we know that this step will not eliminate the problem altogether.

We believe the steps we have taken will substantially reduce our losses from theft. Of course, after we have reviewed the figures at the end of the year, the task force will meet again in January to assess the success of the methods we have used. If you need more details, please let me know.

FIGURE C–2. Chronological Method of Development

C

A logical <u>method of development</u> and an outline will help you avoid presenting your reader with a jumble of isolated thoughts. A method of development and an outline that puts your thoughts in a logical, meaningful sequence brings <u>coherence</u> as well as <u>unity</u> to your writing. Clear <u>transition</u> contributes to clarity by providing the smooth flow that enables the reader to connect your thoughts with one another without conscious effort. See also <u>outlining</u>.

Proper <u>emphasis</u> and <u>subordination</u> are mandatory if you want to achieve clarity. If you do not use those two complementary techniques wisely, all your clauses and sentences will appear to be of equal importance. Your reader will only be able to guess which are most important, which are least important, and which fall somewhere in between. The <u>pace</u> at which you present your ideas is also important to clarity; if the pace is not carefully adjusted to both the topic and the reader, your writing will appear cluttered and unclear.

<u>Point of view</u> establishes through whose eyes or from what vantage point the reader views the subject. A consistent point of view is essential to clarity; if you inappropriately switch from the first person to the third person in midsentence, you are certain to confuse your reader.

Precise <u>word choice</u> contributes to clarity and helps eliminate <u>ambiguity</u> and <u>awkwardness</u>. <u>Vague words</u>, <u>clichés</u>, poor use of <u>idiom</u>, and inappropriate <u>usage</u> detract from clarity.

That <u>conciseness</u> is a requirement of clearly written communication should be evident to anyone who has ever attempted to decipher an insurance policy or a legal contract. Although words are our chief means of communication, more words than necessary can impede clear communication, just as too many cars on a highway can impede traffic. For the sake of clarity, remove unnecessary words from your writing.

clauses

A clause is a group of words that contains a subject and a predicate and that functions as a sentence or as part of a sentence. (See <u>sentence construction</u>.) Every subject-predicate word group in a sentence is a clause, and every sentence must contain at least one independent clause; otherwise, it is a <u>sentence fragment</u>.

A clause that could stand alone as a simple sentence is an *independent clause*.

- *The scaffolding fell* when the rope broke.

A clause that could not stand alone if the rest of the sentence were deleted is a *dependent* (or *subordinate*) *clause*.

- I was at the St. Louis branch *when the decision was made.*

Dependent clauses are useful in making the relationship between thoughts clearer and more succinct than if the ideas were presented in a series of simple sentences or compound sentences.

FRAGMENTED	The recycling facility is located between Millville and Darrtown. Both villages use it. [The two thoughts are of approximately equal importance.]
SUBORDINATED	The recycling facility, *which is located between Millville and Darrtown,* is used by both villages. [One thought is subordinated to the other.]

Subordinate clauses are especially effective for expressing thoughts that describe or explain another statement. Too much <u>subordination</u>, however, can be confusing and produce wordiness. See also <u>conciseness</u>.

- He selected instructors whose classes ~~had a slant that was~~ *were* specifically directed ~~toward students who intended to go into accounting.~~ *at accounting students.*

A clause can be connected with the rest of its sentence by a coordinating <u>conjunction</u>, a subordinating conjunction, a relative <u>pronoun</u>, or a conjunctive <u>adverb</u>.

- It was 500 miles to the facility, *so* we made arrangements to fly. [coordinating conjunction]

- Mission control will have to be alert *because* at launch the space shuttle will contain a highly flammable fuel. [subordinating conjunction]

- Robert M. Fano was the scientist *who* developed the earliest multiple-access computer system at MIT. [relative pronoun]

- We arrived in the evening; *nevertheless,* we began the tour of the facility. [conjunctive adverb]

clichés

Clichés are expressions that have been used for so long that they are no longer fresh but come to mind easily because they are so familiar. Clichés are often wordy as well as vague and can be confusing, especially to nonnative speakers of English. A better, more direct word or phrase is given for each of the following cliches.

C

INSTEAD OF	USE
all over the map	scattered, unfocused
run it up the flagpole	see what others think
last but not least	last, finally

Some writers use clichés in a misguided attempt to appear casual or spontaneous, just as other writers try to impress readers with buzz-words. Although clichés may come to mind easily while you are writing a draft, eliminate them during revision. See also affectation, concise-ness, and international correspondence.

coherence

Writing is coherent when the relationships among ideas are clear to readers. The major components of coherent writing are a logical se-quence of related ideas and clear transitions between these ideas. See also clarity and organization.

Presenting ideas in a logical sequence is the most important re-quirement in achieving coherence. The key to achieving a logical se-quence is the use of a good outline (see outlining). An outline forces you to establish an introduction, a middle (body), and a conclusion. That structure contributes greatly to coherence by enabling you to ex-periment with sequences and to lay out the most direct route to your purpose without digressing.

Thoughtful transition is also essential; without it, your writing can-not achieve the smooth flow from sentence to sentence and from paragraph to paragraph that results in coherence.

Check your draft carefully for coherence during revision. If pos-sible, have someone else review your draft for how well it expresses the relationships between ideas. Such help is especially important in collab-orative writing where team member contributions need to be blended into a coherent document. See also unity.

collaborative writing

Collaborative writing occurs when two or more writers work together to produce a single document for which they share responsibility and decision-making authority. Collaborative writing teams are formed when (1) the size of a project or the time constraints imposed on it re-quire collaboration, (2) the project involves multiple areas of expertise, or (3) the project requires the melding of divergent views into a single perspective that is acceptable to the whole team or to another group.

Tasks of the Collaborative Writing Team

The collaborating team strives to achieve a compatible working relationship by dividing the work in a way that uses each writer's expertise and experience to their collective advantage. The team should also designate a coordinator who will guide the team members' activities, organize the project, and ensure <u>coherence</u> within the document. The coordinator's duties can be determined by mutual agreement or, if the team often works together, assigned on a rotating basis.

Planning. The team collectively identifies the <u>readers</u>, <u>purpose</u>, and <u>scope</u> of the project. The team conceptualizes the document to be produced, creates a broad outline of the document (see <u>outlining</u>), divides it into segments, and assigns each segment to individual team members, often on the basis of expertise. See also <u>meetings</u> and "Five Steps to Successful Writing."

In the planning stage, the team establishes a schedule and sets any writing <u>style</u> standards that the team is expected to follow. The schedule includes due dates for drafts, reviews of the drafts, revisions, and the final document. Milestone deadlines must be met, even if the drafts are not as polished as the individual writers would like: One missed deadline can delay the entire project.

Research and Writing. Planning is followed by <u>research</u> and writing, a period of intense independent activity by members of the team. Each team member researches his or her assigned segment of the document, expands and develops the broad outline, and produces a draft from the detailed outline. See also <u>writing a draft</u>.

Reviewing. Keeping the readers' needs and the document's purpose in mind, each member critically yet diplomatically reviews the other team members' work, from the overall <u>organization</u> to the <u>clarity</u> of each <u>paragraph</u>, and offers advice to help improve the writer's segment. Team members can easily solicit feedback by sharing electronic files. Tracking and commenting features allow the reviewer to show the suggested changes without deleting the original text. The author can then easily accept or reject the proposed changes.

Revising. In this stage, individual writers evaluate their colleagues' reviews and accept, reject, or build on their suggestions. Then, all drafts

C

> 🖱 DIGITAL TIP **REVIEWING COLLABORATIVE DOCUMENTS**
>
> Adobe Acrobat™ and many word-processing packages have options for providing feedback on the drafts of collaborators' documents. You can add text or voice annotations within the text, allowing your readers to read or hear your comments, as well as track changes in your text and allow readers to accept or reject each change. In Acrobat, you can also use a drawing tool to input traditional <u>proofreaders' marks</u>. For more on this topic, see <*bedfordstmartins.com/alredbus*> and select *Digital Tips,* "Reviewing Collaborative Documents."

---

can be consolidated into a final master copy maintained by the team coordinator. See also <u>revision</u>.

Conflict

As you collaborate, be ready to tolerate some disharmony, but temper it with mutual respect. Team members may not agree on every subject, and differing perspectives can easily lead to conflict, ranging from mild differences over minor points to major showdowns. However, creative differences resolved respectfully can energize the team and, in fact, strengthen a finished document by compelling writers to reexamine assumptions and issues in unanticipated ways. See also <u>listening</u>.

Writer's Checklist: Writing Collaboratively

- ☑ Designate one person as the team coordinator.
- ☑ Identify the audience, purpose, and scope of the project.
- ☑ Create a working outline of the document.
- ☑ Assign segments or tasks to each team member.
- ☑ Establish a schedule: due dates for drafts, revisions, and final versions.
- ☑ Agree on a standard reference guide for style and format.
- ☑ Research and write drafts of document segments.
- ☑ Exchange segments for team member reviews.
- ☑ Revise segments as needed.
- ☑ Meet your established deadlines.

collection letters

Collection letters serve two purposes: (1) collecting the overdue bill and (2) preserving the customer relationship. In some states, collection letters may be prepared by attorneys because certain language and state laws must be followed to demand payment.

Most companies use a series of collection letters like the series shown in Figures C–3 through C–5, in which the letters become increasingly demanding and urgent. All letters should be courteous and show a genuine interest in the customer as well as concern for whatever problems may be preventing prompt payment. See also <u>"you" view-point</u>.

The first stage consists of reminders stamped on the invoice ("overdue"), form letters, or brief personal notes. These early reminders should maintain a friendly <u>tone</u> that emphasizes the customer's good credit record until now. As in the example of a first-stage collection letter in Figure C–3, you might suggest that nonpayment may be a result of a simple oversight.

In the second stage, your tone should be firmer and more direct than in the first stage, but it should never be rude, sarcastic, or threatening. Ask directly for payment, and inquire whether some circumstances are preventing payment. Perhaps suggest an installment payment plan if you are able to offer one. Mention the importance of good credit and remind the customer that he or she has always received good value from you. Make it easy to respond by enclosing a return envelope or by offering a toll-free telephone or fax number or a Web address where the customer can pay with a credit card. Notice how the second-stage letter in Figure C–4 is more direct than the first letter, but it is no less polite.

Third-stage collection letters reflect a sense of urgency because the customer has not responded to your previous letters. Although your tone should remain courteous, make your demand for payment explicit, as shown in Figure C–5. Point out how reasonable you have been and urge the customer to pay at once to avoid a collection service or legal action.

C

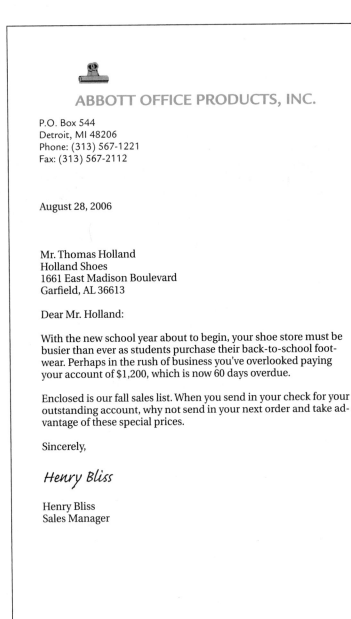

ABBOTT OFFICE PRODUCTS, INC.

P.O. Box 544
Detroit, MI 48206
Phone: (313) 567-1221
Fax: (313) 567-2112

August 28, 2006

Mr. Thomas Holland
Holland Shoes
1661 East Madison Boulevard
Garfield, AL 36613

Dear Mr. Holland:

With the new school year about to begin, your shoe store must be busier than ever as students purchase their back-to-school footwear. Perhaps in the rush of business you've overlooked paying your account of $1,200, which is now 60 days overdue.

Enclosed is our fall sales list. When you send in your check for your outstanding account, why not send in your next order and take advantage of these special prices.

Sincerely,

Henry Bliss

Henry Bliss
Sales Manager

www.abbott.com

FIGURE C–3. First-Stage Collection Letter

ABBOTT OFFICE PRODUCTS, INC.

P.O. Box 544
Detroit, MI 48206
Phone: (313) 567-1221
Fax: (313) 567-2112

December 4, 2006

Mr. Thomas Holland
Holland Shoes
1661 East Madison Boulevard
Garfield, AL 36613

Dear Mr. Holland:

We are concerned that we have not heard from you about your
overdue account of $1,200 even though we have written three
times in the past 90 days. Because you have always been one of our
best customers, we have to wonder if some special circumstances
have caused the delay. If so, please feel free to discuss the matter
with us.

By sending us a check today, you can preserve your excellent credit
record. Because you have always paid your account promptly in the
past, we are sure that you will want to settle this balance now. If
your balance is more than you can pay at present, we will be happy
to work out mutually satisfactory payment arrangements.

Please use the enclosed envelope to send in your check, or call
(800) 526-1945 to discuss your account.

Sincerely,

Henry Bliss

Henry Bliss
Sales Manager

www.abbott.com

FIGURE C–4. Second-Stage Collection Letter

C

ABBOTT OFFICE PRODUCTS, INC.

P.O. Box 544
Detroit, MI 48206
Phone: (313) 567-1221
Fax: (313) 567-2112

March 5, 2007

Mr. Thomas Holland
Holland Shoes
1661 East Madison Boulevard
Garfield, AL 36613

Dear Mr. Holland:

Your account in the amount of $1,200 is now 180 days overdue. You have already received a generous extension of time and, in fairness to our other customers, we cannot permit a further delay in payment.

Because you have not responded to any of our letters, we will be forced to turn your account over to our attorney for collection if we do not receive payment immediately. Such action, of course, will damage your previously fine credit rating.

Why not avoid this unpleasant situation by sending your check in the enclosed return envelope within 10 days or by calling (800) 526-1945 to discuss payment.

Sincerely,

Henry Bliss

Henry Bliss
Sales Manager

www.abbott.com

FIGURE C–5. Third-Stage Collection Letter

colons

The colon (:) is a mark of introduction that alerts readers to the close connection between the preceding statement and what follows.

Colons in Sentences

A colon links independent <u>clauses</u> to words, <u>phrases</u>, clauses, or lists that identify, rename, explain, emphasize, amplify, or illustrate the sentence that precedes the colon.

- Two topics will be discussed: *the new accounting system and the new bookkeeping procedures*. [phrases that identify]

- Only one thing will satisfy Mr. Sturgess: *our finished report*. [appositive (renaming) phrase for <u>emphasis</u>]

- Any organization is confronted with two separate, though related, information problems: *It must maintain an effective internal communication system and an effective external communication system*. [clause to amplify and explain]

- Heart patients should make key lifestyle changes: *stop smoking, exercise regularly, eat a low-fat diet, and reduce stress*. [list to identify and illustrate]

Colons with Salutations, Titles, Citations, and Numbers

A colon follows the salutation in <u>correspondence</u>, even when the salutation refers to a person by first name.

- Dear Professor Jeffers: *or* Dear Georgia:

Colons separate titles from subtitles and separate references to sections of works in citations. See also <u>documenting sources</u>.

- "'We Regret to Inform You': Toward a New Theory of Negative Messages"

- Genesis 10:16 [chapter 10, verse 16]

Colons separate numbers in time references and indicate numerical ratios.

- 9:30 a.m. [9 hours and 30 minutes]

- The cement is mixed with water and sand at 5:3:1. [The colon is read as the word *to*.]

Punctuation and Capitalization with Colons

A colon always goes outside <u>quotation marks</u>.

- This was the real meaning of the manager's "suggestion": Cooperation within our department must improve.

As this example shows, the first word after a colon may be capitalized if the statement following the colon is a complete sentence and functions as a formal resolution or question. If the element following the colon is subordinate, however, use a lowercase letter to begin that element. See also <u>capitalization</u>.

- We have only one way to stay within our present budget: to reduce expenditures for research and development.

Unnecessary Colons

Do not place a colon between a <u>verb</u> and its objects.

- Three fluids that clean pipettes are: water, alcohol, and acetone.

Likewise, do not use a colon between a <u>preposition</u> and its object.

- I may be transferred to: Tucson, Boston, or Miami.

Do not insert a colon after *including, such as,* or *for example* to introduce a simple list.

- Office computers should not be used for activities such as: personal e-mail, Web surfing, Internet shopping, and playing computer games.

One common exception is made when a verb or preposition is followed by a stacked <u>list</u>; however, it may be possible to introduce the list with a complete sentence instead.

- *The following corporations*
  Corporations that manufacture computers include:

Apple	Compaq	Dell
Gateway	IBM	Micron

comma splice

A comma splice is a grammatical error in which two independent <u>clauses</u> are joined by only a <u>comma</u>.

INCORRECT   It was 500 miles to the facility, we arranged to fly.

A comma splice can be corrected in several ways.

1. Substitute a <u>semicolon</u>, a semicolon and a conjunctive <u>adverb</u>, or a comma and a coordinating <u>conjunction</u>.
   - It was 500 miles to the facility; we arranged to fly.
   - It was 500 miles to the facility; *therefore*, we arranged to fly.
   - It was 500 miles to the facility, *so* we arranged to fly.
2. Create two sentences.
   - It was 500 miles to the facility. *We* arranged to fly.
3. Subordinate one clause to the other. (See <u>subordination</u>.)
   - *Because it was 500 miles to the facility*, we arranged to fly.

See also <u>sentence construction</u> and <u>sentence faults</u>.

commas

DIRECTORY

Linking Independent Clauses   92
Enclosing Elements   92
Introducing Elements   93
   Clauses and Phrases   93
   Words and Quotations   93
Separating Items in a Series   94

Clarifying and Contrasting   95
Showing Omissions   95
Using with Numbers and Names   95
Using with Other Punctuation   96
Avoiding Unnecessary Commas   97

Like all <u>punctuation</u>, the comma (,) helps <u>readers</u> understand the writer's meaning and prevents <u>ambiguity</u>. Notice how the comma helps make the meaning clear in the second example.

AMBIGUOUS   To be successful managers with MBAs must continue to learn.

CLEAR   To be successful, managers with MBAs must continue to learn.
[The comma makes clear where the main part of the sentence begins.]

Do not follow the old myth that you should insert a comma wherever you would pause if you were speaking. Although you would pause wherever you encounter a comma, you should not insert a comma wherever you might pause. Effective use of commas depends on an understanding of <u>sentence construction</u>.

Linking Independent Clauses

C

Use a comma before a coordinating <u>conjunction</u> (*and, but, or, nor*, and sometimes *so, yet*, and *for*) that links independent <u>clauses</u>.

- The new microwave disinfection system was delivered, *but* the installation will require an additional week.

However, if two independent clauses are short and closely related—and there is no danger of confusing the reader—the comma may be omitted. Both of the following examples are correct.

- The cable snapped and the power failed.
- The cable snapped, and the power failed.

Enclosing Elements

Commas are used to enclose nonessential information in nonrestrictive clauses, <u>phrases</u>, and parenthetical elements. See also <u>restrictive and nonrestrictive elements</u>.

- Our new factory, *which began operations last month*, should add 25 percent to total output. [nonrestrictive clause]
- The accountant, *working quickly and efficiently*, finished early. [nonrestrictive phrase]
- We can, *of course*, expect their lawyer to call us. [parenthetical element]

Yes and *no* are set off by commas in such uses as the following:

- I agree with you, *yes*.
- *No*, I do not think we can finish by the deadline.

A <u>direct address</u> should be enclosed in commas.

- You will note, *Mark*, that the budget figure matches our estimate.

An <u>appositive</u> phrase (which re-identifies another expression in the sentence) is enclosed in commas.

- Our company, *NT Insurance Group*, won several awards last year.

Interrupting parenthetical and transitional words or phrases are usually set off with commas. See also <u>transition</u>.

- The report, *therefore*, needs to be revised.

Commas are omitted when the word or phrase does not interrupt the continuity of thought.

- I *therefore* suggest that we begin construction.

For other means of punctuating parenthetical elements, see <u>dashes</u> and <u>parentheses</u>.

Introducing Elements

Clauses and Phrases.   Generally, place a comma after an introductory clause or phrase, especially if it is long, to identify where the introductory element ends and the main part of the sentence begins.

- *Because we have not yet reached our hiring goals for the Sales Division,* we recommend the development of an aggressive recruiting program.

A long modifying phrase that precedes the main clause should always be followed by a comma.

- *During the first series of field-performance tests at our Colorado proving ground,* the new engine failed to meet our expectations.

When an introductory phrase is short and closely related to the main clause, the comma may be omitted.

- *In two seconds* a 5°C temperature rise occurs in the test tube.

A comma should always follow an absolute phrase, which modifies the whole sentence.

- *The presentation completed,* we returned to our offices.

Words and Quotations.   Certain types of introductory words are followed by a comma. One example is a transitional word or phrase (*however, in addition*) that connects the preceding clause or sentence with the thought that follows.

- *Furthermore,* we should include college job fairs in our recruiting plans, provided our budget is approved.
- *For example,* this change will make us more competitive in the global marketplace.

When an <u>adverb</u> closely modifies the <u>verb</u> or the entire sentence, it should not be followed by a comma.

- *Perhaps* we can still solve the turnover problem. *Certainly* we should try. [*Perhaps* and *certainly* closely modify each statement.]

A proper <u>noun</u> used in an introductory direct address is followed by a comma, as is an <u>interjection</u> (such as *oh, well, why, indeed, yes,* and *no*).

C

- *Nancy,* enclosed is the article you asked me to review. [direct address]

- *Indeed,* I will ensure that your request is forwarded. [interjection]

Use a comma to separate a direct <u>quotation</u> from its introduction.

- Morton and Lucia White *said,* "People live in cities but dream of the countryside."

Do not use a comma when giving an indirect quotation.

- Morton and Lucia White *said that* people dream of the countryside, even though they live in cities.

Separating Items in a Series

Although the comma before the last item in a series is sometimes omitted, it is generally clearer to include it.

- Random House, Bantam, Doubleday, and Dell were individual publishing companies.
  [Without the final comma, "Doubleday and Dell" might refer to one company or two.]

Phrases and clauses in coordinate series are also punctuated with commas.

- Plants absorb noxious gases, act as receptors of dirt particles, and cleanse the air of other impurities.

When phrases or clauses in a series contain commas, use <u>semicolons</u> rather than commas to separate the items.

- Among those present were John Howard, President of the Howard Paper Company; Thomas Martin, CEO of AIR Recycling, Inc.; and Larry Stanley, President of Northland Papers.

When <u>adjectives</u> modifying the same noun can be reversed and make sense, or when they can be separated by *and* or *or,* they should be separated by commas.

- The aircraft featured a *modern, sleek, swept-wing* design.

When an adjective modifies a phrase, no comma is required.

- She was investigating the *damaged inventory-control system.*
  [The adjective *damaged* modifies the phrase *inventory-control system.*]

Never separate a final adjective from its noun.

- He is a conscientious, honest, reliable/ worker.

Clarifying and Contrasting

Use a comma to separate two contrasting thoughts or ideas.

- The project was finished on time, but not within the budget.

Use a comma after an independent clause that is only loosely related to the dependent clause that follows it or that could be misread without the comma.

- I should be able to finish the plan by July, even though I lost time because of illness.

Showing Omissions

A comma sometimes replaces a verb in certain elliptical constructions.

- Some were punctual; *others, late.*
  [The comma replaces *were.*]

It is better, however, to avoid such constructions in business writing.

Using with Numbers and Names

Commas are conventionally used to separate distinct items. Use commas between the elements of an address written on the same line (but not between the state and the zip code).

- Kristen James, 4119 Mill Road, Dayton, Ohio 45401

A full date that is written in month-day-year format uses a comma preceding and following the year.

- November 30, 2015, is the payoff date.

Do not use commas for dates in the day-month-year format, which is used in many parts of the world and by the U.S. military. See also **international correspondence**.

- Note that 30 November 2015 is the payoff date.

No commas are used if only the day or year is included. See also **dates**.

- The target date of May 2007 is optimistic, so I would like to meet on March 4 to discuss our options.

Use commas to separate the elements of Arabic numbers.

- 1,528,200 feet

C

However, because many countries use the comma as the decimal marker, use spaces or periods rather than commas in international documents.

- 1.528.200 meters *or* 1 528 200 meters

A comma may be substituted for the colon in the salutation of a personal letter or <u>e-mail</u>. Do not, however, use a comma in the salutation of a business letter or e-mail, even if you use the person's first name.

- Dear Marie, [personal letter or e-mail]
- Dear Marie: [business letter or e-mail]

Use commas to separate the elements of geographical names.

- Toronto, Ontario, Canada

Use a comma to separate names that are reversed or that are followed by an <u>abbreviation</u>.

- Smith, Alvin
- Jane Rogers, Ph.D.

Using with Other Punctuation

Conjunctive adverbs (*however, nevertheless, consequently, for example, on the other hand*) that join independent clauses are preceded by a <u>semicolon</u> and followed by a comma. Such adverbs function both as <u>modifiers</u> and as connectives.

- The idea is good; *however,* our budget is not sufficient.

As shown earlier in this entry, use semicolons rather than commas to separate items in a series when the items themselves contain commas.

When a comma should follow a phrase or clause that ends with words in parentheses, the comma always appears outside the closing parenthesis.

- Although we left late (at 7:30 p.m.), we arrived in time for the keynote address.

Commas always go inside <u>quotation marks</u>.

- The display window indicates "*ready,*" but the unit requires an additional warm-up period.

Except with abbreviations, a comma should not be used with a dash, an <u>exclamation mark</u>, a <u>period</u>, or a <u>question mark</u>.

- "Have you finished the project?," I asked.

Avoiding Unnecessary Commas

A number of common writing errors involve placing commas where they do not belong. As stated earlier, such errors often occur because writers assume that a pause in a sentence should be indicated by a comma.

Do not place a comma between a subject and verb or between a verb and its <u>object</u>.

- The location of our booth at this year's conference,/made attracting visitors difficult.
- She has often said,/that one company's failure is another's opportunity.

Do not use a comma between the elements of a compound subject or compound predicate consisting of only two elements.

- The director of the design department,/and the supervisor of the quality-control section were opposed to the new schedules.
- The design director listed five major objections,/and asked that the new schedule be reconsidered.

Do not include a comma after a coordinating conjunction such as *and* or *but*.

- The chairperson formally adjourned the meeting, but,/the members of the committee continued to argue.

Do not place a comma before the first item or after the last item of a series.

- The new products we are considering include,/calculators, scanners, and cameras.
- It was a fast, simple, inexpensive,/process.

Do not use a comma to separate a prepositional phrase from the rest of the sentence unnecessarily.

- We discussed the final report,/on the new project.

---

compare / contrast

When you *compare* things, you point out similarities or both similarities and differences. (He *compared* the two brands before making his choice.) When you *contrast* things, you point out only the differences. (Their speaking styles *contrasted* sharply.) In either case, you compare or contrast only things that are part of a common category.

When *compare* is used to establish a general similarity, it is followed by *to*. (*Compared to* our old copier, the current one is fast.) When *compare* is used to indicate a close examination of similarities or differences, it is followed by *with*. (We *compared* the features of the new copier *with* those of the current one.)

Contrast is normally followed by *with*. (The new policy *contrasts* sharply *with* the earlier one.) When the <u>noun</u> form of *contrast* is used, one speaks of the *contrast between* two things or of one thing being *in contrast to* the other.

- There is a sharp *contrast between* the old and new policies.

- The new policy is *in* sharp *contrast to* the earlier one.

comparison

When you are making a comparison, be sure that both or all of the elements being compared are clearly evident to your reader.

- The Nicom 3 software is better *than the Nicom 2 software*.

The things being compared must be of the same kind.

- A hard-side briefcase offers more protection than *a* fabric *briefcase*.

Be sure to point out the parallels or differences between the things being compared. Do not assume your reader will know what you mean.

- Washington is farther from Boston than *it is from* Philadelphia.

A double comparison in the same sentence requires that the first comparison be completed before the second one is stated.

- The discovery of electricity was one of the great if not the greatest scientific discoveries in history *, if not the greatest*.

Do not attempt to compare things that are not comparable.

- Agricultural experts advise that storage space is reduced by 40 percent compared with baled hay *requires 40 percent less storage space than loose hay requires*.

[*Storage space* is not comparable to *baled hay*.]

comparison method of development

As a **method of development**, comparison points out similarities and differences between the elements of your subject. The comparison method of development can be used effectively, for example, to explain a difficult or an unfamiliar subject by relating it to a simpler or more familiar one.

You must first determine the basis for the **comparison**. For example, if you were comparing bids from contractors for a remodeling project at your company, you most likely would compare such factors as price, previous experience, personnel qualifications, availability at a time convenient for you, and completion date. Once you have determined the basis or bases for comparison, you can determine the most effective way to structure your comparison: whole by whole or part by part.

In the *whole-by-whole method*, all the relevant characteristics of one item are examined before all the relevant characteristics of the next item. The description of typical woodworking glues in Figure C–6 is organized according to the whole-by-whole method. It describes each type of glue and all its characteristics before moving to the next one. This description would be useful for those **readers** who wish to learn about all types of wood glues.

White glue is the most useful all-purpose adhesive for light construction, but it cannot be used on projects that will be exposed to moisture, high temperature, or great stress. Wood that is being joined with white glue must remain in a clamp until the glue dries, which takes about 30 minutes.

Aliphatic resin glue has a stronger and more moisture-resistant bond than white glue. It must be used at temperatures above 50°F. The wood should be clamped for about 30 minutes. . . .

Plastic resin glue is the strongest of the common wood adhesives. It is highly moisture resistant, though not completely waterproof. Sold in powdered form, this glue must be mixed with water and used at temperatures above 70°F. It is slow setting, and the joint should be clamped for four to six hours. . . .

Contact cement is a very strong adhesive that bonds so quickly it must be used with great care. It is ideal for mounting sheets of plastic laminate on wood. It is also useful for attaching strips of veneer to the edges of plywood. Because this adhesive bonds immediately when two pieces are pressed together, clamping is not necessary, but the parts to be joined must be carefully aligned before being placed together. Most brands are flammable, and the fumes can be harmful if inhaled. To meet current safety standards, this type of glue must be used in a well-ventilated area, away from flames or heat.

FIGURE C–6. Whole-by-Whole Method of Comparison

C

If your **purpose** were to help readers consider the various characteristics of all the glues, the information might be arranged according to the *part-by-part method of comparison,* in which the relevant features of the items are compared one by one (as shown in Figure C–7). The part-by-part method could accommodate further comparison—such as temperature ranges, special warnings, and common use, in this case.

Woodworking adhesives are rated primarily according to their bonding strength, moisture resistance, and setting time.

Bonding strength is categorized as very strong, moderately strong, or adequate for use with little stress. Contact cement and plastic resin glue bond very strongly, while aliphatic resin glue bonds moderately strongly. White glue provides a bond least resistant to stress.

The *moisture resistance* of woodworking glues is rated as high, moderate, or low. Plastic resin glues and contact cement are highly moisture resistant, aliphatic resin glues is moderately moisture resistant, and white glue is least moisture resistant.

Setting time for the glues varies from an immediate bond to a four-to-six-hour bond. Contact cement bonds immediately and requires no clamping. Because the bond is immediate, surfaces being joined must be carefully aligned before being placed together. White glue and aliphatic resin glue set in 30 minutes; both require clamping to secure the bond. Plastic resin, the strongest wood glue, sets in four to six hours and also requires clamping.

FIGURE C–7. Part-by-Part Method of Comparison

Comparisons can also be made effectively with the use of <u>tables</u>, as shown in Figure C–8. The advantage of a table is that it provides a quick reference, allowing readers to see and compare all the information at once. The disadvantage is that a table cannot convey as much related detailed information as a narrative description.

	White Glue	**Aliphatic Resin Glue**	**Plastic Resin Glue**	**Contact Cement**
Bonding Strength	Low	Moderate	High	High
Moisture Resistance	Low	Moderate	High	High
Setting Time	Thirty minutes	Thirty minutes	Four to six hours	Bonds on contact
Common Uses	Light construction	General purpose	General purpose	Laminate and veneer to wood

FIGURE C–8. Comparison Using a Table to Illustrate Key Differences

complaint letters

C

The <u>tone</u> of a complaint letter is important; the most effective ones do not sound complaining. If your letter reflects only your annoyance and anger, you may not be taken seriously. Assume that the recipient will be conscientious in correcting the problem. However, anticipate <u>reader</u> reactions or rebuttals.

- I reviewed carefully the "safe operating guidelines" in my user manual before I installed the device.

Without such explanations, readers may be tempted to dismiss your complaint. Figure C–9 on page 102 shows a typical complaint letter.

Although the circumstances and severity of the problem may vary, effective complaint letters generally follow this pattern:

1. Identify the problem or faulty item(s) and include relevant invoice numbers, part names, and dates. Include a copy of the receipt, bill, or contract, and keep the original for your records.
2. Explain logically, clearly, and specifically what went wrong, especially for a problem with a service. (Avoid guessing why you *think* some problem occurred.)
3. State what you expect the reader to do to solve the problem.

Begin by checking to see if the company's Web site provides instructions for submitting a complaint. Otherwise, for large organizations, you may address your complaint to Customer Service. In smaller organizations, you might write to a vice president in charge of sales or service, or directly to the owner. As a last resort, you may find that sending copies of a complaint letter to more than one person in the company will get faster results. See also <u>adjustment letters</u> and <u>refusal letters</u>.

complement / compliment

Complement means "anything that completes a whole" (see also <u>complements</u>). It is used as either a <u>noun</u> or a <u>verb</u>.

- A *complement* of four employees would bring our staff up to its normal strength. [noun]
- The two programs *complement* one another perfectly. [verb]

BAKER HEALTHCARE SYSTEMS

Purchasing Department
501 Main Street
Springfield, OH 45321
(513) 683-8100
Fax (513) 683-8000

September 22, 2006

Manager, Customer Relations
Medical Solutions, Inc.
521 West 23rd Street
New York, NY 10011

Subject: ST3 Diagnostic Scanners

On July 10, I ordered nine ST3 Diagnostic Scanners (order
ST3-1179R). The scanners were ordered from your customer
Web site.

On August 2, I received from your Newark, New Jersey, parts warehouse seven HL monitors. I immediately returned these monitors
with a note indicating the mistake that had been made. However,
not only have I failed to receive the ST3 scanners I ordered, but I
have also been billed repeatedly.

I have enclosed a copy of my confirmation e-mail, the shipping
form, and the most recent bill. If you cannot send me the scanners
I ordered by November 1, please cancel my order.

Sincerely,

Paul Denlinger

Paul Denlinger
Manager
pld@baker.org

Enclosures

FIGURE C–9. Complaint Letter

Compliment means "praise." It too is used as either a noun or a verb.

- The manager's *compliment* boosted staff morale. [noun]
- The manager *complimented* the staff on its efficient job. [verb]

complements

A *complement* is a word, **phrase**, or **clause** used in the predicate of a sentence to complete the meaning of the sentence.

- Pilots fly *airplanes*. [word]
- To live is *to risk death.* [phrase]
- John knew *that he would be late.* [clause]

Four kinds of complements are generally recognized: direct object, indirect object, objective complement, and subjective complement.

A *direct object* is a **noun** or noun equivalent that receives the action of a transitive **verb**; it answers the question *What?* or *Whom?* after the verb.

- I designed *a Web page.* [noun phrase]
- I like *to work.* [verbal]
- I like *it.* [pronoun]
- I like *what I saw.* [noun clause]

An *indirect object* is a noun or noun equivalent that occurs with a direct **object** after certain kinds of transitive verbs such as *give, wish, cause,* and *tell.* It answers the question *To whom or what?* or *For whom or what?*

- We should buy the *office* a *scanner.*
  [*Scanner* is the direct object, and *office* is the indirect object.]

An *objective complement* completes the meaning of a sentence by revealing something about the object of its transitive verb. An objective complement may be either a noun or an **adjective**.

- They call him *a genius.* [noun phrase]
- We painted the building *white.* [adjective]

A *subjective complement*, which follows a linking verb rather than a transitive verb, describes the subject. A subjective complement may be either a noun or an adjective.

- His sister is *a consultant*. [noun phrase]
- His brother is *ill*. [adjective]

See also <u>sentence construction</u>.

compose / constitute / comprise

Compose and *constitute* both mean "make up the whole." The parts *compose* or *constitute* the whole.

- The nine offices *compose* the division.
- Unethical activities *constitute* cause for dismissal.

Comprise means "include," "contain," or "consist of." The whole *comprises* the parts. (The division *comprises* nine offices.)

compound words

A compound word is made from two or more words that function as a single concept. A compound may be hyphenated, written as one word, or written as separate words.

- editor in chief   courthouse   home page
  high-energy   nevertheless   post office
  low-level   online   Web site

If you are not certain whether a compound word should use a <u>hyphen</u>, check a dictionary.

Be careful to distinguish between compound words (*greenhouse*) and words that simply appear together but do not constitute compound words (*green house*). For plurals of compound words, generally add *s* to the last letter (*bookcases* and *Web sites*). However, when the first word of the compound is more important to its meaning than the last, the first word takes the *s* (*editors in chief*). Possessives are formed by adding *'s* to the end of the compound word (the *editor in chief's* desk, the *pipeline's* diameter, the *post office's* hours). See also <u>possessive case</u>.

conciseness

Conciseness means that extraneous words, <u>phrases</u>, <u>clauses</u>, and sentences have been removed from writing without sacrificing <u>clarity</u> or appropriate detail. Conciseness is not a synonym for brevity; a long report may be concise, while its abstract may be brief and concise. Conciseness is always desirable, but brevity may or may not be desirable in a given passage, depending on the writer's purpose. Although concise sentences are not guaranteed to be effective, wordy sentences always sacrifice some of their readability and coherence.

Causes of Wordiness

Modifiers that repeat an idea implicit or present in the word being modified contribute to wordiness by being redundant. See also reason is [because].

basic essentials	*completely* finished
final outcome	*present* status

Coordinated synonyms that merely repeat each other contribute to wordiness.

each and every	*basic and fundamental*
finally and for good	*first and foremost*

Excess qualification also contributes to wordiness.

perfectly clear	*completely* accurate

Expletives, relative pronouns, and relative adjectives, although they have legitimate purposes, often result in wordiness.

WORDY   *There are* [expletive] many Web designers *who* [relative pronoun] are planning to attend the conference, *which* [relative adjective] is scheduled for May 13–15.

CONCISE   Many Web designers plan to attend the conference scheduled for May 13–15.

Circumlocution (a long, indirect way of expressing things) is a leading cause of wordiness. See also gobbledygook.

WORDY   The payment to which a subcontractor is entitled should be made promptly so that in the event of a subsequent contractual dispute we, as general contractors, may not be held in default of our contract by virtue of nonpayment.

CONCISE   Pay subcontractors promptly. Then, if a contractual dispute occurs, we cannot be held in default of our contract because of nonpayment.

When conciseness is overdone, writing can become choppy and ambiguous. (See also telegraphic style.) Too much conciseness can produce a style that is not only too brief but also too blunt, especially in correspondence.

Writer's Checklist: Achieving Conciseness

Wordiness is understandable when you are <u>**writing a draft**</u>, but it should not survive <u>**revision**</u>.

☑ Use <u>**subordination**</u> to achieve conciseness.

* The *five-page* financial report was carefully ~~documented, and it covered~~ *documented.* ~~five pages.~~

☑ Avoid <u>**affectation**</u> by using simple words and phrases.

> **WORDY**   It is the policy of the company to provide Web access to enable employees to conduct the online communication necessary to discharge their responsibilities; such should not be utilized for personal communications or nonbusiness activities.
>
> **CONCISE**   Employee Web access should be used only for appropriate company business.

☑ Eliminate redundancy.

> **WORDY**   Postinstallation testing, which is offered to all our customers at no further cost to them whatsoever, is available with each Line Scan System One purchased from this company.
>
> **CONCISE**   Free postinstallation testing is offered with each Line Scan System One.

☑ Change the passive <u>**voice**</u> to the active voice and the indicative <u>**mood**</u> to the imperative mood whenever possible.

> **WORDY**   Bar codes normally are used when an order is intended to be displayed on a computer, and inventory numbers normally are used when an order is to be placed with the manufacturer.
>
> **CONCISE**   Use bar codes to display the order on a computer, and use inventory numbers to place the order with the manufacturer.

☑ Eliminate or replace wordy introductory phrases or pretentious words and phrases (*in the case of, it may be said that, it appears that, needless to say*).

REPLACE	WITH
in order to; with a view to	to
due to the fact that; for the reason that; owing to the fact that; the reason for	because
by means of; by using; in connection with; through the use of	by; with
at this time; at this point in time; at present; at the present	now

Writer's Checklist: Achieving Conciseness (continued)

☑   Do not overuse **intensifiers**, such as *very, more, most, best, quite, great, really,* and *especially.* Instead provide specific and useful details.

☑   Use the search-and-replace command to find and revise wordy expressions, including *to be* and unnecessary helping **verbs** such as *will.*

conclusions

The conclusion of a document ties the main ideas together and can clinch a final significant point. This final point may, for example, make a prediction or a judgment, summarize the key findings of a study, or recommend a course of action. Figure C–10 is a conclusion from a proposal to reduce health-care costs by increasing employee fitness through health-club subsidies. Notice that it summarizes key points, makes a recommendation, and points out several benefits of implementing the recommendation.

The way you conclude depends on your **purpose**, your **readers'** needs, and the **context**. For example, a committee **report** about possible locations for a new production facility might end with a recommendation that is realistic given the circumstances; a lengthy sales **proposal** might conclude persuasively with a summary of the proposal's salient points and the company's main strong points. The following examples are typical concluding strategies.

RECOMMENDATION
Our findings suggest that you need to alter your marketing to adjust to the changing demographics for your products.

SUMMARY
As this report describes, we would attract more recent graduates with the following strategies:
1. Establish a Web site where students can register and submit online résumés.
2. Increase our advertising in local student newspapers and our attendance at college career fairs.
3. Expand our local co-op program.

JUDGMENT
Based on the scope and degree of the tornado's damage, the current construction code for roofing on light industrial facilities is inadequate.

C

Conclusion and Recommendation

I recommend that ABO, Inc., participate in the corporate membership program at AeroFitness Clubs, Inc., by subsidizing employee memberships. By subsidizing memberships, ABO shows its commitment to the importance of a fit workforce. Club membership allows employees at all five ABO warehouses to participate in the program. The more employees who participate, the greater the long-term savings in ABO's health-care costs. Building and equipping fitness centers at all five warehouse sites would require an initial investment of nearly $2.5 million. These facilities would also occupy valuable floor space—on average, 4,000 square feet at each warehouse. Therefore, this option would be costly.

Enrolling employees in the corporate program at AeroFitness would allow them to receive a one-month free trial membership. Those interested in continuing could then join the club and pay half of the one-time membership fee of $900 and receive a 30 percent discount on the $600 yearly fee. The other half of the membership fee ($450) would be paid for by ABO. If employees leave the company, they would have the option of purchasing ABO's share of the membership to continue at AeroFitness or selling their half of the membership to another ABO employee wishing to join AeroFitness.

Implementing this program will help ABO, Inc., reduce its health-care costs while building stronger employee relations by offering employees a desirable benefit. If this proposal is adopted, I have some additional thoughts about publicizing the program to encourage employee participation. I look forward to discussing the details of this proposal with you and answering any questions you may have.

FIGURE C–10. Conclusion

IMPLICATION

Although our estimate calls for a substantially higher budget than in the three previous years, we believe that it is reasonable given our planned expansion.

PREDICTION

Although I have exceeded my original estimate for equipment, I have reduced my original labor estimate; therefore, I will easily stay within the original bid.

The concluding statement may merely present ideas for consideration, call for action, or deliberately provoke thought.

IDEAS FOR CONSIDERATION
The new prices become effective the first of the year. Price adjustments are routine for the company, but some of your customers will not consider them acceptable. Please bear in mind the needs of both your customers and the company as you implement these price adjustments.

CALL FOR ACTION
Please send us a check for $250 now if you wish to keep your account active. If you have not responded to our previous letters because of some special hardship, I will be glad to work out a solution with you personally.

THOUGHT-PROVOKING STATEMENT
Can we continue to accept the losses incurred by inefficiency? Or should we consider steps to control it now?

Be especially careful not to introduce a new topic when you conclude. A conclusion should always relate to and reinforce the ideas presented earlier in your writing. Moreover, the conclusions must be consistent with what the **introduction** promised the report would examine (its purpose) and how it would do so (its method).

For guidance about the location of the conclusion section in a report, see **formal reports**. For letter and other short closings, see **correspondence** and entries on specific types of documents throughout this book.

conjunctions

A conjunction connects words, phrases, or clauses and can also indicate the relationship between the elements it connects.

A *coordinating conjunction* joins two sentence elements that have identical functions. The coordinating conjunctions are *and, but, or, for, nor, yet,* and *so.*

- Nature *and* technology affect petroleum prices. [joins two **nouns**]

- To hear *and* to listen are two different things. [joins two **phrases**]

- I would like to include the survey, *but* that would make the report too long. [joins two **clauses**]

Coordinating conjunctions in the titles of books, articles, plays, and movies should not be capitalized unless they are the first or last word in the title.

- Our library contains *Consulting and Financial Independence* as well as *So You Want to Improve Your Bottom Line?*

Occasionally, a conjunction may begin a sentence; in fact, conjunctions can be strong transitional words and at times can provide <u>emphasis</u>. See also <u>transition</u>.

- I realize that the project is more difficult than expected and that you have encountered staffing problems. *But* we must meet our deadline.

Correlative conjunctions are used in pairs. The correlative conjunctions are *either . . . or, neither . . . nor, not only . . . but also, both . . . and,* and *whether . . . or.*

- The auditor will arrive *either* on Wednesday *or* on Thursday.

A *subordinating conjunction* connects sentence elements of different relative importance, normally independent and dependent clauses. The most frequently used subordinating conjunctions are *so, although, after, because, if, where, than, since, as, unless, before, that, though,* and *when.*

- I left the office *after* finishing the report.

A *conjunctive adverb* has the force of a conjunction because it joins two independent clauses. The most common conjunctive <u>adverbs</u> are *however, moreover, therefore, further, then, consequently, besides, accordingly, also,* and *thus.*

- The engine performed well in the laboratory; *however,* it failed under road conditions.

connotation / denotation

The *denotations* of a word are its literal meanings, as defined in a dictionary. The *connotations* of a word are its meanings and associations beyond its literal definitions. For example, the denotations of *Hollywood* are "a district of Los Angeles" and "the U.S. movie industry as a whole"; its connotations for many are "romance, glittering success, and superficiality."

Often words have particular connotations for <u>readers</u> within professional groups and organizations. Choose words with both the most accurate denotations and the most appropriate connotations for the <u>context</u>. See also <u>defining terms</u> and <u>word choice</u>.

C

consensus

Because *consensus* means "harmony of opinion" among most of those in a group, the phrases *consensus of opinion* and *general consensus* defeat <u>conciseness</u>. The word *consensus* can be used to refer only to a group, never to one or two people.

* The ~~general~~ consensus ~~of opinion~~ among investors is that the Board of Directors should be replaced.

context

Simply put, context is the environment or circumstances in which writers produce documents and within which <u>readers</u> interpret their meanings. Everything is written in a context, as illustrated in many entries and examples throughout this book. This entry considers specifically the effect of context on documents and suggests how you can be aware of it as you write.

The context for any document, such as a <u>proposal</u> or <u>report</u>, is determined by interrelated events or circumstances both inside and outside an organization.* For example, when you write a proposal to fund a project within your company, the economic condition of that company is part of the context that will determine how your proposal is received. If the company has recently laid off a dozen employees, the management may not be inclined to approve a proposal to expand into a new market—regardless of how well the proposal is written.

When you correspond with someone, the events that prompted you to write shape the context of the message and will affect what you say and how you say it. If you write to a customer in response to a complaint, for example, the <u>tone</u> and approach of your <u>adjustment letter</u> will be determined by the context—what you find when you investigate the issue. Is your company fully or partly at fault? Has the customer incorrectly used a product? contributed to a problem? The answers to such questions reveal the context. Or, if you write <u>instructions</u> for office staff who must use high-volume document-processing equipment, other questions will reveal the context. What are the lighting and other physical conditions near the equipment? Will these physical conditions

*For a detailed illustration of specific documents that have been affected by factors within particular contexts, see Linda Driskill, "Understanding the Writing Context in Organizations," in *Central Works in Technical Communication*, ed. Johndan Johnson-Eilola and Stuart Selber (New York: Oxford UP, 2004), 55–69.

affect the <u>layout and design</u> of the instructions? What potential safety issues might the users encounter?

Each time you write, you should keep in mind and even visualize the context so that you are sure your document will achieve its <u>purpose</u>. The following questions are starting points to help you become aware of the context, how it will influence your approach and your readers' interpretation of what you have written, and how it will affect the decisions you need to make during the writing process. See also "Five Steps to Successful Writing."

- What is your professional relationship with your readers and how might that affect the <u>tone</u>, <u>style</u>, and <u>scope</u> of your writing?
- What is "the story" behind the immediate reason you are writing; that is, what series of events or perhaps previous documents led to your need to write?
- What is the preferred medium of your readers? (See <u>selecting the medium</u>.)
- What specific factors, such as competition, finance, and regulation, are recognized within an organization or a department as important?
- What is the corporate culture in which your readers work, and what are its key values that you might find in its mission statement?
- What are the professional relationships among the specific readers who will receive a document?
- What current events within or outside an organization or a department may influence how readers interpret your writing?
- What national cultural differences might affect your readers' expectations or interpretations of the document? See <u>global communication</u>.

As these questions suggest, context is very specific each time you write and often involves, for example, the history of a specific organization or your past dealings with individual readers.

Context and Openings

Because context is so important, it is often helpful to remind your reader in some way of the context for your writing, as in the following opening for a cover letter to a proposal.

- During our meeting on improving quality last week, you mentioned that we have in the past required usability testing only for documents going to high-profile clients because of the costs involved. As I considered that practice, the idea occurred to me that we might try less extensive usability testing for many of our other clients. Because you suggested that you would welcome new ideas, I have proposed in the attached document a method of limited usability testing for a broad range of clients in order to improve overall quality.

Of course, as described in <u>introductions</u>, providing context for a reader may require only a brief background statement or short reminders.

- Several weeks ago a manager noticed a recurring problem in the software developed by Datacom Systems. Specifically, error messages repeatedly appeared when, in fact, no specific trouble . . .

- Jane, as I promised in my e-mail yesterday, I've attached the personnel budget estimates for the next fiscal year.

As the last example suggests, always provide some context when you send an <u>e-mail</u> with attachments.

continual / continuous

Continual implies "happening over and over" or "frequently repeated." (Writing well requires *continual* practice.) *Continuous* implies "occurring without interruption" or "unbroken." (The *continuous* roar of the machinery was deafening.)

contractions

A contraction is a shortened spelling of a word or phrase with an <u>apostrophe</u> substituting for the missing letter or letters (*cannot/can't; have not/haven't; will not/won't; it is/it's*). Contractions are often used in speech and informal writing; they are generally not appropriate in <u>reports</u>, <u>proposals</u>, and formal <u>correspondence</u>. See also <u>business writing style</u>.

copyright

Copyright establishes legal protection for literary, dramatic, musical, artistic, and other intellectual works in printed or electronic form; it gives the copyright owner exclusive right to reproduce, distribute, perform, or display a work. Copyright protects all original works from the moment of their creation, regardless of whether they are published or contain a notice of copyright (©).

⬛ ETHICS NOTE If you plan to reproduce copyrighted material in your own publication or on your Web site, you must obtain permission from the copyright holder. To do otherwise is a violation of U.S. law. ✦

Permissions

To seek permission to reproduce copyrighted material, you must write to the copyright holder. In some cases it is the author; in other cases it is the editor or publisher of the work. For Web sites, read the site's "terms-of-use" information (if available) and e-mail your request to the appropriate party. State specifically which portion of the work you wish to reproduce and how you plan to use it. The copyright holder has the right to charge a fee and specify conditions and limits of use.

Exceptions

Some copyrighted material may be reproduced without permission. For example, a small amount of material from a copyrighted source may be used, especially for educational purposes, without permission or payment as long as the use satisfies the "fair-use" criteria, as described at the U.S. Copyright Office Web site, <www.copyright.gov/>.

In the workplace, employees often borrow from in-house manuals, reports, and other company documents. Because the company is considered the author of works prepared by its employees on the job, using such boilerplate material is not a violation of copyright.

Works created by or for U.S. government agencies are in the public domain—that is, they are not copyrighted. Such works, including text and **visuals,** can be reproduced without permission unless the information is classified or otherwise protected. As with other material you use in your own work, however, you should give appropriate credit to the source from which material is taken, as described in **plagiarism** and **documenting sources.**

correspondence

DIRECTORY
Writing Style and Accuracy   115
Audience: Tone and Goodwill   116
Writer's Checklist: Using Tone to Build Goodwill   117
Good-News and Bad-News Patterns   118

Openings and Closings   119
Format and Design   120
   Heading   122
   Inside Address   122
   Salutation   122
   Body   125
   Complimentary Closing   125
   Second Page   125
   End Notations   126
Writer's Checklist: Writing Correspondence   127

The process of writing letters or <u>memos</u> (or <u>e-mail</u> that functions as either) involves many of the same steps that go into writing most other documents, as described in "Five Steps to Successful Writing." One important consideration in correspondence is the impression you convey to <u>readers</u>. To convey a professional image—of yourself and your company or organization—take particular care with the <u>tone</u> and <u>style</u> of your writing. See also <u>business writing style</u>.

Writing Style and Accuracy

Correspondence may vary from an informal (or casual) style that you might use with a colleague you know well to a formal (or restrained) style that would be appropriate to a client you do not know.

INFORMAL	It worked! The new process is better than we had dreamed.
RESTRAINED	You will be pleased to know that the new process is more effective than we had expected.

You will probably find yourself using the restrained style more frequently than the casual one. Remember that an overdone attempt to sound casual or friendly can sound insincere. However, do not adopt so formal a style that your writing reads like a legal contract. See <u>affectation</u>.

AFFECTED	Per our dialogue yesterday, we no longer possess an original copy of the brochure requested. Please be advised that a PDF copy is attached to this e-mail.
IMPROVED	We are out of original copies of the brochure we discussed yesterday, so I am attaching a PDF copy to this e-mail.

The improved version is both less stuffy and more concise. Do not be so concise, however, that you become blunt. Responding to a vague written request with "Your request was unclear" or "I don't understand" could offend your reader. Instead, ask for more information and establish goodwill to encourage your reader to provide the information.

- I will need more information before I can answer your request. Specifically, can you give me the title and the date of the report you are looking for?

Although this version is a bit longer, it is more tactful and will elicit a faster response. See also **telegraphic style**.

Check for accuracy: Facts, figures, and dates that are incorrect or misleading may cost time, money, and goodwill. Incorrect punctuation or grammar and unconventional **usage** can undermine your credibility. Remember that when you sign a letter, initial a memo, or press the "send" key for an e-mail, you are accepting responsibility for it. Therefore, allow yourself time to review correspondence carefully before sending it.

Audience: Tone and Goodwill

Correspondence is always more personal than reports or other forms of business writing because it is written directly to another person. To achieve a conversational style, imagine your reader sitting across the desk from you and write to the reader as if you were talking face-to-face.

Take into account your reader's needs and feelings. Ask yourself, "How might I feel if I received this letter?" and then tailor your message accordingly. Remember, an impersonal and unfriendly letter to a customer or client can tarnish the image of you and your business, but a thoughtful and sincere letter can enhance it. Suppose, for example, you received a refund request from a customer who forgot to enclose the receipt with the request. In a response to that customer, you might write the following:

- We must receive the sales receipt before we can process a refund. [The writer's needs are emphasized: "*We* must."]

If you consider how you might keep the customer's goodwill, you might word the request this way:

- Please mail or fax the sales receipt so that we can process your refund. [This is polite, but the writer's needs are emphasized: "so that *we* can process."]

You can put the reader's needs and interests foremost by writing from the reader's perspective. Often, doing so means using the words *you* and *your* rather than *we, our, I,* and *mine*—a technique called the "you" viewpoint. Consider the following revision:

- So you can receive your refund promptly, please mail or fax the sales receipt.
  [The reader's needs are emphasized with *you* and *your*.]

This revision stresses the reader's benefit and interest. By emphasizing the reader's needs, the writer will be more likely to accomplish the **purpose**: to get the reader to act.

Keep in mind that, if overdone, goodwill and the "you" viewpoint can produce writing that is fawning and insincere. Messages that are full of excessive praise and inflated language may be ignored—or even resented—by the reader.

EXCESSIVE	You are just the kind of client that deserves the finest service that anyone can offer—and you deserve our best deal. Knowing how careful you are at making decisions, I know you'll think about the advantages of using our consulting service.
REASONABLE	From our earlier correspondence, I can understand your need for reliable service—we strive to give all our priority clients our full attention. After you have reviewed our proposal, I am confident you will appreciate our "five-star" consulting option.

Writer's Checklist: Using Tone to Build Goodwill

Use the following guidelines to achieve a tone that builds goodwill with your recipients.

☑ Be respectful, not demanding.

DEMANDING	Submit your answer in one week.
RESPECTFUL	I would appreciate your answer within one week.

☑ Be modest, not arrogant.

ARROGANT	My attached report is thorough, and I'm sure that you won't be able to continue without it.
MODEST	The attached report contains details of the refinancing options, and I hope you find it useful.

☑ Be polite, not sarcastic.

SARCASTIC	I just now received the shipment we ordered six months ago. I'm sending it back—we can't use it now. Thanks a lot!

Writer's Checklist: Using Tone to Build Goodwill (continued)

POLITE — I am returning the shipment we ordered on March 12. Unfortunately, it arrived too late for us to be able to use it.

☑ Be positive and tactful, not negative and condescending.

NEGATIVE — Your complaint about our prices is way off target. Our prices are definitely not any higher than those of our competitors.

TACTFUL — Thank you for your suggestion concerning our prices. We believe, however, that our prices are competitive with, and in some cases are below, those of our competitors.

Good-News and Bad-News Patterns

Although the relative directness of correspondence may vary, it is generally more effective to present good news directly and bad news indirectly, especially if the stakes are high.* This principle is based on the fact that readers form their impressions and attitudes very early and that you as a writer may want to subordinate the bad news to reasons that make the bad news understandable. Further, if you are writing international correspondence, be aware that far more cultures are generally indirect in business messages than are direct.

Consider the thoughtlessness and direct rejection in Figure C–11. Although the message is concise and uses the pronouns *you* and *your*, the writer does not consider how the recipient is likely to feel as she reads the rejection. Its pattern is (1) the bad news, (2) an explanation, and (3) the closing.

Dear Ms. Mauer:

Your application for the position of Records Administrator at Southtown Dental Center has been rejected. We have found someone more qualified than you.

Sincerely,

FIGURE C–11. A Poor Bad-News Message

*Gerald J. Alred, "'We Regret to Inform You': Toward a New Theory of Negative Messages," in *Studies in Technical Communication*, ed. Brenda R. Sims (Denton: University of North Texas and NCTE, 1993), 17–36.

A better general pattern for bad news is (1) an opening that provides <u>context</u> (often called a "buffer"), (2) an explanation, (3) the bad news, and (4) a goodwill closing. (See also <u>refusal letters</u>.) The opening introduces the subject and establishes a professional tone. The body provides an explanation by reviewing the facts that make the bad news understandable. Although bad news is never pleasant, information that either puts the bad news in perspective or makes it seem reasonable maintains goodwill between the writer and the reader. The closing should reinforce a positive relationship through goodwill or helpful information. Consider, for example, the courteous rejection shown in Figure C–12. It carries the same disappointing news as does the letter in Figure C–11, but the writer is careful to thank the reader for her time and effort, explain why she was not accepted for the job, and offer her encouragement.

Presenting good news is, of course, easier. Present good news in your opening. By presenting the good news first, you increase the likelihood that the reader will pay careful attention to details, and you achieve goodwill from the start. The pattern for good-news messages should be (1) a good-news opening, (2) an explanation of facts, and (3) a goodwill closing. Figure C–13 is an example of an effective good-news message.

Openings and Closings

To focus the relevance of any correspondence for the reader, identify your subject in the opening.

- Yesterday, I received your letter and the pager, number AJ 50172. I sent the pager to our quality-control department for tests.

Your closing should let the reader know what he or she should do next and reinforce goodwill.

- Thanks again for the report, and let me know if you want me to send you a copy of the test results.

Because a closing is in a position of emphasis, consider it carefully. Before you simply use a routine closing (If you have further questions, please let me know), consider how you might make your closing work for you. It may be helpful to provide prompts to which the reader can respond.

- If you would like further information, such as a copy of the questionnaire we used, please e-mail me at delgado@prn.com.

See also <u>conclusions</u> and <u>introductions</u>.

Southtown Dental Center
3221 Ryan Road   San Diego, CA 92217
Phone: (714) 321-1579   Fax: (714) 321-1222

November 6, 2006

Ms. Barbara L. Mauer
157 Beach Drive
San Diego, CA 92113

Dear Ms. Mauer:

Context
(or "buffer")

Thank you for your time and effort in applying for the position of Records Administrator at Southtown Dental Center.

Explanation
leading to
bad news

Because we need someone who can assume the duties here with a minimum of training, we have selected an applicant with several years of experience.

Goodwill

Your college record is excellent, and I encourage you to apply for another position with us in the future.

Sincerely,

Mary Hernandez

Mary Hernandez
Office Manager

FIGURE C–12. A Courteous Bad-News Message

Format and Design

Although word-processing software provides templates for correspondence, it may not provide specific dimensions and spacing. To achieve a professional appearance, center the letter on the page vertically and horizontally. Although one-inch margins are the default standard in many word-processing programs, it is more important to establish a

C

Southtown Dental Center
3221 Ryan Road   San Diego, CA 92217
Phone: (714) 321-1579   Fax: (714) 321-1222

November 6, 2006

Ms. Barbara L. Mauer
157 Beach Drive
San Diego, CA 92113

Dear Ms. Mauer:

Good news — Please accept our offer of the position of Records Administrator at Southtown Dental Center at the salary of $64,300.

Explanation — If the terms we discussed in the interview are acceptable to you, please come in at 9:30 a.m. on November 15. At that time, we will ask you to complete our benefits form, in addition to . . .

Goodwill — I, as well as the others in the office, look forward to working with you. Everyone was favorably impressed with you during your interview.

Sincerely,

Mary Hernandez

Mary Hernandez
Office Manager

FIGURE C–13. A Good-News Message

picture frame of blank space surrounding the page of text. When you use organizational letterhead stationery, consider the bottom of the letterhead as the top edge of the paper. The right margin should be approximately as wide as the left margin. To give a fuller appearance to very short letters, increase both margins to about an inch and a half.

Use your computer's full-page or print-preview feature to check for proportion.

The two most common formats for business letters are the full-block style shown in Figure C–14 and the modified-block style shown in Figure C–15. In the *full-block style*, which should be used only with letterhead, the entire letter is aligned at the left margin. In the *modified-block style*, the return address, date, and complimentary closing begin at the center of the page and the other elements are aligned at the left margin. All other letter styles are variations of the full-block and modified-block styles.

If your employer requires a particular format, use it. Otherwise, follow the guidelines provided here, and review the examples shown in Figures C–14 and C–15.

Heading.   Place your full return address and the date in the heading. Because your name appears at the end of the letter, it need not be included in the heading. Spell out words like *street, avenue, first,* and *west* rather than abbreviating them. You may either spell out the name of the state in full or use the standard Postal Service abbreviation. The date usually goes directly beneath the last line of the return address. Do not abbreviate the name of the month. Begin the heading about two inches from the top of the page. If you are using company letterhead that gives the address, enter only the date, three lines below the last line of printed copy.

Inside Address.   Include the recipient's full name, title, and address in the inside address, two to six lines below the date, depending on the length of the letter. The inside address should be aligned with the left margin, and the left margin should be at least one inch wide.

Salutation.   Place the salutation, or greeting, two lines below the inside address and align it with the left margin. In most business letters, the salutation contains the recipient's personal title (such as *Mr., Ms., Dr.*) and last name, followed by a colon. If you are on a first-name basis with the recipient, use only the first name in the salutation.

Address women as *Ms.,* unless they have expressed a preference for *Miss* or *Mrs.* However, professional titles (such as *Professor, Senator, Major*) take precedence over *Ms.* If you do not know whether the recipient is a man or a woman, use a title appropriate to the context of the letter. The following are examples of the kinds of salutations you may find suitable: *Dear Customer, Dear Colleague, Dear IT Professional.*

If you are writing to a large company and do not know the name or title of the recipient, you may address the letter to an appropriate department or identify the subject in a subject line and use no salutation.

Letterhead

520 Niagara Street
Braintree, MA 02184

Phone: (781) 787-1175
Fax: (781) 787-1213
E-mail: mail@evans.com

Date

May 16, 2006

Inside
address

Mr. George W. Nagel
Director of Operations
Boston Transit Authority
57 West City Avenue
Boston, MA 02210

Salutation

Dear Mr. Nagel:

Body

Enclosed is our final report evaluating the safety measures for
the Boston Intercity Transit System.

We believe that the report covers the issues you raised in our last
meeting and that you will be pleased with the results. However, if
you have any further questions, we would be happy to meet with
you again at your convenience.

We would also like to express our appreciation to Mr. L. K.
Sullivan of your committee for his generous help during our
trips to Boston.

Compli-
mentary
closing

Sincerely,

Signature

Carolyn Brown

Typed name
Title

Carolyn Brown, Ph.D.
Director of Research

End
notations

CB/ls
Enclosure: Final Safety Report
cc: ITS Safety Committee Members

FIGURE C–14. Full-Block-Style Letter (with Letterhead)

C

Center

Heading
from center
to right

3814 Oak Lane
Dedham, MA 02180
December 8, 2006

Inside
address

Dr. Carolyn Brown
Director of Research
Evans and Associates
Transportation Engineers
520 Niagara Street
Braintree, MA 02184

Salutation

Dear Dr. Brown:

Body

Thank you very much for allowing me to tour your testing facilities. The information I gained from the tour will be of great help to me in preparing the report for my class at Marshall Institute. The tour has also given me some insight into the work I may eventually do as a laboratory technician.

I especially appreciated the time and effort Vikram Singh spent in showing me your facilities. His comments and advice were most helpful.

Complimen-
tary closing
aligned with
heading

Again, thank you.

Sincerely,

Signature

Leslie Warden

Typed name

Leslie Warden

Center

FIGURE C–15. Modified-Block-Style Letter (without Letterhead)

- National Business Systems
  501 West National Avenue
  Minneapolis, MN 55407

  Attention: Customer Relations Department

  I am returning three pagers that failed to operate. . . .

- National Business Systems
  501 West National Avenue
  Minneapolis, MN 55407

  Subject: Defective Parts for SL-100 Pagers

  I am returning three pagers that failed to operate. . . .

When a person's first name could be either feminine or masculine, one solution is to use both the first and last names in the salutation (*Dear Pat Smith:*). Avoid "To Whom It May Concern" because it is impersonal and dated.

For multiple recipients, the following salutations are appropriate:

- Dear Professor Allen and Dr. Rivera: [two recipients]

- Dear Ms. Becham, Ms. Moore, and Mr. Stein: [three recipients]

- Dear Colleagues: [*Members*, or other suitable collective term]

Body.   The body of the letter should begin two lines below the salutation (or any element that precedes the body, such as a subject or an attention line). Single-space within paragraphs, and double-space between paragraphs. To provide a fuller appearance to a very short letter, you can increase the side margins or increase the font size. You can also insert extra space above the inside address, the typed (signature) name, and the initials of the person keying the letter—but do not exceed twice the recommended space for each of these elements.

Complimentary Closing.   Type the complimentary closing two spaces below the body. Use a standard expression like *Sincerely, Sincerely yours,* or *Yours truly.* (If the recipient is a friend as well as a business associate, you can use a less formal closing, such as *Best wishes* or *Best regards* or, simply, *Best.*) Capitalize only the initial letter of the first word, and follow the expression with a comma. Place your full name four lines below, aligned with the closing. On the next line include your business title, if it is appropriate to do so. Sign the letter in the space between the complimentary closing and your name.

Second Page.   If a letter requires a second page, always carry at least two lines of the body text over to that page. Use plain (nonletterhead)

C

paper of quality equivalent to that of the letterhead stationery for the second page. It should have a header with the recipient's name, the page number, and the date. The header can go in the upper left-hand corner or across the page, as shown in Figure C–16.

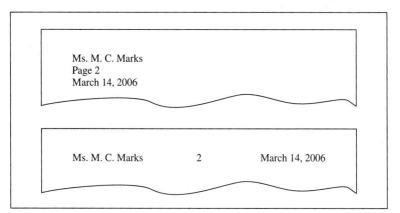

FIGURE C–16. Headers for the Second Page of a Letter

End Notations.   Business letters sometimes require additional information that is placed at the left margin, two spaces below the typed name and title of the writer in a long letter, four spaces below in a short letter.

Reference initials identify the person keying the letter if that person is not the writer. Show the letter writer's initials in capital letters, followed by a slash mark, and then the initials of the person keying the letter in lowercase letters, as shown in Figure C–14. When the writer is also the person keying the letter, no initials are needed.

Enclosure notations indicate that the writer is sending material along with the letter (an invoice, an article, and so on). Note that you must mention the enclosure in the body of the letter. Enclosure notations may take several forms:

- Enclosure: Final Safety Report
- Enclosures (2)
- Enc. or Encs.

Copy notation (cc:) tells the reader that a copy of the letter is being sent to the named recipients (see Figure C–14). Use a blind-copy notation (bcc:) when you do not want the addressee to know that a copy is being sent to someone else. A blind-copy notation appears only on the copy, not on the original (bcc: Dr. Brenda Shelton).

For additional details on letter format and design, you may wish to consult a guide such as *The Gregg Reference Manual* (Tenth Edition) by William A. Sabin.

C

Writer's Checklist: Writing Correspondence

- ☑ Establish your purpose, analyze your reader's needs, determine your **scope**, and consider the context.
- ☑ Prepare an outline, even if it is only a list of points to be covered in the order you want to cover them (see **outlining**).
- ☑ Write the first draft (see **writing a draft**).
- ☑ Allow for a cooling-off period prior to **revision** or seek a colleague's advice, especially for correspondence that addresses a problem.
- ☑ Revise the draft, checking for key problems in **clarity** and **coherence**.
- ☑ Use the appropriate or prescribed format.
- ☑ Check for accuracy: Make sure that all facts, figures, and dates are correct.
- ☑ Check for appropriate **punctuation** and use effective **proofreading** techniques.
- ☑ Remember that when you sign a letter, initial a memo, or send an e-mail, you are accepting responsibility for it.

cover letters

A cover letter (sometimes called a *transmittal*) accompanies a **report**, a **proposal**, an electronic file, or other material that you send to someone by mail, fax, or **e-mail**. It identifies an item that is being sent, the person to whom it is being sent, and the reason that it is being sent; it provides a permanent record for both the writer and the **reader**. For cover letters to **résumés**, see **application letters**.

Your opening should explain what is being sent and, if necessary, why. Then you might highlight or briefly summarize the information enclosed or attached. A cover letter for a proposal, for example, might point out sections in the proposal of particular interest to the reader and go on to present a key point or two explaining why the writer's firm is the best one to do the job. This paragraph could also mention the conditions under which the proposal was prepared, such as limitations of time or budget. The closing paragraph might contain acknowledgments, offer additional assistance, or express the hope that the material will fulfill its purpose.

C

The example in Figure C–17 is brief, to the point, and slightly in-formal because the writer understands that this reader needs no further explanation of the attached document.

From: Philip Snow <psnow@bos.com>
To: Merle Spinnet <mspinnet@ecosys.com>
Sent: Tuesday, May 23, 2006 10:47 AM
Subject: Final Report for Installation of Total Office System

Attachment: 📄 TOS Installation Report.doc

Dear Merle:

Attached is the final report on our installation of your Total Office System. If you have any questions, please call me at the number below (x1206) or reply to this message.

Sincerely,

Philip

Philip Snow, Manager
Sales and Service
Bradenton Office Systems
Customer Services = 800-351-2121

FIGURE C–17. Brief Cover Letter (Sent as E-mail)

The example in Figure C–18 is a bit more detailed and formal; it touches on the manner in which the information was gathered. In this message, the writer wishes to provide **context** to explain a delay as well as to acknowledge those who helped prepare the report. See also **correspondence**.

credible / creditable

Something is *credible* if it is believable. (The statistics in this report are *credible*.) Something is *creditable* if it is worthy of praise or credit. (The accountant did a *creditable* job.)

C

BRADENTON OFFICE SYSTEMS
2573 Penswood Drive
Lansing, MI 48824
www.bofficesystems.com
800-351-2121

May 23, 2006

Merle Spinnet, Purchasing Manager
Ecology Systems and Services
39 Beacon Street
Boston, MA 02106

Dear Mr. Spinnet:

Enclosed is the final report on our installation of your Total Office
System. As the report indicates, this system meets all the specifications you requested and was installed at 12 percent below our
estimated costs.

The report is the result of several meetings with Diana Biel,
Manager of Plant Operations, and her staff as well as an extensive
survey of all your employees. The survey was delayed by the
transfer of key staff in Building A. We believe, however, that you
will find the report useful not only in understanding your particular
installation but also . . .

We would like to thank you for the opportunity to work with you
and your excellent staff. If you have any questions or need more
information, please call me or e-mail me at the address below.

Sincerely,

Philip Snow

Philip Snow, Manager
Sales and Service
psnow@bos.com

Enclosure

FIGURE C–18. Long Cover Letter (for a Report)

criteria / criterion

Criterion is a singular **noun** meaning "an established standard for judging or testing." *Criteria* and *criterions* are both acceptable plural forms of *criterion*, but *criteria* is generally preferred.

critique

A *critique* is a written or an oral evaluation of something. Avoid using critique as a **verb** meaning "criticize."

- Please critique his job description.
  prepare a ^ *of* ^

D

dangling modifiers

Phrases that do not clearly and logically refer to the correct <u>noun</u> or <u>pronoun</u> are called *dangling modifiers*. Dangling modifiers usually appear at the beginning of a sentence as an introductory <u>phrase</u>.

DANGLING	*While eating lunch*, my computer crashed. [*Who* was eating lunch?]
CORRECT	While *I* was eating lunch, my computer crashed.

Dangling modifiers can appear at the end of the sentence as well.

DANGLING	The program gains efficiency by *eliminating the superfluous instructions*. [*Who* eliminates the superfluous instructions?]
CORRECT	The program gains efficiency *when you* eliminate the superfluous instructions.

To correct a dangling modifier, add the appropriate subject to either the dangling modifier or the main <u>clause</u>.

DANGLING	After finishing the research, the proposal was easy to write. [The appropriate subject is *I*, but it is not stated in either the dangling phrase or the main clause.]
CORRECT	After *I* finished the research, the proposal was easy to write. [The pronoun *I* is now the subject of an introductory clause.]
CORRECT	After finishing the research, *I* found the proposal easy to write. [The pronoun *I* is now the subject of the main clause.]

For a discussion of misplaced modifiers, see <u>modifiers</u>.

dashes

The dash (—) can perform all the punctuation duties of linking, separating, and enclosing. The dash, sometimes indicated by two consecutive <u>hyphens</u>, can also indicate the omission of letters. (Mr. A—admitted his error.)

Use the dash cautiously to indicate more <u>emphasis</u>, informality, or abruptness than the other punctuation marks would show. A dash can emphasize a sharp turn in thought.

- The project will end May 15—unless we receive additional funding.

A dash can indicate an emphatic pause.

- The project will begin—after we are under contract.

Sometimes, to emphasize contrast, a dash is used with *but*.

- We completed the survey quickly—*but* the results were not accurate.

A dash can be used before a final summarizing statement or before repetition that has the effect of an afterthought.

- It was hot near the ovens—steaming hot.

Such a statement may also complete the meaning of the <u>clause</u> preceding the dash.

- We try to speak as we write—or so we believe.

Dashes set off parenthetical elements more sharply and emphatically than <u>commas</u>. Unlike dashes, <u>parentheses</u> tend to reduce the importance of what they enclose. Compare the following sentences:

- Only one person—the president—can authorize such activity.
- Only one person, the president, can authorize such activity.
- Only one person (the president) can authorize such activity.

Dashes can be used to set off parenthetical elements that contain commas.

- Three of the applicants—John Evans, Rosalita Fontiana, and Kyong-Shik Choi—seem well qualified for the job.

The first word after a dash is capitalized only if it is a proper <u>noun</u>.

data / datum

In much informal writing, *data* is considered a collective singular <u>noun</u>. In formal and scholarly writing, however, *data* is generally used as a plural, with *datum* as the singular form. Base your decision on whether your readers should consider the data as a single collection or as a group of individual facts. Whatever you decide, be sure that your <u>pronouns</u> and <u>verbs</u> agree in number with the selected <u>usage</u>.

- The *data are* voluminous. *They indicate* a link between cigarette smoking and lung cancer. [formal]

- The *data is* now ready for evaluation. *It is* in the mail. [less formal]

See also <u>agreement</u> and <u>English, varieties of</u>.

dates

In the United States, full dates are generally written in the month-day-year format, with a comma preceding and following the year.

- November 30, 2015, is the payoff date.

Do not use <u>commas</u> in the day-month-year format, which is used in many parts of the world and by the U.S. military.

- Note that 30 November 2015 is the payoff date.

No commas are used if only the month and year or day are included.

- The target date of May 2007 is optimistic, so I would like to meet on March 4 to discuss our options.

When writing days of the month without the year, use the cardinal number (March 4) rather than the ordinal number (March 4th). Of course, in speech or <u>presentations</u>, use the ordinal number ("March fourth").

Avoid the strictly numerical form for dates (11/30/07) because the date is not always immediately clear, especially in <u>international correspondence</u>. Writing out the name of the month makes the entire date immediately clear to all readers.

Centuries often cause confusion with <u>numbers</u> because their spelled-out forms, which are not capitalized, do not correspond with their numeral designations. The twentieth century, for example, is the 1900s: 1900–1999.

When the century is written as a <u>noun</u>, do not use a <u>hyphen</u>.

- During the twentieth century, technology transformed business practices.

When the centuries are written as <u>adjectives</u>, however, use hyphens.

- Twenty-first-century technology relies on dependable power sources.

de facto / de jure

De facto means that something exists or is a fact and therefore is accepted for practical purposes. *De jure* means that something legally exists.

- The law states that no signs should be erected along Highway 127. Store owners have disregarded that law, and many signs exist along Highway 127. The presence of the signs along Highway 127 is *de facto* but not *de jure*—their presence is "a fact," but it is not "lawful."

Limit the use of Latin and legal terms because they can easily become an <u>affectation</u>.

defective / deficient

If something is *defective*, it is faulty. (The wiring was *defective*.) If something is *deficient*, it is lacking or is incomplete in an essential component. (The company was found to be *deficient* in meeting its legal obligations.)

defining terms

Defining key terms and concepts is often essential for <u>clarity</u>. Terms can be defined either formally or informally, depending on your <u>purpose</u>, your <u>readers</u>, and the <u>context</u>.

A *formal definition* is a form of classification. You define a term by placing it in a category and then identifying the features that distinguish it from other members of the same category.

TERM	CATEGORY	DISTINGUISHING FEATURES
An *auction* is	a public sale	in which property passes to the highest bidder through successively increased offers.

An *informal definition* explains a term by giving a more familiar word or phrase as a <u>synonym</u>.

- Plants have a *symbiotic*, or *mutually beneficial*, relationship with certain kinds of bacteria.

State definitions positively; focus on what the term *is* rather than on what it is not.

NEGATIVE	In a legal transaction, *real property* is not personal property.
POSITIVE	*Real property* is legal terminology for the right or interest a person has in land and the permanent structures on that land.

For a discussion of when negative definitions are appropriate, see <u>definition method of development</u>.

Avoid circular definitions, which merely restate the term to be defined and therefore fail to clarify it.

CIRCULAR	*Spontaneous combustion* is fire that begins spontaneously.
REVISED	*Spontaneous combustion* is the self-ignition of a flammable material through a chemical reaction.

In addition, avoid "is when" and "is where" definitions. Such definitions fail to include the category and are too indirect.

- A *contract* is ~~when two or more parties agree to something.~~ *a binding agreement between two or more parties.*

definite / definitive

Definite and *definitive* both apply to what is precisely defined, but *definitive* more often refers to what is complete and authoritative. (Once we receive a *definite* proposal, our attorney can provide a *definitive* legal opinion.)

definition method of development

DIRECTORY
Extended Definition   136
Definition by Analogy   136
Definition by Cause   137
Definition by Components   137
Definition by Exploration of Origin   138
Negative Definition   138

D

Definition is often essential to <u>clarity</u> and accuracy. Although <u>defining terms</u> may be sufficient, at other times definitions need to be expanded through (1) extended definition, (2) definition by analogy, (3) definition by cause, (4) definition by components, (5) definition by exploration of origin, and (6) negative definition. See also <u>methods of development</u>.

Extended Definition

When more than a phrase or a sentence or two is needed to explain an idea, use an extended definition, which explores a number of qualities of the item being defined. How an extended definition is developed depends on your <u>readers'</u> needs and on the complexity of the subject. Readers familiar with a topic might be able to handle a long, fairly complex definition, whereas readers less familiar with a topic might require simpler language and more basic information.

The easiest way to give an extended definition is with specific examples. Examples give readers easy-to-picture details that help them see and thus understand the term being defined.

- Form, which is the shape of landscape features, can best be represented by both small-scale features, such as *trees* and *shrubs*, and by large-scale elements, such as *mountains* and *mountain ranges*.

Definition by Analogy

Another useful way to define a difficult concept, especially when you are writing for nonspecialists, is to use an <u>analogy</u> to link the unfamiliar concept with a simpler or more familiar one. An analogy can help the reader understand an unfamiliar term by showing its similarities with a more familiar term. In the following description of management by objective, notice how the writer develops an analogy to make a point.

- Management by objective has been quite popular, but it is important to remember that carefully selecting objectives is the key to successfully applying this principle. Think, for example, of a golfer who wishes to improve by hitting the ball farther. The golfer sets a goal of hitting every drive as far as possible. Every decision the golfer makes is governed by that goal—hitting the ball as far as possible. The golfer would then be managing his or her game by objective. However, the golfer is shortsighted because golf is as much a game of accuracy as it is of hitting balls for distance. Some of the decisions the golfer makes to hit the ball farther, therefore, might well be counterproductive to achieving the larger goal of obtaining the lowest possible score. In the same way, when a company decides to use a management-by-objective strategy, it must be certain that the objective is appropriate for achieving the desired results.

Definition by Cause

Some terms are best defined by an explanation of their causes, as the following explanation of the term *stagflation* illustrates.

- Traditional economic theory says that a decline in business activity and employment causes the rate of inflation to decrease. However, in the seventies, because of massive increases in energy prices, the economy stagnated while higher energy prices worked their way into the cost of virtually everything, and the currency inflated. To describe that condition, economist Paul Samuelson coined the term *stagflation*.

Definition by Components

Sometimes a formal definition of a concept can be made simpler by breaking the concept into its component parts. In the following example, the formal definition of *fire* is given in the first paragraph, and the component parts are given in the second.

FORMAL DEFINITION	Fire is the visible heat energy released from the rapid oxidation of a fuel. A substance is "on fire" when the release of heat energy from the oxidation process reaches visible light levels.
COMPONENT PARTS	The classic fire triangle illustrates the elements necessary to create fire: *oxygen*, *heat*, and *burnable*

material (fuel). Air provides sufficient oxygen for combustion; the intensity of the heat needed to start a fire depends on the characteristics of the burnable material. A burnable substance is one that will sustain combustion after an initial application of heat to start the combustion.

Definition by Exploration of Origin

Under certain circumstances, the meaning of a term can be clarified and made easier to remember by an exploration of its origin. Medical terms, because of their sometimes unfamiliar Greek and Latin roots, benefit especially from an explanation of this type. Tracing the derivation of a word also can be useful when you want to explain why a word has favorable or unfavorable associations, particularly if your goal is to influence your reader's attitude toward an idea or an activity. See also **persuasion.**

- Efforts to influence legislation generally fall under the head of *lobbying,* a term that once referred to people who prowled the lobbies of houses of government, buttonholing lawmakers and trying to get them to take certain positions. Lobbying today is all of this, and much more, too. It is a respected—and necessary—activity. It tells the legislator which way the winds of public opinion are blowing, and it helps inform [legislators] of the implications of certain bills, debates, and resolutions [that they must face].

  —Bill Vogt, *How to Build a Better Outdoors*

Negative Definition

In some cases, it is useful to point out what something is not to clarify what it is. A negative definition is effective only when the reader is familiar with the item with which the defined item is contrasted. If you say "*x* is not *y*," your readers must understand the meaning of *y* for the explanation to make sense. In a crane operator's manual, for instance, a negative definition is used to show that, for safety reasons, a hydraulic crane cannot be operated in the same manner as a lattice boom crane.

- A hydraulic crane is *not* like a lattice boom crane [a friction machine] in one very important way. In most cases, the safe lifting capacity of a lattice boom crane is based on the *weight needed to tip the machine.* Therefore, operators of friction machines sometimes depend on signs that the machine might tip to warn them of impending danger. This practice is very dangerous with a hydraulic crane. . . .

  —*Operator's Manual* (Model W-180), Harnishfeger Corporation

description

The key to effective description is the accurate presentation of details, whether for simple or complex descriptions. In Figure D–1, notice that the simple description contained in the purchase order includes five specific details in addition to the part number.

PURCHASE ORDER

PART NO.	DESCRIPTION	QUANTITY
IW 8421	Infectious-waste bags, 12″ × 14″, heavy-gauge polyethylene, red double closures with self-sealing adhesive strips	5 boxes containing 200 bags per box

FIGURE D–1. Simple Description

Complex descriptions, of course, involve more details. In describing a mechanical device, for example, describe the whole device and its function before giving a detailed description of how each part works. The description should conclude with an explanation of how each part contributes to the functioning of the whole.

In descriptions intended for **readers** who are unfamiliar with the topic, details are crucial. For these readers, show or demonstrate (as opposed to "tell") primarily through the use of images and details. Notice the use of color, shapes, and images in the following description of a company's headquarters. The writer assumes that the reader knows such terms as *colonial design* and *haiku fountain*.

- Their corporate headquarters, which reminded me of a rural college campus, are located north of the city in a 90-acre lush green wooded area. The complex consists of five three-story buildings of colonial design. The buildings are spaced about 50 feet apart and are built in a U shape surrounding a reflection pool that frames a striking haiku fountain. . . .

You can also use analogy, as described in **figures of speech**, to explain unfamiliar concepts in terms of familiar ones, such as "U shape" in the previous example.

Visuals can be powerful aids in descriptive writing, especially when they show features too intricate to explain completely in words. The

D

Protect Windows and Doors

Protecting windows and doors is one of the most effective actions you can take to reduce your risk of wind damage. High winds and windborne debris can easily break unprotected windows and cause doors to fail. Once wind enters a building, the likelihood of severe structural damage increases, and the contents of the building will be exposed to the elements. The most reliable method of protecting windows and doors is installing permanent storm shutters. Alternatives include using temporary plywood covers, replacing existing glass with impact-resistant glass, and covering existing glass with a protective film.

ROLLDOWN SHUTTER PERMANENTLY ATTACHED TO BUILDING

SHUTTER IS HELD BY GUIDE TRACKS ALONG SIDES OF WINDOW

SHUTTER IS SECURED BY LATCH AT BASE OF GUIDE TRACK

Permanent storm shutters are usually made of aluminum or steel and are attached to a building in such a way that they can be closed quickly before a storm arrives. One type is the "rolldown" shutter (as shown above), which is contained in a housing mounted above the window and lowered when necessary. Manually operated and motor-operated models are available.

FIGURE D–2. Illustrated Description. *Source:* Federal Emergency Management Agency <www.fema.gov>.

example in Figure D–2 illustrates a storm-shutter installation that small businesses can use to protect windows from windborne debris damage. Note that the description concentrates on the types of shutters available and their function. The illustration, with callouts highlighting important features, largely eliminates the need for extensive written details to describe their relationship to one another and their function.

design (*see* layout and design)

despite / in spite of

Although there is no literal difference between *despite* and *in spite of*, *despite* suggests an effort to avoid blame.

- *Despite* our best efforts, the plan failed.
  [We are not to blame for the failure.]

- *In spite of* our best efforts, the plan failed.
  [We did everything possible, but failure overcame us.]

Despite and *in spite of* (both meaning "notwithstanding") should not be blended into *despite of.*

In spite of
- ~~Despite of~~ our best efforts, the plan failed.
  ^

dictionaries

Dictionaries give more than just information about words' meanings. As illustrated in Figure D–3, they often provide words' etymologies (origins and history), forms, pronunciations, <u>spellings</u>, uses as <u>idioms</u>, and functions as <u>parts of speech</u>. For certain words, a dictionary lists <u>synonyms</u> and may also provide illustrations, if appropriate, such as tables, maps, photographs, and drawings. Dictionaries available on CD-ROM and the Web often include a human-voice pronunciation of each word. Excellent sites are also available that translate words from one language to another; one such site is "iTools" at <www.itools.com>.

Desk Dictionaries

Desk dictionaries are often abridged versions of larger dictionaries. There is no single "best" dictionary, but you should choose the most recent edition with upward of 125,000 entries. The following are considered good desk dictionaries.

The American Heritage College Dictionary, 4th ed. with CD-ROM, 2002

Microsoft Encarta World English Dictionary, free online edition at <www.encarta.com>, 2004

Merriam-Webster's Collegiate Dictionary, 11th ed. with CD-ROM, 2003

Random House Webster's College Dictionary, 2nd rev. and updated ed., 2000

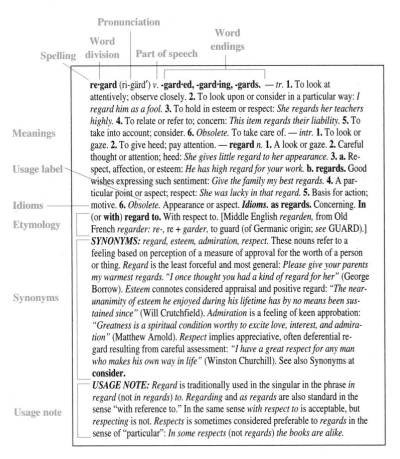

Pronunciation

Word
division

Word
endings

Spelling   Part of speech

Meanings

Usage label

Idioms

Etymology

Synonyms

Usage note

re·gard (ri-gärd′) *v.* **-gard·ed, -gard·ing, -gards.** — *tr.* **1.** To look at attentively; observe closely. **2.** To look upon or consider in a particular way: *I regard him as a fool.* **3.** To hold in esteem or respect: *She regards her teachers highly.* **4.** To relate or refer to; concern: *This item regards their liability.* **5.** To take into account; consider. **6.** *Obsolete.* To take care of. — *intr.* **1.** To look or gaze. **2.** To give heed; pay attention. — **regard** *n.* **1.** A look or gaze. **2.** Careful thought or attention; heed: *She gives little regard to her appearance.* **3. a.** Respect, affection, or esteem: *He has high regard for your work.* **b. regards.** Good wishes expressing such sentiment: *Give the family my best regards.* **4.** A particular point or aspect; respect: *She was lucky in that regard.* **5.** Basis for action; motive. **6.** *Obsolete.* Appearance or aspect. *Idioms.* **as regards.** Concerning. **In** (or **with**) **regard to.** With respect to. [Middle English *regarden,* from Old French *regarder: re-,* re + *garder,* to guard (of Germanic origin; *see* GUARD).]

SYNONYMS: regard, esteem, admiration, respect. These nouns refer to a feeling based on perception of a measure of approval for the worth of a person or thing. *Regard* is the least forceful and most general: *Please give your parents my warmest regards.* "*I once thought you had a kind of regard for her*" (George Borrow). *Esteem* connotes considered appraisal and positive regard: "*The near-unanimity of esteem he enjoyed during his lifetime has by no means been sustained since*" (Will Crutchfield). *Admiration* is a feeling of keen approbation: "*Greatness is a spiritual condition worthy to excite love, interest, and admiration*" (Matthew Arnold). *Respect* implies appreciative, often deferential regard resulting from careful assessment: "*I have a great respect for any man who makes his own way in life*" (Winston Churchill). See also Synonyms at **consider.**

USAGE NOTE: Regard is traditionally used in the singular in the phrase *in regard* (not *in regards*) *to.* *Regarding* and *as regards* are also standard in the sense "with reference to." In the same sense *with respect to* is acceptable, but *respecting* is not. *Respects* is sometimes considered preferable to *regards* in the sense of "particular": *In some respects* (not *regards*) *the books are alike.*

FIGURE D–3. Dictionary Entry

Unabridged Dictionaries

Unabridged dictionaries provide complete and authoritative linguistic information. The printed versions are impractical for desk use because of their size, and the CD and online subscription versions are expensive; libraries make available both versions of these important reference sources.

- *The Oxford English Dictionary*, 2nd ed., is the standard historical dictionary of the English language. Its 20 volumes contain over 500,000 words and give the chronological developments of over 240,000 words, providing numerous examples of uses and sources. It is also available on CD-ROM and online.

- *Webster's Third New International Dictionary, Unabridged,* CD-ROM edition, contains over 450,000 entries. Word meanings are listed in historical order, with the current meaning given last. This dictionary does not list biographical and geographical names, nor does it include usage information.

ESL Dictionaries

English-as-a-second-language (ESL) dictionaries are more helpful to the nonnative speaker than are regular English dictionaries or bilingual dictionaries. The pronunciation symbols in ESL dictionaries are based on the international phonetic alphabet rather than on English phonetic systems, and useful grammatical information is included in both the entries and special grammar sections. In addition, the definitions usually are easier to understand than those in regular English dictionaries; for example, a regular English dictionary defines *opaque* as "impervious to the passage of light," while an ESL dictionary defines the word as "not allowing light to pass through." The definitions in ESL dictionaries also are usually more thorough than those in bilingual dictionaries. For example, a bilingual dictionary might indicate that *obstacle* and *blockade* are synonymous—but not indicate that only *obstacle* can be used for abstract meanings. (Lack of money can be an *obstacle* [not a *blockade*] to a college education.)

The following dictionaries and references provide helpful information for nonnative speakers of English.

Longman Advanced American Dictionary with CD-ROM, 2002

Longman Dictionary of American English with CD-ROM, 2004

Longman American Idioms Dictionary with CD-ROM, Karen Stern, 2000

Oxford American Wordpower Dictionary for Learners of English, Ruth Urbom, 1998

Subject Dictionaries

For the meanings of words too specialized for a general dictionary, a subject dictionary is useful. Subject dictionaries define terms used in a particular field, such as business, geography, architecture, or consumer affairs. Definitions in subject dictionaries are generally more detailed and comprehensive than those found in general dictionaries. One well-known example is *Black's Law Dictionary* (West).

Although subject dictionaries are specialized and offer detailed definitions of field-specific terms, they are written in language that is straightforward enough to be understood by nonspecialists.

differ from / differ with

Differ from suggests that two things are not alike. (Our earlier proposal *differs from* the current one.) *Differ with* indicates disagreement between persons. (The architect *differed with* the contractor on the proposed site.)

different from / different than

In formal writing, the preposition *from* is used with *different*. (The Quantum PC is *different from* the Macintosh computer.) *Different than* is used when it is followed by a clause. (The job cost was *different than* we had estimated it.)

direct address

Direct address refers to a sentence or phrase in which the person being spoken or written to is explicitly named. It is often used in speech and in e-mail messages. Notice that the person's name in a direct address is set off by commas.

- *John*, call me as soon as you arrive at the airport.
- Call me, *John*, as soon as you arrive at the airport.

discreet / discrete

Discreet means "having or showing prudent or careful behavior." (Because the matter was personal, he asked Bob to be *discreet*.) *Discrete* means something is "separate, distinct, or individual." (Accountants must complete ten *discrete* columns on the ledger.)

disinterested / uninterested

Disinterested means "impartial, objective, unbiased."

- Like good judges, researchers should be passionately interested in the problems they tackle but completely *disinterested* when they seek to solve those problems.

Uninterested means simply "not interested."

- Despite Asha's enthusiasm, her manager remained *uninterested* in the project

division-and-classification method of development

An effective <u>method of development</u> for a complex subject is either to divide it into manageable parts and then discuss each part separately (division) or to classify (or group) individual parts into appropriate categories and discuss each category separately (classification). See also <u>instructions</u> and <u>process explanation</u>.

Division

You might use division to describe a physical object, such as the parts of a fax machine; to examine an organization, such as a company; or to explain the components of a system, such as the Internet. The emphasis in division as a method of development is on breaking down a complex whole into a number of like units—it is easier to consider smaller units and to examine the relationship of each to the other than to attempt to discuss the whole. The basis for division depends, of course, on your subject and your <u>purpose</u>.

If you were a financial planner describing the types of mutual funds available to your investors, you could divide the variety available into three broad categories: money market funds, bond funds, and stock funds. Such division would be accurate, but it would be only a first-level grouping of a complex whole. The three broad categories could, in turn, be subdivided into additional groups based on investment strategy, as follows:

Money market funds
- Taxable money market
- Tax-exempt money market

Bond funds
- Taxable bonds
- Tax-exempt bonds
- Balanced (mix of stocks and bonds)

Stock funds
- Balanced
- International growth

- Equity-income
- Domestic growth
- Growth and income
- Small-capitalization
- Aggressive growth
- Specialized

Specialized stock funds could be further subdivided as follows:

Specialized funds
- Communications
- Energy
- Environmental services
- Financial services
- Gold
- Health services
- Technology
- Utilities
- Worldwide capital goods

Classification

The process of classification is the grouping of a number of units (such as people, objects, or ideas) into related categories. Consider the following list:

triangular file	steel tape ruler	needle-nose pliers
vise	pipe wrench	keyhole saw
mallet	tin snips	C-clamps
rasp	hacksaw	plane
glass cutter	ball-peen hammer	steel square
spring clamp	claw hammer	utility knife
crescent wrench	folding extension ruler	slip-joint pliers
crosscut saw	tack hammer	utility scissors

To group the items in the list, you would first determine what they have in common. The most obvious characteristic they share is that they all belong in a carpenter's tool chest. With that observation as a starting point, you can begin to group the tools into related categories. Pipe wrenches belong with slip-joint pliers because both tools grip objects. The rasp and the plane belong with the triangular file because all three tools smooth rough surfaces. By applying this kind of thinking to all the items in the list, you can group (classify) the tools according to function (Figure D–4).

To classify a subject, you must first sort the individual items into the largest number of comparable groups. For explaining the functions of carpentry tools, the classifications (or groups) in Figure D–4 (smoothing, hammering, measuring, gripping, and cutting) are excellent. For recommending which tools a new homeowner should buy first, however, those classifications are not helpful—each group contains tools that a new homeowner might want to purchase right away. To give homeowners advice on purchasing tools, you probably would

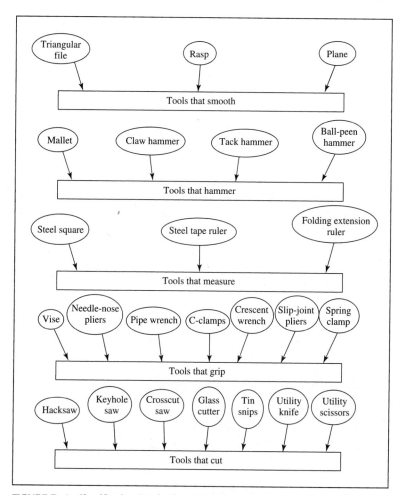

FIGURE D–4. Classification (Tools Placed into Categories)

classify the types of repairs they most likely will have to do (plumbing, painting, etc.). That classification could serve as a guide to tool purchase.

Once you have established the basis for the classification, apply it consistently, putting each item in only one category. For example, it might seem logical to classify needle-nose pliers as both a tool that cuts and a tool that grips because most needle-nose pliers have a small section for cutting wires. However, the primary function of needle-nose pliers is to grip. So listing them only under "tools that grip" would be consistent with the basis used for listing the other tools.

D   documentation

The word *documentation* refers to the formal credit given to sources used or quoted in research papers, trade journal articles, and <u>reports</u>— that is, in <u>documenting sources</u>. (See also <u>bibliographies</u>, <u>copyright</u>, and <u>plagiarism</u>.) The term *documentation* may also refer to information that is recorded, or documented, on paper or in electronic files. The <u>brochures</u> and <u>instructions</u> that companies provide to customers are examples of documentation. Even <u>flowcharts</u> and <u>drawings</u> are considered documentation.

documenting sources

DIRECTORY
APA Documentation   150
    APA In-Text Citations   150
    APA Documentation Models   151
    APA Sample Pages   155
CMS Documentation   157
    CMS Footnotes and Endnotes   157
    CMS Documentation Models   157
    CMS Sample Pages   162
MLA Documentation   164
    MLA In-Text Citations   164
    MLA Documentation Models   164
    MLA Sample Pages   168
Other Style Manuals   170

Documenting sources achieves three important purposes:

- It allows readers to locate and consult the sources used and to find further information on the subject.
- It enables writers to support their assertions and <u>arguments</u> in such documents as <u>proposals</u>, <u>reports</u>, and trade journal articles.
- It helps writers to give proper credit to others and thus avoid <u>plagiarism</u> by identifying the sources of facts, ideas, <u>quotations</u>, and paraphrases. See also <u>paraphrasing</u>.

This entry shows citation models and sample pages for three principal documentation systems: APA, *CMS*, and MLA. The following examples compare these three styles for citing a book by one author: *Management Challenges for the 21st Century* by Peter F. Drucker, which was published in 2001 by HarperBusiness in New York.

D

- The American Psychological Association (APA) system of citation is often used in the social sciences. It is referred to as an author/date method of documentation because parenthetical in-text citations and a references list (at the end of the paper) in APA style emphasize the author(s) and date of publication so that the currency of the research is clear.

APA IN-TEXT CITATION

(Author's Last Name, Year)

(Drucker, 2001)

APA REFERENCES ENTRY

Author's Last Name, Initials. (Year). *Title in italics*. Place of Publication: Publisher.

Drucker, P. F. (2001). *Management challenges for the 21st century*. New York: HarperBusiness.

- The system set forth in the *Chicago Manual of Style* (*CMS*) is often used in business, communications, economics, and history. The *CMS* system of footnotes (at the bottom of the page) or endnotes (at the end of the document) and a bibliography plainly identifies the sources of information.

CMS FOOTNOTES/ENDNOTES

Footnote number. Author's First Name Last Name, *Title in Italics* (Place of Publication: Publisher, Date of Publication), Pages.

1. Peter F. Drucker, *Management Challenges for the 21st Century* (New York: HarperBusiness, 2001), 22–23.

CMS BIBLIOGRAPHY ENTRY

Author's Last Name, First Name. *Title in Italics*. Place of Publication: Publisher, Date of Publication.

Drucker, Peter F. *Management Challenges for the 21st Century*. New York: HarperBusiness, 2001.

- The Modern Language Association (MLA) system is used in the humanities. MLA style uses parenthetical in-text citations and a list of works cited, and places greater importance on the pages on which cited information can be found than on the publication date.

MLA IN-TEXT CITATION

(Author's Last Name Page Number)

(Drucker 162)

MLA WORKS-CITED ENTRY

Author's Last Name, First Name. Title Underlined. Place of Publication:

   Publisher, Date of Publication.

Drucker, Peter F. Management Challenges for the 21st Century. New York:

   HarperBusiness, 2001.

These systems are described in full detail in the following style manuals:

   American Psychological Association. *Publication Manual of the American Psychological Association.* 5th ed. Washington, D.C.: American Psychological Association, 2001. See also <www.apastyle.org>.

   The Chicago Manual of Style. 15th ed. Chicago: University of Chicago Press, 2003. See also <www.press.uchicago.edu/Misc/ Chicago/cmosfaq/about.html>.

   Gibaldi, Joseph. *MLA Handbook for Writers of Research Papers.* 6th ed. New York: Modern Language Association of America, 2003. See also <www.mla.org>.

For additional bibliographic advice and documentation models for types of sources not included in this entry, consult these style manuals or those listed at the end of this entry under "Other Style Manuals." See also bibliographies and research.

APA Documentation

APA In-Text Citations.   APA parenthetical documentation within the text of a paper gives a brief citation—in parentheses—of the author, year of publication, and relevant page numbers if it helps locate a passage in a lengthy document.

- World War II was the occasion of radar's first application in warfare, and Great Britain led the way in radar research (Butrica, 2000).

- According to Butrica (2000), the use of radar as an offensive and a defensive warfare agent made World War II the "first electronic war" (p. 2).

When APA parenthetical citations are needed midsentence, place them after the closing quotation marks and continue with the rest of the sentence.

- The "first electronic war" (Butrica, 2000, p. 2) was fought as much in the research laboratory as on the battlefield.

If the APA parenthetical citation follows a block quotation, place it after the final punctuation mark.

- . . . a close collaboration with the physics and technology staff is essential. (Minsky, 2000)

When a work has two authors, cite both names joined by an ampersand: (Maddie & Khoshaba, 2005). For the first citation of a work with three, four, or five authors, include all names. For subsequent citations and for works with six or more authors, include only the last name of the first author followed by *et al.* (not italicized). When two or more works by different authors are cited in the same parentheses, list the citations alphabetically and use semicolons to separate them: (Maddie & Khoshaba, 2005; Prague, 2003).

APA Documentation Models

BOOKS

Single Author

Van Grembergen, W. (2001). *Information technology evaluation methods and management.* New York: Idea.

Multiple Authors

Testerman, J. O., Kuegler, T. J., Jr., & Dowling, P. J., Jr. (2000). *Web advertising and marketing* (3rd ed.). Rocklin, CA: Prima.

Corporate Author

Ernst and Young. (2001). *Ernst and Young's retirement planning guide* (3rd ed.). New York: Wiley.

Edition Other Than First

Van Horne, J. C. (2000). *Financial market rates and flows* (6th ed.). New York: Prentice Hall.

Multivolume Work

Standard and Poor. (2004). *Standard and Poor's register of corporations, directors and executives* (Vols. 1-3). New York: McGraw-Hill.

Work in an Edited Collection

Griswold, C. L. (2002). Happiness and Cypher's choice: Is ignorance bliss? In W. Irwin (Ed.), *The Matrix and philosophy* (pp. 126-137). Chicago: Open Court.

D

APA

Encyclopedia or Dictionary Entry

Gibbard, B. G. (2003). Particle detector. In *World Book encyclopedia* (Vol. 15, pp. 186–187). Chicago: World Book.

ARTICLES IN PERIODICALS (*See also* Electronic Sources)
Magazine Article

Limp, F. (2001, June). Enterprise deployment. *Business Geographics*, *26*, 18–27.

Journal Article

Loza, J. (2004). Business-community partnerships: The case for community organization capacity building. *Journal of Business Ethics*, *53*, 297–311.

Newspaper Article

Loftus, P. (2004, August 31). Small business: Enterprise. *Wall Street Journal*, p. B4.

Article with an Unknown Author

CFOs remain optimistic on economy. (2004, September 27). *The Business Journal*, p. 33.

ELECTRONIC SOURCES
Entire Web Site

The APA recommends that at minimum, a reference to a Web source should provide a document title or description, a date (of the publication or retrieval of the document), an address (URL) that links directly to the document or section, and an author, whenever possible. On the rare occasion that you need to cite multiple pages of a Web site (or the entire site), provide a URL that links to the site's homepage.

Association for Business Communication. (2004). Retrieved September 20, 2004, from http://www.businesscommunication.org [no period after URLs]

Document on a Web Site, with an Author

Locker, K. O. (2002). *The history of the ABC*. Retrieved September 20, 2004, from the Association for Business Communication Web site: http://www.businesscommunication.org/about/history/history.html

Document on a Web Site, with a Corporate Author

General Motors. (2003). *Company profile*. Retrieved September 20, 2004, from http://www.gm.com/company/corp_info/profiles/

Document on a Web Site, with an Unknown Author

Forgotten inventors. (2001). PBS Online. Retrieved September 20, 2004,
    from http://www.pbs.org/wgbh/amex/telephone/sfeature/
    index.html

Article or Other Work from a Database

Goldbort, R. C. (2001, March). Scientific writing as an art and as a
    science. *Journal of Environmental Health, 63*(7), pp. 22–25. Retrieved
    September 20, 2004, from Expanded Academic ASAP database.

Article in an Online Periodical

Tiernen, R. (2001, April 18). Waiting for wireless. *SmartMoney.com.*
    Retrieved September 20, 2004, from http://www.smartmoney
    .com/techmarket/index.cfm?story=20010418

E-mail Message

Personal communications (including e-mail and messages from
discussion groups and electronic bulletin boards) are not cited in
an APA reference list. They can be cited in the text as follows: "According to J. D. Kahl (personal communication, October 2, 2001),
Web pages need to reflect. . . ."

Publication on CD-ROM

Money 2004. (2004). [CD-ROM]. Redmond, WA: Microsoft.

MULTIMEDIA SOURCES (Electronic and Print)
Map or Chart

Asia. (2001). [Map]. Maps.com. Retrieved April 20, 2001, from
    http://www.maps.com/explore/atlas/political/asia.html

Wisconsin. (2000). [Map]. Chicago: Rand.

Film or Video

Lawrence, D. (Director), & Christopher, J. (Editor). (2001). *Emergency
    film group video* [Video]. Retrieved April 20, 2001, from http://www
    .efilmgroup.com/video1.rm

Massingham, G. (Director), & Christopher, J. (Editor). (2003). *Introduction
    to hazardous chemicals* [Motion picture]. Edgartown, MA: Emergency
    Film Group.

Radio or Television Program

Norris, R. (Host). (2001, April 3). Energy supplies. *All things considered*
    [Radio broadcast]. Boston: WGBH. Retrieved April 20, 2001, from
    http://www.npr.org/programs/atc

Novak, R. (Host). (2001, April 16). Do Americans really want a tax cut? *CNN: Crossfire* [Television broadcast]. Washington, DC: CNN.

OTHER SOURCES

Published Interview

Gates, B. (2000, April 17). The view from the very top [Interview]. *Newsweek, 135,* 36–39.

Personal Communications

Personal communications such as letters, interviews, e-mail, and messages from discussion groups and electronic bulletin boards are not cited in an APA reference list. They can be cited in the text as follows: "According to J. D. Kahl (personal communication, October 2, 2001), Web pages need to reflect. . . ."

Brochure or Pamphlet

Library of Congress. U.S. Copyright Office. (2004). *Copyright registration for online works* [Brochure]. Washington, DC: U.S. Government Printing Office.

Government Document

U.S. Department of Energy. (2004). *The August 14, 2003, blackout one year later* (Technical Publication No. 137-2004-12176). Washington, DC: U.S. Government Printing Office.

Report Published in a Collection

Jacobs, R. L. (2003). Structured on-the-job training: unleashing employee experience in the workplace (Report No. ED-474710). *ERIC, 346082,* 1–28.

Report Published Separately

Bertot, J. C., & McClure, C. R. (2000). *Public libraries and the Internet 2000: Summary findings and data tables.* Washington, DC: U.S. Government Printing Office.

Unpublished Data

Wisniewski, K., & Hussar, D. (2002). [Oregon small business statistics, by county]. Unpublished raw data.

APA Sample Pages

Shortened title and page number.

One-inch margins. Text double-spaced.

This report examines the nature and disposition of the 3,458 ethics cases handled companywide by CGF's ethics officers and managers during 2004. The purpose of such reports is to provide the Ethics and Business Conduct Committee with the information necessary for assessing the effectiveness of the first year of CGF's Ethics Program (Davis, Marks, & Tegge, 2001). According to Matthias Jonas (2004), recommendations are given for consideration "in planning for the second year of the Ethics Program" (p. 152).

The Office of Ethics and Business Conduct was created to administer the Ethics Program. The director of the Office of Ethics and Business Conduct, along with seven ethics officers throughout CGF, was given the responsibility for the following objectives, as described by Rossouw (1997):

Long quote indented five to seven spaces, double-spaced, without quotation marks.

Communicate the values, standards, and goals of CGF's Program to employees. Provide companywide channels for employee education and guidance in resolving ethics concerns. Implement companywide programs in ethics awareness and recognition. Employee accessibility to ethics information and guidance is the immediate goal of the Office of Business Conduct in its first year. (p. 1543)

The purpose of the Ethics Program, established by the Committee, is to "promote ethical business conduct through open communication and compliance with company ethics standards" (Jonas, 2001, p. 89). To accomplish this purpose, any ethics policy must ensure

In-text citation gives name, date, and page number.

confidentiality and anonymity for employees who raise genuine ethics concerns. The procedure developed at CGF guarantees

FIGURE D–5. APA Sample Page

D

APA

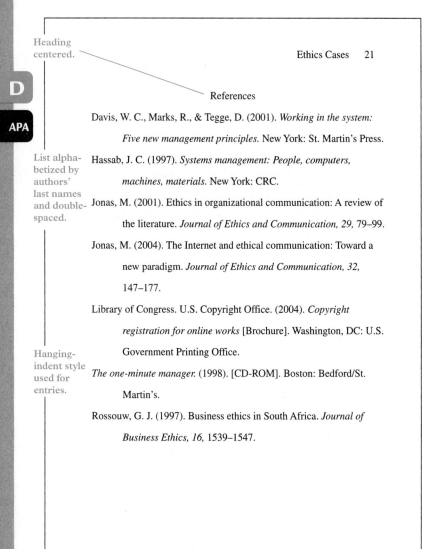

Heading centered.

Ethics Cases   21

References

Davis, W. C., Marks, R., & Tegge, D. (2001). *Working in the system:*
    Five new management principles. New York: St. Martin's Press.

List alpha-
betized by
authors'
last names
and double-
spaced.

Hassab, J. C. (1997). *Systems management: People, computers,*
    machines, materials. New York: CRC.

Jonas, M. (2001). Ethics in organizational communication: A review of
    the literature. *Journal of Ethics and Communication, 29,* 79–99.

Jonas, M. (2004). The Internet and ethical communication: Toward a
    new paradigm. *Journal of Ethics and Communication, 32,*
    147–177.

Library of Congress. U.S. Copyright Office. (2004). *Copyright*
    registration for online works [Brochure]. Washington, DC: U.S.
    Government Printing Office.

Hanging-
indent style
used for
entries.

The one-minute manager. (1998). [CD-ROM]. Boston: Bedford/St.
    Martin's.

Rossouw, G. J. (1997). Business ethics in South Africa. *Journal of*
    Business Ethics, 16, 1539–1547.

FIGURE D–6. APA Sample List of References

CMS Documentation

CMS *Footnotes and Endnotes.* *CMS* footnote and endnote citations give superscript numerals within the text that correspond to numbered footnotes (appearing at the bottom of the page where referenced) or endnotes (listed on a separate page at the end of the paper).

Place superscript numbers at the end of the quotation or sentence after the punctuation marks. Indent the first line of the footnote or endnote entry five spaces (½ inch). Use the number corresponding to the text, but do not make it superscript. Include the author's name (first name first), title, publication information (enclosed in parentheses), and page number(s), separated by commas.

- The year 1776 can be considered a watershed; political events in that year spawned the industrial revolution and, in turn, the burgeoning modern economy.[4]

-     4. Mark Skousen, *The Making of Modern Economics: The Lives and the Ideas of the Great Thinkers* (Armonk, N.Y.: M. E. Sharpe, 2001), 15.

In subsequent footnotes or endnotes from the same source, use the author's last name, a shortened version of the title, and the page number (4. Skousen, *Modern Economics*, 381).

CMS *Documentation Models*

BOOKS

Single Author*

    1. Wim Van Grembergen, *Information Technology Evaluation Methods and Management* (New York: Idea, 2001), 29.

Van Grembergen, Wim. *Information Technology Evaluation Methods and Management.* New York: Idea, 2001.

Two or Three Authors

    2. Joshua O. Testerman, Thomas J. Kuegler Jr., and Paul J. Dowling Jr., *Web Advertising and Marketing*, 3rd ed. (Rocklin, Calif.: Prima, 2000), 120.

Testerman, Joshua O., Thomas J. Kuegler Jr., and Paul J. Dowling Jr. *Web Advertising and Marketing.* 3rd ed. Rocklin, Calif.: Prima, 2000.

Four or More Authors

    3. Michael A. Lewis et al., eds. *Ecotoxicology and Risk Assessment for Wetlands* (Pensacola, Fla.: Society of Environmental Toxicology and Chemistry, 1999), 277.

*Examples are shown for both footnotes and reference pages.

Lewis, Michael A., Gary W. Dickson, Rebecca L. Powell, Marcia K. Nelson, and Mary G. Henry, eds. *Ecotoxicology and Risk Assessment for Wetlands*. Pensacola, Fla.: Society of Environmental Toxicology and Chemistry, 1999.

Corporate Author

4. Ernst and Young, *Ernst and Young's Retirement Planning Guide*, 3rd ed. (New York: Wiley, 2001).

Ernst and Young. *Ernst and Young's Retirement Planning Guide*. 3rd ed. New York: Wiley, 2001.

Edition Other Than First

5. James C. Van Horne, *Financial Market Rates and Flows*, 6th ed. (New York: Prentice Hall, 2000).

Van Horne, James C. *Financial Market Rates and Flows*. 6th ed. New York: Prentice Hall, 2000.

Multivolume Work

6. Standard and Poor, *Standard and Poor's Register of Corporations, Directors and Executives,* 3 vols. (New York: McGraw-Hill, 2004).

Standard and Poor. *Standard and Poor's Register of Corporations, Directors and Executives*. 3 vols. New York: McGraw-Hill, 2004.

Work in an Edited Collection

7. Charles L. Griswold, "Happiness and Cypher's Choice: Is Ignorance Bliss?" in *The Matrix and Philosophy*, ed. William Irwin, 136 (Chicago: Open Court, 2002).

Griswold, Charles L. "Happiness and Cypher's Choice: Is Ignorance Bliss?" In *The Matrix and Philosophy*, edited by William Irwin, 126–37. Chicago: Open Court, 2002.

Encyclopedia or Dictionary Entry

8. *World Book Encyclopedia*, 2003 ed., s.v. "particle detector."

Well-known reference books, such as encyclopedias and dictionaries, are not included in the bibliography.

ARTICLES IN PERIODICALS (*See also* Electronic Sources)
Magazine Article

9. Fred Limp, "Enterprise Deployment," *Business Geographics*, June 2001, 19.

Limp, Fred. "Enterprise Deployment." *Business Geographics*, June 2001, 18–27.

Journal Article

10. Jehan Loza, "Business-Community Partnerships: The Case for Community Organization Capacity Building," *Journal of Business Ethics* 53 (2004): 298.

Loza, Jehan. "Business-Community Partnerships: The Case for Community Organization Capacity Building." *Journal of Business Ethics* 53 (2004): 287–311.

Newspaper Article

11. Patrick Loftus, "Small Business: Enterprise," *Wall Street Journal*, August 31, 2004, sec. B.

Loftus, Patrick. "Small Business: Enterprise." *Wall Street Journal*, August 31, 2004, sec. B.

Article with an Unknown Author

12. "CFOs Remain Optimistic on Economy," *Business Journal*, September 27, 2004, 33.

"CFOs Remain Optimistic on Economy." *Business Journal*, September 27, 2004, 33.

ELECTRONIC SOURCES
Entire Web Site

13. Association for Business Communication. *Association for Business Communication*, 2004, http://www.businesscommunication.org.

Association for Business Communication. *Association for Business Communication*. 2004. http://www.businesscommunication.org.

Short Work from a Web Site, with an Author

14. Kitty O. Locker, "The History of the ABC," *Association for Business Communication*, 2002, http://www.businesscommunication.org/about/history/history.html.

Locker, Kitty O. "The History of the ABC." *Association for Business Communication*. 2002. http://www.businesscommunication.org/about/history/history.html.

Short Work from a Web Site, with a Corporate Author

15. General Motors, "Company Profile," *General Motors*, 2003, http://www.gm.com/company/corp_info/profiles/.

General Motors. "Company Profile." *General Motors*. 2003. http://www.gm.com/company/corp_info/profiles/.

D

CMS

Short Work from a Web Site, with an Unknown Author

16. "Forgotten Inventors," *PBS Online*, 2001, http://www.pbs.org/wgbh/amex/telephone/sfeature/index.html.

"Forgotten Inventors." *PBS Online*. 2001. http://www.pbs.org/wgbh/amex/telephone/sfeature/index.html.

Article or Other Work from a Database

17. Robert C. Goldbort, "Scientific Writing as an Art and as a Science," *Journal of Environmental Health* 63, no. 7 (2001): 22. http://infotrac.galegroup.com/.

Goldbort, Robert C. "Scientific Writing as an Art and as a Science." *Journal of Environmental Health* 63, no. 7 (2001): 22. http://infotrac.galegroup.com/.

Article in an Online Periodical

18. Robert Tiernen, "Waiting for Wireless," *SmartMoney.com*, http://www.smartmoney.com/techmarket/index.cfm?story=20010418.

Tiernen, Robert. "Waiting for Wireless." *SmartMoney.com*. http://www.smartmoney.com/techmarket/index.cfm?story=20010418.

E-mail Message

19. Jonathan D. Kahl, "Re: Web page," e-mail message to author, October 1, 2001.

Kahl, Jonathan D. "Re: Web page." October 1, 2001. Personal e-mail.

E-mail messages are usually cited in text; they should rarely be included in a bibliography.

MULTIMEDIA SOURCES (Print and Electronic)

Map or Chart

20. *Wisconsin*, map (Chicago: Rand, 2000).

Wisconsin. Map. Chicago: Rand, 2000.

Film or Video

21. *Introduction to Hazardous Chemicals*, dir. Gordon Massingham, ed. Jane Christopher, Emergency Film Group, Edgartown, MA, 2003, videocassette.

Introduction to Hazardous Chemicals. Directed by Gordon Massingham, edited by Jane Christopher. Emergency Film Group, Edgartown, MA, 2003. Videocassette.

Television Program

22. Mark Malloch Brown, interview by Charlie Rose, *The Charlie Rose Show*, PBS, December 6, 2001.

Brown, Mark Malloch. Interview. By Charlie Rose. *The Charlie Rose Show*. PBS, December 6, 2001.

OTHER SOURCES

Published Interview

23. Bill Gates, "The View from the Very Top," interview, *Newsweek*, April 17, 2000, 46.

Gates, Bill. "The View from the Very Top." Interview. *Newsweek*, April 17, 2000, 46.

Personal Interview

24. Mahmood Sariolgholam, interview by author, tape recording, November 29, 2000, Berkeley, Calif.

Sariolgholam, Mahmood. Interview by author. Tape recording. November 29, 2000. Berkeley, Calif.

Personal Letter

25. Monica Pascatore, letter to author, April 10, 2002.

Pascatore, Monica. Letter to author. April 10, 2002.

Personal letters should rarely be listed in a bibliography.

Brochure or Pamphlet

26. Library of Congress, U.S. Copyright Office, *Copyright Registration for Online Works* (Washington, D.C.: GPO, 2004), 10.

Library of Congress. U.S. Copyright Office. *Copyright Registration for Online Works*. Washington, D.C.: GPO, 2004.

Government Document

27. U.S. Department of Energy, *The August 14, 2003, Blackout One Year Later* (Washington, D.C.: GPO, 2004), 27.

U.S. Department of Energy. *The August 14, 2003, Blackout One Year Later*. Washington, D.C.: GPO, 2004.

Report Published in a Collection

29. Ronald L. Jacobs, "Structured On-the-Job Training: Unleashing Employee Experience in the Workplace (Report No. ED-474710)," *ERIC* 346082 (2003): 13.

Jacobs, Ronald L. "Structured On-the-Job Training: Unleashing Employee Experience in the Workplace (Report No. ED-474710)," *ERIC* 346082 (2003): 1–28.

Report Published Separately

28. John Carlo Bertot and Charles R. McClure, *Public Libraries and the Internet 2000: Summary Findings and Data Tables* (Washington, D.C.: GPO, 2000).

Bertot, John Carlo, and Charles R. McClure. *Public Libraries and the Internet 2000: Summary Findings and Data Tables*. Washington, D.C.: GPO, 2000.

CMS *Sample Pages*

Litzinger 14

Author's last name (optional) and page number.

This report examines the nature and disposition of the 3,458 ethics cases handled companywide by CGF's ethics officers and managers during 2004. The purpose of such reports is to provide the Ethics and Business Conduct Committee with the information necessary for assessing the effectiveness of the first year of CGF's Ethics Program.[1] According to Matthias Jonas, recommendations are given for consideration "in planning for the second year of the Ethics Program."[2]

One-inch margins. Text double-spaced.

The Office of Ethics and Business Conduct was created to administer the Ethics Program. The director of the Office of Ethics and Business Conduct was given the responsibility for the following objectives, as described by Rossouw:

Long quote indented, set in smaller font size, without quotation marks.

> Communicate the values, standards, and goals of CGF's Program to employees. Provide companywide channels for employee education and guidance in resolving ethics concerns. Implement companywide programs in ethics awareness and recognition. Employee accessibility to ethics information and guidance is the immediate goal of the Office of Business Conduct in its first year.[3]

The purpose of the Ethics Program, according to Jonas, is to "promote ethical business conduct through open communication and compliance with company ethics standards."[4] To accomplish this

Raised superscripts in text correspond to footnotes or endnotes. First line of each entry indents five spaces.

1. W. C. Davis, Roland Marks, and Diane Tegge, *Working in the System: Five New Management Principles* (New York: St. Martin's, 2001), 142.

2. Matthias Jonas, "The Internet and Ethical Communication: Toward a New Paradigm," *Journal of Ethics and Communications* 32 (Fall 2004): 152.

3. George J. Rossouw, "Business Ethics in South Africa." *Journal of Business Ethics* 16 (Spring 1997): 1543.

4. Matthias Jonas, "Ethics in Organizational Communication: A Review of the Literature," *Journal of Ethics and Communication* 29 (Summer 2001): 89.

FIGURE D–7. *CMS* Sample Page (with Footnotes)

Litzinger 21

Heading
centered.

Bibliography

Association for Business Communication. *Association for Business
Communication.* August 2004. http://www
.businesscommunication.org.

List alpha-
betized by
authors' last
names and
double-
spaced.

Davis, W. C., Roland Marks, and Diane Tegge. *Working in the
System: Five New Management Principles.* New York:
St. Martin's, 2001.

Hassab, Joseph C. *Systems Management: People, Computers,
Machines, Materials.* New York: CRC, 1997.

Jonas, Matthias. "Ethics in Organizational Communication:
A Review of the Literature." *Journal of Ethics and
Communication* 29 (Summer 2001): 79–99.

Hanging-
indent style
used for
entries.

———. "The Internet and Ethical Communication: Toward a New
Paradigm." *Journal of Ethics and Communication* 32 (Fall
2004): 147–77.

Library of Congress. U.S. Copyright Office. *Copyright Registration
for Online Works.* Washington, D.C.: GPO, 2004.

The One-Minute Manager. CD-ROM. Boston: Bedford/St. Martin's,
1998.

Rossouw, George J. "Business Ethics in South Africa." *Journal of
Business Ethics* 16 (Spring 1997): 1539–47.

Sariolgholam, Mahmood. Interview by author. Tape recording.
November 29, 2000. Berkeley, Calif.

FIGURE D–8. *CMS* Sample Bibliography

D

MLA

MLA Documentation

MLA In-Text Citations.   MLA parenthetical citation within the text of a paper gives a brief citation—in parentheses—of the author and relevant page numbers, separated only by a space.

- The results of these studies have led even the most conservative managers to adopt technologies that will "catapult the industry forward" (Peterson 183–84).

- As Peterson writes, preparing a videotape of measurement methods is cost-effective and can expedite training (151). [If the author is cited in the text, include only the page numbers in parentheses.]

If the parenthetical citation refers to a long, indented quotation, place it outside the punctuation of the last sentence.

- . . . a close collaboration with the physics and technology staff is essential. (Minsky 42)

If no author is named or if you are using more than one work by the same author, give a shortened version of the title in the parenthetical citation, unless you name the title in the text (a "signal phrase"). A citation for Thomas J. Peterson's book *The Pursuit of Wow: Every Person's Guide to Topsy-Turvy Times* would appear as (Peterson, Pursuit 93).

MLA Documentation Models

BOOKS
Single Author
Van Grembergen, Wim. Information Technology Evaluation Methods and Management. New York: Idea, 2001.

Multiple Authors
Testerman, Joshua O., Thomas J. Kuegler, Jr., and Paul J. Dowling, Jr. Web Advertising and Marketing. 3rd ed. Rocklin, CA: Prima, 2000.

Corporate Author
Ernst and Young. Ernst and Young's Retirement Planning Guide. 3rd ed. New York: Wiley, 2001.

Edition Other Than First
Van Horne, James C. Financial Market Rates and Flows. 6th ed. New York: Prentice Hall, 2000.

Multivolume Work
Standard and Poor. Standard and Poor's Register of Corporations, Directors and Executives. 3 vols. New York: McGraw, 2004.

Work in an Edited Collection

Griswold, Charles L. "Happiness and Cypher's Choice: Is Ignorance
  Bliss?" The Matrix and Philosophy. Ed. William Irwin. Chicago:
  Open Court, 2002. 126–37.

Encyclopedia or Dictionary Entry

Gibbard, Bruce G. "Particle Detector." World Book Encyclopedia.
  2003 ed.

ARTICLES IN PERIODICALS (*See also* Electronic Sources)

Magazine Article

Limp, Fred. "Enterprise Development." Business Geographics June
  2001: 19.

Journal Article

Loza, Jehan. "Business-Community Partnerships: The Case for
  Community Organization Capacity Building." Journal of
  Business Ethics 53 (2004): 287–311.

Newspaper Article

Loftus, Patrick. "Small Business: Enterprise." Wall Street Journal 31 Aug.
  2004: B4.

Article with an Unknown Author

"CFOs Remain Optimistic on Economy." Business Journal 27 Sept.
  2004: 33.

ELECTRONIC SOURCES

Entire Web Site

The MLA recommends that at minimum, a reference to a Web
source should provide a document title or description, the date of
the publication (posted or updated), the date that the publication
was retrieved, an address (URL) that links directly to the document or section, and an author, whenever possible.

Association for Business Communication. Aug. 2004. Assn. for
  Business Communication. 20 Sept. 2005 <http://www
  .businesscommunication.org/>.

Short Work from a Web Site, with an Author

Locker, Kitty O. "The History of the Association for Business
  Communication." Association for Business Communication.
  Oct. 2002. Assn. for Business Communication. 20 Sept. 2004
  <http://www.businesscommunication.org/about/history/
  history.html>.

Short Work from a Web Site, with a Corporate Author
General Motors. "Company Profile." General Motors. 2003. 20 Sept.
    2004 <http://www.gm.com/company/corp_info/profiles/>.

Short Work from a Web Site, with an Unknown Author
"Forgotten Inventors." Forgotten Inventors. PBS Online. 2001. 19 Apr.
    2001 <http://www.pbs.org/wgbh/amex/telephone/sfeature/
    index.htm>.

Article from a Database
Goldbort, Robert C. "Scientific Writing as an Art and as a Science."
    Journal of Environmental Health 63.7 (2001): 22. Expanded
    Academic ASAP. InfoTrac. Salem State Coll. Lib., Salem, MA.
    19 Apr. 2001 <http://infotrac.galegroup.com>.

Article in an Online Periodical
Tiernan, Robert. "Waiting for Wireless." SmartMoney.com 18 Apr. 2001.
    19 Apr. 2001 <http://www.smartmoney.com/techmarket/
    index.cfm?story=20010418>.

Publication on CD-ROM
Money 94. CD-ROM. Redmond, WA: Microsoft, 2004.

E-mail Message
Kahl, Jonathan D. "Re: Web page." E-mail to the author. 2 Oct. 2001.

MULTIMEDIA SOURCES (Print and Electronic)
Map or Chart
Wisconsin. Map. Chicago: Rand, 2000.

Film or Video
Massingham, Gordon, dir., and Jane Christopher, ed. Introduction to
    Hazardous Chemicals. Videocassette. Edgartown, MA: Emergency
    Film Group, 2003.

Television Interview
Brown, Mark Malloch. Interview. The Charlie Rose Show. By Charlie Rose.
    Public Broadcasting System. 6 Dec. 2001.

OTHER SOURCES
Published Interview
Gates, Bill. "The View from the Very Top." Interview. Newsweek 17 Apr.
    2000: 36–39.

Personal Interview

Sariolgholam, Mahmood. Personal interview. 29 Nov. 2000.

Personal Letter

Pascatore, Monica. Letter to the author. 10 Apr. 2002.

Brochure or Pamphlet

Library of Congress. US Copyright Office. Copyright Registration for Online Works. Washington: GPO, 2004.

Government Document

United States. Dept. of Energy. The August 14, 2003, Blackout One Year Later. Technical Pub. 137-2004-12176. Washington: GPO, 2004.

Report Published in a Collection

Jacobs, Ronald L. "Structured On-the-Job Training: Unleashing Employee Experience in the Workplace." *ERIC* 346082 (2003): 1–28. ED-474710.

Report Published Separately

Bertot, John Carlo, and Charles R. McClure. Public Libraries and the Internet 2000: Summary Findings and Data Tables. Washington: GPO, 2000.

Lecture or Speech

McKinney, Scott. Lecture. Demarest Hall, Hobart and William Smith Colls., Geneva, NY. 3 May 2002.

Krug, Steve. "Don't Make Me Think: The Art of Designing User-Friendly Websites." New England School of Art & Design at Suffolk U. Boston Public Lib. 3 Apr. 2001.

MLA Sample Pages

Litzinger 14

Author's last
name and
page num-
ber.

This report examines the nature and disposition of the 3,458 ethics

cases handled companywide by CGF's ethics officers and managers

during 2004. The purpose of such reports is to provide the Ethics

and Business Conduct Committee with the information necessary for

assessing the effectiveness of the first year of CGF's Ethics Program

(Davis, Marks, and Tegge 142). According to Matthias Jonas, recom-

mendations are given for consideration "in planning for the second

year of the Ethics Program" ("Internet" 152).

One-inch
margins.
Text
double-
spaced.

The Office of Ethics and Business Conduct was created to ad-

minister the Ethics Program. The director of the Office of Ethics and

Business Conduct, along with seven ethics officers throughout CGF,

was given the responsibility for the following objectives, as de-

scribed by Rossouw:

> Communicate the values, standards, and goals of CGF's
>
> Program to employees. Provide companywide channels
>
> for employee education and guidance in resolving ethics
>
> concerns. Implement companywide programs in ethics
>
> awareness and recognition. Employee accessibility to
>
> ethics information and guidance is the immediate goal of
>
> the Office of Business Conduct in its first year. (1543)

Long quote
indented one
inch (or 10
spaces),
double-
spaced, with-
out quotation
marks.

The purpose of the Ethics Program, according to Jonas, is to "pro-

mote ethical business conduct through open communication and

compliance with company ethics standards" ("Ethics" 89). To ac-

complish this purpose, any ethics policy must ensure confidentiality

In-text cita-
tions give
author
name and
page num-
ber. Title
used when
multiple
works by
same au-
thor cited.

FIGURE D–9. MLA Sample Page

Litzinger 21

Works Cited

Association for Business Communication. Aug. 2004. Assn. for

Business Communication. 16 Mar. 2005 <http://www

.businesscommunication.org/>.

Davis, W. C., Roland Marks, and Diane Tegge. Working in the

System: Five New Management Principles. New York:

St. Martin's, 2001.

Hassab, Joseph C. Systems Management: People, Computers,

Machines, Materials. New York: CRC, 1997.

Jonas, Matthias. "Ethics in Organizational Communication:

A Review of the Literature." Journal of Ethics and

Communication 29 (2001): 79–99.

---. "The Internet and Ethical Communication: Toward a New

Paradigm." Journal of Ethics and Communication 32 (2004):

147–77.

Library of Congress. US Copyright Office. Copyright Registration for

Online Works. Washington: GPO, 2004.

The One-Minute Manager. CD-ROM. Boston: Bedford, 1998.

Rossouw, George J. "Business Ethics in South Africa." Journal of

Business Ethics 16 (1997): 1539–47.

Sariolgholam, Mahmood. Personal interview. 29 Nov. 2000.

Heading centered.

List alphabetized by authors' last names or title and doublespaced.

Hanging-indent style used for entries.

FIGURE D–10. MLA Sample List of Works Cited

Other Style Manuals

Many professional societies, publishing companies, and other organizations publish manuals that prescribe bibliographic reference formats for their publications or for publications in their fields. Many of these style manuals are well known and widely used.

Business

American Management Association. *The AMA Style Guide for Business Writing.* New York: AMACOM, 1996. See also <www.amanet.org>.

Government Documents

United States Government Printing Office. *Style Manual.* Washington, D.C.:U.S. Government Printing Office, 2000. See also <www.gpo.gov>.

Journalism

Goldstein, Norm, ed. *Associated Press Stylebook and Briefing on Media Law.* 36th ed. New York: Associated Press, 2002. See also <www.ap.org>.

Law

Harvard Law Review et al. *The Bluebook: A Uniform System of Citation.* 17th ed. Cambridge: Harvard Law Review Association, 2000. See also <www.legalbluebook.com>.

Medicine

American Medical Association. *American Medical Association Manual of Style.* 9th ed. Baltimore:Williams, 1998. See also <www.ama-assn.org>.

Political Science

American Political Science Association. *Style Manual for Political Science.* Rev. ed. Washington, D.C.: APSA, 2001. See also <www.apsanet.org>.

Science

Council of Science Editors. *Scientific Style and Format: The CBE Manual for Authors, Editors, and Publishers.* 6th ed. New York: Cambridge University Press, 1994. See also <www.councilscienceeditors.org>.

Social Work

National Association of Social Workers. *An Author's Guide to Social Work Journals.* 4th ed. Washington, D.C.: National Association of Social Workers Press, 1997. See also <www.naswpress.org>.

D

double negatives

A double negative is the use of an additional negative word to reinforce an expression that is already negative. In writing and speech, avoid such constructions.

> **UNCLEAR**   We don't have none.
>   [This sentence literally means that we have some.]
> **CLEAR**   We have none.

Barely, *hardly*, and *scarcely* cause problems because writers sometimes do not recognize that those words are already negative.

- The corporate policy ~~doesn't~~ ˢhardly cover the problem.

Not unfriendly, *not without*, and similar constructions are not double negatives because in such constructions two negatives are meant to suggest the gray area between negative and positive meanings. Be careful how you use such constructions; they can be confusing to the reader and should be used only if they serve a purpose.

- He is *not unfriendly.*
  [He is neither hostile nor friendly.]

- It is *not without* regret that I offer my resignation.
  [I have mixed feelings rather than only regret.]

The correlative **conjunctions** *neither* and *nor* may appear together in a clause without creating a double negative, so long as the writer does not attempt to use the word *not* in the same clause.

- It was ~~not~~ *neither*, as a matter of fact, ~~neither~~ his duty nor his desire to fire the employee.

- It was not, as a matter of fact, ~~neither~~ *either* his duty ~~nor~~ *or* his desire to fire the employee.

D

- She ~~did not~~ neither ~~care~~ about nor ~~notice~~ the error.
  cared ^   *noticed* ^

Negative forms are full of traps that often entice writers into <u>logic errors</u>, as illustrated in the following example:

ILLOGICAL   The book reveals *nothing* that has *not* already been published in some form, but some of it is, I believe, very little known.

In this sentence, "some of it" logically can refer only to "*nothing* that has *not* already been published." The sentence can be corrected by stating the idea in more <u>positive writing</u>.

LOGICAL   Everything in the book has been published in some form, but some of it is, I believe, very little known.

drawings

A drawing can show an object's appearance or illustrate <u>instructions</u>. It can emphasize the significant parts or functions of a device or product, omit what is not significant, and focus on details or relationships that a <u>photograph</u> cannot reveal. Think about your need for drawings during the <u>preparation</u> and <u>research</u> stages of writing. Include them in your <u>outline</u>, indicating approximately where each should appear throughout the outline with "drawing of . . ." enclosed in brackets. For integrating drawings into your text, see <u>visuals</u>.

The types of drawings discussed in this entry are conventional line drawings, exploded-view drawings, cutaway drawings, and clip-art images. Each type of drawing has unique advantages—the type of drawing you use should be determined by its <u>purpose</u> and what your <u>readers</u> might need or expect.

A conventional line drawing, like in Figure D–11, is appropriate if your readers need a representation of an object's general appearance or an overview of a series of steps.

An exploded-view drawing, like that in Figure D–12, can be useful when you need to show the proper sequence in which parts fit together or to show the details of individual parts. Figure D–12 shows a page from a manual for purchasers of a Xerox machine, instructing them to safely unpack the machine and its key parts.

A cutaway drawing, like the one in Figure D–13, can be useful when you need to show the internal parts of a device or structure and illustrate their relationship to the whole.

Fit and Rise

Flap   Button Through

Cuff   Hem

FIGURE D–11. Conventional Line Drawings (from a Retail Catalog)

D

Installation

As you unpack the WorkCentre, familiarize yourself with its contents. After the WorkCentre is installed, and the Ready Indicator is lit, the WorkCentre is ready to make copies.

IMPORTANT: Save the carton and packing materials. They should be used to repack the WorkCentre if it has to be shipped for servicing or in case you move.

Power cord

IEEE-1284 Parallel Cable *

Packing material

User documentation/ Installation CD

Drum cartridge (installed in the machine)

Starter toner cartridge

* Note: To ensure reliability of the WorkCentre use the IEEE-1284 compliant parallel cable that is supplied with the machine. Only cables labeled "IEEE-1284" can be used with your WorkCentre.

FIGURE D–12. Exploded-View Drawing

If you need only general-interest images to illustrate <u>newsletters</u> and <u>brochures</u> or to create <u>presentation</u> slides, use noncopyrighted clip-art drawings from your word-processing program or from thousands of noncopyrighted Web and library sources. Figure D–14 shows examples of clip-art images.

D

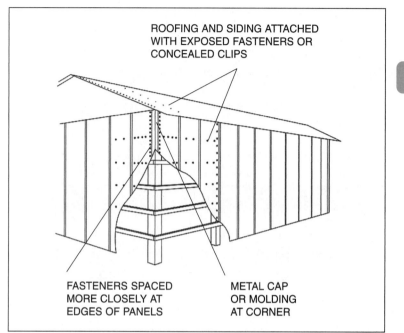

ROOFING AND SIDING ATTACHED
WITH EXPOSED FASTENERS OR
CONCEALED CLIPS

FASTENERS SPACED
MORE CLOSELY AT
EDGES OF PANELS

METAL CAP
OR MOLDING
AT CORNER

FIGURE D–13. Cutaway Drawing

FIGURE D–14. Clip-Art Images

⚡ ETHICS NOTE Be careful not to use drawings from copyrighted sources without permission and proper documentation, especially from the Web—the same <u>copyright</u> laws that apply to printed material also apply to Web-based graphics. See also <u>documenting sources</u> and <u>plagiarism</u>. ✦

D

Writer's Checklist: Creating and Using Drawings

☑ Seek the help of professional graphics specialists for drawings that require a high degree of accuracy and precision.

☑ Show equipment and other objects from the point of view of the person who will use them.

☑ When illustrating a subsystem, show its relationship to the larger system of which it is a part.

☑ Draw the different parts of an object in proportion to one another or indicate that certain parts are enlarged.

☑ When a sequence of drawings is used to illustrate a process, arrange them from left to right or from top to bottom on the page.

☑ Label parts in the drawing so that the text references to them are clear and consistent.

☑ Depending on the complexity of what is shown, label the parts themselves, as in Figure D–12, or use a letter/number key.

☑ Refer to the figure in the text and do not place the figure prior to that text reference.

due to / because of

Due to (meaning "caused by") is acceptable following a linking <u>verb</u>.

- His short temper was *due to* stress from the project.

Due to is not acceptable, however, when it is used with a nonlinking verb to replace *because of*.

- He left work ~~due to~~ illness.
  because of

E

each

When *each* is used as a subject, it takes a singular <u>verb</u> or <u>pronoun</u>.

- *Each* of the reports *is* to be submitted ten weeks after *it* is assigned.

When *each* refers to a plural subject, it takes a plural verb or pronoun. See also <u>agreement</u>.

- The reports *each have* company logos on *their* covers.

The phrase *each and every* is redundant. See also <u>conciseness</u>.

economic / economical

Economic refers to the production, development, and management of material wealth. (The euro had an *economic* impact on several countries.) *Economical* simply means "not wasteful or extravagant." (Employees should be as *economical* as possible in their equipment purchases.)

editing (*see* revision *and* proofreading)

e.g. / i.e.

The abbreviation *e.g.* stands for the Latin *exempli gratia*, meaning "for example"; *i.e.* stands for the Latin *id est*, meaning "that is." Because the English expressions (*for example* and *that is*) are clear to all <u>readers</u>, avoid the Latin *e.g.* and *i.e.* <u>abbreviations</u> except to save space in notes and <u>visuals</u>.

If you must use *i.e.* or *e.g.*, punctuate them as follows. If *i.e.* or *e.g.* connects two independent clauses, a <u>semicolon</u> should precede it and a <u>comma</u> should follow it.

- The conference reflected international viewpoints; *i.e.*, Germans, Italians, Japanese, Pakistanis, and Americans gave presentations.

If *i.e.* or *e.g.* connects a <u>noun</u> and an <u>appositive</u>, a comma should precede it and follow it.

- The conference included speakers from five countries, *i.e.*, Germany, Italy, Japan, Pakistan, and the United States.

Do not italicize either abbreviation.

ellipses

An ellipsis is the omission of words from quoted material; it is indicated by three spaced <u>periods</u> called *ellipsis points* (. . .). When you use ellipsis points, omit marks of internal punctuation at the point of omission, unless they are necessary for <u>clarity</u> or the omitted material comes at the end of a quoted sentence.

ORIGINAL TEXT	"Promotional material is sometimes charged for, particularly in high volume distribution to schools, although prices for these publications are much lower than the development costs when all factors are considered."
WITH OMISSION AND ELLIPSIS POINTS	"Promotional material is sometimes charged for . . . although prices for these publications are much lower than the development costs. . . ."

Notice in the preceding example that the final period is retained and what remains of the quotation is grammatically complete. When the omitted part of the quotation is preceded by a period, retain the period and add the three ellipsis points after it, as in the following example.

ORIGINAL TEXT	"Of the 172 major ethics cases reported, 57 percent were found to involve unsubstantiated concerns. Misinformation was the cause of unfounded concerns of misconduct in 72 cases. Forty-four cases, or 26 percent of the total cases reported, involved incidents partly substantiated by ethics officers as serious misconduct."

WITH OMISSION AND ELLIPSIS POINTS	"Of the 172 major ethics cases reported, 57 percent were found to involve unsubstantiated concerns. . . . Forty-four cases, or 26 percent of the total cases reported, involved incidents partly substantiated by ethics officers as serious misconduct."

Do not use ellipsis points when the beginning of a quoted sentence is omitted. Notice in the following example that the comma is dropped to prevent a grammatical error. See also quotations.

- The ethics report states that "26 percent of the total cases reported involved incidents partly substantiated by ethics officers as serious misconduct."

e-mail

DIRECTORY
Review and Confidentiality   179
Writer's Checklist: Observing Workplace Netiquette   180
Design Considerations   181
Salutations, Closings, and Signature Blocks   182
Writer's Checklist: Managing Your E-mail   184

E-mail (or email) functions in the workplace as a medium to send information, elicit discussions, collect opinions, and transmit documents and files of all types electronically. Although e-mail may take the form of informal notes, you should generally follow the same guidelines for writing style and strategy described in the entries correspondence and memos. See also selecting the medium.

Review and Confidentiality

E-mail is such a quick and easy way to communicate that you need to work to avoid the temptation of sending a first draft without revision. As with all correspondence, your message should include all crucial details and be free of grammatical or factual errors, ambiguities, or unintended implications. See proofreading.

   Be especially careful when sending messages to superiors in your organization or to people outside the organization. Time you spend reviewing your e-mail before you send it can save a great deal of time and embarrassment correcting misunderstandings caused by a careless message. One helpful strategy is to write the draft and revise your e-mail before filling in the "To" line with the address of your recipient. Be careful as well to observe the rules of netiquette (Inter*net* + *etiquette*) in the *Writer's Checklist* that follows.

⚡ ETHICS NOTE Keep in mind the issue of confidentiality when sending e-mail. Remember, e-mail can be intercepted by someone other than the intended recipient, and e-mail messages are never truly deleted. Most companies back up and save all company e-mail and are legally entitled to monitor e-mail. Companies can also be compelled legally to provide e-mail in a court of law. Consider the content of all your messages in the light of these possibilities, and carefully review your text before you click "Send." ✦

Writer's Checklist: Observing Workplace Netiquette

To maintain a high level of professionalism in workplace e-mail, observe the rules of netiquette.

☑ Use company e-mail only for appropriate business.

- Do not send or forward jokes or humorous stories, use **biased language**, or discuss office gossip.
- Do not send *flames* (e-mails that contain abusive, obscene, or derogatory language) to attack someone.
- Do not send *spam* (mass-distributed e-mail that often promotes personal projects and interests).

☑ Respond to incoming e-mail promptly. If you receive an assignment by e-mail that will take a few days or longer to complete, send a courtesy response saying so.

☑ Be scrupulous about typing e-mail addresses and otherwise ensuring that the intended recipient gets the message.

☑ Send an attachment only after verifying that your recipient wants or needs the file and that your recipient's software will accept it.

☑ Include a message that functions as a **cover letter** for all e-mails with attachments.

☑ Consider posting a large file at an Internet server and supplying the file's address so that your recipient may download the file at his or her convenience.

☑ Do not write in ALL UPPERCASE LETTERS; such a message is difficult to read and is considered the equivalent of shouting. Likewise, do not write in all lowercase letters; it is considered lazy and too informal for professional work.

☑ Avoid e-mail abbreviations used in personal e-mail and chat rooms (BTW for *by the way*, for example).

Writer's Checklist: Observing Workplace Netiquette (continued)

☑ Do not use emoticons (keyboard characters used to create sideways faces conveying emotions) for business and professional e-mail. For advice on providing typographic emphasis, review the next section on design considerations.

DIGITAL TIPS **SENDING AN E-MAIL ATTACHMENT**

Large files, like graphics, slow the transmission speed of e-mail messages, and the recipient's software or Internet provider may not be able to accept large attachments. Consider using a compression software utility like WinZip at <http://winzip.com/>, which can reduce the file size by 80 percent or more. **Caution:** Viruses can be embedded in e-mail attachments, so regularly update your virus-scanning software and do not open attachments from anyone you do not know. For more on this topic, see <*bedfordstmartins.com/alredbus*> and select *Digital Tips,* "Sending an E-mail Attachment."

Design Considerations

Some e-mail systems allow you to use sophisticated typographical features, such as various fonts and bullets. These options increase your e-mail file size and may display unpredictably in other e-mail systems. Unless you are sure your recipient's software will display your formatted message correctly, set your e-mail software to send messages in "plain text" and use alternative highlighting devices. For example, capital letters or asterisks, used sparingly, can substitute for boldface, italics, and underlines as <u>emphasis</u>.

- Dr. Wilhoit's suggestions benefit doctors AND patients.
- Although the proposal is sound in *theory*, it will never work in *practice*.

Intermittent underlining can replace solid underlining or italics when referring to published works in an e-mail message.

- My report follows the format given in _The Business Writer's Handbook_.

Keep in mind the following additional design considerations when sending e-mail.

- Break the text into short paragraphs to avoid dense blocks of text.

E

- Consider providing an overview at the top in a brief paragraph for messages that run longer than a screen of text.

- Send as attachments documents containing such formatted elements as tables and bulleted lists that do not transmit well in e-mails.

- Place your response to someone else's message at the beginning (or top) of the e-mail window so that recipients can see your response immediately.

- When replying to a message, quote only relevant parts. If your system does not distinguish the quoted text, note it with a greater-than symbol (>).

- Use the "cc:" (copy) and "bcc:" (blind copy) address lines sparingly and thoughtfully because some recipients use their placement in the address lists to filter their mail. See also **correspondence**.

- Provide a concise phrase in the subject line that describes the topic of your message; recipients use subject lines to prioritize and file their incoming messages. See also **memos**.

Salutations, Closings, and Signature Blocks

E-mail can function as a letter, memo, or personal note; therefore, you must adapt your salutation and complimentary closing to your **readers** and **context**. Unless your employer requires certain forms, use the following guidelines:

- When e-mail functions as a traditional letter, use the standard letter salutation (*Dear Ms. Tucker:* or *Dear Docuform Customer:*) and a closing (*Best wishes,* or *Sincerely,*).

- When e-mail functions as a memo to a large group within an organization or a formal announcement to a group, you do not need a salutation or closing.

- When e-mail functions as a memo to individuals or small groups inside an organization, you may wish to adopt a more personal greeting (*Dear Andy,* or *Dear Project Colleagues,*).

- When e-mail functions as a personal note to a friend or close colleague, you can use an informal greeting or only a first name (*Hi Mike,* or *Hello Jenny,* or *Bill,*) and a closing (*Take care,* or *Cheers,*).

Be aware that in some cultures, business correspondents do not use first names as quickly as they do in American correspondence. See **international correspondence**.

Because e-mail does not provide letterhead with standard addresses and contact information, many companies and individual writers include *signature blocks* (also called *signatures*) at the bottom of their messages. Signature blocks, which writers can preprogram to appear on every e-mail they send, supply information that company letterhead usually provides as well as links to Web sites. If your organization requires a certain format, adhere to that standard. Otherwise, use the pattern shown in Figure E–1.

E

```
==============================
Daniel J. Vasquez, Publications Manager     ←    Name and Title
Medical Information Systems                 ←    Department or Division
TechCom Corporation                         ←    Company Name
P.O. Box 5413   Salinas, CA 93962           ←    Mailing Address
Office Phone 888-229-4511 (x 341)           ←    Phone Number
General Office Fax 888-229-1132             ←    Fax Number
www.tcc.com                                 ←    Web Address (URL)
==============================
```

FIGURE E–1. E-mail Signature Block

For signature blocks, consider the following guidelines:

- Include as few lines as possible. Most netiquette guides advocate using five lines or fewer, but more are acceptable in business correspondence because it typically requires more contact information.
- Keep line length to 60 characters or fewer to avoid unpredictable line wraps.
- Test your signature block in plain-text e-mail systems to verify your format; centered text and vertical lines may look fine in one system but chaotic in another.
- Use highlighting cues, such as <u>hyphens</u>, equal signs, and white space, to separate the signature from the message.
- Avoid using quotations, aphorisms, and other messages ("May the Force be with you") in professional signatures.

DIGITAL TIPS LEAVING AN AWAY-FROM-DESK MESSAGE

Many e-mail systems allow you to create an away-from-desk automatic response. Your message should inform senders when you are expected back and, if necessary, whom they can contact in your absence. To learn how to set up an automatic response, see *<bedfordstmartins.com/alredbus>* and select *Digital Tips*, "Leaving an Away-from-Desk Message."

Writer's Checklist: Managing Your E-mail

☑ Check your in-box several times each day; try to clear your in-box by the end of the day.

☑ Set priorities for reading e-mail by skimming sender names and subject lines.

☑ Review all messages on a subject before you respond, so you don't waste time responding to an issue that is no longer relevant.

☑ Learn the advanced features of your system so that you can use filters that organize messages as they arrive.

☑ Create electronic folders for e-mail, using personal names and key topics.

☑ Copy yourself or save sent copies of important e-mails in your electronic folders.

☑ Use the search command to find topics and individual names.

☑ Print and file hard copies of crucial e-mail messages that are complex or that you will need for meetings.

☑ Keep an up-to-date address book.

emphasis

Emphasis is the principle of stressing the most important ideas in writing. It can be achieved with the careful use of position, climactic order, sentence length, sentence type, active **voice**, **repetition**, **intensifiers**, direct statements, long **dashes**, and mechanical devices.

Achieving Emphasis

Position. Place the idea in a conspicuous position. The first and last words of a sentence, **paragraph**, or document stand out in **readers'** minds.

- Moon craters are important to understanding the earth's history because they reflect geological history.

This sentence emphasizes *moon craters* simply because the term appears at the beginning of the sentence and *geological history* because it is at the end of the sentence. See also **subordination**.

Climactic Order. List the ideas or facts within a sentence in sequence from least to most important. See also **lists**.

- Over subsequent weeks the Human Resources Department worked diligently, management showed tact and patience, and the employees demonstrated remarkable support for the policy changes.

Sentence Length.   Vary sentence length strategically. A very short sentence that follows a very long sentence or a series of long sentences stands out in the reader's mind, as in the short sentence ("We must cut costs") that ends the following paragraph. See **sentence construction**.

- We have already reviewed the problem the accounting department has experienced during the past year. We could continue to examine the causes of our problems and point an accusing finger at all the culprits beyond our control, but in the end it all leads to one simple conclusion. We must cut costs.

Sentence Type.   Vary sentences by using a compound sentence, a complex sentence, or a simple sentence. See **sentence variety**.

- The report submitted by the committee was carefully illustrated, and it covered five pages of single-spaced copy.
  [This compound sentence carries no special emphasis because it contains two coordinate independent clauses.]
- The committee's report, which was carefully illustrated, covered five pages of single-spaced copy.
  [This complex sentence emphasizes the size of the report.]
- The carefully illustrated report submitted by the committee covered five pages of single-spaced copy.
  [This simple sentence emphasizes that the report was carefully illustrated.]

Active Voice.   Use the active voice to emphasize the performer of an action: Make the performer the subject of the **verb**.

- Our department designed the new system.
  [The performer, *our department*, is the subject of the verb, *designed*.]

Repetition.   Repeat keywords and key phrases, as in the use of the word *remains* and the phrase *come and go* in the following sentence.

- Similarly, atoms *come and go* in a molecule, but the molecule *remains*; molecules *come and go* in a cell, but the cell *remains*; cells *come and go* in a body, but the body *remains*; persons *come and go* in an organization, but the organization *remains*.
  —Kenneth Building, *Beyond Economics*

Intensifiers.   Although you can use intensifiers (*most, much, very*) for emphasis, this technique is so easily abused that it should be used with caution.

- The final proposal is *much* more persuasive than the first one.

Direct Statements.   Use direct statements, such as "most important," "foremost," or someone's name in a <u>direct address</u>.

- Most important, keep in mind that everything you do affects the company's bottom line.
- John, I believe we should rethink our plans.

Long Dashes.   Use a dash to call attention to a particular word or statement.

- The job will be done — after we are under contract.

Mechanical Devices.   Use *italics*, **bold type**, <u>underlining</u>, and CAPITAL LETTERS — but use them sparingly because overuse can create visual clutter. See also <u>layout and design</u>, <u>capitalization</u>, and <u>italics</u>.

English as a second language

DIRECTORY
Count and Mass Nouns   187
Articles   187
Gerunds and Infinitives   188
Adjective Clauses   189
Present Perfect Verb Tense   189
Present Progressive Verb Tense   189
ESL Entries   190

Learning to write well in a second language takes a great deal of effort and practice. The most effective way to improve your command of written English is to read widely beyond the reports and professional articles your job requires, such as magazines, newspapers, articles, novels, biographies, and any other writing that interests you. In addition, listen carefully to native speakers on television, on radio, and in person. Do not hesitate to consult a native speaker of English, especially for important writing tasks, such as <u>e-mails</u>, <u>memos</u>, and <u>reports</u>. Focus on those particular areas of English that give you trouble. See also <u>global communication</u>.

Count and Mass Nouns

Count nouns refer to things that can be counted (tables, pencils, projects, reports). *Mass nouns* (also called *noncount nouns*) identify things that cannot be counted (electricity, water, air, loyalty, information). This distinction can be confusing with words like *electricity* and *water*. Although we can count kilowatt-hours of electricity and bottles of water, counting becomes inappropriate when we use the words *electricity* and *water* in a general sense, as in "*Water* is an essential resource." Following is a list of common mass **nouns**.

acid	coffee	information	precision
advice	education	knowledge	research
air	electricity	loyalty	technology
anger	equipment	machinery	transportation
biology	furniture	money	water
business	health	news	weather
clothing	honesty	oil	work

The distinction between whether something can or cannot be counted determines the form of the noun to use (singular or plural), the kind of article that precedes it (*a*, *an*, *the*, or no article), and the kind of limiting <u>adjective</u> it requires (such as *fewer* or *less* and *much* or *many*). See also <u>fewer/less</u>.

Articles

This discussion of <u>articles</u> applies only to common nouns (not to proper nouns, such as the names of people) because count and mass nouns are always common nouns.

The general rule is that every count noun must be preceded by an article (*a*, *an*, *the*), a demonstrative adjective (*this*, *that*, *these*, *those*), a possessive adjective (*my*, *your*, *her*, *his*, *its*, *their*), or some expression of quantity (such as *one*, *two*, *several*, *many*, *a few*, *a lot of*, *some*, *no*). The article, adjective, or expression of quantity appears either directly in front of the noun or in front of the whole noun phrase.

- Beth read *a* report last week. [article]
- *Those* reports Beth read were long. [demonstrative adjective]
- *Their* report was long. [possessive adjective]
- *Some* reports Beth read were long. [indefinite adjective]

The articles *a* and *an* are used with count nouns that refer to one item of the whole class of like items.

- Matthew has *a* pen.
  [Matthew could have *any* pen.]

The article *the* is used with nouns that refer to a specific item that both the reader and the writer can identify.

E

- Matthew has *the* pen.
  [Matthew has a *specific* pen that is known to both the reader and the writer.]

When making generalizations with count nouns, writers can either use *a* or *an* with a singular count noun or use no article with a plural count noun. Consider the following generalization using an article.

- An egg is a good source of protein.
  [any egg, all eggs, eggs in general]

However, the following generalization uses a plural count noun with no article.

- Eggs are good sources of protein.
  [any egg, all eggs, eggs in general]

When you are making a generalization with a mass noun, do not use an article in front of the mass noun.

- Sugar is bad for your teeth.

Gerunds and Infinitives

Nonnative writers of English are often puzzled by which form of a <u>verbal</u> (a verb used as another part of speech) to use when it functions as the direct object of a <u>verb</u>—or a **complement**. No structural rule exists for distinguishing between the use of an infinitive and a gerund as the object of a verb. Any specific verb may take an infinitive as its object, others may take a gerund, and yet others take either an infinitive or a gerund. At times, even the base form of the verb is used.

- He enjoys *working*. [gerund as a complement]
- She promised *to fulfill* her part of the contract.
  [infinitive as a complement]
- The president had the manager *assign* her staff to another project.
  [basic verb form as a complement]

To make such distinctions accurately, rely on what you hear native speakers use or what you read. You might also consult a reference book for ESL students.

Adjective Clauses

Because of the variety of ways adjective clauses are constructed in different languages, they can be particularly troublesome for nonnative writers of English. The following guidelines will help you form adjective clauses correctly.

Place an adjective clause directly after the noun it modifies.

- The tall woman *who is standing across the room* is a vice president of the company ~~who is standing across the room.~~

The adjective clause *who is standing across the room* modifies *woman*, not *company*, and thus comes directly after *woman*.

Avoid using a relative pronoun with another pronoun in an adjective clause.

- The man who ~~he~~ sits at that desk is my boss.

Present Perfect Verb Tense

In general, use the present perfect __tense__ to refer to events completed in the past that have some implication for the present.

PRESENT PERFECT   She *has revised* that report three times.
[She might revise it again.]

When a specific time is mentioned, however, use the simple past.

SIMPLE PAST   I *wrote* the letter yesterday morning.
[The action, *wrote*, does not affect the present.]

Use the present perfect with a *since* or *for* phrase to describe actions that began in the past and continue in the present.

- This company *has been* in business *for* seventeen years.
- This company *has been* in business *since* 1985.

Present Progressive Verb Tense

The present progressive tense is especially difficult for those whose native language does not use this tense. The present progressive tense is used to describe some action or condition that is ongoing (or in progress) in the present and may continue into the future.

PRESENT   I *am searching* for an error in the document.
PROGRESSIVE   [The search is occurring now and may continue.]

In contrast, the simple present tense more often relates to habitual actions.

SIMPLE   I *search* for errors in my documents.
PRESENT   [I regularly search for errors, but I am not
               necessarily searching now.]

See "ESL Tips for Using the Progressive Form" in the entry <u>tense</u>.

ESL Entries

Most of the entries in this handbook may interest writers of English as a second language; however, the specific entries listed in the Contents by Topic under "ESL Trouble Spots" address issues that often cause problems.

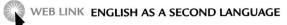

WEB LINK **ENGLISH AS A SECOND LANGUAGE**

For Web sites and electronic grammar exercises intended for speakers of English as a second language, see *<bedfordstmartins.com/alredbus>* and se-lect *Links for Handbook Entries* and *Exercise Central*.

English, varieties of

Written English includes two broad categories: standard and non-standard. Standard English is used in business, industry, government, education, and all professions. It has rigorous and precise criteria for <u>capitalization</u>, <u>punctuation</u>, <u>spelling</u>, and <u>usage</u>.

Nonstandard English does not conform to such criteria; it is often regional in origin, or it reflects the special usages of a particular ethnic or social group. As a result, although nonstandard English may be vigorous and colorful, its usefulness as a means of communication is limited to certain <u>contexts</u> and to people already familiar and comfortable with it in those contexts. It rarely appears in printed material except for special effect. Nonstandard English is characterized by inexact or inconsistent punctuation, capitalization, spelling, diction, and usage choices; thus, you should avoid using it in workplace writing.

Colloquial English

Colloquial English is spoken English or writing that uses words and expressions common to casual conversation (We need to get him up to speed). Colloquial English is appropriate to some kinds of writing (personal letters, notes, some <u>e-mail</u>) but not to most workplace writing.

Dialectal English

Dialectal English is a social or regional variety of the language that is comprehensible to people of that social group or region but may be incomprehensible to outsiders. Dialect, which is usually nonstandard English, involves distinct <u>word choice</u>, grammatical forms, and pronunciations. For example, residents of southern Louisiana who descended from French colonists speak a dialect often referred to as Cajun.

Localisms

A localism is a regional wording or phrasing. For example, a large sandwich on a long split roll is variously known throughout the United States as a *hero, hoagie, grinder, poor boy, submarine,* and *torpedo.* Such words normally should be avoided in workplace writing because not all readers will be familiar with the local meanings.

Slang

Slang is an informal vocabulary composed of <u>figures of speech</u> and colorful words used in humorous or extravagant ways. There is no objective test for slang, and many standard words are given slang applications. For instance, slang may be a familiar word used in a new way (*chill* meaning "relax"), or it may be a new word (*wonk* meaning "someone who works or studies excessively").

Most slang is short-lived and has meaning only for a narrow audience. Sometimes, however, slang becomes standard because the word fills a legitimate need. *Skyscraper* and *date* (as in "go on a date"), for example, were once considered slang expressions. Nevertheless, although slang may be valid in informal and personal writing or fiction, it generally should be avoided in workplace writing. See also <u>jargon</u> and <u>business writing style</u>.

equal / unique / perfect

Logically, *equal* (meaning "having the same quantity or value as another"), *unique* (meaning "one of a kind"), and *perfect* (meaning "a state of highest excellence") are words with absolute meanings and therefore should not be compared. However, colloquial usage of *more* and *most* as **modifiers** of *equal, unique,* and *perfect* is so common that an absolute prohibition on such use is impossible.

● Our system is *more unique* [or *more perfect*] than theirs.

Some writers try to overcome the problem by using *more nearly equal (more nearly unique, more nearly perfect).* When clarity and preciseness are critical, the use of comparative degrees with *equal, unique,* and *perfect* can be misleading. It is best to avoid using comparative degrees with absolute terms. See also **comparison.**

> **MISLEADING**   Ours is a *more equal* percentage split than theirs.
>
> **PRECISE**   Our percentage split is 51–49; theirs is 54–46.

etc.

Etc. is an abbreviation for the Latin *et cetera,* meaning "and others" or "and so on." Therefore, do not use the redundant phrase *and etc.* Likewise, do not use *etc.* at the end of a series introduced by the phrases *such as* and *for example*—those phrases already indicate unnamed items of the same category. Use *etc.* with a logical progression (1, 2, 3, etc.) and when at least two items are named.

● The sorting machine processes coins (~~for example~~ pennies, nickels, ~~and~~ etc.), and then packages them for redistribution.

Otherwise, avoid *etc.* because the reader may not be able to infer what other items a list might include.

> **VAGUE**   He will bring legal pads, paper clips, etc., to the trade show.
>
> **CLEAR**   He will bring legal pads, paper clips, and other office supplies to the trade show.

Do not italicize *etc.*

ethics in writing

Ethics refers to the choices we make that affect others for good or ill. Ethical issues are inherent in writing and speaking because what we write and say can influence others. Further, how we express ideas affects our **readers'** perceptions of us and our company's ethical stance.

⬙ ETHICS NOTE Obviously, no book can describe how to act ethically in every situation, but this entry describes some typical ethical lapses to watch for during **revision**.* In other entries throughout this book, ethical issues are highlighted using the symbols surrounding this paragraph. ✦

Avoid language that attempts to evade responsibility. Some writers use the passive **voice** because they hope to avoid responsibility or obscure an issue.

- It has been decided. [*Who* has decided?]

- Several mistakes were made. [*Who* made them?]

Avoid deceptive language. Do not use words with more than one meaning to circumvent the truth. Consider the company document that stated, "A nominal charge will be assessed for using our facilities." When clients objected that the charge was actually very high, the writer pointed out that the word *nominal* means "the named amount" as well as "very small." In that situation, clients had a strong case in charging that the company was attempting to be deceptive. Various **abstract words**, technical and legal **jargon**, and **euphemisms** are unethical when they are used to mislead readers or to hide a serious or dangerous situation, even though technical or legal experts could interpret them as accurate. See also **word choice**.

Do not deemphasize or suppress important information. Not including information that a reader would want to have, such as potential safety hazards or hidden costs for which a customer might be responsible, is unethical. Such omissions may also be illegal. Use **layout and design** features like type size, bullets, lists, and footnotes to highlight information that is important to readers. Do not hide information in dense paragraphs with small type and little white space, as is common in credit-card contracts. Such a design will defeat all but the most persistent readers.

Do not emphasize misleading or incorrect information. Similarly, avoid the temptation to highlight a feature or service that readers would find attractive but that is available only with some product models or at extra cost. (See also **logic errors** and **positive writing**.) Readers could justifiably object that you have given them a false impression to sell a product or service, especially if you also deemphasize the extra cost or other special conditions.

In general, treat others—individuals, companies, groups—with fairness and with respect. Avoid language that is biased, racist, or sexist or that perpetuates stereotypes. See also **biased language**.

*Adapted from Brenda R. Sims, "Linking Ethics and Language in the Technical Communication Classroom," *Technical Communication Quarterly* 2.3 (Summer 1993): 285–99.

Finally, be aware that both <u>plagiarism</u> and violations of <u>copyright</u> are not only unethical but also can have serious legal and professional consequences for you in the classroom and on the job. You should review those entries carefully to make sure you have a clear understanding of these issues.

E

Writer's Checklist: Writing Ethically

Ask yourself the following questions:

☑ *Am I willing to take responsibility, publicly and privately, for what the document says?* Will you stand behind what you have written to your employer? to your family and friends?

☑ *Is the document honest and truthful?* Scrutinize findings and conclusions carefully. Make sure that the data support them.

☑ *Am I acting in my employer's best interest? my client's or the public's best interest? my own best long-term interest?* Have someone outside your company review and comment on what you have written.

☑ *Does the document violate anyone's rights?* Have people from different backgrounds review your writing.

☑ *Am I ethically consistent in my writing?* Apply consistently the principles outlined here and those you have assimilated throughout your life to meet this standard.

☑ *What if everybody acted or communicated in this way?* If you were the intended audience, would the message be acceptable and respectful?

If the answers to these questions do not come easily, consider seeking the advice of a trusted colleague to review and comment on what you have written. If information is confidential and you have serious concerns, consider a review by the company's legal staff or attorney.

euphemisms

A euphemism is an inoffensive substitute for a word or phrase that could be distasteful, offensive, or too blunt: *passed away* for *died*; *previously owned* or *preowned* for *used*; *lay off* or *downsize* for *terminate* or *fire*. Used judiciously, euphemisms can help you avoid embarrassing or offending someone.

 ETHICS NOTE Euphemisms can also hide the facts of a situation (*incident* or *event* for *accident*) or be a form of <u>affectation</u> if used carelessly. Avoid them especially in <u>international correspondence</u> and other forms of <u>global communication</u> where their meanings could be not only confusing but also misleading. See also <u>ethics in writing</u>. ✦

everybody / everyone

Both *everybody* and *everyone* are usually considered singular and take singular <u>verbs</u> and <u>pronouns</u>.

● *Everyone* here *leaves* at 4:30 p.m.

● *Everybody* at the meeting made *his or her* proposal separately.

However, the meaning can be obviously plural.

● *Everyone* thought the report should be revised, and I really couldn't blame *them*.

Although normally written as one word, *everyone* is written as two words to emphasize each individual in a group. (*Every one* of the team members contributed to this discovery.) See also <u>agreement</u>.

exclamation marks

The exclamation mark (!) indicates strong feeling, urgency, elation, or surprise (Hurry! Great! Wow!). (See also <u>interjections</u>.) However, it cannot make an argument more convincing, lend force to a weak statement, or call attention to an intended irony.

An exclamation mark can be used after a whole sentence or an element of a sentence.

● This meeting—please note it well!—concerns our budget deficit.

When used with <u>quotation marks</u>, the exclamation mark goes outside, unless what is quoted is an exclamation.

● The manager yelled, "Get in here!" Then Ben, according to Ray, "jumped like a kangaroo"!

In <u>instructions</u>, the exclamation mark is often used in cautions and warnings (Danger! Stop!). See also <u>emphasis</u>.

executive summaries

An executive summary consolidates the principal points of a <u>report</u> or <u>proposal</u>, as in Figure E-2. Executive summaries differ from <u>abstracts</u> in that <u>readers</u> scan abstracts to decide whether to read the work in

Reported Ethics Cases — 2005

EXECUTIVE SUMMARY

This report examines the nature and disposition of the 3,458 ethics cases handled by the CGF Aircraft Corporation's ethics officers and managers during 2005. The purpose of this report is to provide CGF's Ethics and Business Conduct Committee with the information necessary for assessing the effectiveness of the first year of the company's Ethics Program.

Background
Effective January 1, 2005, the Ethics and Business Conduct Committee (the Committee) implemented a policy and procedures for the administration of CGF's new Ethics Program. The purpose of the Ethics Program, established by the Committee, is to "promote ethical business conduct through open communication and compliance with company ethics standards." The Office of Ethics and Business Conduct was created to administer the Ethics Program. The director of the Office of Ethics and Business Conduct, along with seven ethics officers throughout the corporation, was given the responsibility for the following objectives:

- Communicate the values and standards for CGF's Ethics Program to employees.

- Inform employees about company policies regarding ethical business conduct.

- Establish companywide channels for employees to obtain information and guidance in resolving ethics concerns.

- Implement companywide ethics-awareness and education programs.

Employee accessibility to ethics information and guidance was available through managers, ethics officers, and an ethics hotline.

Ethics Cases
Major ethics cases were defined as those situations potentially involving serious violations of company policies or illegal conduct. Examples of major ethics cases included cover-up of defective workmanship or use of defective parts in products; discrimination in hiring and promotion; involvement in monetary or other kickbacks; sexual harassment; disclosure of proprietary or company information; theft; and use of corporate Internet resources for inappropriate purposes, such as conducting personal business, gambling, or access to pornography.

1

FIGURE E–2. Executive Summary

Reported Ethics Cases — 2005

Minor ethics cases were defined as including all reported concerns not classified as major ethics cases. Minor ethics cases were classified as informational queries from employees, situations involving coworkers, and situations involving management.

Conclusions
The effectiveness of CGF's Ethics Program during the first year of implementation is most evidenced by (1) the active participation of employees in the program and the 3,458 contacts employees made regarding ethics concerns through the various channels available to them, and (2) the action taken in the cases reported by employees, particularly the disposition of the 30 substantiated major ethics cases. Disseminating information about the disposition of ethics cases, particularly information about the severe disciplinary actions taken in major ethics violations, sends a message to employees that unethical or illegal conduct will not be tolerated.

Recommendations
Based on these conclusions, recommendations for planning the second year of the Ethics Program are (1) continuing the channels of communication now available in the Ethics Program, (2) increasing financial and technical support for the Ethics Hotline, the most highly utilized mode of contact in the ethics cases reported in 2005, (3) disseminating this report in some form to employees to ensure their awareness of CGF's commitment to uphold its Ethics Policies and Procedures, and (4) implementing some measure of recognition for ethical behavior, such as an "Ethics Employee of the Month" award to promote and reward ethical conduct.

2

FIGURE E–2. Executive Summary (*continued*)

full. However, an executive summary may be the only section of a longer work read by many readers, so it must accurately and concisely reflect the original document. It should restate the document's <u>purpose</u>, <u>scope</u>, methods, findings, <u>conclusions</u>, and recommendations as well as explain how results were obtained or the reasons for the recommendations. Executive summaries tend to be about 10 percent of the length of the documents they summarize and generally follow the same sequence.

Write the executive summary so that it can be read independently of the report or proposal. Executive summaries may occasionally include a figure, table, or footnote if that information is essential to the summary. Do not refer by number to figures, tables, or references contained elsewhere in the document. The sample executive summary in Figure E–2 is from a formal report on the disposition of ethics cases in an aircraft corporation.

Writer's Checklist: Writing Executive Summaries

- ☑ Write the executive summary after you have completed the original document.
- ☑ Avoid using terminology that may not be familiar to your intended audience.
- ☑ Spell out all uncommon symbols and **abbreviations**.
- ☑ Make the summary concise, but do not omit transitional words and phrases (*however, moreover, therefore, for example, in summary*).
- ☑ Include only information discussed in the original document.
- ☑ Place the executive summary at the very beginning of the body of the report, as described in **formal reports**.

expletives

An expletive is a word that fills the position of another word, phrase, or clause. *It* and *there* are common expletives.

- *It* is certain that he will be promoted.

In the example, the expletive *it* occupies the position of subject in place of the real subject, *that he will be promoted*. Expletives are sometimes necessary to avoid **awkwardness**, but they are commonly overused, and most sentences can be better stated without them.

- *Many* ~~There were many~~ *were* orders lost because of a computer virus.
  ^   ^

In addition to its use as a grammatical term, the word *expletive* means an exclamation or oath, especially one that is obscene.

explicit / implicit

An *explicit* statement is one expressed directly, with precision and clarity.

- He gave us *explicit* directions to the Wausau facility.

An *implicit* meaning is one that is not directly expressed.

- Although the CEO did not mention the lawsuit directly, the company's commitment to ethical practices was *implicit* in her speech.

exposition

Exposition, or *expository writing*, informs readers by presenting facts and ideas in direct and concise language; it usually relies less on colorful or figurative language than does writing meant to be expressive or persuasive. Expository writing attempts to explain to readers what the subject is, how it works, and how it relates to something else. Exposition is aimed at the readers' understanding rather than at their imagination or emotions; it is a sharing of the writer's knowledge. Exposition aims to provide accurate, complete information and to analyze it for the readers.

Because it is the most effective form of discourse for explaining difficult subjects, exposition is widely used in **reports**, **memos**, and other types of business writing. To use exposition effectively, you must have a thorough knowledge of your subject. As with all writing, how much of that knowledge you pass on to your **readers** depends on the readers' needs and your **purpose**.

F

fact

Expressions containing the word *fact* ("due to the *fact* that," "except for the *fact* that," "as a matter of *fact*," or "because of the *fact* that") are often wordy substitutes for more accurate terms.

- ~~Due to the fact that~~ *Because* the sales force has a high turnover rate, sales have declined.

Do not use the word *fact* to refer to matters of judgment or opinion.

- ~~It is a fact that~~ *In my opinion,* sales are poor in the Midwest because of insufficient market research.

The word *fact* is, of course, valid when facts are what is meant.

- Our tests uncovered numerous *facts* to support your conclusion.

See also **conciseness** and **logic errors**.

fax (*see* **selecting the medium**)

feasibility reports

When organizations consider a new project—developing a new product or service, expanding a customer base, purchasing equipment, or moving operations—they first try to determine the project's chances for success. A feasibility report presents evidence about the practicality of a proposed project based on specific criteria. It answers such questions as the following: Is new construction or development necessary? Is sufficient staff available? What are the costs? What are the legal ramifications? Based on the findings of this analysis, the writer offers logical conclusions and recommends whether the project should be carried out. When feasibility reports stress specific steps that should be taken as a result of a study of a problem or an issue, they are often referred to as *recommendation reports*. In the condensed feasibility report shown in Figure F–1, a business consultant conducts a feasibility study to determine how to upgrade a company's computer system and Internet capability.

Before beginning to write a feasibility report, analyze your <u>readers</u>' needs and the <u>purpose</u> of your study. Then write a purpose statement, such as "The purpose of this study is to determine the feasibility of expanding our Pacific Rim operations." See also <u>brainstorming</u> and <u>collaborative writing</u>.

Report Sections

Feasibility reports vary in length from several pages for small projects to dozens for very large projects. Regardless of length, every feasibility report should contain an <u>introduction</u>, a body, a <u>conclusion</u>, and a recommendation. See also <u>proposals</u> and <u>formal reports</u> for further advice on creating these sections.

Introduction.   The introduction states the purpose of the report, describes the circumstances that led to the report, and includes any pertinent background information. It may also discuss the <u>scope</u> of the report, any procedures or methods used in the analysis of alternatives, and any limitations of the study.

Body.   The body of the report presents a detailed review of all the alternatives under consideration. Examine each alternative according to specific criteria, such as cost and financing, availability of staff, and other relevant requirements, identifying the subsections with <u>headings</u> to guide readers.

Conclusion.   The conclusion interprets the available options and points to one option as the best or most feasible.

Recommendation.   The recommendation section clearly presents the writer's opinion on which alternative best meets the criteria as summarized in the conclusion.

 WEB LINK **SAMPLE FEASIBILITY REPORTS**

For links to full feasibility reports, see <*bedfordstmartins.com/alredbus*> and select *Links for Handbook Entries.*

Introduction

The purpose of this report is to determine which of two proposed options would best enable Darnell Business Forms Corporation to upgrade its file servers and its Internet capacity to meet its increasing data and communication requirements.

Background.   In October 2004, the Information Development Group put the MACRON System into operation. Since then, the volume of processing transactions has increased fivefold (from 1,000 to 5,000 updates per day). This increase has severely impaired system response time; in fact, average response time has increased from 10 seconds to 120 seconds. Further, our new Web-based client services system has increased exponentially the demand for processing speed and access capacity.

Scope.   We have investigated two alternative solutions to provide increased processing capacity: (1) purchase of an additional Aurora processor to supplement the one in operation, and (2) purchase of an Icardo 60 with expandable peripherals to replace the Aurora processor currently in operation. The two alternatives are evaluated here, according to both cost and expanded capacity for future operations.

Additional Aurora Processor

Purchasing a second Aurora processor would require increased annual maintenance costs, salary for a second computer specialist, increased energy costs, and a one-time construction cost for necessary remodeling and installing Internet connections.

Annual maintenance costs	$35,000
Annual costs for computer specialist	75,000
Annual increased energy costs	7,500
Total annual operating costs	$117,500
Construction cost (one-time)	50,000
Total first-year costs	$167,500

The installation and operation of another Aurora processor are expected to produce savings in system reliability and readiness.

System Reliability.   An additional Aurora would reduce current downtime periods from four to two per week. Downtime recovery averages 30 minutes and affects 40 users. Assuming that 50 percent of users require system access at a given time, we determined that the following reliability savings would result:

2 downtimes × 0.5 hours × 40 users × 50% × $50/hour overtime × 52 weeks
= $52,000 annual savings.

[*The feasibility report would also discuss the second option—purchase of the Icardo 60 and its long-term savings.*]

FIGURE F–1. Feasibility Report

Conclusion
A comparison of costs for both systems indicates that the Icardo 60 would cost
$2,200 more in first-year costs.

	Aurora	Icardo 60
Net additional operating costs	$56,300	$84,000
One-time construction costs	50,000	24,500
First-year total	$106,300	$108,500

Installation of an additional Aurora processor would permit the present information-
processing systems to operate relatively smoothly and efficiently. It would not,
however, provide the expanded processing capacity that the Icardo 60 processor
would for implementing new subsystems required to increase processing speed
and Internet access.

Recommendation
The Icardo 60 processor should be purchased because of the long-term savings and
because its additional capacity and flexibility will allow for greater expansion in the
future.

3

F

FIGURE F–1. Feasibility Report (*continued*)

few / a few

In certain contexts, *few* carries more negative overtones than does the
phrase *a few*.

> **NEGATIVE**   There are *few* helpful ideas in the report.
> **POSITIVE**   There are *a few* helpful ideas in the report.

fewer / less

Fewer refers to items that can be counted (count nouns).

- *Fewer* employees took the offer than we expected.

Less refers to mass quantities or amounts (mass nouns).

- Because we had *less* rain this year, the crop yield decreased.

See also <u>English as a second language</u> and <u>nouns</u>.

figuratively / literally

Literally means "actually" and is often confused with *figuratively*, which means "metaphorically." To say that someone "literally turned green with envy" would mean that the person actually changed color.

- In the winner's circle the jockey was, *figuratively* speaking, ten feet tall.
- When he said, "Let's bury our competitors," he did not mean it *literally*.

Avoid the use of *literally* to reinforce the importance of something.

- She was ~~literally~~ the best of the applicants.

figures of speech

A figure of speech is an imaginative expression that often compares two things that are basically not alike but have at least one thing in common. For example, if a device is cone-shaped and has an opening at the narrow end, you might say that it looks like a volcano.

Figures of speech can clarify the unfamiliar by relating a new concept to one with which readers are familiar. In that respect, they help establish understanding between the specialist and the nonspecialist. Figures of speech can also help translate the abstract into the concrete; in the process of doing so, they can also make writing more colorful and graphic. (See also abstract/concrete words.) A figure of speech must make sense, however, to achieve the desired effect.

> ILLOGICAL   Without the fuel of tax incentives, our economic
> engine would operate less efficiently.
> [It would not operate at all without fuel.]

Figures of speech also must be consistent to be effective.

- We must get our sales program *back on course*, and we are counting
  steer the effort.
  on you to ~~carry the ball.~~

A figure of speech should not overshadow the point the writer is trying to make. In addition, it is better to use no figure of speech at all than to use a trite one. A surprise that comes "like a bolt out of the blue" seems stale and not much of a surprise at all. See also clichés.

Types of Figures of Speech

Analogies are comparisons that show the ways in which two objects or concepts are similar, often used to make one of them easier to understand. The following example explains a computer search technique by comparing it to the use of keywords in a dictionary.

- The search technique used in *indexed sequential processing* is similar to a search technique you might use to find the page on which a particular word is located in a dictionary. You might scan the keywords located at the top of each dictionary page that identify the first and last words on each page until you find the keywords that encompass the word you seek. Indexed sequential processing works the same way with computer files.

Hyperboles are gross exaggerations used to achieve an effect or <u>emphasis</u>.

- We were *dead* after working all night on the report.

Litotes are understatements, for emphasis or effect, achieved by denying the opposite of the point you are making.

- Two hundred dollars is not a small price for a book.

Metaphors are figures of speech that point out similarities between two things by treating them as though they were the same thing.

- He is the department's *utility infielder*.

Metonyms are figures of speech that use one aspect of a thing to represent it, such as *the blue* for the sky and *wheels* for a car.

- The *hard-hat* sector of the labor force was especially hurt by the terms of the contract.

Personification is a figure of speech that attributes human characteristics to nonhuman things or abstract ideas. We might refer, for example, to the *birth* of a planet or apply emotions to machines.

- She said that she was frustrated with the *stubborn* computer system.

Similes are direct comparisons of two essentially unlike things, linking them with the word *like* or *as*.

- His feelings about his competitor are so bitter that in recent conversations with his staff he returned to the subject compulsively, *like someone scratching an itch*.

Avoid figures of speech in <u>global communication</u> and <u>international correspondence</u> because those in other cultures may translate figures of speech literally and be confused by their meanings.

fine

When used in expressions such as "I feel *fine*" or "a *fine* day," *fine* is colloquial and, like the word *nice*, is too vague for business writing. Use the word *fine* to mean "refined," "delicate," or "pure."

- A *fine* film of oil covered the surface of the water.
- *Fine* crystal is made in Austria.
- She made a *fine* distinction between the two possible meanings of the disputed passage.

first / firstly

First and *firstly* are both adverbs. Avoid *firstly* in favor of *first*, which sounds less stiff than *firstly*. The same is true of other ordinal <u>numbers</u>, such as *second*, *third*, and so on.

flowcharts

A flowchart is a diagram using symbols, words, or pictures to show the stages of a process in sequence from beginning to end. A flowchart provides an overview of a process and allows the reader to identify its essential steps quickly and easily. Flowcharts can take several forms. The steps might be represented by labeled blocks, as shown in Figure F–2; pictorial symbols, as shown in Figure F–3; or ISO (International Organization for Standardization) symbols, as shown in Figure F–4.

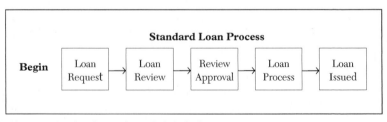

FIGURE F–2. Flowchart Using Labeled Blocks

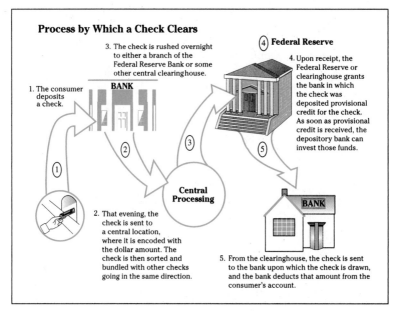

FIGURE F–3. Flowchart Using Pictorial Symbols

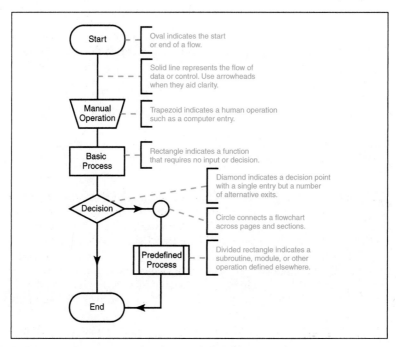

FIGURE F–4. Common ISO Flowchart Symbols (with Annotations)

Writer's Checklist: Creating Flowcharts

☑ Label each step in the process or identify each step with labeled blocks, pictorial representations, or standardized symbols.

☑ Follow the standard flow directions: left to right and top to bottom. When the flow is otherwise, indicate that with arrows.

☑ Include a key (or callouts) if the flowchart contains symbols your **readers** may not understand.

☑ Use standardized symbols for flowcharts that document computer programs and other information-processing procedures, as set forth in *Information Processing—Documentation Symbols and Conventions for Data, Program and System Flowcharts, Program Network Charts, and System Resources Charts*, ISO publication 5807-1985 (E).

For advice on integrating flowcharts into your text, see **visuals**. See also **global graphics**.

---

footnotes (*see* documenting sources)

---

forceful / forcible

Although *forceful* and *forcible* are both **adjectives** meaning "characterized by or full of force," *forceful* is usually limited to persuasive ability and *forcible* to physical force.

- John made a *forceful* presentation at the committee meeting.
- The police report listed three *forcible* entries into the building.

---

foreign words in English

The English language has a long history of borrowing words from other languages. Most borrowing occurred so long ago that we seldom recognize the borrowed terms (also called *loan words*) as being of foreign origin (*kindergarten* from German, *animal* from Latin, *church* from Greek).

Words not likely to be familiar to **readers** or not fully assimilated into the English language are set in **italics** (*sine qua non, coup de grâce, in res, in camera*). Most dictionaries offer guidance, although you should also be guided by the **context**. Even when foreign words have been fully assimilated, they often retain their diacritical marks (cliché, résumé, vis-à-vis). As foreign words are absorbed into English, their plural forms give way to English plurals (*agenda* becomes *agendas* and *formulae* becomes *formulas*).

Generally, foreign expressions should be used only if they serve a real need. (See also **e.g./i.e.** and **etc.**) The overuse of foreign words in an attempt to impress your reader or achieve elegance is **affectation**. Effective communication can be accomplished only if your readers understand what you write; therefore, choose foreign expressions only when they make an idea clearer.

foreword / forward

Although the pronunciation is the same, the spellings and meanings of these two words are quite different. The word *foreword* is a **noun** meaning "introductory statement at the beginning of a book or other work." (The former CEO wrote a *foreword* for the annual report.) The word *forward* is an **adjective** or **adverb** meaning "at or toward the front."

- Move the lever to the *forward* position on the panel. [adjective]
- Turn the dial until the needle begins to move *forward*. [adverb]

form letters

A form letter is a type of **correspondence** (including **e-mail**) in which the identical message is sent to more than one person; only the name and address of the recipient differ from letter to letter. The recipients' names and addresses are stored in a database and merged with the text of the letter. The letters are then e-mailed or printed and mailed to the individuals addressed. Messages that vary slightly from reader to reader are called *guide letters* and are discussed later in this entry.

When to Use Form Letters

Form letters are ideal for simultaneously reaching hundreds or thousands of customers, clients, or employees with announcements and other information. In fact, **sales letters** are usually mass-produced as form letters. Form letters are also useful for situations that occur regularly, such as responses to inquiries, standard orders, acknowledgments of orders, and early-stage **collection letters**. (See also **acknowledgment letters** and **inquiries and responses**.) Of course, if a particular situation calls for a more personal response (such as an **adjustment letter** in response to a complaint), a form letter is not the best choice. Most people resent impersonal treatment when they believe they deserve in-dividual attention.

For routine circumstances, an undisguised form letter results in a more positive response than does a form letter that masquerades as a personal message but contains inappropriate wording. Furthermore, few customers object to form letters for recurring circumstances be-cause it is easy to decipher the necessary information from them. For example, a computer company may send purchasers a brief form letter or e-mail to let them know their computers have been shipped and when to expect delivery.

Writing Form Letters

By using the principles of correspondence and the <u>"you" viewpoint</u>, you can produce a form letter tailored to your potential <u>readers</u> and to your <u>purpose</u>. Even though your readers know they are reading a form letter, you should give each reader the feeling that the letter fits his or her situation. Avoid broadcasting that the message is a form.

GENERAL   Whether you live in Maine or California, you can visit our Web site or get 24-hour personal assistance at our toll-free number.
[This sentence announces that it is aimed at a wide audience.]

PERSONAL   If you have a problem with your MAX-PC and cannot find the answer in the User's Guide, visit our Web site or get 24-hour personal assistance at the following toll-free number.
[This sentence seems aimed more at the individual reader.]

Form letters that do not need to be disguised often use a "headline lead" to replace the standard salutation, as shown in Figure F–5. By

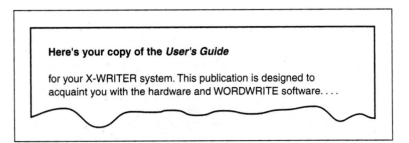

Here's your copy of the *User's Guide*

for your X-WRITER system. This publication is designed to acquaint you with the hardware and WORDWRITE software. . . .

FIGURE F–5. Headline Lead

"talking" directly to the reader, you can make form letters less stiff and impersonal. Some form letters can be personalized by adding a typed or handwritten postscript. However, if you suspect that the reader would resent a form letter, even if it is personalized, either write an individual letter or use a guide letter.

Writing Guide Letters

A guide letter (or e-mail) is individually written and composed of several optional sentences or paragraphs that can be interchanged to produce a variety of letters. In effect, writing a guide letter is like selecting a meal in a cafeteria: You compose the letter by selecting and then arranging previously written parts rather than writing sentences from scratch.

Guide letters are ideal in recurring circumstances that require more personal or varied responses than form letters provide. They are useful, for example, when you wish either to tailor parts of the letter for particular readers or to construct sets of letters from standardized parts, as in application letters, reference letters, refusal letters, and some memos. Because guide letters are formed from various prewritten parts, they require careful preparation. In most cases, an office can create sets of guide-letter files containing paragraphs labeled with a code, often combinations of letters and numbers (A-1, A-2, B-1, B-2, and so on). The writer can determine the parts and the order in which they should appear for a particular letter. When preparing such letters, make sure you provide adequate transitions between sentences and adjust the tone for your readers.

Although those who produce high volumes of letters benefit most from using form and guide letters, anyone can adopt these concepts. By saving each correspondence you write and by refining the language on each new occasion, you can create a bank of form and guide letters that will save you time and effort.

formal reports

DIRECTORY
Front Matter   212   Back Matter   215
Body   214   Sample Formal Report   216

Formal reports are usually written accounts of major projects that require substantial research, and they often involve more than one writer. See also collaborative writing.

Most formal reports are divided into three primary parts—front matter, body, and back matter—each of which contains a number of elements. The number and arrangement of the elements may vary, depending on the subject, the length of the report, and the kinds of material covered. Further, many organizations have a preferred style for formal reports and furnish guidelines for report writers to follow. If you are not required to follow a specific style, use the <u>format</u> recommended in this entry. The following list includes most of the elements a formal report might contain, in the order they typically appear. (The items shown with page numbers appear in the sample formal report on pages 217–33.) Often, a <u>cover letter</u> or <u>memo</u> (only for internal documents) precedes the front matter and identifies the report by title, the person or persons to whom it is being sent, and the reason it was written, as shown on page 217.

FRONT MATTER
Title page (218)
Abstract (219)
Table of contents (220)
List of figures
List of tables
Foreword
Preface
List of abbreviations and symbols

BODY
Executive summary (221–22)
Introduction (223–25)
Text (including headings) (226–30)
Conclusions (231–32)
Recommendations (231–32)
Explanatory notes
References (or Works Cited) (233)

BACK MATTER
Appendixes
Bibliography
Glossary
Index

Front Matter

The front matter serves several functions: It gives <u>readers</u> a general idea of the writer's <u>purpose</u>; it gives an overview of the type of information in the report; and it lists where specific information is covered in the report. Not all formal reports include every element of front matter described here. A title page and table of contents are usually mandatory, but the scope of the report and its intended audience determine whether the other elements are included.

Title Page.   Although the formats of title pages may vary, they often include the following items:

- *The full title of the report.* The title describes the topic, <u>scope</u>, and purpose of the report, as described in <u>titles</u>.
- *The name of the writer(s), principal investigator(s), or compiler(s).* Sometimes contributors identify themselves by their job title in the organization or by their tasks in contributing to the report (Olivia Jones, Principal Investigator).
- *The date or dates of the report.* For one-time reports, the date shown is the date the report is distributed. For periodic reports (monthly, quarterly, or yearly), the subtitle shows the period that the report covers. Elsewhere on the title page, the date shown is the date the report is distributed.
- *The name of the organization for which the writer(s) works.*
- *The name of the organization to which the report is being submitted.* This information is included if the report is written for a customer or client.

The title page, as in the example on page 218, although unnumbered, is considered page i. The back of the title page, which is blank and unnumbered, is considered page ii, and the abstract falls on page iii. The body of the report begins with Arabic number 1, and a new chapter or large section typically begins on a new right-hand (odd-numbered) page. Reports with printing on only one side of each sheet can be numbered consecutively regardless of where new sections begin. Center page numbers at the bottom of each page throughout the report.

Abstract.   An <u>abstract</u>, which normally follows the title page, highlights the major points of the report, as shown on page 219, enabling readers to decide whether to read the report.

Table of Contents.   A <u>table of contents</u> lists all the major sections or <u>headings</u> of the report in their order of appearance, as shown on page 220, along with their page numbers.

List of Figures.   When a report contains more than five figures, list them, along with their page numbers, in a separate section, beginning on a new page immediately following the table of contents. Number figures consecutively with Arabic numbers. Figures include all <u>visuals</u>

contained in the report—<u>drawings</u>, <u>photographs</u>, <u>maps</u>, charts, and <u>graphs</u>.

List of Tables.   When a report contains more than five <u>tables</u>, list them, along with their titles and page numbers, in a separate section immediately following the list of figures (if there is one). Number tables consecutively with Arabic numbers.

Foreword.   A foreword is an optional introductory statement about a formal report or book that is written by someone other than the author(s). The foreword author is usually an authority in the field or an executive of the organization sponsoring the report. That author's name and affiliation appear at the end of the foreword, along with the date it was written. The foreword generally provides background information about the publication's significance and places it in the context of other works in the field. The foreword precedes the preface when a work has both.

Preface.   The preface, another type of optional introductory statement, is written by the author(s) of the formal report. It may announce the work's purpose, scope, and <u>context</u> (including any special circumstances leading to the work). A preface may also specify the audience for a work, contain acknowledgments of those who helped in its preparation, and cite permission obtained for the use of copyrighted works. See also <u>copyright</u>.

List of Abbreviations and Symbols.   When the report uses numerous <u>abbreviations</u> and symbols that readers may not be able to interpret, the front matter may include a section that lists symbols and abbreviations with their meanings.

Body

The body is the section of the report that describes in detail the methods and procedures used to generate the report, demonstrates how results were obtained, describes the results, draws conclusions, and, if appropriate, makes recommendations.

Executive Summary.   The body of the report begins with the <u>executive summary</u> (if included), which provides a more complete overview of the report than an abstract does. As shown on pages 221–22, the executive summary states the report's purpose, provides background information, and describes the scope of the report; it also summarizes conclusions and recommendations.

Introduction.   The <u>introduction</u> gives readers any general information, such as the report's purpose and scope, necessary to understand the detailed information in the rest of the report (see pages 223–25).

Text.   The text of the body presents, as appropriate, the details of how the topic was investigated, how a problem was solved, what alternatives were explored, and how the best choice among them was selected. This information is enhanced by the use of visuals, tables, and references that both clarify the text and persuade the reader.

Conclusions.   The <u>conclusions</u> section pulls together the results of the research and interprets the findings of the report, as shown on pages 231–32.

Recommendations.   Recommendations, which are sometimes combined with the conclusions, as is true on pages 231–32, state what course of action should be taken based on the earlier arguments and conclusions of the study. The recommendations section may state, for example, "We should pursue new markets in . . ." or "I recommend we expand our marketing efforts on the Internet by. . . ."

Explanatory Notes.   Occasionally, reports contain notes that amplify terms or points for some readers that would be a distraction for others. If such notes are not included as footnotes on the page where the term or point appears, they may appear in a final "Notes" section.

References (or Works Cited).   A list of references or works cited appears in a separate section if the report refers to material in, or quotes directly from, a published work or other research sources, including online sources. If your employer has a preferred reference style, follow it; otherwise, use one of the guidelines provided in the entry <u>documenting sources</u>. For a relatively short report, place the references at the end of the body of the report, as shown on page 233. For a report with a number of sections or chapters, place the reference section at the end of each major section or chapter. In either case, title the reference or works-cited section as such and begin it on a new page. If a particular reference appears in more than one section or chapter, repeat it in full in each appropriate reference section. See also <u>plagiarism</u> and <u>quotations</u>.

Back Matter

The back matter of a formal report contains supplementary material, such as where to find additional information about the topic (bibliography), and expands on certain subjects (appendixes). Other back-matter elements define the terms used (glossary) and provide information on how to easily locate information in the report (index). For very large formal reports, back-matter sections may be individually numbered.

Appendixes.   An <u>appendix</u> clarifies or supplements the body with information that is too detailed or lengthy for the primary audience but that is relevant to secondary audiences.

Bibliography.   A <u>bibliography</u> is an alphabetical list of all sources that were consulted (not just those cited) in researching the report. A bibliography is not necessary if the reference listing contains a complete list of sources.

Glossary.   A <u>glossary</u> is an alphabetical list of specialized terms used in the report and their definitions.

Index.   An index is an alphabetical list of all the major topics and subtopics discussed in the report. It cites the page numbers where discussion of each topic can be found and allows readers to find information on topics quickly and easily. The index is always the final section of a report. See also <u>indexing</u>.

DIGITAL TIPS   **CREATING STYLES AND TEMPLATES**

In most word-processing programs, you can create styles — sets of formatting characteristics for text elements such as headings, paragraphs, and lists — that allow you to automate much of the work of formatting your report. Once you have specified your styles, save them as a template and use it each time you create a formal report. For step-by-step instructions, see *<bedfordstmartins.com/alredbus>* and select *Digital Tips*, "Creating Styles and Templates."

Sample Formal Report

Figure F–6 shows the typical sections of a formal report. Keep in mind that the number and arrangement of the elements vary, depending on the specific subject and requirements of an organization or a client.

CGF Aircraft Corporation
Memo

To: Members of the Ethics and Business Conduct Committee   *SL*
From: Susan Litzinger, Director of Ethics and Business Conduct
Date: March 4, 2005
Subject: Reported Ethics Cases, 2004

Enclosed is "Reported Ethics Cases: Annual Report, 2004." This
report, required by CGF Policy CGF-EP-01, contains a review of the
ethics cases handled by CGF ethics officers and managers during
2004, the first year of our Ethics Program.

Identifies topic

The ethics cases reported are analyzed according to two categories:
(1) major ethics cases, or those potentially involving serious violations of company policy or illegal conduct, and (2) minor ethics
cases, or those that do not involve serious policy violations or illegal
conduct. The report also examines the mode of contact in all of the
reported cases and the disposition of the substantiated major ethics
cases.

Briefly sum-
marizes
content

It is my hope that this report will provide the Committee with the
information needed to assess the effectiveness of the first year of
CGF's Ethics Program and to plan for the coming year. Please let me
know if you have any questions about this report or if you need any
further information. I may be reached at (555) 211-2121 and by
e-mail at sl@cgf.com.

Offers
contact
information

Enc.

FIGURE F–6. Formal Report (Cover Memo). Reprinted and adapted by permission of
Susan Litzinger, a student at Pennsylvania State University, Altoona.

F

Full title

REPORTED ETHICS CASES
2004 Annual Report

Author's
name and
job title

Prepared by Susan Litzinger
Director of Ethics and Business Conduct

Report Distributed March 4, 2005

Prepared for
The Ethics and Business Conduct Committee
CGF Aircraft Corporation

Company
name

No page
number

FIGURE F–6. Formal Report (*continued*) (Title Page)

Reported Ethics Cases — 2004

ABSTRACT

This report examines the nature and disposition of 3,458 ethics cases handled companywide by CGF Aircraft Corporation's ethics officers and managers during 2004. The purpose of this annual report is to provide the Ethics and Business Conduct Committee with the information necessary for assessing the effectiveness of the Ethics Program's first year of operation. Records maintained by ethics officers and managers of all contacts were compiled and categorized into two main types: (1) major ethics cases, or cases involving serious violations of company policies or illegal conduct, and (2) minor ethics cases, or cases not involving serious policy violations or illegal conduct. This report provides examples of the types of cases handled in each category and analyzes the disposition of 30 substantiated major ethics cases. Recommendations for planning for the second year of the Ethics Program are (1) continuing the channels of communication now available in the Ethics Program, (2) increasing financial and technical support for the Ethics Hotline, (3) disseminating the annual ethics report in some form to employees to ensure employee awareness of the company's commitment to uphold its Ethics Policies and Procedures, and (4) implementing some measure of recognition for ethical behavior to promote and reward ethical conduct.

Summarizes purpose

Methods and scope

Conclusions and recommendations

Lowercase Roman numerals used on front matter pages.

iii

FIGURE F–6. Formal Report (*continued*) (Abstract)

Reported Ethics Cases — 2004

Uniform
heading
styles

TABLE OF CONTENTS

F

ABSTRACT   iii

EXECUTIVE SUMMARY   1

INTRODUCTION   3

Indented
subheads

    Ethics and Business Conduct Policies and Procedures   3
    Confidentiality Issues   4
    Documentation of Ethics Cases   4
    Major/Minor Category Definition and Examples   5

ANALYSIS OF REPORTED ETHICS CASES   6

Page number
for each
entry

    Reported Ethics Cases, by Major/Minor Category   6
    Major Ethics Cases   6
    Minor Ethics Cases   8
    Mode of Contact   9

CONCLUSIONS AND RECOMMENDATIONS   11

WORKS CITED   13

iv

FIGURE F-6. Formal Report (*continued*) (Table of Contents)

Reported Ethics Cases — 2004

EXECUTIVE SUMMARY

States purpose

This report examines the nature and disposition of the 3,458 ethics cases handled by the CGF Aircraft Corporation's ethics officers and managers during 2004. The purpose of this report is to provide CGF's Ethics and Business Conduct Committee with the information necessary for assessing the effectiveness of the first year of the company's Ethics Program.

Effective January 1, 2004, the Ethics and Business Conduct Committee (the Committee) implemented a policy and procedures for the administration of CGF's new Ethics Program. The purpose of the Ethics Program, established by the Committee, is to "promote ethical business conduct through open communication and compliance with company ethics standards." The Office of Ethics and Business Conduct was created to administer the Ethics Program. The director of the Office of Ethics and Business Conduct, along with seven ethics officers throughout the corporation, was given the responsibility for the following objectives:

Provides background information

- Communicate the values and standards for CGF's Ethics Program to employees.

- Inform employees about company policies regarding ethical business conduct.

- Establish companywide channels for employees to obtain information and guidance in resolving ethics concerns.

- Implement companywide ethics-awareness and education programs.

Employee accessibility to ethics information and guidance was available through managers, ethics officers, and an ethics hotline.

Major ethics cases were defined as those situations potentially involving serious violations of company policies or illegal conduct. Examples of major ethics cases included cover-up of defective workmanship or use of defective parts in products; discrimination in hiring and promotion; involvement in monetary or other kickbacks; sexual harassment; disclosure of proprietary or company information; theft; and use of corporate Internet resources for inappropriate purposes, such as conducting personal business, gambling, or access to pornography.

Describes scope

1

FIGURE F–6. Formal Report (*continued*) (Executive Summary)

F

Reported Ethics Cases—2004

Minor ethics cases were defined as including all reported concerns not classified as major ethics cases. Minor ethics cases were classified as informational queries from employees, situations involving coworkers, and situations involving management.

Summarizes conclusions

The effectiveness of CGF's Ethics Program during the first year of implementation is most evidenced by (1) the active participation of employees in the program and the 3,458 contacts employees made regarding ethics concerns through the various channels available to them, and (2) the action taken in the cases reported by employees, particularly the disposition of the 30 substantiated major ethics cases. Disseminating information about the disposition of ethics cases, particularly information about the severe disciplinary actions taken in major ethics violations, sends a message to employees that unethical or illegal conduct will not be tolerated.

Includes recommendations

Based on these conclusions, recommendations for planning the second year of the Ethics Program are (1) continuing the channels of communication now available in the Ethics Program, (2) increasing financial and technical support for the Ethics Hotline, the most highly utilized mode of contact in the ethics cases reported in 2004, (3) disseminating this report in some form to employees to ensure their awareness of CGF's commitment to uphold its Ethics Policies and Procedures, and (4) implementing some measure of recognition for ethical behavior, such as an "Ethics Employee of the Month" award to promote and reward ethical conduct.

Executive summary is about 10 percent of report length

2

FIGURE F–6. Formal Report (*continued*) (Executive Summary)

Reported Ethics Cases — 2004

INTRODUCTION

Opening states purpose

This report examines the nature and disposition of the 3,458 ethics cases handled companywide by CGF's ethics officers and managers during 2004. The purpose of this report is to provide the Ethics and Business Conduct Committee with the information necessary for assessing the effectiveness of the first year of CGF's Ethics Program. Recommendations are given for the Committee's consideration in planning for the second year of the Ethics Program.

Ethics and Business Conduct Policies and Procedures

Subheads signal shifts in topic

Effective January 1, 2004, the Ethics and Business Conduct Committee (the Committee) implemented Policy CGF-EP-01 and Procedure CGF-EP-02 for the administration of CGF's new Ethics Program. The purpose of the Ethics Program, established by the Committee, is to "promote ethical business conduct through open communication and compliance with company ethics standards" (CGF, "Ethics and Conduct").

The Office of Ethics and Business Conduct was created to administer the Ethics Program. The director of the Office of Ethics and Business Conduct, along with seven ethics officers throughout CGF, was given the responsibility for the following objectives:

- Communicate the values, standards, and goals of CGF's Ethics Program to employees.

- Inform employees about company ethics policies.

List identifies key points

- Provide companywide channels for employee education and guidance in resolving ethics concerns.

- Implement companywide programs in ethics awareness, education, and recognition.

- Ensure confidentiality in all ethics matters.

Employee accessibility to ethics information and guidance became the immediate and key goal of the Office of Ethics and Business Conduct in its first year of operation. The following channels for contact were set in motion during 2004:

3

FIGURE F–6. Formal Report *(continued)* (Introduction)

Reported Ethics Cases — 2004

- Managers throughout CGF received intensive ethics training; in all ethics situations, employees were encouraged to go to their managers as the first point of contact.

- Ethics officers were available directly to employees through face-to-face or telephone contact, to managers, to callers using the ethics hotline, and by e-mail.

- The Ethics Hotline was available to all employees, 24 hours a day, 7 days a week, to anonymously report ethics concerns.

Confidentiality Issues

CGF's Ethics Policy ensures confidentiality and anonymity for employees who raise genuine ethics concerns. Procedure CGF-EP-02 guarantees appropriate discipline, up to and including dismissal, for retaliation or retribution against any employee who properly reports any genuine ethics concern.

Documentation of Ethics Cases

The following requirements were established by the director of the Office of Ethics and Business Conduct as uniform guidelines for the documentation by managers and ethics officers of all reported ethics cases:

- Name, position, and department of individual initiating contact, if available

Includes
detailed   - Date and time of contact
methods
- Name, position, and department of contact person

- Category of ethics case

- Mode of contact

- Resolution

Managers and ethics officers entered the required information in each reported ethics case into an ACCESS database file, enabling efficient retrieval and analysis of the data.

4

FIGURE F–6. **Formal Report** (*continued*) (Introduction)

Reported Ethics Cases — 2004

Major/Minor Category Definition and Examples

Major ethics cases were defined as those situations potentially involving serious violations of company policies or illegal conduct. Procedure CGF-EP-02 requires notification of the Internal Audit and the Law Departments in serious ethics cases. The staffs of the Internal Audit and the Law Departments assume primary responsibility for managing major ethics cases and for working with the employees, ethics officers, and managers involved in each case.

Examples of situations categorized as major ethics cases:

- Cover-up of defective workmanship or use of defective parts in products
- Discrimination in hiring and promotion
- Involvement in monetary or other kickbacks from customers for preferred orders
- Sexual harassment
- Disclosure of proprietary customer or company information
- Theft
- Use of corporate Internet resources for inappropriate purposes, such as conducting private business, gambling, or gaining access to pornography

Organized by decreasing order of importance

Minor ethics cases were defined as including all reported concerns not classified as major ethics cases. Minor ethics cases were classified as follows:

- Informational queries from employees
- Situations involving coworkers
- Situations involving management

5

FIGURE F–6. Formal Report (*continued*) (Introduction)

Reported Ethics Cases—2004

ANALYSIS OF REPORTED ETHICS CASES

Reported Ethics Cases, by Major/Minor Category

CGF ethics officers and managers companywide handled a total of 3,458 ethics situations during 2004. Of these cases, only 172, or 5 percent, involved reported concerns of a serious enough nature to be classified as major ethics cases (see Figure 1). Major ethics cases were defined as those situations potentially involving serious violations of company policy or illegal conduct.

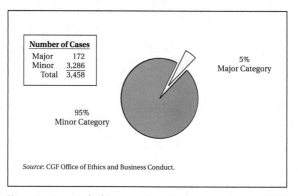

Number of Cases	
Major	172
Minor	3,286
Total	3,458

5%
Major Category

95%
Minor Category

Source: CGF Office of Ethics and Business Conduct.

Figure 1.   Reported ethics cases, by major/minor category in 2004.

Major Ethics Cases

Of the 172 major ethics cases reported during 2004, 57 percent, upon investigation, were found to involve unsubstantiated concerns. Incomplete information or misinformation most frequently was discovered to be the cause of the unfounded concerns of misconduct in 98 cases. Forty-four cases, or 26 percent of the total cases reported, involved incidents partly substantiated by ethics officers as serious misconduct; however, these cases

6

Text introduces figure

Number and title identify figure

F

Reported Ethics Cases — 2004

were discovered to also involve inaccurate information or unfounded issues of misconduct.

Only 17 percent of the total number of major ethics cases, or 30 cases, were substantiated as major ethics situations involving serious ethical misconduct or illegal conduct (CGF, "2004 Ethics Hotline Results") (see Figure 2).

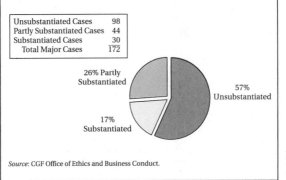

Unsubstantiated Cases	98
Partly Substantiated Cases	44
Substantiated Cases	30
Total Major Cases	172

26% Partly Substantiated

57% Unsubstantiated

17% Substantiated

Source: CGF Office of Ethics and Business Conduct.

Identifies source of information

Figure 2.   Major ethics cases in 2004.

Of the 30 substantiated major ethics cases, seven remain under investigation at this time, and two cases are currently in litigation. Disposition of the remainder of the 30 substantiated reported ethics cases included severe disciplinary action in five cases: the dismissal of two employees and the demotion of three employees. Seven employees were given written warnings, and nine employees received verbal warnings (see Figure 3).

7

FIGURE F–6. Formal Report (*continued*) (Body)

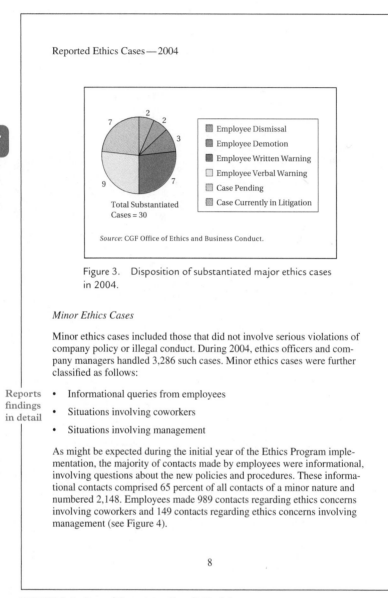

Reported Ethics Cases—2004

Total Substantiated Cases = 30

Employee Dismissal
Employee Demotion
Employee Written Warning
Employee Verbal Warning
Case Pending
Case Currently in Litigation

Source: CGF Office of Ethics and Business Conduct.

Figure 3.   Disposition of substantiated major ethics cases in 2004.

Minor Ethics Cases

Minor ethics cases included those that did not involve serious violations of company policy or illegal conduct. During 2004, ethics officers and company managers handled 3,286 such cases. Minor ethics cases were further classified as follows:

Reports
findings
in detail

- Informational queries from employees

- Situations involving coworkers

- Situations involving management

As might be expected during the initial year of the Ethics Program implementation, the majority of contacts made by employees were informational, involving questions about the new policies and procedures. These informational contacts comprised 65 percent of all contacts of a minor nature and numbered 2,148. Employees made 989 contacts regarding ethics concerns involving coworkers and 149 contacts regarding ethics concerns involving management (see Figure 4).

8

FIGURE F–6. Formal Report (*continued*) (Body)

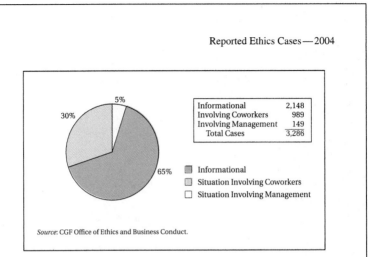

Reported Ethics Cases—2004

Informational	2,148
Involving Coworkers	989
Involving Management	149
Total Cases	3,286

■ Informational
■ Situation Involving Coworkers
□ Situation Involving Management

Source: CGF Office of Ethics and Business Conduct.

Figure 4.   Minor ethics cases in 2004.

Mode of Contact

The effectiveness of the Ethics Program rested on the dissemination of information to employees and the provision of accessible channels through which employees could gain information, report concerns, and obtain guidance. Employees were encouraged to first go to their managers with any ethical concerns, because those managers would have the most direct knowledge of the immediate circumstances and individuals involved.

Other channels were put into operation, however, for any instance in which an employee did not feel able to go to his or her manager. The ethics officers companywide were available to employees through telephone conversations, face-to-face meetings, and e-mail contact. Ethics officers also served as contact points for managers in need of support and assistance in handling the ethics concerns reported to them by their subordinates.

The Ethics Hotline became operational in mid-January 2004 and offered employees assurance of anonymity and confidentiality. The Ethics Hotline was accessible to all employees on a 24-hour, 7-day basis. Ethics officers companywide took responsibility on a rotational basis for handling calls reported through the hotline.

9

Reported Ethics Cases — 2004

In summary, ethics information and guidance was available to all employees during 2004 through the following channels:

- Employee to manager
- Employee telephone, face-to-face, and e-mail contact with ethics officer
- Manager to ethics officer
- Employee Hotline

The mode of contact in the 3,458 reported ethics cases was as follows (see Figure 5):

- In 19 percent of the reported cases, or 657, employees went to managers with concerns.
- In 9 percent of the reported cases, or 311, employees contacted an ethics officer.
- In 5 percent of the reported cases, or 173, managers sought assistance from ethics officers.
- In 67 percent of the reported cases, or 2,317, contacts were made through the Ethics Hotline.

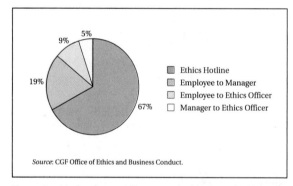

Source: CGF Office of Ethics and Business Conduct.

Figure 5.   Mode of contact in reported ethics cases in 2004.

10

In the left margin:

F

Bulleted lists help organize and summarize information

Reported Ethics Cases — 2004

CONCLUSIONS AND RECOMMENDATIONS

Pulls together findings

The effectiveness of CGF's Ethics Program during the first year of implementation is most evidenced by (1) the active participation of employees in the program and the 3,458 contacts employees made regarding ethics concerns through the various channels available to them, and (2) the action taken in the cases reported by employees, particularly the disposition of the 30 substantiated major ethics cases.

One of the 12 steps to building a successful Ethics Program identified by Frank Navran in *Workforce* magazine is an ethics communication strategy. Navran explains that such a strategy is crucial in ensuring

Uses sources for support

that employees have the information they need in a timely and usable fashion and that the organization is encouraging employee communication regarding the values, standards and the conduct of the organization and its members. (Navran 119)

The 3,458 contacts by employees during 2004 attest to the accessibility and effectiveness of the communication channels that exist in CGF's Ethics Program.

An equally important step in building a successful ethics program is listed by Navran as "Measurements and Rewards," which he explains as follows:

In most organizations, employees know what's important by virtue of what the organization measures and rewards. If ethical conduct is assessed and rewarded, and if unethical conduct is identified and dissuaded, employees will believe that the organization's principals mean it when they say the values and code of ethics are important. (Navran 121)

Disseminating information about the disposition of ethics cases, particularly information about the severe disciplinary actions taken in major ethics violations, sends a message to employees that unethical or illegal conduct will not be tolerated. Making public the tough-minded actions taken in cases of ethical misconduct provides "a golden opportunity to make other employees aware that the behavior is unacceptable and why" (Ferrell and Gardiner 129).

Interprets findings

11

FIGURE F–6. Formal Report (*continued*) (Conclusions and Recommendations)

Reported Ethics Cases — 2004

With these two points in mind, I offer the following recommendations for consideration for plans for the Ethics Program's second year:

Recommends specific steps

- Continuation of the channels of communication now available in the Ethics Program

- Increased financial and technical support for the Ethics Hotline, the most highly utilized mode of contact in the reported ethics cases in 2004

- Dissemination of this report in some form to employees to ensure employees' awareness of CGF's commitment to uphold its Ethics Policy and Procedures

- Implementation of some measure of recognition for ethical behavior, such as an "Ethics Employee of the Month," to promote and reward ethical conduct

To ensure that employees see the value of their continued participation in the Ethics Program, feedback is essential. The information in this annual review, in some form, should be provided to employees. Knowing that the concerns they reported were taken seriously and resulted in appropriate action by Ethics Program administrators would reinforce employee involvement in the program. While the negative consequences of ethical misconduct contained in this report send a powerful message, a means of communicating the *positive* rewards of ethical conduct at CGF should be implemented. Various options for recognition of employees exemplifying ethical conduct should be considered and approved.

Links recommendations to company goal

Continuation of the Ethics Program's successful 2004 operations, with the implementation of the above recommendations, should ensure the continued pursuit of the Ethics Program's purpose: "to promote a positive work environment that encourages open communication regarding ethics and compliance issues and concerns."

12

FIGURE F–6. Formal Report (*continued*) (Conclusions and Recommendations)

Reported Ethics Cases—2004

WORKS CITED

CGF. "Ethics and Conduct at CGF Aircraft Corporation." 1 Jan. 2004.

 11 Feb. 2005. <www.cgfac.com/aboutus/ethics.html>.

---. "2004 Ethics Hotline Investigation Results." 15 Jan. 2005. 11 Feb.

 2005. <www.cgfac.com/html/ethics.html>.

Ferrell, O. C., and Gareth Gardiner. <u>In Pursuit of Ethics: Tough</u>

 <u>Choices in the World of Work</u>. Springfield, IL: Smith Collins,

 1991.

Kelley, Tina. "Corporate Prophets, Charting a Course to Ethical

 Profits." <u>New York Times</u> 8 Feb. 1998: BU12.

Navran, Frank. "12 Steps to Building a Best-Practices Ethics

 Program." <u>Workforce</u> Sept. 1997: 117–22.

13

FIGURE F–6. Formal Report (*continued*) (Works Cited)

format

Format refers to both the organization of information in a document and the physical arrangement of information on the page.

In one sense, format refers to the fact that some types of job-related writing, such as <u>formal reports</u> and <u>correspondence</u>, are characterized by conventions that govern the scope and placement of information. For example, in formal reports, the <u>table of contents</u> precedes the preface but follows the title page and the <u>abstract</u>. Likewise, although variations exist, parts of letters—such as inside address, salutation, and complimentary closing—typically are arranged in standard patterns.

Format also refers to the general physical appearance (as discussed in <u>layout and design</u>) of a finished document, whether printed or electronic. See also <u>e-mail</u> and <u>Web design</u>.

former / latter

Former and *latter* should be used to refer to only two items in a sentence or paragraph.

* The president and his aide emerged from the conference, the *former* looking nervous and the *latter* looking glum.

Because these terms make the reader look to previous material to identify the reference, they complicate reading and are best avoided.

forms design

Forms provide an economical and uniform way to gather, record, and evaluate data. They help respondents provide necessary information in the form of standardized answers that are easy for you to evaluate and tabulate. Figures F–7 and F–8 are two examples of forms.

Preparing a Form

An effective form makes it easy for one person to supply information and for another person to retrieve, record, and interpret that information. Ideally, a form should be self-explanatory to someone seeing it for the first time. When preparing a form, determine the kind of information you are seeking and arrange the questions in a logical order. See also <u>questionnaires</u>.

Annual Reappointment Form   Effective July 1, 20___ to June 30, 20___

CHILDREN'S MEDICAL CENTER
1735 Chapel Street
Toledo, Ohio 43692

NAME:

List appointments or offices held, teaching positions, independent studies in medical or dental societies or other medical organizations, and any other professional recognitions you would like to have included in your file:

_____

_____   Open-
                                                              ended
_____   ques-
                                                              tions
_____

_____

_____

_____

Do you wish a change in your privileges? Yes ☐ No ☐ If so, specify: Labeled boxes

Have there been any changes in your board specialties? Yes ☐ No ☐
        If yes: Date of Change _____
                Specialty Board _____

Signature _____
Date _____   Signature
                                   and date

WHITE: Committee Chair   BLUE: Human Resources   Routing
PINK: Employee   instructions

FIGURE F–7. Form (for Staff Reappointment)

Choosing Online or Paper.   Many organizations are moving their forms online. Forms especially well suited for online use include job applications, conference or seminar registrations, medical records, and order forms. Web-based and other online forms both standardize respondents' interfaces and link to databases that tabulate and interpret data. Online forms ensure that the form will be completed correctly

104-M S A

Section 125 Flexible Spending Account (FSA) Claim Form

Form
title

Employee Name: _____

Social Security Number: _____-____-_____

Writing
lines

Name of Employer: _____

Employee Signature: _____

Instruc-
tions

Complete section below for medical, dental, or vision reimbursement

CLAIM TYPE I: MEDICAL CARE ACCOUNT

Amount of Expense Incurred: $_____

Dates of Services: From: _____ To: _____

Instruc-
tions

Complete section below for reimbursement of care for your dependent provided by a child-care facility, adult dependent-care center, or caretaker

CLAIM TYPE II: DEPENDENT-CARE ACCOUNT

Amount of Expense Incurred: $_____

Name of Dependent-Care Provider: _____

Provider Social Security or Federal ID Number: _____-____-_____

Mail or fax form with documentation to:
Specialized Benefit Services, Inc.
P. O. Box 498
Framingham, MA 01702
Fax: (508) 877-1182
For additional claim forms: www.sbsclaims.com

Mailing
and contact
information

FIGURE F–8. Form (for a Medical Claim)

because their programs do not accept a form until all the necessary fields are completed. In addition, using online forms can eliminate the problems associated with distributing and collecting forms. However, using online forms can be difficult for people with limited computer literacy or access, so consider your <u>readers</u> carefully before opting to collect your responses online. See also <u>Web design</u>.

Writing Instructions.   Place instructions at the beginning of the form or at the beginning of each section of the form and use <u>headings</u> or other design elements, such as the boldface type and shading in Figure F–8, to attract the readers' attention. When necessary, place instructions for distributing the various copies of multiple-copy forms at the bottom of the form and repeat them on every copy of the form, as in Figure F–7. Instructions for mailing or faxing the form should be clearly indicated, as in Figure F–8.

Choosing Response Types.   Forms should ask questions in ways that are best suited to the types of data you hope to collect. The two main types of questions are open-ended questions and closed-ended questions.

- *Open-ended questions* allow respondents the freedom to choose their own words. Such questions are most appropriate if you wish to elicit answers you may not have anticipated (as in a complaint form) or if there are too many possible answers to use a multiple-choice format. However, the responses to open-ended questions are difficult to tabulate and analyze.
- *Closed-ended questions* provide a list of answers from which the respondent can select, limiting the range of possible responses. When you want to make sure you receive a standardized, easy-to-tabulate response, use any of the types of closed-ended questions that follow:
  - *Multiple choice*: Choose one (or sometimes more) from a preset list of options.
  - *Ranked choice*: Rank items according to preference, such as selecting vacation days or choosing job assignments.
  - *Forced choice*: Choose between two preset options, such as yes/no or male/female.

Wording Captions.   Questions are normally presented as captions. Keep them brief, specific, and to the point; avoid unnecessary repetition by combining related information under an explanatory heading.

WORDY	What make of car (or vehicle) do you drive? _____
	What year was it manufactured? _____
	What model is it? _____
	What is the body style? _____
CONCISE	Vehicle Information
	Make _____ Year _____
	Model _____ Body Style _____

If a requested date is other than the date on which the form is being filled out, the caption should read, for example, "Effective date" or "Date issued," rather than simply "Date." (See Figure F–7.) As in all writing, put yourself in your reader's place and imagine what sort of requests would be clear.

Sequencing Data.   At the top of the form, clearly indicate preliminary information, such as the name of your organization, the title of your form, and any reference number. In the main portion of the form, include the entries you need to obtain the necessary data. At the end of the form, include space for a signature and a date.

Arrange requests for information in an order that will be the most logical to the person filling out the form.

- Sequence entries to fit the subject matter. For instance, a form requesting reimbursement for travel expenses would logically begin with the first day of the week (or month) and end with the last day of the appropriate period.

- If the response to one item is based on the response to another item, be sure the items appear in the correct order.

- Group requests for related information together whenever possible.

- For ease of reading, arrange entries from left to right and from top to bottom.

  ETHICS NOTE Information gathered on forms can be of a sensitive or personal nature, so make sure to present questions in a way that is not invasive or illegal. Unless otherwise indicated on the form, the person filling out the form should have the expectation of confidentiality. If you are concerned about issues of confidentiality or legality, check your organization's policy or seek your instructor's advice. ✦

Designing a Form

You can design computer-generated forms specific to your needs with form-design-and-management software or with word-processing software. However you prepare the final version of a form, pay particular attention to design details, especially to the placement of entry lines and the amount of space allowed for responses.

Entry Lines.   A form can be designed so that the person filling it out provides information on a writing line, in a writing block, or in square boxes. A *writing line* is simply a rule with a caption, as shown in Figure F–8.

A *writing block* is essentially the same as a writing line, except that each entry is enclosed in a ruled block, making it impossible for the respondent to associate a caption with the wrong line, as shown in Figure F–9. Some writing blocks arrange the captions horizontally, as in Figure F–9; other writing blocks list captions vertically, as shown in Figure F–10.

When it is possible to anticipate all likely responses, you can make the form easy to fill out by writing the question on the form, supplying a labeled box for each possible answer, and asking the respondent to

FIGURE F–9. Writing Block for a Form

FIGURE F–10. Vertical Captions for a Form

check the appropriate boxes. Such a design also makes it easy to tabulate the data. Be sure your questions are both simple and specific.

● Would your department order another MAX-PC?   Yes ☐ No ☐

Spacing. Provide enough space to enable the person filling out the form to enter the data. Insufficient writing space makes it difficult for people to respond, resulting in responses that are hard to read. Reading responses that are too tightly spaced or that snake around the side of the form can cause eyestrain and errors. To ensure the usability of the form, have a coworker fill one out before printing the final version.

fortuitous / fortunate

When an event is *fortuitous*, it happens by chance or accident and without plan. Such an event may be lucky, unlucky, or neutral.

● My encounter with the general manager in Denver was entirely *fortuitous*; I had no idea he was there.

When an event is *fortunate*, it happens by good fortune or happens favorably.

● Our chance meeting had a *fortunate* outcome.

fragments (*see* sentence fragments)

functional shift

Many words shift easily from one **part of speech** to another, depending on how they are used. When they do, the process is called a *functional shift*, or a shift in function.

● It takes ten minutes to *walk* from the sales office to the accounting department. However, the long *walk* from the sales office to the accounting department reduces efficiency.
[*Walk* shifts from **verb** to **noun**.]

● I talk to the Chicago office on the *phone* every day. He was concerned about the office *phone* expenses. He will *phone* the home office from London.
[*Phone* shifts from noun to **adjective** to verb.]

- *After* we discuss the project, we will begin work. *After* lengthy discussions, we began work. The partners worked well together forever *after*.
[*After* shifts from <u>conjunction</u> to <u>preposition</u> to <u>adverb</u>.]

<u>Jargon</u> is often the result of functional shifts. In hospitals, for example, an *attending physician* is referred to simply as the "attending" (a shift from an adjective to a noun). Likewise, in nuclear plant construction, a *reactor containment building* is called a "containment" (a shift from an adjective to a noun). Do not shift the function of a word indiscriminately merely to shorten a phrase or an expression. See also <u>affectation</u> and <u>conciseness</u>.

F

G

garbled sentences

A garbled sentence is one that is so tangled with structural and grammatical problems that it cannot be repaired. Garbled sentences often result from an attempt to squeeze too many ideas into one sentence.

- My job objectives are accomplished by my having a diversified background which enables me to operate effectively and efficiently, consisting of a degree in computer science, along with twelve years of experience, including three years in Staff Engineering-Packaging sets a foundation for a strong background in areas of analyzing problems and assessing economical and reasonable solutions.

Do not try to patch such a sentence; rather, analyze the ideas it contains, list them in a logical sequence, and then construct one or more entirely new sentences.

An analysis of the preceding example yields the following five ideas:

- My job requires that I analyze problems to find economical and workable solutions.
- My diversified background helps me accomplish my job.
- I have a computer-science degree.
- I have twelve years of job experience.
- Three of these years have been in Staff Engineering-Packaging.

Using those five ideas—together with <u>parallel structure</u>, <u>sentence variety</u>, <u>subordination</u>, and <u>transition</u>—the writer might have described the job as follows:

- My job requires that I analyze problems to find economical and workable solutions. Both my education and experience help me achieve this goal. Specifically, I have a computer-science degree and twelve years of job experience, three of which have been in the Staff Engineering-Packaging Department.

See also <u>clarity</u>, <u>mixed constructions</u>, and <u>sentence construction</u>.

gender

In English grammar, *gender* refers to the classification of <u>nouns</u> and <u>pronouns</u> as masculine, feminine, and neuter. The gender of most words can be identified only by the choice of the appropriate pronoun (*he*, *she*, *it*). Only these pronouns and a select few nouns (*buck/doe*) or noun forms (*heir/heiress*) reflect gender. Many such nouns have been replaced by single terms for both sexes. See also <u>biased language</u> and <u>he/she</u>.

Gender is important to writers because they must be sure that nouns and pronouns within a grammatical construction agree in gender.

(ESL) TIPS FOR ASSIGNING GENDER

The English language has an almost complete lack of gender distinctions. That can be confusing for a nonnative speaker of English whose native language may assign gender. In the few cases in which English does make a gender distinction, there is a close connection between the assigning of gender and the sex of the subject. The few instances in which gender distinctions are made in English are summarized as follows:

Subject pronouns	he/she
Object pronouns	him/her
Possessive adjectives	his/her(s)
Some nouns	king/queen, boy/girl, bull/cow, etc.

When a noun, such as *doctor*, can refer to a person of either sex, you need to know the sex of the person to which the noun refers to determine the gender-appropriate pronoun.

- The doctor gave *her* patients advice. [Doctor is female.]
- The doctor gave *his* patients advice. [Doctor is male.]

When the sex of the noun antecedent is unknown, be sure to follow the guidelines for nonsexist writing in the entry <u>biased language</u>. (*Note:* Some English speakers refer to vehicles and countries as *she*, but contemporary usage favors *it*.)

A pronoun, for example, must agree with its noun antecedent in gender. We must refer to a woman as *she* or *her*, not as *it*; to a man as *he* or *him*, not as *it*; to a barn as *it*, not as *he* or *she*. See also **agreement**.

general and specific methods of development

General and specific **methods of development** proceed either from general information to specific details or from specific information to a general conclusion. As with all methods of development, rarely does a writer rely on only one method throughout a document. Most documents blend methods and use combinations of methods.

General to Specific

The general-to-specific development (see Figure G–1) is especially useful for teaching **readers** about something with which they are not

Subject: Expanding Our Supplier Base for Computer Chips

General statement

On the basis of information presented at the supply meeting on April 14, we recommend that the company initiate relationships with computer-chip manufacturers. Several events make such an action necessary.

Supporting information

Our current supplier, Datacom, is experiencing growing pains and is having difficulty shipping the product on time. Specifically, we can expect a reduction of between 800 and 1,000 units per month for the remainder of this fiscal year. The number of units should stabilize at 15,000 units per month thereafter.

Specific details

Domestic demand for our computers continues to grow. Demand during the current fiscal year is up 500,000 units over the last fiscal year. Our sales projections for the next five years show that demand should peak next year at about 830,000 units given the consumer demand, which will increase exponentially.

Finally, our expansion into Eastern European and Asian markets will require additional shipments of at least 750,000 units per quarter for the remainder of this fiscal year. Sales Department projections put global computer sales at double that rate, or 1,500,000 units per fiscal year, for the next five years.

FIGURE G–1. General-to-Specific Method of Development

familiar because you can begin with generally known information and lead to new and increasingly specific details. This method can also be used to support a general statement with facts or examples that validate the statement. For example, if you begin your writing with the general statement "Companies that diversify are more successful than those that do not," you could follow that statement with examples and statistics that prove to the reader that companies that diversify are, in fact, more successful than companies that do not.

A memo or short report organized entirely in a general-to-specific sequence discusses only one point. All other information in the document supports the general statement, as in Figure G–1 from a memo about locating additional computer-chip suppliers.

Specific to General

Specific-to-general development is especially useful when you wish to persuade skeptical readers of a general principle with an accumulation of specific details and evidence that reach a logical <u>conclusion</u>. It carefully builds its case, often with examples and analogies in addition to facts or statistics, and does not actually make its point until the end. (See also <u>order-of-importance method of development</u>.) Figure G–2 is an example of the specific-to-general method of development.

Specific details	Recently, a government agency studied the use of passenger-side air bags in 4,500 accidents involving nearly 7,200 front-seat passengers of the vehicles involved. Nearly all the accidents occurred on routes that had a speed limit of at least 40 mph. Only 20 percent of the adult front-seat passengers were riding in vehicles equipped with passenger-side air bags. Those riding in vehicles not equipped with passenger-side air bags were more than twice as likely to be killed as passengers riding in vehicles that were so equipped.
General conclusion	A conservative estimate is that 40 percent of the adult front-seat passenger-vehicle deaths could be prevented if all vehicles came equipped with passenger-side air bags. Children, however, should always ride in the backseat because other studies have indicated that a child can be killed by the deployment of an air bag. If you are an adult front-seat passenger in an accident, your chances of survival are far greater if the vehicle in which you are riding is equipped with a passenger-side air bag.

FIGURE G–2. Specific-to-General Method of Development

global communication

The prevalence of global communication technology, international trade agreements, and the emergence of Europe as a giant single market means that the ability to communicate with audiences from varied cultural backgrounds is essential. The audiences for such communications include clients, business partners, and colleagues.

Entries such as **meetings** and **résumés** in this book are based on U.S. cultural patterns. The treatment of such topics might be very different in other cultures where leadership styles, persuasive strategies, and even legal constraints differ. As illustrated in **international correspondence,** organizational patterns, forms of courtesy, and ideas about efficiency can vary significantly from culture to culture. What might be seen as direct and efficient in the United States could be seen as blunt and even impolite in other cultures. The reasons behind these differing ways of viewing communication are complex. Those who study cultures have found various ways to measure cultural differences, such as individual versus group orientation, the importance of saving face, and conceptions of time.

Anthropologist Edward T. Hall, a pioneer in cross-cultural research, developed the concept of "contexting" to assess the predominant communication style of a culture.* By "context," Hall means how much or how little an individual assumes another person understands about a subject under discussion. In a very low-context communication, the participants assume they share little knowledge and must communicate in great detail. Low-context cultures tend to assume little prior knowledge on the part of those with whom they communicate; thus thorough documentation is important—written agreements (contracts) are expected, and rules are spelled out in detail.

In a high-context communication, the participants already understand the context and thus do not feel a need to exchange much background information. High-context cultures depend on shared history (or context) to relate to each other. Thus, words and written contracts are not so important, while personal relationships are paramount. Of course, no culture is entirely high or low context; rather, these concepts can be helpful in understanding the predominant communication style of a particular culture.†

Obviously, cultural differences and the reasons behind them are often so subtle that only someone who is very familiar with a culture

---

*Edward Twitchell Hall and Mildred Reed Hall, *Understanding Cultural Differences: Germans, French and Americans* (Yarmouth, Maine: Intercultural Press, 1990).

†Gerald J. Alred, "Teaching in Germany and the Rhetoric of Culture," *Journal of Business and Technical Communication* 11.3 (July 1997): 353–78.

can explain the effect those differences may have on others from that culture. For that reason, it is best to consult with someone from your intended audience's culture during **preparation** for writing or for a **presentation**. Although many resources are available, the following books are useful starting points:

Andrews, Deborah C. *Technical Communication in the Global Community*. 2nd ed. Upper Saddle River, N.J.: Prentice-Hall, 2000.

Scollon, Ron, and Suzanne Wong Scollon. *Intercultural Communication: A Discourse Approach*. 2nd ed. Cambridge, Mass.: Basil Blackwell, 2001.

Varner, Iris, and Linda Beamer. *Intercultural Communication in the Global Workplace*. 3rd ed. New York: McGraw-Hill/Irwin, 2004.

Victor, David A. *International Business Communication*. New York: HarperCollins, 1992.

Writer's Checklist: Communicating Globally

☑ Acknowledge diversity within your organization. Discussing the differing cultures within your company or region will reinforce the idea that people can interpret verbal and nonverbal communications differently.

☑ Invite global and intercultural communication experts to speak at your workplace. Companies in your area may have employees who could be resources for cultural discussions.

☑ Understand that the key to effective communication with global audiences is recognizing that cultural differences, despite the challenges they may present, offer opportunities for growth for both you and your organization.

☑ Consult with someone from your intended audience's culture. Many phrases, gestures, and visual elements are so subtle that only someone who is very familiar with the culture can explain the effect they may have on others from that culture. See also **global graphics**.

WEB LINK **INTERCULTURAL RESOURCES**

Intercultural Press is a source of publications aimed at specific cultures as well as a wide variety of subjects from cross-cultural theory to international business. For links to this and other resources for global communication, see <bedfordstmartins.com/alredbus> and select *Links for Handbook Entries*.

global graphics

In the global business and technological environment, <u>graphs</u> and other <u>visuals</u> require the same careful attention given to other aspects of <u>global communication</u>. The complex cultural connotations of visuals challenge writers to think beyond their own experience as illustrated in Figures G–3 and G–4.

Symbols, images, and even colors are not free from cultural associations—they depend on <u>context</u>, and context is culturally determined. For instance, in North America, a red cross is commonly used as a symbol for first aid or hospital. In Muslim countries, however, a cross (red or otherwise) represents Christianity, whereas a crescent (usually green) signifies first aid or hospital. A manual for export to Honduras could indicate "caution" by using a picture of a person touching a finger below the eye. In France, however, that gesture means "You can't fool me."

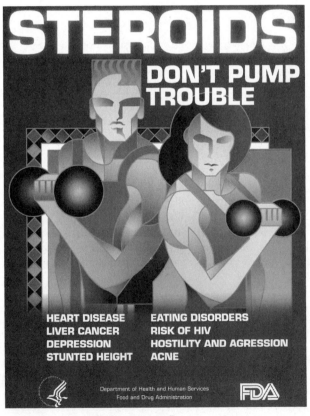

FIGURE G–3. Graphic for a U.S. Audience

FIGURE G–4. Graphic for a Global
Audience

G

Figure G–3 shows a graphic warning weight lifters against the use of steroids. The drawings may be appropriate for U.S. audiences and others. However, the image would be highly inappropriate in many cultures where the image of a partially clothed man and woman in close proximity would be contrary to deeply held cultural beliefs and even laws about the public depiction of men and women. Figure G–4, however, depicts weight lifters by using a neutral icon that avoids the connotations associated with more realistic images of people.

These examples suggest why international groups, such as the International Organization for Standardization (ISO), have established agreed-upon symbols, such as those shown in Figure G–5, designed for public signs, guidebooks, and manuals.

Careful attention to the connotations that visual elements may have for a diverse audience makes translations easier, prevents embarrassment, and earns respect for the company and its products and services. See also **presentations**.

FIGURE G–5. ISO Symbols

Writer's Checklist: Communicating with Global Graphics

- ☑ Consult with someone or test your use of graphics with those from your intended audience's country who can recognize and explain the effect that visual elements will have on **readers**.

- ☑ Organize visual information for the intended audience. For example, North Americans tend to read visuals from left to right in clockwise rotation. Middle Eastern cultures read visuals from right to left in counterclockwise rotation.

- ☑ Be sure that the graphics have no unintended religious implications.

- ☑ Carefully consider how you depict people in visuals. Nudity in advertising, for example, is generally acceptable in Europe but much less so in North America and Asia. In some cultures, showing even isolated bare body parts can alienate audiences.

- ☑ Use outlines or neutral abstractions to represent human beings. For example, use stick figures and avoid representing men and women.

- ☑ Examine how you display body positions in signs and visuals. Body positioning can carry unintended cultural meanings very different from your own. For example, some Middle Eastern cultures regard the display of the soles of one's shoes to be disrespectful and offensive.

- ☑ Choose neutral colors (or those you know are appropriate) for your graphics. Generally, black-and-white and gray-and-white illustrations work well. Colors can be problematic. For example, in North America, Europe, and Japan, red indicates danger. In China, however, red symbolizes joy. In Europe and North America, blue generally has a positive connotation; in Japan, blue represents villainy.

- ☑ Check your use of punctuation marks, which are as language specific as symbols. For example, in North America, the question mark generally represents the need for information or the help function in a computer manual or program. In many countries, that symbol has no meaning at all.

- ☑ Create simple visuals and use consistent labels for all visual items. In most cultures, simple shapes with fewer elements are easier to read.

- ☑ Explain the meaning of icons or symbols. Include a **glossary** to explain technical symbols that cannot be changed, such as company logos.

glossaries

A glossary is an alphabetical list of definitions of specialized terms used in a **formal report**, a manual, or other long document.

If you are writing a document that will go to readers who are not familiar with specialized or technical terms you use, you may want to include a glossary. If you do, keep the entries concise and be sure they are written in language that all your readers can understand.

- *Amortize*: Write off an expenditure by prorating over a specific period.

Arrange the terms alphabetically, with each entry beginning on a new line. The definitions then follow the terms, dictionary style. In a formal report, the glossary appears after the appendix(es) and bibliography, and it begins on a new page.

Including a glossary does not relieve you of the responsibility of defining terms in the text that your reader will not know when those terms are first mentioned.

G

gobbledygook

Gobbledygook is writing that suffers from an overdose of traits guaranteed to make it stuffy, pretentious, and wordy. Such traits include the overuse of big and mostly abstract words, affectation (especially long variants), buzzwords, inappropriate jargon, clichés, euphemisms, stacked modifiers, and vague words. Gobbledygook is writing that attempts to sound official (officialese), legal (legalese), or scientific; it tries to make a "natural elevation of the geosphere's outer crust" out of a molehill. Consider the following statement from an auto repair release form.

LEGALESE	I hereby authorize the above repair work to be done along with the necessary material and hereby grant you and/or your employees permission to operate the car or truck herein described on streets, highways, or elsewhere for the purpose of testing and/or inspection. An express mechanic's lien is hereby acknowledged on above car or truck to secure the amount of repairs thereto.
DIRECT	You have my permission to do the repair work listed on this work order and to use the necessary material. You may drive my vehicle to test its performance. I understand that you will keep my vehicle until I have paid for all repairs.

See also clarity, conciseness, and word choice.

good / well

Good is an <u>adjective</u>, and *well* is an <u>adverb</u>.

ADJECTIVE   Janet presented a *good* plan.
ADVERB   The plan was presented *well*.

Well also can be used as an adjective to describe health (a *well* child, *wellness* programs). See also <u>bad/badly</u>.

G

grammar

Grammar is the systematic description of the way words work together to form a coherent language. In that sense, it is an explanation of the structure of a language. However, grammar is popularly taken to mean the set of rules that governs how a language ought to be spoken and written. In that sense, it refers to the <u>usage</u> conventions of a language.

Those two meanings of grammar—how the language functions and how it ought to function—are easily confused. To clarify the distinction, consider the expression *ain't*. Unless used intentionally to add colloquial flavor, *ain't* is unacceptable because its use is considered nonstandard. Yet taken strictly as a **part of speech**, the term functions perfectly well as a verb. Whether it appears in a declarative sentence (I ain't going) or an interrogative sentence (Ain't I going?), it conforms to the normal pattern for all verbs in the English language. Although readers may not approve of its use, they cannot argue that it is ungrammatical in such sentences.

To achieve <u>clarity</u>, you need to know both grammar (as a description of the way words work together) and the conventions of usage. Knowing the conventions of usage helps you select the appropriate over the inappropriate word or expression. (See also <u>word choice</u>.) A knowledge of grammar helps you diagnose and correct problems arising from how words and phrases function in relation to one another. For example, knowing that certain words and phrases function to modify other words and phrases gives you a basis for correcting those <u>modifiers</u> that are not doing their job. Understanding <u>dangling modifiers</u> helps you avoid or correct a construction that obscures the intended meaning. In short, an understanding of grammar and its special terminology is valuable chiefly because it enables you to recognize and correct problems so that you can communicate clearly and precisely.

For a complete list of grammar entries, see the Contents by Topic.

WEB LINK **GETTING HELP WITH GRAMMAR**

For helpful Web sites and grammar exercises, see *<bedfordstmartins.com/
alredbus>* and select *Links for Handbook Entries* and *Exercise Central.*

---

graphs

DIRECTORY
Line Graphs   253
Bar Graphs   255
Pie Graphs   256
Picture Graphs   258
Writer's Checklist: Creating Graphs   258

A graph presents numerical data in visual form and offers several advantages over presenting data within the text or in <u>tables</u>. Trends,
movements, distributions, comparisons, and cycles are more readily apparent in graphs than they are in tables. However, although graphs present data in a more comprehensible form than tables do, they are less
precise. For that reason, graphs are often accompanied by tables that
give exact data. The types of graphs described in this entry include line
graphs, bar graphs, pie graphs, and picture graphs. For advice on integrating graphs within text, see <u>visuals</u>; for information about using presentation graphics, see **presentations**.

Line Graphs

A line graph shows the relationship between two variables or sets of
numbers by plotting points in relation to two axes drawn at right angles.
The vertical axis usually represents amounts, and the horizontal axis
usually represents increments of time. Line graphs that portray more
than one set of variables (double-line graphs) allow for comparisons
between two sets of statistics for the same period of time. You can
emphasize the difference between the two lines by shading the space
between them, as shown in Figure G–6.

  ◼ ETHICS NOTE Be especially careful to proportion the vertical and
horizontal scales so that they give a precise presentation of the data that
is free of visual distortion. To do otherwise is not only inaccurate but
potentially unethical. (See <u>ethics in writing</u>.) In Figure G–7, the graph

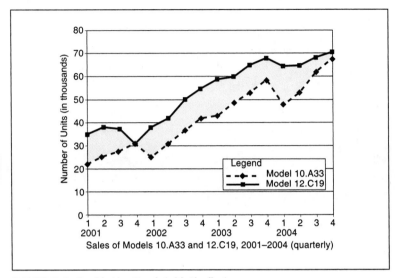

FIGURE G–6. Double-Line Graph (with Shading)

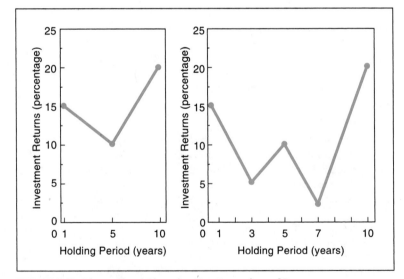

FIGURE G–7. Distorted and Distortion-Free Expressions of Data on the left gives the appearance of a slight decline followed by a steady increase in investment returns because the scale is compressed, with some of the years selectively omitted. The graph on the right represents the trend more accurately because the years are evenly distributed without omissions. ✦

Bar Graphs

Bar graphs consist of horizontal or vertical bars of equal width, scaled in length to represent some quantity. They are commonly used to show (1) quantities of the same item at different times, (2) quantities of different items at the same time, and (3) quantities of the different parts of an item that make up a whole (in which case, the segments of the bar graph must total 100 percent). The horizontal graph in Figure G–8 shows the quantities of different items for the same period of time.

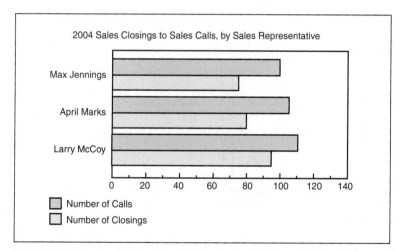

FIGURE G–8. Bar Graph (Quantities of Different Items During a Fixed Period)

Bar graphs can also show the different portions of an item that make up the whole, as shown in Figure G–9. Such a bar graph is divided according to the appropriate proportions of the subcomponents of the item. This type of graph, also called a *column graph* when constructed vertically, can indicate multiple items. Where such items represent parts of a whole, as in Figure G–9, the segments in the bar graph must total 100 percent. Note that in addition to labels, each subdivision of a bar

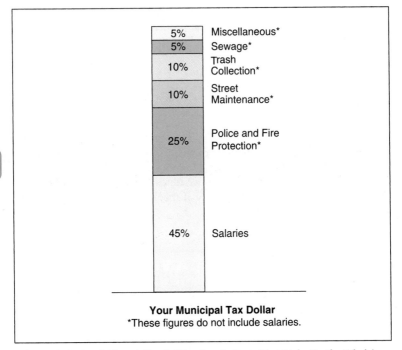

FIGURE G–9. Bar (Column) Graph (Showing the Parts That Make Up the Whole)

graph must be marked clearly by color, shading, or cross-hatching, with a key or labels that identify the subdivisions represented. Be aware that three-dimensional graphs can make sections seem larger than the amounts they represent.

Pie Graphs

A pie graph presents data as wedge-shaped sections of a circle. The circle equals 100 percent, or the whole, of some quantity, and the wedges represent how the whole is divided. Many times, the data shown in a bar graph could also be depicted in a pie graph. For example, Figure G–9 shows percentages of a whole in bar-graph form. In Figure G–10, the same data are converted into a pie graph, dividing "Your Municipal Tax Dollar" into wedge-shaped sections that represent percentages. Pie graphs also provide a quicker way of presenting information that can be shown in a table; in fact, a table with a more detailed breakdown of the same information often accompanies a pie graph.

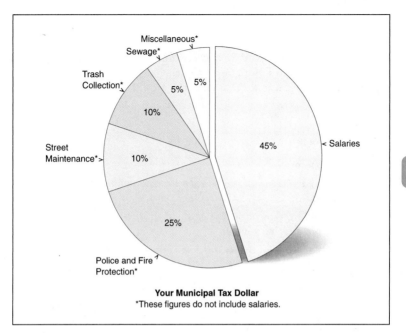

FIGURE G–10. Pie Graph (Showing Percentages of the Whole)

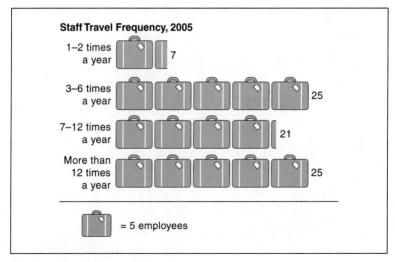

FIGURE G–11. Picture Graph

Picture Graphs

Picture graphs are modified bar graphs that use pictorial symbols of the item portrayed. Each symbol corresponds to a specified quantity of the item, as shown in Figure G–11 on page 257. Note that for precision and clarity, the picture graph includes the total quantity following the symbols.

Writer's Checklist: Creating Graphs

G

FOR ALL GRAPHS

☑ Use, as needed, a key or legend that lists and defines symbols (see Figure G–6).

☑ Include a source line under the graph at the lower left when the data comes from another source.

☑ Place explanatory footnotes directly below the figure caption or label (see Figures G–9 and G–10).

FOR LINE GRAPHS

☑ Indicate the zero point of the graph (the point where the two axes intersect).

☑ Insert a break in the scale if the range of data shown makes it inconvenient to begin at zero.

☑ Divide the vertical axis into equal portions, from the least amount at the bottom (or zero) to the greatest amount at the top.

☑ Divide the horizontal axis into equal units from left to right. If a label is necessary, center it directly beneath the scale.

☑ Make all lettering read horizontally if possible, although the caption or label for the vertical axis is usually positioned vertically (see Figure G–6).

FOR BAR GRAPHS

☑ Show either horizontal bars or vertical columns.

☑ Differentiate among the types of data each bar or column or part of a bar or column represents by color, shading, or cross-hatching.

☑ Avoid three-dimensional graphs when they make sections seem larger than the amounts they represent.

FOR PIE GRAPHS

☑ Make sure that the complete circle is equivalent to 100 percent.

☑ Sequence the wedges clockwise from largest to smallest, beginning at the 12 o'clock position, whenever possible.

Writer's Checklist: Creating Graphs (continued)

☑ Limit the number of items in the pie graph to avoid clutter and to ensure that the slices are thick enough to be clear.

☑ Give each wedge a distinctive color, pattern, shade, or texture.

☑ Label each wedge with its percent value and keep all call-outs (labels that identify the wedges) horizontal.

☑ Detach a slice, as shown in Figure G–10, if you wish to draw attention to a particular segment of the pie graph.

FOR PICTURE GRAPHS

☑ Use picture graphs to add interest to **presentations** and documents, such as **newsletters**, that are aimed at wide audiences.

☑ Choose symbols that are easily recognizable. See also **global graphics**.

☑ Let each symbol represent a specific number of units.

☑ Indicate larger quantities by using more symbols, instead of larger symbols, because relative sizes are difficult to judge accurately.

H

he / she

The use of either *he* or *she* to refer to both sexes excludes half of the population. (See also **biased language**.) To avoid this problem, you could use the phrases *he or she* and *his or her*. (Whoever is appointed will find *his or her* task difficult.) However, *he or she* and *his or her* are clumsy when used repeatedly, as are *he/she* and similar constructions. One solution is to reword the sentence to use a plural **pronoun**; if you do, change the **nouns** or other pronouns to match the plural form.

- *Administrators* *their jobs* *they understand*
  ~~The administrator~~ cannot do ~~his or her job~~ until ~~he or she~~
  ~~understands~~ the organization's culture.

In other cases, you may be able to avoid using a pronoun altogether.

- *the*
  Whoever is appointed will find ~~his or her~~ task difficult.

Of course, a pronoun cannot always be omitted without changing the meaning of a sentence.

Another solution is to omit troublesome pronouns by using the imperative **mood**.

- *Submit all* *s*
  ~~Everyone must submit his or her~~ expense report by Monday.

headers and footers

A *header* in a **report** or other document appears at the top of each page, and a *footer* appears at the bottom of each page. Headers or footers may include such elements as the document name, the topic (or subtopic) of a section, the date of the document, the page number, and other identifying information to help **readers** keep track of where they are in the document. Keep your headers and footers concise—too much information in them can create visual clutter.

Although the information included in headers and footers varies greatly from one organization to the next, the header and footer shown in Figure H–1 are fairly typical. For headers used in letters and memos, see **correspondence**.

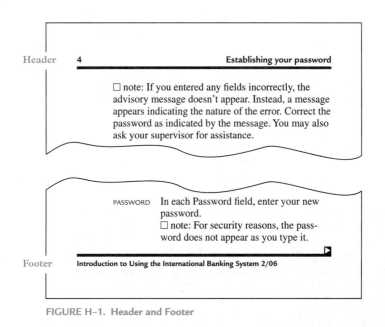

FIGURE H–1. Header and Footer

headings

Headings (also called *heads*) are titles or subtitles within the body of a document that help **readers** find information, divide the material into comprehensible segments, highlight the main topics, and signal topic changes. A **formal report** or **proposal** may need several levels of headings to indicate major divisions, subdivisions, and even smaller units. However, avoid using more than three levels of headings. See also **layout and design**.

Headings typically represent the major topics of a document. In a short document, you can use the major divisions of your outline as headings; in a longer document, you may need to use both major and minor divisions.

General Heading Style

No one format for headings is correct. Often a company settles on a standard format, which everyone in the company follows. Sometimes a customer for whom a report or proposal is being prepared requires a particular format. In the absence of specific guidelines, follow the system illustrated in Figure H–2. See also <u>layout and design</u>.

H

First-
level
head

DISTRIBUTION CENTER LOCATION REPORT

The committee initially considered 30 possible locations for the proposed new distribution center. Of these, 20 were eliminated almost immediately for one reason or another (unfavorable zoning regulations, inadequate transportation infrastructure, etc.). Of the remaining ten locations, the committee selected for intensive study the three that seemed most promising: Chicago, Minneapolis, and Salt Lake City. We have now visited these three cities, and our observations and recommendations follow.

Second-
level
head

CHICAGO
Of the three cities, Chicago presently seems to the committee to offer the greatest advantages, although we wish to examine these more carefully before making a final recommendation.

Third-
level
head

Selected Location
Though not at the geographic center of the United States, Chicago is the demographic center to more than three-quarters of the U.S. population. It is within easy reach of our corporate headquarters in New York. And it is close to several of our most important suppliers of components and raw materials—those, for example, in Columbus, Detroit, and St. Louis. Several factors were considered essential to the location, although some may not have had as great an impact on the selection. . . .

Fourth-
level
heads

Air Transportation.   Chicago has two major airports (O'Hare and Midway) and is contemplating building a third. Both domestic and international air-cargo service are available. . . .

Sea Transportation.   Except during the winter months when the Great Lakes are frozen, Chicago is an international seaport. . . .

Rail Transportation.   Chicago is served by the following major railroads. . . .

FIGURE H–2. Headings Used in a Document

Decimal Numbering System

Some documents, such as **policies and procedures,** benefit from the decimal numbering system for ease of cross-referencing sections. The decimal numbering system uses a combination of numbers and decimal points to differentiate among levels of headings. The following example shows the correspondence between different levels of headings and the decimal numbers used:

1. FIRST-LEVEL HEADING
    1.1 Second-level heading
    1.2 Second-level heading
        1.2.1 Third-level heading
        1.2.2 Third-level heading
            1.2.2.1 Fourth-level heading
            1.2.2.2 Fourth-level heading
    1.3 Second-level heading
2. FIRST-LEVEL HEADING

Although decimal headings are indented in an outline or a **table of contents,** they are flush with the left margins when they function as headings in the body of a report. Every heading starts on a new line, with an extra line of space above and below the heading.

Writer's Checklist: Using Headings

☑ Use headings to signal a new topic. Use a lower-level heading to indicate a new subtopic within the larger topic.

☑ Make headings concise but specific enough to be informative, as in Figure H–2.

☑ Avoid too many or too few headings or levels of headings; too many clutter a document, and too few fail to provide recognizable structure.

☑ Ensure that headings at the same level are of relatively equal importance and have **parallel structure**.

☑ Subdivide sections only as needed; when you do, try to subdivide them into at least two lower-level headings.

☑ Do not leave a heading as the final line of a page. If two lines of text cannot fit below a heading, start the section at the top of the next page.

☑ Do not allow a heading to substitute for discussion; the text should read as if the heading were not there.

hyphens

The hyphen (-) serves both to link and to separate words. The hyphen, for example, joins **compound words** (able-bodied, self-contained, self-esteem) and forms compound **numbers** from twenty-one through ninety-nine and fractions when they are written out (three-quarters). Two consecutive hyphens indicate a **dash**.

Hyphens Used with Modifiers

Two- and three-word <u>modifiers</u> that express a single thought are hyphenated when they precede a <u>noun</u>.

- It was a *well-written* report.

However, a modifying phrase is not hyphenated when it follows the noun it modifies.

- The report was *well written.*

If each of the words can modify the noun without the aid of the other modifying word or words, do not use a hyphen.

- a *new laser* printer

If the first word is an <u>adverb</u> ending in *-ly*, do not use a hyphen.

- a *privately held* company

A hyphen is always used as part of a letter or number modifier.

- 9-inch, A-frame

In a series of unit modifiers that all have the same term following the hyphen, the term following the hyphen need not be repeated throughout the series; for greater smoothness and brevity, use the term only at the end of the series.

- The third-, fourth-, and fifth-floor rooms were recently painted.

Hyphens Used with Prefixes and Suffixes

A hyphen is used with a <u>prefix</u> when the root word is a proper noun.

- pre-Columbian, anti-American, post-Newtonian

A hyphen may be used when the prefix ends and the root word begins with the same vowel.

- re-enter, anti-inflammatory

A hyphen is used when *ex-* means "former."

- ex-president, ex-spouse

A hyphen may be used to emphasize a prefix.

- He is *anti-change.*

The <u>suffix</u> *-elect* is hyphenated.

- president-elect

Hyphens and Clarity

The presence or absence of a hyphen can alter the meaning of a sentence.

AMBIGUOUS   We need a biological waste management system.

That sentence could mean one of two things: (1) We need a system to manage "biological waste," or (2) We need a "biological" system to manage waste.

CLEAR   We need a *biological-waste* management system.

CLEAR   We need a biological *waste-management* system.

To avoid confusion, some words and modifiers should always be hyphenated. *Re-cover* does not mean the same thing as *recover*, for example; the same is true of *re-sent* and *resent*, *re-form* and *reform*, *re-sign* and *resign*.

Other Uses of the Hyphen

Hyphens should be used between letters showing how a word is spelled.

- In his e-mail, he misspelled *believed* as b-e-l-e-i-v-e-d.

A hyphen can stand for *to* or *through* between letters and numbers (pages 44-46, the Detroit-Toledo Expressway, A-L and M-Z).

Writer's Checklist: Using Hyphens to Divide Words

☑ Do not divide one-syllable words.

☑ Divide words at syllable breaks, which you can determine with a dictionary.

☑ Do not divide a word if only one letter would remain at the end of a line or if fewer than three letters would start a new line.

☑ Do not divide a word at the end of a page; carry it over to the next page.

☑ If a word already has a hyphen in its spelling, divide the word at the existing hyphen.

☑ Do not use a hyphen to break a URL or an e-mail address at the end of a line because it may confuse readers who could assume that the hyphen is part of the address.

I

idioms

An idiom is a group of words that has a special meaning apart from its literal meaning. Someone who "runs for office" in the United States, for example, need not be an athlete. The same candidate would "stand for office" in the United Kingdom. Because such expressions are specific to a culture, nonnative speakers must memorize them.

Idioms are often constructed with <u>prepositions</u> that follow <u>adjectives</u> (*similar to*), <u>nouns</u> (*need for*), and <u>verbs</u> (*approve of*). Some idioms can change meaning slightly with the preposition used, as in *agree to* ("consent") and *agree with* ("in accord"). The following are typical idioms that give nonnative speakers trouble.

call off [cancel]	hand in [submit]
call on [visit a client]	hand out [distribute]
cross out [draw a line through]	keep on [continue]
do over [repeat a task]	leave out [omit]
drop in on [visit unexpectedly]	look up [research a subject]
figure out [solve a problem]	put off [postpone]
find out [discover information]	run into [meet by chance]
get through with [finish]	run out of [deplete supply]
give up [quit]	watch out for [be careful]

Idioms often provide helpful shortcuts. In fact, they can make writing more natural and vigorous. Avoid them, however, if your writing is to be translated into another language or read in other English-speaking countries. Because no system can fully explain such usages, you must check <u>dictionaries</u> or usage guides to interpret their meaning. See also <u>international correspondence</u> and <u>English as a second language</u>.

WEB LINK **PREPOSITIONAL IDIOMS**

For links to helpful lists of common pairings of prepositions with nouns, verbs, and adjectives, see <*bedfordstmartins.com/alredbus*> and select *Links for Handbook Entries*.

illegal / illicit

If something is *illegal*, it is prohibited by law. If something is *illicit*, it is prohibited by either law or custom. *Illicit* behavior may or may not be *illegal*, but it does violate social convention or moral codes and therefore usually has a clandestine or immoral <u>connotation</u>. (The employee's *illicit* sexual behavior caused a scandal, but the company's attorney concluded that no *illegal* acts were committed.)

illustrations (*see* **visuals**)

imply / infer

If you *imply* something, you hint or suggest it. (Her e-mail *implied* that the project would be delayed.) If you *infer* something, you reach a conclusion based on evidence or interpretation. (The manager *inferred* from the e-mail that the project would be delayed.)

in / into

In means "inside of"; *into* implies movement from the outside to the inside. (The equipment was *in* the test chamber, so she reached *into* the chamber to adjust it.)

in order to

Most often, *in order to* is a meaningless filler phrase that is dropped into a sentence without thought. See also <u>conciseness</u>.

- ~~In order to~~ improve our profit margin, we must increase our client base. [*To* inserted at start; caret before *client base.*]

However, the phrase *in order to* is sometimes essential to the meaning of a sentence.

- If the vertical scale of a graph line would not normally show the zero point, use a horizontal break in the graph *in order to* include the zero point.

In order to also helps control the <u>pace</u> of a sentence, even when it is not essential to the meaning of the sentence.

● The committee must know the estimated costs *in order to* evaluate the feasibility of the project.

in terms of

When used to indicate a shift from one kind of language or terminology to another, the phrase *in terms of* can be useful.

● *In terms of* gross sales, the year has been relatively successful; however, *in terms of* net income, it has been discouraging.

When simply dropped into a sentence because it easily comes to mind, *in terms of* is meaningless <u>affectation</u>. See also <u>conciseness</u>.

● She was thinking ~~in terms~~ of subcontracting much of the work.

indexing

An index is an alphabetical list of all the major topics and sometimes subtopics in a written work. It cites the pages where each topic can be found and allows <u>readers</u> to find information on particular topics quickly and easily, as shown in Figure I–1. The index always comes at the very end of the work. Many Web sites also provide linked subject indexes to the content of the sites.

The key to compiling a useful index is selectivity. Instead of listing every possible reference to a topic, select references to passages where the topic is discussed fully or where a significant point is made about it.

```
monitoring programs, 27–44 ─────────── Main entry
     aquatic, 42
     ecological, 40                   Subentries
     meteorological, 37
          operational, 39
          preoperational, 37          Sub-subentries
     radiological, 30
     terrestrial, 41, 43–44           Subentries
     thermal, 27
```

FIGURE I–1. Index Entry (with Main Entry, Subentries, and Sub-subentries)

For index entries like those in Figure I–1, choose key terms that best represent a topic. Key terms are those words or phrases that a reader would most likely look for in an index. For example, the key terms in a reference to the development of legislation about environmental-impact statements would probably be *legislation* and *environmental-impact statement,* not *development.* In selecting terms for index entries, use chapter or section titles only if they include such key terms. For index entries on <u>tables</u> and <u>visuals,</u> use the words from their titles that will function as key terms a reader might seek. Create alphabetical Web site indexes from links to topics in subsites throughout the larger site.

DIGITAL TIPS CREATING AN INDEX

Word-processing software can provide a quick and efficient way to create an alphabetical subject index of your document. Review the document to identify entries: the words, phrases, figure captions, or symbols that you wish to index. Then, following your software's instructions, highlight and code these entries. In Microsoft Word, for example, you can mark a key-word and the software will automatically mark all other instances of the word. The software sorts the coded entries, eliminates duplications, and arranges them alphabetically with their page numbers in a separate section at the end of the document. You can also create headings for each alphabetic grouping of the index (A, B, C, etc.).

Your draft index will still need careful review and revisions, but using the software to create the first draft can certainly save time. For further instructions, see *<bedfordstmartins.com/alredbus>* and select *Digital Tips,* "Creating an Index."

---

indiscreet / indiscrete

Indiscreet means "lacking in prudence or sound judgment." (His public discussion of the proposed merger was *indiscreet.*) *Indiscrete* means "not divided or divisible into parts." (The separate departments, once combined, become *indiscrete.*) See also <u>discreet/discrete</u>.

individual

Individual is most appropriate when used as an <u>adjective</u> to distinguish a single person from a group. (The *individual* employee's obligations are detailed in the policy manual.) Using *individual* as a <u>noun</u> is an

affectation. Use *people* or another appropriate term. See also **persons/ people**.

- Several ~~individuals on~~ ^{members of} the committee did not vote.

ingenious / ingenuous

Ingenious means "marked by cleverness and originality." (Seon Ju's *ingenious* solution led to her promotion.) *Ingenuous* means "straightforward" or "characterized by innocence and simplicity." (The *ingenuous* co-op students bring fresh perspectives to the company.)

inquiries and responses

The purpose of writing an inquiry letter or **e-mail** is often to obtain answers to specific questions, as in Figure I–2, which shows a college student's requests for specific information from an official at a power company. Inquiries may either benefit the **reader** (as in requests for information about a product that a company has advertised) or benefit the writer (as in the student's e-mail in Figure I–2). Inquiries that primarily benefit the writer require the use of **persuasion** and special consideration of your readers' needs. See also **correspondence**.

Writing Inquiries

Inquiries need to be specific, clear, and concise in order to receive a prompt, helpful reply. To achieve those goals, keep in mind these guidelines:

- Phrase your questions so that the reader will immediately know the type of information you are seeking, why you need it, and how you will use it.
- If possible, present your questions in a numbered list to make it easy for your reader to respond to them.
- Keep the number of questions to a minimum to improve your chances of receiving a prompt response.
- Offer some inducement for the reader to respond, such as promising to share the results of what you are doing. See also **"you" viewpoint**.
- Promise to keep responses confidential, if appropriate.

From: Kathryn J. Parsons <kjp@fly.ud.edu>
To: Jane E. Metcalf <metcalf@mvpc.org>
Sent: 18 March 2005 09:23:45 -0500 (EDT)
Subject: Inquiry on Heating Systems

Dear Ms. Metcalf:

Could you please send me some information on heating systems for a computerized, energy-efficient house that a team of architecture students at the University of Dayton is designing?

The house, which contains 2,000 square feet of living space (17,600 cubic feet), meets all the requirements in your brochure "Insulating for Efficiency." We need the following information, based on the southern Ohio climate:

1. The proper-size heat pump for such a home.
2. The wattage of the supplemental electrical heating units required.
3. The estimated power consumption and rates for those units for one year.

We will be happy to send you our preliminary design report. If you have questions or suggestions, please contact me at kjp@fly.ud.edu or call 513-229-4598.

Thank you for your help.

Kathryn Parsons

FIGURE I-2. Inquiry

In the closing, thank the reader for taking the time to respond. In addition, make it convenient for the recipient to respond by providing contact information, such as a phone number or an e-mail address, as shown in Figure I-2.

Responding to Inquiries

When you receive an inquiry, determine whether you have both the information and the authority to respond. If you have received an inquiry that you feel you cannot answer, find out who can and forward the inquiry to that person. Notify the writer that you have forwarded the inquiry, as shown in Figure I-3. When an inquiry is forwarded, the

From: Jane E. Metcalf <metcalf@mvpc.org>
To: Kathryn J. Parsons <kjp@fly.ud.edu>
Sent: Mon, 21 March 2005 11:42:25 -0500 (EDT)
Subject: RE: Inquiry on Heating Systems

Dear Kathryn Parsons:

Thank you for inquiring about the heating system we recommend for use in homes designed according to the specifications outlined in our brochure "Insulating for Efficiency."

Because I cannot answer your specific questions, I have forwarded your inquiry to Michael Wang, Engineering Assistant in our Development Group. He should be able to answer the questions you have raised. You should be hearing from him shortly.

Best wishes,

Jane E. Metcalf

Jane E. Metcalf, Director of Public Information
Miami Valley Power Company
P.O. Box 1444 ~ Miamitown, OH 45733
Office 513-264-4800 ~ Fax 513-264-4889
Web ~ www.enersaving.com

FIGURE I–3. Response to an Inquiry (Indicating That It Has Been Forwarded)

person who replies should state in the first paragraph of the response why someone else is answering the original inquiry.

If you are the right person in your organization to respond, answer as promptly as you can, and be sure to answer every question asked, as shown in Figure I–4. How long and how detailed your response should be depends on the nature of the question and the information the writer provides.

From: Michael Wang <mwang@mvpc.org>
To: Kathryn J. Parsons <kjp@fly.ud.edu>
Sent: 28 March 2005 16:09:22 -0500 (EDT)
Subject: RE: Inquiry on Heating Systems

Dear Ms. Parsons:

Jane Metcalf forwarded to me your inquiry of March 18 about the house that your architecture team is designing. I can estimate the heating requirements of a typical home of 17,600 cubic feet as follows:

1. For such a home, we would generally recommend a heat pump capable of delivering 40,000 BTUs, such as our model AL-42 (17 kilowatts).
2. With the AL-42's efficiency, you don't need supplemental heating units.
3. Depending on usage, the AL-42 unit averages between 1,000 and 1,500 kilowatt-hours from December through March. To determine the current rate for such usage, check with Dayton Power and Light Company.

I can give you an answer that would apply specifically to your house based on its particular design (such as number of stories, windows, and entrances). If you send me more details, I will be happy to provide more precise figures for your interesting project.

Sincerely,

Michael Wang

Engineering Assistant
mwang@mvpc.org

FIGURE I–4. Response to an Inquiry

inside / inside of

In the phrase *inside of,* the word *of* is redundant and should be omitted.

- The switch is just inside ~~of~~ the door.

Using *inside of* to mean "in less time than" is colloquial and should be avoided in writing.

- They were finished *inside of* an hour.
  in less than

instructions

Business writers often prepare many kinds of instructions to coworkers. (See also __policies and procedures__.) Instructions that are clear and easy to follow can build goodwill because they help __readers__ complete tasks efficiently and prevent miscommunication. To write effective instructions, you must thoroughly understand the process or system you are describing. Finally, keep in mind that the most effective instructions often combine written elements and visual elements that reinforce each other. See also __process explanation__.

Writing Instructions

Consider your readers' level of knowledge. If all your readers have good backgrounds in the topic, you can use fairly specialized terms. If that is not the case, use plain language or include a __glossary__ for specialized terms that you cannot avoid.

Clear and easy-to-follow instructions are written as commands in the imperative __mood__, active __voice__, and (whenever possible) present __tense__.

- ~~The~~ insurance request ~~will be signed by the employee.~~
  Sign the

Although __conciseness__ is important in instructions, __clarity__ is essential. You can make sentences shorter by leaving out some __articles__ (*a, an, the*), some __pronouns__ (*you, this, these*), and some __verbs__, but such sentences may result in __telegraphic style__ and be harder to understand. For example, the first version of the following instruction for submitting a medical claim is confusing.

CONFUSING   Submit claim negotiated to HR with statement from attending.

CLEAR   Submit the claim to be negotiated to the Human
Resources Office with the statement of the attending
physician who prescribed the treatment.

One good way to make instructions easy to follow is to divide them into short, simple steps in their proper sequence. Steps can be organized with words (*first, next, finally*) that indicate time or sequence.

- *First*, determine the problem the customer is having with the computer. *Next*, observe the system in operation. *At that time*, question the operator until you are sure that the problem has been explained completely. *Then* analyze the problem and make any necessary adjustments.

You can also use numbers, as in the following:

- 1. Open the top cover and remove the toner cartridge.
  2. Use the green handle to lift the paper access plate.
  3. Slowly and carefully pull the paper out of the printer.

Consider using the numbered- or bulleted-list feature of your word-processing software to create sequenced steps.

Plan ahead for your reader. If the instructions in step 2 will affect a process in step 9, say so in step 2. Sometimes your instructions have to make clear that two operations must be performed simultaneously. Either state that fact in an introduction to the specific instructions or include both operations in one step.

CONFUSING   1. Hold down the CONTROL key.
2. Press the RETURN key before releasing the
CONTROL key.

CLEAR   1. While holding down the CONTROL key, press
the RETURN key.

Alert your readers to any potentially hazardous materials (or actions) before they reach the step for which the material is needed.

If your instructions involve a great many steps, break them into stages, each with a separate heading so that each stage begins again with step 1. Using headings as dividers is especially important if your reader is likely to be performing the operation as he or she reads the instructions.

Illustrating Instructions

Illustrations should be developed together with the text, especially for complex instructions that benefit from visuals that foster clarity and conciseness. Such visuals as drawings, flowcharts, maps, and photographs enable your reader to identify relationships more easily than long explanations.

Consider the <u>layout and design</u> of your instructions to most effectively integrate visuals. Highlight important visuals as well as text by making them stand out from the surrounding text. Consider using boxes and boldface or distinctive headings. Experiment with font style, size, and color to determine which devices are most effective.

The instructions in Figure I–5 guide the reader through the steps of "paper orientation" for loading a printer paper tray. Notice that the

Paper Orientation

For Tray 1, load paper with the side to be printed facing up and the top, short edge toward the printer.

Figure 1   Paper Orientation for Tray 1

For all other trays, load paper with the side to be printed facing down and the top edge toward you.

Figure 2   Paper Orientation for All Other Trays

FIGURE I–5. Illustrated Instructions

arrow and magnified view help show users how to load paper correctly into the two paper-tray feeders.

Finally, to test the accuracy and clarity of your instructions, ask someone who is not familiar with the task to follow your directions. A first-time user can spot missing steps or point out passages that should be worded more clearly.

Writer's Checklist: Writing Instructions

- ☑ Use the imperative mood and the active voice.
- ☑ Use short sentences and simple present tense as much as possible.
- ☑ Avoid **jargon** that your readers might not know, including undefined **abbreviations**.
- ☑ Do not use elegant variation (two different words for the same thing). See also **affectation**.
- ☑ Eliminate any **ambiguity**.
- ☑ Use effective visuals and highlighting devices.
- ☑ Test your instructions by having someone else follow them while you observe.

insure / ensure / assure

Insure, ensure, and *assure* all mean "make secure or certain." *Assure* refers to people, and it alone has the connotation of setting a person's mind at rest. (I *assure* you that the promotional material will arrive on time.) *Ensure* and *insure* mean "make secure from harm." Only *insure* is widely used in the sense of guaranteeing the value of life or property.

- We need all the data to *ensure* the success of the project.
- We should *insure* the contents of the warehouse.

intensifiers

Intensifiers are **adverbs** that emphasize degree, such as *very, quite, rather, such,* and *too.* Although intensifiers serve a legitimate and necessary function, unnecessary intensifiers can weaken your writing. Eliminate those that do not make an obvious contribution or replace them with specific details.

- The team was ~~quite~~ happy to ~~receive the very good news~~ *learn* that it

  had been awarded a ~~rather substantial~~ *$10,000* monetary prize for its

  design.

Some words (such as *perfect, impossible,* and *final*) do not logically permit intensification because, by definition, they do not allow degrees of comparison. Although <u>usage</u> often ignores that logical restriction, to ignore it is, strictly speaking, to defy the basic meanings of such words. See also <u>conciseness</u> and <u>equal/unique/perfect</u>.

interface

An *interface* is a surface that provides a common boundary between two bodies or areas. The bodies or areas may be physical (the *interface* of a person and a computer screen) or conceptual (the *interface* of mathematics and economics). Do not use *interface* as a substitute for the verb *cooperate, interact,* or even *work.* See also <u>affectation</u> and <u>buzzwords</u>.

interjections

An interjection is a word or phrase standing alone or inserted into a sentence to exclaim or to command attention. Grammatically, it has no connection to the sentence. An interjection can be strong (*Hey! Ouch! Wow!*) or mild (*oh, well, indeed*). A strong interjection is followed by an <u>exclamation mark</u>.

- *Wow!* Profits more than doubled last quarter.

A weak interjection is followed by a <u>comma</u>.

- *Well,* we need to rethink the proposal.

An interjection inserted into a sentence usually requires a comma before it and after it.

- We must, *indeed,* rethink the proposal.

Because they get their main expressive force from sound, interjections are more common in speech than in writing. Use them sparingly.

international correspondence

Business <u>correspondence</u> varies among cultures. Organizational patterns, persuasive strategies, forms of courtesy, formality, and ideas about efficiency vary from country to country. For example, in the United States, direct, concise correspondence may demonstrate courtesy by not wasting another person's time. In many Asian cultures, such directness and brevity may seem rude to <u>readers</u>, suggesting that the writer wishes to spend as little time as possible corresponding with the reader. Likewise, where an American writer might consider one brief letter sufficient to communicate a request, a writer in another culture may expect an exchange of three or four longer letters to pave the way for action. The features and communication styles of specific cultures are complex; the entry <u>global communication</u> provides information and resources for cross-cultural study. See also <u>global graphics</u>.

Cultural Differences in Correspondence

When you read correspondence from businesspeople in other cultures or countries, be alert to differences in such features as customary expressions, openings, and closings. Japanese business writers, for example, have traditionally used indirect openings that reflect on the season, compliment the reader's success, and offer hopes for the reader's continued prosperity. Consider as well deeper issues, such as how writers from other cultures express bad news. Japanese writers have also traditionally expressed negative messages, such as <u>refusal letters</u> indirectly to avoid embarrassing the recipient. Such differences are often based on cultural perceptions of time, face-saving, and expectations.

WEB LINK GOOGLE'S INTERNATIONAL DIRECTORY

Google's International Business and Trade Directory provides an excellent starting point for searching the Web for information related to customs, communication, and international standards. See <*bedfordstmartins.com/ alredbus*> and select *Links for Handbook Entries*.

Cross-Cultural Examples

Figures I–6 and I–7 on pages 280 and 281 are a draft and a final version of a letter written by an American businessman to a Japanese businessman. The draft in Figure I–6 does not include enough politeness strategies important to Japanese culture in the opening and closing, and it

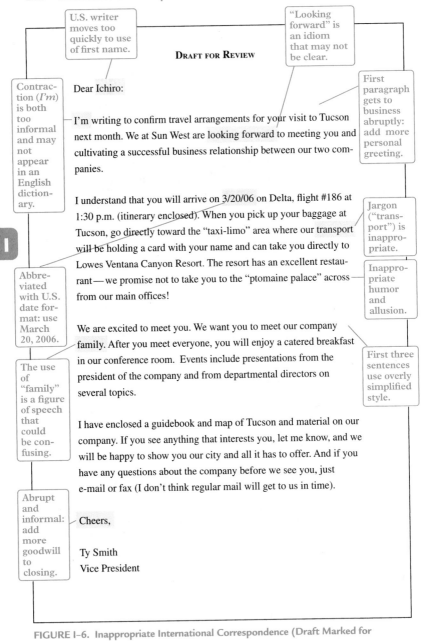

Draft for Review

U.S. writer moves too quickly to use of first name.

"Looking forward" is an idiom that may not be clear.

Contraction (*I'm*) is both too informal and may not appear in an English dictionary.

First paragraph gets to business abruptly: add more personal greeting.

Dear Ichiro:

I'm writing to confirm travel arrangements for your visit to Tucson next month. We at Sun West are looking forward to meeting you and cultivating a successful business relationship between our two companies.

I understand that you will arrive on 3/20/06 on Delta, flight #186 at 1:30 p.m. (itinerary enclosed). When you pick up your baggage at Tucson, go directly toward the "taxi-limo" area where our transport will be holding a card with your name and can take you directly to Lowes Ventana Canyon Resort. The resort has an excellent restaurant—we promise not to take you to the "ptomaine palace" across from our main offices!

Abbreviated with U.S. date format: use March 20, 2006.

Jargon ("transport") is inappropriate.

Inappropriate humor and allusion.

We are excited to meet you. We want you to meet our company family. After you meet everyone, you will enjoy a catered breakfast in our conference room. Events include presentations from the president of the company and from departmental directors on several topics.

The use of "family" is a figure of speech that could be confusing.

First three sentences use overly simplified style.

I have enclosed a guidebook and map of Tucson and material on our company. If you see anything that interests you, let me know, and we will be happy to show you our city and all it has to offer. And if you have any questions about the company before we see you, just e-mail or fax (I don't think regular mail will get to us in time).

Abrupt and informal: add more goodwill to closing.

Cheers,

Ty Smith
Vice President

FIGURE I-6. **Inappropriate International Correspondence (Draft Marked for Revision)**

Sun West Corporation, Inc.

2565 North Armadillo
Tucson, AZ 85719
Phone: (602) 555-6677
Fax: (602) 555-6678   sunwest.com

February 28, 2006

Ichiro Katsumi
Investment Director
Toshiba Investment Company
1-29-10 Ichiban-cho
Tokyo 105, Japan

Dear Mr. Katsumi:

I hope that you and your family are well and prospering in the new year. We at Sun West Corporation are very pleased that you will be coming to visit us in Tucson this month. It will be a pleasure to meet you, and we are very gratified and honored that you are interested in investing in our company.

So that we can ensure that your stay will be pleasurable, we have taken care of all of your travel arrangements. You will

- Depart Narita–New Tokyo International Airport on Delta Airlines flight #75 at 1700 on March 20, 2006.
- Arrive at Los Angeles International Airport at 1050 local time and depart for Tucson on Delta flight #186 at 1205.
- Arrive at Tucson International Airport at 1330 local time on March 20.
- Depart Tucson International Airport on Delta flight #123 at 1845 on March 27.
- Arrive in Salt Lake City, Utah, at 1040 and depart on Delta flight #34 at 1115.
- Arrive in Portland, Oregon, at 1210 local time and depart on Delta flight #254 at 1305.
- Arrive in Tokyo at 1505 local time on March 28.

If you need additional information about your travel plans or information on Sun West Corporation, please call, fax, or e-mail me directly at tsmith@ sunwest.com. That way, we will receive your message in time to make the appropriate changes or additions.

FIGURE I–7. Appropriate International Correspondence

Mr. Ichiro Katsumi   2   February 28, 2006

After you arrive in Tucson, a chauffeur from Skyline Limousines will be waiting for you at Gate 12. He or she will be carrying a card with your name, will help you collect your luggage from the baggage claim area, and will then drive you to the Loews Ventana Canyon Resort. This resort is one of the most prestigious in Tucson, with spectacular desert views, high-quality amenities, and one of the best golf courses in the city. The next day, the chauffeur will be back at the Ventana at 0900 to drive you to Sun West Corporation.

We at Sun West Corporation are very excited to meet you and introduce you to all the staff members of our hardworking and growing company. After you meet everyone, you will enjoy a catered breakfast in our conference room. At that time, you will receive a schedule of events planned for the remainder of your trip. Events include presentations from the president of the company and from departmental directors on

- The history of Sun West Corporation
- The uniqueness of our products and current success in the marketplace
- Demographic information and the benefits of being located in Tucson
- The potential for considerable profits for both our companies with your company's investment

We encourage you to read through the enclosed guidebook and map of Tucson. In addition to events planned at Sun West Corporation, you will find many natural wonders and historical sites to see in Tucson and in Arizona in general. If you see any particular event or place that you would like to visit, please let us know. We will be happy to show you our city and all it has to offer.

Again, we are very honored that you will be visiting us, and we look forward to a successful business relationship between our two companies.

Sincerely,

Ty Smith

Ty Smith
Vice President

Enclosures (2)

FIGURE I-7. Appropriate International Correspondence (*continued*) uses an inappropriately informal salutation with the recipient's first name (*Dear Ichiro:*). This draft contains <u>idioms</u> (*looking forward, company family*), <u>jargon</u> (*transport will be holding . . .*), **contractions** (*I'm, don't*), informal language (*just e-mail or fax, Cheers*), and humor and allusion (*"ptomaine palace" across from our main offices*).

Compare that letter to the one in Figure I–7, which is written in language that is literal and specific. The letter begins with concern about the recipient's family and prosperity because that opening honors traditional Japanese patterns in business correspondence. The letter is free of slang, idioms, and jargon. The sentences are shorter, bulleted lists are used to break up the paragraphs, contractions are not used, and months are spelled out.

When you are writing for international readers, rethink the ingrained habits that define how you express yourself, learn as much as you can about the cultural expectations of others, and focus on politeness strategies that demonstrate your respect for readers. Doing so will help you achieve <u>clarity</u> and mutual understanding with international readers.

Writer's Checklist: Writing International Correspondence

- ☑ Observe the guidelines for courtesy, such as those in the *Writer's Checklist: Using Tone to Build Goodwill* in **correspondence** on page 114.

- ☑ Write clear and complete sentences: Unusual word order or rambling sentences will frustrate and confuse readers. See **garbled sentences**.

- ☑ Avoid an overly simplified style that may offend or affectation that may confuse the reader. See also **English as a second language**.

- ☑ Avoid humor, irony, and sarcasm; they are easily misunderstood outside their cultural context.

- ☑ Do not use idioms, jargon, slang expressions, unusual **figures of speech**, or **allusions** to events or attitudes particular to American life.

- ☑ Consider whether necessary technical terminology can be found in abbreviated English-language dictionaries; if it cannot, carefully define such terminology.

- ☑ Do not use contractions or **abbreviations** that may not be clear to international readers.

- ☑ Avoid excessive informality, such as using first names too quickly.

- ☑ Write out **dates**, whether in the month-day-year style (June 11, 2006, not 6/11/06) used in the United States or the day-month-year style (11 June 2006, not 11/6/06) used in many other parts of the world.

☑ Specify time zones or refer to international standards, such as Greenwich Mean Time (GMT) or Coordinated Universal Time (UTC).

☑ Where possible, use international measurement standards, such as the metric system (18°C, 14 cm, 45 kg, and so on). See also **global graphics**.

☑ Ask someone from your intended audience's culture to review your draft before you complete your final **proofreading**.

Internet research (*see* **research**)

interviewing for information

The process of interviewing for information can be divided into three parts: (1) determining the proper person to interview, (2) preparing for the interview, and (3) conducting the interview.

Determining the Proper Person to Interview

Many times, your subject or **purpose** logically points to the proper person to interview for information. If you were writing about using the Web to market a software-development business, you would want to interview someone with extensive experience in Web marketing as well as someone who has built a successful business developing software. The following sources can help you determine the appropriate person to interview: (1) workplace colleagues or faculty in appropriate academic departments, (2) information from the Internet, (3) local chapters of professional societies, and (4) yellow or business pages of the local telephone directory. For advice on finding sources, see **research**.

Preparing for the Interview

Before the interview, learn as much as possible about the person you are going to interview and the organization for which he or she works. When you contact the prospective interviewee, explain who you are, why you would like an interview, the subject and purpose of the interview, and how much time it will take. You should also let your interviewee know that you will allow him or her to review your draft.

After you have made the appointment, prepare a list of questions to ask your interviewee. Avoid vague, general questions. A question such as "What do you think of the Internet?" is too general to elicit useful information. It is more helpful to ask specific but open-ended questions, such as the following: "Some local professionals in your field are making extensive use of the Internet for helping clients. How has the Internet helped your organization?"

Conducting the Interview

Arrive promptly for the interview and be prepared to guide the discussion. The following *Writer's Checklist: Interviewing Successfully* should help you to do so. During the interview, take only memory-jogging notes that will help you recall the conversation later; do not ask your interviewee to slow down so that you can take detailed notes. As the interview is reaching a close, take a few minutes to skim your notes and ask the interviewee to clarify anything that is ambiguous. Immediately after leaving the interview, use your memory-jogging notes to help you mentally review the interview and record your detailed notes. Do not postpone this step. No matter how good your memory is, you will forget some important points if you do not do this at once. See also **note-taking**.

Writer's Checklist: Interviewing Successfully

- ☑ Be pleasant but purposeful. You are there to get information, so don't be timid about asking leading questions on the subject.

- ☑ Use the list of questions you have prepared, starting with the less controversial aspects of the topic to get the conversation started and then going on to the more controversial aspects.

- ☑ Let your interviewee do most of the talking. Remember that the interviewee is the expert. See also **listening**.

- ☑ Be objective. Don't offer your opinions on the subject. You are there to get information, not to debate.

- ☑ Some answers prompt additional questions; ask them as they arise.

- ☑ Don't get sidetracked. If the interviewee strays too far from the subject, ask a specific question to direct the conversation back on track.

- ☑ If you use a tape recorder, do not let it lure you into relaxing so that you neglect to ask crucial questions.

- ☑ After thanking the interviewee, ask permission to contact him or her again to clarify a point or two as you complete your interview notes.

interviewing for a job

A job interview may last 30 minutes, an hour, or several hours. Sometimes, an initial job interview is followed by a series of additional interviews that can last a half or full day. Often, just one or two people conduct a job interview, but, at times, a group of four or more might do so. Job interviews can take place in person, by phone, or by teleconference. Because it is impossible to know exactly what to expect, it is important that you be well prepared. See also <u>application letters</u>, <u>job search</u>, and <u>résumés</u>.

Before the Interview

The interview is not a one-way communication. It presents you with an opportunity to ask questions of your potential employer. In preparation, learn everything you can about the company before the interview. Use the following questions as a guide.

- What kind of organization (e.g., nonprofit, government) is it?
- How diversified is the organization?
- Is it locally owned?
- Does it provide a product or service? If so, what kind?
- How large is the business? How large are its assets?
- Is the owner self-employed? Is the company a subsidiary of a larger operation? Is it expanding?
- How long has it been in business?
- Where will you fit in?

You can obtain information from current employees, the Internet, company publications, and the business section of back issues of local newspapers (available in the library or online). You may be able to learn the company's size, sales volume, product line, credit rating, branch locations, subsidiary companies, new products and services, building programs, and other such information from its annual reports and from publications such as *Moody's Industrials, Dun and Bradstreet, Standard and Poor's,* and *Thomas' Register,* as well as other business reference sources a librarian might suggest. Ask your interviewer about what you cannot find through your own <u>research</u>. Now is your chance to demonstrate your interest and make certain you are considering a healthy and growing company.

Try to anticipate the questions your interviewer might ask, and prepare your answers in advance. Be sure you understand a question before answering it, and avoid responding too quickly with a rehearsed answer—be prepared to answer in a natural and relaxed manner. Interviewers typically ask the following questions:

- What are your short-term and long-term occupational goals?
- Where do you see yourself five years from now?
- What are your major strengths and weaknesses?
- Do you work better with others or alone?
- How do you spend your free time?
- Describe an accomplishment you are particularly proud of.
- Why are you leaving your current job?
- Why do you want to work for this company?
- Why should I hire you?
- What salary and benefits do you expect?

Many employers use behavioral interviews. Rather than traditional, straightforward questions, the behavioral interview focuses on asking the candidate to provide examples or respond to hypothetical situations. Interviewers who use behavior-based questions are looking for specific examples from your experience. Prepare for the behavioral interview by recollecting challenging situations or problems that were successfully resolved. Examples of behavior-based questions include the following:

- Tell me about a time when you experienced conflict on a team.
- If I were your boss and you disagreed with a decision I made, what would you do?
- How have you used your leadership skills to bring about change?
- Tell me about a time when you failed.

Arrive for your interview on time, or even ten or fifteen minutes early—you may be asked to fill out an application or other paperwork before you meet your interviewer. Always bring extra copies of your résumé and samples of your work (if applicable). If you are asked to complete an application form, read it carefully before you write and proofread it when you are finished. The form provides a written record for company files and indicates to the company how well you follow directions and complete a task.

During the Interview

The interview actually begins before you are seated: What you wear and how you act make a first impression. In general, dress simply and conservatively, avoid extremes in fragrance and cosmetics, and be well-groomed.

Behavior.   First, thank the interviewer for his or her time, express your pleasure at meeting him or her, and remain standing until you are offered a seat. Then sit up straight (good posture suggests self-assurance), look directly at the interviewer, and try to appear relaxed and confident. During the interview, you may find yourself feeling a little nervous. Use that nervous energy to your advantage by channeling it into the alertness that you will need to listen and respond effectively. Do not attempt to take extensive notes during the interview, although it is acceptable to jot down a few facts and figures on a small pad. See also <u>listening</u>.

Responses.   When you answer questions, do not ramble or stray from the subject. Say only what you must to answer each question properly and then stop, but avoid giving just yes or no answers—they usually do not allow the interviewer to learn enough about you. Some interviewers allow a silence to fall just to see how you will react. The burden of conducting the interview is the interviewer's, not yours—and he or she may interpret your rush to fill a void in the conversation as a sign of insecurity. If such a silence makes you uncomfortable, be ready to ask an intelligent question about the company.

If the interviewer overlooks important points, bring them up. However, let the interviewer mention salary first, if possible. Doing so yourself may indicate that you are more interested in the money than the work. However, make sure you are aware of prevailing salaries and benefits in your field. See <u>salary negotiations</u>.

Interviewers look for a degree of self-confidence and an applicant's understanding of the field, as well as genuine interest in the field, the company, and the job. Ask questions to communicate your interest in the job and company. Interviewers respond favorably to applicants who can communicate and present themselves well.

Conclusion.   At the conclusion of the interview, thank the interviewer for his or her time. Indicate that you are interested in the job (if true) and try to get an idea of the company's hiring time frame. Reaffirm friendly contact with a firm handshake.

After the Interview

After you leave the interview, jot down the pertinent information you obtained, as it may be helpful in comparing job offers. As soon as possible following a job interview, send the interviewer a note of thanks in a brief letter or <u>e-mail</u>. Such notes often include the following:

- Your thanks for the interview and to individuals or groups that gave you special help or attention during the interview
- The name of the specific job for which you interviewed
- Your impression that the job is attractive
- Your confidence that you can perform the job well
- An offer to provide further information or answer further questions

Figure I–8 shows a typical example of follow-up correspondence.

If you are offered a job you want, accept the offer verbally and write a brief letter of acceptance as soon as possible—certainly within a week. If you do not want the job, write a refusal letter, as described in **acceptance/refusal letters**.

From: etreadwell@juno.com (Elaine Treadwell)
To: vallone@adbroker.com
Subject: Re: Employment Interview
Sent: 23 June 05 3:59:56 PM Eastern Daylight Time

Dear Mr. Vallone:

Thank you for the informative and pleasant interview we had yesterday. Please extend my thanks to Mr. Wilson of the Media Group as well.

I came away from our meeting most favorably impressed with Adams Brokerage. I find the position of financial adviser to be an attractive one and feel confident that my qualifications would enable me to perform the duties to everyone's advantage.

If I can answer any further questions, please let me know.

Sincerely yours,

Elaine Treadwell

Elaine Treadwell
9672 Patton Drive
Lincoln, NE 68504
(308) 841-9782

FIGURE I–8. Follow-up Correspondence

introductions

DIRECTORY

Routine Openings　290
Opening Strategies　291
　Objective　291
　Problem Statement　291
　Scope　291
　Background　291
　Summary　292

Interesting Detail　292
Definition　292
Anecdote　292
Quotation　293
Forecast　293
Persuasive Hook　293
Full-Scale Introductions　293

This entry discusses opening strategies for short and routine types of **correspondence**, such as **memos** and **e-mail**, and large writing projects, such as **formal reports** and major **proposals**. See also **conclusions**.

Routine Openings

Not every document needs a fully developed introduction or opening. When your **readers** are already familiar with your subject, or if what you are writing is short, a brief or routine opening, as shown in the following examples, will provide adequate **context**.

CORRESPONDENCE
Dear Mr. Ignatowski:
You will be happy to know that we have corrected the error in your bank balance. The new balance shows . . .

PROGRESS REPORT LETTER
Dear Dr. Chang:
To date, 18 of the 20 specimens you submitted for analysis have been examined. Our preliminary analysis indicates . . .

LONGER PROGRESS REPORT
PROGRESS REPORT ON REWIRING THE SPORTS ARENA
The rewiring program at the Sports Arena is proceeding ahead of schedule. Although the costs of certain equipment are higher than our original bid, we expect to complete the project without exceeding our budget because the speedy completion will save labor costs.
Work Completed
As of August 15, we have . . .

E-MAIL
Jane, as I promised in my e-mail yesterday, I've attached the human resources budget estimates for fiscal year 2006.

Opening Strategies

Opening strategies are aimed at focusing the readers' attention and motivating them to read the entire document.

Objective.   In reporting on a project, you might open with a statement of the project's objective so the readers have a basis for judging the results.

- The primary goal of this project was to develop new techniques to solve the problem of waste disposal. Our first step was to investigate . . .

Problem Statement.   One way to give readers the perspective of your report is to present a brief account of the problem that led to the study or project being reported.

- Several weeks ago a manager noticed a recurring problem in the software developed by Datacom Systems. Specifically, error messages repeatedly appeared when, in fact, no specific trouble. . . . After an extensive investigation, we found that Datacom Systems . . .

For proposals or formal reports, of course, problem statements may be more elaborate and a part of the full-scale introduction, which is discussed later in this entry.

Scope.   You may want to present the <u>scope</u> of your document in your opening. By providing the parameters of your material, the limitations of the subject, or the amount of detail to be presented, you enable your readers to determine whether they want or need to read your document.

- This pamphlet provides a review of the requirements for obtaining an FAA pilot's license. It is not intended as a textbook to prepare you for the examination itself; rather, it outlines the steps you need to take and the costs involved.

Background.   The background or history of a subject may be interesting and lend perspective and insight to a subject. Consider the following example from a newsletter describing the process of oil drilling:

- From the bamboo poles the Chinese used when the pyramids were young to today's giant rigs drilling in hundreds of feet of water, there has been considerable progress in the search for oil. But whether in ancient China or a modern city, underwater or on a mountaintop, the objective of drilling has always been the same — to manufacture a hole in the ground, inch by inch.

Summary. You can provide a summary opening by describing in abbreviated form the results, conclusions, or recommendations of your article or report. Be concise: Do not begin a summary by writing "This report summarizes. . . ."

> **CHANGE**   This report summarizes the advantages offered by the photon as a means of examining the structural features of the atom.
>
> **TO**   As a means of examining the structure of the atom, the photon offers several advantages.

Interesting Detail. Often an interesting detail will gain the readers' attention and arouse their curiosity. Readers of an <u>annual report</u> for a manufacturer of telescopes and scientific instruments, for example, may be persuaded to invest if they believe that the company is developing innovative, cutting-edge products.

- The rings of Saturn have puzzled astronomers ever since they were discovered by Galileo in 1610 using the first telescope. Recently, even more rings have been discovered. . . .

  Our company's Scientific Instrument Division designs and manufactures research-quality, computer-controlled telescopes that promise to solve the puzzles of Saturn's rings by enabling scientists to use multicolor differential photometry to determine the rings' origins and compositions.

Definition. Although a definition can be useful as an opening, do not define something with which the reader is familiar or provide a definition that is obviously a contrived opening (such as "Webster defines *technology* as . . ."). A definition should be used as an opening only if it offers insight into what follows.

- *Risk* is often a loosely defined term. In this report, risk refers to a qualitative combination of the probability of an event and the severity of the consequences of that event. In fact, . . .

Anecdote. An anecdote can be used to attract and build interest in a subject that may otherwise be mundane; however, this strategy is best suited to longer documents and <u>presentations</u>.

- In his poem "The Calf Path," Sam Walter Foss tells of a wandering, wobbly calf trying to find its way home at night through the lonesome woods. It made a crooked path, which was taken up the next day by a lone dog. Then "a bellwether sheep pursued the trail over vale and steep, drawing behind him the flock, too, as all good bellwethers do." At last the path became a country road; then a lane that bent and turned and turned again. The lane became a village street, and at last the main street of a flourishing city. The poet ends by saying, "A hundred thousand men were led by a calf, near three centuries dead."

Many companies today follow a "calf path" because they react to events rather than planning. . . .

Quotation. Occasionally, you can use a quotation to stimulate interest in your subject. To be effective, however, the quotation must be pertinent—not some loosely related remark selected from a book of quotations.

- Richard Smith, founder of PCS Corporation, recently said, "I believe that managers need to be more 'people smart' than ever before. The management style of today involves much more than just managing the operations of a department—it requires understanding the personalities that comprise a corporation."[3] His statement represents a growing feeling among corporate leaders that . . .

Forecast. Sometimes you can use a forecast of a new development or trend to arouse the reader's interest.

- In the not-too-distant future, we may be able to use a hand-held medical diagnostic device similar to those in science fiction to assess the complete physical condition of accident victims. This project and others are now being developed at The Seldi Group, Inc.

Persuasive Hook. While all opening strategies contain persuasive elements, the hook uses **persuasion** most overtly. A **brochure** touting the newest innovation in tax-preparation software might address readers as follows:

- Welcome to the newest way to do your taxes! TaxPro EZ ends the headache of last-minute tax preparation with its unique Web-Link feature.

Full-Scale Introductions

The purpose of a full-scale introduction is to give readers enough general information about the subject to enable them to understand the details in the body of the document. An introduction should accomplish any or all of the following:

- *State the subject.* Provide background information, such as definition, history, or theory, to provide context for your readers.
- *State the purpose.* Make your readers aware of why the document exists and whether the material provides a new perspective or clarifies an existing perspective.

- *State the scope.* Tell readers the amount of detail you plan to cover.
- *Preview the development of the subject.* Especially in a longer document, outline how you plan to develop the subject. Providing such information allows readers to anticipate how the subject will be presented and helps them evaluate your conclusions or recommendations.

Consider writing an opening or introduction last. Many writers find that it is only when they have drafted the body of the document that they have a full enough perspective on the subject to introduce it adequately.

investigative reports

Investigative <u>reports</u> may be written for a variety of reasons—most often in response to a request for information. You might be asked, for instance, to determine how your Web site compares to those of competing companies in your industry or to learn the level of satisfaction among your customers. An investigative report gives a precise analysis of a topic and offers <u>conclusions</u>, as is the case of the investigative report shown in Figure I–9.

Open the report with a statement of its primary and (if any) secondary <u>purposes</u>, then define the <u>scope</u> of your investigation. If the report includes a survey of opinions, indicate the number of people surveyed, income categories, occupations, and other identifying information. (See also <u>questionnaires</u>.) Include any information that is pertinent in defining the extent of the investigation. Then report your findings and, if necessary, discuss their significance in the report with your conclusions.

Sometimes the person requesting the investigative report may ask you to make recommendations as a result of your findings. In that case, the report may be referred to as a *recommendation report*. See also <u>feasibility reports</u>.

italics

Italics is a style of type used to denote <u>emphasis</u> and to distinguish foreign expressions, book titles, and certain other elements. *This sentence is printed in italics.* Italic type is signaled by underlining in manuscripts submitted for publication or where italic font is not available (see also <u>e-mail</u>). You may need to italicize words that require special emphasis in

Memo

To: Noreen Rinaldo, Training Manager
From: Charles Lapinski, Senior Instructor   *CL*
Date: February 7, 2006
Subject: Adler's Basic English Program

As requested, I have investigated Adler Medical Instruments' (AMI's) Basic English Program to determine whether we might adopt a similar program.

The purpose of AMI's program is to teach medical technologists outside the United States who do not speak or read English to understand procedures written in a special 800-word vocabulary called *Basic English*. This program eliminates the need for AMI to translate its documentation into a number of different languages. The Basic English Program does not attempt to teach the medical technologists to be fluent in English but, rather, to recognize the 800 basic words that appear in Adler's documentation.

Course Analysis
The course teaches technologists a basic medical vocabulary in English; it does not provide training in medical terminology. Students must already know, in their own language, the meaning of medical vocabulary (e.g., the meaning of the word *hemostat*). Students must also have basic knowledge of their specialty, must be able to identify a part in an illustrated parts book, must have used AMI products for at least one year, and must be able to read and write in their own language.

Students are given an instruction manual, an illustrated book of equipment with parts and their English names, and pocket references containing the 800 words of the Basic English vocabulary plus the English names of parts. Students can write the corresponding word in their language beside the English word and then use the pocket reference as a bilingual dictionary. The course consists of 30 two-hour lessons, each lesson introducing approximately 27 words. No effort is made to teach pronunciation; the course teaches only recognition of the 800 words, which include 450 nouns, 70 verbs, 180 adjectives and adverbs, and 100 articles, prepositions, conjunctions, and pronouns.

Course Success
The 800-word vocabulary enables the writers of documentation to provide medical technologists with any information that might be required because the subject areas are strictly limited to usage, troubleshooting, safety, and operation of AMI medical equipment. All nonessential words (*apple*, *father*, *mountain*, and so on) are eliminated, as are most synonyms (for example, *under* appears, but *beneath* does not).

Conclusions and Recommendations
AMI's program appears to be quite successful, and a similar approach could also be appropriate for us. I see two possible ways in which we could use some or all of the elements of AMI's program: (1) in the preparation of our student manuals or (2) as AMI uses the program.

I think it would be unnecessary to use the Basic English methods in the preparation of manuals for *all* of our students. Most of our students are English speakers to whom an unrestricted vocabulary presents no problem.

As for our initiating a program similar to AMI's, we could create our own version of the Basic English vocabulary and write our instructional materials in it. Because our product lines are much broader than AMI's, however, we would need to create illustrated parts books for each of the different product lines.

FIGURE I–9. Investigative Report

a sentence. (Contrary to projections, sales have *not* improved.) Do not overuse italics for emphasis, however. (This will hurt *you* more than *me*.)

Foreign Words and Phrases

Foreign words and phrases are italicized (*bonjour, guten tag*, the sign said "*Se habla español*"). Foreign words that have been fully assimilated into English need not be italicized (cliché, etiquette, vis-à-vis, de facto, résumé). When in doubt about the treatment of a word, consult a current dictionary. See also **foreign words in English**.

Titles

Italicize the **titles** of separately published documents, such as books, periodicals, newspapers, pamphlets, brochures, legal cases, movies, and television programs.

- The book *Turning Workplace Conflicts into Collaboration* was reviewed in the *New York Times*.

Abbreviations of such titles are italicized if their spelled-out forms would be italicized.

- The *NYT* is one of the nation's oldest newspapers.

Italicize the titles of compact discs, videotapes, plays, long poems, paintings, sculptures, and long musical works.

CD-ROM	*Computer Security Tutorial on CD-ROM*
PLAY	Arthur Miller's *Death of a Salesman*
LONG POEM	T. S. Eliot's *The Wasteland*
MUSICAL WORK	Gershwin's *Porgy and Bess*

Use **quotation marks** for parts of publications, such as chapters of books and articles or sections within periodicals.

Proper Names

The names of ships, trains, and aircraft (but not the companies or governments that own them) are italicized (U.S. aircraft carrier *Independence*, U.S. space shuttle *Endeavour*). Craft that are known by model or serial designations are not italicized (DC-7, Boeing 747).

Words, Letters, and Figures

Words, letters, and figures discussed as such are italicized.

- The word *inflammable* is often misinterpreted.
- The *S* and *6* keys on my keyboard do not function.

Subheads

Subheads in a report are sometimes italicized.

- *Training Managers.* We are leading the way in developing first-line managers who not only are professionally competent but . . .

See also <u>headings</u> and <u>layout and design</u>.

its / it's

Its is a possessive <u>pronoun</u> and does not use an <u>apostrophe</u>. *It's* is a <u>contraction</u> of *it is*.

- *It's* important that the sales department meet *its* quota.

See also <u>expletives</u> and <u>possessive case</u>.

J

jargon

Jargon is a highly specialized slang that is unique to an occupational or a professional group. Jargon is at first understood only by insiders; over time, it may become known more widely. For example, human resources professionals adopted the term *head-hunting* to describe the recruitment of executive personnel. If all your readers are members of a particular occupational group, jargon may provide an efficient means of communicating. However, if you have any doubt that your entire <u>audience</u> is part of such a group, avoid using jargon. See also <u>affectation</u>, <u>functional shift</u>, and <u>gobbledygook</u>.

job descriptions

Most large companies and many small ones use formal job descriptions to specify the duties of and requirements for many of the jobs in the firm. Job descriptions fulfill several important functions: They provide information on which equitable salary scales can be based; they help management determine whether all functions within a company are adequately supported; and they let both prospective and current employees know exactly what is expected of them. Together, all the job descriptions in a firm present a picture of the organization's structure.

Sometimes middle managers are given the task of writing job descriptions for their employees. In many organizations, though, employees are required to draft their own job descriptions, which supervisors then check and approve.

Although job-description formats vary from organization to organization, they commonly contain the following sections:

- The *accountability* section identifies, by title only, the person to whom the employee reports.

- The *scope of responsibilities* section provides an overview of the primary and secondary functions of the job and states, if applicable, who reports to the employee.
- The *specific duties* section gives a detailed account of the specific duties of the job as concisely as possible.
- The *personal requirements* section lists the required or preferred education, training, experience, and licensing for the job.

The job description shown in Figure J–1 is typical. It never mentions the person holding the job described; it focuses, instead, on the job and the qualifications required to fill the position.

PUBLICATIONS MANAGER
GCW Systems

Accountability
Reports directly to the Vice President, Advertising and Public Relations.

Scope of Responsibilities
The Publications Manager plans, coordinates, and supervises the design and development of sales brochures, advertisements, Web sites, and customer manuals required to support the sale, installation, and maintenance of company products and services. The manager is responsible for the administration of the Publications Department. The supervisor of customer publications, the supervisor of internal publications, and the division Webmaster report to the Publications Manager.

Specific Duties
- Directs an organization currently comprising 20 people, including supervisors, writers, designers, and production staff
- Screens, selects, and hires qualified applicants for the department
- Prepares a formal orientation program to familiarize trainees with the production of printed materials
- Evaluates the performance of and determines the salary adjustments for all department employees
- Plans documentation to support new and existing products
- Subcontracts publications and acts as a purchasing agent when needed
- Offers editorial advice to supervisors
- Develops and manages an annual budget for the Publications Department
- Recommends new and appropriate uses for the department within the company

Requirements
- B.A. or equivalent background and experience
- Minimum of three years' professional writing experience and a general knowledge of design and current production software
- Minimum of two years' management experience and a knowledge of the general principles of management
- Strong interpersonal skills

FIGURE J–1. Job Description

Writer's Checklist: Writing Job Descriptions

☑ Before attempting to write your job description, list all the different tasks you do in a week or a month. Otherwise, you will almost certainly leave out some of your duties.

☑ Focus on content. Remember that you are describing your job, not yourself.

☑ List your duties in decreasing order of importance. Knowing how your various duties rank in importance makes it easier to set valid job qualifications.

☑ Begin each statement of a duty with a **verb** and be specific. Write "Greet and assist customers" rather than "Take care of customers."

☑ Review existing job descriptions that are considered well written.

J

job search

Whether you are applying for your first job or want to change careers entirely, begin by assessing your skills, interests, and abilities, perhaps through **brainstorming**.* Next, consider your career goals and values. For instance, do you prefer working independently or collaboratively? Do you enjoy public settings? meeting people? How important are career stability and location? Finally, ask yourself what you would most like to be doing in the immediate future, in two years, and in five years.

Once you have reflected and brainstormed about the job that is right for you, a number of sources can help you locate the job you want. Of course, you should not rely on any one of these sources exclusively:

• Networking
• Campus career services
• Web resources
• Advertisements
• Trade and professional journal listings
• Private (or temporary) employment agencies
• Letters of inquiry

*A good source for stimulating your thinking is the most recent edition of *What Color Is Your Parachute? A Practical Manual for Job-Hunters & Career-Changers* by Richard Nelson Bolles, published by Ten Speed Press.

Keep a file during your job search of dated job ads, copies of <u>application letters</u> and <u>résumés</u>, and the names of important contacts. This collection can serve as a future resource and reminder. See also <u>interviewing for a job</u> and <u>salary negotiations</u>.

Networking

Networking involves communicating with people who might provide useful advice or may know of potential jobs in your interest areas. They may include people already working in your chosen field, contacts in professional organizations, professors, family members, or friends. Use your contacts to expand your network of contacts. Consider that of all open positions, an estimated 80 percent are filled through networking.*

Campus Career Services

A visit to a college career-development center is another good way to begin your job search. Government, business, and industry recruiters often visit campus career offices to interview prospective employees; recruiters also keep career counselors aware of their companies' current employment needs and submit <u>job descriptions</u> to them. Not only can career counselors help you select a career, they can also put you in touch with the best, most current resources—identifying where to begin your search and saving you time. Career-development centers often hold workshops on résumé preparation and offer other job-finding resources on their Web sites.

Web Resources

Using the Web can enhance your job search in a number of ways. First, you can consult sites that give advice about careers, job seeking, and résumé preparation. Second, you can learn about businesses and organizations that may hire employees in your area by visiting their Web sites. Such sites often list job openings, provide instructions for applicants, and offer other information, such as employee benefits. Third, you can learn about jobs in your field and post your résumé for prospective employers at employment databases, such as Monster.com or America's Job Bank. Fourth, you can post your résumé at your personal Web site. Although posting your résumé at an employment database will undoubtedly attract more potential employers, including your résumé at your own site has benefits. For example, you might provide a link to your site in e-mail correspondence or provide your Web site's URL in an inquiry letter to a prospective employer. If you use a personal Web

*From *JobStar Central*, an online job-search guide hosted by the *Wall Street Journal* at <http://jobstar.org>.

site, however, it should contain only material that would be of interest to prospective employers, such as examples of your work, awards, and other professional items.

Employment specialists suggest that you spend time on the Web in the evening or early morning so that you can focus on in-person contacts during working hours.

WEB LINK **FINDING A JOB**

For job-hunting tips, sample documents, and links to the sites mentioned in this entry, see <*bedfordstmartins.com/alredbus*> and select *Finding an Internship or Job* and *Links for Handbook Entries*.

Advertisements

Many employers advertise in the classified sections of newspapers and on their own Web sites. For the widest selection of help-wanted listings, look in the Sunday editions or the help-wanted Web pages of local and big-city newspapers. Use the search options they provide or the general strategies for database searches discussed in the entry **research**.

A human-relations specialist interested in training, for example, might find the specialty listed under "Human Resources" or "Consulting Services." Depending on a company's or government agency's needs, the listing could be even more specific, such as "Software Education Specialist" or "Learning and Development Coordinator."

As you read the ads, take notes on salary ranges, job locations, job duties and responsibilities, and even the terminology used in the ads to describe the work. A knowledge of keywords and key expressions that are generally used to describe a particular type of work can be helpful when you prepare your résumé and letters of application.

Trade and Professional Journal Listings

In many industries, associations publish periodicals of interest to people working in the industry. Such periodicals (print and online) often contain job listings. To learn about the trade or professional associations for your occupation, consult resources on the Web, such as Google's Directory of Professional Organizations or online resources offered by your library or campus career office. You may also consult the following references at a library: *Encyclopedia of Associations, Encyclopedia of Business Information Sources*, and *National Directory of Employment Services*.

Private (or Temporary) Employment Agencies

Private employment agencies are profit-making organizations that are in business to help people find jobs—for a fee. Reputable agencies provide you with job leads, help you organize your job search, and supply information on companies doing the hiring. A staffing agency, or temporary placement agency, could match you with an appropriate temporary or permanent job in your field. Temporary work for an organization for which you might want to work permanently is an excellent way to build your network while continuing your job search.

Choose an employment or a temporary-placement agency carefully. Some are well established and reputable; others are not. Check with your local Better Business Bureau and your college career office before you sign an agreement with a private employment agency. Further, be sure you understand who is paying the agency's fee. Often the employer pays the agency's fee; however, if you have to pay, make sure you know exactly how much. As with any written agreement, read the fine print carefully.

Letters of Inquiry

If you would like to work for a particular firm, write and ask whether it has any openings for people with your qualifications. Normally, you can send the letter to the department head, the director of human resources, or both; for a small firm, however, write to the head of the firm.

Other Sources

Local, state, and federal government agencies offer many employment services. Local government agencies are listed in telephone and Web directories under the name of your city, county, or state.

K

kind of / sort of

The phrases *kind of* and *sort of* should be used only to refer to a class or type of things.

- We require a special *kind of* training to ensure employee safety.

Do not use *kind of* or *sort of* to mean "rather," "somewhat," or "somehow." That usage can lead to vagueness; it is better to be specific.

VAGUE	It was *kind of* a bad year for the company.
SPECIFIC	The company's profits fell 10 percent last year.

know-how

The informal term *know-how*, meaning "special competence or knowledge," should be avoided in formal writing <u>style</u>.

- The applicant has impressive marketing ~~know-how.~~ *skill.*

L

lay / lie

Lay is a transitive <u>verb</u>—a verb that requires a direct object to complete its meaning—that means "place" or "put."

- We will *lay* the foundation of the building one section at a time.

The past-tense form of *lay* is *laid.*

- We *laid* the first section of the foundation last month.

The perfect-tense form of *lay* is also *laid.*

- Since June, we *have laid* all but two sections of the foundation.

Lay is frequently confused with *lie,* which is an intransitive verb—a verb that does not require an object to complete its meaning—that means "recline" or "remain."

- Injured employees should *lie* down and remain still until the EMTs arrive.

The past-tense form of *lie* is *lay.* This form causes the confusion between *lie* and *lay.*

- The injured employee *lay* still for approximately five minutes.

The perfect-tense form of *lie* is *lain.*

- The injured employee *had lain* still for approximately five minutes before the EMTs arrived.

layout and design

DIRECTORY

Typography   306
   Typeface and Type Size   306
   Type Style and Emphasis   307

Page-Design Elements   308
   Justification   308
   Headings   308

Headers and Footers 308

Lists 308

Columns 309

White Space 310

Color 310

Visuals 310

Icons 310

Captions 310

Rules 310

Page Layout and Thumbnails 311

The layout and design of a document can make even the most complex information accessible and give <u>readers</u> a favorable impression of the writer and the organization. To accomplish those goals, a design should help readers find information easily; offer a simple and uncluttered presentation; and highlight structure, hierarchy, and order. The design must also fit the <u>purpose</u> of the document and its <u>context</u>. For example, if clients are paying a high price for consulting services, they may expect a sophisticated, polished design; if employees inside an organization expect management to be frugal, they may accept—even expect—an economical and standard company design.

Effective design is based on visual simplicity and harmony and can be achieved with careful selection of typography, page-design elements, and appropriate visuals, as well as thoughtful layout of text and visual components on a page.

Typography

Typography refers to the style and arrangement of type on a page. A complete set of all the letters, numbers, and symbols available in one typeface (or style) is called a *font*. The letters in a typeface have a number of distinctive characteristics, as shown in Figure L–1.

Typeface and Type Size. For most on-the-job writing, select a typeface primarily for its legibility. Avoid typefaces that may distract

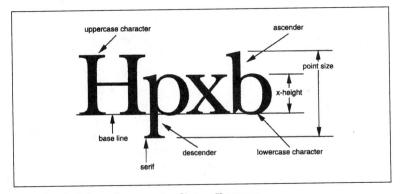

FIGURE L–1. Primary Components of Letter Characters

readers. Instead, choose popular typefaces with which readers are familiar, such as Times Roman, Garamond, or Gill Sans. Avoid using more than two typefaces in the text of a document. For certain documents, however, such as <u>newsletters</u>, you may wish to use distinctively different typefaces to provide contrast among various elements like headlines, headings, inset quotes, and sidebars. Always experiment before making final decisions, and keep in mind your <u>audience</u>.

One way typefaces are characterized is by the presence or absence of serifs. Serif typefaces have projections, as shown in Figure L–1; sans serif styles do not. (*Sans* is French for "without.") The text of this book is set in Plantin, a serif typeface. Although sans serif type has a modern look, serif type is easier to read, especially in the smaller sizes. Sans serif, however, works well for headings (like the entry titles in this book) and for Web sites and other documents read on-screen.

Ideal font sizes for the main text of paper documents range from 10 to 12 points. However, for some elements or documents, you may wish to select typeface sizes that are smaller (as in footnotes) or larger (as in headlines for <u>brochures</u>). See Figure L–2 for a visual comparison of type sizes in a serif typeface.

6 pt. This size might be used for dating a source.
8 pt. This size might be used for footnotes.
10 pt. This size might be used for figure captions.
12 pt. This size might be used for main text.
14 pt. This size might be used for headings.

FIGURE L–2. Type Sizes (6- to 14-Point)

Your readers and the distance from which they will read a document should help determine type size. For example, instructions that will rest on a table at which the reader stands require a larger typeface than a document that will be read up close. For **presentations** and <u>writing for the Web</u>, preview your document to see the effectiveness of your choice of point sizes and typefaces.

Type Style and Emphasis. One method of achieving <u>emphasis</u> through typography is to use capital letters. HOWEVER, LONG STRETCHES OF ALL UPPERCASE LETTERS ARE DIFFICULT TO READ. (See also <u>e-mail</u>.) Use all uppercase letters only in short spans, such as in headings. Likewise, use <u>italics</u> sparingly because *continuous italic type reduces legibility and thus slows readers.* Of course, italics are useful if your aim is to slow readers, as in cautions and warnings. **Boldface**, used in moderation, may be the best cuing device because it is visually different yet retains the customary shapes of letters and numbers.

Page-Design Elements

Thoughtfully used design elements can not only provide emphasis but also give a document visual logic by highlighting organization. Consistency and moderation are important—use the same technique to highlight a particular feature throughout your document and be careful not to overuse any single technique. The following typical elements can be used to make your document accessible and effective: justification, headings, headers and footers, lists, columns, white space, and color. Some of these elements are illustrated in Figure L–3.

Justification.   Left-justified (ragged-right) margins are generally easier to read than full-justified margins, especially for text using standard margins on $8\frac{1}{2}'' \times 11''$ pages. Left-justified is also better if full justification causes your word-processing software to insert irregular spaces between words, producing unwanted white space or unevenness in blocks of text. Full-justified text is more appropriate for publications aimed at a broad readership that expects a more formal, polished appearance. Full justification is also useful with multiple-column formats because the spaces between the columns (called *alleys*) need the definition that full justification provides.

Headings.   Headings reveal the organization of a document and help readers decide which sections they need to read. You should provide typographic contrast between headings and the base text with either a different typeface or a different style (bold, italic, caps, etc.). Headings are often effective in **boldface** or in a sans serif typeface that contrasts with a base text in a serif typeface.

Headers and Footers.   A header in a report, letter, or other document appears at the top of each page, and a footer appears at the bottom of each page. Document pages may have headers or footers or both that include such elements as the topic or subtopic of a section, identifying number, the date the document was written, page number, and the document name. Keep your headers and footers concise—too much information in them can create visual clutter. For headers used in letters and memos, see correspondence.

Lists.   Lists are an effective way to highlight words, phrases, and short sentences. Lists are particularly useful for presenting certain types of

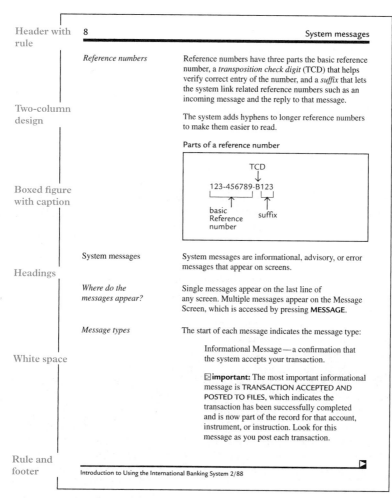

FIGURE L–3. Sample Page Illustrating Layout and Design Choices

The labels on the figure read:

- Header with rule
- Two-column design
- Boxed figure with caption
- Headings
- White space
- Rule and footer

The sample page contents:

8   System messages

Reference numbers

Reference numbers have three parts the basic reference number, a *transposition check digit* (TCD) that helps verify correct entry of the number, and a *suffix* that lets the system link related reference numbers such as an incoming message and the reply to that message.

The system adds hyphens to longer reference numbers to make them easier to read.

Parts of a reference number

TCD
↓
123-456789-B123

basic Reference number   suffix

System messages

System messages are informational, advisory, or error messages that appear on screens.

Where do the messages appear?

Single messages appear on the last line of any screen. Multiple messages appear on the Message Screen, which is accessed by pressing **MESSAGE**.

Message types

The start of each message indicates the message type:

Informational Message—a confirmation that the system accepts your transaction.

⊠**important:** The most important informational message is TRANSACTION ACCEPTED AND POSTED TO FILES, which indicates the transaction has been successfully completed and is now part of the record for that account, instrument, or instruction. Look for this message as you post each transaction.

Introduction to Using the International Banking System 2/88

information, such as steps in sequence, materials or parts needed, concluding points, and recommendations.

Columns.   As you design pages, consider how columns may improve the readability of your document. A single-column format works well with larger typefaces, double spacing, and left-justified margins. For smaller typefaces and single-spaced lines, the two-column structure keeps text columns narrow enough so that readers need not scan back and forth across the width of the entire page for every line. A word on a line by itself at the end of a column is called an *orphan*. A single word carried over to the top of a column or page is called a *widow*. Avoid both.

White Space.   White space visually frames information and breaks it into manageable chunks. For example, white space between paragraphs helps readers see the information in each paragraph as a unit. White space between sections can also serve as a visual cue to signal that one section is ending and another is beginning.

Color.   Color and screening (shaded areas on a page) can distinguish one part of a document from another or unify a series of documents. They can set off sections within a document, highlight examples, or emphasize warnings. In tables, screening can highlight column titles or sets of data to which you want to draw the reader's attention.

Visuals

Readers notice visuals before they notice text, and they notice larger visuals before they notice smaller ones. Thus, the size of an illustration suggests its relative importance. For newsletter articles and publications aimed at wide audiences, consider especially the proportion of the illustration to the text. Magazine designers often use the three-fifths rule: Page layout is more dramatic and appealing when the major element (photograph, drawing, or other illustration) occupies three-fifths rather than half the available space. The same principle can be used to enhance the visual appeal of a report.

Illustrations can be gathered in one place (for example, at the end of a report), but placing them in the text closer to their accompanying explanations makes them more effective. Using illustrations in the text also provides visual relief. For advice on the placement of illustrations, see the *Writer's Checklist: Creating and Integrating Visuals* (pages 561–62).

Icons.   Visuals that are especially useful for Web design are icons, which are pictorial representations of concepts. Commonly used icons include the national flags used for Web pages to symbolize different language versions of a document. To be effective, icons must be simple and easily recognized or defined, as shown in the entry global graphics.

Captions.   Captions are titles that highlight or describe visuals or blocks of text. Captions often appear below or above figures and tables and in the left or right margins next to blocks of text.

Rules.   Rules are vertical or horizontal lines used to create boxes for visuals or divide one area of the page from another. They can effectively highlight elements and make information more accessible. Rules and boxes, for example, set off visuals from surrounding explanations or highlight warning statements from the steps in <u>instructions</u>.

Page Layout and Thumbnails

Page layout involves combining typography, design elements, and visuals on a page to make a coherent whole. The flexibility of your design is affected by your design software, your method of printing the document, and your budget.

Before you spend time positioning actual text and visuals on a page, especially for documents like brochures, you may want to create a thumbnail sketch, in which blocks indicate the placement of elements. You can go further by roughly assembling all the thumbnail pages to show the size, shape, form, and general style of a large document. Such a mock-up, called a *dummy*, allows you to see how a finished document will look.

WEB LINK DESIGNING DOCUMENTS

Word-processing programs offer many options for improving the layout-and-design elements of your document. For a tutorial on these options, see <*bedfordstmartins.com/alredbus*> and select *Tutorials*, "Designing Documents with a Word Processor." For step-by-step instructions for setting margins, alignment, columns, and other design elements, select *Digital Tips*, "Laying Out a Page."

---

lend / loan

Both *lend* and *loan* can be used as <u>verbs</u>, but *lend* is more common. (You can *lend* [or *loan*] them the money if you wish.) Unlike *lend*, *loan* can be a noun. (The bank approved our *loan.*)

letters (*see* correspondence and e-mail)

liable / libel

Liable means "legally subject to" or "responsible for."

- Employers are held *liable* for their employees' actions.

Libel refers to "anything circulated in writing or pictures that injures someone's good reputation." When someone's reputation is injured in speech, the term is *slander*.

- When an editorial accused our board of directors of bribery, the board sued the newspaper for *libel*.

- If the mayor supports the bribery charge in her speech tonight, we will accuse her of *slander*.

In workplace writing, *liable* should retain its legal meaning. Where a condition of probability is intended, use *likely*.

- Rita is ~~liable~~ *likely* to be promoted.

library research (*see* research)

like / as

To avoid confusion between *like* and *as*, remember that *like* is a **preposition** and *as* (or *as if*) is a **conjunction**. Use *like* with a **noun** or **pronoun** that is not followed by a **verb**.

- The new supervisor behaves *like* a novice.

Use *as* before **clauses**, which contain verbs.

- He responded *as* we expected he would.

- It seemed *as if* the presentation would never end.

Like and *as* are used in **comparisons**: *Like* is used in elliptical constructions that omit the verb, and *as* is used when the verb is retained.

- He adapted to the new system *like* a duck to water.

- He adapted to the new system *as* a duck adapts to water.

listening

Effective listening enables the listener to understand the directions of an instructor, the message in a speaker's **presentation**, the goals of a manager, and the needs and wants of customers. Above all, it lays the foundation for cooperation. Productive communication occurs when both the speaker and the listener focus clearly on the content of the message and attempt to eliminate as much interference as possible.

Fallacies About Listening

Most people assume that because they can hear they know how to listen. In fact, *hearing* is passive, whereas *listening* is active. Hearing voices in a crowd or a ringing telephone requires no analysis and no active involvement. We hear such sounds without choosing to listen to them — we have no choice but to hear them. Listening, however, requires taking action, interpreting the message, and assessing its worth. Listening also requires that you consider the context of messages and the differences in meaning that may be the result of differences in the speaker's and the listener's occupation, education, culture, sex, race, or other factors. See also biased language, connotation/denotation, English as a second language, global communication, idioms, international correspondence and jargon.

Active Listening

To listen actively, you should (1) make a conscious decision to listen actively, (2) define your purpose for listening, (3) take specific actions to listen more efficiently, and (4) adapt to the situation.

Step 1: Make a Conscious Decision. The first step to active listening is simply making up your mind to do so. Active listening requires a conscious effort, something that does not come naturally. To listen actively, the well-known precept is true: "Seek first to understand and *then* to be understood."*

Step 2: Define Your Purpose. Knowing why you are listening can go a long way toward managing the most common listening problems: drifting attention, formulating your response while the speaker is still talking, and interrupting the speaker. To help you define your purpose for listening, ask yourself these questions:

- What kind of information do I hope to get from this exchange, and how will I use it?

- What kind of message do I want to send while I am listening? (Do I want to portray understanding, determination, flexibility, competence, or patience?)

- What factors — boredom, daydreaming, anger, impatience — might interfere with listening during the interaction? How can I keep these factors from placing a barrier between the speaker and me?

*Stephen R. Covey, *The 7 Habits of Highly Effective People: Powerful Lessons in Personal Change*, 15th ed. (New York: Free Press, 2004).

Step 3: Take Specific Actions.   Becoming an active listener requires a willingness to become a responder rather than a reactor. A *responder* is a listener who slows down the communication to be certain that he or she is accurately receiving the message sent by the speaker. A *reactor* simply says the first thing that comes to mind, without checking to make sure that he or she accurately understands the message. Take the following actions to help you become a responder and not a reactor.

- Make a conscious effort to be impartial when evaluating a message. For example, do not dismiss a message because you dislike the speaker or are distracted by the speaker's appearance, mannerisms, or accent.

- Slow down the communication by asking for more information or by <u>paraphrasing</u> the message received before you offer your thoughts. Paraphrasing lets the speaker know you are listening, gives the speaker an opportunity to clear up any misunderstanding, and keeps you focused.

- Listen with empathy by putting yourself in the speaker's position. When people feel they are being listened to empathetically, they tend to respond with appreciation and cooperation, thereby improving the communication.

- To help you stay focused on what the speaker is saying, take notes while you are listening. <u>Note-taking</u> not only communicates your attentiveness to the speaker, it also reinforces the message and helps you remember it.

Step 4: Adapt to the Situation.   The requirements of active listening differ from one situation to another. For example, when you are listening to a lecture, you may be listening only for specific information. However, if you are on a team project that depends on everyone's contribution, you need to listen at the highest level so that you can gather information as well as pick up on nuances the other speakers may be communicating. See also <u>collaborative writing</u>.

lists

Lists can save <u>readers</u> time by allowing them to see at a glance specific items, questions, or directions. Lists also help readers by breaking up complex statements and by allowing key ideas to stand out, as in Figure L–4.

Before we agree to hold the regional sales meeting at the Brent Hotel, we should make sure the hotel facilities provide the following:

- Business center with phones, faxes, Internet access, and copying services for the conference committee
- Ground-floor exhibit area large enough for thirty 8-foot-by-15-foot booths
- Eight meeting rooms to accommodate 25 people each
- Internet access, projection screens for presentations, and overhead projectors in each room
- Ballroom and dining facilities for 250 people

To confirm that the Brent Hotel is our best choice, we should tour the facilities during our stay in Kansas City.

FIGURE L–4. Bulleted List in a Paragraph

Writer's Checklist: Using Lists

☑ List only comparable items and use **parallel structure**.

☑ Use only words, phrases, or short sentences of the same general length.

☑ Provide **context** by introducing each list, typically with a complete sentence followed by a **colon**.

☑ Ensure **coherence** by providing for adequate **transition** before and after a list.

☑ Use bullets, as opposed to numbers, when rank or sequence is not important.

☑ Do not overuse lists or include too many items, as in pages or **presentation** slides that contain only lists.

logic errors

Logic is essential to convincing **readers** that your conclusions are valid. Errors in logic can undermine the point you are trying to communicate and your credibility. (See also **persuasion**.) Typical logic errors include *lack of reason, sweeping generalizations, non sequiturs, false cause, biased or suppressed evidence, fact versus opinion,* and *loaded arguments.*

Lack of Reason

When a statement is contrary to the reader's common sense, that statement is not reasonable. If, for example, you stated, "New York is a small town," your reader might immediately question your statement. However, if you stated, "Although New York's population is over eight million, it is composed of neighborhoods that function as small towns," your reader could probably accept the statement as reasonable.

Sweeping Generalizations

Sweeping generalizations are statements that are too broad or all-inclusive to be supportable; they generally enlarge an observation about a small group to refer to an entire population. A flat statement, such as "Management is never concerned about employees," ignores any examples of management that show concern for employees. Using such generalizations weakens your credibility.

Non Sequiturs

A non sequitur is a statement that does not logically follow a previous statement.

- I cleared off my desk, and the report is due today.

The missing link in these statements is that the writer cleared his or her desk to make space for materials to help finish the report today. In your own writing, be careful that you do not allow logical gaps that produce non sequiturs.

False Cause

A false cause (also called *post hoc, ergo propter hoc*) refers to the logical fallacy that because one event followed another event, the first somehow caused the second.

- I didn't bring my umbrella today. No wonder it is now raining.
- Because we now have our board meetings at the Education Center, our management turnover rate has declined.
  [Holding meetings at the Education Center may not have any relationship to the declining management turnover rate.]

Such errors in reasoning can happen when the writer hastily concludes that two events are related without examining the causal connections between them.

Biased or Suppressed Evidence

◀ ETHICS NOTE A conclusion reached as a result of biased or suppressed evidence—self-serving data, questionable sources, purposely omitted or incomplete facts—is both illogical and unethical. Suppose you are preparing a report on the acceptance of a new policy among employees. If you distribute questionnaires only to those who think the policy is effective, the resulting evidence will be biased. If you purposely ignore employees who do not believe the policy is effective, you will be suppressing evidence. Intentionally ignoring relevant data that might not support your position not only produces inaccurate results but is unethical. See also **ethics in writing**. ✦

Fact Versus Opinion

Distinguish between fact and opinion. Facts include verifiable data or statements, whereas opinions are personal conclusions that may or may not be based on facts. For example, it is verifiable that distilled water boils at 100°C; that it tastes better or worse than tap water is an opinion. Distinguish the facts from your opinions in your writing so that your readers can draw their own conclusions.

Loaded Arguments

When you include an opinion in a statement and then reach conclusions that are based on that statement, you are loading the argument. Consider the following opening for a memo:

- I have several suggestions to improve the poorly written policy manual. First, we should change . . .

Unless everyone agrees that the manual is poorly written, readers may reject a writer's entire message because they disagree with this loaded premise. Do not load arguments in your writing; conclusions reached with loaded statements are weak and can produce negative reactions in readers who detect the loading.

WEB LINK   **UNDERSTANDING AN ARGUMENT**

Dr. Frank Edler of Metropolitan Community College in Omaha, Nebraska, offers a tutorial in recognizing the logical components of an argument and thinking critically. See *<bedfordstmartins.com/alredbus>* and select *Links for Handbook Entries.*

loose / lose

Loose is an <u>adjective</u> meaning "not fastened" or "unrestrained." (He found a *loose* wire.) *Lose* is a <u>verb</u> meaning "be deprived of" or "fail to win." (I hope we do not *lose* the contract.)

lowercase and uppercase letters
(*see* **capitalization**)

L

M

malapropisms

A malapropism is a word that sounds similar to the one intended but is ludicrously wrong in the <u>context</u>.

INCORRECT   Our employees are no longer *sedimentary* now that we have a fitness center.

CORRECT   Our employees are no longer *sedentary* now that we have a fitness center.

Intentional malapropisms are sometimes used in humorous writing; unintentional malapropisms can embarrass a writer. See also <u>figures of speech</u>.

maps

Maps are often used to show specific geographic features (roads, mountains, rivers, and the like). They can also illustrate geographic distributions of population, climate patterns, corporate branch offices, and so forth. The map in Figure M–1 on page 320, from an environmental assessment, shows the overlapping geographic areas served by three electric utilities in Missouri, Iowa, and Illinois. Note that the map contains a figure number and title, scale of distances, key (or legend), compass, and distinctive highlighting for emphasis. Maps are often used in <u>reports</u>, <u>proposals</u>, <u>brochures</u>, and other documents in which readers need to know the location or geographic orientation of buildings and other facilities.

Writer's Checklist: Creating and Using Maps

☑ Follow the general guidelines discussed in <u>visuals</u> for placement of maps.

☑ Label each map clearly, and assign each map a figure number if it is one of a number of illustrations.

Figure 12. Location of Service Areas of Three Utilities

Source: The U.S. Nuclear Regulatory Commission

FIGURE M–1. Map

Writer's Checklist: Creating and Using Maps (continued)

☑ Clearly identify all boundaries in the map. Eliminate unnecessary boundaries.

☑ Eliminate unnecessary information that may clutter a map. For example, if the purpose of the map is to show population centers, do not include mountain elevations, rivers, or other physical features.

☑ Include a scale of miles/kilometers or feet/meters to give your readers an indication of the map's proportions.

☑ Indicate which direction is north with an arrow or compass symbol.

☑ Emphasize key features by using color, shading, dots, cross hatching, or other appropriate symbols.

☑ Include a key, or legend, that explains what the different colors, shadings, or symbols represent.

WEB LINK MAPS AND MAPPING INFORMATION

The University of Iowa Libraries offer a useful site with links to online maps and other types of mapping and cartographic resources. See *<bedfordstmartins.com/alredbus>* and select *Links for Handbook Entries.*

---

maybe / may be

Maybe (one word) is an **adverb** meaning "perhaps." (*Maybe* the legal staff can resolve this issue.) *May be* (two words) is a **verb** phrase. (It *may be* necessary to hire a specialist.)

media / medium

M

Media is the plural of *medium* and should always be used with a plural **verb**.

- Many communication *media are* available today.

- The Internet *is* a multifaceted *medium*.

meetings

Meetings allow people to share information and collaborate to produce better results than exchanges of **e-mail** messages or other means would allow. (See also **selecting the medium**.) Like a **presentation**, a successful meeting requires planning and preparation.

Planning a Meeting

For a meeting to be successful, determine the focus of the meeting, decide who should attend, and choose the best time and place to hold it. Prepare an agenda for the meeting and determine who should take the minutes.

Determine the Purpose of the Meeting.   The first step in planning a meeting is to focus on the desired outcome. Ask yourself the following question to help you determine the **purpose** of the meeting: What should participants know, believe, do, or be able to do as a result of attending the meeting?

Once you have focused your desired outcome, use the information to write a purpose statement for the meeting that answers the questions *what* and *why.*

● The purpose of this meeting is to gather ideas from the sales force [*what*] in order to create a successful sales campaign for our new scanner [*why*].

Decide Who Should Attend.   Schedule a meeting for a time when all or most of the key people can be present. If a meeting must be held without some key participants, ask those people prior to the meeting for their contributions or invite them to participate by speakerphone. Of course, the meeting minutes should be distributed to everyone, including significant nonattendees.

Choose the Meeting Time.   The time of day and the length of the meeting can influence its outcome. Consider the following when you are planning a meeting:

- People need Monday morning to focus on the week's work after the weekend.
- People need Friday afternoon to complete tasks that must be finished before the weekend.
- Long meetings should include adequate breaks to allow participants to check their messages, make phone calls, and refresh themselves.
- Meetings held during the last 15 minutes of the day will be quick, but few people will remember what happened.
- Speakerphone participants may need consideration for their time zones.

Choose the Meeting Location.   Having a meeting on your own premises can give you an advantage: You feel more comfortable, which, along with your guests' newness to their surroundings, may help you get an edge. Holding the meeting on someone else's premises, however, can signal cooperation. For balance, especially when people are meeting for the first time or are discussing sensitive issues, having a meeting at a neutral site may be the best solution. No one gains an advantage in off-site meetings, and attendees often feel freer to participate.

Establish the Agenda.   A tool for focusing the group, the agenda is an outline of what the meeting will address. Always prepare an agenda for a meeting, even if it is only an informal list of main topics. Ideally, the agenda should be distributed to attendees a day or two before the meeting. For a longer meeting in which participants are required to make a presentation, try to distribute the agenda a week or more in advance.

The agenda should list the attendees, the meeting time and place, and the topics you plan to discuss. If the meeting includes presentations, list the time allotted for each speaker. Finally, indicate an approximate length for the meeting so that participants can plan the rest of their day. Figure M–2 shows a typical agenda.

Sales Meeting Agenda

Purpose:	To get input for a sales campaign for the new software
Date:	May 12, 2006
Place:	Conference Room E
Time:	9:30 a.m.–11:00 a.m.
Attendees:	Advertising Manager, Sales Manager and Reps, Customer Service Manager

Topic	Presenter	Time
The Software	Bob Arbuckle	9:30–9:45
The Campaign	Maria Lopez	9:45–10:00
The Sales Strategy	Mary Winifred	10:00–10:15
Discussion	Led by Dave Grimes	10:15–11:00

FIGURE M–2. Meeting Agenda

If the agenda is distributed in advance of the meeting, it should be accompanied by a memo or an e-mail informing people of the following:

- The purpose of the meeting
- The date and place
- The meeting start and stop times
- The names of the people invited
- Instructions on how to prepare

Figure M–3 on page 324 shows a cover memo sent as an e-mail to accompany an agenda.

Assign the Minute-Taking.   Delegate the minute-taking to someone other than the leader. The minute-taker should record major decisions made and tasks assigned. To avoid misunderstandings, the

From: Susan McLaughlin <smclaughlin@
millenniumscanners.com>
To: Advertising Manager, Sales Manager, Sales
Representatives, Customer Service Manager
Sent: Thur, 05 May 2006 13:30:12 EST
Subject: Sales Meeting (May 12 at 9:30 a.m.)

Attachments: 📄 Sales Meeting Agenda.doc (29 KB)

Purpose of the Meeting

The purpose of this meeting is to get your ideas for the upcoming introduction and sales campaign for our new software.

Date, Time, and Location

Date: May 12, 2006
Time: 9:30 a.m.–11:00 a.m.
Place: Conference Room E (go to the ground floor, take a right off the elevator, third door on the left)

Attendees

Those addressed above

Meeting Preparation

Everyone should be prepared to offer suggestions on the following topics:

· Sales features of the new software
· Techniques for selling the software
· Customer profile of potential buyers
· FAQs — questions customers may ask
· Anticipated support services

Agenda

Please see the attached document.

FIGURE M–3. E-mail to Accompany an Agenda

minute-taker must record each assignment, the person responsible for it, and the date on which it is due.

For a standing committee, it is best to rotate the responsibility of taking minutes. See also **minutes of meetings** and **note-taking**.

Conducting the Meeting

Assign someone to write on a board or project a computer image of information that needs to be viewed by everyone present.

During the meeting, keep to your agenda; however, allow room for differing views, and foster an environment in which participants listen respectfully to one another. Create a productive environment.

- Consider the feelings, thoughts, ideas, and needs of others — do not let your own agenda blind you to other points of view.
- Help other participants feel valued and respected by <u>listening</u> to them and responding to what they say.
- Respond positively to the comments of others whenever possible.
- Consider communication styles and approaches that are different from your own, particularly those from other cultures. See also <u>global communication</u>.

Deal with Conflict.   Despite your best efforts, conflict is inevitable. However, conflict is potentially valuable; when managed positively, it can stimulate creative thinking by challenging complacency and showing ways to achieve goals more efficiently or economically. See <u>collaborative writing</u>.

Members of any group are likely to vary greatly in their personalities and attitudes, and you may encounter people who approach meetings differently. Consider the following tactics for the interruptive, negative, rambling, overly quiet, and territorial personality types.

- The *interruptive person* rarely lets anyone finish a sentence and may intimidate the group's quieter members. Tell that person in a firm but nonhostile tone to let the others finish in the interest of getting everyone's input. By addressing the issue directly, you signal to the group the importance of putting common goals first.
- The *negative person* has difficulty accepting change and often considers a new idea or project from a negative point of view. Such negativity, if left unchecked, can demoralize the group and suppress enthusiasm for new ideas. If the negative person brings up a valid point, however, ask for the group's suggestions to remedy the issue being raised. If the negative person's reactions are not valid or are outside the agenda, state the necessity of staying focused on the agenda and perhaps recommend a separate meeting to address those issues.
- The *rambling person* cannot collect his or her thoughts quickly enough to verbalize them succinctly. Restate or clarify this person's ideas. Try to strike a balance between providing your own interpretation and drawing out the person's intended meaning.
- The *overly quiet person* may be timid or may just be deep in thought. Ask for this person's thoughts, being careful not to

embarrass the person. In some cases, you can have a quiet person jot down his or her thoughts and give them to you later.

- The *territorial person* fiercely defends his or her group against real or perceived threats and may refuse to cooperate with members of other departments, companies, and so on. Point out that although such concerns may be valid, everyone is working toward the same overall goal and that goal should take precedence.

Close the Meeting.   Just before closing the meeting, review all decisions and assignments. Paraphrase each to help the group focus on what they have agreed to do and to ensure that the minutes will be complete and accurate. Now is the time to raise questions and clarify any misunderstandings. Set a date by which everyone at the meeting can expect to receive copies of the minutes. Finally, thank everyone for participating, and close the meeting on a positive note.

Writer's Checklist: Planning and Conducting Meetings

- ☑ Develop a purpose statement for the meeting to focus your planning.
- ☑ Invite only those essential to fulfilling the purpose of the meeting.
- ☑ Select a time and place convenient to all those attending.
- ☑ Create an agenda and distribute it a day or two before the meeting.
- ☑ Assign someone to take meeting minutes.
- ☑ Ensure that the minutes record key decisions; assignments; due dates; and the date, time, and location of the follow-up meeting.
- ☑ Follow the agenda to keep everyone focused.
- ☑ Respect the views of others and how they are expressed.
- ☑ Review strategies in this entry for handling conflict and attendees whose style of expression may prevent getting everyone's best thinking.
- ☑ Close the meeting by reviewing key decisions and assignments.

memos

Memos are used within organizations to report results, instruct employees, announce policies, disseminate information, and delegate responsibilities. Whether sent on paper, as <u>e-mails,</u> or as attachments to e-mails, memos provide a record of decisions made and actions taken. They also can play a key role in the management of many organizations because managers use memos to inform and motivate employees. See also <u>selecting the medium</u>.

Writing Memos

Many of the principles discussed in <u>correspondence</u> and the "Five Steps to Successful Writing" apply to writing memos.

Development and Protocol. To produce an effective memo, outline it first, even if you simply jot down points to be covered and then order them logically. With careful preparation, your memos will be both concise and adequately developed. Adequate development of your thoughts is crucial to the <u>clarity</u> of your message, as the following example indicates.

ABRUPT	Be more careful on the loading dock.
DEVELOPED	To prevent accidents on the loading dock, follow these procedures: 1. Check . . . 2. Load only . . . 3. Replace . . .

Although the abrupt version is concise, it is not as clear and specific as the developed revision. Do not assume your <u>readers</u> will know what you mean. Readers who are in a hurry may misinterpret a vague memo. See also <u>conciseness</u>.

Although such practices vary, be alert to the protocol of addressing and sending memos in your organization. Consider who should receive a memo and in what order — senior managers, for example, take precedence over junior managers. If rank does not apply, alphabetizing recipients by last name is safe. Who should be copied on a memo is a sensitive matter, and you need to learn both the formal and informal practices in an organization. The best general advice, however, is to copy only those who need to see the information.

M

WEB LINK **WRITING MEMOS**

For links to articles about when to write memos and tips for following organization protocol, see <*bedfordstmartins.com/alredbus*> and select *Links for Handbook Entries.*

Openings. Although <u>methods of development</u> vary, a memo normally begins with a statement of its main point. Consider the following example:

- Because of the recent hacker attack on our Web site, I recommend that we no longer post the e-mail addresses of our loan officers. This practice . . .

When your reader is not familiar with the subject or with the background of a problem, provide an introductory paragraph before stating the main point of the message. Doing so is especially important in memos that will serve as records of crucial information. Generally, longer or complex subjects benefit most from more thorough **introductions**. However, even when you are writing a short message about a familiar subject, remind readers of the **context**. In the following example, words that provide context are shown in *italics*.

- *As Maria Lopez recommended*, I reviewed the office reorganization plan. I like most of the features; however, . . .

Do not state the main point first when (1) the reader is likely to be highly skeptical or (2) you are disagreeing with your superiors. In such cases, a more persuasive tactic is to state the problem first, then present the specific points supporting your final recommendation. See also **persuasion** and **refusal letters**.

Writing Style and Tone.   Whether your memo is formal or informal depends entirely on your readers and your **purpose**. A message to a coworker who is also a friend is likely to be informal, while an internal proposal to several readers or to someone two or three levels higher in your organization is likely to be more formal. Consider the following versions of a statement:

TO AN EQUAL	I can't go along with the plan because I think it has serious logistical problems. First, . . .
TO A SUPERIOR	The logistics of moving the department may pose serious problems. First, . . .

A message that gives instructions to a subordinate should also be relatively formal, impersonal, and direct, unless you are trying to reassure or praise. When writing to subordinates, remember that *managing* does not mean *dictating*. If you are too formal, sprinkling your writing with fancy words, you may seem stuffy and pompous. In fact, **affectation** may both irritate and baffle readers, cause a loss of time, and produce costly errors. Consider the unintended secondary messages the following notice conveys:

- It has been decided that the office will be open the day after Thanksgiving.

"It has been decided" not only sounds impersonal but also communicates an authoritarian, management-versus-employee **tone**. The passive **voice** also suggests that the decision-maker does not want to say "I have decided" and thus be identified. One solution is to remove the first part of the sentence.

- The office will be open the day after Thanksgiving.

The best solution, however, would be to suggest both that there is a good reason for the decision and that employees are privy to (if not a part of) the decision-making process.

- Because we must meet the December 15 deadline for submitting the Bradley Foundation proposal, the office will be open the day after Thanksgiving.

By subordinating the bad news (the need to work on that day), the writer focuses on the reasoning behind the decision to work. Employees may not necessarily like the message, but they will at least understand that the decision is not arbitrary and is tied to an important deadline.

Lists and Headings.   Lists can give impact to important points by making it easier for your reader to quickly grasp information. Be careful, however, not to overuse lists. A message that consists almost entirely of lists is difficult to understand because it forces the reader to connect the separate and disjointed items on the page. Further, lists lose their effectiveness when they are overused.

Headings are another attention-getting device, particularly in long memos. They divide material into manageable segments, call attention to main topics, and signal a shift in topic. Readers can scan the headings and read only the section or sections appropriate to their needs.

M

Closings.   A memo closing can accomplish many important tasks, such as building positive relationships with readers, encouraging colleagues and employees, and letting recipients know what you will do or what you expect of them.

- I will discuss the problem with the marketing consultant and let you know by Monday what we are able to change.

Although routine statements are sometimes unavoidable (Thanks again for your help), make your closing work for you by providing specific prompts to which the reader can respond. See also **conclusions**.

- If you would like further information, such as a copy of the questionnaire we used, please let me know.

Format and Design

Memo formats and conventions vary greatly. Although no single standard exists, Figure M–4 on page 330 shows a typical 8½″ × 11″ format with a printed company name. When memos require more than one page, use a second page header, as shown in Figure C–16 on page 126.

PROFESSIONAL PUBLISHING SERVICES
MEMORANDUM

TO: Barbara Smith, Publications Manager
FROM: Hannah Kaufman, Vice President   *HK*
DATE: April 14, 2006
SUBJECT: Schedule for ACM Electronics Brochures

ACM Electronics has asked us to prepare a comprehensive set of
brochures for its Milwaukee office by August 8, 2006. We have worked
with electronics firms in the past, so this job should be relatively easy to
prepare. My guess is that the job will take nearly two months. Ted Harris
has requested time and cost estimates for the project. Fred Moore in
production will prepare the cost estimates, and I would like you to
prepare a tentative schedule for the project.

Additional Personnel

In preparing the schedule, check the status of the following:
   • Production schedule for all staff writers
   • Availability of freelance writers
   • Availability of dependable graphic designers
Ordinarily, we would not need to depend on outside personnel; however,
because our bid for the *Wall Street Journal* special project is still under
consideration, we could be short of staff in June and July. Further, we have
to consider vacations that have already been approved.

Time Estimates

Please give me time estimates by April 18. A successful job done on time
will give us a good chance to obtain the contract to do ACM Electronics'
annual report for its stockholders' meeting this fall.

I know your staff can do the job.

cc: Ted Harris, President
     Fred Moore, Production Editor

FIGURE M–4. Typical Memo Format

Subject Lines.   Subject lines announce the topic; because they also aid filing and later retrieval, they must be specific and accurate.

VAGUE   Subject: Tuition Reimbursement

VAGUE   Subject: Time-Management Seminar

SPECIFIC   Subject: Tuition Reimbursement for Time-Management Seminar

Capitalize all major words in a subject line, except <u>articles</u>, <u>prepositions</u>, and <u>conjunctions</u> with fewer than five letters unless they are the first or last words. Remember that the subject line should not substitute for an opening that provides context for the message.

Signature.   If you are sending a printed memo, the final step is signing or initialing it, a practice that lets readers know that you approve of its contents. Where you sign or initial the memo depends on the practice of your organization. Figure M–4 shows a typical placement of initials.

methods of development

A logical method of development satisfies the readers' need for shape and structure in a document, whether it is an <u>e-mail</u>, a <u>report</u>, or a Web page. It helps you as a writer move smoothly and logically from the <u>introduction</u> to a <u>conclusion</u>.

M

Choose the method or, as is often the case, a combination of methods that best suits your subject, your <u>readers</u>, and your <u>purpose</u>. Following are the most common methods, each of which is discussed in further detail in its own entry.

- <u>Cause-and-effect method of development</u> begins with either the cause or the effect of an event. This approach can be used to develop a <u>report</u> that offers a solution to a problem, beginning with the problem and moving on to the solution or vice versa.

- <u>Chronological method of development</u> emphasizes the time element of a sequence, as in a <u>trouble report</u> that traces events as they occurred in time.

- <u>Comparison method of development</u> is useful when writing about a new topic that is in many ways similar to another topic that is more familiar to your readers.

- <u>Definition method of development</u> extends definitions with additional details, examples, comparisons, or other explanatory devices. See also <u>defining terms</u>.

- Division-and-classification method of development either separates a whole into component parts and discusses each part separately (*division*) or groups parts into categories that clarify the relationship of the parts (*classification*).
- General and specific methods of development proceed either from general information to specific details or from specific information to a general conclusion.
- Order-of-importance method of development presents information in either decreasing order of importance, as in a proposal that begins with the most important point, or increasing order of importance, as in a presentation that ends with the most important point.
- Sequential method of development emphasizes the order of elements in a process and is particularly useful when writing step-by-step instructions.
- Spatial method of development describes the physical appearance of an object or area (such as a room) from top to bottom, inside to outside, front to back, and so on.

Rarely does a writer rely on only one of these methods. In fact, documents often blend methods of development and most large documents use combinations of methods. For example, in describing the organization of a company, you might use elements from three methods of development. You could divide the larger topic (the company) into departments (division and classification), arrange the departments by their order of importance within the company (order of importance), and present their manufacturing operations in the order they occur (sequential). As this example illustrates, when outlining a document, you may base your major division on one primary method of development appropriate to your purpose, and then subordinate other methods to it.

minutes of meetings

Organizations and committees keep official records of their meetings; such records are known as *minutes*. Because minutes are often used to settle disputes, they must be accurate, complete, and clear. When approved, minutes of meetings are official and can be used as evidence in legal proceedings. An example of minutes is shown in Figure M–5.

Keep your minutes brief and to the point. Except for recording motions, which must be transcribed word for word, summarize what occurs and paraphrase discussions. To keep the minutes concise, follow

NORTH TAMPA MEDICAL CENTER

Minutes of the Monthly Meeting
Medical Audit Committee

DATE: June 26, 2006

PRESENT: G. Miller (Chair), C. Bloom, J. Dades, K. Gilley,
           D. Ingoglia (Secretary), S. Ramirez

ABSENT: D. Rowan, C. Tsien, C. Voronski, R. Fautier, R. Wolf

Dr. Gail Miller called the meeting to order at 12:45 p.m. Dr. David Ingoglia
made a motion that the June 2, 2006, minutes be approved as distributed.
The motion was seconded and passed.

The committee discussed and took action on the following topics.

(1) TOPIC: Meeting Time

Discussion: The most convenient time for the committee to meet.
Action taken: The committee decided to meet on the fourth Tuesday of
every month, at 12:30 p.m.

FIGURE M-5. Minutes of a Meeting

M

a set format, and use <u>headings</u> for each major point discussed. See also
<u>note-taking</u>.

Avoid abstractions and generalities; always be specific. Refer to
everyone in the same way—a lack of consistency in titles or names may
suggest a deference to one person at the expense of another. Avoid
<u>adjectives</u> and <u>adverbs</u> that suggest good or bad qualities, as in "Mr.
Sturgess's *capable* assistant read the *comprehensive* report to the sub-
committee." Minutes should be objective and impartial.

If a member of the committee is to follow up on something and
report back to the committee at its next meeting, clearly state the person's name and the responsibility he or she has accepted.

Writer's Checklist: Preparing Minutes of Meetings

Include the following in meeting minutes:

- ☑ The name of the group or committee holding the meeting
- ☑ The topic of the meeting
- ☑ The kind of meeting (a regular meeting or a special meeting called
  to discuss a specific subject or problem)

Writer's Checklist: Preparing Minutes of Meetings (continued)

☑ The number of members present and, for committees or boards of ten or fewer members, their names

☑ The place, time, and date of the meeting

☑ A statement that the chair and the secretary were present or the names of any substitutes

☑ A statement that the minutes of the previous meeting were approved or revised

☑ A list of any reports that were read and approved

☑ All the main motions that were made, with statements as to whether they were carried, defeated, or tabled (vote postponed), and the names of those who made and seconded the motions (motions that were withdrawn are not mentioned)

☑ A full description of resolutions that were adopted and a simple statement of any that were rejected

☑ A record of all ballots with the number of votes cast for and against resolutions

☑ The time the meeting was adjourned (officially ended) and the place, time, and date of the next meeting

☑ The recording secretary's signature and typed name and, if desired, the signature of the chairperson

mission statements

A mission statement articulates an organization's unique reason for being and attempts to motivate its stakeholders (employees, customers, and stockholders) to pursue common goals. A good mission statement can achieve a focused allocation of organizational resources by posing such tough questions as, Why do we exist? What is our business? What are we trying to accomplish? A good mission statement can be an important factor in the success of an organization.

Different media may be used to distribute mission statements. They may be disseminated through multiple media: included in an organization's **annual report**, printed on parchment suitable for framing, published in a pamphlet, or posted on an organization's Web site. Figure M–6 shows a typical mission statement.

Writing a Mission Statement

Most mission statements have certain elements in common, such as a statement of purpose, a description of the organization's line of busi-

BARTLETT BANKARD MISSION STATEMENT

Mission

The strategic objective of Bartlett Bankard Corporation is to build high-performance, full-service community banks where people matter.

We offer and deliver competitive product lines that meet targeted customer needs and expectations while maintaining asset quality, capital strength, and earnings performance. We provide those products only when we are able to deliver them with the service and quality our customers deserve. For the Corporation to continue to fulfill these goals, we must be able to guarantee that the four cornerstones of our success—our customers, our employees, our communities, and our shareholders—are always firmly in place.

We must respond to:

Our customers:	They are our business. We will provide them with the products they want and need.
Our employees:	They are The Bank. Our customers know them as The Bank. We will provide them with the training, the working environment, and the recognition that encourage and promote growth.
Our communities:	Their success is our success. As a corporation and personally as individuals, we will meet the financial and public service needs of our communities.
Our shareholders:	They are the owners of the Corporation and, as our shareholders, they are entitled to a fair return on their investment.

FIGURE M–6. Mission Statement

ness, and an acknowledgment of important large groups like customers, employees, and stockholders. Following is a list of various goals that mission statements may be aimed to achieve. Some, or indeed all, may apply to a particular organization. Mission statements can do the following:

- Reflect an organization's purpose, function, and primary reason for existing.
- Guide the development and execution of organizational strategies.

- Offer benchmarks toward which long-range goals can be targeted and against which progress can be measured.

- Build and communicate company values over periods of time, thus providing an organization and its employees with a sense of identity.

- Distinguish an organization from others of the same type and identify the scope of the organization's operations in product and market terms.

Before beginning to write a mission statement, get approval of your general approach from top management. Then determine who will write the draft. In a small organization, the top person normally writes it. In a large organization, it is often written by a committee that includes a representative from every interested group (customers, employees, and stockholders).

Gather as much information as possible about your organization and its goals by interviewing top management and researching annual reports and other company documents. If you have a committee to help you, use **brainstorming** to answer the following questions that will help you understand the **context** of the mission statement:

- Why was our organization established?

- Who are our customers and clients? What needs do we meet?

- What image do we want our products and services to project?

- What message do we want to send the community, customers, stockholders, and employees about the organization?

- Where do we see our organization in five or ten years?

- What does our organizational culture need to be to get us there?

When you have answered these questions, create an outline (see **outlining**) and then **write a draft**. As you write, try to find words and phrases that capture the essence of the organization's purpose and goals, and avoid **jargon, buzzwords,** platitudes, meaningless superlatives, and overuse of the word *quality*. If you overload your mission statement with platitudes and superlatives, you will move **readers** to cynicism rather than persuading them. A mission to "Be the best computer manufacturer in the world" sounds good, but "Beat Gateway!" is a good deal more definable, measurable, and actionable—and it is guaranteed to motivate. To test the appropriateness of an assertion in your mission statement, ask whether anyone could reasonably disagree with it. If not, it is probably a platitude. Can you imagine anyone disagreeing with "To provide the best value for the money"?

When you are satisfied with your draft, circulate it to selected reviewers (involving as many employees, customers, and stockholders as possible, in order to give everyone a sense of ownership). Then revise the draft based on the feedback you receive.

Format and Length

The format and the length of a mission statement should be determined by what the organization wants to say about itself and how it wants to say it. The length may vary from a pithy one-sentence statement, such as a pet food company's concise "To enhance the well-being of dogs and cats," to multiple pages that begin with a mission statement and continue with a statement of the company's vision, values, philosophy, objectives, and strategies. Avoid letting the mission statement get too long, however, because readers will more readily remember a relatively short statement and incorporate its values into their daily business activities and planning. See also **business plans**.

mixed constructions

A mixed construction is a sentence in which the elements do not sensibly fit together. The problem may be a **grammar** error, a **logic error**, or both.

M

- Because the copier wouldn't start ~~explains why~~ we had to call a technician.

The original sentence mixes a subordinate **clause** (*Because the copier wouldn't start*) with a **verb** (*explains*) that attempts to incorrectly use the subordinate clause as its subject. The revision correctly uses the **pronoun** *we* as the subject of the main clause. See also **sentence construction**.

modifiers

Modifiers are words, phrases, or clauses that expand, limit, or make otherwise more specific the meaning of other elements in a sentence. Although we can create sentences without modifiers, we often need the detail and clarification they provide.

WITHOUT MODIFIERS	Production decreased.
WITH MODIFIERS	*Automobile* production decreased *rapidly.*

Most modifiers function as **adjectives** or **adverbs**. Adjectives describe qualities or impose boundaries on the words they modify.

- *noisy* machinery, *ten* automobiles, *this* printer, *an* animal

An adverb modifies an adjective, another adverb, a <u>verb</u>, or an entire <u>clause</u>.

- Under test conditions, the brake pad showed *much* less wear than it did under actual conditions.
  [The adverb *much* modifies the adjective *less.*]

- The redesigned brake pad lasted *much* longer.
  [The adverb *much* modifies another adverb, *longer.*]

- The wrecking ball hit the wall of the building *hard.*
  [The adverb *hard* modifies the verb *hit.*]

- *Surprisingly*, the motor failed even after all the durability and performance tests it had passed.
  [The adverb *surprisingly* modifies an entire clause: *the motor failed.*]

Adverbs are <u>intensifiers</u> when they increase the impact of adjectives (*very* fine, *too* high) or adverbs (*very* slowly, *rather* quickly). Be cautious using intensifiers; their overuse can lead to vagueness and hence to inaccuracies.

Stacked (Jammed) Modifiers

Stacked modifiers are strings of modifiers preceding <u>nouns</u> that make writing unclear or difficult to read.

- Your *staffing-level authorization reassessment* plan should result in a major improvement.

The noun *plan* is preceded by three long modifiers, a string that forces the reader to slow down to interpret its meaning. Stacked modifiers are often the result of an overuse of <u>buzzwords</u> or <u>jargon</u>. See how breaking up the stacked modifiers makes the example easier to read.

- Your plan for reassessing the staffing-level authorizations should result in a major improvement.

Misplaced Modifiers

A modifier is misplaced when it modifies the wrong word or phrase. A misplaced modifier can cause <u>ambiguity</u>.

- We *almost* lost all of the parts.
  [The parts were *almost* lost but were not.]

- We lost *almost* all of the parts.
  [Most of the parts were in fact lost.]

To avoid ambiguity, place modifiers as close as possible to the words they are intended to modify. Likewise, place phrases near the words they modify. Note the two meanings possible when the phrase is shifted in the following sentences:

- The equipment *without the accessories* sold the best.
  [Different types of equipment were available, some with and some without accessories.]

- The equipment sold the best *without the accessories.*
  [One type of equipment was available, and the accessories were optional.]

Place clauses as close as possible to the words they modify.

> REMOTE   We sent the brochure to several local firms *that had four-color art.*
>
> CLOSE   We sent the brochure *that had four-color art* to several local firms.

Squinting Modifiers

A squinting modifier is one that can be interpreted as modifying either of two sentence elements simultaneously, thereby confusing readers about which is intended. See also <u>dangling modifiers</u>.

- We agreed *on the next day* to make the adjustments.
  [Did they agree *to make the adjustments on the next day?* Or *on the next day,* did they agree to make the adjustments?]

A squinting modifier can sometimes be corrected simply by changing its position, but often it is better to rewrite the sentence.

- We agreed that *on the next day* we would make the adjustments.
  [The adjustments were to be made on the next day.]

- *On the next day,* we agreed that we would make the adjustments.
  [The agreement was made on the next day.]

M

---

mood

The grammatical term *mood* refers to the <u>verb</u> functions that indicate whether the verb is intended to make a statement or ask a question, give a command, or express a hypothetical possibility.

The *indicative mood* states a fact, gives an opinion, or asks a question.

- The setting *is* correct.
- *Is* the setting correct?

The *imperative mood* expresses a command, suggestion, request, or plea. In the imperative mood, the implied subject *you* is not expressed. (*Install* the system today.)

The *subjunctive mood* expresses something that is contrary to fact, conditional, hypothetical, or purely imaginative; it can also express a wish, a doubt, or a possibility. In the subjunctive mood, *were* is used instead of *was* in clauses that speculate about the present or future, and the base form (*be*) is used following certain verbs, such as *propose, request,* or *insist.* See also progressive <u>tense</u>.

- If we *were* to close the sale today, we would meet our monthly quota.
- The senior partner insisted that she [I, you, we, they] *be* in charge of the project.

The most common use of the subjunctive mood is to express clearly that the writer considers a condition to be contrary to fact. If the condition is not considered to be contrary to fact, use the indicative mood.

M

(ESL) TIPS FOR DETERMINING MOOD

In written and especially in spoken English, the tendency increasingly is to use the indicative mood where the subjunctive traditionally has been used. Note the differences between traditional and contemporary usage in the following examples.

Traditional (formal) use of the subjunctive mood

- I wish he *were* here now.
- If I *were* going to the conference, I would room with him.
- I requested that she *show* up on time.

Contemporary (informal) use of the indicative mood

- I wish he *was* here now.
- If I *was* going to the conference, I would room with him.
- I requested that she *shows* up on time.

In formal business and technical writing, it is best to use the more traditional expressions.

SUBJUNCTIVE   If I *were* president of the firm, I would change several hiring policies.

INDICATIVE   Although I *am* president of the firm, I don't feel that I control every aspect of its policies.

Ms. / Miss / Mrs.

Ms. is widely used in business and public life to address or refer to a woman, especially if her marital status is either unknown or irrelevant to the <u>context</u>. Traditionally, *Miss* is used to refer to an unmarried woman, and *Mrs.* is used to refer to a married woman. Some women may indicate a preference for *Ms.*, *Miss*, or *Mrs.*, which you should honor. If a woman has an academic or a professional title, use the appropriate form of address (*Doctor*, *Professor*, *Captain*) instead of *Ms.*, *Miss*, or *Mrs.* See also <u>biased language</u>.

mutual / common

Common is used when two or more persons (or things) share something or possess it jointly.

M

- We have a *common* desire to make the program succeed.
- Our departments have *common* office space.

Mutual may also mean "shared" (*mutual* friend, of *mutual* benefit), but it usually implies something given and received reciprocally and is used with reference to only two persons or parties.

- Melek respects Roth, and from my observations the respect is *mutual*.
  [Roth also respects Melek.]

N

narration

Narration is the presentation of a series of events in a prescribed (often chronological) sequence. Much narrative writing explains how something happened: a laboratory study, a site visit, an accident, the decisions in an important meeting. See also trip reports and trouble reports.

Effective narration rests on two key writing techniques: the careful, accurate sequencing of events and a consistent point of view on the part of the narrator. Narrative sequence and essential shifts in the sequence are signaled in three ways: chronology (clock and calendar time), transitional words pertaining to time (*before, after, next, first, while, then*), and verb tenses that indicate whether something has happened (past tense) or is under way (present tense). The point of view indicates the writer's relation to the information being narrated as reflected in the use of person. Narration usually expresses a first- or third-person point of view. First-person narration indicates that the writer is a participant, and third-person narration indicates that the writer is writing about what happened to someone or something else.

The narrative shown in Figure N–1 describes the financial climate for investors over the course of one year. The chronology is carefully specified throughout the narrative by month or by quarter, as the events require. The narrator uses the first person throughout (*we wrote*), as is appropriate for a newsletter whose function is to give advice. The chronology of past events (*In September, we said . . .*) shifts to the present (*Stocks and bonds are behaving more as commodity markets have in the past*), as the narrative shifts from past to current market performance.

Although narration often exists in combination with other forms of discourse, once a narrative is under way, it should not be interrupted by lengthy explanations or analyses. Explain only what is necessary for readers to follow the events.

A REVIEW OF THE YEAR'S FINANCIAL CLIMATE

We wrote in April, "As the reality of the crunch unfolds, the market is apt to react emotionally, with violent selling waves followed by equally dramatic periods of short covering. Investors should take advantage of the current market upswing to liquidate low-quality stocks and bonds. Market downdrafts should be used to purchase securities of the highest quality."

May Through July

In May, we introduced the "Watchlist," a group of companies where both annual and quarterly financial ratios were experiencing some deterioration in their balance sheets and financial ratios.

In June, we introduced the "Buy 90% T-bills plus 10% calls" as a defensive strategy preferable to holding equities. We also recommended:

1. getting fully overwritten
2. buy/writing on high-quality securities
3. buying puts aggressively

In July, we said, "This stop/go monetary policy works to increase the inherent volatility and risk in equity and debt markets alike. Therefore, the most appropriate view seems to be that of the informed, negatively biased, but agile contrarian who is willing to don a bullish cap when bearish market forces seem spent." That month we also introduced the "Brignoli Method" of dynamic vs. static method of option overwriting.

September

In September, we said, "While none of us expected the kind of powerful rally we have had in mid-August, . . . it's time to begin looking the other way. While the market still shows few signs of a near-term top, some defensive posturing is in order." We then focused on synthetic puts (sell stock/buy calls deep in the money as a way to protect recent gains) in order to participate in any further upside, and yet limit downside risk.

Current Assessment

We would have done better being bullish and abandoning all caution. By being cautious, we participated in a lot of the upside with more limited downside risk, paying some insurance along the way. Nevertheless, we were uncomfortable riding this kind of roller coaster without seat belts or safety nets. Perhaps the Fed's decision to bail the system out means there is no other stance but a bullish one. Yet, it's hard to gauge just how long this reprieve will last.

Stocks and bonds are behaving more as commodity markets have in the past. Typically, commodity prices move between enormous extremes both up and down. What's more, each extreme tends to have little connection to fundamental reality or value. Indeed, psychology tends to be the driving force behind such market moves.

N

FIGURE N–1. Narration

> ## nature

Nature, when used to mean "kind" or "sort," is vague. Avoid this usage in your writing. Say exactly what you mean.

- The ~~nature of~~ the contract caused the problem.
  exclusionary clause in ∧

> ## needless to say

Although the phrase *needless to say* sometimes occurs in speech and writing, you can either eliminate the phrase or comment on a statement to follow with a more descriptive word.

- ~~Needless to say,~~ departmental cutbacks have meant decreased efficiency.
  Understandably, ∧

> ## newsletter articles

If your organization publishes a <u>newsletter,</u> you may be asked to contribute an article on a subject in your area of expertise. In fact, an article is a good way to promote your work or your department.

Before you begin to write, consider the traditional *who, what, where, when,* and *why* of journalism (*Who* did it? *What* was done? *Where* was it done? *When* was it done? *Why* was it done?) and then add *how,* which may be of as much interest to your colleagues as any of the five *w*'s.

Next, determine whether the company has an official policy or position on your subject. If so, adhere to it as you prepare your article. If there is no company policy, determine as nearly as you can management's attitude toward your subject.

Gather several fairly recent issues of the newsletter and study the <u>style</u> and <u>tone</u> of the writing and the approach used for various kinds of subjects. Understand those perspectives before you begin to work on your own article. Ask yourself the following questions about your subject: What is its significance to the organization? What is its significance to my coworkers? The answers to those questions should help you establish the style, tone, and approach for your article and also heavily influence your conclusion. See also <u>context.</u>

Research for a newsletter article frequently consists of <u>interviewing for information.</u> Interview everyone concerned with your subject. Get all available information and all points of view. Be sure to give maximum credit to the maximum number of people by quoting statements from those involved in projects and naming those who have developed initiatives. See also quotations.

Figure N–2 shows an article written for *Connection*, a newsletter produced by Ken Cook Company and distributed to current and prospective clients. This article describes an innovative approach, called

FIGURE N–2. Newsletter Article

"see through" photography, which was used for the parts catalog of a fitness equipment manufacturer. Notice the inset photograph of a stair-climber, which is intended to draw readers to the article. By describing the innovative see through approach as well as the preeminent reputation of the fitness equipment manufacturer, the article positions Ken Cook Company at the leading edge of product support publications.

Writer's Checklist: Writing Newsletter Articles

Writing a newsletter article requires a more journalistic approach than writing a **report**. Because newsletters are usually not required reading, you do not have a captive audience. See also **emphasis**.

- ☑ Write an intriguing **title** to catch the **readers'** attention; **rhetorical questions** often work well.

- ☑ Include eye-catching **photographs** or **visuals** that entice your audience to read the lead **paragraph** of your **introduction**. See also **layout and design**.

- ☑ Fashion a lead, or first paragraph, that will encourage further reading. The first paragraph generally makes the **transition** from the title to the substantive body of the article.

- ☑ Offer a well-developed presentation of your subject to hold the readers' interest all the way to the end of the article.

- ☑ Write a **conclusion** that emphasizes the significance of your subject to your audience and stresses the points you want your readers to retain.

- ☑ Follow the steps listed in the Checklist of the Writing Process as you prepare your newsletter article.

N

newsletters

Newsletters are publications that are designed to inform and to create and sustain interest and membership in an organization. They can also be used to sell products and services. The two main types of newsletters are organizational newsletters and subscription newsletters.

Organizational newsletters like the one shown in Figure N–3 are sent to employees or members of an association to keep them informed about issues regarding their company or group, such as the development of new products or policies, or the accomplishments of individuals or teams. Stories in organizational newsletters can also urge members to take a specific action. For example, a health club's newsletter

Ken Cook Co.

www.kencook.com

Partners in Product Documentation   April 2003

KEN COOK CO. A FORD TIER 1 SUPPLIER

Ford Motor Company awarded Ken Cook Co. a Tier 1 Supplier status in December, 2002. This prestigious qualification allows the company to expand services to automobile manufacturers under the Ford umbrella. Tier 1 status was awarded because of a 20 year relationship with Volvo Cars of North America, a member of Ford's Premier Automotive Group.

"I'm a strong supporter of Ken Cook Co. and am pleased to see them become a Tier 1 supplier. KCC is an invaluable partner to Volvo and this action secures the integrity of our relationship," says Barry Morse, service operations specialist for Volvo Cars.

Over the 20 year period, Ken Cook Co. has provided technical documentation services to the Rockleigh, NJ automobile manufacturer. Comprehensive services include dealer support programs, data management, publication development and replication, call center operations, online order fulfillment, warehousing and custom distributions of technical documentation.

"We've been very successful in helping Volvo support their dealer and service network. We are currently in the final stages of completing a web-based project to address EPA and CARB requirements affecting the automotive industry," said Bruce Radtke, Ken Cook Co. account executive responsible for managing the Volvo account. The website, which will make service related information available on a subscription basis to both Volvo dealer and independent repair shops, was launched April 1st, 2003.

Visit the Volvo Cars service support website at www.volvotechinfo.com.

"Achieving the designation of a Tier 1 supplier is a significant milestone for our company and a testament to

> "I'm a strong supporter of Ken Cook Co. and am pleased to see them become a Tier 1 supplier. KCC is an invaluable partner to Volvo and this action secures the integrity of our relationship."
>
> **Barry Morse,** service operations specialist for Volvo Cars of North America

the strong relationship we have built with Volvo," says Ken Cook, president of Ken Cook Co. "With a successful business model already in place, our vision is to share our expertise in technical information management and provide other Ford companies with the programs and services Volvo has found indispensable."

Other companies within the Ford Premier Automotive Group include Jaguar, Land Rover and Aston Martin.

VOLVO

FEATURES

Ken Cook Co. A Ford Tier 1 Supplier..................1

Ken Cook Co. Receives ISO 9001:2000 Certification 2

The Benefits of Working With an ISO Certified Vendor..........2

NCAE Elects Cook to Board 3

Ken Cook Elected to NASM Board................3

One Department, One Goal.....4

FIGURE N–3. Company Newsletter (Front Page)

could describe new equipment being installed, its purpose, and how to use it.

Subscription newsletters are designed to attract and build a readership interested in buying specific products or services or in learning more about investing or financial matters. Subscribers are buying information, and they expect a certain level of value for their money. For example, a person with experience in the stock market could create a financial newsletter and charge subscribers a monthly fee for the investing advice in that newsletter; a person who collects movie memorabilia could create an online newsletter that includes stories about ways to find and sell rare movie posters.

Before you begin to develop a newsletter, decide on its specific **purpose** and the specific **readers** you will be targeting; then make sure the newsletter's appearance and editorial choices create a sense of identification among the readership. Because newsletters often involve different individuals who work on design, content, and project management, see **collaborative writing**. See also **persuasion** and **promotional writing**. If you are asked to contribute an article to a newsletter, see **newsletter articles**.

You will need to acquire a mailing list (names and addresses of your readers), and you will need to decide on the most strategic way to get the newsletter to the readers, whether through interoffice mail, the post office, or online. Because it can be time-consuming and technically problematic to send out hundreds or thousands of online newsletters by yourself, you may also need to subscribe to a list-hosting service.

As you develop and edit articles, you need to **research** the topics and interview relevant sources. As you research trade journals, business and technology magazines, newspapers, or the Internet, find specific angles for the articles that will appeal to your select audience. Attempt to provide content that they will not read elsewhere. Other strategies include interviewing and profiling customers or your employees. Be aware that your fact-checking needs to be meticulous. Unlike the general readership of a newspaper, newsletter readers are often specialists in their fields. Because newsletters are often distributed to branches and clients abroad, see **global communication** and **global graphics**. See also **interviewing for information**.

As shown in Figures N–2 and N–3, a newsletter's format should be simple and consistent, yet visually appealing to your readership. Use the active **voice** and a conversational **tone**. Boldface names of customers or association members included in your articles to identify them and bring attention to their contributions. Use **headings** and bullets to break up the text and make the newsletter easy to read. Keep your sentences simple and paragraphs short. See **conciseness** and **layout and design**.

Using word-processing or desktop-publishing software, create newspaper columns and one or two **visuals** per page that complement the text. On the front page, identify the organization, include the date, volume and issue numbers, and a contents box. Depending on the length and quantity of the text and **photographs** or other visuals to be included, newsletters are usually $8\frac{1}{2}'' \times 11''$ or $17'' \times 22''$ pages folded in half. If your budget is generous and the scale of your project is substantial, consider using a professional printer to produce your newsletter.

nominalizations

A nominalization is a weak <u>verb</u> (*make, do, conduct, perform*) combined with a <u>noun</u>, when the verb form of the noun would communicate the same idea more directly and concisely.

- The quality assurance team will ~~perform an evaluation of~~ the new software.

  evaluate ∧

If you use nominalizations solely to make your writing sound more formal, the result will be <u>affectation</u>. You may occasionally have an appropriate use for a nominalization. For example, you might use a nominalization to slow the <u>pace</u> of your writing. See also <u>conciseness</u> and <u>business writing style</u>.

none

None can be considered either a singular or a plural <u>pronoun</u>, depending on the context. See also <u>agreement</u>.

- *None* of the material *has* been ordered.
  [Always use a singular <u>verb</u> with a singular <u>noun</u>, in this case, "material."]
- *None* of the clients *has* been called yet.
  [Use a singular verb even with a plural noun (*clients*) if the intended emphasis is on the idea of *not one*.]
- *None* of the clients *have* been called yet.
  [Use a plural verb if you intend *none* to refer to all clients.]

For <u>emphasis</u>, substitute *no one* or *not one* for *none* and use a singular verb.

- We paid the retail price for three of the machines, ~~none~~ of which was worth the money.

  not one ∧

nor / or

Nor always follows *neither* in sentences with continuing negation. (They will *neither* support *nor* approve the plan.) Likewise, *or* follows *either* in sentences. (The firm will accept *either* a short-term *or* a long-term loan.)

Two or more singular subjects joined by *or* or *nor* usually take a singular <u>verb</u>. However, when one subject is singular and one is plural, the verb agrees with the subject nearer to it. See also <u>conjunctions</u> and <u>parallel structure</u>.

SINGULAR   Neither the *architect* nor the *client was* happy with the design.

PLURAL   Neither the *architect* nor the *clients were* happy with the design.

SINGULAR   Neither the *architects* nor the *client was* happy with the design.

note-taking

The purpose of note-taking is to summarize and record information you extract during <u>research</u>. (For taking notes at a meeting, see <u>minutes of meetings</u>.) The challenge in taking notes is to condense someone else's thoughts into your own words without distorting the original thinking. As you extract information, let your knowledge of the <u>audience</u> and the <u>purpose</u> of your writing guide you.

◪ ETHICS NOTE   Resist copying your source word for word as you take notes; instead, paraphrase the author's idea or concept. You must do more than just change a few words in the original passage; otherwise, you will be guilty of <u>plagiarism</u>. See also <u>paraphrasing</u>. ✦

On occasion, when your source concisely sums up a great deal of information or points to a trend important to your subject, you are justified in directly quoting the source and incorporating it into your document. If you use a direct quote, enclose the material in <u>quotation marks</u> in your notes. In your finished writing, provide the source of your quotation. As a general rule, you will rarely need to quote anything longer than a paragraph. See also <u>documenting sources</u>.

When taking notes on abstract ideas, as opposed to factual data, do not sacrifice clarity for brevity—notes expressing concepts can lose their meaning if they are too brief. The critical test is whether a week later you understand the note and can recall the significant ideas of the passage. Consider the information in the following paragraph:

Long before the existence of bacteria was suspected, techniques were in use for combating their influence in, for instance, the decomposition of meat. Salt and heat were known to be effective, and these do in fact kill bacteria or prevent them from multiplying. Salt acts by the osmotic effect of extracting water from the bacterial cell fluid. Bacteria are less easily destroyed by osmotic action than are animal cells because their cell walls are constructed in a totally different way, which makes them much less permeable.

The paragraph says essentially three things:

1. Before the discovery of bacteria, salt and heat were used to combat the effects of bacteria.
2. Salt kills bacteria by extracting water from their cells by osmosis, hence its use in curing meat.
3. Bacteria are less affected by the osmotic effect of salt than are animal cells, because bacterial cell walls are less permeable.

If your readers' needs and your objective involved tracing the origin of the bacterial theory of disease, you might want to note that salt was traditionally used to kill bacteria long before people realized what caused meat to spoil. It might not be necessary to your topic to say anything about the relative permeability of bacterial cell walls.

You should record notes in a way you find efficient. Some find various shareware note and index programs useful. However, jotting notes on 3 × 5 inch index cards is often more flexible, and the cards are especially useful for <u>outlining</u> complex and long-term projects.*

Writer's Checklist: Taking Notes

☑ Ask yourself the following questions: What information do you need to fulfill your purpose? What are the needs of your <u>readers</u>?

☑ Record only the most important ideas and concepts. Be sure to record all vital names, dates, and definitions.

☑ When in doubt about whether to take a note, consider the difficulty of finding the source again should you want it later.

☑ Use <u>quotations</u> when sources summarize a great deal of information or point to important trends.

☑ Ensure proper credit: Record the author, title, publisher, place, page number, URL, and date of publication or retrieval. (On subsequent notes from the same source, include only the author and page number.)

☑ Use your own shorthand and record notes in a way that you find efficient, whether in an electronic document or on index cards.

☑ Photocopy or download pages and highlight passages that you intend to quote.

☑ Check your notes for accuracy against the original material before moving on to another source.

N

*Peter Walsh, *How to Organize Just About Everything* (New York: Free Press, 2004).

nouns

DIRECTORY
Types of Nouns   352
Noun Functions   352
Collective Nouns   353
Plural Nouns   353

A noun names a person, place, thing, concept, action, or quality.

Types of Nouns

The two basic types of nouns are proper nouns and common nouns. *Proper nouns,* which are capitalized, name specific people, places, and things (H. G. Wells, Boston, United Nations, Nobel Prize). See also capitalization.

Common nouns, which are not capitalized unless they begin sentences, name general classes or categories of persons, places, things, concepts, actions, and qualities (writer, city, organization, award). Common nouns include collective nouns, concrete nouns, abstract nouns, count nouns, and mass nouns.

Collective nouns are common nouns that indicate a group or collection. They are plural in meaning but singular in form (audience, jury, brigade, staff, committee). (See the subsection Collective Nouns on page 353 for advice on using singular or plural forms with collective nouns.)

Concrete nouns are common nouns used to identify those things that can be discerned by the five senses (paper, keyboard, glue, nail, grease).

Abstract nouns are common nouns that refer to things that cannot be discerned by the five senses (loyalty, pride, valor, peace, devotion).

Count nouns are concrete nouns that identify things that can be separated into countable units (desks, envelopes, printers, pencils, books).

Mass nouns are concrete nouns that identify things that cannot be easily separated into countable units (water, air, electricity, oil, cement). See also English as a second language.

Noun Functions

Nouns function as subjects of verbs, direct and indirect objects of verbs and prepositions, subjective and objective complements, or appositives.

- The *metal* failed during the test. [subject]
- The bricklayer cemented the *blocks* efficiently. [direct object of a verb]
- The state presented our *department* a safety award. [indirect object]
- The event occurred within the *year*. [object of a preposition]
- A dynamo is a *generator*. [subjective complement]
- The regional manager was appointed *chairperson*. [objective complement]
- George Thomas, the *treasurer*, gave his report last. [appositive]

Words normally used as nouns can also be used as **adjectives** and **adverbs**.

- It is *company* policy. [adjective]
- He went *home*. [adverb]

Collective Nouns

When a collective noun refers to a group as a whole, it takes a singular verb and pronoun.

- The staff *was* divided on the issue and could not reach *its* decision until May 15.

When a collective noun refers to individuals within a group, it takes a plural verb and pronoun.

- The staff *returned* to *their* offices after the conference.

A better way to emphasize the individuals on the staff would be to use the phrase *the staff members*.

- The staff members *returned* to *their* offices after the conference.

Treat organization names and titles as singular.

- LRM Associates *has* grown 30 percent in the last three years; *it* will move to a new facility in January.

Plural Nouns

Most nouns form the plural by adding -*s*.

- dolphin/dolphins, pencil/pencils

Nouns ending in *ch*, *s*, *sh*, *x*, and *z* form the plural by adding -*es*.

- search/searches, glass/glasses, wish/wishes, six/sixes, buzz/buzzes

Nouns that end in a consonant plus *y* form the plural by changing the *y* to -*ies*.

- delivery/deliveries

Some nouns ending in *o* add -*es* to form the plural, but others add only -*s*.

- tomato/tomatoes, dynamo/dynamos

Some nouns ending in *f* or *fe* add -*s* to form the plural; others change the *f* or *fe* to -*ves*.

- cliff/cliffs, fife/fifes, hoof/hooves, knife/knives

Some nouns require an internal change to form the plural.

- woman/women, man/men, mouse/mice, goose/geese

Some nouns do not change in the plural form.

- many *fish*, several *deer*, fifty *sheep*

Hyphenated and open compound nouns form the plural in the main word.

- sons-in-law, high schools, editors in chief

Compound nouns written as one word add -*s* to the end.

- two *tablespoonfuls*

If you are unsure of the proper usage, check a dictionary. See <u>possessive case</u> for a discussion of how nouns form possessives.

number (grammar)

Number is the grammatical property of <u>nouns</u>, <u>pronouns</u>, and <u>verbs</u> that signifies whether one thing (singular) or more than one (plural) is being referred to. (See also <u>agreement</u>.) Nouns normally form the plural by simply adding -*s* or -*es* to their singular forms.

- *Partners* in successful *businesses* are not always personal friends.

Some nouns require an internal change to form the plural.

- woman/women, man/men, goose/geese, mouse/mice

All pronouns except *you* change internally to form the plural.

- I/we, he/they, she/they, it/they

By adding *-s* or *-es*, most verbs show the singular of the third **person**, present **tense**, indicative **mood**.

- he *stands*, she *works*, it *goes*

The verb *be* normally changes form to indicate the plural.

SINGULAR	I *am* ready to begin work.
PLURAL	We *are* ready to begin work.

numbers

DIRECTORY
Numerals or Words   355
Plurals 356
Measurements   356
Fractions 356
Money 356

Time   357
Dates   357
Addresses   357
Documents   358

The standards for using numbers vary; however, unless you are following an organizational or a professional style manual, observe the following guidelines.

Numerals or Words

Write numbers from zero to ten as words, and write numbers above ten as numerals.

- I rehearsed my presentation *three* times.
- The association added *150* new members.

Spell out numbers that begin a sentence, however, even if they would otherwise be written as figures.

- *One hundred and fifty* people attended the meeting.

If spelling out such a number seems awkward, rewrite the sentence so that the number does not appear at the beginning.

Spell out approximate and round numbers.

- We've had *over a thousand* requests this month.

In most writing, spell out small ordinal numbers, which express degree or sequence (first, second; but 27th, 42nd), when they are single words (our nineteenth year), or when they modify a century (the twenty-first century). However, avoid ordinal numbers in <u>dates</u> (use March 30 or 30 March, not March 30th).

Plurals

Indicate the plural of numerals by adding -s (7s, the late 1990s). Form the plural of a written number (like any noun) by adding -s or -es or by dropping the y and adding -ies (elevens, sixes, twenties). See also **apostrophes**.

Measurements

Express units of measurement as numerals (3 miles, 45 cubic feet, 9 meters). When numbers run together in the same phrase, write one as a numeral and the other as a word.

- The order was for ~~12~~ *twelve* 6-foot tables.

Generally give percentages as numerals and write out the word *percent*, except when the number is in a table. (Approximately *85 percent* of the land has been sold.)

Fractions

Express fractions as numerals when they are written with whole numbers (27½ inches, 4¼ miles). Spell out fractions when they are expressed without a whole number (one-fourth, seven-eighths). Always write decimal numbers as numerals (5.21 meters).

Money

In general, use numerals to express exact or approximate amounts of money.

- We need to charge *$28.95* per unit.
- The new system costs *$60,000*.

Use words to express indefinite amounts of money.

- The printing system may cost *several thousand dollars*.

Use numerals and words for rounded amounts of money over one million dollars.

- The contract is worth *$6.8 million*.

Use numerals for more complex or exact amounts.

* The corporation paid *$2,452,500* in taxes last year.

For amounts under a dollar, ordinarily use numerals and the word *cents* (The pens cost *50 cents* each), unless other figures that require dollar signs appear in the same sentence.

* The business-card holders cost *$10.49* each, the pens cost *$.50* each, and the pencil-cup holders cost *$6.49* each.

ESL TIPS FOR PUNCTUATING NUMBERS

Some rules for punctuating numbers in English are summarized as follows.

Use a comma to separate numbers with four or more digits into groups of three, starting from the right (*5,289,112,001* atoms).

Do not use a comma in years, house numbers, zip codes, and page numbers.

* June *2005*
* *92401* East Alameda Drive
* The zip code is *91601*.
* Page *1204*

Use a period to represent the decimal point (*4.2* percent, *$3,742,097.43*). See also global communication and global graphics.

Time

Divide hours and minutes with <u>colons</u> when *a.m.* or *p.m.* follows (7:30 a.m., 11:30 p.m.). Do not use colons with the 24-hour system (0730, 2330). Spelled out time is not followed by *a.m.* or *p.m.* (seven o'clock in the evening).

Dates

In the United States dates are usually written in a month-day-year sequence (August 11, 2006). Never use the strictly numerical form for dates (8/11/06) because the date is not immediately clear, especially in international correspondence.

Addresses

Spell out numbered streets from one to ten unless space is at a premium (East Tenth Street). Write building numbers as numerals. The only exception is the building number *one* (One East Monument Street). Write highway numbers as numerals (U.S. 40, Ohio 271, I-94).

Documents

In manuscripts, page numbers are written as numerals, but chapter and volume numbers may appear as numerals or words (Page 37, Chapter 2 or Chapter Two, Volume 1 or Volume One). Express figure and table numbers as numerals (Figure 4, Table 3).

Do not follow a word representing a number with a numeral in parentheses that represents the same number. Doing so is redundant.

- Send five ~~(5)~~ copies of the report.

N

O

objects

The three kinds of objects are direct objects, indirect objects, and objects of <u>prepositions</u>. All objects are <u>nouns</u> or noun equivalents: <u>pronouns</u>, <u>verbals</u>, and noun <u>phrases</u> and <u>clauses</u>. See also <u>complements</u>.

Direct Object

A direct object answers the question *what?* or *whom?* about a <u>verb</u> and its subject.

- We sent a *full report.* [We sent *what?*]
- Bill telephoned the *client.* [Bill telephoned *whom?*]

Indirect Object

An indirect object is a noun or noun equivalent that occurs with a direct object after certain kinds of transitive verbs, such as *give, wish, cause,* and *tell.* The indirect object answers the question *to whom or what?* or *for whom or what?* The indirect object always precedes the direct object.

- We sent the *general manager* a full report.
  [*Report* is the direct object; the indirect object, *general manager,* answers the question, "We sent a full report *to whom?*"]

Object of a Preposition

The object of a preposition is a noun or pronoun that is introduced by a preposition, forming a prepositional phrase.

- At the *meeting,* the district managers approved the contract.
  [*Meeting* is the object, and *at the meeting* is the prepositional phrase.]

OK / okay

The expression *okay* (also spelled *OK*) is common in informal writing, but it should be avoided in <u>reports</u> and most <u>correspondence</u>.

- Mr. Sturgess ~~gave his okay to~~ the project.
  approved

on / onto / upon

On is normally used as a preposition meaning "attached to" or "located at." (Install the shelf *on* the north wall.) *Onto* implies movement to a position on or movement up and on. (The commuters surged *onto* the platform.)

Similarly, *on* stresses a position of rest (A book lay *on* the table), and *upon* emphasizes movement or a condition (Final payment will be made *upon* completion).

one

When used as an indefinite <u>pronoun</u>, *one* may help you avoid repeating a <u>noun</u>. (We need a new plan, not an old *one*.) *One* is often redundant in phrases in which it restates the noun, and it may take the proper emphasis away from the <u>adjective</u>.

- The training program was not ~~a unique one.~~
  unique.

One can also be used in place of a noun or personal pronoun in a statement. (*One* cannot ignore *one's* physical condition.) Using *one* in that way is formal and impersonal; in any but the most formal writing, you should address your reader directly and personally as *you*. (*You* cannot ignore *your* physical condition.) See also <u>point of view</u>.

one of those . . . who

A dependent <u>clause</u> beginning with *who* or *that* and preceded by *one of those* takes a plural <u>verb</u>.

- She is *one of those* managers *who are* concerned about their writing.

- This is *one of those* policies *that make* no sense when you examine them closely.

In those two examples, *who* and *that* refer to plural antecedents (*managers* and *policies*) and thus take plural verbs (*are* and *make*). See also <u>agreement</u>.

If the phrase *one of those* is preceded by *the only*, however, the verb should be singular.

- She is *the only one of those* managers *who is* concerned about her writing.
  [The verb is singular because its subject, *who*, refers to a singular antecedent, *one*. If the sentence were reversed, it would read, "Of those managers, she is *the only one who is* concerned about her writing."]

- This is *the only one of those* policies *that makes* no sense when you examine it closely.
  [If the sentence were reversed, it would read, "Of those policies, this is *the only one that makes* no sense when you examine it closely."]

only

The word *only* should be placed immediately before the word or phrase it modifies. See also <u>modifiers</u>.

- We ~~only~~ lack *only* financial backing.

Be careful with the placement of *only* because it can change the meaning of a sentence.

- *Only* he said that he was tired.
  [He alone said that he was tired.]

- He *only* said that he was tired.
  [He actually was not tired, although he said he was.]

- He said *only* that he was tired.
  [He said nothing except that he was tired.]

- He said that he was *only* tired.
  [He said that he was nothing except tired.]

order-of-importance method of development

The order-of-importance <u>method of development</u> is a particularly effective and common organizing strategy. This method can use one of two ordering strategies — decreasing order, which is often best for written documents, and increasing order, which is especially effective for oral <u>presentations</u>.

Decreasing Order

Decreasing order begins with the most important fact or point, then moves to the next most important, and so on, ending with the least important. This order is especially appropriate for a **memo** or other **correspondence** addressed to a busy decision-maker (see Figure O–1), who may be able to reach a decision after considering only the most important points. In a **report** addressed to various **readers,** some of whom may be interested in only the major points and others who may need all the information, decreasing order may be ideal for your **purpose.**

The advantages of decreasing order are that (1) it gets the reader's attention immediately by presenting the most important point first,

---

Memorandum

To: Tawana Shaw, Director, Human Resources Department
From: Frank W. Nemitz, Chief, Claims Department   *FWN*
Date: November 20, 2006
Subject: Selection of Chief of the Claims Processing Section

I have assessed the candidates for Chief of the Claims Processing Section as you requested, and the following are my evaluations.

Top-Ranked Candidate
The most qualified candidate is Michelle Bryant, acting chief of that section. In her 12 years in the Claims Department, Ms. Bryant has gained wide experience in all facets of its operations. She has maintained a consistently high production record and has demonstrated the skills and knowledge required for the supervisory duties she is now handling. She has continually been rated "outstanding" in all categories in her job-performance appraisals. However, her supervisory experience is limited to her present three-month tenure as acting chief of the section, and she lacks the college degree required by the job description.

Second-Ranked Candidate
Michael Bastick, Claims Coordinator, my second choice, also has strong potential for the position. An able administrator, he has been with the company for seven years. Further, he is enrolled in a management-training course at Metro State University's downtown campus. I have ranked him second because he lacks supervisory experience and because his most recent work has been with the department's maintenance and supply components. He would be the best person to take over many of Michelle Bryant's responsibilities if she were made full-time Chief of the Claims Processing Section.

Third-Ranked Candidate
Jane Fine, my third-ranked candidate, has shown herself to be a skilled administrator in her three years with the Claims Processing Section. Despite her obvious potential, she does not yet have the breadth of experience in claims processing that is required to manage the Claims Processing Section. Jane Fine also lacks on-the-job supervisory experience.

FIGURE O–1. Decreasing Order-of-Importance Method of Development

(2) it makes a strong initial impression, and (3) it ensures that even the most hurried reader will not miss the most important point.

Increasing Order

Increasing order begins from the least important point or fact, then progresses to the next more important, and builds finally to the most important or strongest point.

Increasing order of importance is effective for writing in which (1) you want to save your strongest points until the end or (2) you need to build the ideas point by point to an important <u>conclusion</u> (see Figure O–2). Many oral presentations benefit especially from increasing

From: Harry Mathews <matthews@appliedsciences.com>
To: Sun-Hee Kim <kim@appliedsciences.com>
Sent: Friday, May 19, 2006 9:29 AM
Subject: Recruiting Qualified Data Input Operators

As our company continues to expand, and with the planned opening of the Lakeland Facility late next year, we need to increase and refocus our recruiting program to keep our company staffed with qualified data input operators. Below is my analysis of possible recruiting options.

Business School Recruitment
Over the past three years, we have relied on our in-house internship program and on local and regional business school graduates to fill these positions. Although our in-house internship program provides a qualified pool of potential employees, business school enrollments in the area have in the past provided candidates who are already trained. Each year, however, fewer business school graduates are being produced, and even the most vigorous Career Day recruiting has yielded disappointing results.

Military Veteran Recruitment
In the past, we relied heavily on the recruitment of skilled veterans from all branches of the military. This source of qualified applicants all but disappeared when the military offered attractive reenlistment bonuses for skilled operators in uniform. As a result, we need to become aggressive in our attempts to reach this group through advertising. I would like to meet with you soon to discuss the details of a more dynamic recruiting program for skilled operators leaving the military.

I am certain that with the right recruitment campaign, we can find the skilled employees essential to our expanding role in electronics products and consulting.

O

FIGURE O–2. Increasing Order-of-Importance Method of Development order because it leaves the <u>audience</u> with the strongest points freshest in their minds. The disadvantage of increasing order, especially for written documents, is that it begins weakly, and the reader or listener may become impatient or distracted before reaching your main point. In the example given in Figure O–2, the writer begins with the least productive source of applicants and builds up to the most productive source.

organization

Organization is essential to the success of any writing project, from a <u>formal report</u> to a <u>Web design</u> or an effective <u>presentation</u>. Good organization is achieved by <u>outlining</u> and by using a logical and appropriate <u>method of development</u> that suits your subject, your <u>readers</u>, and your <u>purpose</u>.

During the organization stage of the writing process, you must consider a <u>layout and design</u> that will be helpful to your reader and a <u>format</u> appropriate to your subject and purpose. If you intend to include <u>visuals</u> with your writing, consider them as you create your outline, especially if they need to be prepared by someone else while you are writing and revising the draft. See also "Five Steps to Successful Writing."

organizational charts

An organizational chart shows how the various components of an organization are related to one another. This type of <u>visual</u> is useful when you want to give your <u>readers</u> an overview of an organization or to display the lines of authority within it, as in Figure O–3.

The title of each organizational component (office, section, division) is placed in a separate box. The boxes are then linked to a central authority, as shown in Figure O–3. If your readers need the information, include the name of the person and position title in each box.

As with all illustrations, place the organizational chart as close as possible to but not preceding the text that refers to it.

outlining

An outline is the skeleton of the document you are going to write; at the least, it should list the main topics and subtopics of your subject in a logical <u>method of development</u>.

FIGURE O-3. Organizational Chart

Advantages of Outlining

An outline provides structure to your writing by ensuring that it has a beginning (<u>introduction</u>), a middle (body), and an end (<u>conclusion</u>). Using an outline offers many other benefits.

- Larger and more complex subjects are easier to handle because an outline breaks them into manageable parts.
- Like a road map, an outline indicates a starting point and keeps you moving logically so that you do not lose your way before you arrive at your conclusion.
- Parts of an outline are easily moved around so that you can select the most effective arrangement of your ideas.
- Creating a good outline frees you from concerns of <u>organization</u> while you are <u>writing a draft</u>.
- An outline enables you to provide <u>coherence</u> and <u>transition</u> so that one part flows smoothly into the next without omitting important details.
- <u>Logic errors</u> are much easier to detect and correct in an outline than in a draft.
- An outline helps with <u>collaborative writing</u> because it enables a team to refine a project's <u>scope</u>, divide responsibilities, and maintain focus.

Types of Outlines

Two types of outlines are most common: short topic outlines and lengthy sentence outlines. A *topic outline* consists of short phrases arranged to reflect your primary method of development. A topic outline is especially useful for short documents such as letters, <u>e-mails</u>, or memos. See also <u>correspondence</u>.

For a large writing project, create a topic outline first, and then use it as a basis for creating a sentence outline. A *sentence outline* summarizes each idea in a complete sentence that may become the topic sentence for a paragraph in the rough draft. If most of your notes can be shaped into topic sentences for paragraphs in your rough draft, you can be relatively sure that your document will be well organized. See also <u>note-taking</u> and <u>research</u>.

Creating an Outline

When you are outlining large and complex subjects with many pieces of information, the first step is to group related notes into categories. Sort the notes by major and minor division headings. Use an appropriate method of development to arrange items and label them with Roman numerals. For example, the major divisions for this discussion of outlining could be as follows:

I. Advantages of outlining
II. Types of outlines
III. Creating an outline

The second step is to establish your minor points by deciding on the minor divisions within each major division. Arrange your minor points using a method of development under their major division and label them with capital letters.

II. Types of outlines
   A. Topic outlines   ⎤ Division and Classification
   B. Sentence outlines   ⎦
III. Creating an outline
   A. Establish major and minor divisions. ⎤
   B. Sort notes by major and minor divisions. ⎟ Sequential
   C. Complete the sentence outline. ⎦

You will often need more than two levels of headings. If your subject is complicated, you may need three or four levels of headings to better organize all of your ideas in proper relationship to one another. In that event, use the following numbering scheme:

I. First-level heading
  A. Second-level heading
    1. Third-level heading
      a. Fourth-level heading

The third step is to mark each of your notes with the appropriate Roman numeral and capital letter. Arrange the notes logically within each minor heading, and mark each with the appropriate, sequential Arabic number. As you do, make sure your organization is logical and your headings have **parallel structure**. For example, all the second-level headings under "III. Creating an outline" are complete sentences in the active **voice**.

Treat **visuals** as an integral part of your outline, and plan approximately where each should appear. Either include a rough sketch of the visual or write "illustration of . . ." at each place. As with other information in an outline, freely move, delete, or add visuals as needed.

The outline samples shown earlier use a combination of numbers and letters to differentiate the various levels of information. You could also use a decimal numbering system, such as the following, for your outline.

  1. FIRST-LEVEL HEADING
    1.1 Second-level heading
    1.2 Second-level heading
      1.2.1 Third-level heading
      1.2.2 Third-level heading
        1.2.2.1 Fourth-level heading
        1.2.2.2 Fourth-level heading
    1.3 Second-level heading
  2. FIRST-LEVEL HEADING

This system should not go beyond the fourth level because the numbers get too cumbersome beyond that point. In many documents, such as **policies and procedures**, the decimal numbering system is carried over from the outline to the final version of the document for ease of cross-referencing sections.

Create your draft by converting your notes into complete sentences and **paragraphs**. If you have a sentence outline, the most difficult part

---

DIGITAL TIPS **CREATING AN OUTLINE**

Using the outline feature of your word-processing software permits you to format your outline automatically—fill in, rearrange, and update your outline, as well as create an alphanumeric or a decimal numbering outlining style. For step-by-step instructions, see <*bedfordstmartins.com/alredbus*> and select *Digital Tips*, "Creating an Outline."

of the writing job is over. However, whether you have a topic or a sentence outline, remember that an outline is not set in stone; it may need to change as you write the draft, but it should always be your point of departure and return.

outside [of]

In the phrase *outside of*, the word *of* is redundant.

- Place the equipment outside ~~of~~ the meeting room.

Do not use *outside of* to mean "aside from" or "except for."

- ~~Outside of~~ his frequent absences, Jim has a good work record.
  Except for

over [with]

In the expression *over with*, the word *with* is redundant; such words as *completed* or *finished* often better express the thought.

- The conference room is available when the managers' meeting is

  over ~~with.~~

- The conference room is available when the managers' meeting is
  ~~over with.~~
  finished.

P

pace

Pace is the speed at which you present ideas to the reader. Your goal should be to achieve a pace that fits your **readers**, **purpose**, and subject. The more knowledgeable the reader is about the subject, the faster your pace can be. Be careful, though, not to lose control of the pace. In the first version of the following passage, facts are piled on top of each other at a rapid pace. In the second version, even though its length is no greater, the same facts are presented in two more easily assimilated sentences. In addition, the second version achieves a different and more desirable **emphasis**.

RAPID	The corporate records database (CRD) contains every employee's full name, home address, Social Security number, and current job classification and is intended to help individual departments and offices process records for every one of the 21,000 employees worldwide.
CONTROLLED	The corporate records database (CRD) contains identifying information for every one of the 21,000 employees worldwide. The CRD, which enables individual departments and offices to process employee records, contains every employee's full name, home address, social security number, and current job classification.

paragraphs

A paragraph performs three functions: (1) It develops the unit of thought stated in the topic sentence; (2) it provides a logical break in the material; and (3) it creates a visual break on the page, which signals a new topic.

Topic Sentence

A topic sentence states the paragraph's main idea; the rest of the paragraph supports and develops that statement with related details. The topic sentence is often the first sentence because it tells the reader what the paragraph is about.

- *The cost of training new employees is high.* In addition to the cost of classroom facilities and instructors, an organization must pay employees their regular salary while they sit in the classroom. For the companies to break even on the investment in their professional employees, they must stay in the job for which they have been trained for at least one year.

The topic sentence is usually most effective early in the paragraph, but a paragraph can lead up to the topic sentence, which is sometimes done to achieve <u>emphasis</u>.

- Energy does far more than simply make our daily lives more comfortable and convenient. Suppose you wanted to stop—and reverse—the economic progress of this nation. What would be the surest and quickest way to do it? Find a way to cut off the nation's oil resources! . . . The economy would plummet into the abyss of national economic ruin. *Our economy, in short, is energy-based.*
  — *The Baker World* (Los Angeles: Baker Oil Tools)

On rare occasions, the topic sentence may logically fall in the middle of a paragraph.

- . . . [It] is time to insist that science does not progress by carefully designed steps called "experiments," each of which has a well-defined beginning and end. *Science is a continuous and often a disorderly and accidental process.* We shall not do the young psychologist any favor if we agree to reconstruct our practices to fit the pattern demanded by current scientific methodology.
  —B. F. Skinner, "A Case History in Scientific Method"

Paragraph Length

A paragraph should be just long enough to deal adequately with the subject of its topic sentence. A new paragraph should begin whenever the subject changes significantly. A series of short, undeveloped paragraphs can indicate poor <u>organization</u> and sacrifice unity by breaking a single idea into several pieces. A series of long paragraphs, however, can fail to provide the reader with manageable subdivisions of thought. Paragraph length should aid the reader's understanding of ideas.

Occasionally, a one-sentence paragraph is acceptable if it is used as a transition between longer paragraphs or as a one-sentence <u>introduction</u> or <u>conclusion</u> in <u>correspondence</u>.

Writing Paragraphs

Careful paragraphing reflects the writer's logical organization and helps the reader follow the writer's thoughts. A good working outline makes it easy to group ideas into appropriate paragraphs. (See also <u>outlining</u>.) Although paragraphs can vary from their outlines, the following partial topic outline plots the course of the subsequent paragraphs:

TOPIC OUTLINE (PARTIAL)
I. Advantages of Chicago as location for new facility
   A. Transport infrastructure
      1. Rail
      2. Air
      3. Truck
      4. Sea (except in winter)
   B. Labor supply
      1. Engineering and scientific personnel
         a. Similar companies in area
         b. Major universities
      2. Technical and manufacturing personnel
         a. Community college programs
         b. Custom programs

RESULTING PARAGRAPHS
Probably the greatest advantage of Chicago as a location for our new facility is its excellent transport facilities. The city is served by three major railroads. Both domestic and international air cargo service is available at O'Hare International Airport; Midway Airport's convenient location adds flexibility for domestic air cargo service. Chicago is a major hub of the trucking industry, and most of the nation's large freight carriers have terminals there. Finally, except in the winter months when the Great Lakes are frozen, Chicago is a seaport, accessible through the St. Lawrence Seaway.

Chicago's second advantage is its abundant labor force. An ample supply of engineering and scientific staff is assured not only by the presence of many companies engaged in activities similar to ours but also by the presence of several major universities in the metropolitan area. Similarly, technicians and manufacturing personnel are in abundant supply. The colleges in the Chicago City

P

College system, as well as half a dozen other two-year colleges in the outlying areas, produce graduates with associate's degrees in a wide variety of technical specialties appropriate to our needs. Moreover, three of the outlying colleges have expressed an interest in developing off-campus courses attuned specifically to our requirements.

Paragraph Unity and Coherence

A good paragraph has <u>unity</u> and <u>coherence</u>, as well as adequate development. *Unity* is singleness of purpose, based on a topic sentence that states the core idea of the paragraph. When every sentence in the paragraph develops the core idea, the paragraph has unity.

Coherence is holding to one point of view, one attitude, one tense; it is the joining of sentences into a logical pattern. A careful choice of transitional words ties ideas together and thus contributes to coherence in a paragraph. Notice how the boldfaced italicized words tie together the ideas in the following paragraph.

TOPIC SENTENCE   *Over the past several months, I have heard complaints about the Merit Award Program.* **Specifically,** many employees feel that this program should be linked to annual **salary increases.** They believe that **salary increases** would provide a much better incentive than the current $500 to $700 cash awards for exceptional service. **In addition,** these **employees believe** that their supervisors consider the cash awards a satisfactory alternative to salary increases. Although I don't think this practice is widespread, the fact that the **employees believe** that it is justifies a reevaluation of the Merit Award Program.

Simple enumeration (*first, second, then, next,* and so on) also provides effective <u>transition</u> within paragraphs. Notice how the boldfaced italicized words and phrases give coherence to the following paragraph.

- Most adjustable office chairs have nylon tubes that hold metal spindle rods. To keep the chair operational, lubricate the spindle rods occasionally. **First,** loosen the set screw in the adjustable bell. **Then** lift the chair from the base. **Next,** apply the lubricant to the spindle rod and the nylon washer. **When you have finished,** replace the chair and tighten the set screw.

parallel structure

Parallel sentence structure requires that sentence elements that are alike in function be alike in grammatical form as well. This structure achieves an economy of words, clarifies meaning, expresses the equality of the ideas, and achieves <u>emphasis</u>. Parallel structure assists <u>readers</u> because it allows them to anticipate the meaning of a sentence element on the basis of its construction.

Parallel structure can be achieved with words, <u>phrases</u>, or <u>clauses</u>.

- If you want to earn a satisfactory grade in the training program, you must be *punctual, courteous,* and *conscientious.* [parallel words]

- If you want to earn a satisfactory grade in the training program, you must recognize the importance *of punctuality, of courtesy,* and *of conscientiousness.* [parallel phrases]

- If you want to earn a satisfactory grade in the training program, *you must arrive punctually, you must behave courteously,* and *you must study conscientiously.* [parallel clauses]

Correlative <u>conjunctions</u> (*either . . . or, neither . . . nor, not only . . . but also*) should always use parallel structure. Both parts of the pairs should be followed immediately by the same grammatical form: two similar words, two similar phrases, or two similar clauses.

- Viruses carry either *DNA* or *RNA,* never both. [parallel words]

- Clearly, neither *serological tests* nor *virus isolation studies* alone would have been adequate. [parallel phrases]

- Either *we must increase our production efficiency* or *we must decrease our production goals.* [parallel clauses]

To make a parallel construction clear and effective, it is often best to repeat an <u>article</u>, a <u>pronoun</u>, a helping <u>verb</u>, a <u>preposition</u>, a subordinating conjunction, or the mark of an infinitive (*to*).

- The association has *a* mission statement and *a* code of ethics.

- He was promoted *because* he was industrious, *because* he was inventive, and *because* he was an effective team leader.

Parallel structure is especially important in creating <u>lists</u>, outlines, <u>tables of contents</u>, and <u>headings</u>, because it lets readers know the relative value of each item in a table of contents and each heading in the body of a document. See also <u>outlining</u>.

Faulty Parallelism

Faulty parallelism results when joined elements are intended to serve equal grammatical functions but do not have equal grammatical form. Faulty parallelism sometimes occurs because a writer tries to compare items that are not comparable.

> **NOT PARALLEL** The company offers special college training to help nonexempt employees move into professional careers like engineering management, software development, service technicians, and sales trainees.
> [Notice faulty comparison of occupations—*engineering management* and *software development*—to people—*service technicians* and *sales trainees*.]

To avoid faulty parallelism, make certain that each element in a series is similar in form and structure to all others in the same series.

> **PARALLEL** The company offers special college training to help nonexempt employees move into professional careers like *engineering management, software development, technical services,* and *sales.*

paraphrasing

Paraphrasing is restating or rewriting in your own words the essential ideas of another writer. The following example is an original passage explaining the concept of object blur. The paraphrased version restates the essential information of the passage in a form appropriate for a <u>report</u>.

> **ORIGINAL** One of the major visual cues used by pilots in maintaining precision ground reference during low-level flight is that of object blur. We are acquainted with the object-blur phenomenon experienced when driving an automobile. Objects in the foreground appear to be rushing toward us, while objects in the background appear to recede slightly.
> —Wesley E. Woodson and Donald W. Conover, *Human Engineering Guide for Equipment Designers*

> **PARAPHRASED** Object blur refers to the phenomenon by which observers in a moving vehicle report that foreground objects appear to rush at them, while

background objects appear to recede slightly (Woodson & Conover, 1964).

ETHICS NOTE Because the paraphrase does not quote the source word for word, <u>quotation marks</u> are not used. However, paraphrased material should be credited because the *ideas* are taken from someone else. See also <u>ethics in writing</u>, <u>note-taking</u>, <u>plagiarism</u>, and <u>quotations</u>. ✦

parentheses

Parentheses are used to enclose explanatory or digressive words, phrases, or sentences. Material in parentheses often clarifies or defines the preceding text without altering its meaning.

- She severely bruised her tibia (or shinbone) in the accident.

Parenthetical information may not be essential to a sentence—in fact, parentheses deemphasize the enclosed material—but it may be helpful to some readers.

Parenthetical material does not affect the punctuation of a sentence, and any punctuation (such as a <u>comma</u> or <u>period</u>) should appear following the closing parenthesis.

- She could not fully extend her knee because of a torn meniscus (or cartilage), and she suffered pain from a severely bruised tibia (or shinbone).

When a complete sentence within parentheses stands independently, the ending punctuation goes inside the final parenthesis.

- The project director listed the problems her staff faced. (This was the third time she had complained to the board.)

For some constructions, however, you should consider using <u>subordination</u> rather than parentheses.

- The scans showed little damage *, which pleased the attending physician,* ~~(the attending physician was pleased),~~ but later tests revealed extensive bruising.

Parentheses also are used to enclose numerals or letters that indicate sequence.

- The following sections deal with (1) preparation, (2) research, (3) organization, (4) writing, and (5) revision.

Do not follow spelled-out <u>numbers</u> with numerals in parentheses representing the same numbers.

* Send five ~~(5)~~ copies of the report.

Use <u>brackets</u> to set off a parenthetical item that is already within parentheses.

* We should be sure to give Emanuel Foose (and his brother Emilio [1812–1882]) credit for his part in founding the institute.

See also <u>documenting sources</u> and <u>quotations</u>.

parts of speech

The term *parts of speech* describes the class of words to which a particular word belongs according to its function in a sentence (naming, asserting, describing, joining, acting, modifying, exclaiming). Many words can function as more than one part of speech. See also <u>functional shift</u>.

PART OF SPEECH	FUNCTION
<u>noun</u>, <u>pronoun</u>	naming/referring
<u>verb</u>	asserting
<u>adjective</u>, <u>adverb</u>	describing/modifying
<u>conjunction</u>, <u>preposition</u>	joining/linking
<u>interjection</u>	exclaiming

P

party

In legal language, *party* refers to an individual, a group, or an organization. (The injured *party* sued my client.) The term is inappropriate in all but legal writing; when you are referring to a person, use the word *person*.

* The ~~party~~ *person* whose file you requested is here now.

Party is, of course, appropriate when it refers to a group. (Jim arranged a tour of the facility for the members of our *party*.)

passive voice (*see* voice)

per

When *per* is used to mean "for each," "by means of," "through," or "on account of," it is appropriate (*per* annum, *per* capita, *per* diem, *per* head). When used to mean "according to" (*per* your request, *per* your order), the expression is jargon and should be avoided.

- *we discussed,*
  As per our discussion, I will send revised instructions.

percent / percentage

Percent is normally used instead of the symbol % (only 15 *percent*), except in tables, where space is at a premium. *Percentage*, which is never used with numbers, indicates a general size (only a small *percentage*).

periods

A period usually indicates the end of a declarative or an imperative sentence. Periods also link when used as leaders (as in rows of periods in tables of contents) and indicate omissions when used as ellipses. Periods are also used to end questions that are actually polite requests, or instructions to which an affirmative response is assumed. (Will you call me as soon as he arrives.) See also sentence construction.

P

Periods in Quotations

Use a comma, not a period, after a declarative sentence that is quoted in the context of another sentence.

- "There is every chance of success," she stated.

A period is conventionally placed inside quotation marks. See also quotations.

- He stated clearly, "My vote is yes."

Periods with Parentheses

Place a period outside the final parenthesis when a parenthetical element ends a sentence.

- The institute was founded by Harry Denman (1902–1972).

Place a period inside the final parenthesis when a complete sentence stands independently within <u>parentheses</u>.

- The project director listed the problems her staff faced. (This was the third time she had complained to the board.)

Other Uses of Periods

Use periods after initials in names (Wilma T. Grant, J. P. Morgan). Use periods as decimal points with <u>numbers</u> (27.3 degrees Celsius, $540.26, 6.9 percent). Use periods to indicate certain <u>abbreviations</u> (Ms., Dr., Inc.). When a sentence ends with an abbreviation that ends with a period, do not add another period. (Please meet me at 3:30 p.m.) Use periods following the numerals in a numbered list and following lists with complete sentences.

- 1. Enter your name and PIN.
  2. Enter your address with zip code.
  3. Enter your home telephone number.

Period Faults

P

The incorrect use of a period is sometimes referred to as a *period fault.* When a period is inserted prematurely, the result is a <u>sentence fragment</u>.

FRAGMENT   After a long day at the office during which we finished the quarterly report. We left hurriedly for home.

SENTENCE   After a long day at the office, during which we finished the quarterly report, we left hurriedly for home.

When two independent clauses are joined without any punctuation, the result is a *fused,* or *run-on, sentence.* Adding a period between the clauses is one way to correct a <u>run-on sentence</u>.

RUN-ON   Bill was late for ten days in a row Ms. Sturgess had to fire him.

CORRECT   Bill was late for ten days in a row. Ms. Sturgess had to fire him.

Other options are to add a comma and a coordinating **conjunction** (*and, but, for, or, nor, so, yet*) between the clauses, to add a **semicolon,** or to add a semicolon with a conjunctive **adverb,** such as *therefore* or *however.*

person

Person refers to the form of a personal **pronoun** that indicates whether the pronoun represents the speaker, the person spoken to, or the person or thing spoken about. A pronoun representing the speaker is in the *first* person. (*I* could not find the answer in the manual.) A pronoun that represents the person or people spoken to is in the *second* person. (*You* will be a good manager.) A pronoun that represents the person or people spoken about is in the *third* person. (*They* received the news quietly.) The following list shows first-, second-, and third-person pronouns. See also **case, number,** and **one.**

PERSON	SINGULAR	PLURAL
First	I, me, my, mine	we, us, our, ours
Second	you, your, yours	you, your, yours
Third	he, him, his, she, her, hers, it, its	they, them, their, theirs

personal / personnel

Personal is an **adjective** meaning "of or pertaining to an individual person" (a *personal* problem). *Personnel* is a **noun** meaning a "group of people engaged in a common job" (military *personnel*). Be careful not to use *personnel* when the word you need is *persons, people,* or a more descriptive word.

- The remaining ~~personnel~~ *employees* will be moved next Thursday.

persons / people

The word *persons* is used to refer to a specific category or number of people, often in legal or official contexts. (Admittance is limited to *persons* age 18 and over.) In all other contexts, use *people.* (We need more qualified *people* to fill the vacant positions.)

persuasion

Persuasive writing attempts to convince the <u>reader</u> to adopt the writer's point of view or take a particular action. Much workplace writing uses persuasion to reinforce ideas that readers already have, to convince readers to change their current ideas, or to lobby for a particular suggestion or policy (as in Figure P–1). You may find yourself pleading for safer working conditions, justifying the expense of a new program, or writing a <u>proposal</u> for a large purchase. See also <u>audience</u> and <u>purpose</u>.

In persuasive writing, the way you present your ideas is as important as the ideas themselves. You must support your appeal with logic and a sound presentation of facts, statistics, and examples. See also <u>logic errors</u>.

A writer also gains credibility, and thus persuasiveness, through the readers' impressions of the document's appearance. For this reason, consideration of <u>layout and design</u> is important, especially in documents such as <u>résumés</u>.

A persuasive technique, which is especially important in <u>correspondence</u> and <u>e-mail</u> to customers and clients, is called the <u>"you" viewpoint</u>. The "you" viewpoint places your readers' interest and perspective foremost by often, but not always, using the words *you* and *your* rather then *we, our, I,* and *mine.* It is based on the principle that your readers are naturally more concerned about their own needs than they are about those of the writer or organization.

⚡ ETHICS NOTE Avoid ambiguity: Do not wander from your main point, and above all never make false claims. You should also acknowledge any real or potentially conflicting opinions; doing so allows you to anticipate and overcome objections and builds your credibility. See also <u>ethics in writing</u> and <u>promotional writing</u>. ✦

The <u>memo</u> shown in Figure P–1 was written to persuade the marketing staff to accept and participate in a change to a new computer system. Notice that not everything in this memo is presented in a positive light. Change brings disruption, and the writer acknowledges that fact. See also <u>"you" viewpoint</u>.

Interoffice Memo

TO: Marketing Staff
FROM: Harold Kawenski, MIS Administrator *HK*
DATE: April 21, 2006
SUBJECT: Plans for the Changeover to the New Computer System

As you all know, the merger with Datacom has resulted in dramatic growth in our workload—a 30 percent increase in our customer support services during the last several months. To cope with this expansion, we will soon install the NRT/R4 server and QCS Enterprise software with Web-based applications.

Let me briefly describe the benefits of this system and the ways we plan to help you cope with the changeover.

The QCS system will help us access up-to-date marketing and product information when we need it. This system will speed processing dramatically and give us access to all relevant company-wide databases. Because we anticipate that our workload will increase another 30 percent in the next several months, we need to get the QCS system online and working smoothly as soon as possible.

The changeover to this system, unfortunately, will cause some disruption at first. We will need to transfer many of our legacy programs and software applications to the new system. In addition, all of us will need to learn to navigate in the R4 and QCS environments. Once we have made these adjustments, however, I believe we will welcome the changes.

To help everyone cope with the changeover, we will offer training sessions that will begin next week. I have attached a sign-up form with specific class times. We will also provide a technical support hotline at extension 4040, which will be available during business hours, e-mail support at qcs-support@conco.com, and online help documentation.

I would like to urge you to help us make a smooth transition to the QCS system. Please e-mail me with your suggestions or questions about the impact of the changeover on your department. I look forward to working with you to make this system a success.

Enclosure: Training Session Schedule

P

FIGURE P–1. Persuasive Memo

phenomenon / phenomena

A *phenomenon* is an observable thing, fact, or occurrence (a natural *phenomenon*). Its plural form is *phenomena*.

photographs

Photographs are effective in catching the <u>readers</u>' attention and adding personal relevance to such documents as <u>brochures</u>, <u>newsletters</u>, <u>annual reports</u>, and other <u>promotional writing</u>. Photographs are also an effective way to illustrate products in a print catalog or on a Web site. They are often used for instructions and may be the best way to show the appearance of an object, although they cannot depict the internal workings of a mechanism or below-the-surface details of objects or structures. Such details are better represented in <u>drawings</u>.

Figure P–2 shows a photograph from an interactive Web presentation for buyers of corporate aircraft. This photograph is one in a series

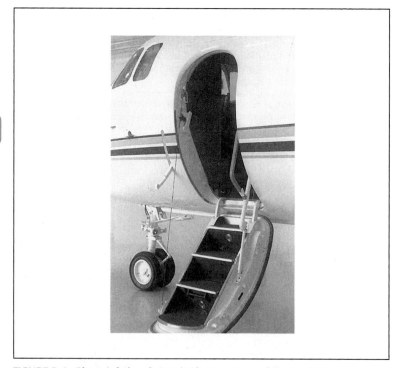

FIGURE P–2. Photo (of Aircraft Door). Photo courtesy of Ken Cook Company.

that simulates a pilot's "walk-around"—a procedure in which pilots visually examine an aircraft in a 360-degree safety inspection prior to takeoff. In this photo, the stair steps are lowered to help show the relative size of the aircraft.

For <u>reports</u>, treat photographs as you do other <u>visuals</u>. Give the photograph a figure number, call-outs (labels) to identify key features, and a caption, if needed. Position the figure number and caption so that the reader can view them and the photograph from the same orientation.

⚡ ETHICS NOTE Be careful to avoid <u>plagiarism</u> by appropriately <u>documenting sources</u> for photographs and to obtain <u>copyright</u> permission if you plan to publish photographs that you do not take yourself. ✦

phrases

DIRECTORY
Prepositional Phrases   384
Participial Phrases   384
Infinitive Phrases   385
Gerund Phrases   386
Verb Phrases   386
Noun Phrases   386

Phrases are groups of words within sentences that are based on <u>nouns</u>, nonfinite <u>verb</u> forms, or verb combinations without subjects. See also <u>clauses</u> and <u>sentence construction</u>.

P

- She encouraged her staff *by her calm confidence.* [phrase]

A phrase may function as an <u>adjective</u>, an <u>adverb</u>, a noun, or a verb.

- The subjects *on the agenda* were all discussed. [adjective]
- We discussed the project *with great enthusiasm.* [adverb]
- *Working hard* is her way of life. [noun]
- The chief engineer *should have been notified.* [verb]

Even though phrases function as adjectives, adverbs, nouns, or verbs, they are normally named for the kind of word around which they are constructed—<u>preposition</u>, participle, infinitive, gerund, verb, or noun. A phrase that begins with a preposition is a *prepositional phrase*, a phrase that begins with a participle is a *participial phrase*, and so on. For typical verb phrases and prepositional phrases that give speakers of <u>English as a second language</u> trouble, see <u>idioms</u>.

Prepositional Phrases

A preposition is a word that shows relationship and combines with a noun or <u>pronoun</u> (its <u>object</u>) to form a modifying phrase. A prepositional phrase, then, consists of a preposition plus its object and the object's modifiers.

- *After the meeting*, the district managers adjourned *to the executive dining room*.

Prepositional phrases, because they normally modify nouns or verbs, usually function as adverbs or adjectives. A prepositional phrase may function as an adverb of motion (Turn the dial four degrees *to the left*) or an adverb of manner (Answer customers' questions *in a courteous fashion*). A prepositional phrase may function as an adverb of place and may appear in different places in the sentence.

- *In home and office computer systems*, security is essential.
- Security is essential *in home and office computer systems*.

Prepositional phrases may function as adjectives; when they do, they follow the nouns they modify.

- Garbage *with a high protein content* can be processed into animal food.

Be careful when you use prepositional phrases because separating a prepositional phrase from the noun it modifies can cause <u>ambiguity</u>.

AMBIGUOUS	*The woman* standing by the security guard *in the gray suit* is our division manager.
CLEAR	*The woman in the gray suit* who is standing by the security guard is our division manager.

Watch as well for the overuse of prepositional phrases where <u>modifiers</u> would be more economical.

OVERUSED	The man *with gray hair in the blue suit with pin-stripes* is the former president *of the company*.
ECONOMICAL	The *gray-haired* man in the *blue pin-striped* suit is the former *company* president.

Participial Phrases

A participle is any form of a verb that is used as an adjective. A participial phrase consists of a participle plus its object and its modifiers.

- The division *having the largest sales increase* will win the award.

The relationship between a participial phrase and the rest of the sentence must be clear to the reader. For that reason, every sentence containing a participial phrase must have a noun or pronoun that the participial phrase modifies; if it does not, the result is a dangling participial phrase.

Dangling Participial Phrases.   A dangling participial phrase occurs when the noun or pronoun that the participial phrase is meant to modify is not stated but only implied in the sentence. See also **dangling modifiers**.

DANGLING	*Being unhappy with the job*, his efficiency suffered. [His efficiency was not unhappy with the job; what the participial phrase really modifies—*he*—is not stated but merely implied.]
CORRECT	*Being unhappy with the job*, he grew less efficient. [Now what that participial phrase modifies—*he*—is explicitly stated.]

Misplaced Participial Phrases.   A participial phrase is misplaced when it is too far from the noun or pronoun it is meant to modify and so appears to modify something else. Such an error can make the writer look ridiculous.

MISPLACED	We saw a large warehouse *driving down the highway*.
CORRECT	*Driving down the highway*, we saw a large warehouse.

Infinitive Phrases

An infinitive is the bare form of a verb (go, run, talk) without the restrictions imposed by **person** and **number**. An infinitive is generally preceded by the word *to* (which is usually a preposition but in this use is called the *sign*, or *mark*, of the infinitive). An infinitive phrase consists of the word *to* plus an infinitive and any objects or modifiers.

- *To succeed in this field*, you must be willing *to assume responsibility*.

Do not confuse a prepositional phrase beginning with *to* with an infinitive phrase. In an infinitive phrase, *to* is followed by a verb; in a prepositional phrase, *to* is followed by a noun or a pronoun.

PREPOSITIONAL PHRASE	We went *to the building site*.
INFINITIVE PHRASE	Our firm tries *to provide a comprehensive training program*.

The implied subject of an introductory infinitive phrase should be the same as the subject of the sentence. If it is not, the phrase is a dangling modifier. In the following example, the implied subject of the infinitive is *you* or *one*, not *practice.*

- To learn a new language, ~~practice is needed.~~
  you must practice.

Gerund Phrases

A gerund is a <u>verbal</u> ending in *-ing* that is used as a noun. A gerund phrase consists of a gerund plus any objects or modifiers and always functions as a noun.

SUBJECT	*Preparing an annual report* is a difficult task.
DIRECT OBJECT	She liked *chairing the committee.*

Verb Phrases

A verb phrase consists of a main verb and its helping verb.

- He *is* [helping verb] *working* [main verb] hard this summer.

Words can appear between the helping verb and the main verb of a verb phrase. (He *is **always** working.*) The main verb is always the last verb in a verb phrase.

Questions often begin with a verb phrase. (*Will* he *audit* their account?) The adverb *not* may be appended to a helping verb in a verb phrase. (He *did not work* today.)

Noun Phrases

A noun phrase consists of a noun and its modifiers. (Have *the two new employees* fill out *these forms.*)

P

plagiarism

Plagiarism is the use of someone else's unique ideas without acknowledgment, or the use of someone else's exact words without <u>quotation marks</u> and appropriate credit. Plagiarism is considered to be the theft of someone else's creative and intellectual property and is not accepted in business, science, journalism, academia, and other fields. See also <u>ethics in writing</u>.

Quoting a passage—including cutting and pasting a passage from the Internet into your work—is permissible only if you enclose the passage in quotation marks and properly cite the source. For detailed guidance on quoting correctly, see <u>quotations</u>. If you intend to publish, reproduce, or distribute material that includes quotations from published works, including Web sites, you may need to obtain written permission from the <u>copyright</u> holders of those works.

Likewise, you may paraphrase the words and ideas of another *if you document your source*. (See also <u>paraphrasing</u> and <u>documenting sources</u>.) Although you do not enclose paraphrased ideas or materials in quotation marks, you must document their sources. Paraphrasing a passage without citing the source is permissible only when the information paraphrased is common knowledge.

Common knowledge generally refers to information that is widely known and readily available in handbooks, manuals, atlases, and other references. For example, the "law of supply and demand" is common knowledge and is found in virtually every economics and business textbook. Common knowledge also refers to information within a specific field that is generally known and understood by most others in that field—even though it is not widely known by those outside the field. An indication that something is common knowledge is whether it is repeated in multiple sources without citation. The best advice is, when in doubt, document.

🔹 ETHICS NOTE In the workplace, employees often borrow from in-house manuals, reports, and other company documents. Using such boilerplate material is neither plagiarism nor a violation of copyright. ✦

⚙ WEB LINK **AVOIDING PLAGIARISM**

For a tutorial on using sources correctly, see <*bedfordstmartins.com/alredbus*> and select *Tutorials*, "The St. Martin's Tutorial on Avoiding Plagiarism." For links to other helpful resources, select *Links for Handbook Entries*.

---

point of view

Point of view is the writer's relation to the information presented, as reflected in the use of grammatical <u>person</u>. The writer usually expresses point of view in first-, second-, or third-person personal <u>pronouns</u>. Use of first person indicates that the writer is a participant or an observer. Use of second or third person indicates that the writer is giving directions, <u>instructions</u>, or advice, or writing about other people or something impersonal.

FIRST PERSON	*I* scrolled down to find the settings option.
SECOND PERSON	*You* must scroll down to find the settings option.
	Scroll down to find the settings option. [*You* is understood.]
THIRD PERSON	*He* scrolled down to find the settings option.

Consider the following sentence, revised from an impersonal to a more personal point of view. Although the meaning of the sentence does not change, the revision indicates that people are involved in the communication.

- ~~It is regrettable~~ that the equipment shipped on the 12th is ~~unacceptable.~~
  I regret ... *we cannot accept* ...

Many people think they should avoid the pronoun *I* in business writing. Such practice, however, often leads to awkward sentences, with people referring to themselves in the third person as *one* or as *the writer* instead of as *I*.

- ~~The writer believes~~ that this project will be completed by July.
  I believe

However, do not use the personal point of view when an impersonal point of view would be more appropriate or more effective because you need to emphasize the subject matter over the writer or the reader. In the following example, it does not help to personalize the situation; in fact, the impersonal version may be more tactful.

PERSONAL	I received objections to my proposal from several of your managers.
IMPERSONAL	Several managers have raised objections to the proposal.

Whether you adopt a personal or an impersonal point of view depends on the **purpose** and the **readers** of the document. For example, in an informal **e-mail** to an associate, you would most likely adopt a personal point of view. However, in a **report** to a large group, you would probably emphasize the subject by using an impersonal point of view.

⬛ ETHICS NOTE In **correspondence** on company stationery, use of the pronoun *we* may be interpreted as reflecting company policy, whereas *I* clearly reflects personal opinion. Which pronoun to use should be decided according to whether the matter discussed in the letter is an individual (*I*) or a corporate (*we*) concern.

- *I* understand your frustration with the price increase, but *we* must now add the import tax to the sales price. ✦

> **ESL** TIPS FOR STATING AN OPINION
>
> In some cultures, stating an opinion in writing is considered impolite or unnecessary, but in the United States, readers expect to see a writer's opinion stated clearly and explicitly. The opinion should be followed by specific examples to help the reader understand the writer's point of view.

policies and procedures

A *policy* states an organization's position on a subject; a *procedure* provides <u>instructions</u> for carrying out the policy. They are often written at the same time, usually by top or middle managers. Policies and procedures are subjected to a careful review process, often by legal staff. Writing these documents requires careful thought and planning as well as precise language and <u>word choice</u> so that the policies and procedures are clear and understandable.

Policies

A statement of policy may be preceded by an explanation of the policy's purpose or rationale. Specific details then follow in numbered sections as in the following company policy regarding tuition refunds.

1. TUITION REFUND POLICY
    1.1 The Tuition Refund Plan is available only to full-time staff.
    1.2 To receive a refund, an individual must be employed by the company at the time of enrollment and at the completion of the course. Should an individual's employment be terminated because of a reduction of staff, fees will be refunded for approved courses upon their satisfactory completion.
    1.3 Satisfactory completion means that the employee has completed the course work and has achieved a grade at least one level above passing. If a course is not satisfactorily completed, reimbursement may be deferred if the employee, upon completion of the degree, attains a cumulative grade average of at least C (B for most graduate-degree programs).

Policies may be kept in loose-leaf binders or posted on an organization's intranet Web site, so they can be easily referred to and updated.

Procedures

Procedures provide a step-by-step explanation of how to carry out a policy. They provide instructions not only for employees but also for managers who must ensure that the company's policy is properly implemented.

To prepare for writing procedures, keep track of who must do what. An easy and effective way is to create a chart, as shown in Figure P–3. Draw a vertical line down a page. Label the left column "Actor" and the right "Directions." Under "Actor," list who must perform the action in each step; under "Directions," describe each step of the procedure. Describe each step fully and in the correct sequence. In effect, the list serves as an outline for the procedure you will write. The draft created from the chart in Figure P–3 might look like the example that follows it.

Actor	Directions
Employee	Determines his or her eligibility for degree program, gains manager's approval, and submits request to Human Resources (HR)
Human Resources Department	Reviews request and, if reason is not obvious, asks manager to justify, in writing, the benefits of approving the degree program
Employee	Completes Sections I and II of Form F-6970
Human Resources Department	Sends form to employee's supervisor and department head for approval
Employee	Submits proof of course enrollment and fee payment to HR for reimbursement

FIGURE P–3. Procedures Chart

P

1. PROCEDURES
    1.1 Degree Approval
        1.1.1 An employee who meets school requirements and is interested in receiving tuition refunds should gain the approval of his or her manager and submit the request to the Human Resources Department. Human Resources may ask the manager to justify, in writing, the benefits of approving the degree request if the reason is not obvious.
        1.1.2 After agreement has been reached, the employee should complete Sections I and II of Form F-6970. After Human Resources has obtained two levels of management approval—from the employee's supervisor and

the head of the department—it approves the employee's enrollment in the degree program.

1.1.3 The employee who has been granted approval must submit proof of course enrollment and payment of course
fees to Human Resources for tuition reimbursement.

positive writing

Presenting positive information as though it were negative is confusing
to <u>readers</u>.

NEGATIVE   If the error does *not* involve data transmission, the
backup function will *not* be used.

In this sentence, the reader must reverse two negatives to understand
the exception that is being stated. (See also <u>double negatives</u>.) The following sentence presents the exception in a positive and straightforward manner.

POSITIVE   The backup function is used only when the error
involves data transmission.

⬆ ETHICS NOTE Negative facts or conclusions, however, should be
stated negatively; stating a negative fact or conclusion positively is deceptive because it can mislead the reader.

DECEPTIVE   In the first quarter of this year, employee exposure to
airborne lead was within 10 percent of acceptable
state health standards.

ACCURATE   In the first quarter of this year, employee exposure to
airborne lead was 10 percent below acceptable state
health standards.

See also <u>ethics in writing</u>. ✦
Even if what you are saying is negative, do not use more negative
words than necessary.

NEGATIVE   We are withholding your shipment because we have
not received your payment.

POSITIVE   We will forward your shipment as soon as we receive
your payment.

See also <u>**correspondence**</u> and <u>**"you" viewpoint**</u>.

possessive case

A <u>noun</u> or <u>pronoun</u> is in the possessive case when it represents a person, place, or thing that possesses something. Possession is generally expressed with an <u>apostrophe</u> and an *s* (the *report's* title), with a prepositional <u>phrase</u> using *of* (the title *of the report*), or with the possessive form of a pronoun (*our* report).

Practices vary for some possessive forms, but the following guidelines are widely used. Above all, be consistent.

Singular Nouns

Most singular nouns show the possessive case with *'s*.

- a *manager's* office

  an *employee's* job satisfaction

  the *company's* stock value

  the *witness's* testimony

  the *bus's* schedule

When pronunciation with *'s* is difficult or when a multisyllable noun ends in a *z* sound, you may use only an apostrophe.

- *New Orleans'* convention hotels

Plural Nouns

Plural nouns that end in *-s* or *-es* show the possessive case with only an apostrophe.

- the *managers'* reports

  the *employees'* paychecks

  the *companies'* joint project

  the *witnesses'* reports

  the *buses'* schedules

Plural nouns that do not end in *-s* show the possessive with *'s*.

- *children's* clothing, *women's* resources, *men's* room

Apostrophes are not used in official names (*Consumers* Union) or for words that may appear to be possessive nouns but function as <u>adjectives</u> (a *computer peripherals* supplier).

Compound Nouns

Compound words form the possessive with *'s* following the final letter.

- the *vice president's* proposal, the *editor in chief's* desk

Plurals of some compound expressions are often best expressed with a prepositional phrase (presentations *of the editors in chief*).

Coordinate Nouns

Coordinate nouns show joint possession with *'s* following the last noun.

- *Fischer and Goulet's* partnership was the foundation of their business.

Coordinate nouns show individual possession with *'s* following each noun.

- The difference between *Barker's* and *Washburne's* test results was statistically insignificant.

Possessive Pronouns

The possessive pronouns (*its, whose, his, her, our, your, their*) are also used to show possession and do not require apostrophes. (Even good systems have *their* flaws.) Only the possessive form of a pronoun should be used with a gerund (a noun formed from an *-ing* **verb**).

- The safety officer insisted on *our* wearing protective clothing. [*Wearing* is the gerund.]

P

Possessive pronouns are also used to replace nouns. (The responsibility was *theirs*.) See also <u>its/it's</u>.

Indefinite Pronouns

Some indefinite pronouns (*all, any, each, few, most, none, some*) form the possessive case with the **preposition** *of*.

- Both desks were stored in the warehouse, but water ruined the surface *of each*.

Other indefinite pronouns (*everyone, someone, anyone, no one*), however, use *'s*.

- *Everyone's* contribution is welcome.

prefixes

A prefix is a letter or group of letters placed in front of a root word that changes the meaning of the root word. When a prefix ends with a vowel and the root word begins with a vowel, the prefix is often separated from the root word with a <u>hyphen</u> (*re-enter, pro-active, anti-inflammatory*). Some words with the double vowel are written without a hyphen (*cooperate*) and others with or without a hyphen (*re-elect* or *reelect*).

Prefixes, such as *neo-* (derived from a Greek word meaning "new"), are often hyphenated when used with a proper <u>noun</u> (*neo-Keynesianism*). Such prefixes are not normally hyphenated when used with common nouns, unless the base word begins with the same vowel (*neonatal, neo-orthodoxy*).

A hyphen may be necessary to clarify the meaning of a prefix; for example, *reform* means "correct" or "improve," and *re-form* means "change the shape of." When in doubt, check a current <u>dictionary</u>.

preparation

The preparation stage of the writing process is essential. By determining the <u>readers'</u> needs, your primary <u>purpose</u>, the <u>context</u>, and the <u>scope</u> of coverage, you understand the information you will need to gather during <u>research</u>. See also "Five Steps to Successful Writing."

P

Writer's Checklist: Preparing to Write

☑ Determine who your readers are and learn certain key facts about them — their knowledge, attitudes, and needs relative to your subject.

☑ Determine the document's primary purpose: What exactly do you want your readers to know, believe, or be able to do when they have finished reading your document?

☑ Consider the context of your message and how it will affect your writing.

☑ Establish the scope of your document — the type and amount of detail you must include — not only by understanding your readers' needs and purpose but also by considering any external constraints, such as word limits for trade journal articles or the space limitations of Web pages. See also <u>writing for the Web</u>.

☑ Select the medium appropriate to your readers and purpose. See also <u>selecting the medium</u>.

prepositions

A preposition is a word that links a <u>noun</u> or <u>pronoun</u> (the preposition's <u>object</u>) to another sentence element by expressing such relationships as direction (*to, into, across, toward*), location (*at, in, on, under, over, beside, among, by, between, through*), time (*before, after, during, until, since*), or position (*for, against, with*). Together, the preposition, its object, and the object's <u>modifiers</u> form a prepositional <u>phrase</u> that acts as a modifier.

- Answer customers' questions *in a courteous manner.*
  [The prepositional phrase *in a courteous manner* modifies the <u>verb</u> *answer.*]

The object of a preposition (the word or phrase following the preposition) is always in the objective <u>case</u>. When the object is a compound, both nouns and pronouns should be in the objective case. For example, the phrase "between you and *me*" is frequently and incorrectly written as "between you and *I.*" *Me* is the objective form of the pronoun, and *I* is the subjective form.

Many words that function as prepositions also function as <u>adverbs</u>. If the word takes an object and functions as a connective, it is a preposition; if it has no object and functions as a modifier, it is an adverb.

PREPOSITIONS	The manager sat *behind* the desk *in* her office.
ADVERBS	The customer lagged *behind*; then he came *in* and sat down.

Certain verbs, adverbs, and adjectives are used with certain prepositions (interested *in*, aware *of*, equated *with*, adhere *to*, capable *of*, object *to*, infer *from*). See also <u>idioms</u>.

Prepositions at the End of a Sentence

A preposition at the end of a sentence can be an indication that the sentence is awkwardly constructed.

- ~~The~~ branch office ~~is where she was at.~~
  She was at the .

However, if a preposition falls naturally at the end of a sentence, leave it there. (I don't remember which file name I saved it *under.*)

Prepositions in Titles

Capitalize prepositions in <u>titles</u> when they are the first or last words, or when they contain more than four letters (unless you are following a style that recommends otherwise). See also <u>capitalization</u>.

P

- The newspaper column "*In* My Opinion" included a review of the article "New Concerns *About* Distance Education."

Preposition Errors

Do not use redundant prepositions, such as "off *of*," "in back *of*," "inside *of*," and "at *about*."

| EXACT | The client arrived at ~~about~~ four o'clock. |
| APPROXIMATE | The client arrived ~~at~~ about four o'clock. |

Avoid unnecessarily adding the preposition *up* to verbs.

- Call ~~up and~~ _{to} see if he is in his office.

Do not omit necessary prepositions.

- He was oblivious _{to} and not distracted by the view from his office window.

See also __conciseness__ and __English as a second language__.

---

presentations

DIRECTORY

Determining Your Purpose   396
Analyzing Your Audience   397
Gathering Information   397
Structuring the Presentation   397
Using Visuals   400

*Writer's Checklist: Using Visuals
   in a Presentation*   402
Delivering a Presentation   403
*Writer's Checklist: Preparing for
   and Delivering a Presentation*   405

The steps required to prepare an effective presentation parallel the steps you follow to write a document. As with writing a document, determine your __purpose__ and analyze your __audience__. Then gather the facts that will support your point of view or proposal and logically organize that information. Presentations do, however, differ from written documents in a number of important ways. They are intended for listeners, not readers. Because you are speaking, your manner of delivery, the way you organize the material, and your supporting __visuals__ require as much attention as your content.

Determining Your Purpose

Every presentation is given for a purpose, even if it is only to share information. To determine the primary purpose of your presentation, use the following question as a guide: What do I want the audience to know, to believe, or to do when I have finished the presentation? Based on the answer to that question, write a purpose statement that answers the *what?* and *why?* questions.

- The purpose of my presentation is to convince my company's chief information officer of the need to improve the appearance, content, and customer use of our company's Web site [*what*] so that she will be persuaded to allocate additional funds for site-development work in the next fiscal year [*why*].

Analyzing Your Audience

Once you have determined the desired end result of the presentation, you need to analyze your audience so that you can tailor your presentation to their needs. (See **readers**.) Ask yourself these questions about your audience:

- What is your audience's level of experience or knowledge about your topic?
- What is the general educational level and age of your audience?
- What is your audience's attitude toward the topic you are speaking about, and—based on that attitude—what concerns, fears, or objections might your audience have?
- Do any subgroups in the audience have different concerns or needs?
- What questions might your audience ask about this topic?

Gathering Information

Once you have focused the presentation, you need to find the facts and arguments that support your point of view or the action you propose. As you gather information, keep in mind that you should give the audience only what will accomplish your goals; too much detail will overwhelm them, and too little will not adequately inform your listeners or support your recommendations. For detailed guidance about gathering information, see **research**.

Structuring the Presentation

When structuring the presentation, focus on your audience. Listeners are freshest at the outset and refocus their attention near the end. Take advantage of that pattern. Give your audience a brief overview of your presentation at the beginning, use the body to develop your ideas, and end with a summary of what you covered and, if appropriate, a call to action. See also **methods of development**.

P

The Introduction.   Include in the <u>introduction</u> an opening that focuses your audience's attention, such as in the following examples.

- You have to write an important report, but you'd like to incorporate lengthy handwritten notes from several meetings you
  attended. Your scanner will not read these notes, and you will have
  to type many pages. You groan because that seems an incredible
  waste of time. Have I got a solution for you! [*Definition of a
  problem*]

- As many as 50 million Americans have high blood pressure. [*An
  attention-getting statement*]

- Would you be interested in a full-sized computer keyboard that is
  waterproof and noiseless, and can be rolled up like a rubber mat?
  [*A rhetorical question*]

- As I sat at my computer one morning, deleting my eighth spam
  message of the day, I decided that it was time to take action to
  eliminate this time-waster. [*A personal experience*]

- According to researchers at the Massachusetts Institute of Technology, "Garlic and its cousin, the onion, confer major health
  benefits—including fighting cancer, infections, and heart disease."
  [*An appropriate quotation*]

Following your opening, use the introduction to set the stage for
your audience by providing an overview of the presentation, which can
include general or background information that will be needed to understand any more detailed information in the body of your presentation. It can also show how you have organized the material.

- This presentation analyzes three high-volume, on-demand printers
  for us to consider purchasing. Based on a comparison of all three,
  I will recommend the one I believe best meets our needs. To do so,
  I'll discuss the following five points:
  1. Why we need a high-volume printer [*the problem*]
  2. The basics of on-demand technology [*general information*]
  3. The criteria I used to compare the three printer models
     [*comparison*]
  4. The printer models I compared and why [*possible solutions*]
  5. The printer I propose we buy [*proposed solution*]

The Body.   If applicable, present the evidence that will persuade the
audience to agree with your conclusions and act on them. (See <u>persua-
sion</u>.) If there is a problem, demonstrate that it exists and offer a solution or range of possible solutions. For example, if your introduction
stated that the problem is low profits, high costs, outdated technology,
or high employee absenteeism, you could use the following approach.

1. Prove your point.
   a. Marshal the facts and data you need.
   b. Present the information using easy-to-understand visuals.
2. Offer solutions.
   a. "Increase profits by lowering production costs."
   b. "Cut overhead to reduce costs or abolish specific programs or product lines."
   c. "Replace outdated technology or upgrade existing technology."
   d. "Offer employees more flexibility in their work schedules or other incentives."
3. Anticipate questions ("How much will it cost?") and objections ("We're too busy now—when would we have time to learn the new software?") and incorporate the answers into your presentation.

The Closing.   Fulfill the goals of your presentation in the closing. If your purpose is to motivate the listeners to take action, ask them to do what you want them to do; if your purpose is to get your audience to think about something, summarize what you want them to think about. Many presenters make the mistake of not actually closing—they simply quit talking, shuffle papers, and then walk away.

Because your closing is what your audience is most likely to remember, use that time to be strong and persuasive. Consider the following possible closing.

- Based on all the data, I believe that the Worthington TechLine 5510 Production Printer best suits our needs. It produces 40 pages per minute more than its closest competitor and provides modular systems that can be upgraded to support new applications. The Worthington is also compatible with our current computer network, and staff training at our site is included with our purchase. Although the initial cost is higher than that for the other two models, the additional capabilities, compatibility with most standard environments, and lower maintenance costs make it a better value.

   I recommend we allocate the funds necessary for this printer by the 15th of this month in order to be well prepared for the production of next quarter's customer publications.

The closing brings the presentation full circle and asks the audience to fulfill the purpose of the presentation—exactly what a <u>conclusion</u> should do.

Transitions.   Planned <u>transitions</u> should appear between the introduction and the body, between points in the body, and between the body and the closing. Transitions are simply a sentence or two to let the audience know that you are moving from one topic to the next. They also prevent a choppy presentation and provide the audience with assurance that you know where you are going and how to get there.

- Before getting into the specifics of each printer I compared, I'd like to present the benefits of networked, on-demand printers in general. That information will provide you with the background you'll need to compare the differences among the printers and their capabilities discussed in this presentation.

It is also a good idea to pause for a moment after you have delivered a transition between topics to let your listeners shift gears with you. Remember, they do not know your plan.

Using Visuals

Well-planned <u>visuals</u> not only add interest and emphasis to your presentation, they also clarify and simplify your message because they communicate clearly, quickly, and vividly. Charts, graphs, and illustrations greatly increase audience understanding and retention of information, especially for complex issues and technical information that could otherwise be misunderstood or overlooked.

You can create and present the visual components of your presentation by using a variety of media—flip charts, whiteboard or chalkboard, overhead transparencies, slides, or computer presentation software. See also <u>layout and design</u>.

Flip Charts.   Flip charts are ideal for smaller groups in a conference room or classroom and are also ideal for <u>brainstorming</u> with your audience.

Whiteboard or Chalkboard.   The whiteboard or chalkboard common to classrooms is convenient for creating sketches and for jotting notes during your presentation. If your presentation requires extensive notes or complex <u>drawings</u>, create them before the presentation to save time and to minimize audience restlessness.

Overhead Transparencies.   With transparencies you can create a series of overlays to explain a complex device or system, adding (or removing) the overlays one at a time. You can also lay a sheet of paper over a list of items on a transparency, uncovering one item at a time as you discuss it, to focus audience attention on each point in the sequence.

Presentation Software.   Presentation software, such as PowerPoint, Corel Presentations, and Freelance Graphics, lets you create your presentation on your computer. You can develop charts and graphs with data from spreadsheet software or locate visuals on the Web, and then import those files into your presentation. This software also offers standard templates and other features that help you design effective visuals and integrated text. Enhancements include a selection of typefaces, highlighting devices, background textures and colors, and clip-art images. Images can also be printed out for use as overhead transparencies or handouts. Avoid using too many enhancements, however, which may distract viewers from your message. Figure P–4 shows slides for a brief presentation.

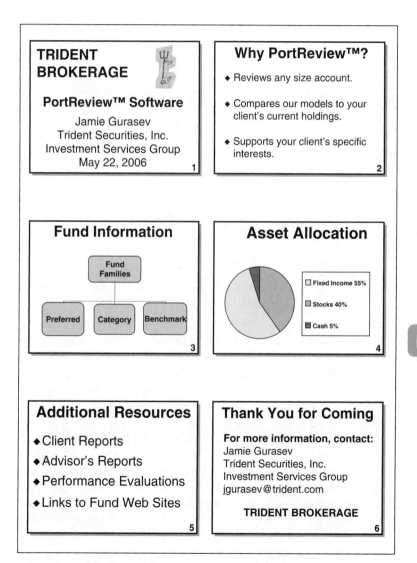

FIGURE P–4. Slides for a Brief Presentation

Rehearse your presentation using your electronic slides, and practice your transitions from slide to slide. Also practice loading your presentation and anticipate any technical difficulties that might arise. Should you encounter a technical snag during the presentation, stay calm and give yourself time to solve the problem. If you cannot solve the problem, move on without the technology. As a backup, carry a printout of your electronic presentation as well as an extra electronic copy on a storage medium.

WEB LINK   PREPARING PRESENTATION SLIDES

For a helpful tutorial on creating effective slides, see <*bedfordstmartins.com/ alredbus*> and select *Tutorials*, "Preparing Presentation Slides." For links to additional information and tutorials for using presentation software, select *Links for Handbook Entries*.

Writer's Checklist: Using Visuals in a Presentation

☑ Use text sparingly in visuals. Use bulleted or numbered <u>lists</u>, keeping them in **parallel structure** and with balanced content. Use numbers if the sequence is important and bullets if it is not.

☑ Limit the number of bulleted or numbered items to 5 or 6 per visual. Each visual should contain no more than 40 to 45 words. Any more will clutter the visual and force you to use a smaller font that could impair the audience's ability to read it.

☑ Make your visuals consistent in type style, size, and spacing.

☑ Use a type size visible to members of the audience in the back of the room. Type should be boldface and no smaller than 30 points. For headings, 45- or 50-point type works even better.

☑ Use graphs and charts to show data trends. Use only one or two illustrations per visual to avoid clutter and confusion.

☑ Make the contrast between your text and the background sharp. Use light backgrounds with dark lettering and avoid textured or decorated backgrounds.

☑ Use no more than 12 visuals per presentation. Any more will tax the audience's concentration.

☑ Match your delivery of the content to your visuals. Do not put one set of words or images on the screen and talk about the previous visual or, even worse, the next one.

☑ Do not read the text on your visual word for word. Your audience can read the visuals; they look to you to explain the key points in detail.

Delivering a Presentation

Once you have outlined and drafted your presentation and prepared your visuals, you are ready to practice your presentation and delivery techniques.

Practice. Familiarize yourself with the sequence of the material—major topics, notes, and visuals—in your outline. Once you feel comfortable with the content, you are ready to practice the presentation itself.

PRACTICE ON YOUR FEET AND OUT LOUD. Try to practice in the room where you will give the presentation. Practicing on-site helps you get the feel of the room: the acoustics, the lighting, the arrangement of the chairs, the position of electrical outlets and switches, and so forth. Practice out loud to make clear exactly how long your presentation will take, highlight problems such as awkward transitions, and help eliminate verbal tics, such as "um," "you know," and "like."

PRACTICE WITH YOUR VISUALS AND TEXT. Integrate your visuals into your practice sessions to help your presentation go more smoothly. Operate the equipment (computer, slide projector, or overhead projector) until you are comfortable with it. Decide if you want to use a remote control or to have someone else advance your slides. Even if things go wrong, being prepared and practiced will give you the confidence and poise to continue.

Delivery Techniques That Work. Your delivery is both audible and visual. In addition to your words and message, your nonverbal communication affects your audience. Be animated—your words will make an impression and have more staying power when they are delivered with physical and vocal animation. If you want listeners to share your point of view, show enthusiasm for your topic. The most common delivery techniques include making eye contact; using movement and gestures; and varying voice inflection, projection, and pace.

EYE CONTACT. The best way to establish rapport with your audience is through eye contact. In a large audience, directly address those people who seem most responsive to you in different parts of the room. Doing that helps you establish rapport with your listeners by holding their attention and gives you important visual cues that let you know how your message is being received. Are people engaged and actively listening, or are they looking around or staring at the floor? Such cues tell you that you may need to speed up or slow down the pace of your presentation.

MOVEMENT.   Animate the presentation with physical movement. Take a step or two to one side after you have been talking for a minute or so. That type of movement is most effective at transitional points in your presentation between major topics or after pauses or emphases. Too much movement, however, can be distracting, so try not to pace.

Another way to integrate movement into your presentation is to walk to the screen and point to the visual as you discuss it. Touch the screen with the pointer and then turn back to the audience before beginning to speak (remember the three *t*'s: touch, turn, and talk).

GESTURES.   Gestures both animate your presentation and help communicate your message. Most people gesture naturally when they talk; nervousness, however, can inhibit gesturing during a presentation. Keep one hand free and use that hand to gesture.

VOICE.   Your voice can be an effective tool in communicating your sincerity, enthusiasm, and command of your topic. Use it to your advantage to project your credibility. *Vocal inflection* is the rise and fall of your voice at different times, such as the way your voice naturally rises at the end of a question ("You want it *when?*"). A conversational delivery and eye contact promote the feeling among members of the audience that you are addressing them directly. Use vocal inflection to highlight differences between key and subordinate points in your presentation.

PROJECTION.   Most speakers think they are projecting more loudly than they are. Remember that your presentation is ineffective for anyone in the audience who cannot hear you. If listeners must strain to hear you, they may give up trying to listen. Correct projection problems by practicing out loud with someone listening from the back of the room.

PACE.   Be aware of the speed at which you deliver your presentation. If you speak too fast, your words will run together, making it difficult for your audience to follow. If you speak too slowly, your listeners will become impatient and distracted.

Presentation Anxiety.   Everyone experiences nervousness before a presentation. Survey after survey reveals that for most people dread of public speaking ranks among their top five fears. Instead of letting fear inhibit you, focus on channeling your nervous energy into a helpful stimulant. The best way to master anxiety is to know your topic thoroughly—knowing what you are going to say and how you are going to say it will help you gain confidence and reduce anxiety as you become immersed in your subject.

Writer's Checklist: Preparing for and Delivering a Presentation

☑ Practice your presentation with visuals; practice in front of listeners, if possible.

☑ Visit the location of the presentation ahead of time to familiarize yourself with the surroundings.

☑ Prepare a set of notes that will trigger your memory during the presentation.

☑ Make as much eye contact as possible with your audience to establish rapport and maximize opportunities for audience feedback.

☑ Animate your delivery by integrating movement, gestures, and vocal inflection into your presentation. However, keep your movements and speech patterns natural.

☑ Speak loudly and slowly enough to be heard and understood.

☑ Do not read the text on your visuals word for word; explain the key points in detail.

For information and tips on communicating with cross-cultural audiences, see **global communication**, **global graphics**, and **international correspondence**.

press releases

Companies and organizations write press releases (or *news releases*) to announce new products and services, new policies, special events (such as branch openings, company anniversaries, mergers, and grand openings), management changes, and sponsorship of social-action and cultural programs. The purpose of a press release is both to inform the public about the company and its products and services and to promote a favorable image. Even the announcement of what might be regarded as an unfavorable event, such as the closing of a division, can put a company in a good light by demonstrating candor, the ability to act effectively in a crisis, or the potential long-term benefits of a change. Large corporations and institutions usually have their own public relations staffs or use outside agencies. However, if you work for a small company without public relations resources, you may be called on to write a press release.

The press release should be clear, concise, and written with particular attention to the five *w*'s: *who*, *what*, *where*, *when*, and *why*. Begin the first paragraph with the place and date of the announcement, as shown in Figure P–5 on page 406. Write the release using the decreas-ing **order-of-importance method of development**. Put all

---

News Release

BENTLEY PLASTICS
3535 Michigan Avenue ■ Chicago, IL 60653

Contact: Marjorie Kohls
E-mail: mkohls@bentley.com
Phone: (312) 712-1946
Fax: (312) 712-1950

FOR IMMEDIATE RELEASE

Mark Williams Joins Bentley Plastics as Vice President

Chicago, Illinois, May 22, 2006: Marketing expert and author Mark Williams has been appointed Vice President for Marketing at Bentley Plastics, a manufacturer of polymer tubing and coils. He will direct the Illinois and Indiana district sales offices and coordinate overseas distribution through the company's Singapore office. Williams will travel extensively throughout Southeast Asia while developing marketing channels for Bentley.

Formerly, Williams was director of services with International Marketing Associates, a consulting group in New York. While at IMA, he developed a computer-based marketing center that linked textile firms in the United States, Finland, and Great Britain. A graduate of the Columbia University Graduate School of Business, Williams is the author of *Marketing Dynamics*, an informal examination of psychological appeals to the buying public. The book has been used in marketing classrooms at several universities.

Bentley Plastics, headquartered in Chicago, has main plants in Skokie, Illinois, and Gary, Indiana. Since 1978, Bentley has also been producing tubing for French distribution through the firm of Jourdan and Sons, Paris.

# # #

FIGURE P–5. Press Release

critical information in the first paragraph, information of the next level of importance in the second paragraph, and so on. Editors may need to make your release fit the space they have available; if they must cut your release, they will delete the last paragraph first, and then the next to last, and so on. Make sure your facts are accurate and be careful to define any unfamiliar terms.

Releases are usually sent to local newspapers, television and radio stations, and other special groups, such as trade publications or professional associations. Send the release to a specific person whenever possible. Otherwise, try to address the news release to a particular editor, such as to the business editor or the technology editor. See also **newsletter articles**.

Writer's Checklist: Preparing Press Releases

☑ Print the release on company stationery with a minimum of one-inch margins on each side of the page.

☑ Provide contact information for the person who can supply further details.

☑ Use boldface type for the headlines and double-space text for easy reading and editing.

☑ Use *-more-* centered at the bottom of the page when you need to indicate that another page follows.

☑ Allow one blank line and center # # # or *-30-* or *-End-* to indicate where the press release ends.

WEB LINK WRITING PRESS RELEASES

For links to Web sites that offer tips, samples, and resources for writing press releases, see <*bedfordstmartins.com/alredbus*> and select *Links for Handbook Entries*.

---

principal / principle

Principal, meaning "an amount of money on which interest is earned or paid" or "a chief official in a school or court proceeding," is sometimes confused with *principle,* which means "a basic truth or belief."

- The bank will pay 6.5 percent on the *principal.*
- He sent a letter to the *principal* of the high school.
- She is a person of unwavering *principles.*

Principal is also an adjective, meaning "main" or "primary." (My *principal* objection is that it will be too expensive.)

process explanation

A process explanation may describe the steps in a process, an operation, or a procedure, such as the steps necessary to start a small business. The **introduction** often presents a brief overview of the process or lets <u>readers</u> know why it is important for them to become familiar with the process you are explaining. Be sure to define terms that readers might not understand and provide <u>visuals</u> to clarify the process. See also <u>defining terms</u> and <u>instructions</u>.

In describing a process, use transitional words and phrases to create unity within <u>paragraphs,</u> and select <u>headings</u> to mark the <u>transition</u> from one step to the next. Notice in Figure P–6 how obtaining a company tuition refund is described as a step-by-step process.

Tuition Refund Process

1. PROCEDURES

  1.1 Degree Approval

      1.1.1 An employee who meets school requirements and is interested in receiving tuition refunds should gain the approval of his or her manager and submit the request to the Human Resources Department. Human Resources may ask the manager to justify, in writing, the benefits of approving the degree request if the reason is not obvious.

      1.1.2 After agreement has been reached, the employee should complete Sections I and II of Form F-6970. After Human Resources has obtained two levels of management approval—from the employee's supervisor and the head of the department—it approves the employee's enrollment in the degree program.

      1.1.3 The employee who has been granted approval must submit proof of course enrollment and payment of course fees to Human Resources for tuition reimbursement.

FIGURE P–6. Process Explanation

P

progress and activity reports

Progress reports keep <u>readers</u> informed about major workplace projects, whereas *activity reports* focus on the ongoing work of individual employees. Both are sometimes called *status reports*.

Progress Reports

A progress report provides information about a project—its status, whether it is on schedule and within budget, and so on. Progress reports are often submitted by a contracting company to a client company, as shown in Figure P–7. They are used mainly for projects that

Hobard Construction Company
9032 Salem Avenue
Lubbock, TX 79409

www.hobardcc.com
(808) 769-0832
Fax: (808) 769-5327

August 15, 2006

Walter M. Wazuski
County Administrator
109 Grand Avenue
Manchester, NH 03103

Dear Mr. Wazuski:

Subject: Progress Report 8 for July 1–July 29, 2006

The renovation of the County Courthouse is progressing on schedule and within budget. Although the cost of certain materials is higher than our original bid indicated, we expect to complete the project without exceeding the estimated costs because the speed with which the project is being completed will reduce overall labor expenses.

Costs
Materials used to date have cost $78,600, and labor costs have been $193,000 (including some subcontracted plumbing). Our estimate for the remainder of the materials is $59,000; remaining labor costs should not exceed $64,000.

Work Completed
As of July 29, we had finished the installation of the circuit-breaker panels and meters, the level-one service outlets, and all the subfloor wiring. The upgrading of the courtroom, the upgrading of the records-storage room, and the replacement of the air-conditioning units are in the preliminary stages.

Work Schedule
We have scheduled the upgrading of the courtroom to take place from August 29 to October 7, the upgrading of the records-storage room from October 11 to November 18, and the replacement of the air-conditioning units from November 21 to December 16. We see no difficulty in having the job finished by the scheduled date of December 23.

Sincerely yours,

Tran Nuguélen

Tran Nuguélen
ntran@hobardcc.com

P

involve many steps over a period of time and are issued at regular intervals to state what has been done and what remains to be done. Progress reports help keep projects running smoothly by helping managers assign work, adjust schedules, allocate budgets, and order supplies and equipment. All progress reports for a particular project should have the same <u>format</u>.

The <u>introduction</u> to the first progress report should identify the project, any methods and necessary materials and other expenditures, and the date by which the project is expected to be completed. Subsequent reports summarize the progress acheived since the preceding report as well as list the steps that remain to be taken.

The body of the progress report should describe the project's status, including details such as schedules and costs. The body also includes a statement of the work completed and perhaps an estimate of future progress.

The report ends with <u>conclusions</u> and recommendations about changes in the schedule, materials, techniques, and so on.

Activity Reports

Within an organization, employees often submit activity reports on the progress of ongoing projects. Managers may combine the activity reports of several individuals or teams into larger activity reports and, in turn, submit those larger reports to their own managers. The activity report shown in Figure P–8 was submitted by a manager (Wayne Tribinski) who supervises 11 employees; the reader of the report (Kathryn Hunter) is Tribinski's manager.

Because the activity report is issued periodically (usually monthly) and contains material familiar to its <u>readers</u>, it normally needs no introduction or conclusion, although it may need a brief opening to provide <u>context</u>. Although the format varies from company to company, the following sections are typical: Current Projects, Current Problems, Plans for the Next Period, and Current Staffing Level (for managers).

INTEROFFICE MEMO

Date: June 6, 2006
To: Kathryn Hunter, Director of IT
From: Wayne Tribinski, Manager, Applications Programs   *WT*
Subject: Activity Report for May 2006

We are dealing with the following projects and problems, as of May 31.

Projects

1. For the *Software Training Mailing Campaign*, we anticipate producing a set of labels for mailing software training information to customers by June 10.
2. The *Search Project* is on hold until the PL/I training has been completed, probably by the end of June.
3. The project to provide a database for the *Information Management System* has been expanded in scope to provide a database for all training activities. We are rescheduling the project to take the new scope into account.

Problems

The *Information Management System* has been delayed. The original schedule was based on the assumption that a systems analyst who was familiar with the system would work on this project. Instead, the project was assigned to a newly hired systems analyst who was inexperienced and required much more learning time than expected.

Bill Michaels, whose activity report is attached, is correcting a problem in the *CNG Software.* This correction may take a week.

Plans for Next Month

- Complete the *Software Training Mailing Campaign.*
- Resume the *Search Project.*
- Restart the project to provide a database on information management with a schedule that reflects its new scope.
- Write a report to justify the addition of two software developers to my department.
- Congratulate publicly the recipients of Meritorious Achievement Awards: Bill Thomasson and Nancy O'Rourke.

Current Staffing Level

Current staff: 11
Open requisitions: 0

Attachment

FIGURE P–8. Activity Report

promotional writing

Promotional writing is vital to the success of any company or organization; high-quality, state-of-the-art products or services are of little value if customers and clients do not know they exist. The specific types of promotional writing discussed in this book include brochures, newsletters, press releases, proposals, sales letters, and writing for the Web. See also Web design.

Although you may not be a marketing or public relations specialist, you may be asked to prepare promotional (or marketing) materials, especially if you work for a small organization or are self-employed. Even at a large company, you may help prepare a brochure, a Web page, or a department newsletter. See also collaborative writing.

Several elements are central to promotional writing:

- *Understanding your audience.* Analyzing the needs, interests, concerns, and makeup of your audience is crucial.
- *Understanding the principles of persuasion.* Good promotional writing must gain attention, build interest, reduce resistance, and motivate readers to act.
- *Making information both easy to find and visually appealing.* You need to make the most effective use of organization as well as layout and design. You need to select the most appropriate visuals and integrate them with the text.
- *Writing with clarity, coherence, and conciseness.* No matter how attractive the design, if readers do not understand the message, you will not achieve your purpose. To make information accessible, of course, you must thoroughly understand the product or service you are promoting—to do so may require research.

⚡ ETHICS NOTE Because readers are persuaded only if they believe the source is credible, you need to be careful not to overstate claims and avoid possible logic errors. See also ethics in writing and persuasion. ✦

Keep in mind that many other documents described in this book often include the additional or secondary purpose of promoting an organization. For example, adjustment letters, which are usually concerned with resolving a specific problem, offer opportunities to promote your organization. Likewise, progress and activity reports provide an opportunity to promote the value of your work in an organization.

pronoun reference

A pronoun should refer clearly to a specific antecedent. Avoid vague and uncertain references.

- We got the account after we wrote the proposal. *, which was a big one,* ~~It was a big one.~~

For <u>coherence</u>, place pronouns as close as possible to their antecedents—distance increases the likelihood of <u>ambiguity</u>.

- The office building next to City Hall *, praised for its architectural design, is* ~~is praised for its architectural design.~~

A general (or broad) reference or one that has no real antecedent is a problem that often occurs when the word *this* is used by itself.

- He deals with personnel problems in his work. This *experience* helps him in his personal life.

Another problem is a hidden reference, which has only an implied antecedent.

- A high-lipid, low-carbohydrate diet is "ketogenic" because it favors *the* ~~their~~ formation *of ketone bodies*.

Do not repeat an antecedent in parentheses following the pronoun. If you feel you must identify the pronoun's antecedent in that way, rewrite the sentence.

AWKWARD The senior partner first met Bob Evans when he (Evans) was a trainee.

IMPROVED Bob Evans was a trainee when the senior partner first met him.

For advice on avoiding pronoun-reference problems with gender, see <u>biased language</u>.

P

pronouns

DIRECTORY
Case   415
Gender   416
Number   417
Person   417

A pronoun is a word that is used as a substitute for a <u>noun</u> (the noun for which a pronoun substitutes is called the *antecedent*). Using pronouns in place of nouns relieves the monotony of repeating the same noun over and over. See also <u>pronoun reference</u>.

Personal pronouns refer to the person or people speaking (*I, me, my, mine; we, us, our, ours*); the person or people spoken to (*you, your, yours*); or the person, people, or thing(s) spoken of (*he, him, his; she, her, hers; it, its; they, them, their, theirs*). See also <u>person</u> and <u>point of view</u>.

- If *their* figures are correct, *ours* must be in error.

Demonstrative pronouns (*this, these, that, those*) indicate or point out the thing being referred to.

- *This* is my desk. *These* are my coworkers. *That* will be a difficult job. *Those* are incorrect figures.

Relative pronouns (*who, whom, which, that*) perform a dual function: (1) They take the place of nouns, and (2) they connect and establish the relationship between a dependent <u>clause</u> and its main clause.

- The department manager decided *who* would be hired.

Interrogative pronouns (*who, whom, what, which*) are used to ask questions.

- *What* is the trouble?

Indefinite pronouns specify a class or group of persons or things rather than a particular person or thing (*all, another, any, anyone, anything, both, each, either, everybody, few, many, most, much, neither, nobody, none, several, some, such*).

- Not *everyone* liked the new procedures; *some* even refused to follow them.

A *reflexive pronoun*, which always ends with the suffix *-self* or *-selves*, indicates that the subject of the sentence acts upon itself. See also <u>sentence construction</u>.

- The electrician accidentally shocked *herself.*

The reflexive pronouns are *myself, yourself, himself, herself, itself, oneself, ourselves, yourselves,* and *themselves. Myself* is not a substitute for *I* or *me* as a personal pronoun.

- Victor and ~~myself~~ *I* completed the report on time.

- The assignment was given to Ingrid and ~~myself~~ *me.*

Intensive pronouns are identical in form to the reflexive pronouns, but they perform a different function: Intensive pronouns emphasize their antecedents.

- I *myself* asked the same question.

Reciprocal pronouns (one another, each other) indicate the relationship of one item to another. *Each other* is commonly used when referring to two persons or things and *one another* when referring to more than two.

- Lashell and Kara work well with *each other.*
- The crew members work well with *one another.*

Case

Pronouns have forms to show the subjective, objective, and possessive cases, as shown in the entry <u>case</u>.

A pronoun that is used as the subject of a clause or sentence is in the subjective case (*I, we, he, she, it, you, they, who*). The subjective case is also used when the pronoun follows a linking <u>verb</u>.

- *She* is my boss.
- My boss is *she.*

A pronoun that is used as the object of a verb or **preposition** is in the objective case (*me, us, him, her, it, you, them, whom*).

- Ms. Davis hired Tom and *me.* [object of verb]
- Between *you* and *me,* she's wrong. [object of preposition]

A pronoun that is used to express ownership is in the **possessive case** (*my, mine, our, ours, his, her, hers, its, your, yours, their, theirs, whose*).

- He took *his* notes with him on the business trip.
- We took *our* notes with us on the business trip.

P

ESL **TIPS FOR USING POSSESSIVE PRONOUNS**

In many languages, possessive pronouns agree in number and gender with the nouns they modify. In English, however, possessive pronouns agree in number and gender with their antecedents. Check your writing carefully for agreement between a possessive pronoun and the word, phrase, or clause to which it refers.

- The *woman* brought *her* brother a cup of soup.
- *Robert* sent *his* mother flowers on Mother's Day.

A pronoun appositive takes the case of its antecedent.

- Two systems analysts, Joe and *I*, were selected to represent the company.
  [*Joe and I* is in apposition to the subject, *systems analysts*, and must therefore be in the subjective case.]
- The manager selected two representatives—Joe and *me*.
  [*Joe and me* is in apposition to *two representatives*, which is the object of the verb, *selected*, and therefore must be in the objective case.]

If you have difficulty determining the case of a compound pronoun, try using the pronoun singly.

- In his letter, Eldon mentioned *him* and *me*.

  In his letter, Eldon mentioned *him*.

  In his letter, Eldon mentioned *me*.
- *They* and *we* must discuss the terms of the merger.

  They must discuss the terms of the merger.

  We must discuss the terms of the merger.

When a pronoun modifies a noun, try it without the noun to determine its case.

- [*We/Us*] pilots fly our own planes.

  We fly our own planes.
  [You would not write, "*Us* fly our own planes."]
- He addressed his remarks directly to [*we/us*] technicians.

  He addressed his remarks directly to *us*.
  [You would not write, "He addressed his remarks directly to *we*."]

Gender

A pronoun must agree in gender with its antecedent. A problem sometimes occurs because the masculine pronoun has traditionally been used to refer to both sexes. To avoid the sexual bias implied in such usage, use *he or she* or the plural form of the pronoun, *they*.

- *All*   *they choose.*
  ~~Each~~ may stay or go as ~~he~~ chooses.

P

As in this example, when the singular pronoun (*he*) changes to the plural (*they*), the singular indefinite pronoun (*each*) must also change to its plural form (*all*). See also <u>biased language</u>.

Number

Number is a frequent problem with only a few indefinite pronouns (*each, either, neither,* and those ending with *-body* or *-one,* such as *anybody, anyone, everybody, everyone, nobody, no one, somebody, someone*) that are normally singular and so require singular verbs and are referred to by singular pronouns.

- As *each member arrives* for the meeting, please hand *him or her* a copy of the confidential report. *Everyone* must return the copy before *he or she* leaves. *Everybody* on the committee *understands* that *neither* of our major competitors *is* aware of the new process we have developed.

Person

Third-person personal pronouns usually have antecedents.

- Gina presented the report to the members of the board of directors. *She* [Gina] first summarized *it* [the report] for *them* [the directors] and then asked for questions.

First- and second-person personal pronouns do not normally require antecedents.

- *I* like my job.
- *You* were there at the time.
- *We* all worked hard on the project.

P

---

proofreaders' marks

Publishers have established symbols called *proofreaders' marks* that writers and editors use to communicate in the production of publications. Familiarity with those symbols makes it easy for you to communicate your changes to others. Figure P–9 on page 418 lists standard proofreaders' marks.

MARK/SYMBOL	MEANING	EXAMPLE	CORRECTED TYPE
	Delete	the ~~manager's~~ report	the report
	Insert	the report	the manager's report
	Let stand	the ~~manager's~~ report	the manager's report
	Capitalize	the monday meeting	the Monday meeting
	Lowercase	the Monday Meeting	the Monday meeting
	Transpose	the cover lettre	the cover letter
	Close space	a loud speaker	a loudspeaker
	Insert space	a loudspeaker	a loud speaker
	Paragraph	...report. The meeting...	...report. The meeting...
	Run in with previous line or paragraph	...report. The meeting...	...report. The meeting...
	Italicize	the New York Times	the *New York Times*
	Boldface	Use boldface sparingly.	Use **boldface** sparingly.
	Insert period	I wrote the e-mail	I wrote the e-mail.
	Insert comma	However we cannot...	However, we cannot...
	Insert hyphen	clear cut decision	clear-cut decision
	Insert em dash	Our goal productivity	Our goal—productivity
	Insert colon	We need the following	We need the following:
	Insert semicolon	we finished we achieved	we finished; we achieved
	Insert quotation marks	He said, I agree.	He said, "I agree."
	Insert apostrophe	the managers report	the manager's report

FIGURE P–9. Proofreaders' Marks

proofreading

Computer grammar checkers and spell checkers, while a help to proof-reading, can make writers overconfident. If a typographical error results in a legitimate English word (for example, *coarse* instead of *course*), the spell checker will not flag the misspelling. Therefore, you still must proofread your work carefully—both on-screen and on paper. You may find some of the tactics discussed in <u>revision</u> useful when proofreading; in fact, you may find passages during proofreading that will require fur-ther revision.

Whether the material you proofread is your own writing or that of someone else, consider proofreading in several stages. Although you need to tailor the stages to the specific document and to your own problem areas, the following *Writer's Checklist* should provide a useful starting point for proofreading.

Writer's Checklist: Proofreading in Stages

FIRST-STAGE REVIEW

☑ Appropriate **format**, as for **reports** or **correspondence**

☑ Typographical consistency (**headings**, spacing, fonts)

☑ Correct numbering of figures and **tables**

SECOND-STAGE REVIEW

☑ Specific **grammar** and **usage** problems

☑ Appropriate **punctuation**

☑ Correct **abbreviations** and **capitalization**

☑ Correct **spelling** (especially names and places)

☑ Complete Web or **e-mail** addresses

☑ Accurate data in tables and **lists**

☑ Cut-and-paste errors; for example, a result of moved or deleted text and numbers

FINAL-STAGE REVIEW

☑ Survey of your overall goals: **readers'** needs and **purpose**

☑ Appearance of the document (see **layout and design**)

☑ Review by a trusted colleague, especially for crucial documents (see **collaborative writing**)

Consider using standard **proofreaders' marks** for proofreading someone else's document.

> **DIGITAL TIPS PROOFREADING FOR FORMAT CONSISTENCY**
>
> Viewing whole pages on-screen is an effective way to check formatting, spacing, and typographical consistency, as well as the general appearance of documents. For comparing layouts, view multiple pages or "tile" separate documents side by side. For instructions, see <*bedfordstmartins.com/alredbus*> and select *Digital Tips*, "Proofreading for Format Consistency."

proposals

DIRECTORY

Strategies   420
   Audience and Purpose   420
   Project Management   421
Proposal Structure   421
   Short Proposals   421
   Long Proposals   421
Internal Proposals   423
   Routine Internal Proposals   423

Formal Internal Proposals   424
External Proposals   424
   Solicited Proposals   424
   Unsolicited Proposals   427
   Sales Proposals   428
   Grant and Research Proposals   428
Writer's Checklist: Writing Persuasive
   Proposals   440

A proposal is a document written to persuade <u>readers</u> to follow a plan or course of action that you believe will solve a problem or fulfill a need. (See also <u>persuasion</u>.) You may send a proposal to others within your organization (an internal proposal) or to potential customers or clients outside the organization (an external or a sales proposal). A proposal may be written in response to a <u>request for proposals</u> (RFP) that describes a particular need. Often, you will collaborate with others in preparing a proposal. See <u>collaborative writing</u>.

Strategies

Regardless of the type of proposal you write, begin by considering its <u>audience</u> and <u>purpose</u>, the project management, and the proposal structure.

Audience and Purpose.   A proposal offers a plan to fill a need, and readers will evaluate your plan based on how well you answer their questions about what you are proposing to do, how and when you plan to do it, and how much it will cost. Because proposals often require more than one level of approval, take all your readers into account as you answer their questions. Consider especially their levels of technical knowledge of the subject. For example, if your primary reader is an expert on your subject but a supervisor who must also approve the proposal is not, provide an <u>executive summary</u> written in nontechnical language. You might also include a <u>glossary</u> of terms used in the body of the proposal or an <u>appendix</u> that explains highly detailed information in nontechnical language. If your primary reader is not an expert but a supervisor is, write the proposal with the nonexpert in mind and include an appendix that contains the technical details.

Writing a persuasive and even complex proposal can be simplified by composing a concise statement of exactly the problem or opportunity that your proposal is designed to address. Stating the problem or opportunity concisely helps you and your readers understand the value, scope, and limitations of your proposed solution.

Project Management.   Proposal writers are often faced with writing high-quality, persuasive proposals under tight organizational deadlines. Breaking the task down into manageable parts is the key to accomplishing your goal. For example, you might set your own deadlines for completing various sections of the proposal or for scheduling the stages of the writing process, as described in "Five Steps to Successful Writing."

Proposal Structure

Proposals vary widely in length, formality, and structure.

Short Proposals.   A short or medium-length proposal typically consists of an introduction, a body, and a conclusion.

INTRODUCTION.   The introduction should state the purpose and scope of your proposal, as well as the problem you propose to solve and your solution to it. It should also indicate the dates on which you propose to begin and complete work, any special benefits of your proposed approach, and the cost of the project. For a sales (external) proposal, refer to any previous positive associations your organization has had with the potential client or customer.

BODY.   The body should offer the details of your solution to the problem and explain (1) the product or service you are offering, (2) how the job will be done, (3) how you will perform the work and any special materials you may use, (4) a schedule when each phase of the project will be completed, and (5) a breakdown of project costs.

CONCLUSION.   The conclusion should persuasively resell your proposal by emphasizing the benefits of your solution, product, or service over any competing ideas. Also include details about the time period during which the proposal is valid. Effective conclusions show confidence in your solution, your appreciation for the opportunity to submit the proposal, and your willingness to provide further information, as well as encouraging your reader to act on your proposal.

Long Proposals.   The sections that follow are found in longer, more formal proposals. The number of sections in any particular proposal depends on the audience, the purpose, and the scope of the proposal, as well as on the standard practice within an organization.

Typically, however, the sections can be grouped into *front matter*, *body* (which includes the introduction and conclusion), and *back matter*. For more information on many of the following components, see **formal reports**.

FRONT MATTER

- *Cover Letter or Letter of Transmittal.* In the **cover letter**, express appreciation for the opportunity to submit your proposal, any assistance from the customer, and any previous positive associations. Then summarize the proposal's recommendations and express confidence that they will satisfy the customer's needs.
- *Title Page.* Include the **title** of the proposal, the date, the organization to which it is being submitted, and your company name.
- *Table of Contents.* Include a **table of contents** in longer proposals to guide readers to important **headings**, which should be listed according to beginning page numbers.
- *List of Figures.* If your proposal has six or more figures, include a list of figures with captions as well as figure and page numbers. See **visuals**.

BODY

- *Executive Summary.* Briefly summarize the proposal's highlights in persuasive, nontechnical language for decision-makers.
- *Introduction.* Explain the reasons for the proposal; emphasize reader benefits; and, when appropriate, discuss your understanding of the problem.
- *Background or Problem.* Describe the problem or opportunity your proposal addresses. To make your proposal more persuasive, your problem statement should illustrate how your proposal will benefit your client's organization.
- *Product Description.* If your proposal offers products as well as services, include a general description of the products and any technical specifications.
- *Detailed Solutions (Rationale).* Explain in a detailed section that will be read by technical specialists exactly how you plan to do what you are proposing.
- *Cost Analysis.* Itemize the estimated costs of all the products and services you are offering.
- *Delivery Schedule.* Outline how you will accomplish the work and show a timetable for each phase of the project.

- *Staffing.* Summarize the expertise (education, experience, and certifications) of key personnel who will work on the project. Include their <u>résumés</u> in an appendix.

- *Site Preparation.* If your recommendations include modifying the customer's physical facilities, include a site-preparation description that details the required modifications.

- *Training Requirements.* If the products and services you are proposing require training the customer's employees, specify the required training and its cost.

- *Statement of Responsibilities.* To prevent misunderstandings about what you and your customer's responsibilities will be, state those responsibilities.

- *Organizational Sales Pitch.* Describe your company, its history, and its present position in the industry. An organizational sales pitch is designed to sell your company and its general capability in the field. It promotes the company and concludes the proposal on an upbeat, persuasive note.

- *Authorization Request and Deadline.* Close with a request for approval and a deadline that explains how long the proposed prices are valid.

- *Conclusion.* Include a persuasive conclusion that summarizes the proposal's key points and stresses your company's strong points.

BACK MATTER

- *Appendixes.* Provide résumés of key personnel or material of interest to some readers, such as statistical analyses, organizational charts, and workflow diagrams.

- *Bibliography.* List all sources consulted to prepare the proposal. See <u>bibliographies</u> and <u>documenting sources</u>.

- *Glossary.* If your proposal contains terms that will be unfamiliar to your intended audience, list and define them in the glossary.

Internal Proposals

Two common types of internal proposals are often distinguished from each other by the frequency with which they are written and by the degree of change proposed.

Routine Internal Proposals. Routine internal proposals are most frequent and typically include small spending requests, requests for permission to hire new employees or increase salaries, and requests to attend conferences or purchase new equipment. In writing routine proposals, follow the introduction-body-conclusion format for short proposals on page 421, and highlight any benefits to be realized.

Formal Internal Proposals.　Formal internal proposals are usually proposals to commit relatively large sums of money. They have various names, but the most common designation is a *capital appropriations request* or a *capital appropriations proposal.*

The introduction to a formal internal proposal should persuasively establish that a problem exists that needs a solution and provide any background information your reader needs to help him or her make the decision in question. The introduction should also briefly describe any supporting evidence you are including, such as a feasibility study you may have conducted. See also **feasibility reports**.

The body of a formal internal proposal should offer a practical solution to the problem; compare possible alternatives; respond to possible objections; and describe all the equipment, property, or services you are proposing to purchase and their key benefits to the organization. You should include any justifications for each expenditure: the calculated return on investment or the internal rate of return; the volume of use over, for example, the next two years; the product life expectancy, technical support, or warranties; and the most economical purchasing option.

The conclusion should emphasize the benefits of what you are proposing and express your willingness to provide any further information that may be required. Figure P–10 shows a formal internal proposal. The writer of the proposal responded to management's concern about the issue of reducing company health-care costs. The writer, Leslie Galusha, concluded that helping employees improve their fitness would be a major step in solving the problem of escalating health-care costs. She examined government data and researched through personal visits and interviews the approaches of other companies.

External Proposals

External proposals to be submitted to other companies or organizations could be either solicited or unsolicited.

Solicited Proposals.　Solicited proposals are prepared in response to a request for goods or services. Procuring organizations that would like competing companies to bid for a job commonly issue a request for proposals (RFP) or an invitation for bids (IFB).

An IFB is commonly issued by government agencies to solicit bids on clearly defined products or services. An IFB is restrictive, binding the bidder to produce an item that meets the exact requirements of the agency. The goods or services to be procured are defined in the IFB by references to performance standards stated in specifications. Bidders must be prepared to prove that their product will meet all requirements of the specifications.

In contrast to an IFB, an RFP is flexible. Often an RFP will define a problem and allow those who respond to suggest possible solutions. Sometimes, RFPs are presented in several stages: (1) development of a concept, (2) construction of a prototype or mock-up, and (3) production of the device or plan selected.

The procuring organization generally publishes its RFP or IFB in trade journals, on its Web site, or in a specialized venue such as Federal Business Opportunities at <www.fedbizopps.gov/>.

ABO, Inc.
Interoffice Memo

To: Joan Marlow, Director, Human Resources Division
From: Leslie Galusha, Chief   *LG*
          Employee Benefits Department
Date: June 13, 2006
Subject: Employee Fitness and Health-Care Costs

Health-care and workers'-compensation insurance costs at ABO, Inc., have risen 100 percent over the last five years. In 2001, costs were $5,675 per employee per year; in 2006, they have reached $11,560 per employee per year. This doubling of costs mirrors a national trend, with health-care costs anticipated to continue to rise at the same rate for the next ten years. Controlling these escalating expenses will be essential. They are eating into ABO's profit margin because the company currently pays 70 percent of the costs for employee coverage.

Healthy employees bring direct financial benefits to companies in the form of lower employee insurance costs, lower absenteeism rates, and reduced turnover. Regular physical exercise promotes fit, healthy people by reducing the risk of coronary heart disease, diabetes, osteoporosis, hypertension, and stress-related problems. I propose that to promote regular, vigorous physical exercise for our employees, ABO implement a health-care program that focuses on employee fitness. . . .

FIGURE P–10. Formal Internal Proposal (Introduction)

Problem of Health-Care Costs

The U.S. Department of Health and Human Services recently estimated that health-care costs in the United States will triple by the year 2015. Corporate expenses for health care are rising at such a fast rate that, if unchecked, in eight years they will significantly erode corporate profits.

Researchers agree that people who do not participate in a regular and vigorous exercise program incur double the health-care costs and are hospitalized 30 percent more days than people who exercise regularly. Nonexercisers are also 41 percent more likely to submit medical claims over $10,000 at some point during their careers than are those who exercise regularly.

My study of Tenneco, Inc., found that the average health-care claim for unfit men was $2,006 per illness compared with an average claim of $862 for those who exercised regularly. For women, the average claim for those who were unfit was $2,535, more than double the average claim of $1,039 for women who exercised. Additionally, Control Data Corporation found that each nonexerciser cost the company an extra $515 a year in health-care expenses.

These figures are further supported by data from independent studies. A model created by the National Institutes of Health (NIH) estimates that the average white-collar company could save $596,000 annually in medical costs (per 1,000 employees) just by promoting wellness. NIH researchers estimated that for every $1 a firm invests in a health-care program, it saves up to $3.75 in health-care costs. Another NIH study of 667 insurance-company employees showed savings of $2.65 million over a five-year period. The same study also showed a 400 percent drop in absentee rates after the company implemented a company-wide fitness program.

Possible Solutions for ABO

The benefits of regular, vigorous physical activity for employees and companies are compelling. To achieve these benefits at ABO, I propose that we choose from one of two possible options: Build in-house fitness centers at our warehouse facilities, or offer employees several options for membership at a national fitness club. The following analysis compares . . .

FIGURE P–10. Formal Internal Proposal (*continued*) (Body)

Joan Marlow   3   June 13, 2006

Conclusion and Recommendation

I recommend that ABO, Inc., participate in the corporate member-ship program at AeroFitness Clubs, Inc., by subsidizing employee memberships. By subsidizing memberships, ABO shows its commitment to the importance of a fit workforce. Club membership allows employees at all five ABO warehouses to participate in the program. The more employees who participate, the greater the long-term savings in ABO's health-care costs. Building and equip-ping fitness centers at all five warehouse sites would require an ini-tial investment of nearly $2.5 million. These facilities would also occupy valuable floor space — on average, 4,000 square feet at each warehouse. Therefore, this option would be very costly.

Enrolling employees in the corporate program at AeroFitness would allow them to receive a one-month free trial membership. Those in-terested in continuing could then join the club and pay half of the one-time membership fee of $900 and receive a 30 percent dis-count on the $600 yearly fee. The other half of the membership fee ($450) would be paid for by ABO. If em-ployees leave the company, they would have the option of purchasing ABO's share of the membership to continue at AeroFitness or selling their half of the membership to another ABO employee wishing to join AeroFitness.

Implementing this program will help ABO, Inc., reduce its health-care costs while building stronger employee relations by offering employees a desirable benefit. If this proposal is adopted, I have some additional thoughts about publicizing the program to encour-age employee participation. I look forward to discussing the details of this proposal with you and answering any questions you may have.

P

FIGURE P–10. Formal Internal Proposal (*continued*) (Conclusion)

Unsolicited Proposals. Unsolicited proposals are submitted to a company without a prior request for a proposal. Companies often oper-ate for years with a problem they have never recognized (unnecessarily high maintenance costs, for example, or poor inventory-control meth-ods). You might prepare an unsolicited proposal if you were convinced that the potential customer could realize substantial benefits by adopting your solution to a problem. Of course, you would need to convince the customer of the need for what you are proposing and that your solution would be the best one. Many unsolicited proposals are preceded by an inquiry to determine potential interest. If you receive a positive response, you would conduct a detailed study of the prospective customer's needs to determine whether you can be of help and, if so, exactly how. You would then prepare your proposal on the basis of your study.

Sales Proposals. A persuasive sales proposal must demonstrate above all that the prospective customer's purchase of the seller's products or services will solve a problem, improve operations, or offer other benefits. Sales proposals vary greatly in size and sophistication—from several pages written by one person, to dozens of pages written collaboratively by several people, to hundreds of pages written by a team of professional proposal writers. A short sales proposal might bid for the construction of a single home, a moderate-length proposal might bid for the installation of a computer network, and a large proposal might bid for the construction of a multimillion-dollar water purification system.

■ ETHICS NOTE Always keep in mind that, once submitted, a sales proposal is a legally binding document that promises to offer goods or services within a specified time and for a specified price. ✦

Your first task in writing a sales proposal is to find out exactly what your prospective customer needs. To do that, survey your potential customer's business, and determine whether your organization can satisfy the customer's needs. Before preparing a sales proposal, try to find out who your principal competitors are. Then compare your company's strengths with those of the competing firms, determine your advantages over your competitors, and emphasize those advantages in your proposal. Figure P–11 shows an example of a major sales proposal, which uses the format recommended for long proposals (but not all elements are shown).

> ◉ WEB LINK **SAMPLE SALES PROPOSALS**
>
> For a complete and annotated version of the proposal shown in Figure P–11, as well as additional sample proposals and the RFP to which Figure P–11 responded, see <*bedfordstmartins.com/alredbus*> and select *Model Documents Gallery.*

Grant and Research Proposals.   Grant and research proposals are written to request the approval of, and usually funding for, particular projects. For example, a professor of education might submit a research or grant proposal to the Department of Education to request funding for research on the relationship of class size to educational performance.

The Waters Corporation
17 North Waterloo Blvd.
Tampa, Florida 33607
Phone: (813) 919-1213   Fax: (813) 919-4411
www.waters.comp.com

September 2, 2006

Mr. John Yeung, General Manager
Cookson's Retail Stores, Inc.
101 Longuer Street
Savannah, Georgia 31499

Dear Mr. Yeung:

The Waters Corporation appreciates the opportunity to respond to Cookson's Request for Proposals dated July 25, 2006. We would like to thank Mr. Becklight, Director of your Management Information Systems Department, for his invaluable contributions to the study of your operations that we conducted before preparing our proposal.

It has been Waters's privilege to provide Cookson's with retail systems and equipment since your first store opened many years ago. Therefore, we have become very familiar with your requirements as they have evolved during the expansion you have experienced since that time. Waters's close working relationship with Cookson's has resulted in a clear understanding of Cookson's philosophy and needs.

Our proposal describes a Waters Interactive Terminal/Retail Processor System designed to meet Cookson's network and processing needs. It will provide all of your required capabilities, from the point-of-sale operational requirements at the store terminals to the host processor. The system uses the proven Retail III modular software, with its point-of-sale applications, and the superior Interactive Terminal, with its advanced capabilities and design. This system is easily installed without extensive customer reprogramming.

FIGURE P–11. Sales Proposal (Cover Letter)

Mr. J. Yeung
Page 2
September 2, 2006

The Waters Interactive Terminal/Retail Processor System, which is compatible with much of Cookson's present equipment, not only will answer your present requirements but will provide the flexibility to add new features and products in the future. The system's unique hardware modularity, efficient microprocessor design, and flexible programming capability greatly reduce the risk of obsolescence.

Thank you for the opportunity to present this proposal. You may be sure that we will use all the resources available to the Waters Corporation to ensure the successful implementation of the new system.

Sincerely yours,

Janet A. Curtain

Janet A. Curtain
Executive Account Manager
General Merchandise Systems
(*JCurtain@netcom.TF.com*)

Enclosure: Proposal

P

FIGURE P–11. Sales Proposal (*continued*) (Cover Letter)

The Waters Proposal   September 2, 2006

EXECUTIVE SUMMARY

The Waters 319 Interactive Terminal/615 Retail Processor System will provide your management with the tools necessary to manage people and equipment more profitably with procedures that will yield more cost-effective business controls for Cookson's.

The equipment and applications proposed for Cookson's were selected through the combined effort of Waters and Cookson's Management Information Systems Director, Mr. Becklight. The architecture of the system will respond to your current requirements and allow for future expansion.

The features and hardware in the system were determined from data acquired through the comprehensive survey we conducted at your stores in February of this year. The total of 71 Interactive Terminals proposed to service your four store locations is based on the number of terminals currently in use and on the average number of transactions processed during normal and peak periods. The planned remodeling of all four stores was also considered, and the suggested terminal placement has been incorporated into the working floor plan. The proposed equipment configuration and software applications have been simulated to determine system performance based on the volumes and anticipated growth rates of the Cookson's stores.

The information from the survey was also used in the cost justification, which was checked and verified by your controller, Mr. Deitering. The cost-effectiveness of the Waters Interactive Terminal/Retail Processor System is apparent. Expected savings, such as the projected 46 percent reduction in sales audit expenses, are realistic projections based on Waters's experience with other installations of this type.

– 1 –

FIGURE P–11. Sales Proposal (*continued*) (Executive Summary)

The Waters Proposal   September 2, 2006

GENERAL SYSTEM DESCRIPTION

The point-of-sale system that Waters is proposing for Cookson's in-cludes two primary Waters products. These are the 319 Interactive Terminal and the 615 Retail Processor.

Waters 319 Interactive Terminal
The primary component in the proposed retail system is the Interactive Terminal. It contains a full microprocessor, which gives it the flexibility that Cookson's has been looking for.

The 319 Interactive Terminal provides you with freedom in sequencing a transaction. You are not limited to a preset list of available steps or transactions. The terminal program can be adapted to provide unique transaction sets, each designed with a logical sequence of entry and pro-cessing to accomplish required tasks. In addition to sales transactions recorded on the selling floor, specialized transactions such as theater-ticket sales and payments can be designed for your customer-service area.

The 319 Interactive Terminal also functions as a credit authorization device, either by using its own floor limits or by transmitting a credit inquiry to the 615 Retail Processor for authorization.

Data-collection formats have been simplified so that transaction editing and formatting are much more easily accomplished. The IS manager has already been provided with documentation on these formats and has outlined all data-processing efforts that will be necessary to transmit the data to your current systems. These projections have been considered in the cost justification.

Waters 615 Retail Processor
The Waters 615 Retail Processor is a minicomputer system designed to support the Waters family of retail terminals. The . . .

[*The proposal next describes the Waters 615 Retail Processor before moving on to the detailed solution section.*]

FIGURE P–11. Sales Proposal (*continued*) (General Description of Products)

PAYROLL APPLICATION

Current Procedure
Your current system of reporting time requires each hourly employee to sign a time sheet; the time sheet is reviewed by the department manager and sent to the Payroll Department on Friday evening. Because the week ends on Saturday, the employee must show the scheduled hours for Saturday and not the actual hours; therefore, the department manager must adjust the reported hours on the time sheet for employees who do not report on the scheduled Saturday or who do not work the number of hours scheduled.

The Payroll Department employs a supervisor and three full-time clerks. To meet deadlines caused by an unbalanced workflow, an additional part-time clerk is used for 20 to 30 hours per week. The average wage for this clerk is $9.00 per hour.

Advantage of Waters's System
The 319 Interactive Terminal can be programmed for entry of payroll data for each employee on Monday morning by department managers, with the data reflecting actual hours worked. This system would eliminate the need for manual batching, controlling, and data input. The Payroll Department estimates conservatively that this work consumes 40 hours per week.

Hours per week	40
Average wage (part-time clerk)	× 9.00
Weekly payroll cost	$360.00
Annual savings	$18,720

Elimination of the manual tasks of tabulating, batching, and controlling can save 0.25 hourly unit. Improved workflow resulting from timely data in the system without data-input processing will allow more efficient use of clerical hours. This would reduce payroll by the 0.50 hourly unit currently required to meet weekly check disbursement.

Eliminate manual tasks	0.25
Improve workflow	0.75
40-hour unit reduction	1.00
Hours per week	40
Average wage (full-time clerk)	11.00
Savings per week	$440.00
Annual savings	$22,880

TOTAL SAVINGS: $41,600

FIGURE P–11. Sales Proposal (*continued*) (Detailed Solution)

COST ANALYSIS

This section of our proposal provides detailed cost information for the Waters 319 Interactive Terminal and the Waters 615 Retail Processor. It then multiplies these major elements by the quantities required at each of your four locations.

319 Interactive Terminal

Equipment	Price	Maint. (1 yr.)
Terminal	$2,895	$167
Journal Printer	425	38
Receipt Printer	425	38
Forms Printer	525	38
Software	220	—
TOTALS	$4,490	$281

[*The cost section goes on to describe other costs to install the system before summarizing the costs.*]

The following table summarizes all costs.

Location	Hardware	Maint. (1 yr.)	Software
Store No. 1	$72,190	$4,975	$3,520
Store No. 2	89,190	6,099	4,400
Store No. 3	76,380	5,256	3,740
Store No. 4	80,650	5,537	3,960
Data Center	63,360	6,679	12,480
Subtotals	$381,770	$28,546	$28,100

TOTAL $438,416

DELIVERY SCHEDULE

Waters is normally able to deliver 319 Interactive Terminals and 615 Retail Processors within 30 days of the date of the contract. This can vary depending on the rate and size of incoming orders.

All the software recommended in this proposal is available for immediate delivery. We do not anticipate any difficulty in meeting your tentative delivery schedule.

FIGURE P–11. Sales Proposal (*continued*) (Cost Analysis and Delivery Schedule)

The Waters Proposal   September 2, 2006

SITE PREPARATION

Waters will work closely with Cookson's to ensure that each site is properly prepared prior to system installation. You will receive a copy of Waters's installation and wiring procedures manual, which lists the physical dimensions, service clearance, and weight of the system components in addition to the power, logic, communications-cable, and environmental requirements. Cookson's is responsible for all building alterations and electrical facility changes, including the purchase and installation of communications cables, connecting blocks, and receptacles.

Wiring
For the purpose of future site considerations, Waters's in-house wiring specifications for the system call for two twisted-pair wires and twenty-two shielded gauges. The length of communications wires must not exceed 2,500 feet.

As a guide for the power supply, we suggest that Cookson's consider the following.

1. The branch circuit (limited to 20 amps) should service no equipment other than 319 Interactive Terminals.
2. Each 20-amp branch circuit should support a maximum of three Interactive Terminals.
3. Each branch circuit must have three equal-size conductors—one hot leg, one neutral, and one insulated isolated ground.
4. Hubbell IG 5362 duplex outlets or the equivalent should be used to supply power to each terminal.
5. Computer-room wiring will have to be upgraded to support the 615 Retail Processor.

–9–

FIGURE P–11. Sales Proposal (*continued*) (Site-Preparation Section)

TRAINING

To ensure a successful installation, Waters offers the following training course for your operators.

Interactive Terminal/Retail Processor Operations
Course number: 8256
Length: three days
Tuition: $500.00

This course provides the student with the skills, knowledge, and practice required to operate an Interactive Terminal/Retail Processor System. Online, clustered, and stand-alone environments are covered.

We recommend that students have a department-store background and that they have some knowledge of the system configuration with which they will be working.

P

FIGURE P–11. Sales Proposal (*continued*) (Training Section)

RESPONSIBILITIES

On the basis of its years of experience in installing information-processing systems, Waters believes that a successful installation requires a clear understanding of certain responsibilities.

Waters's Responsibilities

Generally, it is Waters's responsibility to provide its users with needed assistance during the installation so that live processing can begin as soon thereafter as is practical. The following items describe our specific responsibilities.

- Provide operations documentation for each application that you acquire from Waters.
- Provide forms and other supplies as ordered.
- Provide specifications and technical guidance for proper site planning and installation.
- Provide adviser assistance in the conversion from your present system to the new system.

Cookson's Responsibilities

Cookson's will be responsible for the suggested improvements described earlier, as well as the following.

- Identify an installation coordinator and system operator.
- Provide supervisors and clerical personnel to perform conversion to the system.
- Establish reasonable time schedules for implementation.
- Ensure that the physical site requirements are met.
- Provide personnel to be trained as operators and ensure that other employees are trained as necessary.
- Assume the responsibility for implementing and operating the system.

FIGURE P–11. Sales Proposal (*continued*) (Statement of Responsibilities)

DESCRIPTION OF VENDOR

The Waters Corporation develops, manufactures, markets, installs, and services total business information-processing systems for selected markets. These markets are primarily in the retail, financial, commercial, industrial, health-care, education, and government sectors.

The Waters total system concept encompasses one of the broadest hardware and software product lines in the industry. Waters computers range from small business systems to powerful general-purpose processors. Waters computers are supported by a complete spectrum of terminals, peripherals, and data-communication networks, as well as an extensive library of software products. Supplemental services and products include data centers, field service, systems engineering, and educational centers.

The Waters Corporation was founded in 1934 and presently has approximately 26,500 employees. The Waters headquarters is located at 17 North Waterloo Boulevard, Tampa, Florida, with district offices throughout the United States and Canada.

WHY WATERS?

Corporate Commitment to the Retail Industry
Waters's commitment to the retail industry is stronger than ever. We are continually striving to provide leadership in the design and implementation of new retail systems and applications that will ensure our users of a logical growth pattern.

Research and Development
Over the years, Waters has spent increasingly large sums on research-and-development efforts to ensure the availability of products and systems for the future. In 2005, our research-and-development expenditure for advanced systems design and technological innovations reached the $70-million level.

Leading Point-of-Sale Vendor
Waters is a leading point-of-sale vendor, having installed over 150,000 units. The knowledge and experience that Waters has gained over the years from these installations ensure well-coordinated and effective systems implementations.

FIGURE P–11. Sales Proposal (*continued*) (Vendor Description and Organizational Sales Pitch)

CONCLUSION

Waters welcomes the opportunity to submit this proposal to Cookson's. The Waters Corporation is confident that we have offered the right solution at a competitive price. Based on the hands-on analysis we conducted, our proposal takes into account your current and projected workloads and your plans to expand your facilities and operations. Our proposal will also, we believe, afford Cookson's future cost-avoidance measures in employee time and in enhanced accounting features.

Waters has a proven track record of success in the manufacture, installation, and servicing of retail business information systems stretching over many decades. We also have a demonstrated record of success in our past business associations with Cookson's. We believe that the system we propose will extend and strengthen this partnership.

Should you require additional information about any facet of this proposal, please contact Janet A. Curtain, who will personally arrange to meet with you or arrange for Waters's technical staff to meet with you or send you the information you need.

We look forward to your decision and to continued success in our working relationship with Cookson's.

FIGURE P–11. Sales Proposal (*continued*) (Conclusion)

Many government and private agencies solicit research and grant proposals. The granting agencies usually have their own requirements for the format and content of proposals submitted to them, but the proposals must always be persuasive. Tailor your grant or research proposal to your audience carefully by explaining the project's goals, your plan for achieving those goals, and your qualifications to perform the project.

Writer's Checklist: Writing Persuasive Proposals

- ☑ Analyze your audience carefully to determine how to best meet your readers' needs or requirements.
- ☑ Write a concise purpose statement to clarify your proposal's goals.
- ☑ Emphasize the proposal's benefits to readers and anticipate their questions or objections.
- ☑ Incorporate evidence to support the claims of your proposal.
- ☑ Divide the writing task into manageable segments and develop a work schedule.
- ☑ Review the descriptions of proposal sections and their uses in this entry.
- ☑ Select an appropriate, visually appealing format. (See **layout and design**.)
- ☑ Use a confident, upbeat **tone** throughout the proposal.

pseudo- / quasi-

As a **prefix**, *pseudo-*, meaning "false or counterfeit," is joined to the root word without a **hyphen** unless the root word begins with a capital letter (*pseudo*science, *pseudo*-Keynesian). *Pseudo-* is sometimes confused with *quasi-*, meaning "somewhat" or "partial." Unlike *semi-*, *quasi-* means "resembling something" rather than "half." *Quasi-* is usually hyphenated in combinations (*quasi*-marketing initiatives). See also **bi-/semi-**.

punctuation

Punctuation helps **readers** understand the meaning and relationships of words, phrases, clauses, and sentences. Marks of punctuation link, separate, enclose, indicate omissions, terminate, and classify. Most punctuation marks can perform more than one function. See also **sentence construction**.

The use of punctuation is determined by grammatical conventions and the writer's intention. Understanding punctuation is essential for writers because it enables them to communicate with <u>clarity</u> and precision. See also <u>grammar</u>.

Detailed information on each mark of punctuation is given in its own entry. The following are the 13 marks of punctuation.

<u>apostrophe</u>	'	<u>parentheses</u>	( )
<u>brackets</u>	[ ]	<u>period</u>	.
<u>colon</u>	:	<u>question mark</u>	?
<u>comma</u>	,	<u>quotation marks</u>	" "
<u>dash</u>	—	<u>semicolon</u>	;
<u>exclamation mark</u>	!	<u>slash</u>	/
<u>hyphen</u>	-		

See also <u>abbreviations</u>, <u>capitalization</u>, <u>contractions</u>, <u>dates</u>, <u>ellipses</u>, <u>italics</u>, and <u>numbers</u>.

WEB LINK **PRACTICING PUNCTUATION**

For online exercises on punctuation, see <*bedfordstmartins.com/alredbus*> and select *Exercise Central*.

---

purpose

What do you want your <u>readers</u> to know, to believe, or to do when they have read your document? When you answer that question, you have determined the primary purpose, or objective, of your document. Be careful not to state a purpose too broadly. A purpose such as "to explain a fax machine" is too general to be helpful to you as you write. In contrast, "to instruct the reader how to use the IT-770 fax machine to send and retrieve faxes" is a specific purpose that will help you focus on what you need your document to accomplish. Often the <u>context</u> will help you focus your purpose.

However, the writer's primary purpose is often more complex than simply "to explain" something. To fully understand this complexity, you need to ask yourself not only *why* you are writing the document but *what* you want to influence your reader to believe or to do after reading it. Suppose a writer for a <u>newsletter</u> has been assigned to write an article about cardiopulmonary resuscitation (CPR). In answer to the question *what?* the writer could state the purpose as "to emphasize the importance of CPR." To the question *why?* the writer might respond, "to encourage employees to sign up for evening CPR classes." Putting the answers to the two questions together, the writer's purpose might be stated as, "To write a document that will emphasize the importance of CPR and encourage employees to sign up for evening CPR classes." Note that the primary purpose of the document on CPR was to persuade the readers of the importance of CPR, and the secondary goal was to motivate them to register for a class. Secondary goals often involve such abstract notions as to motivate, to persuade, to reassure, or to inspire your reader. See also **persuasion**.

If you answer the questions *what?* and *why?* and put the answers into writing as a stated purpose that includes both primary and secondary goals, you will simplify your writing task and more likely achieve your purpose. For a **collaborative writing** project, it is especially important to collectively write a statement of your purpose to ensure that the document achieves its goals. Do not lose sight of that purpose as you become engrossed in the other steps of the writing process. See also "Five Steps to Successful Writing."

P

Q

question marks

The question mark (?) has several uses, but it most often ends a sentence that is a direct question or request.

- Where did you put the tax report? [direct question]
- Will you e-mail me if your shipment does not arrive by June 10? [request]

Use a question mark to end a statement that has an interrogative meaning—a statement that is declarative in form but asks a question.

- The tax report is finished? [question in declarative form]

Question marks may follow a series of separate items within an interrogative sentence.

- Do you remember the date of the contract? Its terms? Whether you signed it?

Use a question mark to end an interrogative clause within a declarative sentence.

- It was not until July (or was it August?) that we submitted the report.

Retain the question mark in a title that is being cited, even though the sentence in which it appears has not ended.

- *Can Investments Be Protected?* is the title of her book.

Never use a question mark to end a sentence that is an indirect question.

- He asked me where I put the tax report.

When a question is a polite request or instruction to which an affirmative response is assumed, a question mark is not necessary.

- Will you call me as soon as he arrives. [polite request]

When used with **quotations,** the placement of the question mark is important. When the writer is asking a question, the question mark belongs outside the quotation marks.

- Did she say, "I don't think the project should continue"?

If the quotation itself is a question, the question mark goes inside the quotation marks.

- She asked, "Do we have enough funding?"

If both cases apply—the writer is asking a question and the quotation itself is a question—use a single question mark inside the quotation marks.

- Did she ask, "Do we have enough funding?"

questionnaires

A questionnaire—a series of questions on a particular topic sent out to a number of people—serves the same purpose as an interview but does so on paper, as an **e-mail** attachment, or online. The sample cover memo and questionnaire in Figure Q–1 were sent to employees in a large organization who had participated in a six-month program of flexible working hours.

Questionnaires have several advantages over the personal interview as well as several disadvantages.

Q

ADVANTAGES

- A questionnaire allows you to gather information from more people more quickly than you could by conducting personal interviews.
- It enables you to obtain responses from people who are difficult to reach or who are in various geographical locations.
- Those responding to a questionnaire have more time to think through their answers than when faced with the pressure of composing thoughtful and complete answers to an interviewer.
- The questionnaire may yield more objective data because it reduces the possibility that the interviewer's tone of voice or facial expressions might influence an answer.
- The cost of distributing and tabulating a questionnaire is lower than the cost of conducting numerous personal interviews.

Luxwear Products Corporation
MEMO

To: All Company Employees
From: Nelson Barrett, Director   *NB*
Date: October 17, 2006
Subject: Review of Flexible Working Hours Program

Please complete and return the questionnaire enclosed regarding Luxwear's trial program of flexible working hours. Your answers will help us decide whether we should make the program permanent.

Return the completed questionnaire to Ken Rose, Mail Code 12B, by October 28. Your signature on the questionnaire is not necessary. All responses will be confidential and given serious consideration. Feel free to raise additional issues pertaining to the program.

If you want to discuss any item in the questionnaire, call Pam Peters in the Human Resources Department at extension 8812 or e-mail at pp1@lpc.com.

Enclosure: Questionnaire

Q

FIGURE Q-1. Questionnaire (Cover Memo)

Flexible Working Hours Program
Questionnaire

1. What kind of position do you occupy?

   ☐ Supervisory
   ☐ Nonsupervisory

2. Indicate to the nearest quarter of an hour your starting time under flextime.

   ☐ 7:00 a.m.　　　　☐ 8:15 a.m.
   ☐ 7:15 a.m.　　　　☐ 8:30 a.m.
   ☐ 7:30 a.m.　　　　☐ 8:45 a.m.
   ☐ 7:45 a.m.　　　　☐ 9:00 a.m.
   ☐ 8:00 a.m.　　　　☐ Other (specify) _____

3. Where do you live?

   ☐ Talbot County　　　　☐ Greene County
   ☐ Montgomery County　　☐ Other (specify) _____

4. How do you usually travel to work?

   ☐ Drive alone　　☐ Walk
   ☐ Bus　　　　　　☐ Car pool
   ☐ Train　　　　　☐ Motorcycle
   ☐ Bicycle　　　　☐ Other (specify) _____

5. Has flextime affected your commuting time?

   ☐ Increase: Approximate number of minutes _____
   ☐ Decrease: Approximate number of minutes _____
   ☐ No change

6. If you drive alone or in a car pool, has flextime increased or decreased the amount of time it takes you to find a parking space?

   ☐ Increased　　　　☐ Decreased　　　　☐ No change

7. Has flextime had an effect on your productivity?

   a. Quality of work
   　☐ Increased　　　　☐ Decreased　　　　☐ No change

   b. Accuracy of work
   　☐ Increased　　　　☐ Decreased　　　　☐ No change

   c. Quiet time for uninterrupted work
   　☐ Increased　　　　☐ Decreased　　　　☐ No change

FIGURE Q–1. Questionnaire (*continued*)

8. Have you had difficulty getting in touch with coworkers who are on different work schedules from yours?

☐ Yes ☐ No

9. Have you had trouble scheduling meetings within flexible starting and quitting times?

☐ Yes ☐ No

10. Has flextime affected the way you feel about your job?

☐ Yes ☐ No

If yes, please answer (a) or (b):

a. Feel better about job
☐ Slightly ☐ Considerably

b. Feel worse about job
☐ Slightly ☐ Considerably

11. How important is it for you to have flexibility in your working hours?

☐ Very ☐ Not very ☐ Somewhat ☐ Not at all

12. Has flextime allowed you more time to be with your family?

☐ Yes ☐ No

13. If you are responsible for the care of a young child or children, has flextime made it easier or more difficult for you to obtain babysitting or day-care services?

☐ Easier ☐ More difficult ☐ No change

14. Do you recommend that the flextime program be made permanent?

☐ Yes ☐ No

15. Please describe below or attach any major changes you recommend for the program.

Thank you for your assistance.

FIGURE Q–1. Questionnaire (*continued*)

DISADVANTAGES

- The results of a questionnaire may be slanted in favor of those people who have strong opinions on a subject because they are more likely to respond than those with only moderate views.

- The questionnaire does not allow specific follow-up to answers; at best, a questionnaire can be designed to let one question lead logically to another.

- Distributing questionnaires and waiting for replies may take considerably longer than conducting a personal interview.

See also <u>interviewing for information</u> and <u>research</u>.

Selecting the Recipients

Selecting the proper recipients for your questionnaire is crucial if you are to gather representative and usable data. If you wanted to survey the opinions of large groups in the general population—for example, all medical technologists working in private laboratories or all independent garage owners—your task would not be easy. Because you cannot include everybody in your survey, you need to choose a representative cross section. For example, you would want to include enough people from around the country, respondents of both genders, and people with an assortment of educational training. Only then could you make a generalized statement based on your findings from the sample. (The best sources of information on sampling techniques are market-research and statistics texts.)

WEB LINK   **MARKETING VIRTUAL LIBRARY**

KnowThis.com's Marketing Virtual Library, from Professor Paul Christ of West Chester University in Pennsylvania, is a subject directory of sites related to marketing, market research, and much more. See <*bedfordstmartins.com/ alredbus*> and select *Links for Handbook Entries*.

Preparing the Questions

A key goal in designing the questionnaire is to keep it as brief as possible. The longer a questionnaire is, the less likely the recipient will be to complete and return it. Also, the questions should be easy to understand. A confusing question will yield confusing results, whereas a carefully worded question will be easy to answer. Ideally, recipients should be able to answer most questions with a "yes" or "no" or by checking or circling a choice among several options. Such answers are easy to tabulate and require minimum effort on the part of the respondent, thus increasing your chances of obtaining a response. See also <u>forms design</u>.

- Do you recommend that the flextime program be made permanent?

  ☐ Yes   ☐ No   ☐ No opinion

If you need more information than such questions produce, provide an appropriate range of answers, as in the following example.

- How many hours of overtime would you be willing to work each week?

  ☐ 4 hours   ☐ 8 hours   ☐ Over 10 hours

  ☐ 6 hours   ☐ 10 hours   ☐ No overtime

Questions should be neutral; they should not be worded in such a way as to lead respondents to give a particular answer, which can result in inaccurate or skewed data.

SLANTED   Would you prefer the freedom of a four-day workweek?

NEUTRAL   Would you choose to work a four-day workweek, ten hours a day, with every Friday off?

Writer's Checklist: Designing a Questionnaire

☑ Prepare a **cover letter** (memo or e-mail) explaining who you are, the questionnaire's purpose, the date by which you need a response, and how and where to send the completed questionnaire.

☑ Include a stamped, self-addressed envelope if you are using regular mail.

☑ Construct as many questions as possible for which the recipient does not have to compose an answer.

☑ Include a section on the questionnaire for additional comments, where the recipient may clarify his or her overall attitude toward the subject.

☑ State whether the information provided as well as the recipient's identity will be kept confidential.

☑ Include questions about the respondent's age, gender, education, occupation, and so on, only if such information will be of value in interpreting the answers.

☑ Include your contact information (mailing address, phone number, and e-mail address).

☑ Consider offering some tangible appreciation to those who answer the questionnaire by a specific date, such as a copy of the results or, for a customer questionnaire, a gift certificate.

Q

quid pro quo

Quid pro quo, which is Latin for "one thing for another," suggests mutual cooperation or "tit for tat" in a relationship between two groups or individuals. The term may be appropriate to business and legal contexts if you are sure your <u>readers</u> understand its meaning. (Before approving the plan, we insisted on a fair *quid pro quo.*) See also <u>foreign words in English</u>.

quotation marks

Quotation marks (" ") are used to enclose a direct quotation of spoken or written words. Quotation marks have other special uses, but they should not be used for <u>emphasis</u>.

Direct Quotations

Enclose in quotation marks anything that is quoted word for word (a direct quotation) from speech or written material.

- She said clearly, "I want the progress report by three o'clock."

Do not enclose indirect quotations—usually introduced by the word *that*—in quotation marks. Indirect quotations are paraphrases of a writer's or speaker's words or ideas. See also <u>paraphrasing</u>.

- She said that she wanted the progress report by three o'clock.

■ ETHICS NOTE When you use quotation marks to indicate that you are quoting, do not make any changes or omissions in the quoted material unless you clearly indicate what you have done. For further information on incorporating quoted material and inserting comments, see <u>plagiarism</u> and <u>quotations</u>. ✦

Use single quotation marks (' ') to enclose a quotation that appears within a quotation.

- John said, "Jane told me that she was going to 'stay with the project if it takes all year.' "

Words and Phrases

Use quotation marks to set off special words or terms only to point out that the term is used in context for a unique or special purpose (that is, in the sense of the term *so-called*).

- A remarkable chain of events caused the sinking of the "unsinkable" *Titanic* on its maiden voyage.

Slang, colloquial expressions, and attempts at humor, although infrequent in workplace writing, should seldom be set off by quotation marks.

- Our first six months amounted to a "shakedown cruise." *shakedown cruise.*

Titles of Works

Use quotation marks to enclose <u>titles</u> of reports, short stories, articles, essays, single episodes of radio and television programs, and short musical works (including songs). However, do not use quotation marks for titles of books and periodicals, which should appear in <u>italics</u>.

- His report, "Effects of Government Regulations on Motorcycle Safety," cited the article "No-Fault Insurance and Motorcycles," published in *American Motorcyclist* magazine.

Use quotation marks for parts of publications, such as chapters of books and articles or sections within periodicals.

- "Bad Writing" was an article by Barbara Wallraff in the "On Language" column of the *New York Times.*

Some titles, by convention, are not set off by quotation marks, underlining, or italics, although they are capitalized.

- Professional Writing [college course title], the Bible, the Constitution, Lincoln's Gettysburg Address, the Lands' End Catalog

Punctuation

<u>Commas</u> and <u>periods</u> always go inside closing quotation marks.

- "Reading *Computer World* gives me the insider's view," he says, adding, "It's like a conversation with the top experts."

<u>Semicolons</u> and <u>colons</u> always go outside closing quotation marks.

- He said, "I will pay the full amount"; this statement surprised us.

All other punctuation follows the logic of the context: If the punctuation is part of the material quoted, it goes inside the quotation marks; if the punctuation is not part of the material quoted, it goes outside the quotation marks.

quotations

DIRECTORY
Direct Quotations 452
Indirect Quotations 452
Deletions or Omissions 453
Inserting Material into Quotations 453
Incorporating Quotations into Text 453

Using direct and indirect quotations is an effective way to make or support a point. However, avoid the temptation to overquote during the **note-taking** phase of your **research**; concentrate on summarizing what you read.

◆ ETHICS NOTE When you do use a quotation (or an idea of another writer), cite your source properly. If you do not, you will be guilty of **plagiarism**. For specific details on citation systems, see **documenting sources**. ✦

Direct Quotations

A direct quotation is a word-for-word copy of the text of an original source. Choose direct quotations (which can be of a word, a phrase, a sentence, or, occasionally, a paragraph) carefully and use them sparingly. Enclose direct quotations in **quotation marks** and separate them from the rest of the sentence by a **comma** or **colon**. Use the initial capital letter of a quotation if the quoted material originally began with a capital letter.

- The economist stated, "Regulation cannot supply the dynamic stimulus that in other industries is supplied by competition."

When dividing a quotation, set off the material that interrupts the quotation with commas, and use quotation marks around each part of the quotation.

- "Regulation," he said in a recent interview, "cannot supply the dynamic stimulus that in other industries is supplied by competition."

Indirect Quotations

An indirect quotation is a paraphrased version of an original text. It is usually introduced by the word *that* and is not set off from the rest of the sentence by punctuation marks. See also **paraphrasing**.

● In a recent interview he said that regulation does not stimulate the industry as well as competition does.

Deletions or Omissions

Deletions or omissions from quoted material are indicated by three ellipsis dots (. . .) within a sentence and a period plus three ellipsis points (. . . .) at the end of a sentence.

● "If monopolies could be made to respond . . . we would be able to enjoy the benefits of . . . large-scale efficiency. . . ."

When a quoted passage begins in the middle of a sentence rather than at the beginning, ellipsis dots are not necessary; the fact that the first letter of the quoted material is not capitalized tells the reader that the quotation begins in midsentence.

● Rivero goes on to conclude that "coordination may lessen competition within a region."

Inserting Material into Quotations

When it is necessary to insert a clarifying comment within quoted material, use brackets.

● "The industry is an integrated system that serves an extensive [geographic] area, with divisions existing as islands within the larger system's sphere of influence."

When quoted material contains an obvious error or might be questioned in some other way, insert the expression *sic* (Latin for "thus"), in italic type and enclosed in brackets following the questionable material to indicate that the writer has quoted the material *exactly as it appeared in the original.*

● The company considers the Baker Foundation to be a "guilt-edged [*sic*] investment."

Incorporating Quotations into Text

Quote word for word only when your source concisely sums up a great deal of information or reinforces a point you are making. Quotations must also match logically, grammatically, and syntactically the rest of the sentence and surrounding text. Notice in Figure Q–2 that the quotation blends with the content of the surrounding text, which uses transition to introduce and comment on the quotation.

Depending on the citation system, the style of incorporating quotations varies. For examples of three different styles, see documenting

Q

After reviewing a large number of works in business and technical communication, Alred sees an inevitable connection between theory, practice, and
pedagogy:

> Therefore, theory is necessary to prevent us from being over-
> whelmed by what is local, particular, and temporal. In turn,
> pedagogy both mediates practice and transforms our theory. In-
> deed, one reason I find this work rewarding is that I sense it puts
> me at the intersection of theory, practice, and pedagogy as they
> are involved with writing in the workplace. (ix–x)

The use of the Web today has reinforced this connection because it calls on
the Web page designer to engage in a teaching function as well as reflect on
the practice of Web design. For example, the widespread use of . . .

FIGURE Q–2. Long Quotation (MLA Style)

sources. Figure Q–2 shows MLA style for a long quotation. At the end
of the document, the following entry would appear in the MLA-style
list of works cited as the source of the quotation in Figure Q–2.

- Alred, Gerald J. <u>The St. Martin's Bibliography of Business and
  Technical Communication</u>. New York: St. Martin's, 1997.

Do not rely too heavily on the use of quotations in the final version of
your document. Generally, avoid quoting anything that is longer than
one paragraph.

Q

R

raise / rise

Both *raise* and *rise* mean "move to a higher position." However, *raise* is a transitive <u>verb</u> and always takes an <u>object</u> (*raise* crops), whereas *rise* is an intransitive verb and never takes an object (heat *rises*).

re

Re (and its variant form, *in re*) is business and legal <u>jargon</u> meaning "in reference to" or "in the case of." Although *re* is sometimes used in <u>memos</u> and <u>e-mails</u>, *subject* is a preferable term.

readers

The first rule of effective writing is to *help your readers.* If you overlook this commitment, your writing will not achieve its <u>purpose</u>, either for you or for your business or organization.

Determining Your Readers' Needs

To help your readers, first determine their needs relative to your purpose and goals by asking key questions during <u>preparation</u>.

- Who specifically is your reader? Do you have multiple readers? Who needs to see or use the document?
- What do your readers already know about your subject? What are your readers' attitudes about the subject? (Skeptical? Supportive? Anxious? Bored?)
- What does the <u>context</u> suggest about the readers' expectations for content or <u>layout and design</u>?

R

- Do you need to adapt your message for international readers? If so, see <u>global communication</u>, <u>global graphics</u>, and <u>international correspondence</u>.

In the workplace, your readers are usually less familiar with the subject than you are. You have to be careful, therefore, when writing on a topic that is unique to your area of specialization. Be sensitive to the needs of those whose training or experience lies in other areas; provide definitions of nonstandard terms and explanations of principles that you, as a specialist, take for granted. See also <u>defining terms</u>.

Writing to Individual Readers

When you write to an individual reader, empathize with that reader by considering the <u>"you" viewpoint</u> and writing in an appropriate <u>tone</u>. You may find it useful to visualize that person sitting across from you as you write. Likewise, when you write to a group of readers who are relatively homogeneous, you might create an image of a composite reader and write for *that* reader. You could also list that reader's characteristics (experience, training, attitudes, and work habits, for example) to help you write at the appropriate level. See also <u>business writing style</u>.

Writing for Diverse Audiences

For documents aimed at multiple readers with different needs, consider segmenting the document for different groups of readers: an executive summary for top managers, an appendix with detailed data for technical specialists, and the body for those readers who need to make decisions based on the details. See also <u>formal reports</u> and <u>proposals</u>.

When you have multiple readers with various needs but cannot segment your document, first determine your primary or most important readers—such as those who will make decisions based on the document—and be sure to meet their needs. Then, meet the needs of secondary readers, such as those who need only some of the document's contents, as long as you do not sacrifice the needs of your primary readers. See also <u>correspondence</u>, <u>e-mail</u>, <u>persuasion</u>, and "Five Steps to Successful Writing."

---

really

Really is an <u>adverb</u> meaning "actually" or "in fact." Although both *really* and *actually* are often used as <u>intensifiers</u> for <u>emphasis</u> or sarcasm in speech, avoid such use in writing.

- Did he ~~really~~ finish the report on time?

reason is [because]

Replace the redundant phrase *the reason is because* with *the reason is that* or simply *because*. See also **conciseness**.

reference letters

Writing a reference letter (or letter of recommendation) can range from completing an admission form for a prospective student to composing a detailed description of professional accomplishments and personal characteristics for someone seeking employment. In Figure R–1, a former employer has written a letter for someone who is seeking an advanced position as a researcher.

To write an effective letter of recommendation, you must be familiar enough with the applicant's abilities and performance to offer an evaluation, and you must keep in mind the following.

- Communicate truthfully and without embellishment.
- Address specifically the applicant's skills, abilities, knowledge, and personal characteristics.
- Respond directly to the inquiry, carefully addressing the specific questions asked.
- Identify yourself by name, title or position, employer, and address.

You could begin, as in Figure R–1 on page 458, by stating the circumstances of your acquaintance and how long you have known the person for whom you are writing the letter. You should mention, with as much substantiation as possible, one or two outstanding characteristics of the applicant. Organize the details in your letter using the decreasing **order-of-importance method of development**. Conclude with a brief summary of the applicant's qualifications and a clear statement of recommendation.

◪ ETHICS NOTE When you are asked to serve as a reference or to supply a letter of reference, be aware that applicants have a legal right to examine what you have written about them, unless they sign a waiver. See **correspondence** for letter format and general advice. ✦

refusal letters

A refusal letter delivers a negative message (or bad news) in the form of a letter, a **memo**, or an **e-mail** message. The ideal refusal letter says "no" in such a way that you not only avoid antagonizing your **reader** but also maintain goodwill.

City of Springfield
Legislative Reference Bureau
200 East Main Street
Springfield, AK 99501

(414) 224-5555

January 17, 2006

Mr. Phillip Lester
Human Resources Director
Thompson Enterprises
201 State Street
St. Louis, MO 63102

Dear Mr. Lester:

How long writer has known applicant and the circumstances

As Kerry Hawkin's former employer, I am happy to have the opportunity to recommend her. I've known Kerry for five years, first as an intern in our office and for two years as a full-time research associate. This past year she has remained in contact as she completed graduate school.

Outstanding characteristics of applicant

Our office is the official research arm for the Springfield City Council, so we approved Kerry as an intern not only because of her outstanding grades but also because the university internship coordinator reported that she possessed excellent research skills. Kerry proved her worth in our office as an intern and was offered a full-time position as a research associate to work on projects under my supervision. I found Kerry not only to be a careful researcher but also to be able to complete her assignments on schedule within tight deadlines. The material provided in her well-written reports unfailingly met the requirements for my work and more. During her time in our office, Kerry also proved herself to be a most valued colleague.

I strongly recommend Kerry for her ability to work independently, to organize her time efficiently, and to write clearly and articulately. I regret that we have no position to offer her at this time. Please do not hesitate to let me know if I can provide further information.

Recommendation and summary of qualifications

Sincerely yours,

Michelle Paul

Michelle Paul, Manager
mpaul@springfield.ar.gov

FIGURE R–1. Reference Letter

When the stakes are high, you must convince your reader *before* you present the bad news that your reasons for refusing are logical or understandable. (See also **correspondence**.) Stating a negative message in your opening may cause your reader to react too quickly and dismiss your explanation. The following pattern, used in the message shown in Figure R–2, is an effective way to handle this problem.

1. In the opening, provide a **context** (often called a "buffer").
2. Review the facts leading to the refusal or bad news.
3. Give the negative message based on the facts.
4. In the closing, establish or reestablish a positive relationship.

From:	Nancy Nygaard <nn@bank21.com>
To:	Marsha Coleman <mc2@ntr.com>
Sent:	Friday, February 24, 2006 10:47 AM
Subject:	NTR Check Sorter

Dear Ms. Coleman:

Context

Thank you for your cooperation and your patience with us as we struggled to reach a decision. We believe our long involvement with your company indicates our confidence in your products.

Review of facts and refusal

Based on our research, we found that the Winton Check Sorter has all the features that your sorter offers and, in fact, has two additional features that your sorter does not. The more important one is a backup feature that retains totals in its memory, even if the power fails. The second additional feature is stacked pockets, which are less space-consuming than the linear pockets on your sorter. After much deliberation, therefore, we have decided to purchase the Winton Check Sorter.

Goodwill close

Although we did not select your sorter, we were very favorably impressed with your system and your people. Perhaps we will be able to use other NTR products in the future.

Sincerely,

Nancy Nygaard

R

FIGURE R–2. Refusal Letter (Sent as E-mail)

Your opening can establish a positive and professional <u>tone</u>, for example, by expressing appreciation for your reader's time, effort, or interest.

- The Screening Procedures Committee appreciates the time and effort you spent on your proposal for a new security-clearance procedure.

Next, review the circumstances of the situation sympathetically by placing yourself in the reader's position. Clearly establish the reasons you cannot do what the reader wants — even though you have not yet said you cannot do it. A good explanation, as shown in the following example, should detail the reasons for your refusal so thoroughly that the reader will accept the negative message as a logical conclusion.

- We reviewed the potential effects of implementing your proposed security-clearance procedure company-wide. We asked the Security Systems Department to review the data, surveyed industry practices, sought the views of senior management, and submitted the idea to our legal staff. As a result of this process, we have reached the following conclusions:
  - The cost savings you project are correct only if the procedure could be required universally.
  - The components of your procedure are legal, but most are not widely accepted by our industry.
  - Based on our survey, some components could alienate employees who would perceive them as violating an individual's rights.
  - Enforcing company-wide use would prove costly and impractical.

Do not belabor the negative message — state your refusal quickly, clearly, and as positively as possible.

- For those reasons, the committee recommends that divisions continue their current security-screening procedures.

Close your message in a way that reestablishes goodwill — do not repeat the bad news (avoid writing "Again, we are sorry we cannot use your idea"). You might provide an option, offer a friendly remark, assure the reader of your high opinion of his or her product or service, or merely wish the reader success.

- Because some components of your procedure may apply in certain circumstances, we would like to feature your ideas in the next issue of *The Guardian.* I have asked the editor to contact you next week. On behalf of the committee, thank you for the thoughtful proposal.

For responding to a complaint letter, see <u>adjustment letters</u>. For refusing a job offer, see <u>acceptance/refusal letters</u>.

regarding / with regard to

In *regards to* and *with regards to* are incorrect <u>idioms</u> for *in regard to* and *with regard to*. Both *as regards* and *regarding* are acceptable variants.

- In ~~regards~~ ^regard^ to your last e-mail, I think a meeting is a good idea.

- ~~With regards to~~ ^Regarding^ your last e-mail, I think a meeting is a good idea.

regardless

Always use *regardless* instead of *irregardless*, which expresses a double negative and is nonstandard. The prefix *ir-* renders the base word negative, but *regardless* is already negative, meaning "unmindful."

repetition

The deliberate use of repetition to build a sustained effect or to emphasize a feeling or an idea can be a powerful device. See also <u>emphasis</u>.

- Similarly, atoms *come and go* in a molecule, but the molecule *remains;* molecules *come and go* in a cell, but the cell *remains;* cells *come and go* in a body, but the body *remains;* persons *come and go* in an organization, but the organization *remains.*
   —Kenneth Boulding, *Beyond Economics*

Repeating keywords from a previous sentence or paragraph can also be used effectively to achieve <u>transition</u>.

- For many years, *oil* has been a major industrial energy source. However, *oil* supplies are limited, and other sources of energy must be developed.

Be consistent in the word or phrase you use to refer to something. In business writing, it is generally better to repeat a word (so there will be no question in the reader's mind that you mean the same thing) than to use synonyms to avoid repetition.

SYNONYMS   Several recent *analyses* support our conclusion. These *studies* cast doubt on the feasibility of long-range forecasting. The *reports,* however, are strictly theoretical.

R

CONSISTENT TERMS   Several recent *studies* support our conclusion.
These *studies* cast doubt on the feasibility of
long-range forecasting. They are, however,
strictly theoretical.

Purposeless repetition, however, makes a sentence awkward and
hides its key ideas. See also <u>conciseness</u>.

- She said that the customer ~~said that he~~ was canceling the order.

See also <u>affectation</u>.

reports

A report is an organized presentation of factual information, often
aimed at multiple audiences, that may present the results of an investigation, a trip, or a research project. For any report—whether formal or
informal—assessing the <u>readers</u>' needs is essential. Following is a list
of report entries in this book:

<u>feasibility reports</u> 200   <u>progress and activity reports</u> 408
<u>formal reports</u> 211   <u>trip reports</u> 543
<u>investigative reports</u> 294   <u>trouble reports</u> 544

Formal reports often present the results of long-term projects or
those that involve multiple participants. (See also <u>collaborative writ-
ing</u>.) Such projects may be done either for your own organization or as
a contractual requirement for another organization. Formal reports
generally follow a precise format and include such elements as <u>ab-
stracts</u> and <u>executive summaries</u>. See also <u>proposals</u>.

Informal and short reports normally run from a few paragraphs to a
few pages and ordinarily include only an <u>introduction</u>, a body, a <u>conclu-
sion</u>, and (if necessary) recommendations. Because of their brevity, informal reports are customarily written as <u>correspondence</u>: letters (if sent
outside your organization) and <u>memos</u> or <u>e-mails</u> (if internal).

The introduction announces the subject of the report, states its
<u>purpose</u>, and gives any essential background information. It may also
summarize the conclusions, findings, or recommendations made in the
report. The body presents a clearly organized account of the report's
subject—the results of a test carried out, the status of a project, and so
on. The amount of detail to include depends on the complexity of the
subject and on your readers' familiarity with it.

The conclusion summarizes your findings and tells readers what
you think their significance may be. In some reports, a final, separate
section gives recommendations; in others, the conclusions and the

recommendations sections are combined into one section. This final section makes suggestions for a course of action based on the data you have presented. See also **persuasion**.

research

DIRECTORY
Primary Research   463
Secondary Research   464
Library Research Strategies   464
    Online Catalogs (Locating Books)   465
    Online Databases and Indexes (Locating Articles)   465
    Reference Works   466
Internet Research Strategies   468
    Search Engines   469
Writer's Checklist: Using Search Engines   470
    Web Directories   470
Evaluating Sources   471
    Authority   472
    Accuracy   472
    Bias   473
    Currency   473
Writer's Checklist: Evaluating Print and Online Sources   473

Research is the process of investigation—the discovery of facts. To be focused, research must be preceded by **preparation**, especially consideration of your **readers**, **purpose**, and **scope**. See "Five Steps to Successful Writing."

In an academic setting, your preparatory resources include conversations with your peers, instructors, and especially a research librarian. On the job, your main resources are your own knowledge and experience and that of your colleagues. In business, the most important sources of information may also include market research, **questionnaires** and surveys, focus groups, public meetings, shareholder meetings, and the like. In this setting, begin by **brainstorming** with colleagues about what sources will be most useful to your topic and how you can find them.

Primary Research

Primary research is the gathering of raw data compiled from interviews, direct observation, surveys and questionnaires, focus groups, **meetings**, and the like. In fact, direct observation and interaction are the only ways to obtain certain kinds of information, such as human behavior and the functioning of organizations. You can also conduct primary research on the Internet by participating in discussion groups and newsgroups and by using e-mail to request information from specific audiences.

■ ETHICS NOTE If you are planning research that involves observation, choose your sites and times carefully, and be sure to obtain permission in advance. During your observations, remain as unobtrusive as possible, and keep accurate, complete records that indicate date, time of day, duration of the observation, and so on. Save interpretations of your observations for future analysis. Be aware that observation can be valuable research, but it may also be time-consuming, complicated, and expensive, and you may inadvertently influence the subjects you are observing. ✦

Secondary Research

Secondary research is the gathering of information that has been analyzed, assessed, evaluated, compiled, or otherwise organized into accessible form. Sources include books, articles, reports, Web documents, e-mail discussions, correspondence, minutes of meetings, brochures, and so forth. The following sections, Library Research Strategies (below) and Internet Research Strategies (page 468), provide methods for finding secondary sources.

As you seek information, keep in mind that in most cases the more recent the information, the better. Recently published periodicals and newspapers, as well as academic (.edu), organizational (.org), and government (.gov) Web sites, can be good sources of current information and can include interviews, articles, papers, and conference proceedings. See especially the *Writer's Checklist: Evaluating Print and Online Sources* (page 473).

When a resource seems useful, read it carefully and take notes that include any additional questions about your topic. Some of your questions may eventually be answered in other sources; those that remain unanswered can guide you to further primary research. For example, you may discover that you need to talk with an expert. Not only can someone skilled in a field answer many of your questions, but he or she can also suggest further sources of information. See documenting sources, interviewing for information, listening, note-taking, paraphrasing, and plagiarism.

Library Research Strategies

The library is a gateway to all types of sources—including Internet sources—that can help you find the best, most reliable information. The first step in using library resources, either in an academic institution or in a workplace, is to develop a search strategy appropriate to the information needed for your topic. You may want to begin by meeting with a research librarian who can help you quickly find the best print or online resources for your topic—a brief conversation can focus your research and save you time. In addition, use your library's homepage for access to its catalogs, databases of articles, subject directories to the Web, and more. A sample of a library's homepage is shown in Figure R–3.

Your search strategy depends on the kind of information you are seeking. For example, if you need the latest data offered by government research, check the Web, as described later in this entry. Likewise, if you need a current article on a topic, search an online database—such as InfoTrac—subscribed to by your library. For an overview of a subject, you might turn to an encyclopedia; for historical background, your best resources are books, journals, and primary documents.

FIGURE R–3. Library Homepage

Online Catalogs (Locating Books). An online catalog—accessed through a library terminal and through the Internet—allows you to search a library's holdings, indicates an item's location and availability, and may allow you to arrange an interlibrary loan.

You can search a library's online catalog by author, title, keyword, or subject. The most typical ways of searching for a specific topic are by subject or by keyword. If your search turns up too many results, you can usually narrow it by using the "limit search" or "advanced search" option.

Online Databases and Indexes (Locating Articles). Most libraries subscribe to online databases, such as the following collections of online articles, many of which are available through a library's Web site.

- *InfoTrac*: a collection of databases of articles, many available in full text, which can also provide specialized databases in business, health, and other fields.

- *ProQuest*: a database of articles, many available in full text, which can also provide specialized databases for nursing, biology, and psychology.

- *EBSCOhost*: a database of articles, many available in full text, which can also provide specialized databases in a range of subjects.

- *FirstSearch*: a collection of specialized databases such as WorldCat (library collections) and ArticleFirst (articles, some in full text).

- *Lexis/Nexis Universe*: a collection of databases containing news, business, legal, and congressional information (most in full text).

These databases, sometimes called *periodical indexes*, are excellent resources for articles published within the last ten to twenty years. Some include descriptive abstracts and full texts of articles. To find older articles, you may need to consult a print index, such as the *Readers' Guide to Periodical Literature* and the *New York Times Index*, or a reference librarian. (For more information on print indexes, see "General Guides" in the Reference Works section below.)

To locate articles in a database, conduct a keyword search, as shown in Figure R–4. If your search turns up too many results, refine your search by connecting two search terms with AND—"management AND employment"—or use other options offered by the database, such as a limited, a modified, or an advanced search.

Reference Works.   In addition to articles, books, and Web sources, you may want to consult reference works such as encyclopedias, dictionaries, and atlases for a brief overview of your subject. Bibliographies, which are lists of works written about a topic, can direct you to more specialized sources. Ask your reference librarian to recommend reference works and bibliographies that are most relevant to your topic. Many are available in print, on CD-ROM, and online.

ENCYCLOPEDIAS.   Encyclopedias are comprehensive, multivolume collections of articles arranged alphabetically. Some cover a wide range of subjects, while others, such as *The Encyclopedia of Careers and Vocational Guidance*, 12th ed., edited by Andrew Morkes (Chicago: Ferguson, 2002), focus on specific areas.

DICTIONARIES.   General <u>dictionaries</u> can be compact or comprehensive, unabridged publications. Specialized dictionaries define terms used in a particular field, such as business, computers, architecture, or

Boston Public Library
Expanded Academic ASAP

Help - Search
Dictionary
Title List

Subject guide
Relevance search
Keyword search
Advanced search
Journal search
Start over

Back to ...
Gale Group
Databases
Library

Keyword search

Click in the entry box and enter search term(s)

management AND employment [Search]

Search for words ⊙ in title, citation, abstract ○ in entire article content
Type words to search for. You can use AND, OR, NOT. Results are sorted by date.

Limit the current search: (optional)
☐ to full-text articles:
by date:
to the following journal(s):
to entries containing the word(s):

History

1 (management AND employment)
View 13609 Citations; Modify Search

Expanded Academic ASAP has 12,914,819 articles and was last updated on Jan 5, 2005.

THOMSON
GALE   Copyright and Terms of Use

FIGURE R–4. InfoTrac Search Page

consumer affairs, and offer detailed definitions of field-specific terms, usually written in straightforward language.

HANDBOOKS AND MANUALS.   Handbooks and manuals are typically one-volume compilations of frequently used information in a particular field. They offer brief definitions of terms or concepts, standards for presenting information, procedures for documenting sources, and visuals such as graphs and tables.

BIBLIOGRAPHIES.   Bibliographies list books, periodicals, and other research materials published in areas such as business, medicine, the humanities, and the social sciences.

GENERAL GUIDES.   The annotated *Guide to Reference Books*, 11th ed., by Robert Balay (Chicago: American Library Association, 1996), can help you locate reference books, indexes, and other research materials. The following are specialized indexes. Check your library's homepage or with your reference librarian to find out if your library subscribes to a particular index, and whether it is available online.

Business Periodicals Index, 1958–. Alphabetical subject listing; issued monthly.

Government Reports Announcements and Index, 1965–. Semimonthly index of reports, arranged by subject, author, and report number.

Index to the Times (London), 1790–. Monthly.

Monthly Catalog of U.S. Government Publications, 1895–. Unclassified publications of all federal agencies, listed by subject, author, and report number; issued monthly.

New York Times Index, 1851–. Alphabetical list of subjects covered in *New York Times* articles; issued bimonthly.

Readers' Guide to Periodical Literature, 1900–. Monthly index of about 200 general U.S. periodicals, arranged alphabetically by subject.

Wall Street Journal Index, 1958–. Monthly index of business and financial news covered in the *Journal*.

ATLASES.   Atlases provide representations of the physical and political boundaries of countries, climate, population, or natural resources.

STATISTICAL SOURCES.   Statistical sources are collections of numerical data. They are the best sources for such information as the U.S. gross domestic product, the consumer price index, or the demographic breakdown of the general population.

American Statistics Index. Washington, D.C.: Congressional Information Service, 1978–. Monthly, quarterly, and annual supplements.

United States Bureau of the Census. *Statistical Abstract of the United States*. Washington, D.C.: Government Printing Office, 1879–. Annual (<www.census.gov>).

Internet Research Strategies

The Internet provides access to a staggering amount of information. However, the information on the Web varies widely in its completeness and accuracy, and it can adversely affect the quality and accuracy of your completed project. You need to spend extra time and effort to critically evaluate Internet sources by following the advice in the *Writer's Checklist: Evaluating Print and Online Sources* on page 473.

As comprehensive as search engines and directories may seem, keep in mind that none is complete or objective. Most search sites are incomplete, carrying only a preselected range of content. Many, for example, do not index Adobe PDF files or Usenet newsgroups, and many cannot index databases and other non-HTML-based content. Further, search sites' ranking of the sites they believe will be relevant to you is based on a number of different strategies. Some sites base relevance on how high on the given page your search term appears, on the number of appearances of your term, or on the number of other sites that link to the page. Almost all major search sites now sell high rankings to the highest bidders, so your results may not highlight the pages most relevant to your search. Your best strategy is to research how your favorite search engines work; nearly all provide detailed methodologies on their help pages.

Search Engines.   Search engines—like Google or AltaVista—are machine-generated databases created by "spiders" or "bots" that travel the Web looking for new or updated pages; search engines typically have databases of billions of pages. The following search engines are used widely on the Web:

AltaVista	\<www.altavista.com\>
Excite	\<www.excite.com\>
Google	\<www.google.com\>
Hotbot	\<www.hotbot.lycos.com\>
Lycos	\<www.lycos.com\>
WebCrawler	\<www.webcrawler.com\>
Yahoo!	\<www.yahoo.com\>

Search sites may use a hybrid approach. For example, some search engines, such as Northern Light, at \<www.northernlight.com\>, search not only the Web but also their own database of articles—content that is edited and compiled by staff librarians and not available elsewhere on the Web.

Many search engines allow advanced searches with options that provide more selective results. Figure R–5 shows an advanced search conducted on Google for graduate programs in business management—a search limited to results in English and to sites within the ".edu"

FIGURE R–5. Advanced Google Search

domain. Although search engines vary in what and how they search, you can use some basic strategies, as in the *Writer's Checklist: Using Search Engines*, which follows.

Writer's Checklist: Using Search Engines

☑ Enter words and phrases that are as specific to your topic as possible. For example, if you are looking for information about *nuclear power* and enter only the term *nuclear*, the search will also yield listings for *nuclear* family, *nuclear* medicine, and *nuclear* winter.

☑ Use Boolean operators (AND, OR, NOT) to narrow your search. For example, if you are searching for information on breast cancer and are finding references to nothing but prostate cancer, try "breast AND cancer NOT prostate."

☑ Consider conducting an advanced search (see Figure R–5).

☑ Check any search tips available at the engine you use. For example, some engines allow you to narrow your search by combining phrases with double quotation marks: "Usability testing" will return only pages that have the full compound phrase.

☑ Use a variety of search engines.

☑ Consider using a metasearch engine, such as Dogpile (<www.dogpile.com>) and Metacrawler (<www.metacrawler.com>), if you are interested in obtaining as many hits as possible. Be prepared to refine and narrow your results.

Web Directories.   Directories are human generated, so they index fewer pages than search engines but offer subject directory trees to help organize their content, as shown in Figure R–6. In addition to the subject directories offered by many search engines, the following directories will help you to conduct selective, scholarly research on the Web:

Infomine	<http://infomine.ucr.edu>
The Internet Public Library	<www.ipl.org>
World Wide Web Virtual Library	<www.vlib.org>

The Web includes numerous directories and sites devoted to specific subject areas. Following are some suggested resources for researching a business topic.

Pace University Library Internet Resources	<www.pace.edu/library/links/links.html>
CIO's Resource Centers	<www.cio.com/research>
Inc.com Articles by Topic	<www.inc.com/articles>

The web organized by topic into categories.

Arts
Movies, Music, Television,...

Business
Industries, Finance, Jobs,...

Computers
Hardware, Internet, Software,...

Games
Board, Roleplaying, Video,...

Health
Alternative, Fitness, Medicine,...

Home
Consumers, Homeowners, Family,...

Kids and Teens
Computers, Entertainment, School,...

News
Media, Newspapers, Current Events,...

Recreation
Food, Outdoors, Travel,...

Reference
Education, Libraries, Maps,...

Regional
Asia, Europe, North America,...

Science
Biology, Psychology, Physics,...

Shopping
Autos, Clothing, Gifts,...

Society
Issues, People, Religion,...

Sports
Basketball, Football, Soccer,...

World
Deutsch, Español, Français, Italiano, Japanese, Korean, Nederlands, Polska, Svenska, ...

FIGURE R–6. Google's Main Subject Directory

Yahoo's Business and Economy Directory   <http://dir.yahoo.com/business_and_economy>

LSU Libraries Federal Agencies Directory   <www.lib.lsu.edu/gov/fedgov.html>

FedStats   <www.fedstats.gov>

Some sites combine search engines with directories; for example, Google operates both a standard search engine and directory and a special contributor-generated directory referred to as an "Open Directory" (<http://dmoz.org>).

Evaluating Sources

The easiest way to ensure that information is valid is to obtain it from a reputable source. For Internet sources, be especially concerned about the validity of the information provided. Because anyone can publish on the Web, it is sometimes difficult to determine authorship of a document, and frequently a person's qualifications for speaking on a topic are absent or questionable. The Internet versions of established, reputable journals in medicine, management, engineering, computer software, and the like merit the same level of trust as the printed versions. However, as you move away from established, reputable sites, exercise more caution. Be especially wary of unmoderated discussion groups on Usenet and other public Web forums. Use the following domain abbreviations to help you determine an Internet site sponsor:

.aero	aerospace industry	.mil	U.S. military
.biz	business	.museum	museum
.com	company or individual	.name	individual
.coop	business cooperative	.net	network provider
.edu	college or university	.org	nonprofit
.gov	federal government		organization
.int	international	.pro	professionals
.info	general use		

In addition, keep in mind the following four criteria when evaluating Internet sources: authority, accuracy, bias, and currency.*

Authority.   Because anyone can publish on the Web, it is sometimes difficult to determine authorship of a document, and frequently a person's qualifications for speaking on a topic are absent or questionable. If you do not recognize the author as well known and respected in the field, check the site's "About Us" page or mission statement if available. Following are some possible ways you can determine authority:

- The author's document was listed in or linked from a reliable source or document.

- The document gives substantive biographical information about the author so that you can evaluate his or her credentials, or you can get this information by linking to another document.

- The author is referenced or mentioned positively by another author or organization whose authority you trust.

If the publisher or sponsor is an organization, you may generally assume that the document meets the standards and aims of the group. Consider also:

- The suitability of the organization to address this topic.
- Whether this organization or agency is recognized and respected in the field.
- The relationship of the author to the publisher or sponsor. (Does the document tell you something about the author's expertise or qualifications?)

Accuracy.   Criteria for evaluating accuracy might include the following:

- Other sources that the document relies on are linked to or are included in a bibliography.

*From Leigh Ryan, *The Bedford Guide for Writing Tutors*, 3rd ed. (Boston: Bedford/ St. Martin's, 2002).

- Background information can be verified.
- Methodology is appropriate for the topic.
- With a research project, data that was gathered includes explanations of research methods and interpretations.
- The graphs and visuals are free of distortion.
- The site is modified or updated regularly.

Bias. To determine bias, consider how the <u>context</u> reveals the author's knowledge of the subject and his or her stance on the topic. Check the site for the following:

- The site identifies in some form the audience it targets.
- The site was developed by a recognized academic institution; government agency; or national, international, or commercial organization with an established reputation in the subject area.
- The author shows knowledge of theories, techniques, or schools of thought usually related to the topic.
- The author shows knowledge of related sources and attributes them properly.
- The author discusses the value and limitations of the approach, if it is new.
- The author acknowledges that the subject itself or his or her treatment of it is controversial, if you know that to be the case.

Currency. If currency is important, consider whether the document has a publication or "last updated" date or includes date of copyright, gives dates showing when information was gathered, or gives information about new material when appropriate.

Writer's Checklist: Evaluating Print and Online Sources

R

FOR ALL SOURCES

☑ Is the resource recent enough and relevant to your topic? Is it readily available?

☑ Who is the intended audience? The mainstream public? A small group of professionals?

☑ Who is the author(s)? Is the author(s) an authority on the subject?

☑ Does the author(s) provide enough supporting evidence and document sources so that you can verify the information's accuracy?

☑ Is the information presented in an objective, unbiased way? Are any biases made clear?

☑ Are opinions clearly labeled? Are viewpoints balanced, or are opposing opinions acknowledged?

☑ Are the language, tone, and style appropriate and compelling?

FOR A BOOK

☑ Does the preface or introduction indicate the author's or book's purpose?

☑ Does the table of contents relate to your topic? Does the index contain terms related to your topic?

☑ Are the chapters useful? Skim through one that seems related to your topic — notice especially the introduction, headings, and closing.

FOR AN ARTICLE

☑ Is the publisher of the magazine or other periodical well known?

☑ What is the article's purpose? For a journal article, read the abstract; for a newspaper article, read the headline and lead sentences.

☑ Does the article contain informative diagrams or other visuals that indicate its scope?

FOR A WEB SITE

☑ Does a reputable group or organization sponsor or maintain the site?

☑ Are the purpose and scope of the site clearly stated? Check the "Mission Statement" or "About Us" pages. Are there any disclaimers?

☑ Is the site updated, thus current? Are the links functional and up to date?

☑ Is the documentation authoritative and credible? Check the links to other sources and cross-check facts at other reputable Web sites, such as academic ones.

☑ Is the site well designed? Is the material well written and error-free?

R

⊛ WEB LINK **EVALUATING ONLINE SOURCES**

For a tutorial on evaluating information online, see *<bedfordstmartins.com/ alredbus>* and select *Tutorials*, "Evaluating Online Sources." For links to additional related resources, select *Links for Handbook Entries*.

resignation letters

Resignation letters or <u>memos,</u> as shown in Figures R–7 and R–8, should be as positive as possible, regardless of the reason you are leaving a job. You usually write a resignation letter to your supervisor or to an appropriate person in the Human Resources Department. Use the following guidelines.

- Start on a positive note, regardless of the circumstances under which you are leaving.
- Consider pointing out how you have benefited from working for the company or say something complimentary about the company.
- Comment on something positive about the people with whom you have been associated.
- Explain why you are leaving in an objective, factual tone.
- Avoid angry recriminations, because your resignation will remain on file with the company and could haunt you in the future when you need references.

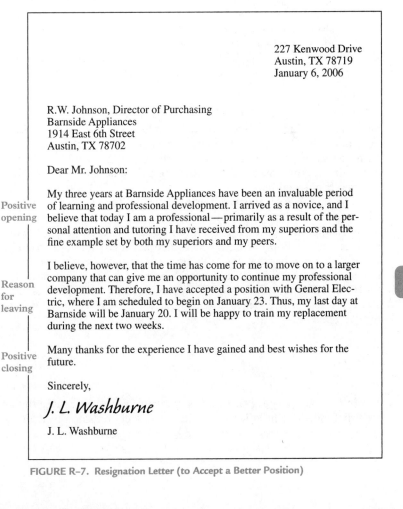

227 Kenwood Drive
Austin, TX 78719
January 6, 2006

R.W. Johnson, Director of Purchasing
Barnside Appliances
1914 East 6th Street
Austin, TX 78702

Dear Mr. Johnson:

Positive opening

My three years at Barnside Appliances have been an invaluable period of learning and professional development. I arrived as a novice, and I believe that today I am a professional—primarily as a result of the personal attention and tutoring I have received from my superiors and the fine example set by both my superiors and my peers.

Reason for leaving

I believe, however, that the time has come for me to move on to a larger company that can give me an opportunity to continue my professional development. Therefore, I have accepted a position with General Electric, where I am scheduled to begin on January 23. Thus, my last day at Barnside will be January 20. I will be happy to train my replacement during the next two weeks.

Positive closing

Many thanks for the experience I have gained and best wishes for the future.

Sincerely,

J. L. Washburne

J. L. Washburne

FIGURE R–7. Resignation Letter (to Accept a Better Position)

MEMORANDUM

To: T. W. Haney, Vice President, Administration
From: L. R. Rupp   *LRR*
Date: February 13, 2006
Subject: Resignation from Winterhaven, effective
          March 3, 2006

Positive opening

My five-year stay with the Winterhaven Company has been a pleasant experience, and I believe that it has been mutually beneficial.

Reason for leaving

Because of the recent restructuring of my job, I have accepted a position with another company that I feel will offer me greater advancement opportunities. I am, therefore, submitting my resignation, to be effective on March 3, 2006.

Positive closing

I have enjoyed working with my coworkers at Winterhaven and wish the company success in the future.

FIGURE R–8. Resignation Memo (Under Negative Conditions)

Your letter or memo should give enough notice to allow your employer time to find a replacement. It might be no more than two weeks, or it might be enough time to enable you to train your replacement. Some organizations may ask for a notice equivalent to the number of weeks of vacation you receive. Check the policy of your employer before you begin your letter.

The sample resignation letter in Figure R–7 is from an employee who is leaving to take a job offering greater opportunities. The memo of resignation in Figure R–8 is written by an employee who is leaving because her position has been reclassified and her supervisor has not supported her advancement, although no personal conflict is mentioned. Notice that it opens and closes positively and that the reason for the resignation is stated without apparent anger or bitterness. For strategies concerning negative messages, see **correspondence** and **refusal letters**.

respective / respectively

Respective is an **adjective** that means "pertaining to two or more things regarded individually." (The committee members returned to their *respective* offices.) *Respectively* is the **adverb** form of *respective*, meaning "singly, in the order designated."

- The first, second, and third prizes in the sales contest were awarded to Maria Juarez, Dan Wesp, and Simone Luce, *respectively*.

Respective and *respectively* are unnecessary if the meaning of individuality is clear.

     Each   *member*   *a report.*
- ~~The~~ committee ~~members~~ prepared ~~their respective reports.~~

restrictive and nonrestrictive elements

Modifying **phrases** and **clauses** may be either restrictive or nonrestrictive. A *nonrestrictive phrase or clause* provides additional information about what it modifies, but it does not restrict the meaning of what it modifies. The nonrestrictive phrase or clause can be removed without changing the essential meaning of the sentence. It is a parenthetical element that is set off by **commas** to show its loose relationship with the rest of the sentence.

NONRESTRICTIVE   The annual report, *which was distributed yesterday*, shows that sales increased 20 percent last year.

A *restrictive phrase or clause* limits, or restricts, the meaning of what it modifies. If it were removed, the essential meaning of the sentence would change. Because a restrictive phrase or clause is essential to the meaning of the sentence, it is never set off by commas.

RESTRICTIVE   All employees *wishing to donate blood* may take Thursday afternoon off.

Writers need to distinguish between nonrestrictive and restrictive elements. The same sentence can take on two entirely different meanings, depending on whether a modifying element is set off by commas (because it is nonrestrictive) or not (because it is restrictive). A slip by the writer can not only mislead **readers** but also embarrass the writer.

MISLEADING   He gave a poor performance evaluation to the staff members who protested to the Human Resources Department.
[This suggests that he gave the poor evaluation because the staff members had protested.]

R

| ACCURATE | He gave a poor performance evaluation to the staff members, who protested to the Human Resources Department. [This suggests that the staff members protested because of the poor evaluation.] |

Use *which* to introduce nonrestrictive clauses and *that* to introduce restrictive clauses.

| NONRESTRICTIVE | After John left the restaurant, *which* is one of the finest in New York, he came directly to my office. |
| RESTRICTIVE | Companies *that* diversify usually succeed. |

résumés

DIRECTORY
Sample Résumés   479
Analyzing Your Background   488
Organizing Your Résumé   488
  Heading   489
  Job Objective   489
  Qualifications Summary   489
  Education   490
  Employment Experience   490
  Related Skills and Abilities   491
  Honors and Activities   491
  References   492
Special Advice for Résumé Preparation   492
  Salary   492
  Returning Job Seekers   492
Electronic Résumés   493
  Web Résumés   493
  Scannable and Plain-Text Résumés   493
  E-mail–Attached Résumés   494

R

A résumé, the key tool of the <u>job search</u>, itemizes the qualifications that you summarize in your <u>application letter</u> (sometimes referred to as a *cover letter*). A résumé* should be limited to one page—or two pages if

---

*A detailed résumé for someone in an academic and scientific area is often called a *curriculum vitae* (also *vita* or *c.v.*). It may include education, publications, projects, grants, and awards as well as a full work history. Outside the United States, the term *curriculum vitae* is often a synonym for the term *résumé*.

you have substantial experience. On the basis of the information in the résumé and application letter, prospective employers decide whether to ask you to come in for an interview. If you are invited to an interview, the interviewer can base specific questions on the contents of your résumé. See also **interviewing for a job**.

Because résumés affect a potential employer's first impression, make sure that yours is well organized, carefully designed, consistently formatted, easy to read, and free of errors. Consider first an **organization** that highlights your strengths and fits your goals, as suggested by the examples shown in this entry. Experiment to determine a **layout and design** that is attractive and uncluttered. Consistency is especially important on a résumé. Be sure to use, for example, the same date formats (5/2006 or May 2006), punctuation, and spacing throughout. **Proofreading** is essential. Verify the accuracy of the information and have someone else review it. Use a quality printer and high-grade paper.

Sample Résumés

The sample résumés in this entry are provided to stimulate your thinking about how to tailor your résumé to your own job search. Before you design and write your résumé, look at as many samples as possible, and then organize and format your own to best suit your previous experience and your professional goals and to make the most persuasive case to your target employers. See also **persuasion**.

- Figure R–9 presents a conventional student résumé in which the student is seeking an entry-level position.
- Figure R–10 shows a résumé with a variation of the conventional headings to highlight professional credentials.
- Figure R–11 presents a student résumé with a format that is appropriately nonconventional because this student needs to demonstrate skills in graphic design for his potential audience.
- Figure R–12 shows a résumé that focuses on the applicant's management experience.
- Figure R–13 focuses on how the applicant advanced and was promoted within a single company.
- Figure R–14 illustrates how an applicant can organize a résumé by combining functional and chronological elements.
- Figure R–15 presents an electronic résumé in ASCII (American Standard Code for Information Interchange) format. Notice how this résumé emphasizes keywords so that potential employers searching online for applicants will be able to find it easily.

R

CAROL ANN WALKER

SCHOOL
148 University Drive
Bloomington, Indiana 47405
(812) 652-4781
caw2@iu.edu

HOME (after June 2006)
1436 West Schantz Avenue
Laurel, Pennsylvania 17322
(717) 399-2712
caw@yahoo.com

OBJECTIVE

Position in financial research, leading to management in corporate finance.

EDUCATION

Bachelor of Science in Business Administration, expected June 2006
Indiana University

Emphasis: Finance   Minor: Professional Writing
Grade Point Average: 3.88 out of possible 4.0
Senior Honor Society

FINANCIAL EXPERIENCE

FIRST BANK, INC., Bloomington, Indiana, 2004
Research Assistant, Summer and Fall Quarters
   Developed long-range planning models for the manager of corporate
   planning.

MARTIN FINANCIAL RESEARCH SERVICES, Bloomington, Indiana, 2003
Financial Audit Intern
   Created a design concept for in-house financial audits and provided re-
   search assistance to staff.
Associate Editor, *Martin Client Newsletter*, 2002–2003
   Wrote articles on financial planning with computer models; developed
   article ideas from survey of business periodicals; edited submissions.

COMPUTER SKILLS

Software: Microsoft Word, Excel, PowerPoint, Pagemaker, QuarkXPress
Hardware: Macintosh, IBM-PC, scanners
Languages: UNIX, JAVA, C++

REFERENCES

Available upon request.

FIGURE R–9. Student Résumé (for an Entry-Level Position)

CHRIS RENAULT, RN

3785 Raleigh Court, #46 • Phoenix, AZ 67903 •
(555) 467-1115 • chris@resumepower.com

Qualifications

➢ *Recent Honors Graduate of Approved Nursing Program*
➢ *Current Arizona Nursing Licensure and BLS Certification*
➢ *Presently Completing Clinical Nurse Internship Program*

Education & Licensure

ARIZONA STATE UNIVERSITY	MOHAVE COMMUNITY COLLEGE
Tempe, AZ	Kingman, AZ
Bachelor of Science in Nursing	**Associate Degree in Nursing (AN)**,
(BSN), 2006	2004
Graduated summa cum laude	Graduated cum laude (GPA 3.5)
(GPA: 4.0)	

Coursework Highlights: Family and Community Nursing, Health-Care
Delivery Models, Health Assessment, Pathology, Microbiology, Nursing
Research, Nursing of Older Adults, Health-Care Ethics

Arizona RN License, 2006
BLS Certification, 2006

Clinical Internship

CAMELBACK MEDICAL CENTER — Phoenix, AZ
Nurse Intern, 2005 to Present

• Accepted into new graduate RN training program and completing in-
depth, eight-month rotation working under a trained preceptor.

• Gaining valuable clinical experience to assume the role of a professional
nurse within an acute-care setting. Rotating through all medical center
areas, including Post Surgical, Orthopedics, Pediatrics, Oncology, Emergency Department, Psychiatric Nursing, Cardiac Telemetry, and Critical Care.

• Developing speed and skill in the day-to-day functions of a staff nurse.
Participating in patient assessment, treatment, medication disbursement, and surgical preparation as a member of the health-care team.

• Earned written commendations from preceptor for *". . . excellent ability
to interact with patients and their families, showing a high degree of
empathy, medical knowledge, and concern for quality and continuity
of patient care."*

Community Involvement

Active Volunteer and Fundraising Coordinator, The American Cancer
Society — Scottsdale, AZ, Chapter (2004 to Present)
Participant, Annual AIDS Walkathon (2001 to 2004) and "Find the Cure"
Breast Cancer Awareness Marathon (2003, 2004)

R

FIGURE R–10. Résumé (Highlighting Professional Credentials). Prepared by Kim
Isaacs, Advanced Career Systems, Inc.

Joshua S. Goodman
222 Morewood Avenue
Pittsburgh, PA 15212
Jgoodman@aol.com

OBJECTIVE

A position as a graphic designer with responsibilities in information design, packaging, and media presentations.

EDUCATION

**Carnegie Mellon University, Pittsburgh, Pennsylvania
BFA in Graphic Design — May 2005.**

*Graphic Design
Corporate Identity
Industrial Design
Graphic Imaging Processes
Color Theory
Computer Graphics
Typography
Serigraphy
Photography
Video Production*

GRAPHIC DESIGN EXPERIENCE

**Assistant Designer • Dyer/Khan, Los Angeles, California
Summer 2003, Summer 2004**
Assistant Designer in a versatile design studio. Responsible for design, layout, comps, mechanicals, and project management.
Clients: Paramount Pictures, Mattel Electronics, and Motown Records.

**Photo Editor • Paramount Pictures Corporation, Los Angeles, California
Summer 2002**
Photo Editor for merchandising department. Established art files for movie and television properties. Edited images used in merchandising. Maintained archive and database.

**Production Assistant • Grafis, Los Angeles, California
Summer 2001**
Production assistant at fast-paced design firm. Assisted with comps, mechanicals, and miscellaneous studio work.
Clients: ABC Television, A&M Records, and Ortho Products Division.

COMPUTER SKILLS

XML, HTML, JavaScript, Forms, Macromedia Dreamweaver 3, Macromedia Flash 4, Photoshop 5.5, Image Ready (Animated GIFs), Corel-DRAW, DeepPaint, iGrafx Designer, MapEdit (Image Mapping), Scanning, Microsoft Access/Excel, QuarkXPress.

ACTIVITIES

Member, Pittsburgh Graphic Design Society; Member, The Design Group.

FIGURE R–11. Student Résumé (for a Graphic Design Job)

ROBERT MANDILLO
7761 Shalamar Drive
Dayton, Ohio 45424
(513) 255-4137
mand@juno.com

OBJECTIVE

A management position in the aerospace industry with responsibility for developing new designs and products.

MANAGEMENT EXPERIENCE

MANAGER, ENGINEERING DRAFTING DEPARTMENT — May 1998–Present
Wright-Patterson Air Force Base, Dayton, Ohio

Supervise 17 drafting mechanics in support of the engineering design staff. Develop, evaluate, and improve materials and equipment for the design and construction of exhibits. Write specifications, negotiate with vendors, and initiate procurement activities for exhibit design support.

SUPERVISOR, GRAPHICS ILLUSTRATORS — June 1985–April 1998
Henderson Advertising Agency, Cincinnati, Ohio

Supervised five illustrators and four drafting mechanics after promotion from Graphics Technician. Analyzed and approved work-order requirements. Selected appropriate media and techniques for orders. Rendered illustrations in pencil and ink. Converted department to CAD system.

EDUCATION

BACHELOR OF SCIENCE IN MECHANICAL ENGINEERING TECHNOLOGY, 1985
Edison State College, Wooster, Ohio

ASSOCIATE'S DEGREE IN MECHANICAL DRAFTING, 1983
Wooster Community College, Wooster, Ohio

PROFESSIONAL AFFILIATION

National Association of Mechanical Engineers and Drafting Mechanics

REFERENCES

References, letters of recommendation, and a portfolio of original designs and drawings available online at <www.juno.com/mand>.

FIGURE R–12. Résumé (Applicant with Management Experience)

CAROL ANN WALKER
1436 West Schantz Avenue
Laurel, Pennsylvania 17322
(717) 399-2712
caw@yahoo.com

FINANCIAL EXPERIENCE

KERFHEIMER CORPORATION, Philadelphia, Pennsylvania

Senior Financial Analyst, June 2001–Present
Report to Senior Vice President for Corporate Financial Planning.
Develop manufacturing cost estimates totaling $30 million annually for
mining and construction equipment with Department of Defense.

Financial Analyst, November 1998–June 2001
Developed $50-million funding estimates for major Department of
Defense contracts for troop carriers and digging and earth-moving
machines. Researched funding options, resulting in savings of
$1.2 million.

FIRST BANK, INC., Bloomington, Indiana

Planning Analyst, September 1993–November 1998
Developed successful computer models for short- and long-range planning.

EDUCATION

Ph.D. in Finance: expected June 2006
The Wharton School of the University of Pennsylvania

M.S. in Business Administration, 1997
University of Wisconsin–Milwaukee
"Executive Curriculum" for employees identified as promising by their
employers.

B.S. in Business Administration (*magna cum laude*), 1993
Indiana University
Emphasis: Finance   Minor: Professional Writing

PUBLISHING AND MEMBERSHIP

Published "Developing Computer Models for Financial Planning," *Midwest Finance Journal* 34.2 (2003): 126–36.

Association for Corporate Financial Planning, Senior Member.

REFERENCES

References and a portfolio of financial plans are available upon request.

———— CAROL ANN WALKER ————

1436 West Schantz Avenue • Laurel, PA 17322
(717) 399-2712 • caw@yahoo.com

Award-Winning Senior Financial Analyst

Astute senior analyst and corporate financial planner with 11 years of experience and proven success enhancing P&L scenarios by millions of dollars. Demonstrated ability to apply critical thinking and sound strategic/economic analysis to multidimensional business issues. Advanced computer skills include Hyperion, SQL, MS Office, and Crystal Reports.

Financial Analyst of the Year, 2004

Recipient of prestigious national award from the Association for Investment Management and Research (AIMR)

Areas of Expertise

- Financial Analysis & Planning
- Forecasting & Trend Projection
- Trend/Variance Analysis
- Comparative Analysis
- Expense Analysis
- Strategic Planning
- SEC & Financial Reporting
- Risk Assessment

Career Progression

KERFHEIMER CORPORATION–Philadelphia, PA   1998 to Present

Senior Financial Analyst, June 2001 to Present
Financial Analyst, November 1998 to June 2001

Rapidly promoted to lead team of 15 analysts in the management of financial/SEC reporting and analysis for publicly traded, $2.3-billion company. Develop financial/statistical models used to project and maximize corporate financial performance. Support nationwide sales team by providing financial metrics, trends, and forecasts.

Key Accomplishments:

- **Developed long-range funding requirements crucial to firm's subsequent capture of $1 billion** in government and military contracts.
- **Facilitated a 45% decrease in company's long-term debt** during several major building expansions through personally developed computer models for capital acquisition.
- **Jointly led large-scale systems conversion to Hyperion**, including personal upload of database in Essbase. Completed conversion without interrupting business operations.

FIGURE R–14. Advanced Résumé (Combining Functional and Chronological Elements). Prepared by Kim Isaacs, Advanced Career Systems, Inc.

———————— CAROL ANN WALKER ————————

Résumé • Page Two

Career Progression (*continued*)

FIRST BANK, INC.–Bloomington, IN   1993 to 1998

Planning Analyst, September 1993 to November 1998

Compiled and distributed weekly, monthly, quarterly, and annual closings/ financial reports, analyzing information for presentation to senior management. Prepared depreciation forecasts, actual-vs.-projected financial statements, key-matrix reports, tax-reporting packages, auditor packages, and balance-sheet reviews.

Key Accomplishments:

- **Devised strategies to acquire over $1 billion at 3% below market rate.**
- **Analyzed financial performance for consistency to plans and forecasts**, investigated trends and variances, and alerted senior management to areas requiring action.
- **Achieved an average 23% return on all personally recommended investments.** Applied critical thinking and sound financial and strategic analysis in all funding options research.

Education

THE WHARTON SCHOOL of the UNIVERSITY OF PENNSYLVANIA– Philadelphia, PA

Ph.D. in Finance Candidate, Expected June 2005

UNIVERSITY OF WISCONSIN–Milwaukee, WI

M.S. in Business Administration, May 1997

INDIANA UNIVERSITY–Bloomington, IN

B.S. in Business Administration, Emphasis in Finance
(*magna cum laude*), May 1993

Affiliations

- Association for Investment Management and Research (AIMR), Member, 2000 to Present
- Association for Corporate Financial Planning (ACFP), Senior Member, 1998 to Present

Portfolio of Financial Plans Available on Request
(717) 399-2712 • caw@yahoo.com

FIGURE R-14. Advanced Résumé (Combining Functional and Chronological Elements) (*continued*)

DAVID B. EDWARDS
6819 Locustview Drive
Topeka, Kansas 66614
(913) 233-1552
dedwards@cpu.fairview.edu

JOB OBJECTIVE
Programmer with writing, editing, and training responsibilities,
leading to a career in information design management.

KEYWORDS
Programmer, Operating Systems, Unipro, Newsletter, Graphics,
Listserv, Professional Writer, Editor, Trainer, Instructor,
Technical Writer, Tutor, Designer, Manager, Information Design.

EDUCATION
** Fairview Community College, Topeka, Kansas
** Associate's Degree, Computer Science, June 2003
** Dean's Honor List Award (six quarters)

RELEVANT COURSE WORK
** Operating Systems Design
** Database Management
** Introduction to Cybernetics
** Technical Writing

EMPLOYMENT EXPERIENCE
** Computer Consultant: September 2003 to Present
Fairview Community College Computer Center: Advised and trained novice
users; wrote and maintained Unipro operating system documentation.
** Tutor: January 2002 to June 2003
Fairview Community College: Assisted students in mathematics and
computer programming.

SKILLS AND ACTIVITIES
** Unipro Operating System: Thorough knowledge of word-processing,
text-editing, and file-formatting programs.
** Writing and Editing Skills: Experience in documenting computer
programs for beginning programmers and users.
** Fairview Community Microcomputer Users Group: Cofounder and
editor of monthly newsletter ("Compuclub"); listserv manager.

FURTHER INFORMATION
** References, college transcripts, a portfolio of computer programs,
and writing samples available upon request.

R

FIGURE R–15. Electronic Résumé (in ASCII Format)

Analyzing Your Background

In preparing to write your résumé, determine what kind of job you are seeking. Then ask yourself what information about you and your background would be most important to a prospective employer. List the following:

- Schools you attended, degrees you hold, your major field of study, academic honors you were awarded, your grade point average, particular academic projects that reflect your best work

- Jobs you have held, your principal and secondary duties in each job, when and how long you held each job, promotions, skills you developed in your jobs that potential employers value and seek in ideal job candidates, projects or accomplishments that reflect your important contributions

- Other experiences and skills you have developed that would be of value in the kind of job you are seeking; extracurricular activities that have contributed to your learning experience; leadership, interpersonal, and communication skills you have developed; any collaborative work you have performed; computer skills you have acquired

Use this information to brainstorm any further key details. Then, based on all the details, decide which to include in your résumé and how you can most effectively present your qualifications.

Organizing Your Résumé

A number of different organizational patterns can be used effectively. The following categories are typical—which you choose should depend on your experience and goals, the employer's needs, and any standard practices in your profession.

R

- Heading (name and contact information)
- Job Objective
- Qualifications Summary
- Education
- Employment Experience
- Related Skills and Abilities
- Honors and Activities
- References

Whether you place education or employment experience first depends on the job you are seeking and on which credentials would strengthen your résumé the most. If you are a recent graduate without much work experience, you would list education first. If you have years of job experience, including jobs directly related to the kind of position you are seeking, you would list employment experience first. In your education and employment sections, use a reverse chronological sequence: List the most recent experience first, the next most recent experience second, and so on.

Heading.   At the top of your résumé, include your name, address, telephone number (home or cell), and e-mail address. Make sure that your name stands out on the page. If you have both a school address and a permanent home address, place your school address on the left side of the page and your permanent home address on the right side of the page. Place both underneath your name, as shown in Figure R–9. Indicate the dates you can be reached at each address (but do not date the résumé itself).

Job Objective.   Some potential employers prefer to see a clear employment objective in résumés. An objective introduces the material in a résumé and helps the reader quickly understand your goal. If you decide to include an objective, use a heading such as "Objective," "Employment Objective," "Career Objective," or "Job Objective." State your immediate goal and, if you know that it will give you an advantage, the direction you hope your career will take. Try to write your objective in no more than three lines, and tailor it to the specific job for which you are applying, as illustrated in the following examples.

- A full-time computer-science position aimed at solving engineering problems and contributing to a management team.

- A position involving meeting the concerns of women, such as family planning, career counseling, or crisis management.

- Full-time management of a high-quality local restaurant.

- A summer research or programming position providing opportunities to use problem-solving skills.

Qualifications Summary.   You may wish to include a brief summary of your qualifications to persuade hiring managers to select you for an interview. Sometimes called a *summary statement* or *career summary*, a qualifications summary can include skills, achievements, experience, or personal qualities that make you especially well suited to the position. You may wish to give this section a heading such as "Profile," "Career Highlights," or simply "Qualifications." Or you may use a headline, as in Figure R–14 ("Award-Winning Senior Financial Analyst").

Education.   List the school(s) you have attended, the degrees you received and the dates you received them, your major field(s) of study, and any academic honors you have earned. Include your grade point average only if it is 3.0 or higher—or include your average in your major if that is more impressive. List courses only if they are unusually impressive or if your résumé is otherwise sparse (see Figures R–10 and R–11). Mention your high school only if you want to call attention to special high-school achievements, awards, projects, programs, internships, or study abroad.

Employment Experience.   Organize your employment experience in reverse chronological order, starting with your most recent job and working backward under a single major heading called "Experience," "Employment," "Professional Experience," or the like. You could also organize your experience functionally by clustering similar types of jobs into one or several sections with specific headings such as "Management Experience" or "Major Accomplishments."

One type of arrangement might be more persuasive than the other, depending on the situation. For example, if you are applying for an accounting job but have no specific background in accounting, you would probably do best to list past and present jobs in chronological order, from most to least recent. If you are applying for a supervisory position and have had three supervisory jobs in addition to two nonsupervisory positions, you might choose to create a single section called "Supervisory Experience" and list only your three supervisory jobs. Or you could create two sections—"Supervisory Experience" and "Other Experience"—and include the three supervisory jobs in the first section and your nonsupervisory jobs in the second section.

The functional résumé groups work experience by types of workplace activities or skills rather than by jobs in chronological order. However, many employers are suspicious of functional résumés because they can be used to hide a poor work history, such as excessive job hopping or extended employment gaps. Functional elements can be combined with a chronological arrangement by using a qualifications summary or skills category, as shown in Figure R–14.

In general, follow these conventions when working on the "Experience" section of your résumé.

- Include jobs or internships when they relate directly to the position you are seeking. Although some applicants choose to omit internships and temporary or part-time jobs, including such experiences can make a résumé more persuasive if they have helped you develop specific related skills.

- Include extracurricular experiences, such as taking on a leadership position in a college organization or directing a community-service project, if they demonstrate that you have developed skills valued by potential employers.

- List military service as a job; give the dates served, the duty specialty, and the rank at discharge. Discuss military duties if they relate to the job you are seeking.

- For each job or experience, list both the job and company titles. Throughout each section, consistently begin with either the job or the company title, depending on which will likely be more impressive to potential employers.

- Under each job or experience, provide a concise description of your primary and secondary duties. If a job is not directly relevant, provide only a job title and a brief description of duties that helped you develop skills valued in the position you are seeking. For example, if you were a lifeguard and now seek a management position, focus on supervisory experience or even experience in averting disaster to highlight your management, decision-making, and crisis-control skills.

- Use action verbs (for example, "managed" rather than "as the manager") and state ideas succinctly, as shown in Figure R–12. Even though the résumé is about you, do not use "I" (for example, instead of "I was promoted to Section Leader," use "Promoted to Section Leader").

- Focus as much as possible on your achievements in your work history (Increased employee retention rate by 16% by developing a training program). Employers want to hire doers and achievers.

Related Skills and Abilities.   Employers are interested in hiring applicants with a variety of skills or the ability to learn new ones fairly quickly. Depending on the position, you might list in a skills section items such as fluency in foreign languages, writing and editing abilities, specialized technical knowledge, or computer skills, including knowledge of specific languages, software, and hardware.

Honors and Activities.   If you have room on your résumé, list any honors and unique activities near the end. Include items such as student or community activities, professional or club memberships, awards received, and published works. Be selective: Do not duplicate information given in other categories, and include only information that supports your employment objective. Provide a heading for this section that fits its contents, such as "Activities," "Honors," "Professional Affiliations," or "Publications and Memberships."

References.   Avoid listing references unless that is standard practice in your profession or your résumé is sparse. You might include a phrase such as "References available upon request" to signal the end of a long résumé, or write "Available upon request" after the heading "References" as a design element to balance a page. In any case, you should have a separate list of references to give to prospective employers after interviews; your list should include the main heading "References for [your name]."

Special Advice for Résumé Preparation

■ ETHICS NOTE   Be truthful. The consequences of giving false information in your résumé are serious. In fact, the truthfulness of your résumé reflects not only on your own ethical stance but also on the integrity with which you would represent the organization. See also **ethics in writing.** ✦

Salary.   Avoid listing the salary you desire in the résumé. On the one hand, you may price yourself out of a job you want if the salary you list is higher than a potential employer is willing to pay. On the other hand, if you list a low salary, you may not get the best possible offer. See **salary negotiations.**

Returning Job Seekers.   If you are returning to the workplace after an absence, most career experts say that it is important to acknowledge the gap in your career. That is particularly true if, for example, you are re-entering the workforce because you have devoted a full-time period to care for children or dependent adults. Do not undervalue such work. Although unpaid, it often provides experience that develops important time-management, problem-solving, organizational, and interpersonal skills. Although gaps in employment can be explained in the application letter, the following examples illustrate how you might reflect such experiences in a résumé. They would be especially appropriate for an applicant seeking employment in a field related to child or health care.

- **Primary Child-Care Provider, 2003 to 2005**
  Provided full-time care to three preschool children at home. Instructed in beginning scholastic skills, time management, basics of nutrition, arts, and swimming. Organized activities, managed household, and served as neighborhood-watch captain.

- **Home Caregiver, 2003 to 2005**
  Provided 60 hours per week in-home care to Alzheimer's patient. Coordinated medical care, developed exercise programs, completed and processed complex medical forms, administered medications, organized budget, and managed home environment.

If you have performed volunteer work during such a period, list that experience. Volunteer work often results in the same experience as does full-time, paid work, a fact that your résumé should reflect, as in the following example.

- **School Association Coordinator, 2003 to 2005**
  Managed special activities of the Briarwood High School Parent-Teacher Association. Planned and coordinated meetings, scheduled events, and supervised fund-drive operations. Raised $70,000 toward refurbishing the school auditorium.

Electronic Résumés

In addition to the traditional paper résumé, you can post a Web-based résumé. You may also need to submit a résumé on disk or through e-mail to a potential employer to be included in an organization's database. As Internet and database technologies converge, remain current with the forms and protocols that employers prefer by reviewing popular job-search sites, such as HotJobs at <http://hotjobs.yahoo.com> and Monster.com at <www.monster.com/>.

Web Résumés. If you plan to post your résumé on your own Web site, keep the following points in mind.

- Follow the general advice for <u>Web design</u>, such as viewing your résumé on several browsers to see how it looks.
- Just below your name, you may wish to provide a series of internal page links to such important categories as "experience" and "education."
- Consider building a multipage site for displaying a work portfolio, publications, reference letters, and the like.
- If privacy is an issue, include an e-mail link ("mailto") at the top of the résumé rather than your home address and phone number.

The disadvantage of posting a résumé at your own Web site is that you must attract the attention of employers on your own. As discussed in the entry <u>job search</u>, commercial services can attract recruiters with their large databases.

Scannable and Plain-Text Résumés. A scannable résumé is normally mailed to an employer in paper form, scanned, and downloaded into a company's searchable database. Such a résumé can be well formatted, but it should not contain decorative fonts, underlining, shading, letters that touch each other, and other features that will not scan easily. Scan such a résumé yourself to make sure there are no problems.

Some employers request ASCII (American Standard Code for Information Interchange) or plain-text résumés via e-mail, which can be added directly into the résumé database without scanning. ASCII résumés also allow employers to read the file no matter what type of software they are using. You can copy and paste such a résumé directly into the body of the e-mail message.

DIGITAL TIPS **PREPARING AN ASCII RÉSUMÉ**

When preparing an ASCII document, proper formatting is critical. For example, you need to insert manual line breaks at 65 characters to prevent long, single lines when the documents are opened in various systems. Further, many word-processing elements such as bullets, underlining, and boldface are incompatible with ASCII, which is limited to letters, numbers, and basic punctuation. For more on this topic, see <*bedfordstmartins.com/ alredbus*> and select *Digital Tips*, "Preparing an ASCII Résumé."

For résumés that will be downloaded into databases, it is good to use nouns rather than verbs to describe experience and skills (*designer* and *management* rather than *designed* and *managed*). You may also include a section in such a résumé titled "Keywords" (or perhaps give a descriptive name, such as "Areas of Expertise"). Keywords, also called *descriptors*, allow potential employers to search the database for qualified candidates. So, be sure to use keywords that are the same as those used in the employer's descriptions of the jobs that best match your interests and qualifications. This section can follow the main heading of your résumé or appear near the end of your résumé. Figure R–15 is an example of an electronic résumé that demonstrates the use of keywords.

E-mail–Attached Résumés. An employer may request or you may prefer to submit a résumé as an e-mail attachment to be printed out by the employer. If so, consider using a relatively plain design and sending the résumé as a rich text format (.rtf) document. Or, if precise design is important, send the résumé as a PDF file that will preserve the fonts, images, graphics, and layout. You can attach this file to an e-mail message that will then serve as your <u>application letter</u>.

WEB LINK **ANNOTATED SAMPLE RÉSUMÉS**

For more examples of résumés with helpful annotations, see <*bedfordstmartins .com/alredbus*> and select *Model Documents Gallery*.

revision

When you revise your draft, read and evaluate it primarily from the point of view of your <u>readers</u>. In fact, revising requires a different frame of mind than <u>writing a draft</u>. To achieve that frame of mind, experienced writers have developed various approaches. For example, some writers print out a draft, double-spaced, and mark up the paper copy. Working on-screen often focuses attention too narrowly on sentence-level problems, causing writers to lose sight of the larger problems of <u>scope</u> and <u>organization</u>. Other tactics include the following:

- Allow a "cooling period" between writing the draft and revision in order to evaluate the draft objectively.
- Read your draft aloud—often, hearing the text will enable you to spot problem areas that need improvement.
- Revise in passes by reading through your draft several times, each time searching for and correcting a different set of problems.

When you can no longer spot improvements, you may wish to give the draft to a colleague for review—especially for projects that are crucial for you or your organization as well as for collaborative projects, as described in <u>collaborative writing</u>.

Writer's Checklist: Revising Your Draft

☑ *Completeness.* Does the document achieve its primary **purpose**? Will it fulfill the readers' needs? Your writing should give readers exactly what they need but not overwhelm them.

☑ *Appropriate introduction and conclusion.* Check to see that your **introduction** frames the rest of the document and your **conclusion** ties the main ideas together. Both should account for revisions to the content of the document.

☑ *Accuracy.* Look for any inaccuracies that may have crept into your draft.

☑ *Unity and coherence.* Check to see that sentences and ideas are closely tied together (**coherence**) and contribute directly to the main idea expressed in the topic sentence of each **paragraph** (**unity**). Provide **transitions** where they are missing and strengthen those that are weak.

☑ *Consistency.* Make sure that **layout and design**, **visuals**, and use of language are consistent. Do not call the same item by one term on one page and a different term on another page.

Writer's Checklist: Revising Your Draft (continued)

☑ *Conciseness.* Tighten your writing so that it says exactly what you mean. Prune unnecessary words, phrases, sentences, and even paragraphs. See **conciseness**.

☑ *Awkwardness.* Look for **awkwardness** in **sentence construction** — especially any **garbled sentences**.

☑ *Ethical writing.* Check for **ethics in writing** and eliminate **biased language**.

☑ *Active voice.* Use the active **voice** unless the passive voice is more appropriate.

☑ *Word choice.* Delete or replace **vague words** and unnecessary **intensifiers**. Check for **affectation** and unclear **pronoun references**. See also **word choice**.

☑ *Jargon.* If you have any doubt that all your readers will understand any **jargon** or special terms you have used, eliminate or define them.

☑ *Clichés.* Replace **clichés** with fresh **figures of speech** or direct statements.

☑ *Grammar.* Check your draft for grammatical errors. Use computer **grammar** checkers with caution. Because they are not always accurate, treat their recommendations only as *suggestions*.

☑ *Typographical errors.* Check your final draft for typographical errors both with your spell checker and with thorough **proofreading** (spell checkers do not catch all errors).

☑ *Other common errors.* Use the search-and-replace command to find and revise wordy phrases, such as *that is, there are, the fact that,* and *to be,* and unnecessary helping **verbs** such as *will*.

DIGITAL TIPS   INCORPORATING TRACKED CHANGES

When colleagues review your document, they can track changes and insert comments within the document itself. Tracking and commenting vary with types and versions of word-processing programs, but in most programs you can view the tracked changes on a single draft or review the multiple drafts of your reviewers' versions. For more on this topic, see <*bedfordstmartins.com/alredbus*> and select *Digital Tips,* "Incorporating Tracked Changes."

---

rhetorical questions

A rhetorical question is a question to which a specific answer is neither needed nor expected. The question is often intended to make an audience think about the subject from a different perspective; the writer or speaker then answers the question in the article or **presenta-tion**. The answer to a rhetorical question such as "Is space exploration worth the cost?" may not be a simple yes or no; it might be a detailed explanation of the pros and cons of the value of space exploration.

The rhetorical question can be an effective opening, and it is often used as a <u>title</u>. By its nature, it is somewhat journalistic and indirect, and therefore should be used judiciously in business writing. For example, although a rhetorical question might be an appropriate opening for a **newsletter article**, it would not be as effective for a **report** or an **e-mail** addressed to a busy manager. When you do use a rhetorical question, be sure it is not trivial, obvious, or forced. The rhetorical question requires that you know your <u>readers</u>.

run-on sentences

A run-on sentence, sometimes called a *fused sentence*, is two or more sentences without punctuation to separate them. The term is also sometimes applied to a pair of independent <u>clauses</u> separated by only a <u>comma</u>, although this variation is usually called a <u>comma splice</u>. See also **sentence construction** and **sentence faults**.

Run-on sentences can be corrected, as shown in the following examples, by (1) making two sentences, (2) joining the two clauses with a <u>semicolon</u> (if they are closely related), (3) joining the two clauses with a comma and a coordinating <u>conjunction</u>, or (4) subordinating one clause to the other.

- The client suggested several solutions *. Some* some are impractical.

- The client suggested several solutions *;* some are impractical.

- The client suggested several solutions *, but* some are impractical.

- The client suggested several solutions *, although* some are impractical.

R

S

salary negotiations

Salary negotiations usually take place either at the end of an interview or after a formal job offer has been made. If possible, delay discussing salary until after you receive a formal written job offer because you will have more negotiating power at that point. See also job search.

Before interviewing for a job, prepare for possible salary negotiations by researching the following:

- The current range of salaries for the work you hope to do at your level (entry? intermediate? advanced?) in your region of the country. Check trade journals and organizations in your field, or ask a reference librarian for help in finding this information. Job listings that include salary can also be helpful.

- Salaries made by last year's graduates from your college or university at your level and in your line of work. Your campus career-development office should have these figures.

- Salaries made by people you know at your level and in your line of work. Attend local organizational meetings in your field or contact officers of local organizations who might have this information or steer you to useful contacts.

If a potential employer requests your salary requirements with a ré-sumé, consider your options carefully. If you provide a salary that is too high, the company might never interview you; if you provide a salary that is too low, you may have no opportunity later in the hiring process to negotiate for a higher salary. However, if you fail to follow the potential employer's directions and omit the requested information, an employer may disqualify you on principle. If you choose to provide salary requirements, always do so in a range (for example, $35,000 to $40,000). See also application letters.

If an interviewer asks your salary requirements toward the end of the job interview, you can try these strategies to delay salary negotiations:

- Say something like "I am sure that this company pays a fair salary for a person with my level of experience and qualifications" or "I am ready to consider your best offer."

- Indicate that you would like to learn more details about the position before discussing salary; point out that your primary goal is to work in a stimulating environment with growth potential, not to earn a specific salary.

- Express generally a strong interest in the position and the organization without referring to the salary.

- Emphasize your unique qualifications (or combination of skills) for the job and what you can do for the company that other candidates cannot.

If the interviewer or company demands to know your salary requirements during a job interview, provide a wide salary range that you know would be reasonable for someone at your level in your line of work in that region of the country. For example, you could say, "I would hope for a salary somewhere between $28,000 and $38,000, but of course this is negotiable."

Once salary negotiations begin, resist the temptation to accept, immediately, the first salary offer you receive. If you have done thorough research, you will know if the first salary offer is at the low, middle, or high end of the salary range for your level of experience in your line of work. If you have little or no experience and receive an offer for a salary at the low end of the range, you will realize that the offer probably is fair and reasonable. Yet, if you receive the same low-end offer but bring considerable experience to the job, you can negotiate for a higher salary that is more reasonable for someone with your background and credentials in your line of work in your region of the country.

Never say that you are unable to accept a salary below a particular figure. To keep negotiations going, simply indicate that you would have trouble accepting the first offer because it was lower than you had expected.

Remember that you are negotiating a package and not just a starting salary. For example, benefits can offer you substantial value. If the starting salary seems low, consider negotiating for some of these possible job perks:

- The chance for an early promotion, thus a higher salary, within a few years

- A particular job title or special job responsibilities that would provide you with impressive chances for career growth

- Tuition credits for continued education

- Payment of relocation costs

- Paid personal leave or paid vacations
- Personal or sick days
- Overtime potential
- Flexible hours
- Health, dental, optical/eye care, disability, and life insurance
- Retirement plans, such as 401(k) and pension plans
- Profit sharing; investment or stock options
- Bonuses or cost-of-living adjustments
- Commuting or parking-cost reimbursement
- Child or elder care
- Discounts on company products and services

You might find it most comfortable to respond to an initial offer in writing and then meet later with the potential employer for further negotiation. If possible, indicate all of your preferences and requirements at one time instead of continually asking for new and different benefits as you negotiate. Throughout this process, focus on what is most important to you (which might differ from what is most important to your friends) and on what you would find acceptable and comfortable.

WEB LINK **SALARY INFORMATION RESOURCES**

For links to Web sites offering useful resources for salary negotiations, see *<bedfordstmartins.com/alredbus>* and select *Links for Handbook Entries.*

sales letters

A sales letter—a printed or an electronic message that promotes a product, service, or business—requires both a thorough knowledge of the product or service and an understanding of the potential customer's needs.

An effective sales letter (1) catches <u>readers</u>' attention, (2) arouses their interest, (3) convinces them that your product or service will fulfill a need or desire, and (4) confidently asks them to take the course of action you suggest. See also <u>correspondence</u>, <u>persuasion</u>, and <u>promotional writing</u>.

The sales message in Figure S–1 is written in a light, friendly <u>tone</u>—sales messages from small, local businesses frequently adopt that tone because their purpose is to make readers feel comfortable about going

Janice's Cycle Shop
775 First Avenue
Ottumwa, IA 52501
(515) 273-5111

April 4, 2005

Mr. Raymond Sommers
350 College Place
Sharpsville, IA 52156

Dear Mr. Sommers:

Are you ready to go bike riding this spring—but your bike isn't?

Janice's Cycle Shop is ready to get your bike in shape for the beautiful days ahead. We'll lubricate all moving parts; check the tires, brakes, chain, lights, horn, and all other accessories; and make any minor repairs—all for only $29.95 with the enclosed coupon.

Just stop in any day, Monday through Saturday, between 8:00 a.m. and 9:00 p.m. We're conveniently located at the corner of First and Walker.

If you bring your bike in before 10:00, you can have it on the road by 5:00!

Ask for Janice, Don, or Lee—we're all here to help you.

Janice Moody

Janice@nc2.com

S

FIGURE S–1. Sales Letter

to the business. Note that such sales letters are sometimes "signed" not by an individual but by the shop itself.

Your first task in writing a sales letter is to determine to whom your message should be sent. One good source of names is a list of your customers; people who have at some time purchased a product or service from you may do so again. Other sources are lists of people who may be interested in similar products or services. Companies that specialize in marketing techniques compile such lists from the membership rolls of professional associations, lists of trade-show attendees, and the like. Because outside lists tend to be expensive, select them with care.

Once you determine who is to receive your sales letter, learn as much as you can about your readers so that you can effectively tell them how your product or service will satisfy their needs. Knowledge of their gender, age, vocation, geographical location, educational level, financial status, and interests will help determine your approach.

Analyze your product or service carefully to determine your strongest psychological sales points. Psychological selling involves stressing a product's benefits, which may be intangible, rather than its physical features. Select the most important psychological selling point about your product or service and build your sales message around it. Show how your product or service will make your readers' jobs easier, increase their status, make their personal lives more pleasant, and so on. Show how your product or service can satisfy your readers' needs or desires, which you identified in your opening. Then describe the physical features of your product in terms of their benefit to your readers. Help your readers imagine themselves using your product or service—and enjoying the benefits of doing so. See also **"you" viewpoint**.

⬧ ETHICS NOTE Be certain that any claim you make in a sales message is valid. To claim that a product is safe guarantees its absolute safety; therefore, say that the product is safe "provided that normal safety precautions are taken." Further, do not exaggerate or speak negatively about a competitor. For further ethical and legal guidelines, visit the Direct Marketing Association at <www.the-dma.org>. See also **ethics in writing**. ✦

S | *Writer's Checklist: Writing Sales Letters*

☑ Attract your readers' attention and arouse their interest in the opening, for example, by describing a product's feature that would appeal strongly to their needs. See also **introductions**.

☑ Convince readers that your product or service is everything you say it is through testimonials, case histories, free-trial use, or a money-back guarantee.

☑ Suggest ways readers can make immediate use of the product or service.

Writer's Checklist: Writing Sales Letters (continued)

☑ Minimize the negative effect price can have on readers.
- Mention the price along with a reminder of the benefits of the product.
- State the price in terms of units rather than sets ($20 per item, not $600 per set).
- Identify the daily, monthly, or even yearly cost based on the estimated life of the product.
- Suggest a series of payments rather than one total payment.
- Compare the cost of your product with that of something readers accept readily (This entire package costs no more than a DVD).

☑ Make it easy and worthwhile for customers to respond: Include a **brochure**, a discount coupon, instructions for phone-in orders, information about free delivery, or a Web address where customers can view special discounts and order online.

scope

Scope is the depth and breadth of detail you include in a document as defined by your **readers**' needs, your **purpose**, and the **context**. For example, if you write a **trip report** about a routine visit to a company facility, your readers may need to know only the basic details and any unusual findings. However, if you prepare a trip report about a visit to a division that has experienced problems and your purpose is to suggest ways to solve those problems, your report will contain many more details, observations, and even recommendations.

You should determine the scope of a document during the **preparation** stage of the writing process, even though you may refine it later. Defining your scope will expedite your **research** and can help determine team members' responsibilities in **collaborative writing**.

Your scope will also be affected by the type of document you are writing as well as the medium you select for your message. For example, government agencies often prescribe the general content and length for **proposals**, and some organizations set limits for the length of **memos** and **e-mails**. See **selecting the medium** and "Five Steps to Successful Writing."

S

selecting the medium

The most important considerations in selecting the most appropriate medium for communicating a message are the expectations of your readers and the purpose as well as the context of the communication. If you need to collaborate with someone to solve a problem or if you need to establish rapport, for example, e-mail exchanges may be far less efficient than a phone call or a face-to-face meeting. However, if you need precise wording or a record of a complex message, communicate in writing. Understanding the typical means of communicating on the job will help you select the most appropriate medium.

Letters on Organizational Stationery

Correspondence in the form of printed letters with handwritten signatures are often the most appropriate choice for formal contacts with new business associates or customers. Letters written on an organization's printed letterhead communicate formality, respect, and authority.

Memos

Memos on printed company stationery or attached to an e-mail are appropriate for internal communication among members of the same organization, even when offices are geographically separated. They have many of the same characteristics as letters, such as formality and authority, but they are used for a wider variety of functions—from formal meeting announcements to short reports.

E-mails

E-mail messages can replace letters and memos when writers are sure they are acceptable to their readers. E-mails can also be a less formal medium to exchange information, elicit discussions, collect opinions, and transmit various electronic documents. Because e-mail recipients can print copies of messages and attachments they receive and easily forward them to others, e-mail requires writers to consider and check messages carefully before clicking the send button.

Faxes

A fax is most useful when speed is essential and when the information—a drawing or signed contract, for example—must be viewed in its original form. Faxes are also useful when the recipient either does not have e-mail or prefers faxed documents. Fax machines in offices can be located in shared areas, so call the intended recipient before you send any confidential or sensitive messages.

Telephone Calls

Telephone exchanges are often best used for answering questions or discussing such matters as the conditions of a contract. Because phone calls enable participants to interpret tone of voice, they can make it easier to resolve misunderstandings, although they do not provide the visual cues possible during face-to-face meetings.

For multiple participants, a conference call may be a less expensive alternative to face-to-face meetings requiring travel. Such conference calls work best when the person coordinating the call works from an agenda shared by all the participants and directs the discussion as if chairing a meeting. Telephone calls in which decisions have been reached should be followed with written confirmation.

Voice Mail

Voice mail allows callers to leave brief messages ("Call me about the deadline for the new project" or "I got the package, so you don't need to call the distributor"). If the message is complicated or contains numerous details, use another medium, such as an e-mail message or a letter. If you want to discuss a subject at length, let the recipient know the subject so that he or she can prepare a response before returning your call. When you leave a message, give your name and contact information.

Face-to-Face Meetings

Face-to-face meetings are most appropriate for initial or early contacts with associates and clients with whom you intend to develop an important, long-term relationship. Meetings may also be best for brainstorming, negotiating, solving a technical problem, or handling a controversial issue. For advice on how to record discussions and decisions, see minutes of meetings.

S

Videoconferencing

Videoconferencing is particularly useful for meetings when travel is impractical. Unlike telephone conference calls, videoconferences have the advantage of allowing participants to see as well as to hear one another. Videoconferences work best with participants who are at ease in front of the camera.

Web Sites

A public Internet or company intranet Web site may be ideal for making available or exchanging information with others. For example, you might make available on your Web site particular documents and files colleagues may need for <u>collaborative writing</u>. Web sites can provide for you and others a home base for resources. See also <u>Web design</u> and <u>writing for the Web</u>.

Instant Messaging

Instant messaging (IM) on a computer or cell phone, although used primarily for personal communication, may be a low-cost alternative to communicating in real time with coworkers, suppliers, and customers—especially in remote locations. Instant messaging often uses online slang and shortened spellings ("u" for "you" and "L8R" for "later"). Instant messaging is obviously limited, and some employers do not consider IM appropriate for business purposes.

semicolons

The semicolon (;) links independent <u>clauses</u> or other sentence elements of equal weight and grammatical rank when they are not joined by a <u>comma</u> and a <u>conjunction</u>. The semicolon indicates a greater pause between clauses than does a comma but not as great a pause as a <u>period</u>.

Independent clauses joined by a semicolon should balance or contrast with each other, and the relationship between the two statements should be so clear that further explanation is not necessary.

- The new Web site was a success; every division reported increased online sales.

Do not use a semicolon between a dependent clause and its main clause.

- No one applied for the position; even though it was heavily advertised.

With Strong Connectives

In complicated sentences, a semicolon may be used before transitional words or <u>phrases</u> (*that is, for example, namely*) that introduce examples or further explanation. See also <u>transition</u>.

- The press understands Commissioner Curran's position on the issue; *that is*, local funds should not be used for the highway project.

A semicolon should also be used before conjunctive <u>adverbs</u> (*therefore, moreover, consequently, furthermore, indeed, in fact, however*) that connect independent clauses.

- The test results are not complete*; therefore,* I cannot make a recommendation.
  [The semicolon in the example shows that *therefore* belongs to the second clause.]

For Clarity in Long Sentences

Use a semicolon between two independent clauses connected by a coordinating conjunction (*and, but, for, or, nor, so, yet*) if the clauses are long and contain other <u>punctuation</u>.

- In most cases, these individuals are executives, bankers, or lawyers*; but* they do not, as the press seems to believe, simply push the button of their economic power to affect local politics.

A semicolon may also be used if any items in a series contain commas.

- Among those present were John Howard, president of the Omega Paper Company*;* Carol Delgado, president of Environex Corporation*;* and Larry Stanley, president of Stanley Papers.

Use <u>parentheses</u> or <u>dashes</u>, not semicolons, to enclose a parenthetical element that contains commas.

- All affected job classifications (receptionist, secretary, transcriptionist, and clerk) will be upgraded this month.

Use a <u>colon</u>, not a semicolon, as a mark of anticipation or enumeration.

- Three decontamination methods are under consideration: a zeolite-resin system, an evaporation system, and a filtration system.

The semicolon always appears outside closing <u>quotation marks</u>.

- The attorney said, "You must be accurate"*;* her client replied, "I will."

S

sentence construction

DIRECTORY
Subjects 508
Predicates 509
Sentence Types 510
    Structure 510
    Intention 510
    Stylistic Use 511
Constructing Effective Sentences 511

A sentence is the most fundamental and versatile tool available to writers. Sentences generally flow from a subject to a <u>verb</u> to any <u>objects</u>, <u>complements</u>, or <u>modifiers</u>, but they can be ordered in a variety of ways to achieve <u>emphasis</u>. When shifting word order for emphasis, however, be aware that word order can make a great difference in the meaning of a sentence.

- He was *only* the accountant.
- He was the *only* accountant.

Subjects

The most basic components of sentences are subjects and predicates. The *subject* of a sentence is a <u>noun</u> or <u>pronoun</u> (and its modifiers) about which the predicate of the sentence makes a statement. Although a subject may appear anywhere in a sentence, it most often appears at the beginning. (*To increase sales* is our goal.) Grammatically, a subject must agree with its verb in <u>number</u>.

- *These departments have* much in common.
- *This department has* several functions.

The subject is the actor in sentences using the active <u>voice</u>.

- *The Webmaster* reported an increase in site visits for May.

A *compound subject* has two or more substantives (nouns or noun equivalents) as the subject of one verb.

- *The president* and *the treasurer* agreed to begin the audit.

S

ESL   TIPS FOR UNDERSTANDING THE SUBJECT OF A SENTENCE

In English, every sentence, except commands, must have an explicit subject.

He established
- *Paul* worked fast. ~~Established~~ the parameters for the project.

In commands, the subject *you* is understood and is used only for emphasis.

- (*You*) Show up at the airport at 6:30 tomorrow morning.

- (*You*) Do your homework, young man. [parent to child]

If you move the subject from its normal position (subject-verb-object), English often requires you to replace the subject with an expletive (*there, it*). In this construction, the verb agrees with the subject that follows it.

- *There are* two files on the desk. [The subject is *files*.]

- *It is* presumptuous for me to speak for Jim.
  [The subject is *to speak for Jim*.]

Time, distance, weather, temperature, and environmental expressions use *it* as their subject.

- *It* is ten o'clock.

- *It* is ten miles down the road.

- *It* seldom snows in Florida.

- *It* is very hot in Jorge's office.

Predicates

The *predicate* is the part of a sentence that makes an assertion about the subject and completes the thought of the sentence.

- Bill *has piloted the corporate jet.*

The *simple predicate* is the verb and any helping verbs (*has piloted*). The *complete predicate* is the verb and any modifiers, objects, or complements (*has piloted the corporate jet*). A *compound predicate* consists of two or more verbs with the same subject.

- The company *tried* but *did not succeed* in that field.

Such constructions help achieve <u>conciseness</u> in writing. A *predicate nominative* is a noun construction that follows a linking verb and renames the subject.

S

- She is my *attorney.* [noun]
- His excuse was *that he had been sick.* [noun clause]

Sentence Types

Sentences may be classified according to *structure* (simple, compound, complex, compound-complex); *intention* (declarative, interrogative, imperative, exclamatory); and *stylistic use* (loose, periodic, minor).

Structure.   A *simple sentence* consists of one independent clause. At its most basic, a simple sentence contains only a subject and a predicate.

- Profits [subject] rose [predicate].

A *compound sentence* consists of two or more independent clauses connected by a comma and a coordinating <u>conjunction</u>, by a <u>semicolon</u>, or by a semicolon and a conjunctive <u>adverb</u>.

- Drilling is the only way to collect samples of the layers of sediment below the ocean floor, *but* it is not the only way to gather information about these strata. [comma and coordinating conjunction]
- The chemical composition of seawater bears little resemblance to that of river water; the various elements are present in entirely different proportions. [semicolon]
- It was 500 miles to the site; *therefore,* we made arrangements to fly. [semicolon and conjunctive adverb]

A *complex sentence* contains one independent clause and at least one dependent clause that expresses a subordinate idea.

- The generator will shut off automatically [independent clause] if the temperature rises above a specified point [dependent clause].

A *compound-complex sentence* consists of two or more independent clauses plus at least one dependent clause.

- Productivity is central to controlling inflation [independent clause]; when productivity rises [dependent clause], employers can raise wages without raising prices [independent clause].

Intention.   A *declarative sentence* conveys information or makes a factual statement. (The motor powers the conveyor belt.) An *interrogative sentence* asks a direct question. (Does the conveyor belt run constantly?) An *imperative sentence* issues a command. (Restart in MS-DOS mode.) An *exclamatory sentence* is an emphatic expression of feeling, fact, or opinion. It is a declarative sentence that is stated with great feeling. (The files were deleted!)

Stylistic Use. A *loose sentence* makes its major point at the beginning and then adds subordinate phrases and clauses that develop or modify that major point. A loose sentence might seem to end at one or more points before it actually does end, as the periods in brackets illustrate in the following sentence.

- It went up[.], a great ball of fire about a mile in diameter[.], an elemental force freed from its bonds[.] after being chained for billions of years.

A *periodic sentence* delays its main ideas until the end by presenting subordinate ideas or modifiers first.

- During the last century, the attitude of the American citizen toward automation underwent a profound change.

A *minor sentence* is an incomplete sentence that makes sense in its context because the missing element is clearly implied by the preceding sentence.

- In view of these facts, is the service contract really useful? *Or economical?*

Constructing Effective Sentences

The subject-verb-object pattern is effective because it is most familiar to <u>readers</u>. In "The company increased profits," we know the subject (*company*) and the object (*profits*) by their positions relative to the verb (*increased*).

An *inverted sentence* places the elements in unexpected order, thus emphasizing the point by attracting the readers' attention.

- A better job I never had. [direct object–subject–verb]
- More optimistic I have never been. [subjective complement–subject–linking verb]
- A poor image we presented. [complement–subject–verb]

Use uncomplicated sentences to state complex ideas. If readers have to cope with a complicated sentence in addition to a complex idea, they are likely to become confused. Just as simpler sentences make complex ideas more digestible, a complex sentence construction makes a series of simple ideas more smooth and less choppy.

Avoid loading sentences with a number of thoughts carelessly tacked together. Such sentences are monotonous and hard to read because all the ideas seem to be of equal importance. Rather, distinguish the relative importance of sentence elements with <u>subordination</u>. See also <u>garbled sentences</u>.

LOADED	We started the program three years ago, only three members were on the staff, and each member was responsible for a separate state, but it was not an efficient operation.
IMPROVED	When we started the program three years ago, only three members were on the staff, each having responsibility for a separate state; however, that arrangement was not efficient.

Express coordinate or equivalent ideas in similar form. The very construction of the sentence helps the reader grasp the similarity of its components, as illustrated in **parallel structure**.

> **ESL TIPS FOR UNDERSTANDING THE REQUIREMENTS OF A SENTENCE**
>
> • A sentence must start with a capital letter.
>
> • A sentence must end with a period, a question mark, or an exclamation point.
>
> • A sentence must have a subject.
>
> • A sentence must have a verb.
>
> • A sentence must conform to subject-verb-object word order (or inverted word order for questions or emphasis).
>
> • A sentence must express an idea that can stand on its own (called the *main*, or *independent*, *clause*).

sentence faults

A number of problems can create sentence faults, including faulty <u>subordination</u>, <u>clauses</u> with no subjects, rambling sentences, omitted <u>verbs</u>, and illogical assertions.

Faulty Subordination

Faulty subordination occurs when a grammatically subordinate element contains the main idea of the sentence or when a subordinate element is so long or detailed that it obscures the main idea. Both of the following sentences are logical, depending on what the writer intends as the main idea and as the subordinate element.

- Although the new filing system saves money, many of the staff are unhappy with it.
  [If the main point is that *many of the staff are unhappy*, this sentence is correct.]

  - The new filing system saves money, although many of the staff are unhappy with it.
  [If the main point is that *the new filing system saves money*, this sentence is correct.]

In the following example, the subordinate element overwhelms the main point.

FAULTY	Because the noise level in the assembly area on a typical shift is as loud as a smoke detector's alarm ten feet away, employees often develop hearing problems.
IMPROVED	Employees in the assembly area often develop hearing problems because the noise level on a typical shift is as loud as a smoke detector's alarm ten feet away.

Missing Subjects

Clauses with no subjects occur when writers inappropriately assume a subject that they do not state in the clause. See also **sentence fragments**.

INCOMPLETE	Your application program can request to end the session after the next command. [Your application program can request *who* or *what* to end the session?]
COMPLETE	Your application program can request *the host program* to end the session after the next command.

Rambling Sentences

Rambling sentences contain more information than the reader can comfortably absorb. The obvious remedy for a rambling sentence is to divide it into two or more sentences. When you do that, put the main message of the rambling sentence into the first of the revised sentences.

S

RAMBLING   The payment to which a subcontractor is entitled should be made promptly in order that in the event of a subsequent contractual dispute we, as general contractors, may not be held in default of our contract by virtue of nonpayment.

DIRECT   Pay subcontractors promptly. Then if a contractual dispute occurs, we cannot be held in default of our contract because of nonpayment.

Missing Verbs

Some sentence faults are created when writers omit a verb.

- I never have and probably never will write the annual report.

    written (inserted above "have and")

Faulty Logic

A sentence is faulty when its predicate makes an illogical assertion about its subject. "Mr. Wilson's *job* is a sales representative" is not logical, but "*Mr. Wilson* is a sales representative" is logical. "Jim's *height* is six feet tall" is not logical, but "*Jim* is six feet tall" is logical. See also **logic errors**.

sentence fragments

A sentence fragment is an incomplete grammatical unit that is punctuated as a sentence.

FRAGMENT   And quit his job.

SENTENCE   He quit his job.

A sentence fragment lacks either a subject or a **verb** or is a subordinate **clause** or **phrase**. Sentence fragments are often introduced by relative **pronouns** (*who, whom, which, that*) or subordinating **conjunctions** (such as *although, because, if, when,* and *while*).

- The new manager instituted several new procedures. ~~Although~~ she didn't clear them with Human Resources.

    , although (inserted)

A sentence must contain a finite verb; **verbals** (nonfinite) do not function as verbs. The following sentence fragments use verbals (*providing, to work*) that cannot function as finite verbs.

FRAGMENT	*Providing* all employees with disability insurance.
SENTENCE	The company *provides* all employees with disability insurance.
FRAGMENT	*To work* a 40-hour week.
SENTENCE	Most of our employees *must work* a 40-hour week.

Explanatory phrases beginning with *such as*, *for example*, and similar terms often lead writers to create sentence fragments.

- The staff wants additional benefits. For example, the use of company cars.

, such as ^

A hopelessly snarled fragment simply must be rewritten. To rewrite such a fragment, pull the main points out of the fragment, list them in the proper sequence, and then rewrite the sentence as illustrated in **garbled sentences**. See also **sentence construction** and **sentence faults**.

sentence variety

Sentences can vary in length, structure, and complexity. As you revise, make sure your sentences have not become tiresomely alike. See also **sentence construction**.

Sentence Length

A series of sentences of the same length is monotonous, so varying sentence length makes writing less tedious to the **reader**. For example, avoid stringing together a number of short independent **clauses**. Either connect them with subordinating connectives, thereby making some dependent clauses, or make some clauses into separate sentences. See also **subordination**.

STRING	The river is 60 miles long, and it averages 50 yards in width, and its depth averages 8 feet.
IMPROVED	The river, which is 60 miles long and averages 50 yards in width, has an average depth of 8 feet.
IMPROVED	The river is 60 miles long. It averages 50 yards in width and 8 feet in depth.

You can often effectively combine short sentences by converting **verbs** into **adjectives**.

S

- The *failed* digital shift indicator ~~failed. It~~ was pulled from the market.

Although too many short sentences make your writing sound choppy and immature, a short sentence can be effective following a long one.

- During the past two decades, many changes have occurred in American life — the extent, durability, and significance of which no one has yet measured. *No one can.*

In general, short sentences are good for emphatic, memorable statements. Long sentences are good for detailed explanations and support. Nothing is inherently wrong with a long sentence, or even with a complicated one, as long as its meaning is clear and direct. Sentence length becomes an element of style when varied for **emphasis** or contrast; a conspicuously short or long sentence can be used to good effect.

Word Order

When a series of sentences all begin in exactly the same way (usually with an **article** and a **noun**), the result is likely to be monotonous. You can make your sentences more interesting by occasionally starting with a modifying word, **phrase**, or clause.

- *To salvage the project*, she presented alternatives when existing policies failed to produce results. [modifying phrase]

However, overuse of this technique itself can be monotonous, so use it in moderation.

Inverted word order can be an effective way to achieve variety, but be careful not to create an awkward construction.

AWKWARD	Then occurred the event that gained us the contract.
EFFECTIVE	Never have sales been so good.

For variety, you can alter normal sentence order by inserting a phrase or clause.

- Titanium fills the gap, *both in weight and in strength,* between aluminum and steel.

The technique of inserting a phrase or clause is good for achieving emphasis, providing detail, breaking monotony, and regulating **pace**.

Loose and Periodic Sentences

A loose sentence makes its major point at the beginning and then adds subordinate phrases and clauses that develop or modify the point. A loose sentence could end at one or more points before it actually does end, as the periods in brackets illustrate in the following example.

- It went up[.], a great ball of fire about a mile in diameter[.], an elemental force freed from its bonds[.] after being chained for billions of years.

A periodic sentence delays its main idea until the end by presenting modifiers or subordinate ideas first, thus holding the readers' interest until the end.

- During the last century, the attitude of Americans toward technology underwent a profound change.

Experiment with shifts from loose sentences to periodic sentences in your own writing, especially during **revision**. Avoid the singsong monotony of a long series of loose sentences, particularly a series containing coordinate clauses joined by **conjunctions**. Subordinating some thoughts to others not only provides emphasis but also makes your sentences more interesting.

sequential method of development

The sequential, or step-by-step, **method of development** is especially effective for explaining a process or describing a mechanism in operation. (See **process explanation**.) It is also the logical method for writing **instructions**, as shown in Figure S–2 on page 518.

The main advantage of the sequential method of development is that it is easy to follow because the steps correspond to the process or operation being described. The disadvantages are that it can become monotonous and does not lend itself well to achieving **emphasis**.

Most methods of development have elements of sequence to a greater or lesser extent. The **chronological method of development**, for example, is also sequential: To describe a trip chronologically, from

S

From: Steven Scott <scott@techline.org>
To: All Hourly Employees <hourly@techline.org>
Sent: Friday, January 27, 2006 2:16 PM
Subject: Flextime Eligibility and Requests

Because Human Resources has received numerous calls about the approval process for using the new "flextime" working schedule, this memo outlines the eligibility requirements and the procedure for requesting flextime.

First, determine if you are eligible to use a flextime schedule. You are eligible if your job does not require you to answer telephones or to be available to the public between the hours of 8:00 a.m. and 5:00 p.m. In addition, you must meet with your department manager to ensure that any necessary duties will be covered during those hours.

After you have established your eligibility, submit a copy of Form FT, signed by your department manager, to Human Resources. We will send the form to your division manager for his or her approval.

Human Resources will notify you when your request is approved or denied. If your request is approved, you may begin your new schedule on the first Monday thereafter. After three weeks, your manager must advise Human Resources in writing that your flextime schedule has not interfered with the smooth functioning of your department.

You may obtain copies of Form FT from Margaret Dienstein in Room 129. If you have any questions, please feel free to contact Margaret at ext. 5648 or mld@techline.org.

FIGURE S–2. Sequential Method of Development (Sent as E-mail)

S

beginning to end, is also to describe it sequentially. The <u>cause and effect method of development</u> may contain certain elements of sequence. For example, a report of the causes leading up to an accident (the effect), might describe those causes in the order they occurred (or their sequence).

service

When used as a <u>verb</u>, *service* means "keep up or maintain" as well as "repair." (Our company will *service* your equipment.) If you mean "provide a more general benefit," use *serve*.

- *serves*
- Our company services the northwest area of the state.

set / sit

Sit is an intransitive <u>verb</u>; it does not, therefore, require an <u>object</u>. (I *sit* by a window in the office.) Its past <u>tense</u> is *sat*. (We *sat* around the conference table.) *Set* is usually a transitive verb, meaning "put or place," "establish," or "harden." Its past tense is *set*.

- Please *set* the trophy on the shelf.
- The jeweler *set* the stone carefully.
- Can we *set* a date for the meeting?
- The high temperature *sets* the epoxy quickly.

Set is occasionally an intransitive verb.

- The new adhesive *sets* in five minutes.

shall / will

Although traditionally *shall* was used to express the future tense with *I* and *we*, *will* is generally accepted with all persons. *Shall* is commonly used today only in questions requesting an opinion or a preference (*Shall* we go?) rather than a prediction (*Will* we go?). It is also used in statements expressing determination (I *shall* return!) or in formal regulations (Applicants *shall* provide a proof of certification).

S

---

sic (*see* **quotations**)

---

slashes

The slash (/) — called a variety of names, including *slant line, diagonal, virgule, bar,* and *solidus* — both separates and shows omission.

The slash can indicate alternatives or combinations.

- David's telephone numbers are 549-2278/2235.

- Check the on/off switch before you leave.

The slash often indicates omitted words and letters.

- miles/hour (miles per hour); w/o (without)

In fractions and mathematical expressions, the slash separates the numerator from the denominator (3/4 for three-fourths; x/y for x over y).

Although the slash is used informally with **dates** (5/11/06), avoid this form in business writing where the date may not be immediately clear, especially in **international correspondence**.

The forward slash often separates items in URL (uniform resource locator) addresses for sites on the Internet (<bedfordstmartins.com/alredbus>). The backward slash is used to separate parts of file names (<c:\myfiles\reports\annual06.doc>).

---

so / so that / such

Avoid *so* as a substitute for *because*. See also **as/because/since**.

- *Because she*
  ~~She~~ reads faster, ~~so~~ she finished before I did.
     ^

Do not replace the phrase *so that* with *so* or *such that*.

- *so that*
  The report should be written ~~such that~~ it can be widely
                              ^
  understood.

Such, an **adjective** meaning "of this or that kind," should never be used as a **pronoun**.

- Our company provides on-site child care, but I do not anticipate
  it.
  using ~~such~~.
        ^

some / somewhat

When *some* functions as an indefinite **pronoun** for a plural count **noun** or as an indefinite **adjective** modifying a plural count noun, use a plural **verb**.

- *Some* of us *are* prepared to work overtime.
- *Some* people *are* more productive than others.

Some is singular, however, when used with mass nouns.

- *Some* stationery *is* sold through our outlet stores.
- Most of the water evaporated, but *some remains.*

When *some* is used as an adjective or a pronoun meaning "an undetermined quantity" or "certain unspecified persons," it should be replaced by the **adverb** *somewhat*, which means "to some extent."

- His writing has improved ~~some.~~ *somewhat.*

some time / sometime / sometimes

Some time refers to a duration of time. (We waited for *some time* before making the decision.) *Sometime* refers to an unknown or unspecified time. (We will visit with you *sometime.*) *Sometimes* refers to occasional occurrences at unspecified times. (He *sometimes* visits the branch offices.)

spatial method of development

The spatial **method of development** describes an object or a process according to the physical arrangement of its features. Depending on the subject, you describe its features from bottom to top, side to side, east to west, outside to inside, and so on. Descriptions of this kind rely mainly on dimension (height, width, length), direction (up, down, north, south), shape (rectangular, square, semicircular), and proportion (one-half, two-thirds). Features are described in relation to one another or to their surroundings, as illustrated in Figure S–3 on page 522, which might be written by a home inspector or crime-scene investigator. The description in Figure S–3 relies on a bottom-to-top, clockwise (south to west to north to east) sequence, beginning with the front door.

S

DESCRIPTION

Interior of Two-Story, Six-Room House

Ground Floor

Front hall and stairwell. The front door faces south and opens into a hallway seven feet deep and ten feet wide. At the end of the hallway is a stairwell that begins on the right-hand (east) side of the hallway, rises five steps to a landing, and reverses direction at the left-hand (west) side of the hallway.

Dining room. To the left (west) of the hallway is the dining room, which measures 15 feet along its southern exposure and ten feet along its western exposure.

Kitchen. North of the dining room is the kitchen, which measures ten feet along its western exposure and 15 feet along its northern exposure.

Bathroom. East of the kitchen, along the northern side of the house, is a bathroom that measures ten feet (west to east) by five feet.

Living room. Parallel to the bathroom is a passageway the same size as the bathroom and leading from the kitchen to the living room. The living room (15 feet west to east by 20 feet north to south) occupies the entire eastern end of the floor.

Second Floor

Hallway. On the second floor, at the top of the stairs, is an L-shaped hallway, five feet wide. The base of the L, over the door, is 15 feet long. The vertical arm of the L is 13 feet long.

Southwest bedroom. To the west of the hall is the southwest bedroom, which measures ten feet along its southern exposure and eight feet along its western exposure.

Northwest bedroom. Directly to the north, over the kitchen, is the northwest bedroom, which measures 12 feet along its western exposure and ten feet along its northern exposure.

S

FIGURE S–3. Spatial Method of Development

The spatial method of development might be used for descriptions of warehouse inventory, **proposals** for landscape work, construction-site **progress and activity reports**, and, in combination with a step-by-step sequence, many types of **instructions**.

spelling

Because spelling errors in your documents will damage your credibility, careful **proofreading** is essential. The use of a spell checker is crucial; however, it will not catch all mistakes, especially those in personal and company names. It cannot detect a spelling error if the error results in a valid word; for example, if you mean *to* but inadvertently type *too*, the spell checker will not detect the error. Likewise, spell checkers will not detect errors in the names of people, places, and organizations. If you are unsure about the spelling of a word, do not rely on guesswork or a spell checker—consult a standard **dictionary** or style guide.

style

A dictionary definition of *style* is "the way in which something is said or done, as distinguished from its substance." Writers' styles are determined by the way writers think and transfer their thoughts to paper—the way they use words, sentences, images, **figures of speech**, and so on.

A writer's style is the way his or her language functions in particular situations. For example, an **e-mail** to a friend would be relaxed, even chatty, in **tone**, whereas a job **application letter** would be more restrained and formal. Obviously, the style appropriate to one situation would not be appropriate to the other. In both situations, the **readers**, the **purpose**, and the **context** determine the manner or style the writer adopts. Beyond an individual's personal style, various kinds of writing have distinct stylistic traits, such as **business writing style**.

Standard English can be divided into two broad categories of style—formal and informal—according to how it functions in certain situations. Understanding the distinction between formal and informal writing styles helps writers use the appropriate style. We must recognize, however, that no clear-cut line divides the two categories and that some writing may call for a combination of the two.

S

Formal Writing Style

A formal writing style can perhaps best be defined by pointing to certain material that is clearly formal, such as scholarly and scientific articles in professional journals, lectures read at meetings of professional societies, and legal documents. Material written in a formal style is usually the work of a specialist writing to other specialists or writing that embodies laws or regulations. As a result, the vocabulary is specialized and precise. The writer's tone is impersonal and objective because the subject matter looms larger in the writing than does the author's personality. (See **point of view**.) A formal writing style does not use **contractions**, slang, or dialect. (See **English, varieties of**.) Because the material generally examines complex ideas, the **sentence construction** may be elaborate.

Formal writing need not be dull and lifeless. By using such techniques as the active **voice** whenever possible, **sentence variety**, and **subordination**, a writer can make formal writing lively and interesting, especially if the subject matter is inherently interesting to the reader.

- Business graphics has emerged as a significant applications area for computer graphics systems. Many business managers today have discovered the availability and potential benefits of computer graphics. Their appeal lies in their ability to generate graphs quickly that summarize the relations inherent in a set of data and to make changes and revisions to the graphs quickly and easily. The ultimate purpose of the resulting graphs is the rapid apprehension (and possible retention) of these relationships.

    However, computers do not automatically create good graphs. They merely provide the tool for doing so quickly and easily. The design of good graphs must be based on a systematic method that plays upon the interaction between the relations or information that we wish to communicate and our perception of these relations.
    — William A. Simcox, "A Design Method
    for Graphic Communication," *ABCA Bulletin* 47

S

Whether you should use a formal style in a particular instance depends on your readers and purpose. When writers attempt to force a formal style when it should not be used, their writing is likely to fall victim to **affectation**, **awkwardness**, and **gobbledygook**.

Informal Writing Style

An informal writing style is a relaxed and colloquial way of writing standard English. It is the style found in most personal e-mail and in some business **correspondence**, nonfiction books of general interest, and mass-circulation magazines. There is less distance between the writer and the reader because the tone is more personal than in a formal writing style. Contractions and elliptical constructions are common. Consider the following passage, written in an informal style, from a nonfiction book.

- Business, like art and science, has been revealed and conceived through the intellect and imagination of people, and it develops or declines because of the intellect and imagination of people.

  In fact, there is no business; there are only people. Business exists only *among* people and *for* people.

  Seems simple enough, and it applies to every aspect of business, but not enough businesspeople seem to get it.

  Reading the economic forecasts and the indicators and the ratios and the rates of this or that, someone from another planet might actually believe that there really are invisible hands at work in the marketplace.

  It's easy to forget what the measurements are measuring. Every number—from productivity rates to salaries—is just a device contrived by people to measure the results of the enterprise of other people. For managers, the most important job is not measurement but motivation. And you can't motivate numbers.

  —James A. Autry, *Love and Profit: The Art of Caring Leadership*

As the example illustrates, the vocabulary of an informal writing style is made up of generally familiar rather than unfamiliar words and expressions, although slang and dialect are usually avoided. An informal style approximates the cadence and structure of spoken English while conforming to the grammatical conventions of written English.

Writers who consciously attempt to create a distinctive style usually defeat their purpose. Attempting to impress readers with a flashy writing style can lead to affectation; attempting to impress them with scientific objectivity can produce a style that is dull and lifeless. Business writing need be neither affected nor dull. It can and should be simple, clear, direct, even interesting—the key is to master basic writing skills and always to keep your readers in mind. What will be both informative and interesting to your **audience**? When that question is uppermost in your mind as you apply the steps of the writing process, you will achieve an interesting and informative writing style. See "Five Steps to Successful Writing."

Writer's Checklist: Developing an Effective Style

☑ Use the active voice — not exclusively but as much as possible without becoming awkward or illogical.

☑ Use **parallel structure** whenever a sentence presents two or more thoughts of equal importance.

☑ Use a variety of sentence structures to avoid a monotonous style.

☑ Avoid stating positive thoughts in negative terms (write "40 percent responded" instead of "60 percent failed to respond"). See also **positive writing** and **ethics in writing**.

☑ Concentrate on achieving the proper balance between **emphasis** and subordination.

subordination

Use subordination to show, by the structure of a sentence, the appropriate relationship between ideas of unequal importance. By putting less important ideas in subordinate **clauses** or **phrases** you emphasize your main idea.

- Pacific Enterprises now employs 500 people. It was founded just three years ago.
  [The two ideas are equally important.]

- Pacific Enterprises, *which now employs 500 people*, was founded just three years ago.
  [The number of employees is subordinated; the founding date is emphasized.]

- Pacific Enterprises, *which was founded just three years ago*, now employs 500 people.
  [The founding date is subordinated; the number of employees is emphasized.]

Effective subordination can be used to achieve **conciseness**, **emphasis**, and **sentence variety**. For example, consider the following sentences.

DEPENDENT CLAUSE	The regional manager's report, *which covered five pages*, was carefully illustrated.
PHRASE	The regional manager's report, *covering five pages*, was carefully illustrated.
SINGLE MODIFIER	The regional manager's *five-page report* was carefully illustrated.

Subordinating **conjunctions** (*because, if, while, when, though*) achieve subordination effectively.

- An increase in local sales is unlikely *because* the local population has declined.

You may use a coordinating conjunction (*and, but, for, nor, or, so, yet*) to concede that an opposite or balancing fact is true; however, a subordinating conjunction (*although, since, while*) can often make the point more smoothly.

- *Although* their bank has a lower interest rate on loans, ours provides a wider range of essential services.

The relationship between a conditional statement and a statement of consequences is clearer if the condition is expressed as a subordinate clause.

- *Because* the bill was incorrect, the customer was angry.

Relative **pronouns** (*who, whom, which, that*) can be used effectively to combine related ideas within sentences.

- The OnlinePro, *which* protects computers from malicious programs and e-mail attachments, makes your system "invisible" to hackers.

Avoid overlapping subordinate constructions that depend on the preceding construction. Overlapping can make the relationship between a relative pronoun and its antecedent less clear.

OVERLAPPING	Shock, *which* often accompanies severe injuries and infections, is a failure of the circulation, *which* is marked by a fall in blood pressure *that* initially affects the skin (*which* explains pallor) and later the vital organs such as the kidneys and brain.
CLEAR	Shock often accompanies severe injuries and infections. Marked by a fall in blood pressure, it is a failure of the circulation, initially to the skin (thus producing pallor) and later to the vital organs like the kidneys and the brain.

S

substantives (*see* sentence construction)

suffixes

A suffix is a letter or letters added to the end of a word to change its meaning in some way. Suffixes can change the part of speech of a word.

NO SUFFIX	The proposal was *thorough*. [adjective]
SUFFIX	The *thoroughness* is obvious. [noun]
SUFFIX	The proposal *thoroughly* described the problem. [adverb]

The suffix *-like* is sometimes added to nouns to make them into adjectives. The resulting compound word is hyphenated only if it is unusual or might not immediately be clear (childlike, lifelike, but dictionary-like, robot-like).

surveys (*see* questionnaires)

synonyms

A synonym is a word that means nearly the same thing as another word does (seller, vendor, supplier). The dictionary definitions of synonyms are very similar, but the connotations may differ. For example, a *seller* may be the same thing as a *supplier*, but the term *supplier* does not suggest a retail transaction as strongly as *seller* does.

Do not try to impress your readers by finding fancy or obscure synonyms in a thesaurus; the result is likely to be affectation. See also connotation/denotation and antonyms.

syntax

Syntax refers to the way that words, phrases, and clauses are combined to form sentences. In English, the most common structure is the subject-verb-object pattern. For more information about the word order of sentences, see sentence construction, sentence faults, sentence fragments, and sentence variety.

S

T

tables of contents

A table of contents is typically included in a document longer than ten pages. It previews what the work contains and how it is organized, and it allows <u>readers</u> looking for specific information to locate sections by page number quickly and easily.

When creating a table of contents, use the major <u>headings</u> and subheadings of your document exactly as they appear in the text, as shown in the entry <u>formal reports</u>. (See the table of contents in Figure F–6 on page 217.) Note that the table of contents is typically placed in the front matter so that it follows the title page and <u>abstract</u>, and precedes the list of tables or figures, the foreword, and the preface.

tables

A table can present data, such as statistics, more concisely than text and more accurately than <u>graphs</u>. A table facilitates precise comparisons of data by organizing it into rows and columns. However, overall trends are more easily conveyed in charts, graphs, and other <u>visuals</u>.

Table Elements

Tables typically include the elements shown in Figure T–1 on page 530.

Table Number. Table numbers are usually Arabic and should be assigned sequentially to the tables throughout the document.

Table Title. The title, which is normally placed just above the table, should describe concisely what the table represents.

Box Head. The box head contains the column headings, which should be brief but descriptive. Units of measurement, where necessary, should be either specified as part of the heading or enclosed in

Table number → Table 1.   Estimated Emissions from Electric Power ← Table title
Generation (tons per gigawatthour)

Box head {

Column headings

Fuel	Sulphur Dioxide	Nitrogen Oxides	Parti-culate Matter	Carbon Dioxide	Volatile Organic Compounds
Eastern coal	1.74	2.90	0.10	1,000	0.06
Western coal	0.81	2.20	0.06	1,039	0.09
Gas	0.003	0.57	0.02	640	0.05
Biomass	0.06	1.25	0.11	0*	0.61
Oil	0.51	0.63	0.02	840	0.03
Wind	0	0	0	0	0
Geothermal	0	0	0	0	0
Hydro	0	0	0	0	0
Solar	0	0	0	0	0
Nuclear	0	0	0	0	0

Stub ← | → Body

Rule →
Footnote → *Net emissions.
Source line → SOURCE: Department of Energy

FIGURE T–1. Elements of a Table

parentheses beneath the heading. Standard <u>abbreviations</u> and symbols are acceptable. Avoid vertical lettering whenever possible.

Stub.   The stub, the left vertical column of a table, lists the items about which information is given in the body of the table.

Body.   The body comprises the data below the column headings and to the right of the stub. Within the body, arrange columns so that the items to be compared appear in adjacent rows and columns. Align the numerical data in columns for ease of comparison, as shown in Figure T–1. Where no information exists for a specific item, substitute a row of dots or a dash to acknowledge the gap.

Rules.   Rules are the lines that separate the table into its various parts. Horizontal rules are placed below the title, below the body of the table, and between the column headings and the body of the table. Tables are usually open at the sides. The columns within the table may be separated by vertical rules only if such lines aid clarity.

Footnotes.   Footnotes are used for explanations of individual items in the table. Symbols (such as * and †) or lowercase letters (sometimes in parentheses) rather than numbers are ordinarily used to key table footnotes because numbers might be mistaken for numerical data or could be confused with the numbering system for text footnotes. See also <u>documenting sources</u>.

T

Source Line.   The source line identifies where the data originated. When a source line is appropriate, it appears below the table. Many organizations place the source line below the footnotes. See also <u>copyright</u> and <u>plagiarism</u>.

Continued Tables.   When a table must be divided so that it can be continued on another page, repeat the column headings and give the table number at the head of each new page with a "continued" label (for example, "Table 3, *continued*").

Informal Tables

To list relatively few items that would be easier for the reader to grasp in tabular form, you can use an informal table, as long as you introduce it properly. Although informal tables do not need titles or table numbers to identify them, they do require column headings that accurately describe the information listed, as shown in Figure T–2.

Dear Customer:
To order replacement parts, use the following part numbers and prices:

Part	Part Number	Price ($)
Diverter valve	2-912	12.50
Gasket kit	2-776	0.95
Adapter	3-212	0.90

FIGURE T–2. Informal Table

telegraphic style

Telegraphic style condenses writing by omitting <u>articles</u>, <u>pronouns</u>, <u>conjunctions</u>, and <u>transitions</u>. Although <u>conciseness</u> is important, especially in <u>instructions</u>, writers sometimes try to achieve conciseness by omitting necessary words. Telegraphic style forces <u>readers</u> to supply the missing words mentally, thus creating the potential for misunderstandings. Compare the following two passages and notice how much easier the revised version reads (the added words are italicized).

TELEGRAPHIC   Per 5/21 e-mail, 12 copies of instruction sheet and questionnaire attached. Report can be completed as soon as above materials received. July filling quickly so let's set date. Please advise.

CLEAR   *As I promised in my May 21* e-mail, attached *are*
               12 copies of *the* instruction sheet and *the* question-
               naire. *We can* complete *the* report as soon as *we*
               receive *the questionnaires. Our* July *calendar is* filling
               quickly, so *we should* set *a meeting* date soon. Please
               suggest a date when you return the questionnaire.

Telegraphic style can also produce <u>ambiguity</u>, as the following example demonstrates.

AMBIGUOUS   The director wants report written by New York office.
               [Does the director want a report that the New York
               office *wrote in the past,* or does the director want the
               New York office *to write a report in the future?*]

CLEAR   The director wants the report *that was* written by
               the New York office.

CLEAR   The director wants the report *to be* written by the
               New York office.

Although you may save yourself work by writing telegraphically, your
readers will have to work that much harder to decipher your meaning.

tenant / tenet

A *tenant* is one who holds or temporarily occupies a property owned by
another person. (The *tenant* was upset by the rent increase.) A *tenet* is
an opinion or principle held by a person, an organization, or a system.
(Competition is a central *tenet* of capitalism.)

tense

DIRECTORY
Past Tense   533   Future Tense   534
Past Perfect Tense   533   Future Perfect Tense   534
Present Tense   533   Shift in Tense   535
Present Perfect Tense   534

Tense is the grammatical term for <u>verb</u> forms that indicate time distinctions. The six tenses in English are past, past perfect, present, present
perfect, future, and future perfect. Each tense also has a corresponding
progressive form.

TENSE	BASIC FORM	PROGRESSIVE FORM
Past	I began	I was beginning
Past perfect	I had begun	I had been beginning
Present	I begin	I am beginning
Present perfect	I have begun	I have been beginning
Future	I will begin	I will be beginning
Future perfect	I will have begun	I will have been beginning

Perfect tenses allow you to express a prior action or condition that continues in a present, past, or future time.

PRESENT PERFECT   I *have begun* to write the annual report and will continue for the rest of the month.

PAST PERFECT   I *had begun* to read the manual when the lights went out.

FUTURE PERFECT   I *will have begun* this project by the time funds are allocated.

Progressive tenses allow you to describe some ongoing action or condition in the present, past, or future.

PRESENT PROGRESSIVE   I *am beginning* to be concerned that we will not meet the deadline.

PAST PROGRESSIVE   I *was beginning* to think we would not finish by the deadline.

FUTURE PROGRESSIVE   I *will be requesting* a leave of absence when this project is finished.

Past Tense

The simple past tense indicates that an action took place in its entirety in the past. The past tense is usually formed by adding -*d* or -*ed* to the root form of the verb. (We *closed* the office early yesterday.)

Past Perfect Tense

The past perfect tense (also called *pluperfect*) indicates that one past event preceded another. It is formed by combining the helping verb *had* with the past-participle form of the main verb. (He *had finished* by the time I arrived.)

Present Tense

The simple present tense represents action occurring in the present, without any indication of time duration. (I *ride* the train.)

A general truth is always expressed in the present tense. (He believes the saying "Time *heals* all wounds.") The present tense can be used to present actions or conditions that have no time restrictions. (Water *boils* at 212 degrees Fahrenheit.) Similarly, the present tense can be used to indicate habitual action. (I *pass* the coffee shop every day.) The present tense is also used for the "historical present," as in newspaper headlines (Dow Jones *Reaches* a High for the Year) or as in references to an author's opinion or a work's contents—even though it was written in the past.

- In *Post-Capitalist Society* (1993), Peter Drucker argues that the educated person will need "to live and work simultaneously in two cultures—that of the 'intellectual,' who focuses on words and ideas, and that of the 'manager,' who focuses on people and work" (215).

Present Perfect Tense

The present perfect tense describes something from the recent past that has a bearing on the present—a period of time before the present but after the simple past. The present perfect tense is formed by combining a form of the helping verb *have* with the past-participle form of the main verb. (We *have finished* the draft and can now revise it.)

Future Tense

The simple future tense indicates a time that will occur after the present. It uses the helping verb *will* (or *shall*) plus the main verb. (I *will finish* the job tomorrow.) Do not use the future tense needlessly; doing so merely adds complexity.

- This system ~~will be~~ *is* explained on page 3.

- When you press this button, the feeder ~~will move~~ *moves* the paper into position.

Future Perfect Tense

The future perfect tense indicates action that will have been completed at the time of or before another future action. It combines *will have* and the past participle of the main verb. (She *will have driven* 1,400 miles by the time she returns.)

Shift in Tense

Be consistent in your use of tense. The only legitimate shift in tense records a real change in time. Illogical shifts in tense will only confuse your <u>readers</u>.

met
- Before he visited the facility, the manager ~~meets~~ with the staff.

ESL TIPS FOR USING THE PROGRESSIVE FORM

The progressive form of the verb is composed of two features: a form of the helping verb *be* and the *-ing* form of the base verb.

PRESENT PROGRESSIVE	I *am updating* the Web site.
PAST PROGRESSIVE	I *was updating* the Web site last week.
FUTURE PROGRESSIVE	I *will be updating* the Web site regularly.

The present progressive is used in three ways:

1. To refer to an action that is in progress at the moment of speaking or writing:
   - The secretary *is taking* the meeting minutes.
2. To highlight that a state or an action is not permanent:
   - The office temp *is helping* us for a few weeks.
3. To express future plans:
   - The summer intern *is leaving* to return to school this Friday.

The past progressive is used to refer to a continuing action or condition in the past, usually with specified limits.

- I *was failing* calculus until I got a tutor.

The future progressive is used to refer to a continuous action or condition in the future.

- We *will be monitoring* his condition all night.

Verbs that express mental activity (*believe, know, see,* and so on) are generally not used in the progressive.

believe
- I ~~am believing~~ the defendant's testimony.

T

that / which / who

The word *that* is often overused and can foster wordiness.

* ~~I think that when~~ this project is finished ~~that~~ you should publish the results.

  (When ... , I think)

However, include *that* in a sentence if it avoids <u>ambiguity</u> or it improves the <u>pace</u>. See also <u>conciseness</u>.

* Some designers fail to appreciate the workers who operate equipment *that* constitute an important safety system.

Use *which*, not *that*, with nonrestrictive clauses (clauses that do not change the meaning of the basic sentence). See also <u>restrictive and nonrestrictive elements</u>.

NONRESTRICTIVE	After John left the law firm, *which* is the largest in the region, he started a private practice.
RESTRICTIVE	Companies *that* diversify usually succeed.

That and *which* should refer to animals and things; *who* should refer to people.

* Companies *that* fund basic research must not expect immediate results.

* The jet stream, *which* flows west to east, usually travels in excess of 67 miles per hour.

* Diane Stoltzfus, *who* retires tomorrow, worked 23 years for the company.

there / their / they're

There is an <u>expletive</u> (a word that fills the position of another word, phrase, or clause) or an <u>adverb</u>.

EXPLETIVE	*There* were more than 1,500 people at the conference.
ADVERB	More than 1,500 people were *there*.

Their is the <u>possessive case</u> form of *they*. (Managers should check *their* e-mail regularly.) *They're* is a <u>contraction</u> of *they are*. (Clients tell us *they're* pleased with our services.)

thesaurus

A thesaurus is a book or an electronic file of words and their <u>synonyms</u> and <u>antonyms</u>, arranged or retrievable by categories. Thoughtfully used, a thesaurus can help you with <u>word choice</u> during the <u>revision</u> phase of the writing process. However, the variety of words it offers may tempt you to choose an inappropriate word for the <u>context</u> or to use an obscure synonym just because it is available. Use a thesaurus only to clarify or refine your meaning, not to impress your <u>readers</u>. (See also <u>affectation</u>.) Never use a word unless you are sure of its meanings; its <u>connotations</u> might be unknown to you and could mislead your readers.

titles

Titles are important because many <u>readers</u> decide whether to read documents—such as <u>reports</u>, <u>e-mails</u>, and <u>newsletter articles</u>—based on their titles. This entry treats both creating titles and referring to them in your writing. For advice on labeling figures and tables, see <u>visuals</u>.

Reports and Long Documents

Titles for reports, <u>proposals</u>, articles, and similar documents should state the document's topic, reflect its <u>tone</u>, and indicate its <u>scope</u> and <u>purpose</u>, as in the following title of an academic article.

- "Using Chaos Theory to Evaluate Small Business Growth Management"

Such titles should be concise but not so short that they are not specific. For example, the title "Chaos Theory and Small Businesses" announces the topic and might be appropriate for a book, but it does not answer important questions that readers of an article would expect, such as "What does the article say about the relationship of chaos theory and small businesses?" and "What aspect of small businesses is related to chaos theory?"

Avoid titles with such redundancies as "Notes on," "Studies on," or "A Report on." However, works like <u>annual reports</u> or <u>feasibility reports</u> should be identified as such in the title because this information specifies the purpose and scope of the report. For titles of periodic or **progress reports**, indicate the dates in a subtitle ("Quarterly Report on Hospital Admission Rates: January–March 2006"). Avoid using **abbreviations**, chemical formulas, and the like in your title unless the work is addressed exclusively to specialists in the field. For multivolume publications, repeat the title on each volume and include the subtitle and number of each volume.

Titles do not use the sentence form, except for titles of articles in **newsletters** and magazines that ask a **rhetorical question**.

- "Is Online Learning Right for You?"

Memos and E-mails

Subject lines of **memos** and e-mails function as titles and should concisely describe the topic of the message. Such titles must be specific and accurate to aid in filing and later retrieval.

VAGUE	Subject: Tuition Reimbursement
SPECIFIC	Subject: Tuition Reimbursement for Time-Management Seminar

Recipients often use subject-line titles to prioritize and file their incoming messages. Although the title in the subject line announces your topic, you should still begin the memo or e-mail with an opening that provides **context** for the message.

Formatting Titles

Capitalization.   Capitalize the initial letters of the first and last words of a title as well as all major words in the title. Do not capitalize articles (*a, an, the*), coordinating conjunctions (*and, but*), or short prepositions (*at, in, on, of*) unless they begin or end the title (*The Lives of a Cell*). Capitalize prepositions in titles if they contain more than four letters (*Between, Because, Until, After*).

Italics.   Use **italics** or underlining when referring to titles of separately published works, such as books, periodicals, newspapers, pamphlets, brochures, legal cases, movies, and television programs.

- *Turning Workplace Conflict into Collaboration* by Joyce Richards was reviewed in the *New York Times.* [book, newspaper]

Abbreviations of such titles are italicized if their spelled-out forms would be italicized.

- The *NYT* is one of the nation's oldest newspapers.

Italicize the titles of compact discs, videotapes, plays, long poems, paintings, sculptures, and long musical works.

CD-ROM	*Computer Security Tutorial on CD-ROM*
PLAY	Arthur Miller's *Death of a Salesman*
LONG POEM	T. S. Eliot's *The Wasteland*
PAINTING	M. C. Escher's *Drawing Hands*
SCULPTURE	Auguste Rodin's *The Thinker*
MUSICAL WORK	Gershwin's *Porgy and Bess*

Quotation Marks.   Use <u>quotation marks</u> when referring to parts of publications, such as chapters of books and articles or sections within periodicals.

* His report, "Effects of Government Regulations on Motorcycle Safety," cited the article "No-Fault Insurance and Motorcycles" published in *American Motorcyclist* magazine.

Titles of reports, essays, short poems, short musical works (including songs), short stories, and single episodes of radio and television programs are also enclosed in quotation marks.

REPORT	"Analysis of Ethics Cases at CGE Corporation"
ESSAY	Ralph Waldo Emerson's "The American Scholar"
SHORT POEM	Robert Frost's "The Road Not Taken"
SONG	Bob Dylan's "Like a Rolling Stone"
SHORT STORY	Nathaniel Hawthorne's "The Birthmark"
TV PROGRAM	"In Depth: Jacques Barzun" on C-Span [episode of *In Depth*]

Special Cases.   Some titles, by convention, are not set off by quotation marks, underlining, or italics. Such titles follow standard practice for capitalization.

* Business Communication [college course title], Amazon.com, Old Testament, Magna Carta, the Constitution, Lincoln's Gettysburg Address, the Lands' End Catalog

T

to / too / two

To, too, and *two* are confused only because they sound alike. *To* is used as a <u>preposition</u> or to mark an infinitive. See <u>verbs</u>.

- Send the report *to* the district manager. [preposition]
- I do not wish *to* attend. [mark of the infinitive]

Too is an <u>adverb</u> meaning "excessively" or "also."

- The price was *too* high. [excessively]
- I, *too*, thought it was high. [also]

Two is a number (*two* buildings, *two* concepts).

tone

Tone is the attitude a writer expresses toward the subject and his or her <u>readers</u>. In workplace writing, tone may range widely—depending on the <u>purpose</u>, situation, <u>context</u>, <u>audience</u>, and even the medium of a communication. For example, in an <u>e-mail</u> message to be read only by an associate who is also a friend, your tone might be casual.

- Your proposal to Smith and Kline is super. We'll just need to hammer out the schedule. If we get the contract, I owe you lunch!

In a <u>memo</u> to your manager or superior, however, your tone might be more formal and respectful.

- I think your proposal to Smith and Kline is excellent. I have marked a couple of places where I'm concerned that we are committing ourselves to a schedule that we might not be able to keep. If I can help in any other way, please let me know.

In a message that serves as a <u>report</u> to numerous readers, the tone would be professional, without the more personal <u>style</u> that you would use with an individual reader.

- The Smith and Kline proposal appears complete and thorough, based on our department's evaluation. Several small revisions, however, would ensure that the company is not committing itself to an unrealistic schedule. These revisions are marked on the copy of the report attached to this message.

The <u>word choice</u>, the <u>introduction</u>, and even the <u>title</u> contribute to the overall tone of your document. For instance, a title such as "Ecological Consequences of Diminishing Water Resources in California" clearly sets a different tone from "What Happens When We've Drained California Dry?" The first title would be appropriate for a report; the second title would be appropriate for a popular magazine or <u>newsletter article</u>. See also <u>correspondence</u>.

transition

Transition is the means of achieving a smooth flow of ideas from sentence to sentence, **paragraph** to paragraph, and subject to subject. Transition is a two-way indicator of what has been said and what will be said; it provides **readers** with guideposts for linking ideas and clarifying the relationship between them.

Transition can be obvious.

- *Having considered* the benefits of a new facility, *we move next* to the question of adequate staffing.

Transition can be subtle.

- *Even if* this facility can be built at a reasonable cost, there *still remains* the problem of adequate staffing.

Either way, you now have your readers' attention fastened on the problem of adequate staffing, exactly what you set out to do.

Methods of Transition

Transition can be achieved in many ways: (1) using transitional words and phrases, (2) repeating keywords or key ideas, (3) using **pronouns** with clear antecedents, (4) using enumeration (1, 2, 3, or first, second, third), (5) summarizing a previous paragraph, (6) asking a question, and (7) using a transitional paragraph.

Certain words and phrases are inherently transitional. Consider the following terms and their functions:

FUNCTION	TERMS
Result	*therefore, as a result, consequently, thus, hence*
Example	*for example, for instance, specifically, as an illustration*
Comparison	*similarly, likewise, in comparison*
Contrast	*but, yet, still, however, nevertheless, on the other hand*
Addition	*moreover, furthermore, also, too, besides, in addition*
Time	*now, later, meanwhile, since then, after that, before that time*
Sequence	*first, second, third, initially, then, next, finally*

Within a paragraph, such transitional expressions clarify and smooth the movement from idea to idea. Conversely, the lack of transitional devices can make for disjointed reading. See also **telegraphic style**.

Transition Between Sentences

You can achieve effective transition between sentences by repeating keywords or key ideas from preceding sentences and by using pronouns that refer to antecedents in previous sentences. Consider the following short paragraph, which uses both of those means.

- Representative of many American university towns is Middletown. *This midwestern town,* formerly *a sleepy farming community,* is today the home of a large and vibrant *academic community.* Attracting students from all over the Midwest, *this university town* has grown very rapidly in the last ten years.

Enumeration is another device for achieving transition.

- The recommendation rests on *two conditions. First,* the department staff must be expanded to handle the increased workload. *Second,* sufficient time must be provided for training the new staff.

Transition Between Paragraphs

The means discussed so far for achieving transition between sentences can also be effective for achieving transition between paragraphs. For paragraphs, however, longer transitional elements are often required. One technique is to use an opening sentence that summarizes the preceding paragraph and then moves on to a new paragraph.

- One property of material considered for manufacturing processes is hardness. Hardness is the internal resistance of the material to the forcing apart or closing together of its molecules. Another property is ductility, the characteristic of material that permits it to be drawn into a wire. Material also may possess malleability, the property that makes it capable of being rolled or hammered into thin sheets of various shapes. Purchasing managers must consider these properties before selecting manufacturing materials for use in production.

  The requirements of hardness, ductility, and malleability account for the high cost of such materials. . . .

Another technique is to ask a question at the end of one paragraph and answer it at the beginning of the next.

- New technology has always been feared because it has at times displaced some jobs. However, it invariably creates many more jobs than it eliminates. Almost always, the jobs eliminated by techno-

logical advances have been menial, unskilled jobs, and workers who have been displaced have been forced to increase their skills, which resulted in better and higher-paying jobs for them. *In view of these facts, is new technology really bad?*
　　Certainly technology has given us unparalleled access to information and created many new roles for employees. . . .

A purely transitional paragraph may be inserted to aid readability.

- The problem of poor management was a key factor that has caused the weak performance of the company.
  Two other setbacks to the company's fortunes also marked the company's decline: the loss of many skilled workers through the early retirement program and the intensification of the rate of employee turnover.
  The early retirement program caused the failure . . .

If you provide logical **organization** and have prepared an outline, your transitional needs will easily be satisfied and your writing will have **unity** and **coherence**. During **revision**, look for places where transition is missing and add it. Look for places where it is weak and strengthen it.

trip reports

A trip report provides a permanent record of a business trip and its accomplishments. It provides managers with essential information about the results of the trip and can enable many employees to benefit from the information. See also **reports**.
　　A trip report is normally written as a **memo** or an **e-mail** and addressed to an immediate superior, as shown in Figure T–3 on page 544. The subject line identifies the destination and dates of the trip. The body of the report explains why you made the trip, whom you visited, and what you accomplished. The report should devote a brief section to each major event and may include a **heading** for each section. You need not give equal space to each event—instead, elaborate on the more important events. Follow the body of the report with the appropriate **conclusions** and recommendations. Finally, if required, attach a record of expenses to the trip report.

T

From: James D. Kerson <jdkerson@psys.com>
To: Roberto Camacho <rcamacho@psys.com>
Sent: Fri, 14 Jan 2005 12:16:30 EST
Subject: Trip to Smith Electric Co., Huntington, West Virginia,
            January 2005

Attachments: 📄 Expense Report.xls (25 KB)

I visited the Smith Electric Company in Huntington, West Virginia, to determine the cause of a recurring failure in a Model 247 printer and to fix it.

Problem
The printer stopped printing periodically for no apparent reason. Repeated efforts to bring it back online eventually succeeded, but the problem recurred at irregular intervals. Neither customer personnel operating the printer nor the local maintenance specialist was able to solve the problem.

Action
On January 3, I met with Ms. Ruth Bernardi, the Office Manager, who explained the problem. My troubleshooting did not reveal the cause of the problem then or on January 4.

Only when I tested the logic cable did I find that it contained a broken wire. I replaced the logic cable and then ran all the normal printer test patterns to make sure no other problems existed. All patterns were positive, so I turned the printer over to the customer.

Conclusion
There are over 12,000 of these printers in the field, and to my knowledge this is the first occurrence of a bad cable. Therefore, I do not believe the logic cable problem found at Smith Electric Company warrants further investigation.

```
==================================
```
James D. Kerson, Maintenance Specialist
Printer Systems, Inc.
1366 Federal St., Allentown, PA 18101
(610) 747-9955 Fax: (610) 747-9956
jdkerson@psys.com
www.psys.com
```
==================================
```

FIGURE T–3. **Trip Report Sent as E-mail (with Attachment)**

trite language (*see* clichés)

T

trouble reports

The trouble report is used to analyze such events as accidents, equipment failures, or health emergencies. For example, the report shown in Figure T–4 describes an accident involving personal injury. The report assesses the causes of the problem and suggests changes necessary to prevent its recurrence. Because it is usually an internal document, the trouble report normally follows a **memo** format. See also **reports**.

In the subject line of the memo, state the precise problem you are reporting. Then, in the body of the report, provide a detailed, precise description of the problem. What happened? Where and when did the problem occur? Was anybody hurt? Was there any property damage? Was there a work stoppage?

⚡ ETHICS NOTE Because insurance claims, workers' compensation awards, and even lawsuits may hinge on the information contained in a trouble report, be sure to include precise times, dates, locations, treatment of injuries, names of any witnesses, and any other crucial information. (Notice the careful use of language and factual detail in Figure T–4.) Be thorough and accurate in your analysis of the problem and support any judgments or conclusions with facts. Be objective: Always use a neutral **tone** and avoid assigning blame. If you speculate about the cause of the problem, make it clear to your **reader** that you are speculating. See also **ethics in writing**. ✦

Consolidated Energy, Inc.

To: Marvin Lundquist, Vice President
          Administrative Services
From: Kalo Katarlan, Safety Officer   *KK*
          Field Service Operations
Date: August 19, 2005
Subject: Field Service Employee Accident on August 5, 2005

The following is an initial report of an accident on Friday, August 5, 2005, involving John Markley that resulted in two days of lost time.

Accident Summary
John Markley stopped by a rewiring job on German Road. Chico Ruiz was working there, stringing new wire, and John was checking with Chico about the materials he wanted for framing a pole. Some tree trimming had been done in the area, and John offered to help remove some of the debris by loading it into the pickup truck he was driving. While John was loading branches into the bed of the truck, a piece broke off in his right hand and struck his right eye.

Accident Details
1. John's right eye was struck by a piece of tree branch. John had just undergone laser surgery on his right eye on Wednesday, August 3, to reattach his retina.
2. John immediately covered his right eye with his hand, and Chico Ruiz gave him a paper towel with ice to cover his eye and help ease the pain.

FIGURE T–4. Trouble Report

7. On Thursday, August 11, John returned to his eye surgeon. Although bruised, his eye was not damaged, and the surgically reattached retina was still in place.

Recommendations

To prevent a recurrence of such an accident, the Safety Department will require the following actions in the future:

- When working around and moving debris such as tree limbs or branches, all service crew employees must wear safety eyewear with side shields.
- All service crew employees must always consider the possibility of shock for an injured employee. If crew members cannot leave the job site to care for the injured employee, someone on the crew must call for assistance from the Service Center. The Service Center phone number is printed in each service crew member's handbook.

FIGURE T–4. Trouble Report (*continued*)

In your **conclusion**, state what has been or will be done to correct the conditions that led to the problem. That may include training in safety practices, improved equipment, protective clothing, and so on.

try to

The phrase *try and* is colloquial for *try to.* For business writing, use *try to.*

- Please try ~~and~~ finish the report on time.
  ^*to*

T

U

unity

Unity is singleness of **purpose** and treatment; a unified **paragraph** or document has a central idea and does not digress into unrelated topics.

The logical sequence provided through **outlining** is essential to achieving unity. An outline enables you to lay out the most direct route from **introduction** to **conclusion,** and it enables you to build each paragraph around a topic sentence that expresses a single idea.

Effective **transition** helps build unity, as well as **coherence,** because transitional terms clarify the relationship of each part to what precedes it.

up

Adding the word *up* to **verbs** often creates a redundant phrase. See also **conciseness.**

- He quickly wrote up the report.

usage

Usage describes the choices we make among the various words and expressions available in our language. The lines between standard English and nonstandard English and between formal and informal English are determined by those choices. Your guideline in any situation requiring such choices should be appropriateness: Is the word or expression you use appropriate to your **readers** and your subject? When it is, you are practicing good usage.

This book contains many entries that focus on various usages. For a complete list of the usage entries, which appear in italics throughout the book, see "Commonly Misused Words and Phrases." An up-to-date **dictionary** is also an invaluable aid in your selection of the right word.

U

> ⊛ WEB LINK ONLINE USAGE AND STYLE GUIDES
>
> Bartleby.com provides classic reference books online, including the *American Heritage Book of English Usage*. For this and additional useful links, see *<bedfordstmartins.com/alredbus>* and select *Links for Handbook Entries*.

utilize

Do not use *utilize* as a long variant of *use*, which is the general word for "employ for some purpose." *Use* will almost always be clearer and less pretentious. See <u>affectation</u>.

U

V

vague words

A vague word is one that is imprecise in the context in which it is used. Some words encompass such a broad range of meanings that there is no focus for their definition. Words such as *real, nice, important, good, bad, contact, thing,* and *fine* are often called *omnibus words* because they can have so many meanings and interpretations. In speech, our vocal inflections help make the meanings of such words clear. Because you cannot rely on vocal inflections when you are writing, avoid using vague words. Be concrete and specific. See also abstract/concrete words and word choice.

VAGUE   It was a *good* meeting. [Why was it good?]

SPECIFIC   The meeting resolved three questions: pay scales, fringe benefits, and workloads.

verbals

Verbals are derived from verbs but function as nouns, adjectives, and adverbs. The three types of verbals are gerunds, infinitives, and participles.

Gerunds

A gerund is a verbal ending in *-ing* that is used as a noun. A gerund can be used as a subject, a direct object, the object of a preposition, a subjective complement, or an appositive.

- *Estimating* is an important managerial skill. [subject]

- I find *estimating* difficult. [direct object]

- We were unprepared for their *coming*. [object of preposition]

- Seeing is *believing*. [subjective complement]

- My primary departmental function, *programming*, occupies about two-thirds of my time on the job. [appositive]

Only the possessive form of a noun or <u>pronoun</u> should precede a gerund.

- *John's* working has not affected his grades.
- *His* working has not affected his grades.

Infinitives

An infinitive is the bare, or uninflected, form of a verb (for example, *go, run, fall, talk, dress, shout*) without the restrictions imposed by <u>person</u> and <u>number</u>. Along with the gerund and the participle, it is one of the nonfinite verb forms. The infinitive is generally preceded by the word *to*, which, although not an inherent part of the infinitive, is considered to be the sign of an infinitive. An infinitive is a verbal and can function as a noun, an adjective, or an adverb.

- *To expand* is not the only objective. [noun]
- These are the instructions *to follow*. [adjective]
- The company struggled *to survive*. [adverb]

The infinitive can reflect two <u>tenses</u>: the present and (with a helping verb) the present perfect.

- to go [present tense]
- to have gone [present perfect tense]

The most common mistake made with infinitives is using the present perfect tense when the simple present tense is sufficient.

- I should not have tried to ~~have~~ go~~gone~~ so early.

Infinitives formed with the root form of transitive verbs can express both active and (with a helping verb) passive <u>voice</u>.

- to hit [present tense, active voice]
- to have hit [present perfect tense, active voice]
- to be hit [present tense, passive voice]
- to have been hit [present perfect tense, passive voice]

A split infinitive is one in which an adverb is placed between the sign of the infinitive, *to*, and the infinitive itself. Because they make up a grammatical unit, the infinitive and its sign are better left intact than separated by an intervening adverb.

V

- To ~~initially~~ build the table in the file, you could input transaction records containing the data necessary to construct the record and table.

However, it may occasionally be better to split an infinitive than to allow a sentence to become awkward, ambiguous, or incoherent.

AMBIGUOUS	She agreed immediately *to deliver* the toxic materials. [This sentence could be interpreted to mean that she agreed immediately.]
CLEAR	She agreed *to* immediately *deliver* the toxic materials. [This sentence is no longer ambiguous.]

Participles

A participle is a verb form that functions as an adjective. Present participles end in *-ing*.

- *Declining* sales forced us to close one branch office.

Past participles end in *-ed, -t, -en, -n,* or *-d.*

- What are the *estimated* costs?
- Repair the *bent* lever.
- Return the *broken* part.
- What are the metal's *known* properties?
- The story, *told* many times before, was still interesting.

The perfect participle is formed with the present participle of the helping verb *have* plus the past participle of the main verb.

- *Having gotten* [perfect participle] a large bonus, the *smiling* [present participle], *contented* [past participle] sales representative worked harder than ever.

A participle cannot be used as the verb of a sentence. Inexperienced writers sometimes make that mistake, and the result is a **sentence fragment**.

- The committee chairperson was responsible. ~~His~~ , *his* vote being the decisive one.

- The committee chairperson was responsible. His vote *was* being the decisive one.

For information on participial and infinitive phrases, see **phrases**.

V

verbs

DIRECTORY
Types of Verbs   552
Forms of Verbs   553
   Finite Verbs   553
   Nonfinite Verbs   553
Properties of Verbs   553
Conjugation of Verbs   555

A verb is a word or group of words that describes an action (The copier *jammed* at the beginning of the job), states how something or someone is affected by an action (He *was disappointed* that the proposal was rejected), or affirms a state of existence (She *is* a district manager now).

Types of Verbs

Verbs are either transitive or intransitive. A *transitive verb* requires a direct <u>object</u> to complete its meaning.

- They *laid* the foundation on October 24.
  [*Foundation* is the direct object of the transitive verb *laid.*]

- Rosalie Anderson *wrote* the treasurer a letter.
  [*Letter* is the direct object of the transitive verb *wrote.*]

An *intransitive verb* does not require an object to complete its meaning. It makes a full assertion about the subject without assistance (although it may have <u>modifiers</u>).

- The engine *ran.*
- The engine *ran* smoothly and quietly.

A *linking verb* is an intransitive verb that links a <u>complement</u> to the subject.

- The carpet *is* stained.
  [*Is* is a linking verb; *stained* is a subjective complement.]

Some intransitive verbs, such as *be, become, seem,* and *appear,* are almost always linking verbs. A number of others, such as *look, sound, taste, smell,* and *feel,* can function as either linking verbs or simple intransitive verbs. If you are unsure about whether one of those verbs is a linking verb, try substituting *seem;* if the sentence still makes sense, the verb is probably a linking verb.

V

- Their antennae *feel* delicate.
  [*Seem* can be substituted for *feel*—thus *feel* is a linking verb.]

- Their antennae *feel* delicately for their prey.
  [*Seem* cannot be substituted for *feel*; in this case, *feel* is a simple intransitive verb.]

Forms of Verbs

Verbs are described as being either finite or nonfinite.

Finite Verbs.   A finite verb is the main verb of a <u>clause</u> or sentence. It makes an assertion about its subject and often serves as the only verb in its clause or sentence. (The telephone *rang*, and the receptionist *answered* it.) See also <u>sentence construction</u>.

A helping verb (sometimes called an *auxiliary verb*) is used in a verb <u>phrase</u> to help indicate <u>mood</u>, <u>tense</u>, and <u>voice</u>. (The phone *had* rung.) Phrases that function as helping verbs are often made up of combinations with the sign of the infinitive, *to* (for example, *am going to*, *is about to*, *has to*, and *ought to*). The helping verb always precedes the main verb, although other words may intervene. (Machines *will* never completely *replace* people.)

Nonfinite Verbs.   Nonfinite verbs are <u>verbals</u>—verb forms that function as <u>nouns</u>, <u>adjectives</u>, or <u>adverbs</u>.

A *gerund* is a noun that is derived from the *-ing* form of a verb. (*Seeing* is *believing*.) An *infinitive*, which uses the root form of a verb (usually preceded by *to*), can function as a noun, an adverb, or an adjective.

- He hates *to complain*. [noun, direct object of *hates*]
- The valve closes *to stop* the flow. [adverb, modifies *closes*]
- This is the proposal *to consider*. [adjective, modifies *proposal*]

A *participle* is a verb form that can function as an adjective.

- The *rejected* proposal was ours.
  [*Rejected* is a verb form that is used as an adjective modifying *proposal*.]

Properties of Verbs

Verbs must (1) agree in <u>person</u> with personal pronouns functioning as subjects, (2) agree in tense and <u>number</u> with their subjects, and (3) be in the appropriate voice.

ⓔ TIPS FOR AVOIDING SHIFTS IN VOICE, MOOD, OR TENSE

To achieve clarity in your writing, you must maintain consistency and avoid shifts. A shift is an abrupt change in voice, mood, or tense. Pay special attention when you edit your writing to check for the following types of shifts.

VOICE

> *he does not permit*
- The captain permits his crew to go ashore, but ~~they are not~~
  them
  ~~permitted~~ to go downtown.
  [The entire sentence is now in the active voice.]

MOOD

- Reboot your computer,/ and ~~you should~~ empty the cache.
  [The entire sentence is now in the imperative mood.]

TENSE

> *fell*
- I was working quickly, and suddenly a box ~~falls~~ off the conveyor
  broke
  belt and ~~breaks~~ my foot.
  [The entire sentence is now in the past tense.]

Person is the term for the form of a personal pronoun that indicates whether the pronoun refers to the speaker, the person spoken to, or the person (or thing) spoken about. Verbs change their forms to agree in person with their subjects.

- I *see* [first person] a yellow tint, but she *sees* [third person] a yellow-green hue.

Tense refers to verb forms that indicate time distinctions. The six tenses are past, past perfect, present, present perfect, future, and future perfect.

Number refers to the two forms of a verb that indicate whether the subject of a verb is singular (The copier *was* repaired) or plural (The copiers *were* repaired).

Most verbs show the singular of the present tense by adding *-s* or *-es* (he *stands*, she *works*, it *goes*), and they show the plural without *-s* or *-es* (they *stand*, we *work*, they *go*). The verb *to be*, however, normally changes form to indicate the singular (I *am* ready) or plural (We *are* ready).

V

Voice refers to the two forms of a verb that indicate whether the subject of the verb acts or receives the action. The verb is in the *active voice* if the subject of the verb acts (The bacteria *grow*); the verb is in the passive voice if it receives the action (The bacteria *are grown* in a petri dish).

Conjugation of Verbs

The conjugation of a verb arranges all forms of the verb so that the differences caused by the changing of the tense, number, person, and voice are readily apparent. Figure V–1 shows the conjugation of the verb *drive*.

TENSE	NUMBER	PERSON	ACTIVE VOICE	PASSIVE VOICE
Present	Singular	1st	I drive	I am driven
		2nd	You drive	You are driven
		3rd	He/she drives	He/she is driven
	Plural	1st	We drive	We are driven
		2nd	You drive	You are driven
		3rd	They drive	They are driven
Present progressive	Singular	1st	I am driving	I am being driven
		2nd	You are driving	You are being driven
		3rd	He/she is driving	He/she is being driven
	Plural	1st	We are driving	We are being driven
		2nd	You are driving	You are being driven
		3rd	They are driving	They are being driven
Present perfect	Singular	1st	I have driven	I have been driven
		2nd	You have driven	You have been driven
		3rd	He/she has driven	He/she has been driven
	Plural	1st	We have driven	We have been driven
		2nd	You have driven	You have been driven
		3rd	They have driven	They have been driven
Present perfect progressive	Singular	1st	I have been driving	I have been being driven
		2nd	You have been driving	You have been being driven
		3rd	He/she has been driving	He/she has been being driven
	Plural	1st	We have been driving	We have been being driven
		2nd	You have been driving	You have been being driven
		3rd	They have been driving	They have been being driven

V

FIGURE V–1. Verb-Conjugation Chart (*continued on next page*)

TENSE	NUMBER	PERSON	ACTIVE VOICE	PASSIVE VOICE
Past	Singular	1st	I drove	I was driven
		2nd	You drove	You were driven
		3rd	He/she drove	He/she was driven
	Plural	1st	We drove	We were driven
		2nd	You drove	You were driven
		3rd	They drove	They were driven
Past progressive	Singular	1st	I was driving	I was being driven
		2nd	You were driving	You were being driven
		3rd	He/she was driving	He/she was being driven
	Plural	1st	We were driving	We were being driven
		2nd	You were driving	You were being driven
		3rd	They were driving	They were being driven
Past perfect	Singular	1st	I had driven	I had been driven
		2nd	You had driven	You had been driven
		3rd	He/she had driven	He/she had been driven
	Plural	1st	We had driven	We had been driven
		2nd	You had driven	You had been driven
		3rd	They had driven	They had been driven
Past perfect progressive	Singular	1st	I had been driving	I had been being driven
		2nd	You had been driving	You had been being driven
		3rd	He/she had been driving	He/she had been being driven
	Plural	1st	We had been driving	We had been being driven
		2nd	You had been driving	You had been being driven
		3rd	They had been driving	They had been being driven
Future	Singular	1st	I will drive	I will be driven
		2nd	You will drive	You will be driven
		3rd	He/she will drive	He/she will be driven
	Plural	1st	We will drive	We will be driven
		2nd	You will drive	You will be driven
		3rd	They will drive	They will be driven
Future progressive	Singular	1st	I will be driving	I will be being driven
		2nd	You will be driving	You will be being driven
		3rd	He/she will be driving	He/she will be being driven
	Plural	1st	We will be driving	We will be being driven
		2nd	You will be driving	You will be being driven
		3rd	They will be driving	They will be being driven

FIGURE V–1. Verb-Conjugation Chart (*continued*)

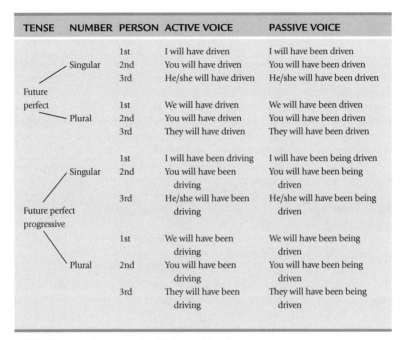

TENSE	NUMBER	PERSON	ACTIVE VOICE	PASSIVE VOICE
Future perfect	Singular	1st	I will have driven	I will have been driven
		2nd	You will have driven	You will have been driven
		3rd	He/she will have driven	He/she will have been driven
	Plural	1st	We will have driven	We will have been driven
		2nd	You will have driven	You will have been driven
		3rd	They will have driven	They will have been driven
Future perfect progressive	Singular	1st	I will have been driving	I will have been being driven
		2nd	You will have been driving	You will have been being driven
		3rd	He/she will have been driving	He/she will have been being driven
	Plural	1st	We will have been driving	We will have been being driven
		2nd	You will have been driving	You will have been being driven
		3rd	They will have been driving	They will have been being driven

FIGURE V–1. Verb-Conjugation Chart (*continued*)

very

The temptation to overuse **intensifiers** like *very* is great. In many sentences, the word can simply be deleted.

- The board was ~~very~~ angry about the newspaper report.

When you do use intensifiers, clarify their meaning. (Retail sales were *very* strong; they were up 43 percent this month.)

via

Via is Latin for "by way of." The term should be used only in routing instructions.

- The package was shipped *via* FedEx.
- Her project was funded ~~via~~ *as a result of* the recent legislation.

visuals

Visuals can express ideas or convey information in ways that words alone cannot by making abstract concepts and relationships concrete. Visuals can show how things look (drawings, photographs, maps), represent numbers and quantities (graphs, tables), depict relationships (flowcharts, schematic diagrams), and show hierarchical relationships (organizational charts). They also highlight important information and emphasize key concepts succinctly and clearly.

Many of the qualities of good writing—simplicity, clarity, conciseness, directness—are equally important in the creation and use of visuals. Presented with clarity and consistency, visuals can help **readers** focus on key portions of your document, presentation, or Web site. Be aware, though, that even the best visual will not be effective without **context**—and most often context is provided by the text that introduces the visual and clarifies its purpose.

The following entries in this book are related to specific visuals and their use in printed and online documents, as well as in **presentations** (see that entry for presentation graphics).

drawings   172
flowcharts   206
formal reports   211
global graphics   248
graphs   253
layout and design   305

maps   319
organizational charts   364
photographs   382
tables   529
Web design   566
writing for the Web   577

Selecting Visuals

Consider your **audience** and your **purpose** carefully in selecting visuals. You would need different illustrations for an automobile owner's manual or an auto dealer's Web site, for example, than you would for a mechanic's diagnostic guide. Figure V–2 can help you select the most appropriate visuals, based on their purposes and special features. Jot down visual options when you are considering your **scope** and **organization**.

◆ ETHICS NOTE Be aware that visuals have the potential of misleading readers when data are selectively omitted or distorted. For example, Figure G–7 on page 254 shows a graph that gives a misleading impression of investment returns because the scale is compressed with some of the years selectively omitted. Visuals that mislead readers at the least call the credibility of you and your organization into question—and they are unethical. The use of misleading visuals can even subject you and your organization to lawsuits. ✦

CHOOSING APPROPRIATE VISUALS

TO SHOW OBJECTS AND SPATIAL RELATIONSHIPS

DRAWINGS CAN . . .

- Depict real objects difficult to photograph
- Depict imaginary objects
- Highlight only parts viewers need to see
- Show internal parts of equipment in cutaway views
- Show how equipment parts fit together in exploded views

PHOTOGRAPHS CAN . . .

- Show actual physical images of subjects
- Record an event in process
- Record the development of phenomena over time
- Record the as-found condition of a situation for an investigation

TO DISPLAY GEOGRAPHIC INFORMATION

MAPS CAN . . .

- Show specific geographic features of an area
- Show distance, routes, or locations of sites
- Show the geographic distribution of information (e.g., populations by region)

TO SHOW NUMERICAL AND OTHER RELATIONSHIPS

TABLES CAN . . .

Divisions	Employees
Research	1,052
Marketing	2,782
Automotive	13,251
Consumer Products	2,227

- Organize information systematically in rows and columns
- Present large numerical quantities concisely
- Facilitate item-to-item comparisons
- Clarify trends and other graphical information with precise data

BAR & COLUMN GRAPHS CAN . . .

- Depict data in vertical bars and horizontal columns for comparison
- Show quantities that make up a whole
- Visually represent data shown in tables

FIGURE V–2. Chart for Choosing Appropriate Visuals (*continued on next page*)

V

LINE GRAPHS CAN . . .	• Show trends over time in amounts, sizes, rates, and other measurements • Give an at-a-glance impression of trends, forecasts, and extrapolations of data • Compare more than one kind of data over the same time period • Visually represent data shown in tables
PICTURE GRAPHS CAN . . .	• Use recognizable images to represent specific quantities • Help nonexpert readers grasp the information • Visually represent data shown in tables
PIE GRAPHS CAN . . .	• Show quantities that make up a whole • Give an immediate visual impression of the parts and their significance • Visually represent data shown in tables or lists

TO SHOW STEPS IN A PROCESS OR RELATIONSHIPS IN A SYSTEM

FLOWCHARTS CAN . . .	• Show how the parts or steps in a process or system interact • Show the stages of an actual or a hypothetical process in the correct direction, including recursive steps

TO SHOW RELATIONSHIPS IN A HIERARCHY

ORGANIZATION CHARTS CAN . . .	• Give an overview of an organization's departmental components • Show how the components relate to one another • Depict lines of authority within an organization

TO SUPPLEMENT OR REPLACE WORDS

SYMBOLS OR ICONS CAN . . .	• Convey ideas without words • Save space and add visual appeal • Transcend individual languages to communicate ideas effectively for international readers

FIGURE V–2. Chart for Choosing Appropriate Visuals (*continued*)

Integrating Visuals with Text

Consider the best locations for visuals before you begin <u>writing a draft</u>. Your goal should be to use visuals where they will best advance your purpose, aid your readers, and integrate smoothly within your text. One way to use visuals wisely is to make their placement a part of your <u>outlining</u> process. At appropriate points in your outline, either make a rough sketch of the visual, if you can, or write "illustration of . . . ," noting the source of the visual and enclosing each suggestion in a text box.

When you write the draft, place visuals as close as possible to the text where they are discussed—in fact, no visual should precede its first text mention. Clarify for readers why each visual is included in the text. The amount of description you should provide will vary, depending on your readers' backgrounds. For example, nonexperts may require lengthier explanations than do experts.

Give each visual a concise <u>title</u> that clearly describes its content. Assign figure and table numbers, particularly if your document contains more than one illustration or table. Then refer to visuals in the text of your document by their figure or table numbers. Refer to graphical illustrations (such as drawings, maps, and photographs) as "figures" and to tables as "tables."

🔲 ETHICS NOTE Obtain written permission to use copyrighted visuals—including images and multimedia material from Web sites—and acknowledge borrowed material in a source line below the caption for a figure and in a footnote at the bottom of a table. Use a site's "Contact Us" page to request approval. Acknowledge your use of any public (uncopyrighted) information, such as demographic or economic data from government publications and Web sites, with a source line. See also <u>copyright</u>, <u>documenting sources</u>, and <u>plagiarism</u>. ✦

Writer's Checklist: Creating and Integrating Visuals

CREATING VISUALS

- ☑ Keep visuals simple: Include only information needed for discussion in the text and eliminate unneeded labels, arrows, boxes, and lines.
- ☑ Position the lettering of any explanatory text or labels horizontally; allow adequate white space within and around the visual.
- ☑ Specify the units of measurement used, make sure relative sizes are clear, and indicate distance with a scale, when appropriate.
- ☑ Use consistent terminology; for example, do not refer to a "proportion" in the text and a "percentage" in the visual.
- ☑ Define <u>abbreviations</u> the first time they appear in the text and in figures and tables. If any symbols are not self-explanatory, include a key.

V

Writer's Checklist: Creating and Integrating Visuals (continued)

☑ Give each visual a concise **title** that clearly describes its content, and assign figure and table numbers if your document contains more than one illustration or table.

INTEGRATING VISUALS

☑ Clarify for readers why each visual is included in the text and provide an appropriate description.

☑ Place visuals as close as possible to the text where they are discussed, but after their first text mention.

☑ Refer to visuals in the text of your document as "figures" or "tables" and by their figure or table numbers.

☑ Consider placing lengthy, detailed visuals in an **appendix** and refer to it in the text.

☑ In documents with more than five illustrations or tables, include a section following the **table of contents** titled "List of Figures" or "List of Tables" that identifies each by number, title, and page number.

☑ Check the editorial guidelines or recommended style manual when preparing visuals for a publication.

voice

In grammar, *voice* indicates the relation of the subject to the action of the **verb**. When the verb is in the *active voice*, the subject acts; when it is in the *passive voice*, the subject is acted upon.

ACTIVE   David Cohen *wrote* the newsletter article.
           [The subject, *David Cohen*, performs the action; the
           verb, *wrote*, describes the action.]

PASSIVE   The newsletter article *was written* by David Cohen.
           [The subject, *the newsletter article*, is acted upon; the
           verb, *was written*, describes the action.]

The two sentences say the same thing, but each has a different emphasis: The first emphasizes *David Cohen*; the second emphasizes *the newsletter article*. In business writing, it is often important to emphasize who or what performs an action. Further, the passive-voice version is indirect because it places the performer of the action behind the verb instead of in front of it. Because the active voice is generally more direct, more concise, and easier for **readers** to understand, use the active voice unless the passive voice is more appropriate, as described on page 564. Whether you use the active voice or the passive voice, be careful not to shift voices in a sentence.

● David Cohen corrected the inaccuracy as soon as ~~it was identified~~
  identified it
  ~~by~~ the editor.
      ^

Using the Active Voice

Improving Clarity.   The active voice improves <u>clarity</u> and avoids confusion, especially in <u>instructions</u> and <u>policies and procedures</u>.

PASSIVE	Sections B and C *should be checked* for errors. [Are they already checked?]
ACTIVE	*Check* sections B and C for errors. [The performer of the action, *you*, is understood: (You) *Check* the sections.]

Active voice can also help avoid <u>dangling modifiers</u>.

PASSIVE	Hurrying to complete the work, the cables *were connected* improperly. [*Who* was hurrying? The implication is the cables were hurrying!]
ACTIVE	Hurrying to complete the work, the technician *connected* the cables improperly. [Here, *hurrying to complete the work* properly modifies the performer of the action: *the technician.*]

Highlighting Subjects.   One difficulty with passive sentences is that they can bury the performer of the action in <u>expletives</u> and prepositional <u>phrases</u>.

PASSIVE	It *was reported by* the testing facility that the new model is defective.
ACTIVE	The testing facility *reported* that the new model is defective.

Sometimes writers using the passive voice fail to name the performer— information that might be missed.

PASSIVE	The problem *was discovered* yesterday.
ACTIVE	The Maintenance Department *discovered* the problem yesterday.

V

Achieving Conciseness. The active voice helps achieve <u>concise-ness</u> because it eliminates the need for an additional helping verb as well as an extra <u>preposition</u> to identify the performer of the action.

> PASSIVE   Arbitrary changes in policy *are resented by* employees.
>
> ACTIVE   Employees *resent* arbitrary changes in policy.

The active-voice version takes one verb (*resent*); the passive-voice version takes two verbs (*are resented*) and an extra preposition (*by*).

Using the Passive Voice

The passive voice is sometimes effective or even necessary. Indeed, for reasons of tact and diplomacy, you might need to use the passive voice to avoid accusing others.

> ACTIVE   Your staff *did not meet* the quota last month.
>
> PASSIVE   The quota *was not met* last month.

◆ ETHICS NOTE Be careful, however, not to use the passive voice to evade responsibility or obscure an issue or information that readers should know.

- Several mistakes *were made*. [*Who* made the mistakes?]
- It *has been decided*. [*Who* has decided?]

See also <u>ethics in writing</u>. ✦

When the performer of the action is either unknown or unimportant, of course, use the passive voice. (The copper mine *was discovered* in 1929.) When the performer of the action is less important than the receiver of that action, the passive voice is sometimes more appropriate. (Ann Bryant *was presented* with an award by the president.)

When you are explaining an operation in which the reader is not actively involved or when you are explaining a process or a procedure, the passive voice may be more appropriate. In the following example, anyone — it really does not matter who — could be the performer of the action.

- Area strip mining *is used* in regions of flat-to-gently rolling terrain, like that found in the Midwest. Depending on applicable reclamation laws, the topsoil *may be removed* from the area *to be mined, stored,* and later *reapplied* as surface material during reclamation of the mined land. After the removal of the topsoil, a trench *is cut* through the overburden to expose the upper surface of the coal to be mined. The overburden from the first cut *is placed* on the unmined land adjacent to the cut. After the first cut *has been completed,* the coal *is removed*.

V

Do not, however, simply assume that any such explanation should be in the passive voice; in fact, as in the following example, the active voice is often more effective.

- In the operation of an internal combustion engine, an explosion in the combustion chamber *forces* the pistons down in the cylinders. The movement of the pistons in the cylinders *turns* the crankshaft.

Ask yourself, "Would it be of any advantage to the reader to know the performer of the action?" If the answer is yes, use the active voice, as in the previous example.

ESL TIPS FOR CHOOSING VOICE

Different languages place different values on active-voice and passive-voice constructions. In some languages, the passive is used frequently; in others, hardly at all. As a nonnative speaker of English, you may have a tendency to follow the pattern of your native language. But remember, even though business writing may sometimes require the passive voice, active verbs are highly valued in English.

V

W

wait for / wait on

Wait on should be restricted in writing to the activities of hospitality and service employees. (We need extra staff to *wait on* customers.) Otherwise, use *wait for.* (Be sure to *wait for* Ms. Sturgess's approval.) See also **idioms**.

Web design

DIRECTORY

Navigation and Pages   567
   Navigation Plan   567
   Page Links   567
   Link Design   568
   Page Layout   569
   Homepages   569
Graphics and Typography   570
Access for People with Disabilities   571
Writer's Checklist: Designing Web Pages   572

You can apply many of the principles covered throughout this book to designing Web sites. As you prepare, carefully consider your **purpose** and **readers'** needs when designing Web pages and assembling those pages to create Web sites. Most organizational sites have well-defined goals, such as reference, marketing, education, or advocacy. Before you begin building your Web pages and sites, create a clear statement of purpose that identifies your target audience.

EXTERNAL SITE   The purpose of this site is to enable our customers to locate product information, place online orders, and contact our customer-service department.

INTERNAL SITE   The purpose of this site is to provide SNR Security Corporation employees, suppliers, and partner organizations with a single, consistent, and up-to-date resource for materials about SNR Security.

W

As the examples suggest, the two general kinds of sites are external and internal. *External sites* target an audience from the entire Internet. *Internal sites* are designed for audiences either on an *intranet* (a network within an organization) that is not accessible to audiences outside that organization or an *extranet* (a password-protected site) available exclusively to trusted partners and suppliers to provide them with common data and documents.

Navigation and Pages

Your main goal when designing a Web site is to establish a predictable environment in which users can comfortably navigate and easily find the information they need. This information should be logically accessible to the user in the fewest possible steps (or clicks). See also **methods of development**.

Navigation Plan.   To design an efficient navigation plan, draft a navigation chart or map of your site early in the process. Figure W–1 on page 568 shows an initial navigation plan for a company Web site.

In Figure W–1 on page 568, each higher-level page (for example, Departments and Divisions) is linked to increasingly specific pages about the company's internal organization (Marketing, Accounting, Customer Relations). Human Resources, although logically a department in the company's organization, is given higher visibility on the homepage because recruiting new employees is important to the company. The site map is preliminary, so it does not yet include areas such as a Privacy Statement, What's New, About Us, or a site search window.

Page Links.   When viewers access Web pages randomly, they often have no context for where they are in the site. One way to orient users is to provide a set of links in graphics or words called a toolbar or button bar, as shown here.

[Home | Search | Order | What's New | About Us]

A toolbar at the top, bottom, or sides of each page serves as a table of contents and shows visitors the top-level structure of your site. Toolbars on each page help you avoid sending users to a dead-end page (one with no link); in fact, every page should, if nothing else, link back to your homepage. You may also incorporate the name of your company or organization and its logo in a banner at the top of each page that links back to your homepage.

Check links to external sites routinely because these sites can change or disappear without your knowledge. Some sites place an icon or EXIT next to outside links to inform users that they are leaving the host site.

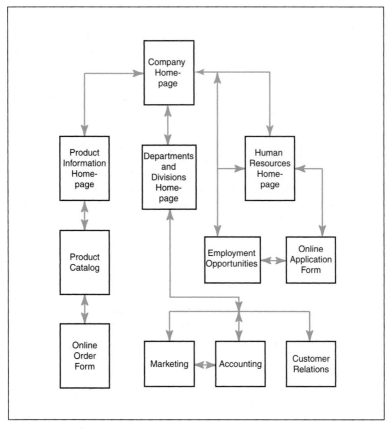

FIGURE W–1. Site Map

Link Design.   Create links to other pages and sites that are related to your visitors' organizational or professional needs and interests. Links to customer service and online order forms are especially useful for cultivating potential customers.

When you identify links, do not write out "Click here for more information." Instead, write the sentence as you normally would, and anchor the link on the most relevant word in the sentence, as illustrated in the following example.

- For information about employment opportunities, visit Human Resources.

Avoid writing paragraphs that are dense with links. Instead, list links alphabetically in groups of about four to seven to make them easier for the viewer to see at a glance.

▶ Accounting
▶ Customer Relations
▶ Marketing
▶ Product Help

In addition to identifying links with words, you can use icons and graphics, as shown in the preceding list; they not only are easy to use but also provide the visual cues Web users expect.

Page Layout.   Most users do not like scrolling down long pages, so pages should contain no more than one or two screens of information. Keep homepages, in particular, to one screen. Many computer monitors and settings do not display more than half of a typical Web page at any one time, allowing only the top four or five inches to be visible. For that reason, place titles, banners, and important graphic elements and information in the upper half of the page (or top 300 pixels).

When a greater amount of information must be covered on a single page, include a concise table of contents at the top of the page linked to specific sections elsewhere on the page. Viewers can select the section they want without having to scroll through the entire page. You can also provide periodic links that return visitors to the top of the page.

Use short narrative passages or lists so that viewers can scan and access the information quickly. See **writing for the Web**.

Your Web pages should include the date they were created or last updated (usually in a footer) so that users can determine whether the information is current. You might also place a New icon next to each new or updated item to alert users to these changes. Be sure to remove the icon after a suitable interval, such as 30 days.

Finally, test your design by viewing it on several different Web browsers as well as on different platforms (including UNIX, Linux, Mac, and Windows). Different software and different platforms can interact unpredictably, and you may be surprised at how different your page can look on systems unlike your own.

Homepages.   A homepage (or *start page*) is an important focus for all pages in your Web site. Many organizational homepages include an image map that functions like a toolbar, linking to other pages in the

W

site. The image map introduces visitors to the overall site design, identifies the purpose of the site, and provides an overview of major content areas. Include links to your site's Privacy Statement and About Us page, which describe your organization. You should also consider including a Contact Us link that provides visitors with your e-mail address and other contact information, as appropriate.

Because a complex homepage graphic can take a minute or longer to download, consider using relatively small graphics files on your homepage, gradually increasing the size of the graphics for pages deeper into your site. Users who go beyond a page or two into a site are more committed and therefore more willing to tolerate longer delays, especially if you offer them warnings that particular pages contain graphics that may take time to download.*

Graphics and Typography

Your audience and purpose should determine the graphic style and theme of your Web site. Although graphic elements provide visual relief from dense text, do not overdo graphics — use graphics that fit the particular audience, purpose, and <u>context</u>. Complex graphics and motion can clutter or slow access to your site. Avoid bold and multiple colors; instead, use lighter colors, especially for backgrounds. Keep in mind that large or high-resolution graphics, like color photographs, can cause long delays as they download to the user's system. For high-resolution graphics, you might use thumbnails (images reduced to 10 to 15 percent of the original file size) that link to the original size image. Consider as well providing a graphics-free option for quicker access.

Aim for consistency in your graphics and typography to establish a sense of unity and to provide consistent visual cues that help visitors find information. Consider creating a cascading style sheet to implement the specifications for fonts, spacing between paragraphs, heading styles, and other elements. *Cascading style sheets* are codes, linked from or included in your HTML (hypertext markup language) that work like templates. You can define the style (color, font, size, emphasis, etc.) for a particular set of HTML tags once, and thereafter every time you use those tags in your site they will look the same. Cascading style sheets are especially helpful for large sites with numerous pages, as you can quickly and easily change your headings by simply changing the style sheet.

---

*The current industry "best practices" recommendation is that a page load in ten seconds or less on a 56K modem.

W

Access for People with Disabilities

Design elements like colorful graphics, animation, and streaming video and audio can be barriers to people with impaired vision or hearing or those who are color-blind. Use the following strategies to meet the needs of such audiences.

- Avoid frames, complex tables, animation, JavaScript, and other design elements incompatible with text-only browsers and adaptive technologies, such as voice or large-print software.

- Provide HTML versions of pages and documents whenever possible because this format is most compatible with the current generation of screen readers.

- Attach text equivalents for graphic or audio elements.

- Design for the color-blind reader by making meaning independent of color. For example, rather than asking users to "Click on the green button for more information," label the button (Click Here) or embed a link in a sentence: "See our catalog for more information."

You may want to consider offering different options for site visitors, such as full-graphics, light-graphics, and text-only versions.

Finally, test your pages using "Bobby," a site that will provide an on-screen analysis of a Web page to ensure its accessibility: <http://bobby.watchfire.com/>.

W

Writer's Checklist: Designing Web Pages

Many of the guidelines on typography in <u>layout and design</u> are applicable to Web pages; however, not all apply, so keep the following in mind:

- ☑ Limit the number of typeface styles as well as colors.
- ☑ Use sans serif fonts for text passages; they are generally legible on computer screens.
- ☑ Use uppercase letters or boldface type sparingly.
- ☑ Use typeface colors that contrast (but do not clash) with background colors.
- ☑ Use underlined text only for links.
- ☑ Separate text from graphics with generous blank space (the equivalent of white space).
- ☑ Limit your text lines to 50 to 70 characters (or 10 to 12 words) for readability.
- ☑ Use <u>heading</u> and subheading styles sparingly and consistently.
- ☑ Block-indent text sections that you expect viewers to read in detail.
- ☑ Test your design by viewing it on alternate browsers and platforms.
- ☑ Check that all your links work, particularly after site changes.
- ☑ Test the load time of your pages using a slow modem.

WEB LINK WEB DESIGN RESOURCES

For Mike Markel's helpful overview of the process and principles of designing Web sites, see *<bedfordstmartins.com/alredbus>* and select *Tutorials,* "Designing for the Web." For links to more tutorials as well as to sites that provide advice for improving accessibility for people with disabilities, select *Links for Handbook Entries.*

---

when / where / that

When and if (or *if and when*) is a colloquial expression that should not be used in writing.

- When ~~and if~~ funding is approved, you will get the position.

- *If*
  ~~When and if~~ funding is approved, you will get the position.

In phrases using the *where . . . at* construction, *at* is unnecessary and should be omitted.

- Where is his office ~~at~~?

Do not substitute *where* for *that* to anticipate an idea or fact to follow.

- I read in the newsletter ~~where~~ *that* sales have increased this quarter.

whether

Whether communicates the notion of a choice. When *whether or not* is used to indicate a choice between alternatives, omit *or not*; it is redundant.

- The client asked whether ~~or not~~ the proposal was finished.

The phrase *as to whether* is clumsy and redundant. Either omit it altogether or use only *whether.*

- ~~As to whether~~ *We have decided to* we ~~will~~ commit to a long-term ~~contract, we have decided to do so.~~ *contract.*

while

While, meaning "during an interval of time," is sometimes substituted for connectives like *and, but, although,* and *whereas.* Used as a connective in that way, *while* often causes ambiguity.

- Ian Evans is sales manager, ~~while~~ *and* Joan Thomas is director of research.

Do not use *while* to mean *although* or *whereas.*

- ~~While~~ *Although* Ryan Patterson wants the job of financial services manager, he has not yet applied for it.

Restrict *while* to its meaning of "during the time that."

- I'll have to catch up on my reading *while* I am on vacation.

W

who / whom

Writers are often unsure whether to use *who* or *whom*. *Who* is the subjective case form, whereas *whom* is the objective case form. When in doubt about which form to use, substitute a personal pronoun to see which one fits. If *he, she,* or *they* fits, use *who.*

- *Who* is the training coordinator?
  [You would say, "*She* is the training coordinator."]

If *him, her,* or *them* fits, use *whom.*

- It depends on *whom*?
  [You would say, "It depends on *them.*"]

who's / whose / of which

Who's is the contraction of *who is.* (*Who's* scheduled today?) *Whose* is the possessive case of *who.* (Consider *whose* budget should be cut.)
  Normally, *whose* is used with persons, and *of which* is used with inanimate objects.

- The employee *whose* car had been towed away was angry.
- Completing the EMBA program is an achievement *of which* to be proud.

If *of which* causes a sentence to sound awkward, *whose* may be used with inanimate objects. (Compare "The business *whose* profits steadily declined" with "The business the profits *of which* steadily declined.")

-wise

Although the <u>suffix</u> *-wise* often seems to provide a tempting shortcut in writing, it leads more often to inept than to economical expression. It is better to rephrase the sentence.

- Our department rates high efficiencywise.
  has a   *efficiency rating.*

The *-wise* suffix is appropriate, however, in instructions that indicate certain space or directional requirements (lengthwise, clockwise).

word choice

Mark Twain once said, "The difference between the right word and almost the right word is the difference between 'lightning' and 'lightning bug.'" The most important goal in choosing the right word in business writing is the preciseness implied by Twain's comment. Vague words and abstract words defeat preciseness because they do not convey the writer's meaning directly and clearly.

VAGUE   It was a *productive* meeting.

PRECISE   The meeting resulted in the approval of the health-care benefits package.

In the first sentence, *productive* sounds specific but conveys little; the revised sentence says specifically what made the meeting "productive." Although <u>abstract words</u> may at times be appropriate to your topic, using them unnecessarily will make your writing difficult to understand.

Being aware of the <u>connotations</u> and denotations of words will help you anticipate <u>readers</u>' reactions to the words you choose. Understanding <u>antonyms</u> (fresh/stale) and <u>synonyms</u> (notorious/infamous) will increase your ability to choose the proper word. Make other <u>usage</u> decisions carefully, especially in technical contexts, such as <u>average/median/mean</u> and <u>biannual/biennial</u>.

Although many of the entries throughout this book will help you improve your word choices and avoid impreciseness, the following entries should be particularly helpful:

<u>affectation</u>	23	<u>euphemisms</u>	194
<u>biased language</u>	53	<u>idioms</u>	266
<u>buzzwords</u>	68	<u>jargon</u>	298
<u>clichés</u>	81	<u>logic errors</u>	315
<u>conciseness</u>	104	<u>vague words</u>	549

A key to choosing the correct and precise word is to keep current in your reading and to be aware of new words in your profession and in the language. In your quest for the right word, remember that there is no substitute for an up-to-date <u>dictionary</u>. See also <u>English as a second language</u>.

WEB LINK **WISE WORD CHOICES**

For online exercises on word choice, see <*bedfordstmartins.com/alredbus*> and select *Exercise Central.*

W

writing a draft

You are well prepared to write a rough draft when you have established your __purpose__ and __readers__' needs, considered the __context__, defined your __scope__, completed adequate __research__, and prepared an outline (whether rough or developed). (See also __outlining__.) Writing a draft is simply transcribing and expanding the notes from your outline into __paragraphs__, without worrying about __grammar__, refinements of language, or __spelling__. Refinement will come with __revision__ and __proofreading__. See also "Five Steps to Successful Writing."

Writing and revising are different activities. Do not let worrying about a good opening slow you down. Instead, concentrate on getting your ideas on paper—now is not the time to polish or revise. Do not wait for inspiration—treat writing a draft as you would any other on-the-job task.

Writer's Checklist: Writing a Rough Draft

☑ Set up your writing area with whatever supplies you need (notepads, pens and pencils, reference material, etc.) to keep going once you get started. Then hang out the "Do Not Disturb" sign.

☑ Avoid the temptation of writing first drafts on the computer without any planning by using a good outline as a springboard to start and keep going.

☑ Keep in mind your readers' needs, expectations, and knowledge of the subject. Doing so will help you write directly to your readers and suggest which ideas need further development.

☑ When you are trying to write quickly and you come to something difficult to explain, try to relate the new concept to something with which the readers are already familiar, as discussed in __figures of speech__.

☑ Start with the section that seems easiest. Your readers will neither know nor care that the middle section of the document was the first section you wrote.

☑ Give yourself a set time (ten or fifteen minutes, for example) in which you write continuously, regardless of how good or bad your writing seems to be. Don't stop when you are rolling along easily—if you stop and come back, you may lose momentum.

☑ Routinely save to your hard drive and create a backup copy of your documents on separate disks or on the company network.

W

Writer's Checklist: Writing a Rough Draft (continued)

☑ Give yourself a small reward — a short walk, a soft drink, a brief chat with a friend, an easy task — after you have finished a section.

☑ Reread what you have written when you return to your writing. Seeing what you have already written can return you to a productive frame of mind.

writing for the Web

In the workplace, those who write content for Web sites are not always the same people who design the sites. This entry provides guidelines only for those writing for an online audience; for more information on site design, see <u>Web design</u>.

⚡ ETHICS NOTE Work with your Webmaster or site administrator to comply with Web policy guidelines as well as technical issues of access and design standards. On campus, consult your instructor or campus computer support staff about standards for posting content. ✦

Crafting Content for the Web

Because most <u>readers</u> scan Web sites for specific information, the way you write and organize your information will greatly affect your readers' understanding. State your important points first, before any detailed supporting information. (This method is called *inverted pyramid organization.*) Keep your writing <u>style</u> simple and straightforward, and avoid such directional cues as "as shown in the example below" that make sense on the printed page but not on a Web screen. Use the following techniques to make your content more accessible to readers.

Headings. Divide your text into short passages, each focusing on one facet of your topic. Use informative <u>headings</u> to help the reader decide at a glance whether to read a passage. Headings also simplify text by highlighting structure and organization, and they signal <u>transitions</u> from one topic to the next.

Lists. Use bullets and numbered <u>lists</u> to break up dense <u>paragraphs,</u> reduce text length, and highlight important content.

Keywords. To help search engines and your audience find your site, use keywords in the first 50 or so words of your text.

W

WITHOUT KEYWORDS   We are proud to introduce a new commemorative coin honoring our bank's founder and president. The item will be available on this Web site after December 3, 2007, which is the 100th anniversary of our first deposit.

WITH KEYWORDS   The new *Reynolds* commemorative coin features a portrait of *George G. Reynolds*, the founder and president of *Reynolds Bank*. The coin can be purchased after December 3, 2007, in honor of the 100th anniversary of the sale of the first *Reynolds* deposit.

Graphics.   Graphics provide visual relief from text and make your site attractive and appealing. Use only <u>visuals</u> that are appropriate for your audience and purpose, however, and use graphics that load quickly.

Hyperlinks.   Use hyperlinks to help readers navigate the information in your site. If a passage of text is longer than two or three screens, create a table of contents of hyperlinks for it at the top of the Web page and link each item to the relevant content further down the page. Avoid hyperlinks within text paragraphs because they can distract readers, make scanning the text difficult, and tempt readers to leave before reaching the end of your content.

Fonts.   Font sizes and styles affect screen legibility. Because computer screens display fonts at lower resolutions than does printed text, sans serif fonts work better for online text passages. Consult your Webmaster about your site's font preferences. Do not use capital letters or boldface type for blocks of text because they slow the reader. For content that contains special characters (such as for mathematical or chemical content), consult your Webmaster about the best way to submit the files for HTML (hypertext markup language) coding or post them as PDF (portable document format) files.

Line Length.   Line length also affects readability because short line lengths reduce the amount of eye movement necessary to scan text. Optimal length is approximately half the width of the screen. To achieve this length, draft text that is between 50 and 70 characters (or between 10 and 12 words) to a line.

Writing for a Global Audience

When you write for public-access sites, eliminate expressions and references that make sense only to someone very familiar with American English. Express <u>dates</u>, clock times, and measurements consistent with international practices. For visuals, choose symbols and icons, colors, representations of human beings, and captions that can be easily understood, as described in **global communication** and **global graphics**. See also **biased language** and **English as a second language**.

Linking to External Sites

Links to outside sites can expand your content. However, review such sites carefully before linking to them. Is the site's author or sponsoring organization reputable? Is its content accurate, current, and unbiased? Does the site date-stamp its content with notices such as "This page was last updated on January 1, 2007"? (For more advice on evaluating Web sites, see **research**.) Link directly to the page or specific area of an outside site that is relevant to your users, and be sure that you provide a clear **context** for why you are sending your readers there.

Posting an Existing Document

If you post files for existing paper documents to a Web site, try to retain the document's original sequence and page layout. If you shorten or revise the original document for posting to the Web, add a notice informing readers that it differs from the printed original.

Regardless of format or version used, be sure to:

- Obtain permission from the **copyright** holder for the use of copyrighted text, **tables**, or images. See also **plagiarism**.
- Ask the Webmaster or site administrator about the preferred file format to submit for coding and posting. On campus, consult your instructor or campus computer support staff.
- Request that the Webmaster optimize any slow-loading graphics files for quick access.
- Review the document internally before it is posted to the public site: Is it the correct version? Is any information missing? Do all links work and go to the right places? See **proofreading**.
- Ask the Webmaster to create a single-file version of the document (a version formatted as a single, long Web page) for readers who will print it to read offline.

⊡ ETHICS NOTE Document sources of information or of help received—text, images, streaming video, and other multimedia material. Seek prior approval before using any copyrighted information. Documenting your sources is not only required, it also bolsters the credibility of your site. To do so, either provide links to your source or use a citation as described in **documenting sources**. ✦

W

DIGITAL TIPS **USING PDF FILES**

Converting documents such as reports, articles, and brochures to PDF files allows you to retain the identical look of the printed documents. The PDF pages will display on screen exactly as they appear on the printed page. Readers can read the document online, download and save it, or print it in whole or in part. For more on this topic, see <bedfordstmartins.com/alredbus> and select *Digital Tips*, "Using PDF Files."

Protecting the Privacy of Users

Put a link on your page to the site's privacy statement, particularly if you solicit comments about your content or have an e-mail link for unsolicited comments for site users. A Privacy Statement informs site visitors about how the site sponsor handles solicited and unsolicited information from individuals, its policy on the use of cookies,* and legal action it takes against hackers. Inform users if you intend to use their information for marketing or to share their information with third parties, and give visitors the option of refusing you permission to use or share their information.

---

*"Cookies" are small files that are downloaded to your computer when you browse certain Web pages. Cookies hold information, such as your user name and password, so you do not need to re-enter it each time you visit the site.

Y

"you" viewpoint

The "you" viewpoint places your <u>readers</u>' interest and perspective foremost. It is based on the principle that your readers are naturally more concerned about their own needs than they are about those of the writer or organization.

The "you" viewpoint often, but not always, means using the words *you* and *your* rather than *we, our, I,* and *mine.* Consider the following sentence that focuses on the needs of the writer and organization (we) rather than on those of the reader.

- *We must receive* your signed invoice before *we can process* your payment.

Even though the sentence uses *your* twice, the words in italics suggest that the <u>point of view</u> centers on the writer's need to receive the invoice in order to process the payment. Consider the following revision, written with the "you" viewpoint.

- *So you can receive* your payment promptly, please send your signed invoice.

Because the benefit to the reader is stressed, the writer is more likely to motivate the reader to act. See also <u>persuasion</u>.

In some instances, as suggested earlier, you may need to avoid using the <u>pronouns</u> *you* and *your* to achieve a positive <u>tone</u> and maintain goodwill. Notice how the first of the following examples—with *your*—seems to accuse the reader, while the second—without *your*—achieves the goals of the "you" viewpoint with <u>positive writing</u>.

ACCUSATORY   *Your* budget makes no allowance for setup costs.

POSITIVE   The budget should include an allowance for setup costs to meet all the concerns of our client.

As this example illustrates, the "you" viewpoint means more than using particular pronouns or adopting a particular writing <u>style</u>. By placing the readers' interests at the center, you can achieve your <u>purpose</u> not only in <u>correspondence</u>, <u>e-mail</u>, and <u>memos</u> but also in <u>proposals</u>, <u>brochures</u>, many <u>reports</u>, and <u>presentations</u>.

your / you're

Your is a possessive <u>pronoun</u> (*your* wallet); *you're* is the contraction of *you are* (*You're* late for the meeting). If you tend to confuse *your* with *you're,* use the search function of your word processor to review both terms during <u>proofreading</u>.

Acknowledgments (continued)

Figure D–12: From Xerox Corporation, *WorkCentre XD Series User Guide*, page 6. Copyright © Xerox Corporation. Used with permission.

Figure D–13: Source: Federal Emergency Management Agency.

Figure D–14: Reprinted with the permission of Corel Corporation.

Figures E–2 and F–6: Reprinted with the permission of Susan Litzinger, a student at Pennsylvania State University, Altoona.

Figure G–3: Source: U.S. Food and Drug Administration.

Figure G–5: Copyright © 2003 by ISO. Reprinted with permission.

Figure L–4: From Gerald J. Alred et al., *The Professional Writer*. Copyright © 1991 by Bedford/St. Martin's. Reprinted with permission of Bedford/St. Martin's.

Figure M–1: Source: U.S. Nuclear Regulatory Commission.

Figures N–2, N–3, and P–2: Copyright © 1998, 2000 by Ken Cook Co. Reprinted with the permission of Ken Cook Company.

Figure R–3: "Library Homepage." Reprinted with the permission of Columbia University Libraries.

Figure R–4: "InfoTrac Search Page." Reprinted with permission.

Figure R–5: "Advanced Google Search." Reprinted with the permission of Google, Inc.

Figure R–6: "Google's Main Subject Directory." Reprinted with the permission of Google, Inc.

Figure R–10: Prepared by Kim Isaacs, Advanced Career Systems, Inc.

Figure R–14: Prepared by Kim Isaacs, Advanced Career Systems, Inc.

"Four Criteria for Evaluating Sources" from Leigh Ryan, *The Bedford Guide for Writing Tutors*, Third Edition, Copyright © 2002 by Bedford/St. Martin's. Reprinted with the permission of Bedford/St. Martin's.

Index

a/an, 1, 47
  as adjectives, 13–14, 15
a few/few, 203
a lot/alot, 2
a while/awhile, 50–51
abbreviations, 2–6
  in abstracts, 9
  acronyms and initialisms, 2, 12
  capitalization of, 72
  commas with, 96
  common scholarly, 5
  defining, 561
  in e-mail, 3, 181
  in international correspondence, 283
  of Latin words, 177–78, 192
  list of, 214
  for measurements, 4
  for organization names, 3–4
  periods with, 378
  for personal names and titles, 4
  plurals of, 3, 41, 42
  spelling out uncommon, 198
  in tables, 530
  in titles of works, 538
  Web resources for, 6
  writer's checklist for, 3
About Us page, in Web design, 570
above, 6
absolute phrases, 93
absolute words, 15, 191–92
absolutely, 6
abstract nouns, 28, 352
abstract words, 6–7
  affectation and, 23
  ethics in using, 193
  figures of speech for clarifying, 204
  as gobbledygook, 251
  impreciseness of, 575
abstracts, 7–9
  vs. executive summaries, 195

  in formal reports, 213, 219
  sample of, 8
  writing style for, 9
academic titles, 4
accept/except, 9
acceptance/refusal letters, for
    employment, 9–11, 289
  samples of, 10, 11
accident reports, 544
accuracy
  in application letters, 46
  in correspondence, 116, 179–80
  of instructions, 277
  of Internet sources, 472–73
  in note-taking, 351
  in résumés, 479
  revising for, 495
accusative case, 74
acknowledgment letters, 11–12
  form letters for, 209
  sample of, 12
acronyms and initialisms, 2, 3, 12
action verbs, 74
  in résumés, 491
active listening, 313–14
active voice, 51, 526, 555, 562
  for conciseness, 106, 564
  for emphasis, 185
  in formal writing, 524
  for highlighting subjects, 563
  for improving clarity, 563
  infinitives and, 550
  for instructions, 274
  for newsletters, 348
  revising for, 496
  in sentence construction, 508
activities section, in résumés, 491
activity reports, 410–11, 412
  sample of, 411
actually, 456

ad hoc, 12–13
adapt/adept/adopt, 13
address, direct. *See* direct address
addresses, street
    commas with, 95
    inside, for letters, 122
    numbers in, 357–58
    in résumés, 489
adept/adopt/adapt, 13
adjective clauses, 17, 189
adjectives, 13–17, 337–38. *See also*
    modifiers
    as absolute words, 15
    adverbs modifying, 21
    articles, 1, 13–14, 47–48
    commas with, 17, 94
    comparison of, 15
    converting verbs into, 515–16
    with count nouns, 187
    demonstrative, 14, 187
    ESL tips for, 16
    indefinite, 15
    irregular, 15
    limiting, 13–15
    nouns as, 17, 353, 392, 528
    numeral, 14
    phrases as, 383, 384–85
    placement of, 15, 16, 17
    possessive, 14, 187
    relative, 105
    used with prepositions, 395
    verbals as, 549, 550, 551, 553
adjustment letters, 17–20, 209
    context in, 111
    full adjustments, 19
    partial adjustments, 19–20
    as promotional writing, 412
    samples of, 18, 20
Adobe Acrobat, 84
Adobe PDF files, 468, 494
    converting documents into, 580
adopt/adapt/adept, 13
advanced searches, 469–70
adverbs, 21–23, 337–38
    commas with, 93
    comparison of, 22
    conjunctive, 22
    intensifiers, 277–78, 338
    irregular, 22

nouns as, 353
ordinal numbers as, 14
phrases as, 383, 384
placement of, 22–23
prepositions confused with, 395
questions answered by, 21
split infinitives and, 550–51
types of, 21–22
used with prepositions, 395
verbals as, 549, 550, 553
affect/effect, 23
affectation, 23–25
    allusions and, 33
    buzzwords, 68
    causes of, 25
    euphemisms, 194
    foreign words as, 134, 209
    formal style as, 115, 524, 525
    as gobbledygook, 251
    legal terms as, 134
    in management memos, 328
    nominalizations as, 349
    overusing abbreviations, 3
    revising for, 496
    wordiness, 49, 106
affinity, 26
aforementioned, 6
aforesaid, 6, 24
age bias, in writing, 55
agenda, for meetings, 323–24
agreement, 26–32. *See also* pronoun-
    antecedent agreement; subject-
    verb agreement
    with collective nouns, 29, 31, 133,
        353
    with data/datum, 133
    with demonstrative adjectives, 14, 31
    with each, 27, 29, 30, 177
    with everybody/everyone, 30–31, 195
    gender, 26–27, 30, 243–44
    with none, 349
    with nor/or, 350
    number, 26–29, 30–31, 354
    with one of those . . . who, 360–61
    with possessive pronouns, 415
    pronoun-antecedent, 26–27, 29–32
    subject-verb, 26, 27–29
ain't, 252
aircraft names, 296

all-capital letters
  in e-mail, 180, 181
  for emphasis, 181, 186, 307
  in Web design, 572, 578
all ready/already, 32
all right/alright, 32
all together/altogether, 32
allude/elude/refer, 32–33
allusion/illusion, 33
allusions, 33
almost/most, 33
also, 34
AltaVista, 469
ambiguity, 34–35
  clarity and, 80
  commas for preventing, 91, 95
  incomplete comparisons, 34–35
  missing or misplaced modifiers,
    34–35, 338–39
  with prepositional phrases, 384
  in pronoun references, 34, 413
  telegraphic style and, 532
  using that for, 536
  word choice and, 35
American Heritage College Dictionary,
    The, 141
American Psychological Association
    (APA) style. See APA style
America's Job Bank, 301
among/between, 53
amount/number, 35
ampersands, 4, 35, 151
an. See a/an
analogy, 205
  definition by, 136–37
  in description, 139
and
  and/or usage, 36
  both . . . and usage, 56, 110
  commas with, 97
anecdote, opening with, 292–93
annotated bibliography, 56
annual reports, 36–40
  board of directors and officers, 38
  design and visuals, 39–40
  financial highlights, 37
  financial statement, 38
  interesting-detail openings, 292
  mission statements, 334

narrative section, 37–38
preparation process, 38–40
statement to stockholders, 37
titles for, 537–38
writer's checklist for, 40
anonymous/unknown authors,
    documenting, 152, 153, 159, 165,
    166
antecedents, 413. See also pronoun
    references; pronoun-antecedent
    agreement
  agreement with pronouns, 26–27,
    29–32, 416–17
  compound, 31–32
  implied, 413
  personal pronouns and, 417
  references to, 34, 412–13
anticipation, punctuation for, 507
antonyms, 41, 537, 575
anxiety, presentation, 404
APA style, 149, 150–56. See also
    documenting sources
  for articles in periodicals, 152, 153
  for books, 151–52
  compared with other styles, 149–50
  documentation models, 151–54
  for electronic sources, 152–53, 154
  in-text citations, 150–51, 155
  for multimedia sources, 153–54
  other sources, 154
  sample list of references, 156
  sample page, 155
apostrophes, 41–42
  in contractions, 41, 113
  forming plurals with, 41–42
  indicating omissions, 41
  showing possession, 41, 75, 392–93
appendixes, 42
  for business plans, 66
  in formal reports, 216
  in proposals, 420, 423
  for technical specialists, 456
  visuals in, 562
application letters, 42–46
  guide letters for, 211
  résumés and, 478–79
  samples of, 43–45
  structure and parts of, 46
  writing style for, 523

appositives, 46–47
  case of, 47, 75, 416
  commas with, 92
  following proper names, 71–72
  gerunds as, 549
  nouns as, 353
arguments
  loaded, 317
  Web resources for, 317
articles (a/an/the), 47–48
  a/an usage, 1, 47
  count nouns and, 187–88
  definite, 47
  eliminating in telegraphic style, 47,
    531
  ESL tips for, 48, 187–88
  indefinite, 1, 47
  as limiting adjectives, 13–14, 15
  in titles of works, 47, 71, 538
  the usage, 47
  when not to use, 48
articles in periodicals. *See also*
    newsletter articles
  APA style for documenting, 152,
    153
  capitalization in titles, 71, 110
  CMS style for documenting,
    158–59, 160
  electronic, documenting, 153, 160,
    166
  evaluating, 474
  MLA style for documenting, 165,
    166
  online databases and indexes for,
    465–66
  titles for, 451, 537–38, 539
  with unknown author, 152, 159, 165
  writing style for, 524
as/because/since, 48–49
as/like, 312
as/than, and pronoun case, 74, 75–76
as much as/more than, 49
as such, 49
as to whether, 573
as well as/both, 49–50
ASCII résumés, 487, 494
assure/insure/ensure, 277
asterisks, 181
atlases, 468
attachments, e-mail, 180, 181, 182

attention-getting statement, opening
    with, 398
attributive adjectives, 15, 17
audience, 50. *See also* readers
  analyzing, for presentations, 397
  assessing, in writing process, x–xi
  tone and, 540
augment/supplement, 50
author/date method of documentation,
    149. *See also* APA style
authority, of Internet sources, 472
authorization request, in proposals, 423
authors, documenting, 55
  corporate, 151, 152, 158, 159, 164,
    166
  of electronic sources, 152–53,
    159–60, 165–66
  multiple, 151, 157–58, 164
  multiple, in citations, 151
  unknown, 152, 153, 159, 165, 166
auxiliary verbs, 553
average/median/mean, 50
awhile/a while, 50–51
awkwardness, 51
  ambiguity and, 35
  expletives and, 198
  formal style and, 524
  inverted word order and, 516
  overuse of as, 49
  revising for, 496
  word choice and, 80
  writer's checklist for eliminating, 51

back matter
  for formal reports, 212, 215–16
  for proposals, 423
background, opening with, 291
bad/badly, 52
bad-news patterns. *See also* negative
    messages
  in correspondence, 118–19, 120
  cultural differences in, 279
  positive writing and, 391
  refusal letters, 457–60
balance/remainder, 52
banners, in Web design, 567, 569
bar graphs, 255–56, 258, 559
barely, 171
bcc: notations, 126, 182
be sure to/be sure and, 52

because, reason is, 457
because/since/as, 48–49
because of/due to, 49, 176
behavioral interviews, 287
being as/being that, 49
beside/besides, 52
between/among, 53
between you and me/between you and
    I, 53, 395
bi-/semi-, 53
biannual/biennial, 53
biased evidence, 317
biased language, 53–55. *See also* sexist
    language
    ethics in writing and, 193
    gender and, 243
    pronoun references and, 413
    revising for, 496
    sexist language, 54–55, 260
biased sources, on Internet, 473
bibliographies, 55–56. *See also*
    documenting sources
    annotated, 56
    in *CMS* style, 149, 157–61, 163
    in formal reports, 216
    organizational names in, 4
    in proposals, 423
    for research, 467
biennial/biannual, 53
bilingual dictionaries, 143
Black's Law Dictionary, 143
blind-copy notations, 126, 182
block indents, in Web design, 572
block quotations
    APA style for, 151
    MLA style for, 454
body
    for formal reports, 212, 214–15,
        226–30
    of presentations, 398–99
    for proposals, 421, 422–23, 424
    for reports, 462
    of tables, 530
body depictions, for global graphics,
    249, 250
body movement, in presentations, 404,
    405
boldface type. *See also* typography
    for emphasis, 186, 308
    for headings, 308

in newsletters, 348
for presentation visuals, 402
in Web design, 572, 578
books
    APA style for documenting, 151–52
    capitalization in titles, 71, 72, 110
    CMS documentation, 157–58
    evaluating, 474
    italics for titles, 296, 451, 538
    MLA style for documenting, 164–65
    online catalogs for, 465
Boolean operators, 470
both/as well as, 49–50
both . . . and, 56, 110
box heads, 529–30
boxes
    for organizational charts, 364
    in page design, 310–11
brackets, 56–57
    for parenthetical items, 56, 376
    for *sic,* 57, 453
brainstorming, 57–58
    during presentations, 400
    for research, 463
    for résumé writing, 488
brochures, 58–62
    designing, 59–61
    as documentation, 148
    documenting, 154, 161, 167
    italics for titles, 296, 538
    with sales letters, 503
    samples of, 59, 60
    types of, 58–59
    visuals for, 172
    Web resources for, 62
    writer's checklist for, 61–62
bulleted lists, 61, 275, 315, 402. *See
    also* lists
business description, in business plans,
    64
business forms. *See* forms design
business image
    brochures for promoting, 58–62
    using visuals, 39
business names
    abbreviations of, 3–4
    ampersands in, 4, 35
    capitalization of, 71
    in salutations, 122–25
    as singular nouns, 353

business names (*continued*)
  on title page, 213, 422
  on Web sites, 567
Business Periodicals Index, 467
business plans, 62–66
  company description and strategy,
    64–65
  financial analysis, 65–66
  format, length, sections in, 63
  market analysis and strategy, 65
  marketing plan, 65
  purpose and audience, 62–63
  supporting documents for, 66
  Web resources for, 66
  writer's checklist for, 66
business style manual, 170
business writing. *See also*
    correspondence; proposals;
    reports; writing style
  active voice for, 562–63
  brochures, 58–62
  business plans, 62–66
  exposition for, 199
  mission statements, 334–37
  newsletters, 344–48
  promotional writing, 412
  style for, 67–68, 523–26
business writing style, 67–68. *See also*
    style; writing style
but, commas with, 97
button bar, in Web design, 567
buzzwords, 68
  as affectation, 23
  as gobbledygook, 251
  in mission statements, 336
  Web resources on, 68

call for action, in conclusions, 109
callouts
  for flowchart symbols, 208
  illustrations with, 140, 259, 383
campus career services, 301
can/may, 69
cannot, 69, 113
capital/capitol, 69
capital appropriations proposals, 424
capitalization, 69–72. *See also* all-capital
    letters
  of abbreviations, 72
  for adjectives of origin, 16

of events and concepts, 71
of first words, 70, 90, 125, 132, 452,
    538
of letters of alphabet, 72
of organizations, 71
of professional and personal titles,
    71–72
of proper nouns, 70, 352
for quotations, 70, 452
of specific groups, 70
of specific places, 71
in subject lines, 71, 331
of titles of works, 47, 71, 109–10,
    395–96, 538
captions
  in business forms, 237–38
  in page design, 310
  with visuals, 383
cardinal adjectives, 14
career counselors, 301
career summary, in résumés, 489
cascading style sheets, in Web design,
    570
case, 72–76, 415–16
  agreement and, 26–27
  of appositives, 47, 75, 416
  objective case, 74, 415
  possessive case, 75, 392–93, 415
  subjective case, 73–74, 415
  tests for determining, 75–76, 416
causal relationships, words expressing,
    48–49
cause
  definition by, 137
  false, 316
cause-and-effect method of
    development, 76–78, 331
  evaluating evidence, 76–77
  linking causes to effects, 77–78
cc: notations, 126, 182
CD-ROM publications
  dictionaries, 141, 142, 143
  documenting, 153, 166
center on/center around, 78
centuries, format for writing, 133–34
chalkboards, 400
chapters and sections
  in annual reports, 37–38
  in business plans, 63
  in feasibility reports, 201

in headers or footers, 308
numbers for, 358
titles of, 72, 296, 451, 539
charts. *See also* visuals
  for annual reports, 40
  documenting, 153, 160, 166
  flowcharts, 206–08, 560
  organizational, 364, 365, 560
  for presentations, 400, 402
Chicago Manual of Style (CMS). *See*
  CMS documentation
choppy writing, 516
chronological method of development,
  78, 79, 331, 517
  in narratives, 342, 343
  for résumés, 490
circular definitions, 135
circumlocution, 105
citations. *See also* documenting sources
  APA style, 149, 150–51
  footnotes and endnotes, 157
  MLA style, 149–50, 164
  sample pages, 155, 168
cite/sight/site, 78
claims
  adjustment letters for, 17–20
  complaint letters, 101, 102
clarity, 78, 80
  active voice for, 563
  in business writing, 67–68
  commas for, 95
  conciseness and, 104
  defining terms for, 134–35, 136
  grammar and usage for, 252
  hyphens and, 265
  in instructions, 274–75
  in promotional writing, 412
  punctuation and, 441
  semicolons for, 507
  transitions for, 541–43
  in visuals, 558
  word choice and, 575
classification, 146–48. *See also* division-
  and-classification method of
  development
clauses, 80–81. *See also* dependent
  clauses; independent clauses
  adjective, 189
  commas with, 92–93
  missing subjects in, 513

restrictive and nonrestrictive,
  477–78
clichés, 81–82
  avoiding, 39
  clarity and, 80
  as figures of speech, 204
  as gobbledygook, 251
  revising for, 496
climactic order, for emphasis, 184–85
clip-art images, 172, 175
closed-ended questions, 237
closings. *See also* conclusions
  for application letters, 46
  in correspondence, 119, 125
  cultural differences in, 279
  for e-mail, 182
  for meetings, 326
  for memos, 329
  for presentations, 399
  for refusal letters, 460
clustering, 57–58
CMS documentation, 157–63
  for articles in periodicals, 158–59, 160
  for books, 157–58
  compared with other styles, 149–50
  documentation models, 157–61
  for electronic sources, 159–60
  footnotes and endnotes, 157
  other sources, 161
  sample bibliography, 163
  sample page, 162
coherence, 82
  clarity and, 80
  outlining and, 365
  in paragraphs, 372
  in promotional writing, 412
  pronoun references and, 413
  revising for, 495
  unity and, 547
collaborative writing, 82–84
  active listening and, 314
  coherence in, 82, 83
  managing conflict, 84
  outlining in, 365
  purpose in, 442
  team tasks in, 83–84
  Web sites for, 506
  writer's checklist for, 84
collection letters, 85–88, 209
  samples of, 86, 87, 88

collective nouns, 352
  agreement and, 29, 31, 133, 353
colloquialisms, 49
  fine as, 206
  as nonstandard English, 191, 524–25
  quotation marks for, 451
colons, 89–90
  capitalization of word following, 70,
    90
  for enumeration, 507
  with numbers, 89
  with quotation marks, 90, 451, 452
  in salutations, 89, 122
  in sentences, 89
  in titles and citations, 89
  unnecessary use of, 90
color
  in brochures, 61
  in global graphics, 248, 250
  in graphs, 256
  in maps, 321
  in page design, 310
  in presentation visuals, 401
  in Web design, 570, 572
color-blind readers, 571
column graphs, 255–56, 559
columns
  in newsletters, 348
  page design for, 308, 309–10
  in tables, 529–30
comma splice, 90–91, 497
commands, 340, 509
commas, 91–97
  with adjectives, 17, 94
  with appositives, 47
  avoiding unnecessary, 97
  for clarifying and contrasting, 95
  for dates, 95, 133
  for enclosing elements, 92–93, 132,
    477
  with interjections, 93–94, 278
  for introducing elements, 93–94
  for items in series, 94, 97
  for linking independent clauses, 22,
    92, 96, 510
  with names, 95–96
  with numbers, 95–96, 357
  for omissions, 95
  with other punctuation, 96

with quotation marks, 94, 377, 451,
    452
common/mutual, 341
common knowledge, 387
common nouns, 70, 352
communication
  global, 246–47
  listening and, 312–14
  selecting the medium and, 504–06
company image. See business image
company names. See business names
comparative form
  absolute words and, 191–92
  of adjectives, 15
  of adverbs, 22
compare/contrast, 97–98
comparison, 98
  determining basis of, 99
  incomplete, 34–35
  like and as for, 312
comparison method of development,
    99–100, 331
complaint letters, 101, 102
  responding to, 17–20, 460
  sample of, 102
complement/compliment, 101, 103
complements, 103–04. See also specific
    types
  linking verbs and, 552
  number agreement and, 28
  sentence construction and, 508, 509
  subjective, 73–74
  types of, 103–04
  verbals as, 188–89
completeness, revising for, 495
complex sentences, 185, 510
compliment/complement, 101–03
complimentary closings
  for business letters, 125
  capitalization in, 70, 125
components, definition by, 137–38
compose/constitute/comprise, 104
compound antecedents, 31–32
compound-complex sentences, 510
compound predicates, 97, 509
compound sentences, 81, 185, 510
compound subjects, 508
  commas with, 97
  possessive case of, 393

pronoun case and, 76, 416
subject-verb agreement and, 29
compound words, 104
hyphens for, 263
plurals of, 354
comprise/compose/constitute, 104
concepts, capitalization of, 71
conciseness, 104–07. *See also* wordiness
in abstracts, 9
active voice for, 564
avoiding bluntness, 115–16
in business writing, 67
causes of wordiness and, 105
clarity and, 67, 80
compound predicates for, 509
in instructions, 274–75
in international correspondence, 279
overdoing, 105
in promotional writing, 412
revising for, 496
subordination and, 526
telegraphic style and, 531–32
using abbreviations, 3
writer's checklist for, 106–07
conclusions, 107–09. *See also* closings
in abstracts, 7, 8
for articles, 346
for feasibility reports, 201
for formal reports, 215, 231–32
lists for, 309
opening with summary of, 292
for progress reports, 410
for proposals, 421, 423, 424, 439
for reports, 462–63
revising, 495
for trip reports, 543
for trouble reports, 546
concrete nouns, 352
concrete words, 6–7
conditional statements, subordination
for, 527
confidentiality
business forms and, 238
e-mail and, 180
conflict
in collaborative writing, 84
in meetings, 325–26
conjugation of verbs, 555–57
conjunctions, 109–10

capitalization and, 71, 110, 331
in compound subjects, 29
eliminating in telegraphic style,
531
types of, 81, 109–10
conjunctive adverbs, 22
for comma splices, 91
commas with, 22, 96
common, 22, 96, 110
in compound sentences, 510
for connecting clauses, 81, 110
for run-on sentences, 379
semicolons with, 507
connotation/denotation, 110
connotations
of synonyms, 528, 537
of visuals, 249
word choice and, 575
consensus, 111
consistency
proofreading for, 419
in repetition, 461–62
in résumé format, 479
revising for, 495
for visuals, 402, 558, 561
in voice, mood, tense, 554
in Web design, 570
constitute/comprise/compose, 104
Contact Us link, in Web design, 570
context, 111–13
in cover letters, 128
design and, 306
global communication and, 246–47
global graphics and, 248
listening and, 313
openings and, 46, 112–13, 328
in preparation stage, 394
purpose and, 441
questions to clarify, 112
readers' expectations and, 455
in refusal letters, 459
scope and, 503
selecting the medium and, 504
style and, 523
tone and, 540
for visuals, 558
word choice and, 7
in writing process, xi–xii
continual/continuous, 113

continued tables, 531
contractions, 113
   apostrophes in, 41
   writing style and, 283, 524, 525
contrast
   commas for, 95
   sentence variety for, 516
contrast/compare, 97–98
conversational style
   in business writing, 67
   in correspondence, 116
   in informal writing, 525
   for newsletters, 348
   nonstandard English, 190–91
"cookies," 580
coordinate nouns, possessive case of,
   393
coordinate series, 94
coordinating conjunctions, 92, 109–10
   for comma splices, 91
   commas with, 92, 97
   in compound sentences, 510
   for connecting clauses, 81, 92, 109
   for run-on sentences, 379, 497
   semicolons with, 507
   in subordination, 527
   in titles of works, 71, 109–10, 538
copy notations, 126, 182
copyright, 113–14. *See also*
   documenting sources
   common knowledge and, 387
   ethics in writing and, 194
   exceptions, 114
   permissions, 114, 214
   plagiarism and, 387
   for visuals, 174, 383
Corel Presentations, 400
corporate names. *See* business names
corporate reports. *See* annual reports
correlative conjunctions, 110
   double negatives and, 171
   in parallel structure, 373
correspondence, 114–27. *See also*
   e-mail; memos
   accuracy of, 116, 179–80
   acknowledgment letters, 11–12
   adjustment letters, 17–20
   application letters, 42–46
   body of, 125
   collection letters, 85–88

common format styles, 122, 123–24
complaint letters, 101, 102
complimentary closings, 125
cover letters, 112–13, 127–28, 129
documenting, 154, 161, 167
e-mail, 179–84
employment acceptance/refusal
   letters, 9–11, 289
end notations, 126
form letters, 209–11
for formal contacts, 504
format and design for, 120–27, 234
good-news/bad-news patterns,
   118–19, 120, 121
goodwill tone for, 116–18
guide letters, 209, 211
headings in, 122
informal reports as, 462
inquiries and responses, 270–73
inside address, 122
international, 279–84
memos, 326–31
methods of development for, 362
names and titles in, 4, 122–25
openings and closings, 119, 290
outlining for, 366
point of view in, 388
reference letters, 457, 458
refusal letters, 457–60
resignation letters, 474–76
sales letters, 500–503
salutations, 122–25
samples of, 118, 120, 121, 123, 124,
   126
second page of, 125–26
writer's checklist for, 127
writing style for, 67, 115–16, 524
cost analysis, in proposals, 422, 434
count nouns, 14, 27, 35, 352
   articles and, 187–88
   ESL tips for, 187
   fewer/less usage and, 203
cover letters, 127–28, 129
   for e-mail attachments, 180
   for formal reports, 212, 217
   for proposals, 422, 429–30
   providing context in, 112–13, 128
   for questionnaires, 449
   samples of, 128, 129
credible/creditable, 128

criteria/criterion, 130
critique, 130
cultural differences. *See also* global
    communication; international
    correspondence
    in communication styles, 246–47, 325
    in directness of messages, 118, 246,
        279
    listening and, 313
currency
    numbers for, 356–57
    of Internet sources, 473, 569
    of secondary sources, 464
curriculum vitae, 478
cutaway drawings, 172, 175

-d ending, 533, 551
dangling modifiers, 131
    active voice and, 563
    ambiguity and, 34
    infinitive phrases as, 386
    participial phrases as, 385
dashes, 132
    for emphasis, 132, 186
    for enclosing elements, 132, 507
    hyphens and, 263
data/datum, 133
databases, online
    APA style for documenting, 153
    CMS style for documenting, 160
    MLA style for documenting, 166
    for periodicals, 465–66
    plain-text résumés for, 493–94
    search strategies, 468–71
dates, 133–34
    apostrophes in, 41
    on business forms, 238
    capitalization of, 71
    commas with, 95, 133
    for international correspondence,
        133, 283, 357, 520
    in letter heading, 122
    numbers in, 356, 357
    plurals of, 42
    slashes in, 520
    in titles, 213, 422, 538
    in Web design, 569
days. *See also* dates
    capitalization of, 71
    format for writing, 95, 133

de facto/de jure, 134
deadlines, in proposals, 423
deceptive language, avoiding, 193, 380,
    391
decimal numbering system
    for headings, 262–63
    for outlining, 367
decimals
    punctuation with, 96, 378
    writing as numbers, 356
declarative sentences, 443, 510
decreasing order-of-importance
    method of development, 332,
        362–63, 457
defective/deficient, 134
defining terms, 134–35. *See also*
    definitions
    expanding definitions, 136
    glossaries and, 251
    for readers, 456
definite/definitive, 135
definite articles, 47–48
definition method of development,
    136–38, 331
definitions. *See also* word meanings
    by analogy, 136–37
    by cause, 137
    circular, 135
    by components, 137–38
    dictionaries for, 141–43
    by exploration of origin, 138
    extended, 136
    formal and informal, 134–35
    in glossaries, 251
    "is when" and "is where," 135
    negative, 135, 138
    opening with, 292
deletions. *See* omissions
delivery schedules, in proposals, 422,
    434
delivery techniques, for presentations,
    403–05
demonstrative adjectives, 14
    count nouns and, 187
    number agreement and, 14,
        31
demonstrative pronouns, 414
denotation/connotation, 110
denotations, and word choice,
    575

dependent clauses, 80–81
  in sentence construction, 510
  sentence faults and, 512–13
  subordinating conjunctions with,
    110
  subordination and, 526–27
description, 139–40
  samples of, 139, 140
descriptive abstracts, 7–9
descriptive adjectives, 13, 15
descriptors, in electronic résumés, 494
design. *See* layout and design
desk dictionaries, 141
desktop publishing software, for layout
  and design, 348
despite/in spite of, 141
detailed solutions, in proposals, 422,
  433
details
  in description, 139
  interesting, opening with, 292
diagonals, 520
dialectal English, 191
dictionaries, 141–43
  bilingual, 143
  desk, 141
  documenting entries, 152, 158, 165
  ESL, 143
  for research, 466–67
  sample entry, 142
  subject, 143
  synonyms in, 528
  unabridged, 142–43
  for usage, 547
  for word choice, 575
differ from/differ with, 144
different from/different than, 144
Digital Tips
  creating an index, 269
  creating an outline, 367
  creating styles and templates, 216
  incorporating tracked changes, 496
  leaving an away-from-desk message,
    183
  preparing an ASCII résumé, 494
  proofreading for format consistency,
    419
  reviewing collaborative documents,
    84

  sending an e-mail attachment, 181
  testing your Web site, 571
  using PDF files, 580
direct address, 144
  commas with, 92, 93–94
  for emphasis, 186
direct objects, 103, 359
  gerunds as, 549
  nouns as, 353
  pronoun case and, 74
  transitive verbs and, 305, 359, 552
  verbals as, 188–89
direct quotations, 452. *See also*
  quotations
  commas with, 94, 452
  quotation marks for, 450
direct statements, for emphasis, 186
disabilities, people with
  bias toward, 55
  Web design for, 571
discreet/discrete, 144
discussion groups, for research, 464,
  471
disinterested/uninterested, 144–45
diverse audiences, writing for, 456
division-and-classification method of
  development, 145–48, 332
document design. *See* layout and design
document elements. *See* report
  elements
document titles. *See* titles of works and
  documents
documentation, 148
documenting sources, 148–70. *See also*
  APA style; authors, documenting;
  CMS documentation; MLA
  style
  APA style, 150–56
  for avoiding plagiarism, 386–87
  bibliographies, 55–56
  CMS style, 157–63
  colon use in, 89
  common abbreviations for, 5
  common knowledge, 387
  comparison of major styles, 149–50
  copyrighted materials and, 114
  footnotes and endnotes, 157
  in formal reports, 215, 233
  in-text citations, 150–51, 164

MLA style, 164–69
  in note-taking, 350, 351
  paraphrasing and, 375, 387
  in proposals, 423
  purposes of, 148
  quotations, 452, 453–54
  samples of, 155–56, 162–63,
    168–69
  style manuals for, 150, 170
  for visuals, 174, 383, 531, 561
  for Web sites, 579
Dogpile, 470
double negatives, 171–72, 391, 461
draft writing, 576–77
  integrating visuals and, 561
  outlining for, 365, 367–68, 576
  revising, 495–96
  wordiness in, 106
  in writing process, xv–xvi
drawings, 172–76, 558. See also visuals
  functions of, 559
  vs. photographs, 172, 382
  types of, 172–75
  writer's checklist for, 175–76
due to/because of, 49, 176
due to the fact, 49
dummy, in page design, 311

each, 177
  gender agreement and, 30
  subject-verb agreement and, 27, 29,
    177, 417
each and every, 177
each other, 415
EBSCOhost, 466
economic/economical, 177
-ed ending, 533, 551
edited collections, documenting, 151,
    158, 165
editing. See proofreading; revision
editions, book, documenting, 151, 158,
    164
education section, of résumé, 490
effect. See cause-and-effect method of
    development
effect/affect, 23
e.g./i.e., 5, 177–78
either . . . or, 110, 349–50
  agreement and, 29, 31–32

double negatives and, 171
  in parallel structure, 373
electronic forms, 235–37
electronic résumés, 301–02, 487,
    493–94
electronic sources. See also Internet
    research strategies
  APA style for documenting, 152–53,
    154
  CMS documentation, 159–60
  evaluating reliability of, 471–74
  MLA style for documenting, 165–66
  online catalogs, 465
  online databases and indexes,
    465–66
  with unknown author, 153, 159
elegant variation, 24
ellipses, 178–79
  periods as, 377
  in quoted material, 453
elliptical constructions
  commas with, 95
  in informal style, 525
elude/allude/refer, 32–33
e-mail, 179–84. See also
    correspondence
  abbreviations in, 3, 181
  for acknowledgment letters, 11–12
  addresses, 180, 184
  away-from-desk messages, 183
  confidentiality and, 180
  cover letters, 127–28
  design considerations, 181–82
  direct address in, 144
  documenting, 153, 154, 160, 166
  form letters, 209–11
  functions of, 179, 182, 504
  guide letters, 211
  informal reports as, 462
  length of, 503
  for meeting agendas, 323–24
  memos as, 326
  netiquette rules, 180–81
  point of view in, 388
  providing context in, 113
  research using, 464
  responding to, 180, 182
  résumés sent via, 494
  reviewing, 179–80

e-mail (*continued*)
  salutations and closings, 182–83
  sending attachments, 180, 181, 182
  signature blocks for, 182–83
  subject line of, 71, 182, 538
  titles for, 538
  tone for, 523, 540
  trip reports as, 543
  writer's checklist for, 180, 184
  writing style for, 67, 180, 182, 191
emoticons, 181
emphasis, 184–86
  active voice for, 185
  clarity and, 80
  climactic order for, 184–85
  of closings, 119
  colons for, 89
  conjunctions for, 110
  dashes for, 132, 186
  direct statements for, 186
  figures of speech for, 205
  highlighting devices for, 181, 186,
    294–96, 307–08
  intensifiers for, 186, 277
  pace and, 369
  parallel structure for, 373
  position for, 184
  really and actually for, 456
  repetition for, 185, 461
  sentence construction and,
    184–85
  sentence variety and, 516
  subordination for, 526
  word order and, 508, 511, 512
employment agencies, 303
employment experience section, of
  résumé, 490–91
employment process
  acceptance/refusal letters, 9–11,
    457–60
  application letters, 42–46
  job descriptions, 298–300
  job interviews, 286–89
  job searches, 300–303
  reference letters, 457
  resignation letters, 474–76
  résumés, 478–94
  returning job seekers, 492–93
  salary negotiations, 288, 498–500
enclosure notations, 126

*Encyclopedia of Careers and Vocational
  Guidance, The* (Morkes), 466
encyclopedias
  documenting entries, 152, 158, 165
  for research, 466
end notations, in correspondence, 126
endnotes. *See* footnotes/endnotes
English, varieties of
  colloquial, 191
  dialectal, 191
  localisms, 191
  nonstandard, 190–91, 547
  slang, 191
  standard, 190, 523, 547
English as a second language (ESL),
  186–90
  adjective clauses, 189
  adjectives, 16
  articles, 48, 187–88
  assigning gender, 243
  avoiding shifts in voice, mood, tense,
    554
  choosing voice, 565
  count and mass nouns, 187–88
  determining mood, 340
  dictionaries, 143
  gerunds and infinitives, 188–89
  possessive pronouns, 415
  present perfect verb tense, 189
  progressive verb tenses, 189–90,
    535
  punctuating numbers, 357
  sentence construction, 512
  subject of sentence, 509
  Web resources for, 190
  in writing process, xi
ensure/assure/insure, 277
entry lines, in forms, 239–40
enumeration
  punctuation for, 507
  for transitions, 372, 541, 542
equal/unique/perfect, 191–92
-er/-est ending, 15, 22
-es ending
  for noun plurals, 354
  for plural numbers, 356
  for verbs, 355, 554
-ese ending, 24
essay titles, 451, 539
etc., 5, 192

ethics in writing, 192–94
　affectation and, 23
　biased language and, 53–55
　biased or suppressed evidence, 317
　for business forms, 238
　copyright and, 114, 174
　e-mail and confidentiality, 180
　euphemisms and, 193, 194
　paraphrasing, 375
　passive voice usage, 193, 564
　persuasive writing, 380
　plagiarism and, 350, 386–87
　for promotional writing, 412
　pronoun usage, 67
　for quotations, 450, 452
　for reference letters, 457
　for research, 464
　for résumés, 492
　revision and, 496
　for sales letters, 502
　for trouble reports, 545
　using graphs, 253–55, 558
　for visuals, 558, 561
　for Web writing, 577, 579
　writer's checklist for, 194
ethnic groups
　bias toward, 55
　capitalization of, 70
etymologies, in dictionaries, 141, 142
euphemisms, 194
　as affectation, 23
　ethics in writing and, 193, 194
　as gobbledygook, 251
evaluating sources, 471–74
events, capitalization of, 71
every
　gender agreement and, 30
　subject-verb agreement and, 29
everybody/everyone, 30–31, 195
evidence
　biased or suppressed, 317
　guidelines for evaluating, 76–77
examples
　in extended definitions, 136
　in general and specific methods of
　　development, 245
except/accept, 9
exclamation marks, 96, 195
　for interjections, 195, 278
exclamatory sentences, 510–11

executive summaries, 195–98
　in business plans, 63
　in formal reports, 214, 221–22
　for management, 456
　placement of, 198
　in proposals, 420, 422, 431
　sample of, 196–97
　writer's checklist for, 198
experience section, of résumé, 490–91
explanatory notes, in formal reports,
　215
explanatory phrases, as sentence
　fragments, 515
expletives, 198, 536
　awkwardness and, 51
　passive voice and, 563
　subject position and, 509
　wordiness and, 105
explicit/implicit, 199
exploded-view drawings, 172, 174
exploration of origin, definition by, 138
exposition, 199
extended definitions, 136
external proposals, 424–40
extranet, 567
eye contact, in presentations, 403,
　405

face-to-face meetings, 505
fact, 200
facts
　in general and specific methods of
　　development, 245
　vs. opinions, 200, 317
fair use, and copyright, 114
false cause, 316
false conclusions, 76
false impressions, and ethics in writing,
　193
family relationships, capitalization of, 72
faulty logic, in sentences, 514
faulty parallelism, 374
faulty subordination, 512–13
faxes, 504–05
feasibility reports, 200–203
　in proposals, 424
　sample of, 202–03
　sections in, 201
　titles for, 537–38
　Web resources for, 201

few/a few, 203
fewer/less, 203
figuratively/literally, 204
figures. *See also* visuals
    list of, 213–14, 422, 562
    numbering, 213, 319, 358, 383, 561
figures of speech, 204–06
    as slang, 191
films
    documenting, 153, 160, 166
    titles of, 71, 110, 296, 538
financial analysis, in business plans,
    65–66
financial statements, in annual reports,
    37, 38
fine, 206
finite verbs, 553
first/firstly, 206
first person, 379
    antecedents and, 417
    in narratives, 342
    point of view, 388
first words, capitalization of, 70, 90,
    125, 132, 452, 538
FirstSearch, 466
flames, e-mail, 180
flip charts, 400
flowcharts, 206–08, 558, 560
focus groups, 463
fonts, 306, 578. *See also* typography
footers, 260–61, 308
footnotes/endnotes, 55. *See also*
    documenting sources
    in *CMS* documentation, 149, 157,
    162
    in formal reports, 215
    for graphs, 258
    for tables, 530
for example
    vs. e.g./i.e., 177
    in sentence fragments, 515
forceful/forcible, 208
forecast, opening with, 293
foreign words in English, 208–09
    ad hoc, 12–13
    affectation and, 23, 134
    de facto/de jure, 134
    italics for, 208, 296
foreword/forward, 209

forewords, in formal reports, 214
form letters, 209–11
    when to use, 209–10
    writing style for, 210–11
formal definitions, 134–35
formal internal proposals, 424, 425–27
formal reports, 211–33, 462. *See also*
    report elements; reports
    back matter, 215–16
    body of, 214–15
    business plans, 63
    format for, 212–16, 234
    front matter, 212–14
    sample of, 216–33
formal style, 524. *See also* writing
    style
    affectation and, 24
    in business writing, 67
    in correspondence, 115, 328–29
    usage and, 547
format, 234. *See also* layout and
    design
    for brochures, 61
    for business plans, 63
    for correspondence, 120–27
    for formal reports, 212–16
    for memos, 329–31
    for newsletters, 348
    for organization, 364
    for progress reports, 410
    proofreading for, 419
    for résumés, 488–92, 493–94
    for titles of works, 538–39
    using templates, 216
former/latter, 6, 234
forms design, 234–40
    layout and design for, 238–40
    online vs. paper, 235–37
    response types, choosing, 237
    samples of, 235, 236
    sequencing data, 238
    wording captions, 237–38
    writing instructions, 237
fortuitous/fortunate, 240
fractions
    numerals vs. words, 356
    slashes in, 520
fragments. *See* sentence fragments
Freelance Graphics, 400

front matter, 529
    for formal reports, 212–14
    for proposals, 422
full-block-style letter, 122, 123
full justification, 308
functional résumé, 490
functional shift, 14, 240–41, 376
fused sentences, 378–79, 497
future perfect tense, 533, 534
future progressive tense, 533, 535
future tense, 534

garbled sentences, 51, 242–43, 496
gathering information. *See also* research
    interviews, 284–85
    for presentations, 397
    questionnaires, 444–49
gender, 243–44. *See also* sexist language
    agreement, 26–27, 30, 243–44,
        416–17
    avoiding, in global graphics, 249
    ESL tips for assigning, 243
    Ms./Miss/Mrs. usage, 122, 341
    of nouns and pronouns, 243–44
    unknown, in salutations, 122, 124
general and specific methods of
        development, 244–45, 332
generalizations, sweeping, 316
geographical features
    capitalization of, 71
    commas with, 96
    visuals for, 319, 559
gerund phrases, 386
gerunds, 386, 549–50, 553
    ESL tips for, 188–89
    object of, and pronoun case, 74
    possessive pronouns with, 393
gestures
    cultural differences in, 247, 248
    in presentations, 404, 405
global communication, 246–47. *See also*
        cultural differences; international
        correspondence
    adapting content for, 456
    context and, 112, 246
    idioms and, 266
    international correspondence,
        279–84
    visuals and graphics for, 248–50

Web design and, 578–79
    Web resources for, 247, 279
    writer's checklist for, 247
global graphics, 248–50
glossaries, 250–51
    in formal reports, 216
    for global communication, 250
    in instructions, 274
    in proposals, 420, 423
goals
    in business plans, 64
    purpose and, 442
gobbledygook, 24, 251, 524
good/well, 252
good-news patterns, in
        correspondence, 118–19, 121
goodwill, establishing
    with acknowledgment letters,
        11–12
    with adjustment letters, 17–20
    in correspondence, 116–18
    informational brochures for, 59
    in refusal letters, 457–59
    writer's checklist for, 117–18
    "you" viewpoint and, 581–82
Google, 469, 471
government agencies
    employment services, 303
    invitation for bids (IFB) from,
        424–25
government publications
    catalog of, 468
    documenting, 154, 161, 167
    as public domain, 114
    style manual for, 170
*Government Reports Announcements and
    Index*, 468
grammar, 252–53
    proofreading for, 418, 419
    revising for, 496
    Web resources for, 253
grant proposals, 428, 440
graphics. *See also* visuals
    in Web design, 569, 570, 578
graphs, 253–59, 558. *See also* visuals
    for annual reports, 40
    avoiding distortion in, 253–55, 558
    bar, 255–56
    in business plans, 65

graphs (*continued*)
　functions of, 559–60
　line, 253–55
　picture, 257, 258
　pie, 256, 257
　for presentations, 402
　vs. tables, 253, 256, 529
　writer's checklist for, 258–59
Gregg Reference Manual, The (Sabin),
　127
groups, capitalization of specific, 70
guide letters, 209, 211
Guide to Reference Books (Balay), 467

had/have, 533, 534, 551
Hall, Edward T., 246
handbooks, for research, 467
hardly, 171
he/him/his, 379, 414
he/she, 260
　gender agreement and, 30, 243–44
　sexist language and, 30, 54, 260,
　　416–17
headers and footers, 260–61, 308
headings, 261–63
　for brochures, 60
　in correspondence, 122
　decimal numbering system, 262–63
　in document design, 308
　general style for, 262
　in instructions, 275
　italics for, 297
　levels of, 261, 263, 366–67
　for meeting minutes, 333
　in memos, 329
　in newsletters, 348
　in outlining, 366–67
　parallel structure for, 373
　for résumés, 489
　in table of contents, 213, 529
　in tables, 529–30
　in trip reports, 543
　typography for, 307
　in Web design, 572, 577
　writer's checklist for, 263
headline leads, 210
helping verbs, 386, 553
her/him, and sexist language, 54
hierarchical relationships, visuals for,
　364, 560

highlighting devices
　for e-mail, 181, 183
　for emphasis, 181, 186, 294–96,
　　307–08
　ethics in writing and, 193
historical terms, 71
homepage design, 569–70
honors and activities section, of
　résumé, 491
HotJobs, 493
humor
　in correspondence, 180
　in global communication, 283
　malapropisms for, 319
　quotation marks for, 451
hyperbole, 205
hyperlinks, in Web design, 567–69, 578,
　579
hyphens, 263–65
　clarity and, 265
　for compound words, 104, 263
　as highlighting cue, 183
　with modifiers, 264
　with prefixes, 264, 394
　with spelled-out numbers, 134, 263
　with suffixes, 264
　for word division, 265

I (personal pronoun)
　between you and . . . , 53, 395
　in business writing, 67, 388
　me/my/mine, 379, 414
　usage in résumés, 491
icons
　functions of, 560
　in global graphics, 250
　in Web design, 310, 568, 569
ideas for consideration, in conclusions,
　109
idioms, 266
　clarity and, 80
　in dictionaries, 141, 142
　faulty, 35
　in global communication, 266, 283
i.e./e.g., 177–78
-ies ending
　for noun plurals, 354
　for plural numbers, 356
if and when, 572
illegal/illicit, 267

illusion/allusion, 33
illustrations. *See* visuals
image maps, in Web design, 569–70
images, in description, 139
imitation, and affectation, 25
imperative mood, 340
    for conciseness, 106
    for instructions, 274
    for nonsexist language, 54–55, 260
imperative sentences, 510
impersonal point of view, 387–88
implications, in conclusions, 108
implicit/explicit, 199
imply/infer, 267
imprecision, and affectation, 25
impression, and affectation, 25
in/into, 267
in order to, 267–68
in re, 455
in regard to, 461
in spite of/despite, 141
in terms of, 268
in-text citations. *See* citations
inasmuch as, 49
increasing order-of-importance method
    of development, 332, 363–64
indefinite adjectives, 15
indefinite articles, 1, 47–48
indefinite pronouns, 414
    one usage, 360
    possessive case of, 393
    subject-verb agreement and, 27,
        417
independent clauses, 80
    in comma splices, 90–91
    connecting, 22, 81, 92, 96, 110, 506,
        507
    in run-on sentences, 378–79, 497
    in sentence construction, 510
Index to the Times (London), 468
indexes, 268–69
    compiling, 268–69
    in formal reports, 216
    periodical, 465–66
    software for creating, 269
    for specialized sources, 467–68
indexing, 268–69. *See also* indexes
indicative mood, 339
    vs. subjunctive mood, 340–41
    wordiness of, 106

indirect objects, 103, 359
    nouns as, 353
    pronoun case and, 74
indirect quotations, 452–53. *See also*
    quotations
    punctuating, 94, 450
indiscreet/indiscrete, 269
individual, 269–70
infer/imply, 267
infinitive phrases, 385–86
infinitives, 385, 550–51, 553
    ESL tips for, 188–89
    split, 550–51
    subject of, and pronoun case, 74
    to as sign of, 385, 550, 553
Infomine, 470
informal definitions, 135
informal reports, 462
informal style, 524–25. *See also* writing
    style
    in correspondence, 115, 328–29
    usage and, 547
informal tables, 531
information sources. *See* Internet
    research strategies; library
    research strategies; research
informational brochures, 58–62
informative abstracts, 7–9
InfoTrac, 466, 467
-ing ending
    gerunds, 549–50, 553
    for present participles, 551
    in progressive form, 535
ingenious/ingenuous, 270
initialisms. *See* acronyms and
    initialisms
initials
    in correspondence, 126, 331
    periods with, 378
initiation, and affectation, 25
inquiries and responses, 270–73
    form letters for, 209
    for job searches, 303
    responding to inquiries, 271–73
    samples of, 271, 272, 273
    for unsolicited proposals, 428
    writing inquiries, 270–71
insecurity, and affectation, 25
inside/inside of, 274
inside address, 122

insofar as, 49
instant messaging (IM), 506
instructions, 274–77
    active voice for, 563
    context of, 111–12
    as documentation, 148
    for forms, 237
    methods of development for, 78,
        332, 517, 523
    point of view in, 387
    procedures as, 390
    sample of, 276
    testing, 277
    visuals for, 172, 275-77
    warnings in, 195
    writer's checklist for, 277
    writing style for, 274–75
insure/ensure/assure, 277
intensifiers, 277–78
    adverbs as, 338
    for emphasis, 186
    overuse of, 6, 107
    really and actually as, 456
    revising for, 496
    very as, 557
intensive pronouns, 415
intention, in sentence construction,
    510–11
interface, 278
interjections, 278
    commas with, 93–94
    exclamation marks with, 195
internal proposals, 423–24, 425–27
international correspondence, 279–84.
        See also global communication
    avoiding euphemisms, 194
    avoiding figures of speech, 206
    context and, 112, 246
    cultural differences and, 279
    dates in, 133, 283, 357, 520
    global communication and, 246–47
    idioms and, 266, 283
    indirect style for, 118, 246, 279
    punctuation for, 250
    salutations for, 182
    samples of, 280, 281–82
    visuals and graphics for, 248–50
    Web resources for, 247, 279
    writer's checklist for, 283–84
    writing style for, 279–83

International Organization for
        Standardization (ISO) symbols
    for flowcharts, 206–08
    for global communication, 249
International System of Units (SI), 4
Internet. See also e-mail; Web design;
        Web resources; Web sites; writing
        for the Web
    domain names, 471–72
    instant messaging, 506
    for mailing newsletters, 348
    online forms, 235–37
    primary research on, 464
    slashes in addresses, 520
    writing for, 577–80
Internet Public Library, The, 470
Internet research strategies, 468–74.
        See also electronic sources
    documenting sources, 152–53, 154,
        159–60, 165–66
    evaluating sources, 471–74, 579
    job searches, 301–02, 493
    library resources, 465
    online databases and indexes,
        465–66
    search engines, 468–70
    Web directories, 470–71
interrogative adverbs, 21
interrogative pronouns, 414
interrogative sentences, 443, 510
interrupting elements, commas with,
    92–93
interruptive person, in group meetings,
    325
interviewing for information,
    284–85
    active listening and, 313–14
    for annual reports, 38–39
    choosing interviewees, 284
    compared with questionnaires, 444,
        448
    conducting interview, 285
    for mission statements, 336
    for newsletter articles, 344–45
    preparation, 284–85
    for research, 463, 464
    writer's checklist for, 285
interviewing for a job, 286–89. See also
        employment process
    application letters, 42–46

behavior and responses during,
    287–88
behavioral interviews, 287
follow-up procedures, 288–89
preparation for, 286–87
résumés and, 479
salary negotiations, 498–99
interviews, documenting, 154, 160,
    161, 166–67
intimidation, and affectation, 25
intranet, 567
intransitive verbs, 305, 552–53
introductions, 290–94. *See also*
    openings
conclusions consistent with, 109
for feasibility reports, 201
for formal reports, 215, 223–25
full-scale, 293–94
for memos, 327–28
opening strategies, 291–93
for presentations, 398
for process explanations, 407–08
for progress reports, 410
for proposals, 421, 422, 424
providing context in, 112–13
for reports, 462
revising, 495
routine openings, 290
setting tone with, 540
introductory elements. *See also*
    sentence openings
commas with, 93–94
dangling modifiers as, 131
eliminating wordy, 106
inverted pyramid organization, 577
inverted sentences
for emphasis, 511, 512
subject-verb agreement and, 27
for variety, 516
investigative reports, 294, 295
sample of, 295
invitation for bids (IFB), 424–25
irregardless, 461
"is when" and "is where" definitions,
    135
ISO symbols. *See* International
    Organization for Standardization
    (ISO) symbols
it
    as expletive, 198, 509

as subject, 509
it/its, 379, 414
italics, 294, 296–97
in e-mail, 181
for emphasis, 186, 294–96, 307–08
for foreign words, 208, 296
for proper names, 296
for subheadings, 297
for titles of works, 296, 538–39
for words, letters, and numbers,
    296
its/it's, 113, 297

jammed modifiers. *See* stacked
    modifiers
jargon, 298
as affectation, 23
ethics in writing and, 193
as functional shift, 241
as gobbledygook, 251
in mission statements, 336
revising for, 496
stacked modifiers and, 338
job descriptions, 298–300
sample of, 299
job interviews. *See* interviewing for a
    job
job objective, in résumés, 489
job search, 300–303. *See also*
    employment process
advertisements, 302
campus career services, 301
employment agencies, 303
networking, 301
résumés, 478–94
trade and professional listings, 302
Web resources, 301–02, 493
writing letters of inquiry, 303
job titles, 72
journalism, style manual for, 170
journals. *See* articles in periodicals;
    periodicals
judgments, in conclusions, 107
justification, in page design, 308

key terms
defining, 134–35
in index, 269
repetition of, 185, 461, 541, 542
for Web writing, 577–78

keys (legends)
    for flowchart symbols, 208
    for graphs, 258
    for maps, 319, 321
    for symbols, 561
keyword searches
    for online databases, 465, 466
    résumé databases and, 494
    using search engines, 470
kind/sort/type, 14, 31
kind of/sort of, 14, 31, 304
know-how, 304

labels, for visuals, 176, 206, 255, 258, 259, 383
lack of reason, 316
language. *See* English; word choice
Latin words. *See also* foreign words in English
    as affectation, 134
    common abbreviations for, 177–78, 192
    via, 557
latter/former, 6, 234
law style manual, 170
lay/lie, 305
layout and design, 305–11. *See also* format; report elements; Web design
    for annual reports, 39–40
    for brochures, 59–61
    for business forms, 237, 238–40
    captions, 310
    color in, 310
    columns, 309–10
    consistency in, 495
    context and, 112
    for correspondence, 120–27
    for e-mail, 181–82, 183
    ethics in writing and, 193
    headers and footers, 308
    headings, 261–63, 308
    for instructions, 276
    justification, 308
    lists, 308–09
    for memos, 329–31
    for newsletters, 348
    for organization, 364
    page-design elements, 308–10, 569
    for persuasion, 380

    for presentation visuals, 400–402
    for promotional writing, 412
    proofreading for, 419
    for proposals, 440
    for résumés, 479
    rules, 310–11
    typography, 306–08
    using thumbnails, 311
    of visuals, 310–11
    Web resources for, 311
    for Web sites, 567–72
    white space, 310
lectures, documenting, 167. *See also* presentations
left-justified (ragged-right) margins, 308
legal case titles, 538
legal terms
    as affectation, 24, 134
    de facto/de jure, 134
    ethics in writing and, 193
    illegal/illicit, 267
    liable/libel, 311–12
    party, 376
    quid pro quo, 450
    re, 455
legalese, 24, 251
legends. *See* keys
lend/loan, 311
length
    for business plans, 63
    of paragraphs, 370–71
    of sentences, 515–16
less/fewer, 203
less/least, 15, 22
letterhead
    correspondence, 120–22, 504
    for formal contacts, 504
    margins on, 121
letters. *See* correspondence; e-mail
letters (alphabet)
    capitalization of, 72
    italics for, 296
    lower case and upper case, *see* capitalization
    plurals of, 41
Lexis/Nexis Universe, 466
liable/libel, 311–12
library research strategies, 464–68. *See also* Internet research strategies; research

library homepage, 465
online catalogs, 465
online databases and indexes, 465–66
reference works, 466–68
specialized indexes, 467–68
lie/lay, 305
-like, 528
like/as, 312
limiting adjectives, 13–15
line drawings, 172, 173
line graphs, 253–55, 258, 560
linking verbs, 52, 73, 552–53
links, in Web design, 567–69, 578, 579
list-hosting service, 348
listening, 312–14
active, 313–14
fallacies about, 313
in interviews, 285, 288
in meetings, 325
lists, 314–15
of abbreviations and symbols, 214
in brochures, 61
climactic order for, 184–85
colons for introducing, 89, 90
in document design, 308–09
of figures and tables, 213–14, 422, 562
in instructions, 275
in memos, 329
numbered and bulleted, 275, 315, 378, 402
organization names in, 4
parallel structure for, 373
in presentations, 315, 402
in Web design, 569, 577
writer's checklist for, 315
literally/figuratively, 204
litotes, 205
loaded arguments, 317
loaded sentences, 511–12
loan/lend, 311
localisms, 191
logic errors, 315–17
awkwardness and, 51
biased or suppressed evidence, 317
correcting, 365
double negatives and, 171–72
fact vs. opinion, 200, 317
false cause, 316
lack of reason, 316

loaded arguments, 317
mixed constructions, 337
non sequiturs, 316
in promotional writing, 412
in sentence construction, 514
sweeping generalizations, 316
long variants, as affectation, 24
Longman Advanced American Dictionary, 143
Longman American Idioms Dictionary, 143
Longman Dictionary of American English, 143
loose/lose, 318
loose sentences, 511, 517
lowercase and uppercase letters. See capitalization
-ly ending, 22, 264

magazines. See also periodicals
documenting articles, 152, 158, 165
visuals in, 310
writing style for, 525
mailing lists, 348
malapropisms, 319
management
describing in business plans, 64–65
job description writing, 298–300
listing in annual reports, 38
progress reports and, 410
use of memos, 326
writing policies and procedures, 390–91
writing style and tone for, 328–29
manuals, for research, 467
maps, 319–21, 558. See also visuals
documenting, 153, 160, 166
functions of, 559
Web resources for, 321
writer's checklist for, 319–21
margins
for brochures, 61
for correspondence, 120–22
in page design, 308
market analysis and strategy, in business plans, 65
market research, 463
marketing. See also promotional writing
sales letters, 500–503
Web resources for, 448

mass nouns, 27, 35, 352
    articles and, 188
    common, 187
    ESL tips for, 187
    fewer/less usage and, 203
may/can, 69
maybe/may be, 321
me
    between you and . . . , 53, 395
    my/mine, 379, 414
mean/average/median, 50
measurements, 529–30
    abbreviations for, 4
    average/median/mean, 50
    in global communication, 284
    numbers for, 356
    subject-verb agreement and, 28
media/medium, 321
median/mean/average, 50
medical terms, defining, 138
medicine style manual, 170
medium. *See* selecting the medium
meetings, 321–26
    closing, 326
    conducting, 324–26
    conflict in, 325–26
    determining attendees, 322
    establishing agenda for, 323–24
    functions of, 505
    location for, 322
    minutes of, 78, 324, 332–34
    planning for, 321–24
    purpose of, 322
    for research, 463
    time and duration of, 322
    writer's checklist for, 326
memos, 326–31. *See also*
        correspondence
    closings for, 329
    as e-mail, 326
    for formal reports, 212, 217
    format and design for, 329–31
    functions of, 504
    guide letters for, 211
    informal reports as, 462
    length of, 503
    lists and headings in, 329
    for meeting agendas, 323–24
    methods of development for, 78, 362
    openings for, 327–28

preparation and development, 327
protocols for sending, 327
resignation, 474–76
sample of, 330
signatures, 331
subject line of, 71, 331, 538
titles for, 538
tone for, 540
trip reports as, 543
trouble reports as, 544–45
Web resources for, 327
writing style for, 67, 328–29
Merriam-Webster's Collegiate Dictionary,
    141
Metacrawler, 470
metaphors, 205
metasearch engines, 470
methods of development, 331–32. *See
    also specific methods*
    cause-and-effect, 76–78
    chronological, 78, 79
    clarity and, 80
    comparison, 99–100
    definition, 136–38
    division-and-classification, 145–48
    general and specific, 244–45
    order-of-importance, 361–64
    for organization, 364
    sequential, 517–18
    spatial, 521–23
    in writing process, xiv
metonyms, 205
*Microsoft Encarta World English
    Dictionary*, 141
milestones, in business plans, 64
mind mapping, 57–58
minor sentences, 511
minutes of meetings, 332–34
    assigning responsibility for, 324
    chronological order for, 78
    sample of, 333
misplaced modifiers, 34–35, 51,
        338–39
misplaced participial phrases, 385
mission statements, 334–37
    in business plans, 64
    format and length of, 337
    guidelines for writing, 334–37
    sample of, 335
mixed constructions, 337

MLA style, 164–69. *See also* documenting sources
  for articles in periodicals, 165, 166
  for books, 164–65
  compared with other styles, 149–50
  documentation models, 164–67
  for electronic sources, 165–66
  in-text citations, 164, 168
  for multimedia sources, 166
  other sources, 166–67
  for quotations, 454
  sample page, 168
  sample works cited, 169, 233
Modern Language Association style.
  See MLA style
modest tone, in correspondence, 117
modified-block-style letter, 122, 124
modifiers, 337–39. *See also* adjectives;
  adverbs
  ambiguous use of, 34–35
  dangling, 131
  hyphens with, 264
  misplaced, 34–35, 51, 338–39
  redundant, 105
  restrictive and nonrestrictive, 477–78
  sentence construction and, 508, 509
  squinting, 339
  stacked (jammed), 16, 17, 51, 338
money, numbers for, 356–57
Monster.com, 301, 493
Monthly Catalog of U.S. Government Publications, 468
months. *See also* dates
  capitalization of, 71
  format for writing, 95, 133
mood, 339–41
  avoiding shifts in, 554
  ESL tips for, 340
  helping verbs and, 553
  imperative, 340
  indicative, 339
  subjunctive, 340–41
more/most
  for comparison, 15, 22, 192
  number agreement and, 27
more than/as much as, 49
most/almost, 33
Ms./Miss/Mrs., 122, 341

multimedia sources
  APA style for documenting, 153–54
  CMS style for documenting, 160
  MLA style for documenting, 166
multiple readers, writing for, 456
multivolume works, documenting, 151, 158, 164
musical works titles, 451, 539
mutual/common, 341

names. *See* business names; names and titles; organization names; proper nouns
names and titles
  abbreviations for, 4
  capitalization of, 71–72
  commas with, 95, 96
  in correspondence, 122–25
  first name usage, 4, 122, 125, 182, 283
  initials, 126, 331, 378
  Ms./Miss/Mrs. usage, 122, 341
  on title page, 213
narration, 78, 342–43
  sample of, 343
narrative section, in annual reports, 37–38
nationalities
  bias toward, 55
  capitalization of, 70
nature, 344
navigation plan, in Web design, 567
needless to say, 344
negative definitions, 135, 138
negative messages. *See also* bad-news patterns
  in correspondence, 118
  international correspondence and, 279
  positive writing and, 391
  refusal letters, 457–60
  resignation letters, 474–76
negative person, 325
negatives, double, 171–72, 391, 461
neither . . . nor, 110, 349–50
  agreement and, 29, 31–32
  double negatives and, 171
  in parallel structure, 373
netiquette rules, for e-mail, 180–81
networking, for job search, 301

New York Times Index, 466, 468
news releases, 405–07
newsgroups, for research, 464, 468
newsletter articles, 344–46. *See also*
      articles in periodicals
   openings for, 497
   sample of, 345
   visuals in, 310, 346
   writer's checklist for, 346
newsletters, 346–48
   format and design for, 348
   sample of, 347
   types of, 346–48
   typography for, 307
   visuals for, 172, 259, 348
newspapers
   for current information sources, 464
   documenting articles, 152, 159, 165
   italics for titles, 296, 538
   online databases and indexes for,
      466, 468
no, commas with, 92
no one/not one, 349
nominalizations, 349
nominative case, 73–74
non sequiturs, 316
none, 349
nonfinite verbs, 553
nonrestrictive elements, 477–78. *See
   also* parenthetical elements
   commas with, 92, 477
   using which with, 478, 536
nonstandard English, 190–91, 547
nor/or, 349–50
   with compound subjects, 29, 31–32
   double negatives and, 171
Northern Light, 469
not
   double negatives and, 171
   in verb phrases, 386
not only . . . but also, 110, 373
note-taking, 350–51
   active listening and, 314
   draft writing and, 576
   for interviews, 285
   meeting minutes, 324, 332–34
   methods for, 351
   outlining and, 366
   paraphrasing, 374–75
   plagiarism and, 350

for presentations, 405
   quotations and, 452
   for research, 464
   writer's checklist for, 351
notes section, in formal reports, 215
noun phrases, 46–47
nouns, 352–54
   abstract, 352
   as adjectives, 17, 353, 392, 528
   collective, 29, 352, 353
   common, 70, 352
   concrete, 352
   coordinate, 393
   count, 14, 27, 35, 187, 352
   for electronic résumés, 494
   ESL tips for, 187
   functions of, 352–53
   gender and, 243–44
   mass, 27, 35, 187, 352
   as objects, 359
   phrases as, 383, 386
   plurals of, 75, 353–54, 392
   possessive case of, 72–73, 75,
      392–93, 550
   pronouns modifying, 416
   proper, 70, 352
   as subject, 508
   types of, 352
   verbals as, 549–50, 553
number (grammar), 345–55. *See also*
      agreement
   indefinite pronouns and, 27, 417
   pronoun-antecedent agreement,
      26–27, 30–31
   subject-verb agreement, 26, 27–29,
      417, 508, 553, 554
number (word)
   number/amount usage, 35
   subject-verb agreement and, 28
numbered lists, 315. *See also* lists
   for inquiries, 270
   in instructions, 275
   periods in, 378
   in presentations, 402
numbering
   decimal headings, 262–63, 367
   in documents, 358
   for figures and tables, 213–14, 319,
      358, 383, 529, 561
   in outlines, 366–67

numbers, 355–58. *See also*
measurements
in addresses, 357–58
as adjectives, 14
colons with, 89
commas with, 95–96, 357
dates, 357
ESL tips for, 358
fractions, 356
hyphens with spelled-out, 134, 263
italics for, 296
measurements, 356
money, 356–57
numerals vs. words, 355–56
ordinal, 14, 206
in parentheses, 358, 375–76
percentages, 377
periods with, 357, 378
plurals of, 42, 356
slashes with, 520
time, 357
numerical data
in appendixes, 42
in general and specific methods of
development, 245
in graphs, 253–59, 559–60
proofreading, 419
sources for, 468
in tables, 529, 559

object of preposition, 359, 395
gerunds as, 549
nouns as, 353
pronoun case and, 74
punctuation for, 90
objective case, 73, 74, 415
objective complements, 103, 353
objectives
opening with, 291
in résumés, 489
objects, 359. *See also* direct objects;
indirect objects; object of
preposition
observation, direct, in research,
463–64
of
with demonstrative adjectives, 14, 31
possessive case using, 392, 393
redundant use of, 274, 368, 396
of which/who's/whose, 574

OK/okay, 360
omissions
apostrophes for, 41
commas for, 95
dashes for, 132
ellipses for, 178–79, 377, 453
ethics in writing and, 193
slashes for, 520
in telegraphic writing, 531–32
omnibus words, 549
on/onto/upon, 360
on account of, 49
on the grounds of/that, 49
one, 360
in business writing, 67, 366
subject-verb agreement and, 27
one another, 415
one of those . . . who, 360–61
online databases. *See* databases,
online
online forms, 235–37
online resources. *See* electronic sources;
Internet research strategies
only, 23, 361
open-ended questions, 237
openings. *See also* introductions
for application letters, 46
for bad-news letters, 119
for correspondence, 119
for international correspondence,
279, 283
for memos, 327–28
for presentations, 398
providing context in, 46, 112–13,
328
for refusal letters, 459
for sales letters, 502
opinions
vs. facts, 200, 317
point of view for, 388–89
or/nor, 349–50
with compound subjects, 29, 31–32
double negatives and, 171
oral presentations. *See* presentations
order-of-importance method of
development, 76, 332, 361–64
for press releases, 405–06
ordinal numbers, 206
as modifiers, 14
spelling out, 356

organization, 364. *See also* methods of
    development
  awkwardness and, 51
  coherence and, 82
  outlining and, 364–68
  paragraph length and, 370–71
  for presentations, 397–400
  for promotional writing, 412
  for résumés, 479, 488–92
  in Web design, 567
  in writing process, xiv–xv
organization names
  abbreviations of, 3–4
  ampersands in, 4, 35
  capitalization of, 71
  in salutations, 122–25
  as singular nouns, 353
organizational charts, 364, 365, 558, 560
organizational newsletters, 346–47
organizational sales pitch, in proposals,
    423, 438
origins, definitions exploring, 138
orphans, 310
our/ours, 379, 414
outlining, 364–68
  advantages of, 365
  brainstorming and, 57
  clarity and, 80
  coherence and, 82
  decimal headings in, 263
  digital tips for, 367
  draft writing and, 365, 367–68, 576
  including visuals, 172, 364, 367, 561
  method of development for, 332
  for organization, 364, 365
  parallel structure for, 367, 373
  steps for creating, 366–68
  transitions and, 543
  types of, 366
  unity and, 547
  writing paragraphs and, 366, 371
  in writing process, xiv–xv
outside [of], 368
over [with], 368
overhead transparencies, 400
overview, in presentations, 398
ownership. *See* possessive case
*Oxford American Wordpower Dictionary
    for Learners of English*, 143

Oxford English Dictionary, The, 142

pace, 369
  clarity and, 80
  inserting clauses or phrases for, 268,
    516
  nominalizations for slowing, 349
  in presentations, 404
page design. *See* layout and design
page links, in Web design, 567–69
page numbers
  in formal reports, 213
  in headers or footers, 260, 308
  number usage for, 357, 358
painting titles, 539
pamphlets
  documenting, 154, 161, 167
  italics for titles, 296, 538
panels, brochure, 59–61
paragraphs, 369–72
  in e-mail, 181
  functions of, 369–70
  hyperlinks within, 569
  length of, 370–71
  outlining, 366, 371
  topic sentence of, 46, 370
  transitional, 541, 543
  transitions between, 542–43
  unity and coherence in, 82, 372,
    495, 547
  writing, 371–72
parallel structure, 9, 373–74, 526
  for both . . . and usage, 56
  faulty parallelism, 374
  for garbled sentences, 242
  for headings, 263
  in lists, 315
  for nonsexist language, 54
  in outlining, 367, 373
  in sentence construction, 512, 526
paraphrasing, 374–75
  active listening and, 314
  documenting sources and, 148,
    387
  indirect quotations as, 450
  in meeting minutes, 332–33
  note-taking and, 350
parentheses, 375–76
  brackets within, 56

commas with, 96
for enclosing elements, 132, 507
numbers in, 357, 375–76
periods with, 375, 378
parenthetical citations. *See* citations
parenthetical elements
brackets for, 56, 376
capitalization of, 72
commas with, 92–93, 477
dashes for, 132, 507
nonrestrictive elements as, 477–78
parentheses for, 375–76, 507
for sentence variety, 516
part-by-part method of comparison,
99, 100
participial phrases, 383, 384–85
dangling and misplaced, 385
participles, 551, 553
ESL tips for, 16–17
parts of speech, 376. *See also specific
parts of speech*
in dictionaries, 141, 142
party, 376
passive voice, 555, 562, 564–65
avoiding responsibility and, 193, 564
awkwardness and, 51
in business writing, 67
infinitives and, 550
in management memos, 328–29
wordiness of, 106, 564
past participles, 16, 551
past perfect tense, 533
past progressive tense, 533, 535
past tense, 189, 533
PDF files. *See* Adobe PDF files
people/persons, 379
per, 377
percent/percentage, 377
perfect/equal/unique, 191–92
perfect participles, 551
perfect tense, 533
periodic sentences, 511, 517
periodical indexes, 7, 465–66
periodicals. *See also* articles in
periodicals
abstracts in, 7
for current information sources, 464
documenting, 152, 158–59, 165
italics for titles, 296, 451, 538

periods, 96, 377–79
for abbreviations, 3, 4
with ellipses, 178–79
with numbers, 358
with parentheses, 375, 378
period faults, 378–79
with quotation marks, 377, 451
for run-on sentences, 378
permissions, for copyrighted material,
114
person, 379
agreement of, 26–27, 553, 554
in narratives, 342
point of view and, 387–89
pronouns and, 417
person/party, 376
personal/personnel, 379
personal communications,
documenting, 154, 161, 167
personal experience, opening with, 398
personal names and titles. *See* names
and titles
personal pronouns, 414
antecedents and, 417
in business writing, 67
person and, 379
point of view and, 387–88
personification, 205
persons/people, 379
persuasion, 380–81
in application letters, 42
in inquiry letters, 270
in openings, 293, 328
in presentations, 398–99
in promotional writing, 412
in résumés, 479
"you" viewpoint and, 581
phenomenon/phenomena, 382
photographs, 382–83, 558. *See also*
visuals
for annual reports, 36, 39
vs. drawings, 172, 382
functions of, 558, 559
phrases, 383–86
commas with, 92–93
functions of, 383–84
gerund, 386
infinitive, 385–86
noun, 386

phrases (*continued*)
    participial, 384–85
    prepositional, 384
    restrictive and nonrestrictive,
        477–78
    verb, 386
pictorial symbols, in flowcharts, 206,
    207
picture graphs, 257, 258, 259, 560
pie graphs, 256, 257, 258–59, 560
place names, 71
plagiarism, 114, 386–87
    copyright and, 114
    documenting sources and, 148
    ethics in writing and, 194
    note-taking and, 350
    quotations and, 450
    Web resources for, 387
plain-text résumés, 493–94
planning. *See also* outlining; preparation
    for brochures, 61
    in collaborative writing, 83
platitudes, in mission statements, 336
play titles, 71, 110, 539
pluperfect, 533
plurals. *See also* number (grammar)
    abbreviations and, 3, 41, 42
    apostrophes for, 41–42
    compound words, 104, 354
    for foreign words, 209
    nouns, 75, 353–54
    of numbers, 42, 356
    possessive case of, 392
poem titles, 539
point of view, 387–89. *See also* person,
    "you" viewpoint
    for business writing, 67
    consistent use of, 80, 372
    for correspondence, 116–17
    for individual readers, 456
    in narratives, 342
    one usage and, 360
    person and, 379
    "you" viewpoint, 581–82
policies and procedures, 389–91
    active voice for, 563
    decimal number heads for, 262–63,
        367
    policies, 389
    procedures, 390–91
    process explanations for, 407–08

polite tone
    in correspondence, 117–18
    in global communication, 279–83
political science style manual, 170
political terms, 71
position, and emphasis, 184
positive writing, 391. *See also* goodwill,
    establishing
    for defining terms, 135
    for double negatives, 172
    style and, 526
    "you" viewpoint and, 581
possessive adjectives, 14
    count nouns and, 187
possessive case, 392–93
    apostrophes for, 41, 392–93
    for compound words, 104
    ESL tips for, 415
    of nouns, 72–73, 75, 392–93
    of pronouns, 73, 75, 392, 393, 415
post hoc, ergo propter hoc, 316
postal service abbreviations, 6, 122
PowerPoint, 400
practicing, presentations, 403, 405
predicate adjectives, 15, 17
predicate nominative, 509–10
predicates, 509–10
    complements in, 103–04
predictions, in conclusions, 108
preface, in formal reports, 214
prefixes, 264, 394
preparation, 394
    for annual reports, 38–40
    determining readers' needs, 455–56
    determining scope, 503
    for global communication, 247
    purpose and, 441–42
    for research, 463
    writer's checklist for, 394
    in writing process, x–xiii
prepositional idioms, 266
prepositional phrases, 359, 383, 384,
    395
    commas with, 97
    overuse of, 384
    passive voice and, 563
    showing possession, 392
prepositions, 384, 395–96. *See also*
    object of preposition
    confused with adverbs, 395
    at end of sentence, 395

errors with, 396
number agreement and, 14, 31
in titles of works, 71, 395–96, 538
present participle, 16, 551
present perfect tense, 533, 534
ESL tips for, 189
infinitives and, 550
present progressive tense, 533
ESL tips for, 189–90, 535
present tense, 190, 533–34
infinitives and, 550
for instructions, 274
presentations, 396–405
analyzing audience for, 397
body of, 398–99
closings, 399
delivery techniques for, 403–05
eye contact during, 403, 405
gathering information for, 397
introductions, 292, 398
methods of development for, 332,
    361, 363–64
practicing, 403, 405
presentation anxiety and, 404
purpose of, 396–97
software for, 400–402
structuring, 397–400
transitions in, 399–400
typography for, 307, 402
using lists in, 315, 402
visuals for, 172, 259, 400–402
writer's checklist for, 402, 405
press releases, 405–07
sample of, 406
pretentious language. *See* affectation
primary research, 463–64
principal/principle, 407
privacy statements, in Web design, 570,
    580
problem statement
opening with, 291, 398
in proposals, 420–21, 422
procedures. *See* policies and procedures
process explanation, 407–08
flowcharts for, 206–08, 560
instructions, 274–77
organization for, 517
sample of, 408
product description
in proposals, 422, 432
in sales letters, 502

professional journals, job listings in,
    302
progress and activity reports, 408–11
openings for, 290
as promotional writing, 412
samples of, 409, 411
titles for, 538
progressive tense, 533
ESL tips for, 189–90, 535
projection, in presentations, 404
promotional writing, 412
press releases, 405–07
sales letters, 500–503
subscription newsletters as, 347–48
pronoun-antecedent agreement, 26–27,
    29–32. *See also* agreement
with compound antecedents, 31–32
in gender, 30, 243–44, 416–17
in number, 30–31
pronoun reference, 412–13. *See also*
    antecedents
ambiguous, 34
revising unclear, 496
pronouns, 413–17. *See also* case;
    indefinite pronouns; personal
    pronouns; pronoun-antecedent
    agreement; relative pronouns
as adjectives, 14
for business writing, 67
case of, 72–76, 415–16
in compound subjects, 76, 416
demonstrative, 414
eliminating in telegraphic style, 531
gender and, 30, 243–44, 416–17
indefinite, 393, 414
intensive, 415
interrogative, 414
number and, 30–31, 417
person and, 379, 414, 417, 554
plurals of, 355
point of view and, 387–88
possessive, 75, 392, 393, 550
reciprocal, 415
reflexive, 414
relative, 414
sexist language and, 30, 54–55, 260,
    416–17
as subject, 508
for transitions, 541, 542
pronunciations, in dictionaries, 141,
    142

proofreaders' marks, 417–18
proofreading, 418–19
    application letters, 46
    e-mail, 179–80
    for spelling, 418, 419, 523
    for typographical errors, 496
    writer's checklist for, 419
proper nouns, 352
    capitalization of, 70
    italics for, 296
proposals, 420–40
    appendixes for, 42
    audience for, 420–21
    business plan, 62–66
    conclusions, 107–09
    context in, 111
    cover letters for, 112–13, 127–28
    executive summaries in, 195–98
    external, 424–40
    formal internal, 424, 425–27
    grant and research, 428, 440
    length of, 503
    methods of development for, 332,
        523
    project management for, 421
    routine internal, 423–24
    sales, 428
    samples of, 425–27, 429–39
    solicited, 424–25
    structure for long, 421–23
    structure for short, 421
    titles for, 537–38
    unsolicited, 427–28
    writer's checklist for, 440
ProQuest, 466
pseudo-/quasi-, 440
public domain works, 114
publication dates
    in headers or footers, 260, 308
    of Internet sources, 473
    for reports, 213
punctuation, 440–41
    apostrophes, 41–42
    brackets, 56–57
    in business writing, 68
    colons, 89–90
    commas, 91–97
    dashes, 132
    ellipses, 178–79

exclamation marks, 195
    for global communication, 250
    hyphens, 263–65
    parentheses, 375–76
    periods, 377–79
    question marks, 443–44
    quotation marks, 450–51
    semicolons, 506–07
    slashes, 520
    Web resources for, 441
purpose, 441–42
    in abstracts, 7, 8
    active listening and, 313
    of brochures, 59
    for business plans, 62–63
    clarity and, 78
    design and, 306
    for feasibility reports, 201
    front matter for defining, 212
    in introduction, 293
    of meetings, 322
    in preparation stage, 394
    for presentations, 396–97
    for proposals, 420–21
    readers and, 455
    scope and, 503
    selecting the medium and, 504
    style and, 523
    in titles, 537
    tone and, 540
    unity and, 547
    for visuals, 558
    for Web design, 566–67
    word choice and, 7
    in writing process, x

qualifications summary, in résumés,
        489
quasi-/pseudo-, 440
question marks, 96, 443–44
questionnaires, 444–49
    advantages and disadvantages of,
        444–48
    biased evidence and, 317
    form design for, 234–40
    for investigative reports, 294
    preparing questions, 448–49
    for research, 463
    sample of, 445–47

selecting recipients for, 448
writer's checklist for, 449
questions
   in business forms, 237
   for interviewing for information,
      284–85
   job interview, 286–87
   pronouns asking, 414
   punctuation for indirect, 443
   punctuation for polite requests,
      443–44
   for research, 464
   rhetorical, 398, 496–97
   as transitions, 541, 542–43
   verb phrases and, 386
   word order for, 512
quid pro quo, 450
quiet person, in group meetings,
      325–26
quotation marks, 450–51
   for direct quotations, 450, 452
   punctuation with, 451, 507
   for titles of works, 296, 451, 539
   for words and phrases, 450–51
quotations, 452–54
   block, 151, 454
   capitalization of first word of, 70,
      452
   colons with, 90, 451, 452
   commas with, 94, 96, 451, 452
   direct, 450, 452
   documenting, 148
   ellipses for omissions, 178–79, 453
   with exclamation marks, 195
   footnotes/endnotes with, 157
   incorporating into text, 453–54
   indirect, 452–53
   inserting words into, 56, 453
   in note-taking, 350, 351
   opening with, 293, 398
   paraphrasing, 374–75, 387
   parenthetical citations following,
      151, 164
   periods in, 377, 451
   plagiarism and, 386–87
   question marks with, 444
   within quotations, 450
   semicolons with, 451, 507
   using *sic*, 57, 453

racial groups
   bias toward, 55
   capitalization of, 70
radio programs
   documenting, 153–54
   titles of, 451
raise/rise, 455
rambling person, in group meetings, 325
rambling sentences, 513–14
*Random House Webster's College
      Dictionary*, 141
re, 455
reactor, in listening, 314
readers (audience), 455–56
   for business plans, 62–63
   of correspondence, 116–18
   defining terms and, 134, 136
   determining needs of, 455–56
   draft writing and, 576
   layout and design and, 306, 307
   pace and, 369
   in preparation stage, 394
   primary, 456
   in promotional writing, 412
   for proposals, 420–21
   purpose and, 441
   for sales letters, 500, 502
   scope and, 503
   selecting the medium and, 504
   usage and, 547
   of Web sites, 566, 571, 577
   writing for diverse, 456
   writing to individual, 456
   "you" viewpoint and, 581–82
Readers' Guide to Periodical Literature,
      466, 468
really, 456
reason is [because], 457
reasoning errors. *See* logic errors
reciprocal pronouns, 415
recommendation letters, 457
recommendation reports, 201, 294
recommendations. *See also* conclusions
   in abstracts, 7, 8
   in conclusions, 107, 108
   for feasibility reports, 201
   lists for, 309
   opening with summary of, 292
   in reports, 215, 231–32, 462–63

redundancy. *See also* repetition
  eliminating, 105, 106
  numbers in parentheses, 357, 376
  one usage as, 360
  with prepositions, 274, 368, 396,
    547
refer/allude/elude, 32–33
reference letters, 457, 458
  guide letters for, 211
  sample of, 458
reference works, 466–68
references
  avoiding above, 6
  in résumés, 492
references list (APA style), 55, 149. *See
    also* APA style; documenting
    sources
  documentation models, 151–54
  in formal reports, 215
  sample page, 156
reflexive pronouns, 414
refusal letters, 457, 459–60
  bad-news patterns for, 118–19, 120
  employment, 10–11
  guide letters for, 211
  samples of, 458, 460
regarding/with regard to, 461
regardless, 461
relative adjectives, 105
relative pronouns, 414
  in adjective clauses, 189
  for combining ideas, 527
  for connecting clauses, 81
  in sentence fragments, 514
  subject-verb agreement and, 28
  that/which/who usage, 536
  wordiness and, 105
religious groups
  bias toward, 55
  capitalization of, 70
remainder/balance, 52
repetition, 461–62
  awkwardness and, 51
  dashes before, 132
  for emphasis, 185, 461
  for transitions, 461, 541, 542
  wordiness from, 105, 106
report elements, 212–16. *See also* layout
    and design
  abstracts, 7–9, 213, 219

appendixes, 42, 216
back matter, 215–16
bibliographies, 55–56, 216
body, 214–15, 226–30, 462
conclusions, 107–09, 215, 231–32,
    462–63
cover letters, 127–28, 129, 212, 217
executive summaries, 195–98, 214,
    221–22
explanatory notes, 215
foreword, 214
front matter, 212–14
glossaries, 216, 250–51
headers and footers, 260–61, 308
headings, 261–63, 308
index, 216
introductions, 215, 223–25, 290–94,
    462
list of abbreviations and symbols,
    214
list of figures and tables, 213–14
page numbers, 213
preface, 214
problem statement, 291
recommendations, 215, 231–32,
    462–63
references/works cited list, 215, 233
sample report, 216–33
table of contents, 213, 220, 234, 529
text, 215
title page, 213, 218
titles, 537–38, 539
visuals, 310, 383
reports, 462–63. *See also* report
    elements
  activity reports, 410–11
  annual reports, 36–40
  context in, 111
  documenting, 154, 161, 167
  feasibility reports, 200–203
  formal reports, 211–33
  investigative reports, 294, 295
  methods of development for, 331,
    362
  point of view in, 388
  progress reports, 408–10
  pronoun usage in, 67
  recommendation reports, 201, 294
  sample of, 216–33
  tone for, 540

trip reports, 78, 543–44
trouble reports, 78, 544–46
types of, 462
requests for proposals (RFP), 420,
    424–25
research, 463–74. *See also* Internet
    research strategies; library
    research strategies
    for collaborative writing, 83
    direct observation, 463–64
    evaluating sources, 471–74
    Internet research strategies,
        468–74
    interviews, 284–85
    library research strategies, 464–68
    for newsletters, 344–45, 348
    note-taking for, 350–51
    for presentations, 397
    primary, 463–64
    for promotional writing, 412
    questionnaires for, 444–49
    reference works for, 466–68
    secondary, 464
    in writing process, xiii–xiv
research methods, in abstracts, 7, 8
research proposals, 428, 440
resignation letters, 474–76
    samples of, 475, 476
respectful tone, in correspondence,
    117
respective/respectively, 476–77
responder, in listening, 314
response letters. *See* inquiries and
    responses
responses
    to e-mail, 180, 182
    in form design, 237
    to inquiries, 271–73
responsibility
    ethics in writing and, 193, 194, 564
    statement of, in proposals, 423, 437
restrictive and nonrestrictive elements,
    477–78. *See also* parenthetical
    elements
résumés, 478–94. *See also* employment
    process
    analyzing background for, 488
    in appendixes, 42, 66
    application letters and, 42–46,
        478–79

electronic, 487, 493–94
    e-mail attached, 494
    ethics in writing, 492
    organization for, 488–92
    posting online, 301–02
    for returning job seekers, 492–93
    salary negotiations and, 492, 498
    samples of, 479–87
    scannable and plain-text, 493–94
    Web resources for, 494
reviewing. *See also* revision
    for biased language, 54
    in collaborative writing, 83
    e-mail, 179–80
revision, 495–96. *See also* reviewing
    achieving conciseness, 106–07
    for clichés, 82
    for coherence, 82
    in collaborative writing, 83–84
    proofreading and, 418–19
    for sentence construction, 496,
        517
    for transitions, 495, 543
    writer's checklist for, 495–96
    in writing process, xv–xvi
rhetorical questions, 496–97
    opening with, 398, 497
    as titles, 497, 538
rise/raise, 455
routine internal proposals, 423–24
rules
    in page design, 310–11
    in tables, 530
run-on sentences, 378–79, 497

-s ending
    for plural nouns, 353, 354
    for plural numbers, 356
    for verbs, 355, 554
salary negotiations, 498–500
    benefits and job perks, 499–500
    job interviews and, 288, 498–99
    résumés and, 492, 498
    Web resources for, 500
sales brochures, 58–62
sales letters, 500–503
    application letters as, 42
    form letters for, 209
    sample of, 501
    writer's checklist for, 502–03

sales pitch, in proposals, 423, 438
sales proposals, 428, 429–39
    sample of 429–39
salutations
    for business letters, 122–25
    capitalization in, 70
    colons in, 89
    commas in, 96
    for e-mail, 182
    first name usage, 122, 125, 182, 283
    in form letters, 210–11
    headline leads, 210
    for international correspondence,
        182, 283
    for multiple recipients, 124
    for unknown gender, 122, 124
sans serif typeface, 307, 572
scarcely, 171
schedules
    chronological order for, 78
    for collaborative writing, 83
    delivery, in proposals, 422, 434
scholarly abbreviations, 5
science style manual, 170
scope, 503
    in abstracts, 7
    in introductions, 201, 291, 294
    in preparation stage, 394
    purpose and, 441–42
    readers and, 455–56
    in titles, 537
    in writing process, xii
screening (shading)
    in graphs, 253, 256
    in maps, 321
    in page design, 310
sculpture titles, 539
search engines, 468–70
second page, of correspondence,
    125–26
second person, 379
    antecedents and, 417
    point of view, 388
secondary research, 464
sections. See chapters and sections
selecting the medium, 504–06
    context and, 112
    scope and, 503
    in writing process, xii–xiii
-self/-selves, 414

semi-/bi-, 53
semicolons, 473, 506–07
    for comma splices, 91
    in compound sentences, 510
    with conjunctive adverbs, 22, 96
    for items in series, 94, 96
    for linking independent clauses, 506,
        507
    in long sentences, 507
    with quotation marks, 451, 507
    for run-on sentences, 379, 497
    with strong connectives, 506–07
sentence construction, 508–12. See also
        sentence types
    avoiding loaded sentences, 511–12
    awkwardness and, 51
    in business writing, 67
    capitalization of first word, 70
    clauses, 80–81
    comma splices, 90–91
    emphasis and, 184–85
    ESL tips for, 509, 512
    in formal style, 524
    garbled sentences, 242–43
    for global communication, 283
    guidelines for effective, 511–12
    intention and, 510–11
    mixed constructions, 337
    period faults, 378–79
    predicates, 509–10
    revising, 496, 517
    run-on sentences, 378–79, 497
    sentence faults, 512–14
    sentence fragments, 514–15
    sentence structures, 510
    sentence variety and, 515–17
    stylistic use and, 511
    subject-verb-object pattern, 508,
        509, 511, 512, 528
    subjects, 508–09
sentence endings
    ESL tips for, 512
    within parentheses, 375, 378
    prepositions, 395
    punctuation for, 195, 377, 378, 443
sentence faults, 512–14
    faulty logic, 514
    faulty subordination, 512–13
    missing subjects, 513
    missing verbs, 514

rambling sentences, 513–14
run-on sentences, 497
sentence fragments, 514–15
    clauses and, 80, 513
    with participles, 551
    period faults and, 378–79
    rewriting, 515
sentence length, and emphasis, 185
sentence openings. *See also*
        introductory elements
    avoiding also, 34
    commas with, 93–94
    conjunctions as, 110
    dangling modifiers, 131
    ESL tips for, 512
    with numbers, 355
sentence outlines, 366
sentence types, 510–11
    complex, 510
    compound, 81, 510
    compound-complex, 510
    declarative, 510
    emphasis and, 185
    exclamatory, 510–11
    imperative, 510
    interrogative, 510
    loose, 511, 517
    minor, 511
    periodic, 511, 517
    simple, 80, 81, 510
sentence variety, 515–17. *See also*
        sentence types
    for formal writing, 524
    for garbled sentences, 242
    length of sentence, 515–16
    loose and periodic sentences for,
        517
    subordination for, 515, 517, 526
    using parenthetical elements, 516
    word order and, 516
sentence word order. *See* inverted
        sentences; word order
sentences, transitions between, 542
sequential method of development,
        332, 517–18
    chronological order, 78
    in flowcharts, 206
    in instructions, 275
    lists for, 309
    in narratives, 342

series of items
    commas with, 94, 97
    etc. with, 192
    parallel structure for, 374
    question marks with, 443
    semicolons with, 94, 96, 507
serif typeface, 307
service, 519
set/sit, 519
sexist language, 54–55. *See also* biased
        language
    imperative mood for, 54–55, 260
    Ms./Miss/Mrs. usage, 122, 341
    occupational descriptions, 54
    pronoun usage, 30, 54–55, 243, 260,
        416–17
    unparallel terms, 54
shall/will, 519, 534
she/he
    gender agreement and, 30, 243–44
    sexist language and, 30, 54, 260,
        416–17
she/her/hers, 379, 414
ship names, 296
short story titles, 451
sic, 5, 57, 453
sight/site/cite, 78
signature blocks, e-mail, 182–83
signatures
    in correspondence, 125
    for memos, 331
similes, 205
simple sentences, 80, 81, 185, 510
since/as/because, 48–49
sit/set, 519
site/cite/sight, 78
site map, in Web design, 567, 568
site preparation, in proposals, 423, 435
skills and abilities section, of résumé,
        491
slang
    as nonstandard English, 191
    quotation marks for, 451
slashes, 520
slides, for presentations, 400–402
so/so that/such, 520
social work style manual, 170
software, for presentations, 400–402.
        See also digital tips; word-
        processing software

solicited proposals, 424–25
solidus (slash), 520
solutions, detailed, in proposals, 422, 433
some/somewhat, 521
some time/sometime/sometimes, 521
sort/type/kind, 14, 31
sort of, 14, 31, 304
source lines, for visuals, 258, 531, 561
sources, citing. *See* documenting sources
sources of information, 463. *See also* research
    evaluating, 471–74
    in writing process, xiii–xiv
spacing
    for brochures, 61
    for forms, 240
    for letter formats, 120–22
    in Web design, 572
    white space, 310
spam, e-mail, 180
spatial method of development, 332, 521–23
spatial relationships, visuals depicting, 559
specific-to-general method of development, 245, 332
speeches, documenting, 167. *See also* presentations
spelled-out words, hyphens for, 265
spelling, 523
    dictionaries for, 141, 142
    proofreading for, 418, 419, 523
    spell checkers, 496, 523
split infinitives, 550–51
squinting modifiers, 339
stacked (jammed) modifiers, 338
    awkwardness and, 51
    as gobbledygook, 251
    order for, 16
    series of nouns as, 17
standard English, 190, 523, 547
standardized symbols, 206–08
statistics. *See* numerical data
status reports, 408
steps. *See* sequential method of development

stereotypes. *See* biased language; sexist language
stockholders statement, in annual reports, 37
stubs, in tables, 530
style, 523–26. *See also* writing style
    formal writing, 524
    informal writing, 524–25
    writer's checklist for, 526
style manuals, 150, 170, 548
style sheets, for Web design, 570
stylistic use, in sentence construction, 511
subheadings, 261, 297. *See also* headings
subject (of document), introducing, 293, 294
subject (of sentence), 508. *See also* subject-verb agreement
    active voice for highlighting, 563
    compound, 508
    ESL tips for, 509, 512
    gerunds as, 549
    nouns as, 353
    position of, 508, 509
    problems with missing, 513, 514
subject dictionaries, 143
subject directories, 470–71
subject lines
    capitalization in, 71, 331
    e-mail, 182, 538
    memo, 331, 538
    for trouble reports, 545
subject-verb agreement, 26, 27–29, 508. *See also* agreement
    abstract nouns and, 28
    with collective nouns, 29, 353
    compound subjects and, 29
    indefinite pronouns and, 27, 417
    with intervening words and phrases, 27
    inverted word order and, 27
    with measurement subjects, 28
    relative pronouns and, 28
    special problem words, 28
    subjective complements and, 28
    titles of works and, 29
    word number and, 28

subject-verb-object pattern, 508, 509, 511, 512, 528
subjective case, 73–74, 415
subjective complements, 103–04
  adjectives as, 17
  gerunds as, 549
  nouns as, 353
  pronouns as, 73–74
  subject-verb agreement and, 28
subjunctive mood, 340–41
subordinate clauses, 80–81. *See also* dependent clauses
subordinating conjunctions
  common, 110
  for connecting clauses, 81, 110
  in sentence fragments, 514
  for subordination, 527
subordination, 9, 526–27
  avoiding overlapping, 527
  awkwardness and, 51
  clarity and, 80
  for comma splices, 91
  for conciseness, 106
  effective use of, 81
  faulty, 512–13
  in formal writing, 524
  for garbled sentences, 242
  for loaded sentences, 512
  for run-on sentences, 497
  for sentence variety, 515, 517, 526
  vs. using parentheses, 375
subscription newsletters, 347–48
substantives, 508
such/so/so that, 520
such as, in sentence fragments, 515
suffixes, 264, 527–28
summaries
  career, 489
  in conclusions, 107
  executive, 195–98
  meeting minutes, 332–33
  for note-taking, 452
  opening with, 292
  for transitions, 541
summarizing statements, dashes before, 132
superlative form
  of adjectives, 15
  of adverbs, 22

supplement/augment, 50
surveys. *See also* questionnaires
  in investigative reports, 294
  questionnaires, 444–49
  for research, 463
sweeping generalizations, 316
symbols
  in flowcharts, 206–08
  functions of, 560
  for global communication, 248, 249, 250
  for graphs, 258, 259
  keys for, 561
  list of, 214
  proofreaders' marks, 417–18
  in tables, 530
synonyms, 528
  coordinated, 105
  for defining terms, 135
  in dictionaries, 141, 142
  in thesaurus, 537
  word choice and, 575
  vs. word repetition, 461–62
syntax, 528

tables, 529–31, 558. *See also* visuals
  in business plans, 65
  for comparisons, 100
  elements of, 529–31
  functions of, 559
  vs. graphs, 253, 256, 529
  informal, 531
  list of, 214, 562
  numbering, 214, 358, 529, 561
  screening (shading) in, 310
tables of contents, 529
  in business plans, 63
  decimal headings in, 263
  in formal reports, 213, 220, 234
  parallel structure for, 373
  placement of, 529
  in proposals, 422
  for Web sites, 567, 569, 578
team writing, 82–84
technical terminology
  affectation and, 23
  ethics in writing and, 193
  in glossaries, 251
  in international correspondence, 283

technical terminology (*continued*)
　jargon, 298
　in proposals, 420
　word choice and, 575
telegraphic style, 531–32
　caution with, 67, 105
　eliminating articles, 47
　in instructions, 274–75
telephone calls, 505
television programs
　documenting, 153–54, 160, 166
　titles of, 296, 451, 538, 539
templates
　cascading style sheets, 570
　for correspondence, 120–21
　for style and format, 216
tenant/tenet, 532
tense, 532–35, 554
　avoiding shifts in, 535, 554
　ESL tips for, 189–90, 535
　helping verbs and, 553
　for infinitives, 550
　in narratives, 342
　present perfect, 189
　present progressive, 189–90
territorial person, in group meetings,
　326
testing. *See* usability testing
text, in formal reports, 215
than/as, and subjective case, 74, 75–76
that
　dual function of, 414
　with indirect quotations, 450,
　452–53
　one of those . . . , 360–61
　for restrictive clauses, 478
that/those
　as demonstrative adjectives, 14, 414
　number agreement and, 14, 28, 31
that/where, 573
that/which/who, 536
the, 13–14, 47
there, as expletive, 198, 509, 536
there/their/they're, 536–37
thesaurus, 537
they/them/their/theirs, 379, 414
third person, 379
　antecedents and, 417
　in narratives, 342

point of view, 388
this/these
　as demonstrative adjectives, 14, 414
　number agreement and, 14, 31
　pronoun references and, 413
thought-provoking statement, in
　conclusions, 109
thumbnails
　in page design, 311
　in Web design, 570
time
　in global communication, 284
　numbers for, 357
time periods, capitalization of, 71
title page
　in business plans, 63
　in formal reports, 213, 218
　in proposals, 422
titles, 537–39. *See also* names and titles;
　titles of works and documents
titles of works and documents, 537–39
　articles in, 47, 71, 538
　capitalization of, 47, 71, 109–10,
　395–96, 538
　colons in, 89
　coordinating conjunctions in, 71,
　109–10, 538
　formatting, 538–39
　importance of, 537
　italics for, 296, 538–39
　memos and e-mails, 181, 538
　prepositions in, 71, 395–96, 538
　question marks in, 443
　quotation marks for, 296, 451, 539
　reports and long documents, 213,
　218, 422, 537–38
　as rhetorical question, 497, 538
　setting tone with, 537, 540
　special cases, 539
　subject-verb agreement and, 29
　for visuals, 561, 562
　in Web design, 569
to
　in prepositional phrases, 385
　as sign of infinitive, 385, 550, 553
to/too/two, 539–40
tone, 540
　in abstracts, 8
　for adjustment letters, 20

for annual reports, 39
building goodwill with, 116–18
for collection letters, 85
for complaint letters, 101
context and, 111, 112
for correspondence, 116–18
for memos, 328–29
for newsletters, 344, 348
for proposals, 440
for refusal letters, 459
for sales letters, 500–502
style and, 523
of titles, 537, 540
"you" viewpoint, 581
toolbars, in Web design, 567
topic outlines, 366, 371
topic sentences, 9, 46, 370
trade journals, job listings in, 302
train names, 296
training requirements, in proposals,
    423, 436
transition, 541–43
    clarity and, 80
    coherence and, 82
    commas and, 92, 93
    conjunctions as, 110
    eliminating in telegraphic style, 531
    enumeration for, 372, 541, 542
    for garbled sentences, 242
    methods of, 541
    in narratives, 342
    outlining and, 365
    for paragraph coherence, 372
    between paragraphs, 542–43
    in presentations, 399–400
    in process explanations, 408
    for quotations, 453
    repeating keywords, 461, 541, 542
    revising for, 495, 543
    semicolons and, 506
    between sentences, 542
    unity and, 543, 547
    for Web writing, 577
    words and phrases for, 541
transitive verbs, 305, 359, 552
transmittals, 127. See also cover letters
transparencies, overhead, 400
trip reports, 78, 543–44
    sample of, 544

trouble reports, 78, 331, 544–46
    sample of, 545–46
    try to, 546
two/to/too, 539–40
type/kind/sort, 14, 31
typographical errors, checking for, 496
typography, 306–08. See also
    highlighting devices
    for brochures, 61
    for electronic résumés, 493–94
    for e-mail, 181
    for emphasis, 307–08
    for presentations, 307, 402
    typeface and type size, 306–07
    in Web design, 570, 572, 578

unabridged dictionaries, 142–43
underlining
    in e-mail, 181
    for emphasis, 186
    for italics, 294
    in Web design, 572
uninterested/disinterested, 144–45
unique/perfect/equal, 191–92
unity, 547
    clarity and, 80
    in paragraphs, 372
    revising for, 495
    transitions and, 543, 547
unpublished data, documenting, 154
unsolicited proposals, 427–28
up, 396, 547
upon/on/onto, 360
uppercase letters. See all-capital letters
us/our/ours, 379, 414
us/we, 379, 414
usability testing
    for global graphics, 250
    for instructions, 277
    for Web design, 569, 571, 572
usage, 547–48
    clarity and, 80
    dictionaries on, 142
    grammar and, 252–53
    Web resources for, 548
utilize/use, 548

vague words, 549
    clarity and, 80

vague words (*continued*)
as gobbledygook, 251
impreciseness of, 575
revising for, 496
verb tense. *See* tense
verbals, 549–51
ESL tips for, 188–89
gerunds, 549–50
infinitives, 550–51
as nonfinite verbs, 553
participles, 551
in sentence fragments, 514–15
verbs, 552–57. *See also* mood; subject-
verb agreement; tense; voice
adding up to, 547
adjectival forms, 16
agreement with subject, 26, 27–29,
553, 554
conjugation of, 555–57
converting into adjectives, 515–16
ESL tips for, 512
finite and nonfinite, 553
forms of, 553
intransitive, 305, 552–53
linking, 552–53
mood of, 339–41
phrases as, 383, 386
plurals of, 355
as predicates, 509
problems with missing, 514–15
properties of, 553–55
tense of, 532–35
transitive, 305, 359, 552
types of, 552–53
used with prepositions, 395
voice of, 562–65
very, 557
via, 557
videoconferencing, 505
videos, documenting, 153, 160, 166
virgule (slash), 520
viruses, in e-mail, 181
vision statements, in business plans, 64
visual logic, in page design, 308
visuals, 558–62
for annual reports, 36, 39–40
in appendixes, 42
boxes for, 310–11
in brochures, 61
in business plans, 65

captions for, 310
for description, 139–40
in dictionaries, 141
as documentation, 148
documenting and copyright of, 174,
383, 531, 561
drawings, 172–76, 559
ethical considerations, 253–55, 558,
561
in executive summaries, 198
flowcharts, 206–08, 560
for global communication,
248–50
graphs, 253–59, 559–60
guidelines for selecting, 558–60
icons, 310
indexing, 269
for instructions, 275–77
integrating with text, 561–62
layout and design for, 310–11
list of figures and tables, 213–14,
422, 562
maps, 319–21, 559
for newsletters, 172, 259, 348
numbering, 213–14, 319, 358, 383,
529, 561
organizational charts, 364, 365,
560
outlining and, 172, 364, 367
photographs, 382–83, 559
presentations and, 400–402, 403
references to, 6
resources for, 467
symbols and icons, 560
tables, 529–31, 559
in Web design, 569, 570, 578
writer's checklist for, 561–62
voice, 555, 562–65. *See also* active
voice; passive voice
active voice, 563–64
avoiding shifts in, 554
ESL tips for, 565
helping verbs and, 553
passive voice, 564–65
in presentations, 404, 405
voice mail, 505

wait for/wait on, 566
Wall Street Journal Index, 468
warnings, in instructions, 195, 275

we
  in business writing, 67, 388
  us/our/ours, 379, 414
Web design, 566–72. *See also* writing
    for the Web
  cascading style sheets, 570
  homepage design, 569–70
  hyperlinks in, 567–69, 578, 579
  icons, 310, 569
  navigation plan for, 567
  page layout, 569
  for people with disabilities, 571
  posting documents, 579–80
  privacy statements, 570, 580
  for résumés, 493
  site map for, 567, 568
  testing, 569, 571, 572
  typography for, 307, 570, 578
  visuals for, 382, 570
  Web resources for, 572
  writer's checklist for, 572
  writing for the Web, 577–80
Web directories, 470–71
Web resources
  for abbreviations and acronyms, 6
  for argument, 317
  for avoiding plagiarism, 387
  for brochures, 62
  for business plans, 66
  on buzzwords, 68
  on copyrights, 114
  dictionaries, 141
  for ESL skills, 190
  for feasibility reports, 201
  for global communication, 247, 279
  for grammar, 253
  for job searches, 301–02
  for layout and design, 311
  for maps, 321
  for marketing, 448
  for memos, 327
  for prepositional idioms, 266
  for presentation slides, 402
  for press releases, 407
  for punctuation, 441
  for résumés, 494
  for salary information, 500
  for sales proposals, 428
  for sending e-mail attachments, 181
  for usage and style guides, 548

  for Web design, 572
  for word choice, 575
Web sites. *See also* Internet
  APA style for documenting, 152–53
  CMS style for documenting, 159
  for current information sources, 464
  evaluating, 474
  functions of, 506
  indexes for, 269
  internal and external, 566–67
  MLA style for documenting, 165–66
  policies posted on, 389
  posting résumés on, 301–02, 493
*Webster's Third New International
    Dictionary, Unabridged*, 143
well/good, 252
when and if, 572
where/that, 573
where . . . at, 573
whether, 573
whether . . . or, 110
which
  dual function of, 414
  for nonrestrictive clauses, 478, 536
  number agreement and, 28
which/who/that, 536
while, 573
white space, 310. *See also* spacing
whiteboards, 400
who, one of those . . . , 360–61
who/that/which, 536
who/whom, 28, 574
who/whom/what/which, 414
who/whom/which/that, 414
whole-by-whole method of
    comparison, 99
who's/whose/of which, 574
widows, 310
will/shall, 519, 534
WinZip, 181
-wise, 574
with regard to/regarding, 461
word choice, 575
  abstract/concrete words, 6–7
  affectation and, 23–24
  ambiguity and, 35, 80
  buzzwords, 68
  clarity and, 68, 80
  clichés, 81–82
  colloquialisms, 191

word choice (*continued*)
connotation/denotation and, 110
deceptive language and, 193
dictionaries for, 141–43, 575
ethics in writing and, 193
figures of speech, 204–06
for global communication, 283
gobbledygook, 251
idioms, 266
jargon, 298
localisms and slang, 191
malapropisms, 319
outdated words, 24
revising for, 496
standard vs. nonstandard English,
190–91
thesaurus for, 537
tone and, 540
usage conventions and, 252, 547–48
vague words, 549
Web resources for, 575
word divisions
in dictionaries, 142
hyphens in, 265
word meanings. *See also* definitions
capitalization and, 70
connotation/denotation in, 110
dictionaries for, 141–43
word order. *See also* sentence
construction
emphasis and, 508, 511
sentence variety and, 516
subject-verb-object pattern, 508,
509, 511, 512, 528
syntax and, 528
word-processing software. *See also*
Digital Tips
backing up files, 576
clip-art images, 172
for collaborative writing, 84
for designing correspondence,
120–22
incorporating tracked changes, 496
for indexing, 269
for layout and design, 311, 348
search-and-replace command, 496
style and format templates, 216
wordiness. *See also* conciseness
affectation and, 24
causes of, 105

in faulty subordination, 512–13
of passive voice, 106, 564
rambling sentences, 513–14
revising for, 496
using that, 536
wordy phrases, 49, 106, 200,
267–68, 344, 384
words used as words
italics for, 296
plurals of, 41
works-cited list (MLA style), 55, 150.
See also documenting sources;
MLA style
documentation models for, 164–67
in formal reports, 215
sample page, 169, 233
World Wide Web Virtual Library, 470
Writer's Checklists
achieving conciseness, 106–07
annual reports, 40
communicating globally, 247
creating and integrating visuals,
561–62
creating and using drawings, 175–76
creating and using maps, 319–21
creating graphs, 258–59
creating sales or informational
brochures, 61–62
designing a questionnaire, 449
designing Web pages, 572
developing an effective style, 526
eliminating awkwardness, 51
interviewing successfully, 285
managing your e-mail, 184
observing workplace netiquette,
180
planning and conducting meetings,
326
preparing business plans, 66
preparing for and delivering a
presentation, 405
preparing to write, 394
proofreading in stages, 419
revising your draft, 495–96
taking notes, 357
using abbreviations, 3
using headings, 263
using lists, 315
using tone to build goodwill,
117–18

using visuals in a presentation, 402
writing collaboratively, 84
writing correspondence, 127
writing ethically, 194
writing executive summaries, 198
writing instructions, 277
writing international
    correspondence, 283–84
writing newsletter articles, 346
writing persuasive proposals, 440
writing sales letters, 502–03
writing a draft, 576–77. *See also* draft
    writing
writing block, in forms, 239
writing for the Web, 577–80. *See also*
    Web design
documenting sources, 579
fonts, 578
for global audiences, 578–79
graphics, 578
headings, 577
hyperlinks, 578, 579
keywords, 577–78
line length, 578
lists, 577
posting documents, 579–80
privacy statements, 570, 580
writing line, in forms, 239
writing process
brainstorming, 57–58
checklist for, xvii–xviii

five steps for success in, ix–xvi
writing a draft, 576–77
writing style
for abstracts, 9
for annual reports, 36, 39
business, 67–68
contractions and, 113
for correspondence, 115–16
for e-mail, 67, 180, 182, 191
formal, 524
for global communication, 279–83
informal, 524–25
for instructions, 274–75
for memos, 328–29
standard vs. nonstandard English,
    190–91
for Web writing, 577
writer's checklist for, 526

years. *See also* dates
apostrophes with, 41
format for writing, 95, 133–34
plurals of, 42
yes, commas with, 92
you/your/yours, 379, 414
"you" viewpoint, 581–82
for business writing, 67
in correspondence, 116–17
in form letters, 210
readers and, 456
your/you're, 582

COMMONLY MISUSED WORDS AND PHRASES

Many entries in this book focus on the standard <u>usage</u> of various words, phrases, and constructions. Use this complete list as a quick reference for finding usage entries, which appear in italics throughout the book.

A

a / an   1
a lot   2
above   6
absolutely   6
accept / except   9
ad hoc   12
adapt / adept / adopt   13
affect / effect   23
affinity   26
all ready / already   32
all right   32
all together / altogether   32
allude / elude / refer   32
allusion / illusion   33
almost / most   33
also   34
amount / number   35
and / or   36
as / because / since   48
as much as / more than   49
as such   49
as well as   49
augment / supplement   50
average / median / mean   50
awhile / a while   50

B

bad / badly   52
balance / remainder   52
be sure to   52
beside / besides   52
between / among   53
between you and me   53
bi- / semi-   53
biannual / biennial   53
both . . . and   56

C

can / may   69
cannot   69
capital / capitol   69
center on   78
cite / sight / site   78

compare / contrast   97
complement / compliment   101
compose / constitute / comprise   104
consensus   111
continual / continuous   113
credible / creditable   128
criteria / criterion   130
critique   130

D

data / datum   133
de facto / de jure   134
defective / deficient   134
definite / definitive   135
despite / in spite of   141
differ from / differ with   144
different from / different than   144
discreet / discrete   144
disinterested / uninterested   144
due to / because of   176

E

each   177
economic / economical   177
e.g. / i.e.   177
equal / unique / perfect   191
etc.   192
everybody / everyone   195
explicit / implicit   199

F

fact   200
few / a few   203
fewer / less   203
figuratively / literally   204
fine   206
first / firstly   206
forceful / forcible   208
foreword / forward   209
former / latter   234
fortuitous / fortunate   240

G

good / well   252

H
he / she   260

I
illegal / illicit   267
imply / infer   267
in / into   267
in order to   267
in terms of   268
indiscreet / indiscrete   269
individual   269
ingenious / ingenuous   270
inside / inside of   274
insure / ensure / assure   277
interface   278
its / it's   297

K
kind of / sort of   304
know-how   304

L
lay / lie   305
lend / loan   311
liable / libel   311
like / as   312
loose / lose   318

M
maybe / may be   321
media / medium   321
Ms. / Miss / Mrs.   341
mutual / common   341

N
nature   344
needless to say   344
none   349
nor / or   349

O
OK / okay   360
on / onto / upon   360
one   360
one of those . . . who   360
only   361
outside [of]   368
over [with]   368

P
party   376
per   377
percent / percentage   377

personal / personnel   379
persons / people   379
phenomenon / phenomena   382
principal / principle   407
pseudo- / quasi-   440

Q
quid pro quo   450

R
raise / rise   455
re   455
really   456
reason is [because]   457
regarding / with regard to   461
regardless   461
respective / respectively   475

S
service   519
set / sit   519
shall / will   519
so / so that / such   520
some / somewhat   521
some time / sometime / sometimes   521

T
tenant / tenet   532
that / which / who   536
there / their / they're   536
to / too / two   539
try to   546

U
up   547
utilize   548

V
very   557
via   557

W
wait for / wait on   566
when / where / that   572
whether   573
while   573
who / whom   574
who's / whose / of which   574
-wise   574

Y
your / you're   582